Human Resource Management

Theory and Practice

Third edition

John Bratton and Jeffrey Gold

Published by
PALGRAVE MACMILLAN
Houndmills, Basingstoke, Hampshire RG21 6XS and
175 Fifth Avenue, New York, N. Y. 10010
Companies and representatives throughout the world

PALGRAVE MACMILLAN is the global academic imprint of the Palgrave Macmillan division of St. Martin's Press, LLC and of Palgrave Macmillan Ltd. Macmillan® is a registered trademark in the United States, United Kingdom and other countries. Palgrave is a registered trademark in the European Union and other countries.

ISBN 0–333–99325–X hardback
ISBN 0–333–99326–8 paperback

This book is printed on paper suitable for recycling and made from fully managed and sustained forest sources.

A catalogue record for this book is available from the British Library.

Library of Congress Catalog Card Number: 2003045982

Editing and origination by Aardvark Editorial, Mendham, Suffolk

11   10   9   8   7   6   5   4   3   2
12   11   10   09   08   07   06   05   04   03

Printed and bound in Great Britain by
Bath Press, Bath

People are the only element with the inherent power to generate value. All the other variables offer nothing but inert potential. By their nature, they add nothing, and they cannot add anything until some human being leverages that potential by putting it into play.

Jac Fitz-enz,
The ROI of Human Capital, 2000, p. xii

After a few years away from their MBA programmes, most managers report that they wish they had focused more on people management skills while in school.

Margaret Wheatley,
Leadership and the New Science, 1994, p. 144

To Carolyn, and our children, Amy, Andrew and Jennie,
who supported me in this and all other endeavours – John Bratton

To Susan and Alma – Jeffrey Gold

Contents in brief

Full contents

List of figures

List of tables

Useful HRM web links

Throughout this text relevant web links are included where appropriate and the companion website includes a thorough and updated index of useful links on all aspects of the subject. This summary is designed as a useful starting point for researching human resource management via the Internet.

HR journals

Asia-Pacific Journal of Human Resources www.sagepub.co.uk/journals/details/j0468.html
HR Magazine (USA) www.shrm.org/hrmagazine/
HR Monthly (Australia) www.ahri.com.au
HR Professional (Canada) www.hrprofessional.org
Human Resource Management International www.tandf.co.uk/journals/online/
   1367-8868.html
Human Resource Management International Digest www.mustafa.emeraldinsight.com
International Journal of Human Resource Management www.tandf.co.uk/journals/online/
   0958-5192.html
Journal of Human Resources www.ssc.wise.edu/jhr/home.html
People Management (UK) www.peoplemanagement.co.uk

Professional HR associations around the world

Australian Human Resources Institute www.ahri.com.au
Canadian Council of Human Resources Associations www.cchra-ccarh.ca
Centrum for Personal & Utveckling (Sweden) www.hrmorg.se
Chartered Institute of Personnel & Development (UK) www.cipd.co.uk
Finnish Association for Human Resource Management www.henryorg.fi
Hong Kong Institute of Human Resource Management www.hkihrm.org
Human Resources Institute of New Zealand www.hrinz.org.nz
Human Resources Norway www.hrnorge.no
Institute of People Management (South Africa) www.ipm.co.za
Japan Society for Human Resource Management www.jshrm.org
National Institute of Personnel Management (India) www20.brinkster.com/nipm
Nederlandse Vereniging voor Personeelbeleid (Netherlands) www.nvp.plaza.nl
Society for Human Resource Management (USA) www.shrm.org
World Federation of Personnel Management Associations www.wfpma.com

Health and safety

Asian-Pacific Regional Network on Occupational Safety and Health Information
www.ilo.org/public/english/region/asro/bangkok/asiaosh
Association of Societies for Occupational Safety and Health (South and Southern Africa)
www.asosh.org/
Canadian Centre for Occupational Health and Safety ccohs.ca
European Agency for Health and Safety at Work uk.osha.eu.int/
Health and Safety Executive (UK) www.hse.gov.uk/
Hong Kong Occupational Safety and Health Association hkosha.org.hk
International Occupational Safety and Health Information Centre www.ilo.org/public/
english/protection/safework/cis
Occupational Safety and Health Administration (USA) www.osha.gov/
National Occupational Health and Safety Commission (Australia) www.nohsc.gov.au/

Human resource planning

Enterprise Resource Planning (USA) www.erpassist.com
Flexibility (UK) www.flexibility.co.uk
HR Focus (South Africa) www.hr-focus.com
Personnel Economics Institute (Sweden) www.fek.su.se/pei/indexe/html
Software Source (established by CIPD) www.softwaresource.co.uk

Recruitment and selection

Association of Online Recruiters (UK) www.aolr.org/
Recruitment and Employment Federation (UK) www.rec.uk.com/

Appraisal and performance management

ACAS 'Appraisal Related Pay' www.acas.org.uk/publications/pub_ab_appraisalpay.html
Performance Management Association www.som.cranfield.ac.uk/som/cbp/pma/
PerformanceReview.com (USA) performancereview.com

Reward management

International Foundation of Employee Benefits Plan www.ifebp.org
New Earnings Survey (UK) www.statistics.gov.uk
Reward Strategies (USA) rewardstrategies.com

Human resource development

Academy of Human Resource Development (USA) www.ahrd.org
Australian National Training Authority www.anta.gov.au
CIPD (UK) www.cipd.co.uk/HRD/
European Mentoring Centre www.mentoringcentre.org/
HRD Gateway (Asia) www.hrdgateway.org/hub1/
Human Resources Development Canada www.hrdc-drhc.gc.ca/common/homex/shtml
Human Resource Development in Europe www.b.shuttle.de/wifo/ehrd/=portal.htm
Investors in People www.iipuk.co.uk
Learning and Skills Council (UK) www.lsc.gov.uk
National Training Directory (South Africa) www.peopledevelopment.co.za

Employee relations

1998 Workplace Employee Relations Survey www.dti.gov.uk/er/emar/1998WERS.htm
Advisory, Conciliation and Arbitration Service www.acas.org.uk/
Australian Industrial Relations Commission www.airc.gov.au
Commission for Conciliation, Mediation and Arbitration (South Africa) www.ccma.org.za
Commonwealth Department of Employment, Workplace Relations and Small Business
    (Australia) www.dewrsb.gov.au
Employee Involvement Association www.eia.com
European Industrial Relations Observatory On-line www.eiro.eurofound.ie/
Institute for Employment Studies www.employment-studies.co.uk/
Industrial Relations Services www.irsonline.co.uk/index_pub.htm
International Labour Organization www.ilo.org/
National Labor Management Association (USA) www.nlma.org/

Trade unions

Australian Council of Trade Unions www.actu.asn.au
Canadian Labour Congress www.clc-ctc.ca
Commonwealth Trade Union Council www.commonwealthtuc.org/members.shtml
Congress of SA Trade Unions (South Africa) cosatu.org.za
European Trade Union Institute www.etuc.org/ETUI/
Indian National Trade Union Congress members.rediff.com/intuc/
International Confederation of Free Trade Unions www.icftu.org/
International Centre for Trade Union Rights www.ictur.labournet.org/
Trades Union Congress (UK) www.tuc.org.uk/

Equal opportunities

American Institute for Managing Diversity www.aimd.org/
Australian Human Rights and Equal Opportunities Commission www.hreoc.gov.au/
Canadian Human Rights Commission www.chrc_ccdp.ca
Commission for Racial Equality (UK) www.cre.gov.uk/
Department of Labour (South Africa) www.labour.gov.za
Equal Opportunities Commision (UK) www.eoc.org.uk/
European Institute for Managing Diversity www.iegd.org/
European Union www.europa.eu.int/
United Nations www.un.org/

Employment law

Australian Employment Law www.dewr.gov.au/
British Employment Law www.emplaw.co.uk www.hmso.gov.uk/acts.htm
European Union Law www.euroli.net/search.html
International Labour Organisation www.ilo.org
South African Employment Law www.labour.gov.za
US Employment Law www.rmlibrary.com/db/lawilabor.htm

About the authors

Dr John Bratton is Associate Professor and teaches at the University of Calgary and the University College of the Cariboo, Canada. He has also taught at Leeds Business School, Leeds Metropolitan University, the University of Bradford and the Open University in the UK and has been a Visiting Professor at the University of Tampere, Finland.

His research interests focus on the politics of technology, leadership and workplace learning and he was the first Director of the University of Calgary's Workplace Learning Research Unit. He has undertaken research on HRM in Japan and Germany and has published widely in journals in Canada, the United Kingdom and the United States. In 2001, he co-chaired the Second International Conference on Researching Work and Learning.

Dr Bratton is a member of the editorial board of the *Journal of Workplace Learning* and is the author of several books, including *Japanization of Work: Managerial Studies in the 1990s*; *New Technology and Employment* (1981) (with Jeremy Waddington), *Workplace Learning: A Critical Introduction* (with T. Pyrch, J. Helm-Mills and P. Sawchuk, Garamond Press (2003)) and *Organizational Leadership* (with K. Grint and D. Nelson, forthcoming).

Jeffrey Gold is Principal Lecturer in Human Resource Management at Leeds Business School, Leeds Metropolitan University, UK and a Visiting Lecturer at the École Supérieure de Commerce, Amiens, France.

He has published widely on human resource development and issues relating to learning at work and is a founding member of the Human Resource Development Unit within Leeds Business School.

Jeff Gold has a strong interest in action learning and the creation of collaborative learning partnerships with organizations to bridge the divide between academic ideas and organization practice. He has acted as a consultant for multinational clients in the USA and Europe.

Dear Student

Thank you for buying *Human Resource Management: Theory and Practice*. This third edition of our best-selling textbook has been written in response to feedback from students and lecturers around the world so you can be confident it has been designed with your needs in mind. Whatever level you are studying at, it provides an accessible but critical introduction to human resource management that will equip you with a comprehensive knowledge and understanding of the latest relevant theories, practices and functional activities of the subject.

The text is structured in four parts which are described in detail in the Preface. Each chapter follows a similar structure in order to help you navigate easily through the text. At the beginning of each chapter we offer quotes from academics or practitioners to show the direct relevance of the chapter topic. The chapter outline and chapter objectives which follow summarize the key concepts that will be covered and the knowledge you will gain.

The main text introduces you to the major concepts and issues before offering critical comment and discussing alternative perspectives. Reflective questions encourage you to think critically about key issues and consider broader consequences than we can cover in the space available. HRM in practice examples illustrate current developments or practices in HRM so you can see the application of theory in the real world. We have included study tips to help you formulate questions about the subject and HRM web links to help you research topics further and appreciate the application of human resource practices in the contemporary workplace.

At the end of each chapter you will find a summary of the chapter content and a list of key concepts. These can be used alongside the chapter outlines and chapter objectives to ensure you have understood the key issues. If you need to recap on any topics, page references are provided to enable you to find the relevant section. There is also a comprehensive glossary at the back of the book. We provide details of further reading sources to enable you to explore the subject further and case studies to highlight the challenges of applying HRM theory in practice. Finally, the practising human resource management assignments offer you the opportunity to develop the key skills needed for professional success.

The companion website to this text can be accessed at **www.palgrave.com/business/ brattonandgold** and provides extensive web links to further resources to help you research the topic, summary lecture notes to accompany each chapter, skill development exercises to improve your professional competencies and a searchable online glossary to check on definitions of key terms. You can also gain access to a guide to enhancing your study skills.

We hope our hands-on approach to learning helps you to make maximum use of the textbook and be successful in your human resource management course and future career. We would welcome any feedback on the text and any suggestions on how we can improve the next edition; please contact us via our email addresses on the companion website.

Good luck with your studies

John Bratton   Jeffrey Gold

Dear Lecturer

Thank you for adopting *Human Resource Management: Theory and Practice*. This third edition incorporates changes we have made teaching our own courses – particularly the use of Internet resources – and the comments and criticisms from the 14 anonymous users and non-users of the second edition, and five more who looked in detail at the manuscript for this book. If you are not familiar with previous editions of the book, the Preface provides a complete explanation of our approach to teaching HRM and the structure and content of the text.

This third edition has been thoroughly updated including new material on: the contemporary context of HRM; new post-Fordism topics within work organization, such as flexibility, postbureacratic work design and the move towards knowledge work; performance in the public sector – New Managerialism, Best Value; a new discussion on e-HR; testing and assessment centres; the growth of workplace learning including knowledge management and e-learning; new material on skills; indirect employee participation and partnership strategies; and new legislation. Reflecting the growing emphasis on delivery value in business, this edition features a new chapter (Chapter 13) on Evaluating Human Resource Management. For a more detailed description of changes in this edition, see New to the third edition of the Preface.

More than ever, *Human Resource Management: Theory and Practice*, Third Edition now not only teaches students but it also elicits their responses. Reflective questions, study tips and discussion questions prompt students to consider key concepts and implications. In addition, the student website for the text offers skill development exercises and other web resources which encourage students to discover more about HRM on their own.

This new edition includes a variety of supporting materials to help you prepare and present the material in the textbook. The web site at **www.palgrave.com/business/brattonandgold** offers downloadable teaching supplements including:

- Lecturer notes, teaching tips and lecture enhancement ideas
- PowerPoint lecture slides for each chapter
- Skill development exercises.

We would welcome any feedback on these new features or any suggestions on how we can improve the next edition. Please contact us via our email addresses.

Best wishes

John Bratton

Jeffrey Gold

Preface

Human Resource Management: Theory and Practice has been written specifically to fulfill the need of introductory undergraduate and graduate courses for an accessible but rigorous, comprehensive analysis of contemporary human resource management.

● Approach

At the beginning of the 21st century, the way people are managed in the workplace presents managers with major challenges. The turbulent business climate, caused by increased global price competitiveness, changing technologies, changing employment legislation, and changing work force composition is challenging managers to utilize their employees more effectively to gain competitive advantage. The change towards more knowledge-based work and the growing acknowledgement that workers are the key to sustainable competitive advantage has strengthened the case for 'new' human resource management initiatives.

In academia, HRM scholars emphasize the strategic role of HRM and detect a 'new agenda' for managing the employment relationship including: new organizational designs, flexible work arrangements, 'psychological contracts', and the development of social partnerships. An important theoretical development, that supports the central tenets of HRM, is the integration of strategic management, organizational restructuring, and adult learning to create a resource-based theory of competitive advantage. In addition, empirical-based data has been gathered, analysed and published on the extensiveness of HRM practices in North American and European organizations. However, running in tandem with the 'new' is evidence of the old order including, 'downsizing', 'rightsizing' – euphemisms for layoffs – a culture of employment insecurity, and job-related stress. 'McWorld' is the symbolic term often used to capture these new realities of globalization which engulf young people in the 21st century workplace. We believe that *Human Resource Management: Theory and Practice* and its companion website will help the student of HRM to make sense of these developments.

Many undergraduate textbooks on the market tend to be more prescriptive than analytical. Academically rigorous and practically relevant, this new edition gives a comprehensive coverage of contemporary theories and concepts in key human resources activities such as recruitment and selection, appraisal, training and development, rewards management and employee relations. Though our aim is to give students a solid working knowledge of HRM, this text also encourages students to think critically and thereby develop a deeper understanding of this important area of management. It reviews and discusses HRM concepts and includes up-to-date references on HRM scholarship. It also has a practical orientation – the `how to' activities of HRM. For example, it discusses how to recruit and select and how to design training programmes.

Human Resource Management: Theory and Practice has been written for an international audience, and draws examples and literature on HRM from Europe, Canada, the United States and other countries. This should help students to compare international developments in HRM and to develop a broader understanding of HRM issues and practices.

● Content

This book is divided into four major parts which are summarized in the plan of the book opposite. These parts are, of course, interconnected as shown by a feedback loop which links HRM practices with the external and internal contexts but, at the same time, they reflect different focuses of study.

Part 1 introduces the whole arena of HRM. Chapter 1 discusses the nature and role of HRM and addresses some of the controversial theoretical issues surrounding the contemporary HRM debate. Chapter 2 examines the notion of strategic HRM and explores various strategic issues such as HRM performance, workplace learning and international HRM.

Part 2 reviews the external contexts that affect human resource management policies and actions inside the organization. The economic, social, political and technology contexts are outlined in Chapter 3 while Chapter 4 discusses changes in organizational structures and job design and Chapter 5 examines employee health and safety issues including workplace stress, workplace violence and sexual harassment.

The discussion in *Parts 1 and 2* provides the context of HRM and prepares the groundwork for *Part 3*.

Part 3 examines the key HR practices including human resource planning, recruitment and selection, appraisal, rewards, and human resource development. The content of each chapter reflects the latest developments in HR practice. In particular, Chapter 6 introduces the concept of e-HR, Chapter 7 highlights the increased use of assessment centres and psychological tests to measure personality and Chapter 8 discusses the international growth of organizational performance appraisal systems for both non-manual and manual workers. In the area of reward or compensation management, Chapter 9 shows that employers have been moving towards a more individualist approach to the wage-effort bargain with merit pay increasingly replacing traditional wage rates. Chapter 10 covers the pivotal component of the HRM model, human resource development, and discusses issues such as the demand for skills, workplace learning, knowledge management and e-learning. Within employee and union relations, Chapter 11 provides evidence that organizations are devoting more resources to employee communication programmes and introducing employee involvement arrangements, and Chapter 12 highlights the major changes that are taking place at worksite and national levels including collective bargaining and partnership strategies.

Part 4 discusses whether human resource practices can be evaluated in terms of organizational effectiveness and human resource effectiveness. Chapter 13 discusses statistical and financial approaches to evaluating HR strategy and high-

Plan of the book

This book is divided into four major parts. These parts are, of course, interconnected as shown by a feedback loop which links HRM practices with the external and internal contexts but, at the same time, they reflect different focuses of study (see below).

PART 1 THE HUMAN RESOURCE MANAGEMENT ARENA

Chapter 1 The nature of human resource management

Chapter 2 Strategic human resource management

PART 2 THE HUMAN RESOURCE MANAGEMENT CONTEXT

Chapter 3 The context of human resource management

Chapter 4 Work and work organization

Chapter 5 Health and safety

PART 3 HUMAN RESOURCE MANAGEMENT PRACTICES

Chapter 6 Human resource planning

Chapter 7 Recruitment and selection

Chapter 8 Appraisal and performance management

Chapter 9 Reward management

Chapter 10 Human resource development

Chapter 11 Employee relations

Chapter 12 Union–management relations

PART 4 THE EVALUATION CONTEXT

Chapter 13 Evaluating human resource management

Chapter 14 Conclusion: Whither HRM?

lights the methodological challenges in measuring HRM-organizational and individual effectiveness.

The plan of the book does not assign values to the relationships between HRM contexts, practices, and outcomes, and therefore it does not claim to be predictive. The model is, however, a useful learning tool that allows the different dimensions of human resource management to be studied within a consistent, general framework upon which this text builds.

● Teaching aids

The textual material is complemented by a number of features to help student learning. These include:

Chapter outlines and chapter objectives guide the student through the material that follows and allow them to check their progress.

HRM in practice examples illustrate current developments or practices in HRM. These are taken from a range of companies and regions to reflect the breadth of application of HR theory.

Reflective questions challenge the student to think analytically and critically and to consider the broader relationships and interactions of the topics under discussion.

Study tips encourage students to challenge mainstream thinking on HRM by formulating critical thinking questions and identifying and evaluating alternative information and perspectives.

HRM web links enable students to download statistical information, follow current international developments in HRM practices, and even to monitor the job market in human resource management.

Chapter summaries provide an abbreviated version of the main concepts and theories which students may find useful for revision and also to check their understanding of the key points.

Key concepts at the end of each chapter are referenced back to their introduction in the text. Students can use these to check they understand all the key terms and recap if necessary.

Discussion questions test students' understanding of core concepts and can be used to promote classroom or group discussion of different perspectives.

Further reading references provide elaboration of key topics discussed in the text.

Chapter case studies demonstrate the application of theoretical material from the text and help the student appreciate the challenges of managing people at work.

Practising human resource management assignments provides individual and group learning activities that focus on skill development so that students can use the HRM theories and concepts they learn to improve their personal and professional lives.

Glossary. A comprehensive glossary (containing more than 150 terms) is provided at the end of the book and on the accompanying website to help the student review and define key terms used in the text.

Bibliography. A bibliography provides the student with a comprehensive list of sources/works cited in the text.

Indices. At the end of the book we provide an author index and a general index to help readers easily search for relevant information or references.

⬤ New to the third edition

Users of previous editions of *Human Resource Management: Theory and Practice* will find that we have retained the overall aims of the previous versions. However, all the material retained from the second edition has been updated and has also been carefully edited to enhance readability. Chapter 2 now includes some discussion of international and comparative HRM, previously covered in the final chapter. Chapter 3 has been renamed and rewritten to provide an up-to-date and thorough discussion of the contemporary context in which HRM operates, while Chapter 4 now includes new post-Fordism topics within work organization, such as flexibility, postbureaucratic work design and the move towards knowledge work. Flexibility is covered again in Chapter 6 along with a new discussion on e-HR. Testing and assessment centres are new in Chapter 7. Chapter 10 has an expanded discussion on workplace learning, including knowledge management and e-learning and also includes new material on skills. Chapters 11 and 12 have both been renamed and now include material on indirect employee participation and partnership strategies. Reflecting the growing emphasis on delivery value in business, this edition features a new chapter (Chapter 13) on Evaluating human resource management which discusses different approaches to researching and evaluating HR strategies. We have also updated relevant legislation, particularly in Chapters 5, 7 and 12.

In addition we have increased the interactive nature of the book with more opportunities for students to check or reinforce their learning and expand their knowledge outside the printed text. The reflective questions, study tips, HRM web links and practising human resource management features described above have all been introduced to enhance the learning experience.

⬤ Companion website

Lecturers who adopt this textbook for student purchase have access to Palgrave's password-protected website (contact your local sales representative for details). The website at **www.palgrave.com/business/brattonandgold** offers downloadable teaching support and other resources including:

- Suggested course outlines to demonstrate how to incorporate the text in your teaching.
- A conversion guide to show you how to change easily from using an alternative text to this *Human Resource Management: Theory and Practice*.
- Lecture notes for each chapter expanding the content in the book and providing advice for teaching each topic. This includes lecture enhancement notes providing new ideas for adding further dimensions to lectures.
- PowerPoint lecture slides for each chapter, including key points and definitions, learning objectives and relevant figures and tables, which you can edit for your own use.

Students also have free access to:

- extensive web links to further resources around the world to help them research topics in more depth
- summary lecture notes to accompany each chapter topic
- skill development exercises to improve their professional competencies
- a searchable online glossary to check on definitions of key terms.

Overall, we are confident that the incorporation of new material and student-focused features will continue to make *Human Resource Management: Theory and Practice* a valuable learning resource. We are also confident that this book will encourage the reader to question, to doubt, to investigate, to be sceptical and to seek different causes when analysing the problems and challenges of managing people in the workplace. We would welcome any feedback on the text or any suggestions on how we can improve the next edition. Please contact us via our email addresses listed on the companion website.

JOHN BRATTON
JEFFREY GOLD

Acknowledgements

This textbook was originally inspired by the teaching and research in which we were involved at Leeds Business School and the University College of the Cariboo, Canada.

The third edition of *Human Resource Management: Theory and Practice* has been improved by the comments and suggestions of colleagues, anonymous reviewers and students. We have endeavoured to incorporate their insights and criticisms to improve this edition. We are particularly indebted to the reviewers: Jane Mason, Department of Business and Management Studies, De Montfort University; Dr Julian Gould-Williams, Cardiff Business School, Cardiff University; Cliff Lockyer, Department of Human Resource Management, University of Strathclyde; Dr Jackie Granleese, School of Management, University of East Anglia; Dr Tahir Nisar, School of Management, University of Southampton.

John Bratton would like to recognize Michelle Jeffery, at the University College of the Cariboo, for her excellent research assistance, and Amy Bratton, University of Calgary, for her help in typing part of the manuscript. Special thanks also to Carolyn Forshaw, at the University College of the Cariboo, who provided so much valuable insight and assistance with the manuscript and the web support material. He also wishes to thank Bernard Igwe, John Dumesnil and Lorne Bellamy, at the University College of the Cariboo, for their friendship and support.

Jeffrey Gold would like to thank Rick Holden, Stuart Watson, John Hamblett, Vicky Harte and Les Hamilton at Leeds Business School for their undying support. He would also like to express his gratitude to Mike Rix at NTP Meridian, Lloyd and Sallie Davies, Howard Pickard and Hugh Clark at LBBC, David Firth at Treefrog, Andrew Choi at WY Business Link, Peter Mullinger at Croda Chemicals and Steve Francis at Simply Fresh Foods.

Finally, we are grateful for the professional advice and support shown by our publishers, Sarah Brown and Helen Bugler, throughout the project.

People Management, from which some of the HRM in practice articles in this book are taken, is the magazine of the Chartered Institute of Personnel and Development, with a circulation of 107,648 every fortnight. It is sent to all CIPD members, and is available on subscription. For details and a sample copy, contact *PM* by phone, on 020 7880 6200, or fax on 020 7336 7635. Alternatively visit them online at www.peoplemanagement.co.uk.

The authors and publishers are grateful to the following for permission to reproduce copyright material:

The Free Press, a Division of Simon & Schuster Adult Publishing Group, for Figure 2.4: from *Competitive Advantage: Creating and Sustaining Superior Performance* by Michael E. Porter. Copyright © 1985, 1998 by Michael E. Porter.

Random House for the extract from *On the Edge* by W. Hutton and A. Giddens, published by Jonathan Cape. Used by permission of The Random House Group Limited.

Globe and Mail for HRM in practice 2.1, 2.3, 3.2, 3.3, 3.4, 3.5, 4.3, 5.3, 9.2, and 12.1. Reprinted by permission.

Suzanne Wintrob for HRM in practice 9.1: from *Globe and Mail*, 2001, February 1.

Taylor & Francis Ltd (http://www.tandf.co.uk/journals) for Tables 1.1 and 1.2: from 'Human resource management and performance: a review and research agenda', David E. Guest (1997) *International Journal of Human Resource Management*, 8(3): 263–76; and for Figure 1.6 by C. Hendry and A. Pettigrew (1990): from *International Journal of Human Resource Management*, 1(1): 17–44.

The *Guardian* for HRM in practice 5.2: by David Henke, 2001, July 30. © The Guardian.

Colin Cottell for HRM in practice 5.1: from the *Guardian*, 2001, July 28.

People Management for HRM in practice 1.1, 1.2, 1.3, 4.2, 6.1, 6.2, 7.1, 7.2, 8.1, 8.2, 9.3, 10.1, 10.3, 11.1, 11.3, 12.2 and 13.3.

Journal of Management for Figure 2.7: adapted from 'Firm resources and sustained competitive advantage' by J. B. Barney (1991), 17(1): 99–120.

Houghton-Mifflin for Figure 2.7: adapted from *Strategic Management and Theory*, 5th edn, by C. Hill and G. Jones (2001).

Bank of England *Quarterly Bulletin* for Figure 3.4: Autumn, 2001 p. 341.

Routledge for Tables 3.3, 3.4, 11.1, 11.2, 12.2 and 12.5: adapted from *All Change at Work?* by N. Millward, A. Bryson and J. Forth (2000); and for Tables 11.1, 11.2, 13.3: adapted from *Britain at Work* by M. Cully, S. Woodland, A. O'Reilly and G. Dix (1999).

TUC Research Department (2002) for Table 12.4.

Personnel Psychology for Figure 7.2: from 'The People Make the Place' by B. Schneider (1987), 40: 437–53; and for Figure 10.2: from 'Transfer of Training: A Review and Directions for Future Research' by T. T. Baldwin and J. K. Ford (1988), 41: 63–105.

Organizational Dynamics for Table 8.4: from 'Implications of Self-Other Rating Agreement for Human Resource Management' by F. J. Yammarino and L. E. Atwater (1997), 25(4): 35–44.

Butterworth for Figures 11.7 and 11.9 from *Selwyn's Law of Employment*, 11th edn, by N. M. Selwyn (2000).

Labour Force Survey Data (2001) for Table 12.1.

June Williamson for HRM in practice 10.2.

Every effort has been made to trace all the copyright-holders, but if any have been inadvertently overlooked the publishers will be pleased to make the necessary arrangements at the first opportunity.

List of abbreviations

ACAS	Advisory, Conciliation and Arbitration Service	HSE	Health and Safety Executive
AEEU	Amalgamated Engineering and Electrical Union	ICT	information and communication technology
AIDS	acquired immune deficiency syndrome	IIP	Investors in People
		ILA	Individual Learning Account
BPR	business process re-engineering	IPD	Institute of Personnel and Development (now CIPD)
CBI	Confederation of British Industry	IPM	Institute of Personnel Management
CIPD	Chartered Institute of Personnel and Development	IPRP	individual performance-related pay
CoP	communities of practice		
CPD	continuous professional development	ISO	International Standards Organization
DETR	Department of the Environment, Transport and the Regions	JCC	joint consultative committee
		JIT	just-in-time
EI	employee involvement	LEC	Local Enterprise Companies
EIRO	European Industrial Relations Observatory	LMC	labour–management committee
		LSC	Learning and Skills Council
ERP	enterprise resource planning	MSF	Manufacturing, Science and Finance union (UK)
EU	European Union		
EWC	European Works Council	NAFTA	North Atlantic Free Trade Agreement
FFM	five-factor model		
GDP	gross domestic product	NGA	National Graphical Association
GPMU	Graphical, Paper and Media Union	NVQ	National Vocational Qualification
		OECD	Organisation for Economic Co-operation and Development
HASAWA	Health and Safety at Work etc. Act 1974	PDP	performance and development plan
HIV	human immunodeficiency virus		
HPWS	high-performing work system	PMS	performance management system
HR	human resources		
HRA	human resource accounting	PODC	planning, organizing, directing and controlling
HRIS	human resource information system		
		QWL	quality of working life
HRM	human resource management	RJP	realistic job preview
HRP	human resource planning	RMT	National Union of Rail, Maritime and Transport Workers
HSC	Health and Safety Commission		

ROI	return on investment	TEC	Training and Enterprise Councils
SBS	sick building syndrome	TQC	total quality control
SHRM	strategic human resource management	TUC	Trades Union Congress
SOGAT	Society of Graphical and Allied Trades	UfI	University for Industry
		VCS	video-conferencing system
STF	Skills Task Force	WERS98	Workplace Employee Relations Survey 1998
SVQ	Scottish Vocational Qualification	WHO	World Health Organization
SWOT	strengths, weaknesses, opportunities and threats		

Part One

The human resource management arena

Chapter one

The nature of human resource management

John Bratton

Human resource management (HRM) is a strategic approach to managing employment relations which emphasizes that leveraging people's capabilities is critical to achieving sustainable competitive advantage, this being achieved through a distinctive set of integrated employment policies, programmes and practices.

'The real sources of competitive leverage [are] the culture and capabilities of your organization that derive from how you manage your people.'[1]

'The whole emphasis on people, as one of the most important competitive advantages a company can create, demands that top management attract, cultivate, and keep the best workforce they can possibly find.'[2]

'The role of [human resources] is becoming as important if not more than any other executive leadership function.'[3]

Chapter outline

Chapter objectives

After studying this chapter, you should be able to:

1. Evaluate the development of human resource management (HRM)
2. Explain the central features of the contract in the employment relationship
3. Summarize the key HRM functions
4. Explain the theoretical issues surrounding the HRM debate
5. Compare and contrast personnel management and HRM as approaches to managing employment relations
6. Explain the different approaches to studying HRM

This book is concerned with managing people at work. The quotations that opened this chapter provide an insight into how the human resource function is viewed by academics and practitioners at the beginning of the 21st century. In recent times, human resource management (HRM) has assumed new prominence because of continuing concerns about global competition, the internationalization of technology and the productivity of labour. It is argued that these market imperatives require managers to change the way in which they manage the employment relationship in order to allow for the most effective utilization of human resources (HR). Managers and academics argue that the traditional approaches to managing workers are inappropriate and 'can no longer deliver the goods' (Betcherman et al., 1994, p. 2). Harnessing workers' full potential and producing the attitudes and behaviour considered necessary for a competitive advantage require three aspects of managerial control to change: organizational design, culture, and HR policies and practices. Current managerial orthodoxy therefore argues the need for a restructuring towards 'flat' hierarchical structures, an enlargement of job tasks with greater employee autonomy, and managerial leadership to shape the more intangible aspects of the workplace, for example beliefs, norms and values. For some, HRM is associated with a set of distinctive 'best' practices that aim to recruit, develop, reward and manage people in ways that create a sustainable commitment to high commitment management, or what North American academics term 'high-performing work systems'.

The seminal book *New Perspectives on Human Resource Management*, edited by John Storey (1989), generated the 'first wave' of debate on the nature and ideological significance of the 'progressive' HRM model. This debate on the alleged shift from personnel management to the HRM model has been particularly fierce among academics in Britain but has also taken place in many other countries (Storey, 1995). By the late 1990s, a 'second wave' of debate emerged with four distinct themes: the significance of the economic and social context in shaping and reshaping the HRM arena; the links between HRM and organizational performance; the new organizational forms and relationships; and the importance of 'knowledge' management and learning in the workplace (Mabey et al., 1998).

The discourse produced normative models, evidence of a direct connection between 'bundles' of best HRM practices and organizational performance (Baker, 1999; Buyens & De Vos, 2001; Hutchinson et al., 2000; Purcell, 1999), and exposed familiar tensions and paradoxes in the HRM model (Sparrow & Marchington, 1998). Since 1998, when we were writing the second edition of this book, the focus of much empirical work has explored the 'added value' of the HRM function and the role of HR professionals within that process. We have acknowledged the importance of this development in HRM research by extending our discussion on this important topic to a whole new chapter. The link between HRM practices and business performance and the role of the HR specialist has been a focus for studies for over a decade (for example Storey, 1992; Tyson & Fell, 1986), but recent work by Caldwell (2001), exploring the HR director's role as a 'change agent', is a reminder that any typology that differentiates the HR role is in reality multifaceted and complex.

The HRM movement has exposed many of the old underlying tensions and paradoxes that have caused some observers to talk of a 'crisis of confidence' in the field (Sparrow & Marchington, 1998), and recent events may indeed justify the crisis in confidence in the HRM metaphor. During the 2001–02 economic recession in the world's largest economy, the USA, most business organizations, rather than look to the HRM elixir for survival, followed the conventional wisdom of business strategy: restructuring, delayering and redundancies. The tensions between HRM rhetoric and reality have led others to emphasize the deep divisions among practitioners concerning the personnel versus HRM debate. Classifying HRM practitioners into three groups – 'believers', 'atheists' and 'agnostics' – Grant and Oswick (1998) conclude that many practitioners who believe in HRM have had their faith 'installed' by the Institute of Personnel and Development (IPD). The IPD is characterized as 'an unwitting preacher' encouraging practitioners to believe in something that is unproven in reality. This chapter examines the complex debate surrounding the nature and significance of the HRM model. To make sense of the HRM discourse, however, it is important for us to briefly examine the history of personnel/HRM.

REFLECTIVE QUESTION

Based upon your reading or own work experience, how can HR specialists help line managers to do their job?

The history of human resource management

In the management literature, there is an awareness that developments in HRM are mediated by product and labour markets, social movements and public policies that are shaped by past patterns of historical development and current societal changes and beliefs. Fashions come and go, and the same might be said about approaches to people management.

Personnel management: an established orthodoxy

The roots of people management can be traced back to the Industrial Revolution in England in the late 18th century, but we will begin our discussion with the economic and political conditions prevailing after the Second World War of 1939–45. The war increased the demand for labour and personnel specialists, and in 1946 those professionals working in people management established the Institute of Personnel Management (IPM). The period 1950–74 was the 'golden age' of Keynesian economic doctrine, evidenced by the post-war Labour government's commitment 'to combine a free democracy with a planned economy' (Coates, 1975, p. 46). After 1951, little changed because the Conservative government was also anxious to foster industrial peace through conciliation, mediation and arbitration (Crouch, 1982). In the 1960s, however, employment laws were passed that encouraged growth in the personnel function. Moreover, British industrial relations were the focus of intense political controversy over the allegedly intolerable level of strikes. The Donovan Commission (1965–68) investigated these developments and recommended, among other things, that management should develop joint (union–management) procedures for the speedy settlement of grievances.

In the 1970s, new legislation promoting sexual equality and standards in employment, combined with the prescriptions contained in the Donovan Commission's report (1968), amplified the status of the personnel function. Parallel to these public policy developments ran the rise of productivity bargaining, which had the effect of extending the personnel manager's function into the 'fabric of the business – the improvement of profitability' (Clegg, 1979, p. 100). The Donovan Commission observed the growth in personnel management. 'From a tiny band of women factory welfare officers in 1914, personnel managers have multiplied to well over ten thousand today, most of them men' (1968, p. 25). A decade later, Brown's (1981) study found that 46 per cent of the manufacturing establishments sampled had personnel officers with some responsibility for 'dealing with trade unions'. Between 1956 and 1989, IPM membership rose from 3979 to 35,548 (Farnham, 1990).

Analysing why men have dominated the HR profession lies outside the scope of this chapter, but Townley (1994) offers one explanation. She argues that gender was a dimension in the relative employment opportunities in the workplace as 'soft' training positions went to women and senior industrial relations negotiating positions devolved to men. The current debate on HRM is heavily gendered: 'Put bluntly, the focus of HRM – an agenda, in the main, prescribed by men – has been "important" men in one field (academia) talking to, reflecting and reporting on "important" men in another (business)' (Townley, 1994, p. 16). If we accept a feminist critique, the gender dimension has also shaped the way in which personnel management and HRM have been constituted as a subject for study (see, for example, Mills & Tancred, 1992).

HRM WEB LINKS

Go to the websites of the HR professional associations (e.g. Australia www.ahri.com.au; Britain www.cipd.co.uk; Canada www.hrpao.org; USA www.shrm.org; South Africa www.ipm.co.za) and click on the 'mission statement' or 'history' sections. Evaluate the information on the site in terms of the material covering the history of personnel management. What are the origins of the association?

The human resource management phenomenon

The 1980s and 90s witnessed a period of radical change in both the context and content of people management. Western economies saw the renaissance of 'market disciplines' and a strong belief that, in terms of economic well-being, too much government was the problem. The new economic orthodoxy insisted that the role of government was mainly to facilitate this laissez-faire agenda (Kuttner, 2000), the rise of radical Conservative governments in Britain and the USA providing the political and economic backdrop to the shift in managerial thought and discourse. Whereas personnel management based its legitimacy and influence on its ability to deal with the uncertainties stemming from full employment and trade union growth, HRM concentrated more attention on internal sources of competitive advantage. The debate on HRM policies and practices focused on 'hard' and 'soft' versions of HRM. The 'hard' version emphasized the term 'resource' and adopted a 'rational' approach to managing employees, that is, viewing employees as any other economic factor, as a cost that had to be controlled. The 'soft' HRM model, however, emphasized the term 'human' and thus advocated investment in training and development and the adoption of 'commitment' strategies to ensure that highly skilled and loyal employees gave the organization a competitive advantage.

For some academics, the HRM model represented a distinctive approach to managing the employment relationship that fitted the new economic order (Bamberger & Meshoulam, 2000; Beer et al., 1984; Betcherman et al., 1994) and heralded the beginnings of a new theoretical sophistication in the area of personnel management (Boxall, 1992). For others, however, the HRM model was characterized as a manipulative form of management control causing work intensification (Wells, 1993), and as a cultural construct concerned with moulding employees to corporate values (Keenoy & Anthony, 1992; Townley, 1994). The HRM 'cottage industry' spawned a spate of books (including the first edition of this text) and articles advocating, analysing or contesting the concept and significance of HRM. The HRM model, among both its advocates and its detractors, came to represent 'one of the most controversial signifiers in managerial debate' (Storey, 1989, p. 4). In 1994, the IPD was formed by the merger of the IPM and the Institute of Training and Development. A recognition of the strategic importance of HRM came in 2000 when the IPD was awarded chartered status and became the Chartered Institute of Personnel and Development (CIPD).

● Management and human resource management

The term 'human resource management' has been the subject of considerable debate, and its underlying philosophy and character are highly controversial. Much of this controversy stems from the absence of a precise formulation of and agreement on its significance (Storey, 1989, 1995a). We obviously need a definition of the subject matter if we are to analyse and understand HRM theory and practice, although we accept that this will be only one of several possible definitions. This is our own attempt at a definition:

> Human resource management (HRM) is a strategic approach to managing employment relations which emphasizes that leveraging people's capabilities is critical to achieving sustainable competitive advantage, this being achieved through a distinctive set of integrated employment policies, programmes and practices.

Human resource management, as we have portrayed it, underlines a belief that people really make the difference; only *people* among other resources have the capacity to generate value. It follows from this premise that human knowledge and skills are a *strategic* resource that needs to be adroitly managed. Another distinguishing feature of HRM relates to the notion of *integration*. A set of employment policies, programmes and practices needs to be coherent and integrated with organizational strategy. It follows, therefore, that if the workforce is so critical for organizational success, the responsibility for HRM activities rests with all *line managers* and should not be left to HR specialists (Schonberger, 1982; Storey, 1992, 1995a, 2001). Since most readers of this textbook will be line managers rather than HR specialists, this book is orientated towards helping people to manage others more effectively and equitably, whether they become line managers or chief executive officers. To grasp the nature and significance of HRM, it is necessary to understand both the management process and the role of HRM within it. Before we do this, however, we should explain why managing the 'human resource' is different from managing other resources.

The meaning of 'human resource'

First and foremost, people in work organizations set overall strategies and goals, design work systems, produce goods and services, monitor quality, allocate financial resources and market products and services. Human beings therefore become a 'human resource', or what economists call human capital by virtue of the roles they assume in the work organization. Employment roles are defined and described in a manner designed to maximize particular employees' contributions to achieving organizational objectives. Schultz (1981), an economist who won the Nobel Prize in 1979, argued that economic development depended on the application of knowledge, calling this aspect of economics 'human capital' and offering this definition (Schultz, 1981, p. 21; quoted in Fitz-enz, 2000, p. xii):

> Consider all human abilities to be either innate or acquired. Every person is born with a particular set of genes, which determines his [sic] innate ability. Attributes of acquired population quality, which are valuable and can be augmented by appropriate investment, will be treated as human capital.

In management terms, 'human capital' or 'human resource' refers to the traits people bring to the workplace – intelligence, aptitudes, commitment, tacit knowledge and skills, and the ability to learn. But the contribution of this human resource to the organization is typically variable and unpredictable. This indeterminacy of an employee's contribution to his or her organization's activities makes the human resource the 'most vexatious of assets to manage' (Fitz-enz, 2000, p. xii).

The open-ended nature of the human component drives much of the research in organizational behaviour. One set of perspectives, drawing on psychology, suggests that the behaviour of people in the workplace is a function of at least four variables: ability, motivation, role perception and situational contingencies (McShane, 2001). Another set of perspectives, drawing on sociology, emphasizes the problematic nature of employment relations – the interrelated problems of 'control' and 'commitment' (Baldamus, 1961; Watson, 1986). Human capital differs from other resources, partly because individuals are endowed with various levels of ability (including aptitudes, skills and knowledge), with differences in personality traits, gender, role perception and experience, and partly as a result of differences in motivation and commitment. In other words, employees differ from other resources because of their ability to evaluate and to question management's actions, and their commitment and cooperation always has to be won. In addition, employees have the capacity to form groups and trade unions to defend or further their own economic interest.

The meaning of 'management'

The term management may be applied to either a social group or a process. When applied to a process, 'management' conjures up a variety of images of managerial work, but it would be misleading to define a manager in terms of the tasks that she or he performs. A homemaker, for example, plans and organizes tasks in the home – does this make him or her a manager (Grint, 1995; Hales, 1986; Stewart, 1998)?

The answer to the question, 'Who is a manager?', depends not upon the tasks undertaken but upon an individual's social position in the organization's hierarchy. A manager is an organizational member who is 'institutionally empowered to determine

HRM IN PRACTICE 1.1

RAIL FIRMS SHUNT 'OLD BR WAY' INTO SIDINGS

NEIL MERRICK *PEOPLE MANAGEMENT*

Great North Eastern Railway (GNER), which operates trains between London and the north-east, celebrated its first birthday earlier this month by announcing that it would spend an extra £1 million on training over the next four years.

The investment, taking the company's annual training budget to £1.25 million, will allow it to place extra emphasis on customer service and to introduce core competencies for managers.

Twenty 'on-board coaches', will work alongside inspectors, caterers and other staff to assist them in meeting new delivery standards. 'Traditionally, managers have told employees what to do,' said Victoria McKechnie, the firm's HR development manager, who worked with many members of the coaching staff when the line was owned by British Rail. 'The idea of appointing coaches is to create a peer group on board the trains that will help to enhance customer service.'

Some of the new money will be spent on a management-training programme, which is being introduced in July to coincide with the new performance management system. The course will revolve around 12 core competencies, including teamworking, creativity and building relationships, that were proposed by managers.

According to McKechnie, the 'old BR way' of sending people on training courses has been abandoned in favour of coaching, mentoring and secondments. Managers and other employees are, with the assistance of the training department, responsible for identifying and meeting their own training needs.

'They want to make safety secondary to revenue-raising,' Harries said. 'It is absolutely critical that, if a train breaks down, the people left in control know what they are doing.'

Midland Main Line (MML) is organising a 'Winning the Future' programme, under which all 600 employees who have direct contact with customers or fill support roles will attend a two-day programme focusing on culture change. About 300 maintenance staff will take part in similar events at their depots.

MML, privatised in April 1996, spends about £800,000 per year on training. Barry Brown, customer services director, hopes that events focusing on culture and attitude change will be held annually, with all staff spending up to five days away from the workplace.

'It's the hearts and minds of front-line managers that have got to change,' he said. 'They are a pivotal influence on the staff below them.'

Richard Greenhill, an IPD vice-president, believes that training is encouraging employees to review traditional roles. 'People can organise themselves more effectively if they are prepared to be flexible and cross boundaries that they didn't cross previously,' he said.

Anglia Railways, privatised in January, has expanded its customer service programme to cover all its 650 staff. The company has also introduced a training scheme for telesales and ticket-office staff. Among the areas covered are proactive selling, such as asking a customer if they want to upgrade to first-class travel. 'In the past, railways have not been very good at selling themselves,' said Peter Meades, Anglia's communications manager.

Laurie Harries, spokesman for the RMT [National Union of Rail, Maritime, and Transport Workers], said that the rail workers' union had always argued for better customer service training, but it was concerned that the rail operators might go too far in ending demarcation. The RMT is opposing proposals under consideration by a Railtrack working party that would see guards spending more time collecting money from passengers, rather than performing other duties.

'They want to make safety secondary to revenue-raising,' Harries said. 'It is absolutely critical that, if a train breaks down, the people left in control know what they are doing.'

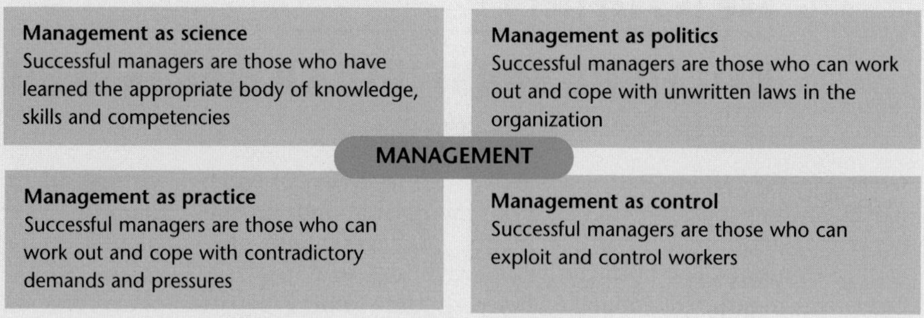

Management as science
Successful managers are those who have learned the appropriate body of knowledge, skills and competencies

Management as politics
Successful managers are those who can work out and cope with unwritten laws in the organization

MANAGEMENT

Management as practice
Successful managers are those who can work out and cope with contradictory demands and pressures

Management as control
Successful managers are those who can exploit and control workers

Figure 1.1 Management as science, politics, control and practice
Source: Based on Watson (1986) and Reed (1989)

and/or regulate certain aspects of the actions of others' (Willmott, 1984, p. 350). Collectively, managers are traditionally differentiated horizontally by their functional activities and vertically by the level at which they are located in their organizational hierarchy. Management has been variously conceptualized as a 'system of authority and administration' to achieve the semblance of congruence and direction in organizations (Mintzberg, 1989, p. 7), as 'art, science, magic and politics' (Watson, 1986, p. 28) and as a process designed to coordinate and control productive activities (for example Reed, 1989; Thompson & McHugh, 2002). In order to study the complex and contradictory nature of managerial work, we will examine various theoretical perspectives, thus developing a more in-depth understanding of the factors that shape the HRM process.

Drawing upon the work of Watson (1986) and Reed (1989), we can identify four major analytical perspectives that have shaped the study of management (Figure 1.1):

1. the science perspective
2. the political perspective
3. the control perspective
4. the practice perspective.

Fayol (1949) articulated the notion that management is a *science*. In his seminal work, Fayol identified a distinct body of knowledge and managerial activities, from **p**lanning and **o**rganizing to **d**irecting and **c**ontrolling – the PODC tradition – which offers an idealized image of management as a rationally designed and operationalized tool for realizing organizational goals.

The *political perspective* provides a view of management that characterizes the workplace as a purposive miniature society with politics pervading all managerial work. By politics, we mean here the power relationships between managers and relevant others, and in turn the capacity of an individual manager to influence others who are in a state of dependence. This perspective on studying management offers an approach that examines individual managers as 'knowledgeable human agents' functioning within a dynamic arena where both organizational resources and outcomes can be substantially shaped by their actions. It reinforces the theoretical and practical importance attached to building alliances and networks of cooperative relationships among organizational members. The political perspective has been criticized for failing to give sufficient attention to 'power struggles' in the workplace (for example

Salaman, 1979; Willmott, 1984), which is the essence of the 'radical' control perspective on management.

The *control perspective* conceptualizes management as a controlling agent that serves the economic imperatives imposed by capitalist market relations. Managerial control is thus *the* central focus of management activity. According to this perspective, management structures and labour strategies are instruments and techniques to control the labour process in order to secure a high level of labour productivity and corresponding profitability. This approach to management has come to be associated with the seminal work of Braverman (1974) and the labour process school, to which his work has given rise. This recognizes the existence of inconsistent organizational designs and management practices, these paradoxical tendencies providing the source of further management strategies that attempt to eradicate the tensions caused by these paradoxes. The most important of these paradoxes is considered to be the simultaneous desire for control over, and yet cooperation and commitment from, workers.

The *practice perspective* sees management as an activity aimed at the continual melioration of diverse, fragmented and usually contested complex practices. According to Reed (1989), it addresses the limitations of the first three perspectives by recognizing that management is indeed a science but, at the same time, involves both a political process and control mechanisms. Furthermore, Reed (1989, p. 21) contends that within the practice perspective, organizations 'generate both structural and processual contradictions that will be reflected within management practice'. Managers will therefore be called upon to secure subordinates' discipline and consent simultaneously, and, given the heterogeneous nature of management, they will be divided over how these mutually incompatible objectives are to be achieved. A nexus of HRM practices and supporting rationales will typically be constructed to provide the mechanisms by which managers strive to secure control over and commitment from their organizational members, in other words ensuring that employees are manageable.

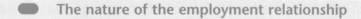

REFLECTIVE QUESTION

What do you think of these four perspectives of management? Do they help to explain managerial behaviour? Do they help us in understanding the uncertainties and conflicts encountered in managing people?

The nature of the employment relationship

The nature of the relationship between individuals and their work organization is clearly an issue of central importance to HRM. Although the term employment relationship appears to be self-explanatory, it contains components that make it different from other contractual relationships. The employment relationship describes dynamic interlocking relations that exist between individuals and their work organizations, research into the employment relationship having drawn attention to relations in the workplace orientated towards the:

- economic
- legal
- social
- psychological.

At its most basic, the employment relationship embraces an *economic* relationship: the 'exchange of pay for work' (Brown, 1988, p. 55). When people enter the workplace, they enter into a *pay–effort bargain*, which places an obligation on both the employer and the employee: in exchange for a wage or salary paid by the employer, the employee is obligated to perform a certain amount of physical or intellectual labour. The pay–effort bargain is relevant for understanding how far the employment relationship is inherently conflictual or consensual. In the capitalist labour market, people sell their labour and seek to maximize their pay. To the employer, pay is a cost that, all things being equal, reduces profit and therefore needs to be minimized. Thus, as Brown (1988, p. 57) states, 'Conflict is structured into employment relations' as logic makes the pay to one group the cost to the other. The 'effort' or 'work' side of the contract also generates tensions and conflict because it is inherently imprecise and indeterminate. The contract permits the employer to buy a *potential* level of physical or intellectual labour, the function of management therefore being to transform this potential into actual value-added labour. HR practices are designed to narrow the gap between employees' potential and actual performance or, as Townley (1994, p. 14) explains:

> Personnel practices measure both the physical and subjective dimensions of labour, and offer a technology which aims to render individuals and their behaviour predictable and calculable ... to bridge the gap between promise and performance, between labour power and labour, and organizes labour into a productive force or power.

The second component of the employment relationship is that it involves a *legal* relationship: a network of common law and statutory rights and obligations affecting both parties to the contract. A contract of employment can be entered into informally or formally; it can emerge as a result of a conversation at the office door, interviews, an exchange of letters or negotiations, and it is in principle subject to the general contractual rules of common law (Selwyn, 2000). A contract freely negotiated between an individual and his or her employer is, according to Wedderburn (1986), central to the understanding of the employment relationship in English law. There is an array of legislation that impacts on the employer–employee relationship and employer–union relationship: the 'right to manage', the 'right not to be unfairly dismissed', the 'right to bargain'. Today, a complex network of UK and European Union statutory rights modifies the employment relationship for employees, a 'floor of rights' that regulates the obligations of the worker and employer even though they are not (for the most part) inserted in formal terms into the employment contract itself. In the event of any violation, legal rights can be enforced by some compulsory mechanism provided by the state (Hepple, 1983). For a more detailed discussion on the legal regulation of the employment relations, see 'The state and the employment relationship' in Chapter 3.

The third distinguishing component of the employment relationship is that it involves a *social* relationship. Managerial and non-managerial employees are not isolated individuals but members of social groups responding to 'social norms' that influence their actions in the workplace. This observation of human behaviour in the workplace, documented since the 1930s, is highly relevant given the increased use of work teams (Cully et al., 1999). Furthermore, unless the employee happens to be an international soccer or hockey celebrity, the employment relationship typically involves an uneven balance of social power between the employer and the employee. The notion in English law of a 'freely' negotiated individual agreement is misleading: in reality, without collective (trade union) or statutory intervention, the most powerful party – the employer – imposes the agreement by 'the brute facts of power' (Wedderburn, 1986, p. 106). The social dimension of the employment relationship thus relates to the issue of power in the workplace.

The fourth component of the employment relationship is a dynamic two-way exchange of perceived promises and obligations between employees and their organization – the *psychological* contract (Guest & Conway, 2002; Herriot, 1998; Kramer & Tyler, 1996; Rousseau, 1995). The concept of the psychological contract was written about in the early 1960s but has in recent years become a 'fashionable' framework within which to study aspects of the employment relationship (Guest & Conway, 2002; Sisson & Storey, 2000). One reason for the increased focus on the more cognitively driven aspects of the employment relationship is corporate restructuring. Organizations seek both flexibility and employee commitment, and the restructuring of many corporations has an increased number of 'non-standard' forms of employment (temporary, part time, contract work), which has led to a 'no-guarantees' attitude among many organizations (Rousseau, 1995). Yet when competitive advantage appears to come from leveraging managerial or 'knowledge' workers' intellectual assets, and when those 'human assets' can walk out of the door to work for a competitor, the notion of employee commitment emphasizes the importance of managing the psychological contract (Rousseau, 1995) and why we need to examine this contemporary concept more fully.

The 'psychological contract' is a metaphor that captures a wide variety of largely unwritten expectations and understandings of the two parties about their mutual obligations. Rousseau (1995, p. 9) defines it as 'individual beliefs, shaped by the organization, regarding the terms of an exchange agreement between individuals and their organization'. Most who debate the concept view it as a two-way exchange of perceived promises and obligations. Guest and Conway (2002, p. 22) have conducted empirical studies on the psychological contract, defining it as 'the perceptions of both parties to the employment relationship – organization and individual – of the reciprocal promises and obligations implied in that relationship'. At the heart of the concept lie levers for individual commitment, motivation and task performance that go *beyond* 'expected outcomes' (Figure 1.2).

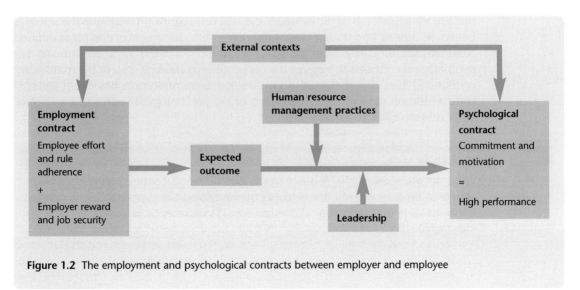

Figure 1.2 The employment and psychological contracts between employer and employee

The concept of the psychological contract has a number of important features that challenge managers. The organization does not always communicate with one voice, and ineffective communication practices are more likely to create different beliefs about the reciprocal promises and obligations (Guest & Conway, 2002). Thus, individual employees will have different perceptions of their psychological contract even when the legal contract is itself identical. Managers will therefore be faced with a multitude of potential psychological contracts within the same organization (Bendal et al., 1998). A second feature of the psychological contract challenging to managers is that it reaffirms the notion that the employment relationship is perceived to be one of exchange, the *promissory* exchange of offers and the mutual obligation to fulfil these offers on the part of the organization and employee. As Rousseau (1995, p. xi) observes, 'Promises about the future are the essence of contracts'. Yet research confirms that senior managers often fail to keep their promises (Guest & Conway, 2002). A third feature of psychological contracts is that they are shaped by the social and economic context, leadership, communication and HR practices. Rousseau (1995; Rousseau & Ho, 2000), for example, has persuasively shown that HR practices shape the day-to-day behaviours of employees and are 'the major means through which workers and their organization contract with each other. HR practices send strong messages to individuals regarding what the organization expects of them and what they can expect in return' (1995, pp. 182–3).

Let us try to illustrate how HR practices create contracts. Eleanor has just graduated from university and is considering applying to Zap Airlines for an entry-level management position. She goes to the company's website and reads in its mission statement 'We are a learning organization'. The job advertisement she reads in the newspaper states 'Excellent career prospects', and at the selection interview Eleanor is told 'We encourage you to complete an MBA'. Two weeks later, Eleanor receives a letter offering her the position and detailing her salary and other terms. Over the first 12 months, she works hard and frequently completes company work at the weekends, she hears stories from co-workers of other employees on the career 'fast track' being promoted, and at the year-end appraisal interview she is reassured 'Keep up the good work and you'll be promoted'. The psychological contract with Eleanor is in effect being conveyed via several communication channels, both written documents (for example mission statement, job advertisement) and oral discussions (for example the selection interview, 'stories' and the appraisal interview). Thus, HR practices and organizational communications create both formal (for example a letter of appointment) and psychological contracts to support the organizational strategy. Recent UK research has emphasized the importance of organizational communication practices: 'Effective communication reduces perceived breach of the psychological contract', assert Guest and Conway (2002, p. 35).

REFLECTIVE QUESTION

What do you think of the concept of the psychological contract? Why does there appear to be more interest in managing the psychological contract? How important is it to manage the psychological contract for (1) non-managerial employees and (2) managerial employees?

● Human resource management functions

HRM encompasses a body of knowledge and a set of policies and practices that shape the nature of work and regulate the employment relationship. Drawing on Squires' (2001) work, these practices suggest three basic questions: What do HRM professionals do? What affects what they do? And how do HR professionals do what they do? To help us answer the first question, we will draw on the work of Millward et al., (1992, 2000) and Ulrich (1997) to identify eight key HRM functions, policies, programmes and practices designed in response to organizational goals and contingencies, and managed to achieve those goals. Each of the eight functions contains alternatives from which managers can choose. The functions are:

- *Planning:* preparing forecasts of future HR needs in the light of an organization's environment, mission and objectives, strategies, and internal strengths and weaknesses, including its structure, culture, technology and leadership.
- *Staffing:* obtaining people with the appropriate skills, abilities, knowledge and experience to fill jobs in the work organization. Key practices are human resource planning, job analysis, recruitment and selection.
- *Developing:* analysing learning requirements to ensure that employees possess the knowledge and skills to perform satisfactorily in their jobs or to advance in the organization. Performance appraisal can identify employees' key skills and 'competencies'.
- *Motivating:* the design and administration of reward systems. HR practices include job evaluation, performance appraisal, pay and benefits.
- *Maintaining:* the administration and monitoring of workplace safety, health and welfare policies to retain a competent workforce and comply with statutory standards and regulations.
- *Managing relationships:* encompasses a range of employee involvement/participation schemes in non-union or union workplaces. In a union environment, this includes negotiating contracts and administrating the collective agreement.
- *Managing change:* this involves helping others to envision the future, communicating this vision, setting clear expectations for performance and developing the capability to reorganize people and reallocate other resources.
- *Evaluating:* designing the procedures and processes that measure, evaluate and communicate the value-added component of HR practices and the entire HR system to the organization.

HRM IN PRACTICE 1.2

NORTHUMBERLAND IS STAR PERFORMER FOR BEST VALUE

EMMA DEEKS, *PEOPLE MANAGEMENT,* 2001, APRIL 5

Northumberland County Council's HR department has been awarded the best possible grade by the Best Value Inspection Service (BVIS) in the first wave of reviews of local government personnel services.

The Best Value regime places a duty on all councils to deliver the most economic, efficient and effective service possible.

Northumberland is the first

local government HR department to achieve three stars. The result was hailed by Terry Gorman, the outgoing president of the Society of Chief Personnel Officers in Local Government, as 'a triumph for local government HR and a model for everyone to aspire to'.

Nick Cook, personnel director at the council, welcomed the inspectors' verdict. 'This is a stunning result. I am delighted for my staff, who have performed exceptionally well over the past years, often in very difficult circumstances,' he said.

Describing the department as 'excellent and likely to improve', Darra Singh, director of the Northern region of BVIS, praised Northumberland's 'positive and active approach to continuous improvement'.

'The personnel service has a track record of leading change and has established and proven arrangements for improving its service,' Singh said.

'This is a stunning result. I am delighted for my staff, who have performed exceptionally well ... often in very difficult circumstances.'

York and Durham councils were also reviewed in this first round, and their HR departments were awarded one and two stars respectively.

Durham's HR department was judged to be 'good but unlikely to improve'. But Paul Boyd, policy and HR manager for Durham County Council, questioned his judgement.

'We've already drawn up a three-year improvement plan and we will improve what needs to be improved,' he told *PM*.

Ian McBride, head of HR at York City Council, whose department was described as 'fair and likely to improve', saw the judgement as 'a bit harsh'. He said that the department 'had improved dramatically since the inspectors' visit'.

Copies of the BVIS reports are available from the Audit Commission's web site (www.audit-commission.gov.uk).

HRM WEB LINKS

Go to the website of the 1998 Workplace Employee Relations Survey – www.dti.gov.uk/er/emar/1998WERS.htm – for data on the job responsibilities of HR specialists. Has there been any change in the functions performed by HR specialists over the past decade? Are they involved in all eight areas of activity described above?

In terms of the second question, 'What affects what they do?', the HR activities that managers undertake vary from one workplace to another depending upon the *contingencies* affecting management. These contingencies can be divided into three broad categories:

● external context
● strategy
● organization.

The external category encompasses economic, political and legal regulations, and social aspects (for a full discussion on this, see Chapter 3), the external variables framing the context for formulating competitive strategies (see Chapter 2). The organization category is subdivided into size, work and structure, and technology (see Chapters 4 and 5). A firm employing a large workforce is, for example, more likely to employ at least one HRM specialist to assist line managers with people-related issues.

It is important to recognize that HR policies and practices are contingent upon external and internal contexts and are highly interrelated. A company responding to competitive pressures may, for example, change its manufacturing strategy by introducing 'self-managed' teams. This will in turn cause changes in recruitment and selection, training and reward priorities – perhaps hiring people perceived to be 'team-players', designing cross-functional training or designing a reward system that encourages the sharing of information and learning. HRM practices therefore aim to achieve two sets of objectives: improving employee performance and enhancing organizational effectiveness.

The third question, 'How do HR professionals do what they do?' requires us to discuss the means or *skills* by which HR practitioners may accomplish their managerial work. Line managers and HR specialists use technical, cognitive and interpersonal processes and skills to accomplish their work (Squires, 2001; Yukl, 2002), fulfilling their role by mentoring and teaching (Agashae & Bratton, 2001; Senge, 1990). Power is important because it is part of the influence process, as are legal procedures. Communication practices and skills convey the formal and psychological contract to employees (Guest & Conway, 2002). Managing the employment relationship will involve a mix of processes and skills, individual managers varying in terms of their capacity or inclination to use them. These processes and skills therefore concern human relationships and go some way to explaining different management styles and the distinction between a manager and a leader (Bratton et al., in press; Kotter, 1990). The three related dimensions of HRM – functions, contingencies and skills – can be brought together and diagrammatically shown in a three-dimensional model (Figure 1.3).

This model implies not only that HRM is a multidimensional activity, but also that any analysis of it has to be multidirectional (Squires, 2001). We might therefore examine the effect of new technology (a contingency) on HR functions, such as training and development, and how such functions are translated into action, such as learning and communication processes. The model is useful in several ways:

- It serves as a pedagogical device that allows the reader to discover and connect specific aspects of HRM within a consistent, general framework.

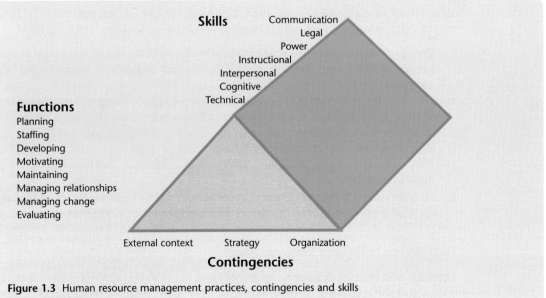

Figure 1.3 Human resource management practices, contingencies and skills
Source: Based upon Squires (2001)

● It offers HR specialists a sense of professional 'identity' by identifying professional functions, processes and skills.

● It helps the HR specialists to look beyond their immediate tasks and become aware of the 'totality of management' (ibid, p. 482).

HRM WEB LINKS

Go to the website of the HR professional associations (e.g. Australia www.ahri.com.au; Britain www.cipd.co.uk; Canada www.hrpao.org; USA www.shrm.org; or South Africa www.ipm.co.za) and click on the 'accreditation and/or certification' button. Using the information you find, compare the practices that HR professionals are formally accredited to undertake with the practices shown in Figure 1.3. Does the information on the website give a comprehensive picture of 'what HRM specialists do'?

● Theoretical perspectives on human resource management

Practice without theory is blind. (Hyman, 1989)

We have so far focused on the meaning of management and the practical contribution that HRM practice makes to the functioning of the modern work organization. We will now turn to an important part of the discourse – the search for the defining features of HRM – by addressing the theoretical perspectives in this area.

Models of human resource management

We can identify five major HRM models that seek to demonstrate analytically the qualitative differences between traditional personnel management and HRM (Beer et al., 1984; Fombrun et al., 1984; Guest, 1987; Hendry & Pettigrew, 1990; Storey, 1992). These models fulfil at least four important intellectual functions for those studying HRM:

1. They provide an analytical framework for studying HRM (for example, situational factors, stakeholders, strategic choice levels and notions of commitment and competence).
2. They legitimate certain HRM practices, a key issue here being the distinctiveness of HRM practices: 'it is not the presence of selection or training but a distinctive approach to selection or training that matters. It is the use of high performance or high commitment HRM practices' (Guest, 1997, p. 273).
3. They provide a characterization of HRM that establishes variables and relationships to be researched.
4. They serve as a heuristic device – something to help us discover and understand the world – for explaining the nature and significance of key HR practices.

The Fombrun, Tichy and Devanna model

The early HRM model developed by Fombrun et al., (1984) emphasizes the interrelatedness and the coherence of HRM activities. The HRM 'cycle' in their model consists

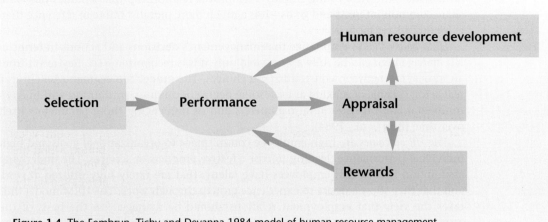

Figure 1.4 The Fombrun, Tichy and Devanna 1984 model of human resource management
Source: Adapted from Fombrun et al. (1984). Reprinted by permission of John Wiley and Sons Ltd

of four key constituent components: selection, appraisal, development and rewards (Figure 1.4), these four human resource activities aiming to increase organizational performance. The weakness of Fombrun et al.'s model lies in its apparently prescriptive nature, with its focus on four HR practices. It also ignores different stakeholder interests, situational factors and the notion of management's strategic choice. The strength of the model is, however, that it expresses the coherence of internal HR policies and the importance of 'matching' internal HR policies and practices to the organization's external business strategy (see Chapter 2). The 'HRM cycle' is also a simple model that serves as a heuristic framework for explaining the nature and significance of key HR practices and the interactions between the factors making up the complex fields of HRM.

The Harvard model

The analytical framework of the Harvard model offered by Beer et al. (1984) consists of six basic components – situational factors, stakeholder interests, HRM policy choices, HR outcomes, long-term consequences and a feedback loop via which the outputs flow directly into the organization and to the stakeholders (Figure 1.5).

The *situational factors* influence management's choice of HR strategy. This normative model incorporates workforce characteristics, management philosophy, labour market regulations, societal values and patterns of unionization, and suggests a meshing of both 'product market' and 'sociocultural logics' (Evans & Lorange, 1989). Analytically, both HRM scholars and practitioners will be more comfortable with contextual variables being included in the model because it conforms to the reality of what they know: 'the employment relationship entails a blending of business and societal expectations' (Boxall, 1992, p. 72).

The *stakeholder interests* recognize the importance of 'trade-offs', either explicitly or implicitly, between the interests of the owners and those of employees and their organizations, the unions. Although the model is still vulnerable to the charge of 'unitarism' – the view of the employer–employee relationship that assumes that both share common interests and goals – it is a much more pluralist frame of reference than is found in later models.

HRM policy choices emphasize that management's decisions and actions in terms of HR management can be fully appreciated only if it is recognized that they result from an interaction between constraints and choices. The model depicts management as a real actor, capable of making at least some degree of unique contribution within environmental and organizational parameters and of influencing those parameters itself over time (Beer et al., 1984).

The *HR outcomes* are high employee commitment to organizational goals and high individual performance, leading to cost-effective products or services. The underlying assumption here is that employees have talents that are rarely fully utilized at work and that they show a desire to experience growth through work. The HRM model thus takes the view that employment relations should be managed on the basis of the assumptions inherent in McGregor's (1960) approach to people-related issues that he called 'Theory Y'.[4]

The *long-term consequences* distinguish between three levels: individual, organizational and societal. At the level of the individual employee, the long-term outputs comprise the psychological rewards that workers receive in exchange for effort. At the organizational level, increased effectiveness ensures the survival of the organization. In turn, as a result of fully utilizing people at work, some of society's goals (for example, employment and growth) are attained at the societal level. A strength of the Harvard model is its classification of inputs and outcomes at both the organizational and the societal level, creating the basis for a critique of comparative HRM (Boxall,

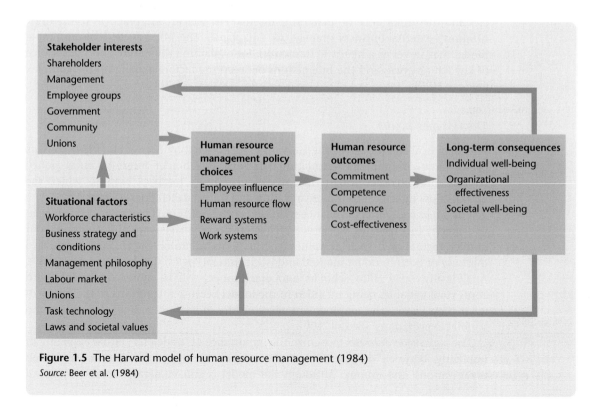

Figure 1.5 The Harvard model of human resource management (1984)
Source: Beer et al. (1984)

1992). A weakness, however, is the absence of a coherent theoretical basis for measuring the relationship between HR inputs, outcomes and performance (Guest, 1997).

The *feedback loop* is the sixth component of the Harvard model. As we have discussed above, situational factors influence HRM policy and choices, but, conversely, long-term outputs can also influence the situational factors, stakeholder interests and HR policies, the feedback loop in Figure 1.5 above reflecting this two-way relationship. The Harvard model clearly provides a useful analytical basis for studying HRM. It also contains elements that are analytical (situational factors, stakeholders, strategic choice levels) and prescriptive (notions of commitment, competence and so on) (Boxall, 1992).

The Guest model

David Guest (1989, 1997) has developed a more prescriptive theoretical framework reflecting the view that a core set of integrated HRM practices can achieve superior individual and organizational performance. According to Guest, HRM differs from personnel management, and he attempts to identify the major assumptions or stereotypes underpinning each approach to employment management (Table 1.1).

HRM is, according to the stereotypes shown in Table 1.1, distinctively different from personnel management because:

- it integrates human resources into strategic management
- it seeks a behavioural commitment to organizational goals
- the perspective is unitary, with a focus on the individual
- it works better in organizations that have an 'organic' structure
- the emphasis is on a full and positive utilization of human resources.

Implicit in the contrasting stereotypes is an assumption that HRM is 'better', but, as Guest (1987, p. 508) correctly states, 'this fails to take account of variations in context

Table 1.1 Points of difference between personnel management (PM) and human resource management (HRM)

	PM compliance	HRM commitment
Psychological contract	Fair day's work for a fair day's pay	Reciprocal commitment
Locus of control	External	Internal
Employee relations	Pluralist Collective Low trust	Unitarist Individual High trust
Organizing principles	Mechanistic Formal/defined roles Top-down Centralized	Organic Flexible roles Bottom-up Decentralized
Policy goals	Administrative efficiency Standard performance Cost minimization	Adaptive work-force Improving performance Maximum utilization

Source: Guest (1987)

Table 1.2 The Guest model of human resource management (HRM)

HRM strategy	HRM practices	HRM outcomes	Behaviour outcomes	Performance outcomes	Financial outcomes
Differentiation (innovation)	Selection		Effort/ motivation	High: Productivity	Profits
	Training	Commitment		Quality Innovation	
Focus (quality)	Appraisal		Cooperation		
	Rewards	Quality		Low:	Return on
Cost (cost- reduction)	Job design		Involvement	Absence Labour turnover Conflict	investment
	Involvement	Flexibility	Organizational citizenship	Customer complaints	
	Status and security				

Source: Guest (1997)

which might limit its effectiveness ... human resource management can most sensibly be viewed as an approach to managing the workforce'.

The central hypothesis of Guest's (1997) model is that if an integrated set of HR practices is applied in a coherent fashion, superior individual performance will result. It also assumes that this will result in superior organizational performance. The Guest model has six components (Table 1.2):

1. an HR strategy
2. a set of HR practices
3. a set of HR outcomes
4. behavioural outcomes
5. a number of performance outcomes
6. financial outcomes.

The model acknowledges the close links between HR strategy and general business strategies in terms of differentiation, focus and cost (see Chapter 2). The 'core' hypothesis, however, is that HR practices should be designed to lead to a set of HR outcomes of 'high employee commitment', 'high quality' and 'flexibility'. Like Beer et al., Guest sees high employee commitment as a critical HR outcome, concerned with the goals of binding employees to the organization and obtaining the behavioural outcomes of increased effort, cooperation and organizational citizenship. Quality refers to all aspects of employee behaviour, which bear directly on the quality of goods and services. Flexibility is concerned with employees' receptiveness to innovation and change. The right-hand side of the model focuses on the link between HR practices and performance. Only when all three HR outcomes – commitment, quality, and flexibility – have been achieved can we expect superior performance outcomes. As Guest (1989, 1997) emphasizes, these HRM goals are a 'package', and 'Only when a coherent strategy, directed towards these four policy goals, fully integrated into business strategy and fully sponsored by line management at all levels is applied will the high productivity and related outcomes sought by industry be achieved' (1990, p. 378).

Guest (1987, 1989, 1997) recognizes a number of conceptual issues associated with the HRM model. The first is that the values underpinning the model are predominantly individualist orientated: 'There is no recognition of any broader concept of pluralism within society giving rise to solidaristic collective orientation' (Guest, 1987, p. 519). The second conceptual issue concerns the status of some of the concepts. The important concept of commitment is, for example, suggested to be 'a rather messy, ill-defined concept' (Guest, 1987, pp. 513–14). A third issue is the explicit link between HRM and performance. This raises the problem of deciding which types of performance indicator to use in order to establish these links (see Chapter 13). It has been argued elsewhere that Guest's model may simply be an 'ideal type' towards which Western organizations can move, thus positing unrealistic conditions for the practice of HRM (Keenoy, 1990, p. 367). It may also make the error of criticizing managers for not conforming to an image that academics have constructed (Boxall, 1992). Furthermore, it presents the HRM model as being inconsistent with collective approaches to managing the employment relationship (Legge, 1989).

In contrast, a strength of the Guest model is that it clearly maps out the field of HRM and classifies the inputs and outcomes. The model is useful for examining the key goals usually associated with the normative models of HRM: strategic integration, commitment, flexibility and quality. Guest's constructed set of theoretical propositions can also improve our understanding of the precise nature of HRM and of the link between HRM and performance, and can be empirically tested by survey-based and case study-based research.

The Warwick model

This model emanates from the Centre for Corporate Strategy and Change at the University of Warwick, especially from two particular researchers, Hendry and Pettigrew (1990). The Warwick model (Figure 1.6) extends the Harvard framework by drawing on its analytical aspects. It takes cognizance of business strategy and HR practices, the external and internal context in which these activities take place, and the processes by which such changes take place, including interactions between changes in both context and content. The strength of the model is that it identifies and classifies important environmental influences on HRM. It maps the connections between the outer (wider environment) and inner (organizational) contexts, and explores how HRM adapts to changes in the context. The implication is that those organizations achieving an alignment between the external and internal contexts will experience superior performance. A weakness of the model is that the process whereby internal HR practices are linked to business output or performance is not developed. The five elements of the model are:

1. outer context
2. inner context
3. business strategy content
4. HRM context
5. HRM content.

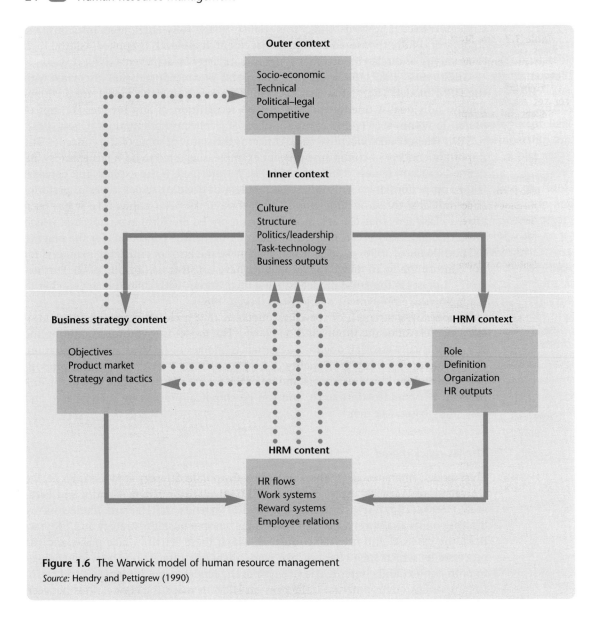

Figure 1.6 The Warwick model of human resource management
Source: Hendry and Pettigrew (1990)

The Storey model

The Storey model attempts to demonstrate the differences between what Storey terms the 'personnel and industrials' and the HRM paradigm by creating an 'ideal type'. He devised the model by reconstructing the 'implicit models' conveyed by some managers during research interviews. We should note that the usage of 'ideal type' is a popular heuristic tool in the social sciences. It is a 'mental construct' and in its conceptual purity cannot be found in any workplace. Its purpose 'is to simplify by highlighting the essential features in an exaggerated way' (Storey, 1992, p. 34). Storey's model characterizes HRM as 'an amalgam of description, prescription, and logical deduction' (2001, p. 6), the four main elements of the model (Table 1.3) being:

Table 1.3 The Storey model of human resource management

Personnel and industrial relations (IR) and human resource management (HRM): the differences

Dimension	Personnel and IR	HRM
Beliefs and assumptions		
Contract	Careful delineation of written contracts	Aim to go 'beyond contract'
Rules	Importance of devising clear rules/mutuality	'Can do' outlook; impatience with 'rules'
Guide to management action	Procedures/consistency control	'Business need'/ flexibility/commitment
Behaviour referent	Norms/custom and practice	Values/mission
Managerial task vis-à-vis labour	Monitoring	Nurturing
Nature of relations	Pluralist	Unitarist
Conflict	Institutionalised	De-emphasised
Standardisation	High (for example 'parity' an issue)	Low (for example 'parity' not seen as relevant)
Strategic aspects		
Key relations	Labour–management	Business–customer
Initiatives	Piecemeal	Integrated
Corporate plan	Marginal to	Central to
Speed of decision	Slow	Fast
Line management		
Management role	Transactional	Transformational leadership
Key managers	Personnel/IR specialists	General/business/line managers
Prized management skills	Negotiation	Facilitation
Key levers		
Foci of attention for interventions	Personnel procedures	Wide-ranging cultural, structural and personnel strategies
Selection	Separate, marginal task	Integrated, key task
Pay	Job evaluation; multiple fixed grades	Performance-related; few if any grades
Conditions	Separately negotiated	Harmonisation
Labour-management	Collective bargaining contracts	Towards individual contracts
Thrust of relations with stewards	Regularised through facilities and training	Marginalised (with exception of some bargaining for change models)
Communication	Restricted flow/indirect	Increased flow/direct
Job design	Division of labour	Teamwork
Conflict handling	Reach temporary truces	Manage climate and culture
Training and development	Controlled access to courses	Learning companies

Source: Storey (1992)

1. beliefs and assumptions
2. strategic aspects
3. role of line managers
4. key levers.

According to the stereotypes depicted in Table 1.3, HRM attempts to increase trust and employee commitment and aims to go 'beyond the contract'. The strategic aspects of Storey's model show HRM as being central to corporate planning. The third component, line management, gives HRM specialists a 'transformational leadership' role in the organization. Research evidence from 15 UK 'core' organizations studied by Storey (1992) suggests that line managers have emerged in almost all cases as the key players on HR issues. The key levers are shown in the lower portion of Storey's model and are issues and techniques that were strongly featured, either explicitly or implicitly, in researcher–manager interviews on HRM. Storey found considerable unevenness in the adoption of these key levers (performance-related pay, harmonization of conditions and the learning company). The 'implicit models' of the managers were used to devise a checklist of 25 key HRM variables to measure the degree of movement from one approach to the other in the 'core' organizations (Storey, 1992).

REFLECTIVE QUESTION

Reviewing the five models, what beliefs and assumptions are implied in them? Look, for example, at the direction of the arrows in Fombrun et al.'s model; what is the message for managers? What similarities and/or differences do you see? How well does each model define the characteristics of HRM?

Personnel management versus human resource management

It should be clear by now that an important part of the debate on HRM centres on the critical question, 'How does HRM differ from the deeply rooted personnel management model?' In the UK in particular, it has proved difficult to arrive at an agreed meaning and significance of HRM. For some, HRM represents a new approach to managing people; for others, it is simply a relabelling and repackaging of 'progressive' personnel management (see, for example, Blyton & Turnbull, 1992; Legge, 1989, 1995; Noon, 1992).

The review of the HRM models suggests that there are differences between HRM and traditional personnel management and that these differences are not just a matter of semantics. This assertion is based upon a number of previously articulated arguments. First, HRM is, in theory at least, integrated into *strategic planning*; as Hendry and Pettigrew (1990, p. 36) state, 'the strategic character of HRM is indeed distinctive'. Second, the HRM model emphasizes the importance of the *'psychological contract'*. Whereas personnel management is built on a legally constructed exchange – 'you do this work for that level of pay' – HRM attempts to build a cognitive construct concerned with developing a 'reciprocal commitment' and an obligation between each of the parties. In this sense, the concept of employee commitment 'lies at the heart of any analysis of HRM' (Guest, 1998, p. 42). Third, the HRM paradigm explicitly emphasizes the importance of *learning* in the workplace. Fourth, HRM overall has focused heavily on the *individual* and the way in which individuals might be motivated and managed to achieve individual and organizational goals. The role of work-place trade union representatives and the collective aspects of relations between the workforce and management are marginalized. The rise in prominence of HRM has coincided with a period of decline in trade union membership (Blyton & Turnbull, 1998), which has led critics of HRM to argue cogently that this approach to employment management represents a renaissance of unitarism or non-union employment strategy (see Chapter 12). Fifth, the theoretical models conceptualize HRM as a *proactive* central strategic management activity that is different from personnel management, with its implied passive connotations. Finally, three of the HRM models make explicit reference to performance outcomes, one compelling claim for HRM being that if organizations adopt this distinctive approach to employment management, the organization's financial 'bottom line' will improve.

The positive claim that a coherent 'bundle' of HR practices will, when aligned with organizational strategy, result in higher performance is an area of continuing research (see Chapter 13). The HRM phenomenon is 'highly controversial', certainly among the academic community, its antecedents, defining characteristics and outcomes being much disputed (Storey, 2001). However, as others have suggested (Legge, 1995; Storey, 1989; 1995a), what may be of more significance is not the message but the messenger: HRM represents the 'discovery' of human capital's potential by senior management and the message itself is being listened to more seriously. The core argument of this chapter is that it is legitimate to define HRM as a particular approach to the management of the employment relationship with a distinctive set of HR policies and practices designed to produce the specific outcome of securing greater employee commitment and organizational performance.

Paradoxes in human resource management

The more critical evaluations of HRM models expose internal paradoxes. Paradox involves ambiguity and inconsistency, two or more positions that each sound reasonable yet conflict or even contradict each other. Paradox is inherent in HRM; Charles Dickens ([1859] 1952, p. 21) described something similar in *A Tale of Two Cities*:

> It was the best of times, it was the worst of times, it was the age of wisdom, it was the age of foolishness, it was the epoch of belief, it was the epoch of incredulity, it was the season of Light, it was the season of Darkness, it was the spring of hope, it was the winter of despair, we had everything before us, we had nothing before us, we were all going direct to heaven, we were all going direct the other way.

For our purposes here, paradox results when managers, in pursuit of a specific organizational goal or goals, call for or carry out actions that are in opposition to the very goal(s) the organization is attempting to accomplish. Critics of the HRM model have drawn upon the Weberian notion (Weber, 1968) of a **paradox of consequences** arising from HR policies and practices. New organizational designs have, for example, been introduced to improve productivity and employee autonomy. On the other hand, the productivity benefits arising from the new organizational forms are accompanied by a number of deleterious consequences on the psychological contract, which have the effect of undermining other espoused goals such as loyalty and commitment. More broadly, there is ambiguity with regard to whether the main role of the HRM function is a 'caring' or a 'controlling' one (Watson, 1986). Townley

(1994), for example, applying the work of Michel Foucault, offers a cogent argument that HR practices produce knowledge about work activities and employees' behaviour that enables the workforce to be more easily controlled; a whole battery of HR practices are designed to make employees more 'governable' and to bring order and stability to organizational life.

Legge's (1995) incisive critique of the HRM phenomenon identifies further ambiguities in the 'soft' and 'hard' schools of HRM. As such, she contrasts the 'rhetoric' and 'reality' of HRM in which, for example, the rhetoric asserting that 'we are all managers now' as a result of 'empowerment' conceals the legitimate question of whether a social group holding privileges and material returns can hold on to power: 'Paradoxically, then, a rhetoric adopted to enhance managerial legitimacy might prove the thin end of the wedge for at least some of its advocates' (Legge, 1995, p. 56). Similarly, the inclusion of the HR director in the strategic management team, the act of 'giving away HR management' to line managers and the outsourcing of more specialized HR activities might ultimately lead to the demise of the HR professional (Caldwell, 2001) – the 'big hat, no cattle' syndrome (Fernie et al., 1994). Armstrong (1989) has argued that short-term accounting controls practised in UK companies might well undermine their long-term HR employee development-orientated goals. In addition, the HRM rhetoric on investment in work-based learning is at odds with the reality of 'HRM's organizationally sponsored ageism', according to Lyon and Glover (1998, p. 65).

One notable feature of much of the HRM literature is the tendency for the research and debate on the HRM model to be gender blind, although more recently there has been more interest in the gender implications of HRM models (Dickens, 1994, 1998). Within that interest, Dickens has suggested that the HRM model might undermine the promotion of equal opportunities and that the gender equality assumption in the HRM model, which emphasizes the value of diversity and individual learning and development, is part of the rhetoric rather than the reality. One of the most important consequences of gender analysis in the HRM approach is theoretically its power to question research findings and analysis that segregate studies of HRM from those of gender divisions in the labour market (Dex, 1988), patriarchal power (Witz, 1986), issues of workplace inequality (Phillips & Phillips, 1993) and 'dual-role' work–family issues (Knights & Willmott, 1996; Platt, 1997). More importantly, however, including the development of gender in the study of the HRM model has the potential to move the HRM debate forward by examining the people who are deemed to be the 'recipients' of HRM theory and practice (Mabey et al., 1998). Throughout this book, we emphasize that paradox is an inherent ongoing part of the employment relationship. By illustrating and explaining the inevitable paradoxes, we hope to encourage a deeper understanding and sensitivity to HR-related issues.

⬤ The extent of human resource management

Another aspect of the HRM debate focuses on the question, 'How many organizations have adopted the new HRM model?' The take-up of HRM-type practices can be assessed using case study and survey research methodologies. A decade ago, there was limited case evidence on the extent to which HRM was practised, the overexposure of a 'regular core' of 123 cases tending to give the impression that more change was taking place than was really the case (Guest, 1990). By the early 1990s, a number of studies provided prima facie evidence of 'a remarkable take-up' of individual HR prac-

HRM IN PRACTICE 1.3

HR SHUNNED BY BOARDS

KAREN HIGGINBOTTOM *PEOPLE MANAGEMENT,* 2002, FEBRUARY 7

Three-quarters of large organisations do not have an HR director on their main board, according to the results of new research revealed exclusively to *People Management.*

Although the most senior HR figures at the majority of larger firms sit on the management board, most are not on the main board. Nonetheless, two-thirds of employers insisted that HR issues are considered at board level as part of their strategic planning.

The situation was criticised by Tony Gale, business solutions HR director at Microsoft Great Plaines, which carried out the study. 'It's essential that HR is involved in the direction of the business. HR opinion must be expressed on the main board.'

> ... only 13 out of 48 UK board members questioned were aware of research linking good people management practices to profitability.

Researchers also looked at the use of e-HR technology. They found more than 85 per cent of large firms used HR management systems for updating personnel records – but that less than half used them to integrate payroll and personnel systems.

Separately, the need for top-level HR representation to explain the business benefits of good HR was confirmed by a new CIPD report. *Voices from the Boardroom* revealed that only 13 out of 48 UK board members questioned were aware of research linking good people management practices to profitability.

'This lack of awareness means that boards are not getting the maximum benefit from linking their business and their people strategies,' said Geoff Armstrong, CIPD director-general.

tices by large British businesses (Storey, 1992, 1995). In addition, Betcherman et al. (1994), Ichniowski et al. (1996) and Storey (1995) provided evidence of a diffusion of HRM across Canada, the USA and Britain. In US establishments, Ichniowski et al.'s (1996) review of longitudinal case studies documented the changes from traditional employment practices to sets of 'innovative' HR practices, Osterman's (1995) national cross-industry survey of American establishments showing that a 'clear majority' of USA business establishments had adopted at least one HRM innovation. Similarly, UK studies found an extensive take-up of the individual elements of HR-type practices in 'mainstream organizations' (Cully et al., 1999; Millward et al., 2000; Storey, 1992, 2001). In the high-tech sector, further studies reported a high degree of strategic integration (McLoughlin & Gourlay, 1992).

Empirical studies, are, however, less supportive of a paradigm shift towards a 'full HRM system', that is, combining different HR practices in a rationale strategic whole. In the UK, Millward et al. (2000) offer some information about the diffusion of the strategic role of HRM. The survey data suggest that HR specialists have less opportunity to incorporate HRM-related issues into wider business plans because fewer appear to be sitting on the board of directors (see also HRM in practice 1.3). In the private sector, HR representation at board level fell from 76 per cent in 1984 to 71 per cent in 1990 and 64 per cent in 1998. Moreover, during the 1990s when the HRM phenomenon was reported to be 'flourishing' this trend accelerated (Millward et al., 2000), reaffirming Sisson's (1995) point that the number of HR 'architects' in the highest levels of decision-making is small. Among major Canadian companies, survey information has revealed that only a minority have adopted the new HRM model: 'the large majority of Canadian firms still follow traditional approaches to human resource management', assert Betcherman et al. (1994, p. 58). Furthermore, studies have reported that US business establishments rarely adopt '*bundles*' [emphasis added] of new HR practices (Ichniowski et al., 1996). In other words, although individual work practice innovations are quite prevalent in most US establishments, the HRM model or 'systems' of innovative HR practice are relatively exceptional.

Over the past decade, there has been incontrovertible evidence of a renaissance of 'individualism' and a fall in the importance attached to 'collectivism' in the management of the employment relationship in UK organizations (Millward et al., 2000). A symbolic desire by employers to move towards 'individually orientated' cultures is represented by the growth of contingency pay (Bacon & Storey, 1993). Many HRM techniques could exist within either an HRM or a traditional personnel management model, depending upon both circumstances and strategic choice (Keenoy, 1990). In addition, the fairly extensive take-up of individual, rather than 'bundles' of, HR practices supports the view that a large proportion of UK organizations are still preoccupied with cost-focus strategies, the so-called 'hard' HRM model (Legge, 1989, 1995; Storey, 2001). In appraising the empirical evidence, there appears to be a disjuncture between knowledge of the HRM model and management practice. Despite many organizations looking for some magic formula that will provide a competitive advantage, relatively few organizations have integrated HRM planning into strategic business planning, a central element in the HRM model.

Studying human resource management

This book presents a detailed examination of definitions, theories, historical development and practices in the field of HRM, and in so doing we expose the differing *standpoints* found in the management literature. Differing standpoints give rise to different perspectives, which in turn provide meaning, legitimacy and justification for people's actions. When people ask, 'What's your perspective on this?', they might just as well be asking, 'What is your own bias on this?' because each perspective is a particular bias, based on how you 'see' the issue and what vested interests are most important to you (Pratt, 1998). Thus, perspectives are a 'lens' through which we view the world of work and organizations. When we refer to a perspective on HRM, we are speaking of an interrelated set of beliefs, values and intentions that legitimize actions.

In our treatment of HRM, we present two standpoints: mainstream and critical. Although there are variations and tensions, *mainstream* management analysis makes a number of assumptions: that the managerial process takes place in rationally designed organizations to accomplish strategic goals, that work organizations are harmonious bodies tending towards a state of equilibrium and order, and that the basic task of managers is to manage resources for formal organizational ends. Thus, the mainstream perspective becomes inseparable from the notion of efficiency. The focus of much of the research and literature on management using this 'lens' relates to finding the 'winning formula' so that more managers can become 'effective' (Thompson & McHugh, 2002). Common to all variations of mainstream perspectives is a failure to connect management processes to the 'master discourse' on market economics and globalization.

In contrast, *critical* perspectives on management set out to discover the ways in which power, control, conflict and legitimacy impact on employment relations. As is the case with mainstream perspectives, critical perspectives are based on numerous theoretical ideas. The starting point is obviously critique per se: the identification of the limitations, paradoxes, contradictions and ideological functions of orthodoxy (see Clegg & Dunkerley, 1980; Mills & Simmons, 1995; Thompson & McHugh, 2002). In critical theory, *historical* and *contextual* considerations are underlined. Consequently, HRM theory and practice can only be understood as part of a management *process* and located within a set of structural contingencies. This approach to studying HRM means more analysis of economic forces, political cultures and communities; it demands multidimensional causal explanations. In writing this text, we do not pretend to be neutral for we have our own bias. But we have found concepts from both mainstream and critical perspectives to be helpful for analysing HRM. We hope that our approach to HRM will encourage readers to question, to be sceptical and to seek multicausality when analysing employment relations in the contemporary workplace.

STUDY TIP

Evaluating more effectively the debate on HRM means having an appreciation that most scholarly writing is 'embedded' within a dominant perspective (Reinharz, 1988). Thus, Reinharz (1988, p. 168) argues, 'we need to treat scientific writing not only as a source of information as defined by the author, but also as a text revealing something about the author'.

Obtain a copy of T. Keenoy's (1990) article 'Human resource management: rhetoric, reality and contradiction', *International Journal of Human Resource Management*, **1**(3), 363–84, and a copy of C. Prahalad and G. Hamel's (1990) article 'The core competencies of the corporation', *Harvard Business Review*, **68**, 79–91. Compare how the authors define HRM and describe its role in the organization. What asides, examples and taken-for-granted assumptions do the authors make? Are the authors 'silent' on some HRM issues (for example gender, discrimination, race/ethnicity, ageism)? After comparing the two articles, to what extent does the text reveal something about the authors' 'lens' or perspective?

Chapter summary

- In this introductory chapter, we have emphasized the primacy of managing people over other resources in the workplace. We have examined the development of HRM and emphasized that it is a product of its times, in the UK and USA the political era of Thatcherism and Reaganism (Guest, 1990). Thus, HRM has reflected an ascendancy of a new political and economic ideology and the changed conditions of national and global capitalism.

- To show the polysemy, the multiplicity of meanings, of the term 'human resource management', we have examined five theoretical models. We have discussed whether HRM now represents a new orthodoxy. The language is certainly different. The US models include those of Fombrun et al. and Beer et al. For Fombrun et al., HRM portrays an approach to managing employment relations that emphasizes the interrelatedness and coherence of HR practices; this was also one of the first models to explicitly suggest that specific bundles of HR practices lead to performance outcomes. The Harvard HRM model provides a useful analytical framework for studying HRM. It contains analytical elements, such as situational factors, stakeholder interests and strategic choice, and prescriptive elements stressing notions of employee commitment and competence.

- We have also examined HRM models developed by UK academics including Guest, Hendry and Pettigrew, and Storey. Guest has identified key features of personnel management and HRM that allow for comparative measurement, his model acknowledging the close links between HR strategy and general business strategies. Like Beer et al., Guest sees high employee commitment as a crucial HRM outcome. The model developed by Hendry and Pettigrew extends the Harvard framework, drawing on its analytical aspects by connecting the outer (wider environment) and inner (organizational) contexts, and exploring how HRM adapts to changes in the context. Storey sees HRM as a combination of description, prescription and logical deduction, his model of HRM focusing on four key elements: beliefs and assumptions, strategy, the role of line managers and key levers. Storey has also identified the 'Jekyll and Hyde' quality of HRM, or what are called 'soft' and 'hard' versions of HRM (Storey, 1989; Sisson and Storey, 2000).

- Whereas personnel management is built on a legally constructed exchange – 'you do this work for that level of pay' – HRM builds a cognitive construct concerned with developing a 'reciprocal commitment' and obligation between each of the parties. Managing the psychological contract is an important task for managers in the contemporary workplace.

- On balance, we consider that the 'soft' HRM metaphor is different from personnel management because it represents a different 'mind set' and approach to managing people in the workplace. In essence, the 'soft', or what others have called 'high-commitment' HRM, sees employees – both managerial and non-managerial – as part of the solution rather than the problem. This distinctive approach may be summed up in this way: people empowered and continuously learning are central to organizational success.

- Paradox is an ongoing part of the employment relationship, and the more critical evaluations of HRM expose internal paradoxes. Throughout this book, we will illustrate and explain some of these inevitable paradoxes to encourage a deeper understanding of HR-related issues.

- Empirical research supports the argument that individual elements of the HRM model have established a secure foothold in UK and US workplaces. We have noted, however, that the significance of the data are open to different interpretations, and the studies do not appear to support the view that there has been a paradigm shift towards a fully integrated strategic HRM model.

- Finally, the HRM discourse should be considered within the wider debates on globalization and competitive advantage, and changing public policy. In the 21st century, the term 'human resource management' continues to be controversial but is central to understanding employment relations.

Key concepts

- Employment relationship
- Human capital
- Human resource management
- Management

- Paradox of consequences
- Personnel management
- Psychological contract
- Theoretical perspectives

Chapter review questions

1. What role does human resource management play in organizations?

2. Explain the development of the HRM profession. Account for the gender structure of the HR function in the UK.

3. To what extent is HRM different from conventional personnel management, or is it simply 'old wine in new bottles'?

Further reading

Caldwell, R. (2001). Champions, adapters, consultants and synergists: The new change agents in HRM. *Human Resource Management Journal*, **11**(3), 39–52.

Dickens, L. (1998). What HRM means for gender equality. *Human Resource Management Journal*, **8**(1), 23–38.

Guest, D. (1990). Human resource management and the American dream'. *Journal of Management Studies*, **27**(4). 377–97.

Legge, K. (1995). *Human resource management: Rhetorics and realities.* London: Macmillan – now Palgrave Macmillan.

Storey, J. (2001). Human resource management today: an assessment'. In J. Storey (ed.), *Human resource management: A critical text* (pp. 3–20). London: Thompson Learning.

Practising human resource management

Searching the web

Enter the website of an HR-related organization (e.g. www.hrhq.com) and an HR-related magazine (e.g. www.peoplemanagement.co.uk). Write a report outlining the key issues facing managers and HR specialists. To what extent, if at all, do the current issues reflect underlying tensions and contradictions within the HR function?

HRM group project

Form a study group of between three and five people, and go to the website of any of the following organizations or one that interests members of the group: Compaq

Computer (www.compaq.com); Airbus Industrie (www.airbus.com); Wal-Mart (www.walmart.com); General Electric (www.gecareers.com/workingforGE/index.cfm); Virgin Airlines (www.virgin.com). Go to the 'company overview' of the site and then look at the HRM department. Evaluate the goals of the HRM department in light of the material contained in this chapter. Write a report that draws out the common features and identifies any key omissions (for example union–management relations). As a guide to your search, ask the following questions: How is the HR department organized? Do the department's activities correspond to the key functional areas outlined in this chapter? Do the values listed here provide a good guideline for managerial behaviour at the company? Do the HR department's objectives emphasize the strategic role of HRM?

Chapter case study

SERVO ENGINEERING

Servo Engineering was founded in 1897 to manufacture mining equipment. Over the next 68 years, the company developed as a leading manufacturer of commercial vehicle components. In 1965, Servo Engineering became a subsidiary of Zipton Holding Ltd, which merged in 1977 with American Ensign. This multinational company has manufacturing plants in the UK, USA and Germany. In 2003, the UK group had four sites in the UK.

In recent years, the company has replaced over half of its conventional and numerical control machines with computer numerical control. In addition, the firm has organized production into six 'self-managed teams' (SMTs). The SMTs are product centred, one, for example, manufacturing a whole component such as a vacuum pump or air compressor. Each SMT operates as a miniature factory within the larger factory and each has sufficient machinery to complete the majority of the manufacturing stages. Processes outside the scope of the SMT are subcontracted to either another SMT or an external contractor. The number of workers in each SMT varies between 12 and 50. The SMT

operates a three-shift system: 6 am to 2 pm, 2 pm to 10 pm, and 10 pm to 6 am. In terms of the division of labour within the SMT, the SMT supervisor has overall responsibility for the SMT, whereas the product-coordinator's job is to ensure the supply of raw materials and parts to meet the SMT production target. The charge-hand acts as progress-chaser. Below the supervisory grades come a hierarchy of manual grades reflecting different levels of training, experience and pay. The setter, for example, is apprentice trained and is paid a skilled rate to set up the machines for the semi-skilled operators. Semi-skilled workers receive little training. In total, the firm employs 442 people. Just over half the workforce belong to the trade union, AMICUS-AEEU for collective-bargaining purposes.

The personnel manager at the factory is George Wyke, who has worked for the company for 25 years. Prior to becoming the personnel manager, he was a union shop steward, but he had no formal personnel management qualifications. The company has given SMT leaders considerable discretion for employee relations. To quote George Wyke:

'What the SMT system has done as far as man-management [sic] is concerned, it has pushed that responsibility further down the chain, into the SMTs. So where somebody wants disciplining, they don't say to the personnel manager: "I want to sack this bastard. What can I do to get rid of him?" They know what they have got to do. The only time they will come to me is to seek advice on whether they are doing it right or wrong.'

Although the level of unemployment is high in the area, the company has had difficulty recruiting 'good' people at its factory in Yorkshire. In addition, absenteeism and turnover have been high.

Absenteeism %	2002	Turnover rates %
5.3	January	34.4
5.7	February	20.4
8.0	March	27.5

The apparent low level of commitment among manual employees can be explained in two ways. First, shop stewards and workers have expressed considerable discontent over the bonus scheme: the standard time allowed to complete a particular task is not considered adequate to earn a 'decent' bonus. Second, the way in which the SMTs were designed has resulted in operatives performing narrow, repetitive tasks, closely supervised. The personnel manager, George Wyke, is due to retire this Christmas. The plant manager, Elizabeth Bell, has been concerned for some time about employee relations in the factory and the management style of George Wyke and some of the SMT leaders. Elizabeth Bell has decided to seek an external candidate to replace the incumbent personnel manager. Gleaning through the ads in newspapers and journals, she has decided to drop the term 'personnel' and advertise for a 'human resource' manager.

Source: Adapted from The motor components company: Japanization in large-batch production. In Bratton, J. (1992). *Japanization at Work*, pp. 103–30 (London: Macmillan – now Palgrave Macmillan).

Discussion questions

1. Describe the main features of George Wyke's approach to managing employment relations. How does Wyke's approach differ from the stereotypical HRM approach?

2. Discuss the contribution that an HRM professional could make to this company.

HR-related skill development

No skill is as important to managers as report-writing. Managers and HR specialists have to write progress reports, proposals, accident reports and evaluation reports to name but a few. You should use a formal report format if your subject matter is important to your organization, if your findings are extensive or if your readership is large or important. Many of the assignments in the section 'Practising human resource management' ask you to write a formal report. Remember that a formal report is, especially if it is to be sent outside the organization, meant to reflect and maintain the organization's professional image. You will develop your skill at report writing by going to our website (www.palgrave.com/business/brattonandgold) and clicking on 'Report Writing'.

Notes

1. Jeffrey Pfeffer, (1998). *The human equation* p. 5.
2. James Champy, (1996). *Reengineering management: The mandate for new leadership* p. 176.
3. Maureen Shaw, (2002, January 16). COE quoted in the *Globe and Mail*, p. M2.
4. According to David McGregor (1960), *The human side of enterprise*, New York: McGraw-Hill, 'people work because they want to work', not because they have to work. Thus, Theory Y view of people assumed that when workers are given challenging assignments and autonomy over work assignments, they will respond with high motivation, high commitment and high performance.

Chapter two

Strategic human resource management

John Bratton

Strategic human resource management is the process of linking the human resource function with the strategic objectives of the organization in order to improve performance.

'If a global company is to function successfully, strategies at different levels need to inter-relate.'[1]

'An organization's [human resource management] policies and practices must fit with its strategy in its competitive environment and with the immediate business conditions that it faces.'[2]

'The [human resources–business strategy] alignment cannot necessarily be characterized in the logical and sequential way suggested by some writers; rather, the design of an HR system is a complex and iterative process.'[3]

Chapter outline

Chapter objectives

After studying this chapter, you should be able to:

1. Explain the meaning of strategic management and give an overview of its conceptual framework

2. Describe the three levels of strategy formulation and comment on the links between business strategy and human resource management (HRM)

3. Explain three models of human resources (HR) strategy: control, resource and integrative

4. Comment on the various strategic HRM themes of the HR–performance link: re-engineering, leadership, workplace learning and trade unions

5. Outline some key aspects of international and comparative HRM

● Introduction

In the first chapter, we examined the theoretical debate on the nature and significance of the human resource management (HRM) model; in this chapter we explore an approach to HRM labelled *strategic human resource management*, or SHRM. By a strategic approach to HRM, we are referring to a managerial process requiring human resource (HR) policies and practices to be linked with the strategic objectives of the organization. Just as the term 'human resource management' has been contested, so too has the notion of SHRM. One aspect for debate is the lack of conceptual clarity (Bamberger & Meshoulam, 2000). Do, for example, the related concepts of SHRM and HR strategy relate to a process or an outcome?

Over the past decade, HR researchers and practitioners have focused their attention on other important questions. First, what determines whether an organization adopts a strategic approach to HRM, and how is HR strategy formulated? Of interest is which organizations are most likely to adopt a strategic approach to HRM. Is there, for example, a positive association with a given set of external and internal characteristics or contingencies and the adoption of SHRM? Another area of interest concerns the policies and practices making up different HR strategies. Is it possible to identify a cluster or 'bundle' of HR practices with different strategic competitive models? Finally, much research productivity in recent years has been devoted to examining the relationship between different clusters of HR practices and organizational performance. Does HR strategy really matter? For organizational practitioners who are looking for ways to gain a competitive advantage, the implication of HR strategic choices for company performance is certainly the key factor.

Before, however, we look at some of the issues associated with the SHRM debate, we need first to examine the strategic management process. This chapter also examines whether it is possible to speak of different 'models' of HR strategy and the degree to which these types of HR strategy systematically vary between organizations. We then consider some issues associated with SHRM, including international and comparative SHRM. As for the question of whether there is a positive association between different HR strategies and organizational performance, we are of the opinion that, given the importance and volume of the research surrounding this issue, the topic warrants an extended discussion (Chapter 13). In the current chapter, we address a number of questions, some essential to our understanding of how work organizations operate in the early 21st century work and the role of HRM therein. How do 'big' corporate decisions impact on HRM? Does the evidence suggest that firms adopting different competitive strategies adopt different HR strategies? How does HRM impact on the 'bottom line'? There is a common theme running through this chapter, much of the HR research pointing out that there are fundamental structural constraints that attest to the complexity of implementing different HRM models.

● Strategic management

The word 'strategy', deriving from the Greek noun *strategus*, meaning 'commander in chief', was first used in the English language in 1656. The development and usage of the word suggests that it is composed of *stratos* (army) and *agein* (to lead). In a management context, the word 'strategy' has now replaced the more traditional term – 'long-term planning' – to denote a specific pattern of decisions and actions

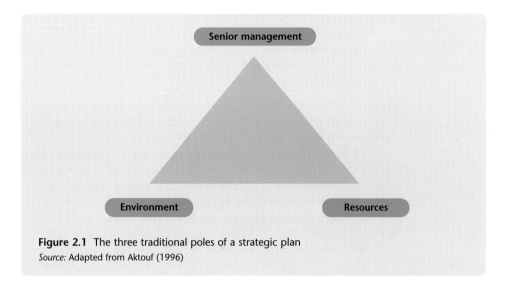

Figure 2.1 The three traditional poles of a strategic plan
Source: Adapted from Aktouf (1996)

undertaken by the upper echelon of the organization in order to accomplish perform-ance goals. Wheelen and Hunger (1995, p. 3) define strategic management as 'that set of managerial decisions and actions that determines the long-run performance of a corporation'. Hill and Jones (2001, p. 4) take a similar view when they define strategy as 'an action a company takes to attain superior performance'. Strategic management is considered to be a continuous activity that requires a constant adjustment of three major interdependent poles: the values of senior management, the environment, and the resources available (Figure 2.1).

HRM IN PRACTICE 2.1

STRATEGY PLANNING HAS SUDDENLY GOT SEXY

GORDON PITT 'THE INS AND OUTS OF MANAGEMENT TOOLS'. *GLOBE AND MAIL*, 1998, JANUARY 8

In the past decade, the North American workplace, as those in Europe, has seen a constant parade of management fads and fashions. In 1993, the top three most popular manage-ment techniques were mission statements, customer satisfac-tion measurement, and total quality management. In 1996, strategic planning, mission statements and benchmarking were the top three management techniques. Of the 409 North American companies surveyed, 89 per cent reported using strate-gic planning in 1996. As one business observer (Pitt, 1998) commented: 'Strategic planning has always been around [but] it suddenly got sexy.'

Model of strategic management

In the descriptive and prescriptive management texts, strategic management appears as a cycle in which several activities follow and feed upon one another. The strategic management process is typically broken down into five steps:

1. mission and goals
2. environmental analysis
3. strategic formulation
4. strategy implementation
5. strategy evaluation.

Figure 2.2 illustrates how the five steps interact. At the corporate level, the strategic management process includes activities that range from appraising the organization's current mission and goals to strategic evaluation.

The first step in the strategic management model begins with senior managers evaluating their position in relation to the organization's current *mission and goals*. The mission describes the organization's values and aspirations; it is the organization's *raison d'être* and indicates the direction in which senior management is going. Goals are the desired ends sought through the actual operating procedures of the organization and typically describe short-term measurable outcomes (Daft, 2001).

Environmental analysis looks at the internal organizational strengths and weak-

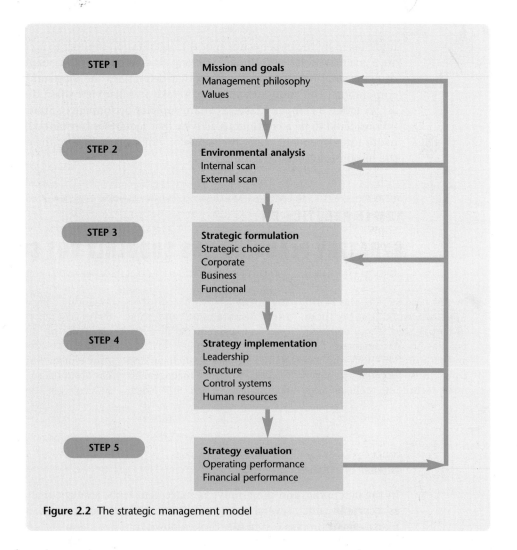

Figure 2.2 The strategic management model

nesses and the external environment for opportunities and threats. The factors that are most important to the organization's future are referred to as strategic factors and can be summarized by the acronym SWOT – **S**trengths, **W**eaknesses, **O**pportunities and **T**hreats.

Strategic formulation involves senior managers evaluating the interaction between strategic factors and making strategic choices that guide managers to meet the organization's goals. Some strategies are formulated at the corporate, business and specific functional levels. The term 'strategic choice' raises the question of *who* makes decisions and *why* they are made (McLoughlin & Clark, 1988). The notion of strategic choice also draws attention to strategic management as a 'political process' whereby decisions and actions on issues are taken by a 'power-dominant' group of managers within the organization. Child (1972, quoted in McLoughlin & Clark, 1988, p. 41) affirms this interpretation of the decision-making process when he writes:

> [W]hen incorporating strategic choice in a theory of organizations, one is recognizing the operation of an essentially political process, in which constraints and opportunities are functions of the power exercised by decision-makers in the light of ideological values.

In a political model of strategic management, it is necessary to consider the distribution of power within the organization. According to Purcell and Ahlstrand (1994, p. 45), we must consider 'where power lies, how it comes to be there, and how the outcome of competing power plays and coalitions within senior management are linked to employee relations'. The strategic choice perspective on organizational decision-making makes the discourse on strategy 'more concrete' and provides important insights into how the employment relationship is managed.

Strategy implementation is an area of activity that focuses on the techniques used by managers to implement their strategies. In particular, it refers to activities that deal with leadership style, the structure of the organization, the information and control systems, and the management of human resources (see Figure 1.2 above). Influential management consultants and academics (for example Champy, 1996; Kotter, 1996) emphasize that leadership is the most important and difficult part of the strategic implementation process.

Strategy evaluation is an activity that determines to what extent the actual change and performance match the desired change and performance.

The strategic management model depicts the five major activities as forming a rational and linear process. It is, however, important to note that it is a *normative* model, that is, it shows how strategic management *should* be done rather than describing what is actually done by senior managers (Wheelen & Hunger, 1995). As we have already noted, the notion that strategic decision-making is a political process implies a potential gap between the theoretical model and reality.

Hierarchy of strategy

Another aspect of strategic management in the multidivisional business organization concerns the level to which strategic issues apply. Conventional wisdom identifies different levels of strategy – a hierarchy of strategy (Figure 2.3):

1. corporate
2. business
3. functional.

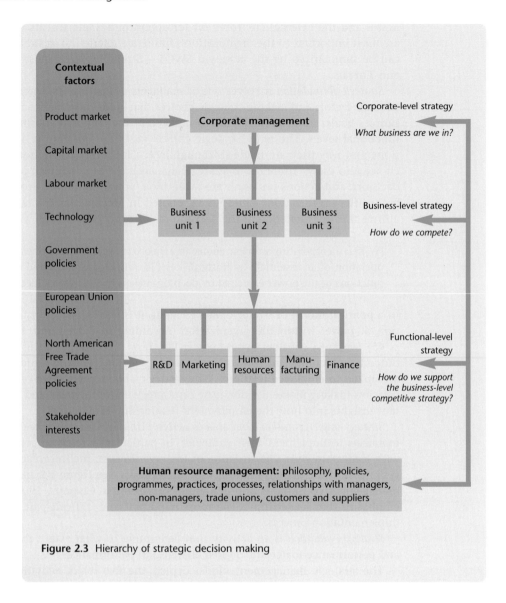

Figure 2.3 Hierarchy of strategic decision making

Corporate-level strategy

Corporate-level strategy describes a corporation's overall direction in terms of its general philosophy towards the growth and the management of its various business units. Such strategies determine the types of business a corporation wants to be involved in and what business units should be acquired, modified or sold. This strategy addresses the question, 'What business are we in?' Devising a strategy for a multidivisional company involves at least four types of initiative:

● establishing investment priorities and steering corporate resources into the most attractive business units

- initiating actions to improve the combined performance of those business units with which the corporation first became involved
- finding ways to improve the synergy between related business units in order to increase performance
- making decisions dealing with diversification.

Business-level strategy

Business-level strategy deals with decisions and actions pertaining to each business unit, the main objective of a business-level strategy being to make the unit more competitive in its marketplace. This level of strategy addresses the question, 'How do we compete?' Although business-level strategy is guided by 'upstream', corporate-level strategy, business unit management must craft a strategy that is appropriate for its own operating situation. In the 1980s, Porter (1980, 1985) made a significant contribution to our understanding of business strategy by formulating a framework that described three competitive strategies: cost leadership, differentiation and focus.

The low-cost leadership strategy attempts to increase the organization's market share by having the lowest unit cost and price compared with competitors. The simple alternative to cost leadership is differentiation strategy. This assumes that managers distinguish their services and products from those of their competitors in the same industry by providing distinctive levels of service, product or high quality such that the customer is prepared to pay a premium price. With the *focus* strategy, managers focus on a specific buyer group or regional market. A market strategy can be narrow or broad, as in the notion of niche markets being very narrow or focused. This allows the firm to choose from four generic business-level strategies – low-cost leadership, differentiation, focused differentiation and focused low-cost leadership – in order to establish and exploit a competitive advantage within a particular competitive scope (Figure 2.4).

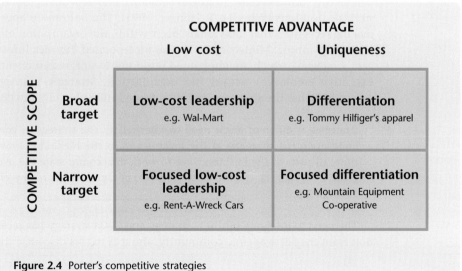

Figure 2.4 Porter's competitive strategies
Source: Adapted from Porter (1985)

Miles and Snow (1984) have identified four modes of strategic orientation: defenders, prospectors, analysers and reactors. *Defenders* are companies with a limited product line and a management focus on improving the efficiency of their existing operations. Commitment to this cost orientation makes senior managers unlikely to explore new areas. *Prospectors* are companies with fairly broad product lines that focus on product innovation and market opportunities. This sales orientation makes senior managers emphasize 'creativity over efficiency'. *Analysers* are companies that operate in at least two different product market areas, one stable and one variable. In this situation, senior managers emphasize efficiency in the stable areas and innovation in the variable areas. *Reactors* are companies that lack a consistent strategy–structure–culture relationship. In this reactive orientation, senior management's responses to environmental changes and pressures thus tend to be piecemeal strategic adjustments. Competing companies within a single industry can choose any one of these four types of strategy and adopt a corresponding combination of structure, culture and processes consistent with that strategy in response to the environment. The different competitive strategies influence the 'downstream' functional strategies.

Functional-level strategy

Functional-level strategy pertains to the major functional operations within the business unit, including research and development, marketing, manufacturing, finance and HR. This strategy level is typically primarily concerned with maximizing resource productivity and addresses the question, 'How do we support the business-level competitive strategy?' Consistent with this, at the functional level, HRM policies and practices support the business strategy goals.

These three levels of strategy – corporate, business and functional – form a hierarchy of strategy within large multidivisional corporations. In different corporations, the specific operation of the hierarchy of strategy might vary between 'top-down' and 'bottom-up' strategic planning. The top-down approach resembles a 'cascade' in which the 'downstream' strategic decisions are dependent on higher 'upstream' strategic decisions (Wheelen & Hunger, 1995). The bottom-up approach to strategy-making recognizes that individuals 'deep' within the organization might contribute to strategic planning. Mintzberg (1978) has incorporated this idea into a model of 'emergent strategies', which are unplanned responses to unforeseen circumstances by non-executive employees within the organization. Strategic management literature emphasizes that the strategies at different levels must be fully integrated. Thus:

> strategies at different levels need to inter-relate. The strategy at corporate level must build upon the strategies at the lower levels in the hierarchy. However, at the same time, all parts of the business have to work to accommodate the overriding corporate goals. (F. A. Maljers, Chairman of the Board of Unilever, quoted by Wheelen & Hunger, 1995, p. 20)

The need to integrate business strategy and HRM strategy has received much attention from the HR academic community, and it is to this discourse that we now turn.

HRM IN PRACTICE 2.2

SENIOR HR EXECUTIVES DECRY LACK OF STRATEGIC INPUT

HR MAGAZINE, 1999, JANUARY, PP. 21–2

Though many HR management gurus have championed the evolving and expanding strategic role of HR professionals, a recent report from the Conference Board of Canada seems to indicate that most HR executives feel they aren't very involved with their companies' strategic plans. The recent survey of 155 senior-level HR executives found that 63 per cent of the respondents felt that 'HR is never, rarely or only sometimes' a major part of their companies' overall strategy. The remaining 37 per cent did feel that HR plays a significant role

> **most HR executives ... aren't very involved with their companies' strategic plans.**

in their companies' strategic planning. According to researchers with the Conference Board, employees at companies that encourage HR participation in strategic planning have a stronger understanding of their functions within the organization. 'There is a strong correlation between those companies that say HR is always linked to the strategic process, and how well the companies' employees understand where the company wants to go', says Brian Hackett, a senior HR specialist with the board.

● Strategic human resource management

The SHRM literature is rooted in 'manpower' (sic) planning, but it was the work of influential management gurus (for example Ouchi, 1981; Peters & Waterman, 1982), affirming the importance of the effective management of people as a source of competitive advantage, that encouraged academics to develop frameworks emphasizing the strategic role of the HR function (for example Beer et al., 1984; Fombrun et al., 1984) and attaching the prefix 'strategic' to the term 'human resource management'. Interest among academics and practitioners in linking the strategy concept to HRM can be explained from both the 'rational choice' and the 'constituency-based' perspective. There is a managerial logic in focusing attention on people's skills and intellectual assets to provide a major competitive advantage when technological superiority, even once achieved, will quickly erode (Barney, 1991; Pfeffer, 1994, 1998a). From a 'constituency-based' perspective, it is argued that HR academics and HR practitioners have embraced SHRM as a means of securing greater respect for HRM as a field of study and, in the case of HR managers, of appearing more 'strategic', thereby enhancing their status within organizations (Bamberger & Meshoulam, 2000; Pfeffer & Salancik, 1977; Powell & DiMaggio, 1991; Purcell & Ahlstrand, 1994; Whipp, 1999).

REFLECTIVE QUESTION

Why have academics and HR professionals embraced SHRM? Is there a strong business case for the strategic approach to HRM, or is it more the case that academics and HR professionals have embraced SHRM out of self-interest? What do you think of these arguments?

Concepts and models

In spite of the increasing volume of research and scholarship, the precise meaning of strategic HRM and HR strategy remains problematic. It is unclear, for example, which one of these two terms relates to an *outcome* or a *process* (Bamberger & Meshoulam, 2000). For Snell et al., (1996, p. 62) 'strategic HRM' is an outcome: 'as organizational systems designed to achieve sustainable competitive advantage through people'. For others, however, SHRM is viewed as a process, 'the process of linking HR practices to business strategy' (Ulrich, 1997, p. 89). Similarly, Bamberger and Meshoulam (2000, p. 6) describe SHRM as 'the process by which organizations seek to link the human, social, and intellectual capital of their members to the strategic needs of the firm'. According to Ulrich (1997, p. 190) 'HR strategy' is the outcome: 'the mission, vision and priorities of the HR function'. Consistent with this view, Bamberger and Meshoulam (2000, p. 5) conceptualize HR strategy as an outcome: 'the pattern of decisions regarding the policies and practices associated with the HR system'. The authors go on to make a useful distinction between senior management's 'espoused' HR strategy and their 'emergent' strategy. The espoused HR strategy refers to the pattern of HR-related decisions made but not necessarily implemented, whereas the emergent HR strategy refers to the pattern of HR-related decisions that have been applied in the workplace. Thus, 'espoused HR strategy is the road map … and emergent HR strategy is the road actually traveled' (Bamberger & Meshoulam, 2000, p. 6). Purcell (2001) has also portrayed HR strategy as 'emerging patterns of action' that are likely to be much more 'intuitive' and only 'visible' after the event.

We begin the discussion of SHRM and HR strategy with a focus on the link between organizational strategy formulation and strategic HR formulation. A range of business–HRM links has been classified in terms of a proactive–reactive continuum (Kydd & Oppenheim, 1990) and in terms of environment–human resource strategy–business strategy linkages (Bamberger & Phillips, 1991). In the 'proactive' orientation, the HR professional has a seat at the strategic table and is actively engaged in strategy formulation. In Figure 2.3 above, the two-way arrows on the right-hand side showing both downward and upward influence on strategy depict this type of proactive model.

At the other end of the continuum is the 'reactive' orientation, which sees the HR function as being fully subservient to corporate and business-level strategy, and organizational-level strategies as ultimately determining HR policies and practices. Once the business strategy has been determined, an HR strategy is implemented to support the chosen competitive strategy. This type of reactive orientation would be depicted in Figure 2.3 above by a *one-way downward arrow* from business- to functional-level strategy. In this sense, a HR strategy is concerned with the challenge of matching the **p**hilosophy, **p**olicies, **p**rogrammes, **p**ractices and **p**rocesses – the 'five Ps' – in a way that will stimulate and reinforce the different employee role behaviours appropriate for each competitive strategy (Schuler, 1989, 1992).

The importance of the environment as a determinant of HR strategy has been incorporated into some models. Extending strategic management concepts, Bamberger and Phillips' (1991) model depicts links between three poles: the environment, human resource strategy and the business strategy (Figure 2.5). In the hierarchy of the strategic decision-making model (see Figure 2.3 above), the HR strategy is influenced by contextual variables such as markets, technology, national government policies, European Union policies and trade unions. Purcell and Ahlstrand (1994) argue, however, that those models which incorporate contextual influences as a mediating

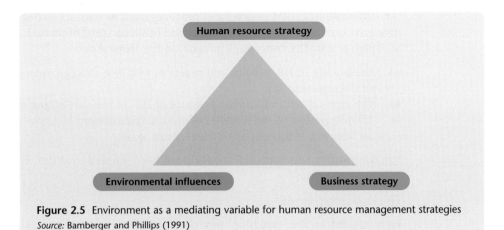

Figure 2.5 Environment as a mediating variable for human resource management strategies
Source: Bamberger and Phillips (1991)

variable of HR policies and practices tend to lack 'precision and detail' in terms of the precise nature of the environment linkages, and that 'much of the work on the linkages has been developed at an abstract and highly generalized level' (p. 36).

In the late 1980s, Purcell made a significant contribution to research on business–HRM strategy. Drawing on the literature on 'strategic choice' in industrial relations (for example Kochan et al., 1986; Thurley & Wood, 1983) and using the notion of a hierarchy of strategy, Purcell (1989) identified what he called, 'upstream' and 'downstream' types of strategic decision. The upstream or 'first-order' strategic decisions are concerned with the long-term direction of the corporation. If a first-order decision is made to take over another enterprise, for example a French company acquiring a water company in southern England, a second set of considerations applies concerning the extent to which the new operation is to be integrated with or separate from existing operations. These are classified as downstream or 'second-order', strategic decisions. Different HR strategies are called 'third-order' strategic decisions because they establish the basic parameters for managing people in the workplace. Purcell (1989, p. 71) wrote, '[in theory] strategy in human resources management is determined in the context of first-order, long-run decisions on the direction and scope of the firm's activities and purpose ... and second-order decisions on the structure of the firm'.

In a major study of HRM in multidivisional companies, Purcell and Ahlstrand (1994) argue that what actually determines HR strategy will be determined by decisions at all three levels and by the ability and leadership style of local managers to follow through goals in the context of specific environmental conditions. Case study analysis has, however, highlighted the problematic nature of strategic choice model-building. The conception of strategic choice might exaggerate the ability of managers to make decisions and take action independent of the environmental contexts in which they do business (Colling, 1995).

Another part of the strategic HRM debate has focused on the integration or 'fit' of business strategy with HR strategy. This shift in managerial thought, calling for the HR function to be 'strategically integrated', is depicted in Beer et al.'s (1984) model of HRM. The authors espoused the need to establish a close two-way relationship or 'fit' between the external business strategy and the elements of the internal HR strategy:

'An organization's HRM policies and practices must fit with its strategy in its competitive environment and with the immediate business conditions that it faces' (Beer et al., 1984, p. 25). The concept of integration has three aspects:

- the linking of HR policies and practices with the strategic management process of the organization
- the internalization of the importance of HR on the part of line managers
- the integration of the workforce into the organization to foster commitment or an 'identity of interest' with the strategic goals.

Not surprisingly, this approach to SHRM has been referred to as the 'matching' model.

The matching model

Early interest in the 'matching' model was evident in Devanna et al.'s (1984) work: 'HR systems and organizational structure should be managed in a way that is congruent with organizational strategy' (p. 37). This is close to Chandler's (1962) distinction between strategy and structure and his often-quoted maxim that 'structure follows strategy'. In the Devanna et al. model, HRM–strategy–structure follow and feed upon one another and are influenced by environmental forces (Figure 2.6).

Similarly, the notion of 'fit' between an external competitive strategy and the internal HR strategy is a central tenet of the HRM model advanced by Beer et al. (1984,

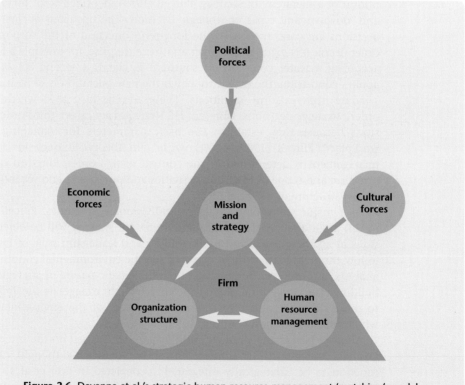

Figure 2.6 Devanna et al.'s strategic human resource management 'matching' model
Source: Devanna et al. (1984)

see Figure 1.5). The authors emphasize the analysis of the linkages between the two strategies and how each strategy provides goals and constraints for the other. There must be a 'fit between competitive strategy and internal HRM strategy and a fit among the elements of the HRM strategy' (Beer et al., 1984, p. 13). The relationship between business strategy and HR strategy is said to be 'reactive' in the sense that HR strategy is subservient to 'product market logic' and the corporate strategy. The latter is assumed to be the independent variable (Boxall, 1992; Purcell & Ahlstrand, 1994). As Miller (1987, cited in Boxall, 1992, p. 66) emphasizes, 'HRM cannot be conceptualized as a stand-alone corporate issue. Strategically speaking it must flow from and be dependent upon the organization's (market oriented) corporate strategy'. There is some theorization of the link between product markets and organizational design, and approaches to people management. Thus, for example, each Porterian competitive strategy involves a unique set of responses from workers, or 'needed role behaviours', and a particular HR strategy that might generate and reinforce a unique pattern of behaviour (Cappelli & Singh, 1992; Schuler & Jackson, 1987). HRM is therefore seen to be 'strategic by virtue of its alignment with business strategy and its internal consistency (Boxall, 1996).

Human resource strategy models

This section examines the link between organization/business strategy and HR strategy. 'Human resource strategies' are here taken to mean the patterns of decisions regarding HR policies and practices used by management to design work and select, train and develop, appraise, motivate and control workers. Studying HR strategies in terms of typologies is appealing to academics because conceptual frameworks or models give HR researchers the ability to compare and contrast the different configurations or clusters of HR practices and further develop and test theory (Bamberger & Meshoulam, 2000).

To appreciate the significance of 'typologies', it is useful to recall the work of Max Weber. This sociologist built his theory through the use of abstractions he called 'ideal types', such as 'bureaucracy'. Weber warned, however, that these abstractions or ideal types never actually exist in the real world; they are simply useful fictions to help us understand the more complex and messy realities found in work organizations. The same is true of HR typologies – they are abstractions that do not necessarily exist in the workplace, but they help the student of management to understand the nature of HR strategies.

Since the early 1990s, academics have proposed at least three models to differentiate between 'ideal types' of HR strategies. The first model examined here, the control-based model, is grounded in the way in which management attempts to monitor and control employee role performance. The second model, the resource-based model, is grounded in the nature of the employer–employee exchange and, more specifically, in the set of employee attitudes, in behaviours and in the quality of the manager–subordinate relationship. A third approach creates an integrative model that combines resource-based and control-based typologies.

The control-based model

The first approach to modelling different types of HR strategy is based on the nature of workplace control and more specifically on managerial behaviour to direct and monitor employee role performance. According to this perspective, management structures and HR strategy are instruments and techniques to control all aspects of work to secure a high level of labour productivity and a corresponding level of profitability. This focus on monitoring and controlling employee behaviour as a basis for distinguishing different HR strategies has its roots in the study of 'labour process' by industrial sociologists.

The starting point for this framework is Marx's analysis of the capitalist labour process and what he referred to as the 'transformation of labour power into labour'. Put simply, when organizations hire people, they have only a *potential* or capacity to work. To ensure that each worker exercises his or her full capacity, managers must organize the tasks, space, movement and time within which workers operate. But workers have divergent interests in terms of pace of work, rewards and job security, and engage in formal (trade unions) and informal (restrictions of output or sabotage) behaviours to counteract management job controls. Workers' own countermanagement behaviour then causes managers to control and discipline the interior of the organization. In an insightful review, Thompson and McHugh (2002, p. 104) comment that, 'control is not an end in itself, but a means to transform the capacity to work established by the wage relation into profitable production'.

What alternative HR strategies have managers used to render employees and their behaviour predictable and measurable? Edwards (1979) identified successive dominant modes of control that reflect changing competitive conditions and worker resistance. An early system of *individual control* by employers exercising direct authority was replaced by more complex structural forms of control: *bureaucratic control* and *technical control*. Bureaucratic control includes written rules and procedures covering work. Technical control includes machinery or systems – assembly line, surveillance cameras – that set the pace of work or monitor employees' behaviour in the workplace. Edwards also argued that managers use a 'divide and rule' strategy, using gender and race, to foster managerial control.

Friedman (1977) structured his typology of HR strategies – *direct control* and *responsible autonomy* – around the notion of differing logics of control depending upon the nature of the product and labour markets. Another organizational theorist, Burawoy (1979), categorized the development of HR strategies in terms of the transition from *despotic* to *hegemonic* regimes. The former was dominated by coercive manager–subordinate relations; the latter provided an 'industrial citizenship' that regulated employment relations through grievance and bargaining processes. The growth of employment in new call centres has recently given rise to a renewed focus of interest on the use of technical control systems: the electronic surveillance of the operator's role performance (Callaghan & Thompson, 2001; Sewell, 1998).

The choice of HR strategy is governed by variations in organizational form (for example size, structure and age), competitive pressures on management and the stability of labour markets, mediated by the interplay of manager–subordinate relations and worker resistance (Thompson & McHugh, 2002). Moreover, the variations in HR strategy are not random but reflect two management logics (Bamberger & Meshoulam, 2000). The first is the logic of direct, *process-based control*, in which the focus is on efficiency and cost containment (managers needing within this domain to monitor and control workers' performance carefully), whereas the second is the logic of indirect *outcomes-based control*, in which the focus is on actual results (within this domain, managers needing to engage workers' intellectual capital, commitment and cooperation). Thus, when managing people at work, control and cooperation coexist, and the extent to which there is any ebb and flow in intensity and direction between *types* of control will depend upon the 'multiple constituents' of the management process.

Implicit in this approach to managerial control is that the logic underlying an HR strategy will tend to be consistent with an organization's competitive strategy (for example Schuler & Jackson, 1987). We are thus unlikely to find organizations adopting a Porterian cost-leadership strategy with an HR strategy grounded in an outcome-based logic. Managers will tend to adopt process-based controls when means–ends relations are certain (as is typically the case among firms adopting a cost-leadership strategy), and outcomes-based controls when means–ends are uncertain (for example differentiation strategy). These management logics result in different organizational designs and variations in HR strategy, which provide the source of inevitable structural tensions between management and employees. It is posited, therefore, that HR strategies contain inherent contradictions (Hyman, 1987; Storey, 1995; Thompson & McHugh, 2002).

REFLECTIVE QUESTION

What do you think of the argument that each type of competitive strategy requires a different HR strategy? Thinking about your own work experience, reflect upon the way in which managers attempted to control your behaviour at work. Was each task closely monitored, or was the focus on actual outcome? To what extent, if at all, were different *types* of managerial control related to the firm's product or service?

The resource-based model

This second approach to developing typologies of HR strategy is grounded in the nature of the reward–effort exchange and, more specifically, the degree to which managers view their human resources as an asset as opposed to a variable cost. Superior performance through workers is underscored when advanced technology and other inanimate resources are readily available to competing firms. The sum of people's knowledge and expertise, and social relationships, has the *potential* to provide non-substitutable capabilities that serve as a source of competitive advantage (Cappelli & Singh, 1992). The various perspectives on resource-based HRM models raise questions about the inextricable connection between work-related learning, the 'mobilization of employee consent' through learning strategies and competitive advantage. Given the upsurge of interest in resource-based models, and in particular the new workplace learning discourse, we need to examine this model in some detail.

The genesis of the resource-based model can be traced back to Selznick (1957), who suggested that work organizations each possess 'distinctive competence' that enables them to outperform their competitors, and to Penrose (1959), who conceptualized the firm as a 'collection of productive resources'. She distinguished between 'physical' and 'human resources', and drew attention to issues of learning, including the knowledge and experience of the management team. Moreover, Penrose emphasized what many organizational theorists take for granted – that organizations are 'heterogeneous' (Penrose, 1959, cited in Boxall, 1996, pp. 64–5). More recently, Barney (1991) has argued that 'sustained competitive advantage' (emphasis added) is achieved not through an analysis of a firm's external market position but through a careful analysis of its skills and capabilities, characteristics that competitors find themselves unable to imitate. Putting it in terms of a simple SWOT analysis, the resource-based perspective emphasizes the strategic importance of exploiting internal 'strengths' and neutralizing internal 'weaknesses' (Barney, 1991).

The resource-based approach exploits the distinctive competencies of a work organization: its resources and capabilities. An organization's *resources* can be divided into tangible (financial, technological, physical and human) and intangible (brand-name, reputation and know-how) resources. To give rise to a distinctive competency, an organization's resources must be both unique and valuable. By *capabilities*, we mean the collective skills possessed by the organization to coordinate effectively the resources. According to strategic management theorists, the distinction between resources and capabilities is critical to understanding what generates a distinctive competency (see, for example, Hill & Jones, 2001). It is important to recognize that a firm may not need a uniquely endowed workforce to establish a distinctive competency as long as it has managerial capabilities that no competitor possesses. This observation may explain why an organization adopts one of the control-based HR strategies.

HRM WEB LINKS

An increasing number of US companies are establishing 'corporate' universities to help to build 'core' competencies. Examples of US corporate universities are Intel University (www.wiche.edu/telecom/resources/sharinginformation), Dell University (www.dell.com/careers) and Motorola University (www.mot.com/MU).

Barney argues that four characteristics of resources and capabilities – value, rarity, inimitability and non-substitutability – are important in sustaining competitive advantage. From this perspective, collective learning in the workplace on the part of managers and non-managers, especially on how to coordinate workers' diverse knowledge and skills and integrate diverse information technology, is a strategic asset that rivals find difficult to replicate. In other words, leadership capabilities are critical to harnessing the firm's human assets. Amit and Shoemaker (1993, p. 37) make a similar point when they emphasize the strategic importance of managers identifying, ex ante, and marshalling 'a set of complementary and specialized resources and capabilities which are scarce, durable, not easily traded, and difficult to imitate' in order to enable the company to earn 'economic rent' (profits). Figure 2.7 summarizes the relationship between resources and capabilities, strategies, and sustained competitive advantage.

REFLECTIVE QUESTION

Based upon your own work experience, or upon your studies of organizations, is continuous learning at the workplace more or less important for some organizations than others? If so, why?

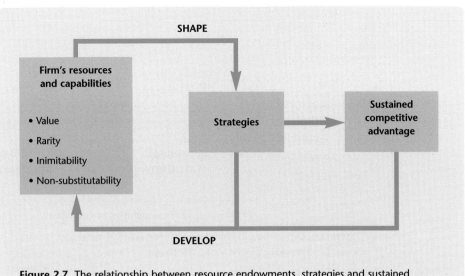

Figure 2.7 The relationship between resource endowments, strategies and sustained competitive advantage
Source: Based on Barney (1991) and Hill and Jones (2001)

The integrative model

Bamberger and Meshoulam (2000) integrate the two main models of HR strategy, one focusing on the strategy's underlying logic of managerial control, the other focusing on the reward–effort exchange. Arguing that neither of the two dichotomous approaches (control- and resource-based models) provides a framework able to encompass the ebb and flow of the intensity and direction of HR strategy, they build a model that characterizes the two main dimensions of HR strategy as involving 'acquisition and development' and the 'locus of control'.

Acquisition and development are concerned with the extent to which the HR strategy develops *internal* human capital as opposed to the *external* recruitment of human capital. In other words, organizations can lean more towards 'making' their workers (high investment in training) or more towards 'buying' their workers from the external labour market (Rousseau, 1995). Bamberger and Meshoulam (2000) call this the 'make-or-buy' aspect of HR strategy.

Locus of control is concerned with the degree to which HR strategy focuses on monitoring employees' compliance with process-based standards as opposed to developing a *psychological* contract that nurtures social relationships, encourages mutual trust and respect, and controls the focus on the outcomes (ends) themselves. This strand of thinking in HR strategy can be traced back to the ideas of Walton (1985), who made a distinction between commitment and control strategies (Hutchinson et al., 2000). As Figure 2.8 shows, these two main dimensions of HR strategy yield four different 'ideal types' of dominant HR strategy:

- commitment
- collaborative
- paternalistic
- traditional.

Figure 2.8 Categorizing human resource management strategies
Source: Based on Bamberger and Meshoulam (2000)

The *commitment HR strategy* is characterized as focusing on the internal development of employees' competencies and outcome control. In contrast, the *traditional HR
strategy*, which parallels Bamberger and Meshoulam's 'secondary' HR strategy, is
viewed as focusing on the external recruitment of competencies and behavioural or
process-based controls. The *collaborative HR strategy*, which parallels Bamberger and
Meshoulam's 'free agent' HR strategy, involves the organization subcontracting work
to external independent experts (for example consultants or contractors), giving
extensive autonomy and evaluating their performance primarily in terms of the end
results. The *paternalistic HR strategy* offers learning opportunities and internal promotion to employees for their compliance with process-based control mechanisms. Each
HR strategy represents a distinctive HR paradigm, or set of beliefs, values and assumptions, that guide managers. Similar four-cell grids have been developed by Lepak and
Snell (1999). Based upon empirical evidence, Bamberger and Meshoulam suggest that
the HR strategies in the diagonal quadrants 'commitment' and 'traditional' are likely
to be the most prevalent in (North American) work organizations.

It is argued that an organization's HR strategy is strongly related to its competitive
strategy. So, for example, the traditional HR strategy (bottom right quadrant) is most
likely to be adopted by management when there is certainty over how inputs are
transformed into outcomes and/or when employee performance can be closely monitored or appraised. This dominant HR strategy is more prevalent in firms with a highly
routinized transformation process, low-cost priority and stable competitive environment. Under such conditions, managers use technology to control the uncertainty
inherent in the labour process and insist only that workers enact the specified core
standards of behaviour required to facilitate undisrupted production. Managerial
behaviour in such organizations can be summed up by the managerial edict 'You are
here to work, not to think!' Implied by this approach is a focus on process-based
control in which 'close monitoring by supervisors and efficiency wages ensure
adequate work effort' (MacDuffie, 1995, quoted by Bamberger & Meshoulam, 2002,
p. 60). The use of the word 'traditional' to classify this HR strategy and the use of a technological 'fix' to control workers should not be viewed as a strategy only of 'industrial'

worksites. Case study research on call centres, workplaces that some organizational theorists label 'post-industrial', reveal systems of technical and bureaucratic control that closely monitor and evaluate their operators (Sewell, 1998; Thompson & McHugh, 2002).

The other dominant HR strategy, the commitment HR strategy (top left quantrant), is most likely to be found in workplaces in which management lacks a full knowledge of all aspects of the labour process and/or the ability to monitor closely or evaluate the efficacy of the worker behaviours required for executing the work (for example single-batch, high quality production, research and development, and health care professionals). This typically refers to 'knowledge work'. In such workplaces, managers must rely on employees to cope with the uncertainties inherent in the labour process and can thus only monitor and evaluate the outcomes of work. This HR strategy is associated with a set of HR practices that aim to develop highly committed and flexible people, internal markets that reward commitment with promotion and a degree of job security, and a 'participative' leadership style that forges a commonality of interest and mobilizes consent to the organization's goals (Hutchinson et al., 2000). In addition, as others have noted, workers under such conditions do not always need to be overtly controlled because they may effectively 'control themselves' (Thompson, 1989; Thompson & McHugh, 2002). To develop cooperation and common interests, an effort–reward exchange based upon investment in learning, internal promotion and internal equity is typically used (Bamberger & Meshoulam, 2000). In addition, such workplaces 'mobilize' employee consent through culture strategies, including the popular notion of the 'learning organization'. As one of us has argued elsewhere (Bratton, 2001, p. 341):

> For organizational controllers, workplace learning provides a compelling ideology in the twenty-first century, with an attractive metaphor for mobilizing worker commitment and sustainable competitiveness ... [And] the learning organization paradigm can be construed as a more subtle way of shaping workers' beliefs and values and behaviour.

HRM IN PRACTICE 2.3

AIRLINE HOPES TO CUT COSTS, REGAIN MARKET SHARE

PATRICK BRETHOUR AND KEITH MCARTHUR, *GLOBE AND MAIL*, 2002, APRIL 20, PP. B1, B6

Air Canada unveiled its long awaited discount carrier yesterday, but warned that customers shouldn't expect fares to immediately be lower than those already offered by Air Canada. Steve Smith, president and chief executive officer of Zip Air Inc., said the new airline is being created to cut Air Canada's costs – not to reduce fares.

'Right now, the price is already low, particularly in this market,' he said, adding that prices could fall over time as the new airline reduced expenses.

Observers see the wholly owned subsidiary as a way for Air Canada to lower labour costs and win back market share it has lost in recent years to Calgary-based WestJet Air-

lines Ltd. Mr Smith said a new business model is emerging in the airline market – as it has in retailing – where lower-cost, no-frills service becomes the norm. He said the full-service model for short flights is 'going the way of the dinosaur.' Zip is aimed at meeting that challenge in the low end of the market, he said.

Zip's costs will be at least 20 per cent lower than those at Air Canada's comparable mainline flights, in part because Zip's employees will be making less money than their counterparts at Air Canada. Mr. Smith said wages will be competitive with Zip's competitors in the low-cost market. 'For the employees, they have to understand that they will be working for zip,' he joked.

Pamela Sachs, president of Air Canada component of the Canadian Union of Public Employees, said the union will mount a legal challenge to Air Canada's attempts to pay so-called B-scale wages to Zip employees. 'Air Canada gives zip by zapping its employees. They are hurting the very people who have worked so hard for them and for so long,' she said.

'They are hurting the very people who have worked so hard for them and for so long ...'

Other cost-cutting measures at Zip include offering snacks instead of meals, providing no in-flight entertainment and operating only one kind of plane. There will also be less room between seats – 32 inches or 33 inches – although the seats will still have more leg room than the smallest seats at WestJet. The reduction, along with the elimination of business-class seats, will allow Zip to add 17 seats to the 100 seats in the Boeing 737-200. (WestJet has 120 seats in its Boeing 737-200s).

The company will operate independently of Air Canada, although it will buy maintenance services from its parent, as well as using the larger company's pilots.

REFLECTIVE QUESTION

How would you describe the HR strategy at Zip Air (HRM in practice 2.3)? How does this HR strategy support the business plan? Do you think that Zip Air will be able to mobilize its employees' competencies and commitment to achieve a competitive advantage?

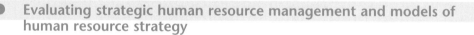

Evaluating strategic human resource management and models of human resource strategy

A number of limitations to current research on SHRM and HR strategy have been identified: the focus on strategic decision-making, the absence of internal strategies and the conceptualization of managerial control.

Existing conceptualizations of SHRM are predicated upon the traditional rational perspective to managerial decision-making – definable acts of linear planning, choice and action – but critical organizational theorists have challenged these assumptions, arguing that strategic decisions are not necessarily based on the output of rational calculation. The assumption that a firm's business-level strategy and HR system have a logical, linear relationship is questionable given the evidence that strategy formulation is informal, politically charged and subject to complex contingency factors (Bamberger & Meshoulam, 2000; Monks & McMackin, 2001; Whittington, 1993). As such, the notion of *consciously* aligning business strategy and HR strategy applies only to the 'classical' approach to strategy (Legge, 1995). Those who question the classical approach to strategic management argue that the image of the manager as a reflective planner and strategist is a myth. Managerial behaviour is more likely to be uncoordinated, frenetic, ad hoc and fragmented (for example Hales, 1986).

The political perspectives on strategic decision-making make the case that managerial rationality is limited by lack of information, time and 'cognitive capacity' as well as that strategic management is a highly competitive process in which managers fiercely compete for resources, status and power. Within such a management milieu, strategies can signal changes in power relationships among managers (Mintzberg et al., 1998). Rather than viewing strategic choices as the outcome of rational decision-making, Johnson (1987, cited in Purcell, 1989, p. 72), among others, argues that 'Strategic decisions are characterized by the political hurly-burly of organizational life with a high incidence of bargaining ... all within a notable lack of clarity in terms of environmental influences and objectives.'

Alternatively, strategic decision-making may be conceptualized as a 'discourse' or body of language-based communication that operates at different levels in the organization. Thus, Hendry (2000) persuasively argues that a strategic decision takes its meaning from the discourse and social practice within which it is located, so a decision must be not only effectively communicated, but also 'recommunicated' until it becomes embodied in action. This perspective reaffirms the importance of conceptualizing management in terms of functions, contingencies and skills and the leadership competence of managers (see Figure 1.3). Whatever insights the different perspectives afford on the strategic management process, critical organizational theorists have suggested that 'strategic' is no longer fashionable in management thought and discourse, having gone from 'buzzword to boo-word' (Thompson & McHugh, 2002, p. 110).

A second limitation of SHRM and HR strategy theory is the focus on the connection between external market strategies and HR function. It is argued that contingency analysis relies exclusively on external marketing strategies (how the firm competes) and disregards the internal operational strategies (how the firm is managed) that influence HR practices and performance (Purcell, 1999). In an industry in which a flexible, customized product range and high quality are the key to profitability, a firm can adopt a manufacturing strategy that allows, via new technology and self-managed work teams, for far fewer people but ones who are functionally flexible, within a commitment HR strategy regime. This was the strategy at Flowpak Engineering (Bratton, 1992). Microelectronics and the use of plastic changed the firm's manufacturing strategy from their being a manufacturer of packaging machinery to an assembler. The technology and manufacturing strategy in this case became the key intervening variable between overall business strategy and HRM.

Drawing upon the work of Kelly (1985), the major limitation of a simple SHRM model is that it privileges only one step in the full circuit of industrial capital. To put it another way, the SHRM approach looks only at the *realization* of surplus value within product markets rather than at complex contingent variables that constitute the full transformation process. As Purcell (1999, p. 37) argues, 'we need to be much more sensitive to processes of organizational change and avoid being trapped in the logic of rational choice'.

Another limitation of most current studies examining SHRM is the conceptualization of managerial control. The basic premise of the typologies of HR strategy approach is that a dominant HR strategy is strongly related to a specific competitive strategy. Thus, the commitment HR strategy is most likely to be adopted when management seek to compete in the marketplace by using a generic differentiation strategy. This might be true, but the notion that a commitment HR strategy follows from a real or perceived 'added-value' competitive strategy is more problematic in practice. Moreover, it is misleading to assume that managerial behaviour is not influenced by the indeterminacy of the employment contract and by how to close the 'gap' between an employee's potential and actual performance level. Reflecting on this problem, Colling (1995, p. 29) correctly emphasizes that '"added-value" [differentiation] strategies do not preclude or prevent the use of managerial control over employees ... few companies are able to operationalize added-value programmes without cost-constraints and even fewer can do so for very long'. Others have gone beyond the 'organizational democracy' rhetoric and acknowledge that 'It is utopian to think that control can be completely surrendered' in the 'postmodern' work organization (Cloke & Goldsmith, 2002, p. 162).

Consistent with our earlier definition of strategy – as a specific pattern of decisions and actions – managers do act strategically, and strategic patterns do emerge over a period of time (Thompson & McHugh, 2002; Watson, 1999). One strategic decision and action might, however, undermine another strategic goal. In a market downturn or recession, for example, there is a tendency for corporate management to improve profitability by downsizing and applying more demanding performance outcomes at the unit level. This pattern of action constitutes a strategy even though manifesting a disjunction between organizational design and employer–employee relations. As Purcell (1989, 1995) points out, an organization pursuing a strategy of acquisition and downsizing might 'logically' adopt an HR strategy that includes the compulsory lay-off of non-core employees and, for the identifiable core of employees with rare attributes, a compensation system based on performance results. In practice, the resource-based approach predicts a sharp differentiation within organizations 'between those with key competencies, knowledge and valued organizational memory, and those more easily replaced or disposed of ' (Purcell, 1999, p. 36). In such a case, the business strategy and HR strategy might 'fit', but, as Legge (1995, p. 126) points out, these HR policies and practices 'although consistent with such a business strategy, are unlikely to generate employee commitment' (1995, p. 126). Thus, achieving the goal of 'close fit' of business and HR strategy can contradict the goal of employee commitment and cooperation.

It is important to emphasize that however committed a group of managers might be to a particular HR strategy (for example the commitment HR strategy), there are external conditions and internal 'structural contradictions' at work that will constrain management action (Boxall, 1992, 1996; Streeck, 1987). The kind of analysis explored here is nicely summed up by Hyman's pessimistic pronouncement that 'there is no "one best way" of managing these contradictions, only different routes to partial failure' (1987, quoted in Thompson & McHugh, 2002, p. 108).

STUDY TIP

Read Chapter 8, Control: concepts and strategies in Thompson and McHugh's (2002) book, *Work organizations: A critical introduction*, 3rd edition. Why and how do organizational theorists contest theories of management control? To what extent do variations in HR strategy reflect the fundamental tension between management's need to control workers' behaviour while tapping into workers' ingenuity and cooperation?

In addition to focusing on the validity of the matching SHRM model and typologies of HR strategy, researchers have identified a number of important themes associated with the notion of SHRM that are discussed briefly here and, with the exception of leadership, more extensively in later chapters. These are:

- HR practices and performance (see also Chapter 13)
- re-engineering (see also Chapter 4)
- leadership
- workplace learning (see also Chapter 10)
- trade unions (see also Chapter 12).

Human resource management practices and performance

Although most HRM models provide no clear focus for any test of the HRM–performance link, the models tend to assume that an alignment between business strategy and HR strategy will improve organizational performance and competitiveness. During the past decade, demonstrating that there is indeed a positive link between particular sets or 'bundles' of HR practices and business performance has become '*the* dominant research issue' (Guest, 1997, p. 264). The dominant empirical questions on this topic ask 'What types of performance data are available to measure the HRM–performance link?' and 'Do "high-commitment-type" HRM systems produce above-average results compared with "control-type" systems?' A number of studies (for example Baker, 1999; Betcherman et al., 1994; Guest, 1997; Hutchinson et al., 2000; Ichniowski et al., 1996; Pfeffer, 1998a) have found that, in spite of the methodological challenges, bundles of HRM practices are positively associated with superior organization performance.

Re-engineering and strategic human resource management

All normative models of HRM emphasize the importance of organizational design. As previously discussed, the 'soft' HRM model is concerned with job designs that encourage the vertical and horizontal compression of tasks and greater worker autonomy. The redesign of work organizations has been variously labelled 'high-performing work systems' (HPWSs), 'business process re-engineering' and 'high-commitment management'. The literature emphasizes core features of this approach to organizational design and management, including a 'flattened' hierarchy, decentralized decision-making to line managers or work teams, 'enabling' information technology, 'strong' leadership and a set of HR practices that make workers' behaviour more congruent with the organization's culture and goals (see Champy, 1996; Hammer, 1997; Hammer & Champy, 1993).

Leadership and strategic human resource management

The concept of managerial leadership permeates and structures the theory and practice of work organizations and hence how we understand SHRM. Most definitions of managerial leadership reflect the assumption that it involves a *process* whereby an individual exerts influence upon others in an organizational context. Within the literature, there is a continuing debate over the alleged differences between a manager and a leader: managers develop *plans* whereas leaders create a *vision* (Kotter, 1996). Much of the leadership research and literature tends to be androcentric in nature and rarely acknowledges the limited representation of ethnic groups and women in senior leadership positions (Townley, 1994). The current interest in alternative leadership paradigms variously labelled 'transformational leadership' (Tichy & Devanna, 1986) and 'charismatic leadership' (Conger & Kanungo, 1988) may be explained by understanding the prerequisites of the resource-based SHRM model. Managers are looking for a style of leadership that will develop the firm's human endowment and, moreover, cultivate commitment, flexibility, innovation and change (Bratton et al., in press; Guest, 1987).

A number of writers (for example Agashae & Bratton, 2001; Barney, 1991; Senge, 1990) make explicit links between learning, leadership and organizational change. It would seem that a key constraint on the development of a resource-based SHRM model is leadership competencies. Apparently, 'most re-engineering failures stem from breakdowns in leadership' (Hammer & Champy, 1993, p. 107), and the 'engine' that drives organizational change is 'leadership, leadership, and still more leadership' (Kotter, 1996, p. 32). In essence, popular leadership models extol to followers the need for working beyond the economic contract for the 'common' good. In contemporary parlance, the 'transformational' leader is empowering workers. To go beyond the rhetoric, however, such popular leadership models shift the focus away from managerial control processes and innate power relationships towards the psychological contract and the individualization of the employment relationship.

Workplace learning and strategic human resource management

Within most formulations of SHRM, formal and informal work-related learning has come to represent a key lever that can help managers to achieve the substantive HRM goals of commitment, flexibility and quality (Beer et al., 1984; Keep, 1989). As such, this growing field of research occupies centre stage in the 'soft' resource-based SHRM model. From a managerial perspective, formal and informal learning can, it is argued, strengthen an organization's 'core competencies' and thus act as a lever to sustainable competitive advantage – having the ability to learn faster than one's competitors is of the essence here (Dixon, 1992; Kochan & Dyer, 1995). There is a growing body of work that has taken a more critical look at workplace learning. Some of these writers, for example, emphasize how workplace learning can strengthen 'cultural control' (Legge, 1995), strengthen the power of those at the 'apex of the organization' (Coopey, 1996) and be a source of conflict when linked to productivity or flexibility bargaining and job control (Bratton, 2001) (Chapter 10).

Trade unions and strategic human resource management

The notion of worker commitment embedded in the HRM model has led writers from both ends of the political spectrum to argue that there is a contradiction between the normative HRM model and trade unions. In the prescriptive management literature, the argument is that the collectivist culture, with its 'them and us' attitude, sits uncomfortably with the HRM goal of high employee commitment and the individualization of the employment relationship. The critical perspective also presents the HRM model as being inconsistent with traditional industrial relations, albeit for very different reasons. Critics argue that 'high-commitment' HR strategies are designed to provide workers with a false sense of job security and to obscure underlying sources of conflict inherent in capitalist employment relations (Godard, 1994). Other scholars, taking an 'orthodox pluralist' perspective, have argued that trade unions and the 'high-performance–high-commitment' HRM model cannot only coexist but are indeed necessary if an HPWS is to succeed (see Betcherman et al., 1994; Guest, 1995; Verma, 1995). What is apparent is that this part of the SHRM debate has been strongly influenced by economic, political and legal developments in the USA and UK over the past two decades (Chapter 3).

International and comparative strategic human resource management

The assumption that SHRM is a strategically driven management process points to its international potentialities. The employment relationship is shaped by national systems of employment legislation and the cultural contexts in which it operates. Thus, as the world of business is becoming more globalized, variations in national regulatory systems, labour markets and institutional and cultural contexts are likely to constrain or shape any tendency towards 'convergence' or a 'universal' model of best HRM practice (Bélanger et al., 1999; Clark & Pugh, 2000; Kidd et al., 2001). This section addresses aspects of the international scene to help us place the discourse on the SHRM model into a wider global context. In doing so, we make a distinction between international HRM and comparative HRM. The subject matter of the former revolves around the issues and problems associated with the globalization of capitalism. Comparative HRM, on the other hand, focuses on providing insights into the nature of, and reasons for, differences in HR practices across national boundaries.

HRM IN PRACTICE 2.4

WOMEN FIND OVERSEAS POSTINGS OUT OF REACH

SHERWOOD ROSS, *GLOBE AND MAIL*, 2001, AUGUST 27, P. M6

Female executives who want plum overseas assignments are forced to break through a 'glass border' – a barrier to foreign postings that is not unlike the glass ceiling that stands in the way of promotions, experts say.

'As global assignments increasingly become prerequisites for advancement, glass borders may impede women's progress before they even reach the glass ceiling,' says Sheilla Wellington, president of Catalyst, an advocacy group to advance women in business. Women hold about 13 per cent of all corporate American expatriate posts, according to a study done by Catalyst. That's a poor showing, says the New York-based group.

Authorities cite a variety of obstacles to women becoming global executives. These include misplaced concerns for the safety and effectiveness of female expatriates, as well as the fact that some women have been given little or no opportunity to obtain experience abroad, even with small projects. Women who are selected 'tend to be younger and single and that tells me employers are probably ruling out married women with children,' says Virginia Hollis, vice-president of sales at Cigna International Expatriate Benefits. Women are victims of 'subtle discrimination,' says Linda Stroh, a professor at the Institute of Human Resources and Industrial Relations at Loyola University, in Chicago.

'It doesn't mean that men are screening women out to work abroad. It's an unawareness that women are capable of going.' Also, male executives do not send women abroad 'in the mistakenly paternalistic belief that they are protecting them from environments that may be difficult or dangerous,' says Jean Lipman-Blumen, professor of public policy and organizational behaviour, at the University of Claremont.

Women hold about 13 per cent of all corporate American expatriate posts.

Change will not come, though, until 'corporate executives at the top become very proactive in reaching out to women to be considered for [overseas] assignments,' predicts Anna Lloyd, president of the Committee of 200, a group that represents more than 430 female business executives.

International human resource management

The majority of international HRM research has focused on issues associated with the cross-national transfer of people, such as how to select and manage expatriate managers in international job assignments (for example Shenkar, 1995; Tung, 1988). A decade ago, it was suggested that much of this work tended to be descriptive and lacked analytical rigour (Kochan et al., 1992) but research and scholarship have made considerable progress over the past 10 years. Recent studies have recognized the importance of linking international HRM with the strategic evolution of the firm, and theoretical models of international HRM have been developed (Scullion, 2001). International HRM has been defined as 'HRM issues, functions and policies and practices that result from the strategic activities of multinational enterprises and that impact the international concerns and goals of those enterprises' (Scullion, 1995, p. 356). International HRM tends to emphasize the subordination of national culture and national employment practices to corporate culture and HRM practices (Boxall, 1995).

The issue of transplanting Western HR practices and values into culturally diverse environments needs to be critically researched. Early 21st century capitalism, when developing international business strategy, faces the perennial difficulty of organizing the employment relationship to reduce the indeterminacy resulting from the unspecified nature of the employment contract (Townley, 1994). If we adopt Townley's approach to international HRM, the role of knowledge to render people in the workplace 'governable' is further complicated in culturally diverse environments. For example, it behoves researchers to examine whether managers and workers in Mexico, Chile, India, Pakistan, South Africa and elsewhere will accept the underlying ideology and embrace the HRM paradigm. In addition, although there is an awareness of the importance of international HRM, further research is needed into the barriers facing women seeking international assignment – the 'glass border' (see HRM in practice 2.4).

HRM WEB LINKS

For further information on cultural diversity go to www.ciber.bus.msu.edu, www.shrm.org/diversity and www.shhrm.org/trends.

Comparative human resource management

As with international HRM, the growth of interest in comparative HRM is linked to the globalization of business. Of considerable interest to HR academics and practitioners is the question of the extent to which an HR strategy that works effectively in one country and culture can be transplanted to others. Recent comparative research suggests that there are significant differences between Asian, European and North American companies with regard to HR strategies (Brewster, 2001; Kidd et al., 2001; Scullion, 2001). Drawing upon Bean's (1985) work on comparative industrial relations, comparative HRM is defined here as a systematic method of investigation relating to two or more countries that has analytical rather than descriptive implications. On this basis, comparative HRM should involve activities that seek to explain the patterns and variations encountered in cross-national HRM rather than being simply a description of HRM institutions and HR practices in selected countries. Simple description, what can be called the 'tourist approach', in which 'the reader is presented with a diverse selection of exotic ports of call and left to draw his own conclusion about their relevance to each other and to the traveller himself [sic]' (Shalev, 1981, quoted by Bean, 1985, p. ii), lacks academic rigour. The case for the study of comparative HRM has been made by a number of HR scholars (for example Bean, 1985; Boxall, 1995; Clark & Pugh, 2000; Moore & Jennings, 1995). In terms of critical research, comparative HRM is relatively underdeveloped.

REFLECTIVE QUESTION

Do you believe that there is increasing convergence in HR practices in (1) Europe and (2) worldwide?

There is, of course, an intellectual challenge and intrinsic interest in comparative studies. They may lead to a greater understanding of the contingencies and processes that determine different approaches to managing people at work. The common assumption found in many undergraduate textbooks is that 'best' HR practice has 'universal' application, but an assumption is untenable since HRM phenomena reflect a different cultural milieu (Boxall, 1995). Comparative HRM studies can provide the basis for reforms in a country's domestic public policy by offering 'lessons' from offshore experience. Furthermore, they can promote a wider understanding of, and foster new insights into, HRM, either by reducing what might appear to be specific and distinctive national characteristics by providing evidence of their occurrence elsewhere or, equally well, by demonstrating what is unique about any set of national HR arrangements. The potential benefits of studying comparative and international HRM have been recognized by both academics and HR practitioners and thus 'can no longer be considered a marginal area of interest' (Clark et al., 2000, p. 17).

Using comparative analysis, Brewster (1993, 1995, 2001) has examined the HRM paradigm from a European perspective. Drawing upon the data from a 3-year survey of 14 European countries, Brewster puts forward the notion of a new 'European HRM model' that recognizes State and trade union involvement in the regulation of the employment relationship. According to Brewster, the European HRM model has a greater potential for 'partnership' between labour and management because, in most European Union states, 'the unions are not seen, and do not see themselves, as "adversaries"' (Brewster, 1995, p. 323). Adopting a 'systemic view' of European national work systems, Clark and Pugh (2000) have argued that, despite economic and political pressures towards convergence, differences in cultural and institutional contexts continue to produce divergent employment relationships. Thus, the Dutch 'feminine' culture encourages the antipathy of Dutch workers towards 'hard' HRM whereas 'Sweden's strong collectivist culture counters the development of an individualistic orientation to the employment relationship' (Clark & Pugh, 2000, p. 96).

Inherent in controversies surrounding the notion of a European model, Asian model or North American model are questions of the limitations and value of cross-national generalizations in HRM (Hyman, 1994). Despite the economic and political pressures from globalization, as it is loosely called, the national diversity of HRM systems remains and is particularly sharp between the developed and the developing world (Lipsig-Mummé, 2001). Building on Tyson and Brewster's (1991) hypothesis, we might have to acknowledge the existence of discrete HRM models both between and within nations, contingent on distinct contextual factors. We have also to recognize that those factors which maintain differences in approaches to managing the employment relationship will continue, albeit with decreasing power (Clark & Pugh, 2000). It is easier to formulate questions than answers, and this section has taken the easier route rather than the more difficult, yet there is value in asking questions. Questions can stimulate reflection and increase our understanding of the HRM paradigm. Our objective has been to do both.

HRM WEB LINKS

For further information on comparative HRM, go to www.hrmguide.co.uk (UK), www.workindex.com/ (USA), www.clc-ctc.ca (Canada) and www.travail.gouv.qc.ca/ (Quebec, Canada).

Chapter summary

- This chapter has examined different levels of strategic management, defining strategic management as a 'pattern of decisions and actions' undertaken by the upper echelon of the company.

- Strategic decisions are concerned with change and the achievement of superior performance, and involve strategic choices. In multidivisional companies, strategy formulation takes place at three levels – corporate, business and functional – to form a hierarchy of strategic decision-making. Corporate and business-level strategies, as well as environmental pressures, dictate the choice of HR policies and practices.

- When reading the descriptive and prescriptive strategic management texts, there is a great temptation to be smitten by what appears to be the linear and absolute rationality of the strategic management process. We draw attention to the more critical literature that recognizes that HR strategic options are, at any given time, partially constrained by the outcomes of corporate and business decisions, the current distribution of power within the organization and the ideological values of the key decision-makers.

- A core assumption underlying much of the SHRM research and literature is that each of the main types of generic competitive strategy used by organizations (for example cost leadership or differentiation strategy) is associated with a different approach to managing people, that is, with a different HR strategy.

● We critiqued here the matching model of SHRM on both conceptual and empirical grounds. It was noted that, in the globalized economy with market turbulence, the 'fit' metaphor might not be appropriate when flexibility and the need for organizations to learn *faster* than their competitors seem to be the key to sustainable competitiveness. We also emphasized how the goal of aligning a Porterian low-cost business strategy with an HRM strategy can contradict the core goal of employee commitment.

● The resource-based SHRM model, which places an emphasis on a company's human resource endowments as a strategy for sustained competitive advantage, was outlined. In spite of the interest in workplace learning, there seems, however, little empirical evidence to suggest that many firms have adopted this 'soft' HR strategic model.

● The final section examined the distinctions between international HRM and comparative HRM. This portrayed international HRM as an area of research and practice related to issues associated with the cross-national transfer of people, for example how to select and manage expatriate managers in international job assignments.

● Comparative HRM was portrayed as a field of inquiry largely concerned with the issue of how well an HR strategy that works effectively in one country and culture can be transplanted to another work site overseas.

● We indicated that international HRM and comparative HRM as fields of inquiry have expanded over the past decade, but more research is needed to test the links between international business strategy and international HRM. Studies need to examine the barriers facing women who seek overseas appointments (see HRM in practice 2.4). Furthermore, research is needed to investigate HR practices in developing countries. The mantra of 'high-commitment' HR practices is hollow and unconvincing when applied to organizational life in the export-processing zones (see HRM in practice 3.1). The next chapter examines some of the environmental factors that underlie managerial decision-making processes in SHRM and international HRM.

Key concepts

- Control-based model
- Differentiation strategy
- Hierarchy of strategy
- HR strategy
- Leadership
- Low-cost leadership

- Resource-based model
- Strategic human resource management
- Strategic management
- Workplace learning

Chapter review questions

1. What is meant by 'strategy'? Explain the meaning of 'first-order' and 'second-order' strategies.

2. Explain Purcell's statement that 'trends in corporate strategy have the potential to render the ideals of HRM unobtainable'.

3. 'Business-level strategies may be constrained by human resource issues but rarely seem to be designed to influence them.' Discuss.

4. What does a 'resource-based' SHRM model of competitive advantage mean? What are the implications for HRM of this competitive strategy?

5. What are the linkages, if any, between SHRM, leadership and learning?

6. Why is it difficult to quantify accurately the HRM–organizational performance link?

7. Explain why recent research suggests that the HRM–organizational performance relationship is clearer and stronger when whole 'systems', rather than individual HRM practices, are considered.

8. What value is gained from studying international HRM and comparative HRM?

Further reading

Brewster, C. (2001). HRM: The comparative dimension. In J. Storey (ed.), *Human resource management: A critical text* (pp. 255–71). London: Thompson Learning.

Clark, T., Grant, D. & Heijltjes, M. (2000). Researching comparative and international human resource management. *International Studies of Management*, **29**(4), 6–23.

Kamoche, K. (1996). Strategic human resource management within a resource-capability view of the firm. *Journal of Management Studies,* **33**(2), 213–33.

Monks, K. & McMackin, J. (2001). Designing and aligning an HR system. *Human Resource Management Journal*, **11**(2), 57–72.

Purcell, J. (2001). The meaning of strategy in human resource management. In J. Storey (ed.), *Human resource management: A critical text* (pp. 59–77). London: Thompson Learning.

Scullion, H. (2001). International human resource management. In J. Storey (ed.), *Human resource management: A critical text* (pp. 288–313). London: Thompson Learning.

Practising human resource management

Searching the web

Enter the website of two luxury-car manufacturers such as Lexus (www.lexususa.com) and Volvo (www.volvo.com), both of which compete in the same strategic group. Scan the websites to determine the key features of each company's business strategy. In what ways are their business-level strategies similar and different? Do the companies include HRM in their business-level strategies? If so, how does each company's HR strategy support its business strategy? Enter the websites of two economy-car manufacturers, for example Ford (www.ford.com) and Hyundai (www.hyundai.com). In what ways are their business-level and HR strategies similar and different from those of the first group?

HRM group project

Form a study group of between three and five people, and search the web for sports equipment retailers such as Balmoral Boards (www.snowboards.net.au), Mountain Equipment Co-operative (www. mec.ca), ProSportUK (www.prosportuk.com) and Sportsmart (www.sportsmart.com). After viewing various company websites, discuss the following scenario:

You are advising a group of partners contemplating opening a new sports retail store in your city. Based on your web search, decide what business strategy can best provide your sports store with a competitive advantage to make it a profitable, ongoing operation.

1. Create a strategic group of sports equipment stores in your city and define their generic strategies (for example cost leadership or differentiation strategy).

2. Identify which sports stores are most successful and why.

3. On the basis of this analysis, decide what kind of sports retail store you would advise your clients to open.

4. On the basis of your understanding of the material in this chapter, decide what kind of HR strategy would best support your chosen business-level strategy and why.

Chapter case study

AIR NATIONAL[4]

Air National's (AN) 1998 Annual Report glowed with optimism. Bradley Smith, CEO, stated in his letter to shareholders, 'As a newly privatized company, we face the future with enthusiasm, confident that we can compete in a deregulated industry.' By April 2000, however, the tone had changed, with a reported pre-tax loss of $93 million. The newly appointed CEO, Clive Warren, announced a major change in the company's business strategy that would lead to a transformation of business operations and HR practices in Europe's largest airline company.

Background

During the early 1980s, civil aviation was a highly regulated market, and competition was managed via close, if not always harmonious, relationships between airlines, their competitors and governments. National flag-carriers dominated the markets, and market shares were determined not by competition but by the skill of their governments in negotiating bilateral 'air service agreements'. These agreements established the volume and distribution of air traffic and thereby revenue. Within these markets, AN dominated other carriers; despite the emergence of new entrants, AN's share of the domestic market in the early 1980s, for example, increased by 60 per cent.

The competition

In the middle of the 1980s, AN's external environment was subjected to two sets of significant change. First, in 1986, AN was privatized by Britain's Conservative government. This potentially reduced the political influence of the old corporation and exposed the new company to competitive forces. Preparation for privatization required a painful restructuring and 'downsizing' of assets and the workforce, driven largely by the need to make the company attractive to initially sceptical investors.

Privatization also offered significant political leverage, which AN was able to deploy to secure further stability in its key product markets. It was this context, rather than the stimulus of market competition, that gave senior management the degree of stability and security needed to plan and implement new business and HRM strategies. The second set of pressures, potentially more decisive, was generated by prolonged economic recession and the ongoing deregulation of civil aviation in Europe and North America.

With these environmental forces, AN attempted to grow out of the recession by adopting a low-cost competitive strategy and joining the industry-wide price war. Bradley Smith, when he addressed his senior management team, stated, 'this strategy requires us to be aggressive in the marketplace and to be diligent in our pursuit of cost reductions and cost minimization in areas like service, marketing and advertising'. The low-cost competitive strategy failed. Passenger numbers slumped by 7 per cent during the late 1980s, contributing to a pre-tax loss. Following the appointment of the new CEO, AN changed its competitive strategy and began to develop a differentiation business strategy (Porter, 1980) or what is also referred to as an 'added-value' strategy.

In 2002, following the September 11 attacks in New York and Washington in which four commercial planes were hijacked and crashed, killing almost 3000 people, international air travel bookings fell sharply. The catastrophes caused the loss of more than 100,000 airline jobs around the world. In addition, early in 2002, new discount airlines started operating in Europe, and there was a costly battle for market share between AN, HopJet Airlines and Tango Airlines.

Air National's new competitive strategy

Under the guidance of the newly appointed CEO, Clive Warren, AN prioritized high-quality customer service, 're-engineered' the company and launched a discount airline that operated as a separate company. The management structure was reorganized to provide a tighter focus on operational issues beneath corporate level. AN's operations were divided into route groups based on five major markets (Exhibit 2.1). Each group was to be headed by a general manager who was given authority over the development of the business, with a particular emphasis on marketing. The company's advertising began also to emphasize the added-value elements of AN's services. New brand names were developed, and new uniforms were introduced for the cabin crews and point-of-service staff.

AN's restructuring also aimed to cut the company's cost base. Aircraft and buildings were sold and persistently unprofitable routes either suspended or abandoned altogether. AN's overall route portfolio was cut by 4 per cent during 2001 alone. Labour costs offered the most significant potential savings, and with 35,000 employees AN's re-engineering included 'one of the biggest redundancy programmes in British history'. Once the redundancy programme was underway, the company was able to focus on product development, marketing, customer service and HR development. The company's sharpened focus on the new 'customer-first' programme prompted a major review of the management of employees and their interface with customers.

Air National's human resources strategy

The competitive and HR strategies pursued by

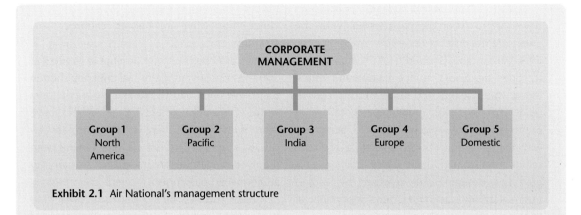

Exhibit 2.1 Air National's management structure

AN mainline business in the wake of this restructuring process, are congruent with an HR strategy that emphasizes employee empowerment and commitment. As Clive Warren stated in a television interview, 'In an industry like ours, where there are no assembly lines or robots, people are our most important asset and our long term survival depends upon how they work as part of a team'. In the closing part of her presentation, Elizabeth Hoffman, AN's Director of Human Resources, outlined the need for a new approach to managing AN's mainline employees: 'We must emphasize to our managers that they must give up control if our employees are to improve their performance' (Exhibit 2.2).

As part of the 'new way of doing things', demarcation between craft groups, such as avionics and mechanical engineers, were removed, and staff were organized into teams of multiskilled operatives led by team leaders. Even those middle managers who supported the new work teams found this approach to managing their subordinates uncomfortable, as one maintenance manager acknowledged: 'The hard part is having to share power. I confess, I like to be able to say yes or no without having to confer all the time and seek consensus from the team.'

AN instituted a series of customer service training seminars and invested in training and development. The senior management also

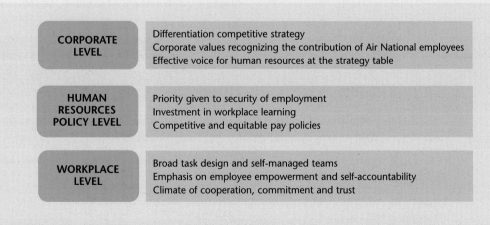

Exhibit 2.2 Key characteristics of Air National's strategic human resource management and empower–developmental approach

developed a 'strategic partnership' with the unions. At the onset of the restructuring process, Clive Warren and Elizabeth Hoffman undertook to 'open the books' to the unions and established team briefings and regular, formal consultation meetings with union representatives. A profit-related pay system was also launched, with the full support of the unions. In addition, senior management held major training programmes, designed and delivered by leading business school academics, on the importance of trust, motivation and 'visionary' leadership.

Running parallel to these developments was the company's concurrent objective of cost reduction. Between 1996 and 2000, AN shed 37 per cent of its workforce, nearly 25 per cent leaving in 1998. Job cuts were managed entirely through voluntary severance and redeployment. The requirement to sustain and improve performance in the face of such job losses produced, however, a preoccupation with productivity levels, and attempts to alter shift patterns sometimes provoked conflict. Disputes were resolved quickly, usually by the company reminding employees of AN's commitment to job security, training and development, and through senior management 'throwing money at the problem'.

GoJet competitive and human resources strategy

AN also launched its GoJet product in November 2002 to take advantage of the dramatic shift by European and North American passengers towards discount airlines. GoJet planes have more seats because there is less room between the seats and the business-class section has been removed, which allows the planes to carry an additional 20 passengers.

GoJet costs will be 20 per cent lower than those of AN's comparable mainline flights partly because GoJet's employees will be paid a lower wage than their counterparts at AN. Clive Warren has, however, said that wages will be competitive with GoJet's competitors in the discount market.

Reviewing the developments, Clive Warren considered that AN had been 'transformed by re-engineering'. Deep in debt in the late 1980s, AN went into profit in the first quarter of 1998 and then suffered a loss in the last quarter of 2001 and the first quarter of 2002. The company's aircraft were flying to 164 destinations in 75 countries from 16 UK airports. 'If we are to maintain our market share in domestic and international passenger traffic we have to have a business plan that recognizes the realities of airline travel in the 21st century', said Warren.

Discussion questions

You are an HR consultant employed by a rival national airline to investigate AN's competitive and HR strategy. Prepare a written report on the following questions:

1. What factors enabled AN's senior management to take a strategic approach to its business and to adopt an empowering-developmental approach to HRM?

2. How useful is the concept of 'strategic choice' in understanding the linkage between AN's competitive and HR strategies?

3. What problems, if any, do you envisage with AN's HR strategy and GoJet's HR strategy? (Re-reading HRM in practice 2.3 might help here.)

HR-related skill development

Case study analysis is an important skill for potential and practising managers to develop: it provides learners with experience of applying strategic management concepts to an organization they have been asked to study or to their own company or organization. Typically, a detailed analysis of a case should include the following: background of the organization, SWOT analysis, nature of the business strategy, an HR system to match its strategy and recommendations. You will develop your skill at analysing a case study by going to www.palgrave.com/business/brattonandgold) and clicking on 'Analysing a Case Study'.

Notes

1. F. A. Maljers, Chairman of the Board of Unilever.
2. Beer et al. (1984). *Managing human assets*, p. 25.
3. Kathy Monks and John McMackin (2001). Designing and aligning an HR system. *Human Resource Management,* **11**(2), pp. 57–72.
4. This case is based on Experiencing turbulence: Competition, strategic choice and the management of human resources in British Airways by Trevor Colling (1995), *Human Resource Management Journal,* **5**(5), pp. 18–32, and articles in the *Globe and Mail* (2002, April 20).

Part Two

The human resource management context

PART 1 THE HUMAN RESOURCE MANAGEMENT ARENA

Chapter 1 The nature of human resource management

Chapter 2 Strategic human resource management

PART 2 THE HUMAN RESOURCE MANAGEMENT CONTEXT

Chapter 3 The context of human resource management

Chapter 4 Work and work organization

Chapter 5 Health and safety

PART 3 HUMAN RESOURCE MANAGEMENT PRACTICES

Chapter 6 Human resource planning

Chapter 7 Recruitment and selection

Chapter 8 Appraisal and performance management

Chapter 9 Reward management

Chapter 10 Human resource development

Chapter 11 Employee relations

Chapter 12 Union–management relations

PART 4 THE EVALUATION CONTEXT

Chapter 13 Evaluating human resource management

Chapter 14 Conclusion: Whither HRM?

Chapter three

The context
of human resource
management

John Bratton

Context refers to all the external forces that exist outside the boundary of the organization and have the potential to affect work organizations and, in turn, shape human resource management strategy, policies and practices.

'Every generation believes it is living through great change, and our generation is no different ... [But] What gives contemporary change its power and momentum is in the economic, political and cultural change summed up by the term "globalization". It is the interaction of extraordinary technological innovation combined with worldwide reach driven by a global capitalism that gives today's change its particular complexion. It has a speed, inevitability and force that it has not had before.'[1]

'An infectious greed seemed to have gripped much of our business community in the late 1990s. It's not that humans have become any more greedy than in generations past. It is that the avenues to express greed have grown so enormously.'[2]

'Until the benefits of globalization are shared more widely, people will continue to rise up against globalization.'[3]

Chapter outline

Chapter objectives

After studying this chapter, you should be able to:

1. Explain the importance of studying context for understanding human resource management (HRM)
2. Discuss ways of conceptualizing the nature of context
3. Identify the external contexts that affect HRM policies and actions
4. Understand the implications of these external contexts for the HRM function

● Introduction

Managing people at work does not take place in a vacuum. Wider economic, techno-logical, political and social forces influence and shape human resource management (HRM) strategy, policies and practices, global and local economic developments some-times having an indirect or a 'multiplier' effect. The electrical giant Siemens, for example, overtakes Philips Electronics, so Philips downsizes and lays off workers. Belt-tightening workers then press for cheaper services from local traders and are prepared to work for lower wages, thereby causing an adjustment in the local labour market and in the HRM decisions and activities of those organizations affected. Williams (1993) is one of a number of theorists who have argued the importance of understanding the relationship between economic stability or instability and HRM, but it is not just the economic context that matters. New manufacturing and service technologies, new processes (for example total quality management and International Organization for Standardization [ISO 9000]) and developments in global telecommunications networks have important ramifications for the labour markets, organizational and work design, and HRM. Furthermore, the employment relationship involves a legal relationship, and how people are managed within the workplace will be influenced by the political and legal climate. Just as significant is the nature of the workforce and demographic changes that affect the broader labour market. Past fluctuations in the birthrate in Anglo-Saxon economies are producing abrupt changes in the composition of the labour force. The proportion of older workers (aged 55 years and above) is beginning to rise as the 'baby-boomers' approach retirement age, and an ageing work-force has significant implications for organizations.

Changes in the economic, technological, political and social contexts impact on managerial behaviour (see Figure 1.3). The attack on the World Trade Center on 11 September 2001 and the crisis in the equity markets in July 2002 are dramatic exam-ples of contextual events that impact on organizations. An analysis of the external environment, the structural changes, the causes of the adjustments and possible outcomes would fill several volumes. In this chapter, however, we clarify what we mean by the term 'context' and assess the causal connections between context and work organizations. In so doing, we provide a modest review of the economic, tech-nological, political and social changes in European and North American economies, and possible ramifications for HRM. The chapter begins with a brief overview of some of the broader changes in global capitalism. This is followed by sections examining developments in labour markets and government interventions, the chapter concluding by considering demographic changes.

REFLECTIVE QUESTION

Go back to Chapter 1 and look at Figure 1.3 (HRM practices, contingencies and skills). Can you think of some recent events that significantly influence the external context of HRM? Why is it important for human resources managers to be informed of external developments?

Conceptions of contexts

A fundamental insight of sociology is that people operate in a social context or environment that has a powerful influence on their behaviour. Organizational theorists have applied this idea to formal work organizations by acknowledging the role of external factors or forces in shaping managerial behaviour. But studying the context is not easy. Over the past three decades, analysts have encompassed more and more elements shaping organizational action and have, moreover, recognized that the causal arrows point in both directions: contexts influence organizations, but organizations also affect contexts (Scott, 2003). The analysis presented here uses an 'open-systems' model to examine the multidimensional and changing nature of context. So what is an open system? A system is a set of interrelated and interdependent parts configured in a manner that produces a unified whole. Cars, plants and societies are said to be systems. That is, they take inputs, transform them and produce an output. Systems may be classified as either 'closed' or 'open' to their environment. Work organizations are said to be open systems in that they acquire inputs (for example materials, energy, people and finance) from the environment, transform them into services or products, and discharge outputs in the form of services, products – and sometimes pollutants – to the external environment. Figure 3.1 illustrates a simple open system. A closed system is one that does not depend on its environment, that is, one that is sealed off from the outside world.

In a broad sense, the context is infinite and includes everything outside the immediate boundaries of the organization. The analysis of external factors is, however, limited to the factors or forces to which the organization is sensitive and to which it must respond to survive (Scott, 2003). Thus, for our purposes, context refers to all the external elements that exist outside the boundary of the organization or 'system' and have the potential to affect and shape formal work organizations and in turn influence HRM strategy, policies and practices. Conceptions of contexts vary by level of analysis as well as by substantive focus (for example economic resources or political

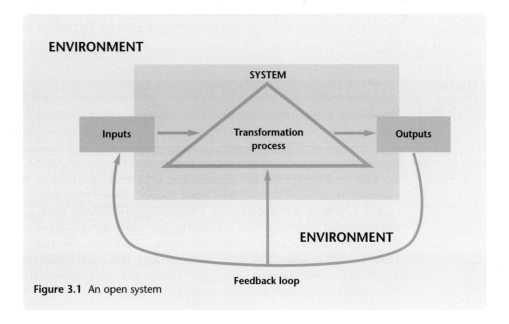

Figure 3.1 An open system

forces). Levels of analysis include the specific organization, the industry level, the spatial level (for example all the organizations in a geographical region) and the global level. The open-system model emphasizes that management action is not separate from the world but is connected to the wider context. As Jaffee (2001, p. 209) states, 'The existing internal structure, strategy, and success of an organization is heavily influenced by environmental forces in which it operates and with which it interacts and competes.' This proposition suggests, first, that those in charge of organizations are externally constrained in their ability to implement any organizational strategy, and second, that any 'one best way' to manage depends on the environment or context in which the organization operates.

The notion that a particular organizational strategy is contingent upon the contextual demands placed upon organizations has been criticized on the grounds of 'environmental determinism' (for example Perrow, 1986). The resource dependency theory advances an alternative to contextual determinism. Rather than viewing organizational controllers as largely passive or impotent in relation to contextual forces, it is emphasized that organizations pursue 'proactive strategies' to overcome contextual constraints (Pfeffer & Salancik, 1978). In essence, it is proposed that it is too simple to regard the influence of context as merely a one-way flow. Senior management will attempt to change the external context or environment. A company might, for example, transfer its operations to where there is little competition or few, if any, health and safety regulations. In addition, workers seek to influence government legislation and regulation by lobbying members of parliament. Thus, the context is a social construct, created at a specific time in history for conducting business. Understanding fully the strategic role of HRM requires an understanding of external contexts. A model for examining the complex and dynamic realities of context and its causal connections with HRM is shown in Figure 3.2 (see also Figure 2.3).

REFLECTIVE QUESTION

Consider how the external context has impacted on an organization you have studied, your own workplace or an organization in which a member of your family is employed. How has the employer or senior management responded to such contextual changes?

STUDY TIP

Underlying the economic–competitive advantage discourse is an emphasis on learning both *for* work and *at* work. As the Organisation for Economic Co-operation and Development (OECD) argues, 'a well educated and well trained population is important for the social and economic well-being of countries' (OECD, 1997, p. 33). Go back to the HRM models presented in Chapter 1, and look at the contextual elements in some of the models. What context elements in the models help to explain why there is a new focus on workplace learning? Why is the notion of workplace learning changing how businesses see themselves? Obtain a copy of the Department for Education and Employment's 1998 report, *The Learning Age* (DfEE, 1998a). What assumptions underpin the report? What are the implications of the report for the HRM function? What contribution can organizations, and in particular the HRM function, make to wider workplace learning?

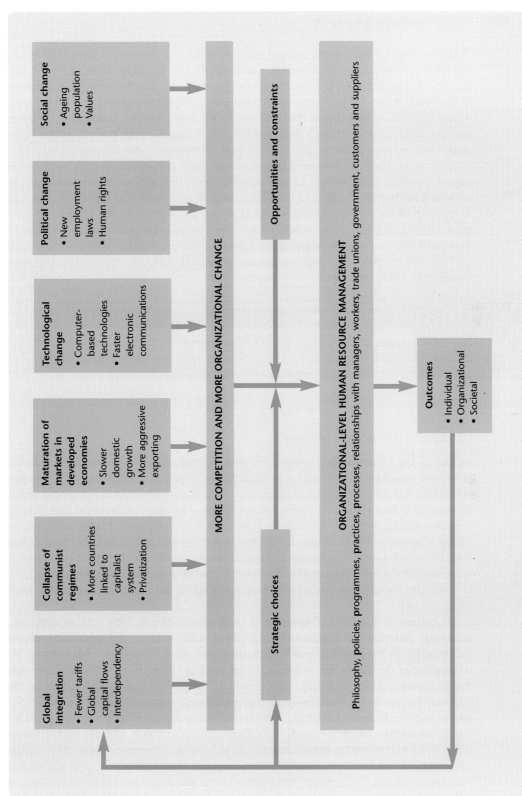

Figure 3.2 A model of the external contexts of human resource management

● The **economic context**

There is a general agreement among commentators that the structure as well as the fundamental dynamics of business has dramatically changed over the past two decades. At the global level, in the advanced capitalist world, the previous dominance of the USA began to give way to a three-way competitive rivalry between North America, the European Union (EU) and the Pacific rim countries, dominated by Japan and the 'four tigers' of Hong Kong, South Korea, Singapore and Taiwan. At the European level, as part of the process of European integration, the EU has introduced a number of measures to remove barriers to free trade and encourage the mobility of capital, services and people. At the national level, in Britain, contextual changes include a further contraction of manufacturing employment, the wide diffusion and acceptance of microprocessor-based technologies, an increase in the amount of part-time work and female employment, higher levels of unemployment and an entrenchment of a political economic paradigm based on the pre-eminence of the individual and the free market. The implementation of similar economic policies can also be observed in North America.

REFLECTIVE QUESTION

Look at the quotes on the economy and global developments at the beginning of the chapter and HRM in practice 3.1. What is your own view on global capitalism – unlimited opportunities for wealth creation or an Orwellian nightmare?

Changes in the world economy

As part of the constructed economic context, 'globalization' is the defining political economic paradigm of our time – it refers to the growing integration of the world's economies whereby a handful of large corporations are permitted to control as much as possible of the natural resources and social life – for example medical care, education and welfare services – in order to pursue their primary goal, that of maximizing profits (Chomsky, 1999). In the 1990s, the idea of 'globalization' became ubiquitous; it was and still is used to capture a range of developments in the world economy. It must also be the most misused term in public discourse today. 'Globalization' is used to cover any activity that crosses international borders, but we need to define the term more precisely.

Globalization refers to a number of overlapping trends. The first is that core economic activities are conducted on a global scale; that is, the manufacturing of commodities or the processing of information takes place in international markets. By the middle of the 1990s, for example, 25 per cent of UK manufacturing capacity was foreign owned (Hutton, 1996). The second trend that defines globalization is the communications revolution, based on microelectronics, satellite telecommunications and network-orientated computer software. The communication revolution provides the infrastructure for new 'global capitalism' (Castells, 2000). Thirdly, globalization refers to a fundamental political change, the implosion of Soviet communism and the relegation of national governments to being the 'gate-keepers' of free unfettered markets. Without competition from communist ideology, post-1989 capitalism 'is much harder, more mobile, more ruthless and more certain about what it needs to make it tick' (Giddens & Hutton, 2000, p. 9). Moreover, the new global electronic capitalism of the 21st century is less controlled and regulated than the industrial capitalism of the 1960s and 70s, which has important ramifications for HRM. Giddens and Hutton call it a 'febrile capitalism' serving the needs of Wall Street and financial and stock markets; 'Its ideology is that shareholder value must be maximized, that labour markets should be 'flexible' and that capital should be free to invest and disinvest in industries and countries at will' (2000, p. 10).

HRM IN PRACTICE 3.1

THREAD THAT COULD SPAN GLOBAL GULF

KEVIN WATKINS, *GUARDIAN*, 2001, JULY 30, P. 21

At the age of 18, with three years' education to her name, Shawaz Begum is an authority on globalization.

Six mornings a week she leaves her crumbling one-room mud home in the slum area of Ashulia on the outskirts of Dhaka, capital of Bangladesh, and walks to a South Korean-owned factory in the export-processing zone. She spends the next 10 hours sewing garments, including Tesco, Pierre Cardin and Harrods shirts, Nike tracksuits and Levi jeans. Is Shawaz Begum a symbol of globalization or a victim of a world trading system that benefits only the rich? Answer: neither. Debates on world trade are becoming polarized. In one corner stand the 'globaphiles', among them the World Bank, the IMF and northern governments, which hold that increased exports are good for the poor. In the other are the 'globaphobes', arguing that trade is inherently exploitive and salvation should be sought in less trade and more self-reliance. In Ashulia, both camps appear equally out of

touch with reality.

Bangladesh is a desperately poor country, with almost half of the population below the poverty line. Yet by comparison with other least developed countries it is a (very) partial success story. In the past 10 years incomes have been rising at more that 2% a year, poverty is falling – albeit far too slowly – and social welfare indicators are improving.

> **What the anti-trade lobby does not understand is that access to northern markets provides real people with opportunities to build a better life.**

Garment exports are crucial. From minuscule beginnings at the end of the 1980s, the sector now generates almost 80% of foreign exchange earnings, about 3.7 billion pounds a year. There are 1.7 million people employed in the industry, three-quarters of them women.

In return for clothing western consumers, Shawaz Begum receives $1.70 for her 10-hour day. This is double what she would earn in the informal sector; it keeps a widowed mother in food and a sister in school.

The more serious problem concerns labour conditions. When Bangladeshi women enter an export-processing zone, they leave their human rights at the gate. Membership of a trade union is illegal, government has relinquished the right to carry out health and safety checks, and compliance with minimum wage and social welfare law is voluntary ...

What the anti-trade lobby does not understand is that access to northern markets provides real people with opportunities to build a better life. Their alter egos in the World Bank and G8 appear equally incapable of grasping that their complacency, hypocrisy, and failure to act on pledges to make globalization work for the poor undermine the credibility of the international trading system.

These broad changes in global capitalism have been the subject of different interpretations. One influential school of thought links the changes to the concept of postmodernism: flexible specialization (Piore & Sabel, 1984), disorganized capitalism (Lash & Urry, 1987), post-Fordism (Hall & Jacques, 1989) and neo-liberalism, or the 'Washington consensus' (Chomsky, 1999). Lash and Urry (1987) argue that Britain and the USA, among other capitalist societies, are moving into an era of 'disorganized capitalism'. The increasing scale of industrial and financial corporations, combined with the growth of a global market, means that national markets have become less regulated by large nationally based corporations, and individual nation-states have less direct control and regulation over large transnational companies. The themes of post-Fordism, flexibility and disorganization are supportive of the broader themes of the diversity of capital, political management, 'post-bureaucratic' and 'postmodern' work organization (Thompson, 1993; Thompson & McHugh, 2002). Others have argued that the changes in the global economy are so profound as to constitute 'multiple revolutions'. In the words of Giddens and Hutton 'The open global economy is a precious acquisition offering opportunity, creativity and wealth. But it is a system ... that is precarious and potentially dangerous – it is on the edge' (2000, p. 214). Still others have emphasized the basic rules of the new global order: 'liberalize trade and finance, let markets set prices ('get prices right'), end inflation ('macroeconomic stability'), privatize.' And, as for the elected government, it should 'get out of the way – hence the population too, insofar as the government is democratic, though the conclusion remains implicit' (Chomsky, 1999, p. 20).

The effects of globalization on income level are readily apparent. Global free trade has enriched a class of senior executives, financial investors and professionals (largely accountants and corporate lawyers). In 1996, the United Nations reported that the assets of the world's 358 billionaires exceeded the combined incomes of 45 per cent of the planet's population (Faux & Mishel, 2000). In 1990, 2.7 billion people were living on less than US$2 a day, whereas in 1998 the number living on less than US$2 daily had increased to an estimated 2.8 billion (Stiglitz, 2002). Moreover, inequality of income and wealth, both within Anglo-Saxon mature countries and between the mature developed and less developed countries, has increased. In the advanced countries, for which comparable data are available, income growth was higher in the 1980s than the 1990s. Over the past two decades, income growth has been substantially below that of the two decades between 1960 and 1980, as shown in Table 3.1.

Table 3.1 Per capita income growth in selected developed countries, 1960–96

| | Annual growth rate per capita income* | | |
	1960–79	1979–89	1989–96
Canada	3.4%	1.8%	–0.1%
France	3.7	1.6	0.8
Germany	3.3	1.9	1.3
UK	2.2	2.2	1.0
USA	2.3	1.5	1.0
* At 1990 price levels and exchange rates			

Source: Faux and Mishel (2000) Table 2, p. 97

Critics of globalization also point to the inherently exploitive nature of global free trade. Klein (2000, p. xvii), for example, brings together the reality of the so-called 'logo-linked' global economy:

This village where some multinationals, far from leveling the global playing field with jobs and technology for all, are in the process of mining the planet's poorest back-country for unimaginable profits. This is the village where Bill Gates lives, amassing a fortune of $55 billion while a third of his workforce is classified as temporary workers, and where competitors are either incorporated into the Microsoft monolith or made obsolete by the latest feat in software bundling. This is the village where we are indeed connected to one another through a web of brands, but the underside of that web reveals designer slums like the one I visited outside Jakarta. IBM claims that its technology spans the globe, and so it does, but often its international presence takes the form of cheap Third World labour producing the computer chips and power sources that drive our machines.

In recent years, a significant theme in the globalization discourse has been the increasingly expressed concern for the current and emerging quality of the natural environment (Egri & Pinfield, 1999: Hertz, 2002). Critics of globalization have argued that global free trade has caused worldwide environmental destruction in an asymmetrical pattern. It has been suggested that as the multinational corporations located in the North control the global economy, it is the South and the underdeveloped countries that are, because of the North's greater economic and political power, disproportionately bearing the environmental burden of the new global capitalism (Shiva, 2000).

HRM IN PRACTICE 3.2

RATIFYING KYOTO ESTIMATED TO COST UP TO 450,000 JOBS

STEVEN CHASE, *GLOBE AND MAIL*, 2002, FEBRUARY 27, P. B6

Ratifying the Kyoto protocol could force plant closing throughout Canada and cost the country's manufacturing sector as many as 450,000 jobs by 2010, the Canadian Manufacturers and Exporters association is warning. 'The cumulative impact of meeting Canada's Kyoto target would be the equivalent of a one-year recession,' the CME says in a report to be released today called 'Pain Without Gain: Canada and the Kyoto Protocol'.

Ottawa is coming under pressure to decide whether Canada will ratify the 1997 Kyoto accord, negotiated in Japan by 150 countries, which requires signatories to cut emissions of global-warming gases by about 6 per cent from 1990 levels by the end of 2012.

The federal government has said it hopes to ratify the deal, but, in the four years since the accord was signed, has yet to develop a detailed plan showing how Canada will meet its Kyoto emissions targets – a delay that's making business groups nervous. 'We've been working on this for over four years of consultation and we still don't have a reliable economic analysis that can tell us what the costs will be,' said the CME chief economist Jayson Myers. The CME's estimate of 450,000 lost manufacturing jobs – or about 20 per cent of the country's manufacturing base of 2.2 million workers – is based in part on the assumption that curbing emissions will impose new costs on businesses and reduce their competitiveness compared to the USA. Being less competitive would cost Canadian companies contracts and jobs, the CME reasons. The CME fears that American companies will beat our Canadian companies for jobs and production if Ottawa ratifies Kyoto. 'The jobs will go south and so will the emissions: the production will just be picked up by another country,' Mr. Myers said.

Meanwhile, the group says new technologies that might enable Canada to painlessly meet targets have not yet been invented. 'The bottom line is that Canada will not be able to achieve its Kyoto target without damaging economic and employment growth,' the CME's report says.

'The bottom line is that Canada will not be able to achieve its Kyoto target without damaging economic and employment growth.'

The federal government, which insists it can meet Kyoto targets, is currently hammering out new estimates of the Kyoto accord's impact on Canada's economy. 'It is possible, in Canada, to remain competitive and yet make sure that our air is not polluted,' Prime Minister Jean Crétien told the House of Commons yesterday.

The CME suggests in its report that perhaps Ottawa would think twice about ratifying the deal. 'It is not clear that the ... Kyoto protocol is the appropriate mechanism for Canada in responding to the challenges of climate change. Our largest trading partner, the United States, is not covered by the agreement. [And] developing countries are not bound to emissions reductions targets either.'

Despite the environmental costs of atmospheric pollution, North American global corporations continue to influence and shape the external context by lobbying against ratifying the Kyoto Protocol on Climate Change (see HRM in practice 3.2). Broad social movements, concerned about global inequality and environmental pollution, have also attempted to influence the external context of business through international conferences, commissioned reports, political lobbying and street protests, for example in Seattle, Genoa, and Quebec.

These issues of growing inequality and atmospheric pollution, among others, are symptomatic of the deep structure of beliefs regarding the consequences of globalization. As Hutton and Giddens (2000) explore in their book, the trajectory of global capitalism is unpredictable. At the time of writing, there is growing concern that the string of accounting deceptions in corporate America – Enron, WorldCom Inc. and Adelphia Communications Corp. – and the implosion of the North American equity markets will permanently destabilize investor confidence and long-term economic growth. In addition, the US accounting scandals have caused the conventional wisdom of the 1990s, that government should abdicate control and initiative to the private business sector, to be questioned. Commenting on President George W. Bush's speech to the business community in July 2002, one business editorial reflected the shift in thinking like this: 'It has become clear that the scandals represent not just a few bad apples, but an entire system of inadequate corporate and financial reporting. If President Bush is serious about getting tough on big business, he must deal with the conflicts that have undermined investors' faith in the markets.'[4]

Changes in the UK economy, 1980–2000

The notion of globalization suggests that all advanced economies face a similar economic context dictated by a common set of global market forces. Compared with other G7 economies (which include the USA, Canada, the UK, Germany, France, Italy and Japan), the UK has, however, a number of economic peculiarities (Hirst &

Thompson, 2000). The changes and the distinctiveness of the UK economy are usually described by opaque economic statistics. In broad terms, looking back over the 1980s, the UK economy started off with a severe recession, particularly in the manufacturing sector in the Midlands and the north of Britain; then, between 1985 and 1987, there was a short period of growth, until 1990 when another recession began that affected businesses and communities in both the north and south of Britain. Real gross domestic product (GDP) increased by 5 per cent and real manufacturing output fell by 2 per cent between 1980 and 1984. The upward path of the GDP remained erratic and concealed the disappearance of large tracts of industrial landscape. Overall, however, real GDP increased by 23 per cent and manufacturing output rose by 25 per cent in the period 1984–90. Over the past decade, 1990–2000, the rate of growth of the GDP at first fell as Britain entered a deep recession in the second quarter of 1990. Thereafter, the economy grew steadily, with unemployment and inflation levels at their lowest levels since 1980 (Millward et al., 2000). There were significant shifts of economic activity and employment from the manufacturing to the service sector, as well as concerns for the future prospects of the production industries.

At the beginning of the 21st century, economic growth fluctuated sharply across most EU Member States. In 2000–01, growth was quite strong, but following the attacks of 11 September 2001 on the New York World Trade Center, the economies of Britain and many other states entered an economic recession, particularly in civil aviation, tourism and related industries. In 2001, manufacturing output in Britain fell by 5.4 per cent, the biggest decline since the recession in autumn 1991, but even with a poor performance in manufacturing, Britain managed to outpace all other members of the G7 economy (*The Economist*, January 26, 2002, p. 51). In the wider EU context, Figure 3.3 shows that average GDP growth was 1.4 per cent in the 15 EU Member States in 2001, down significantly compared with the figure of 3.3 per cent in the 15 Member States for the third quarter of 2000. The 2001–02 recession in the US economy was exacerbated by the accounting scandals in some high-profile American corporations.

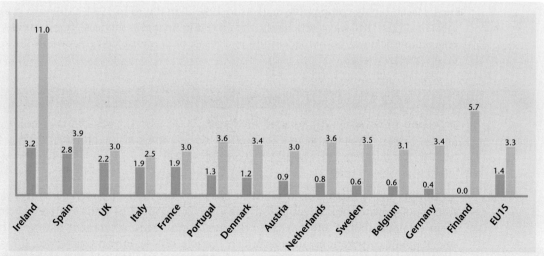

Figure 3.3 Growth in gross domestic product in the European Union (EU) for the third quarters of 2001 and 2000 (percentage change compared with the same period in the previous year)
Source: www.eiro.eurofound.ie

HRM WEB LINKS

Go to the following websites for more information on important economic trends in Britain (www.statistics.gov.uk), Canada (www.statcan.ca/start.html), the EU (www. eiro.eurofound.ie), South Africa (www.statssa.gov.za) and Australia (www.abs. gov.au).

The UK's economic problems, with regards to its competitiveness performance, are measured in terms of its share of the overseas and domestic market. The UK's share of world exports of manufactures fell from approximately 17 per cent in 1960 to about 8 per cent in 1986. Although the volume of international exports of manufactures increased by almost 42 per cent between 1978 and 1987, the volume of UK exports of manufactured goods increased by only 23 per cent (Griffiths & Wall, 1989). In the manufacturing sector, UK output increased by 6 per cent in the period 1979 to 1991 compared with the OECD average (excluding the UK) of 35 per cent. In 1983, UK trade in manufacturing went into deficit for the first time since the Industrial Revolution (Hutton, 1996), the UK being placed 20th out of the 21 OECD economies. The UK's share of total OECD manufacturing output declined from 6.5 per cent in 1979 to 5.2 per cent in 1991; for the period 1979–92, the UK was situated at the bottom of the league (Michie, 1992).

The data collected by Millward et al. (1992, 2000) provide an alternative source of information on important aspects of the changing nature of the economy. Their findings, covering the period 1984 to 1998, show some identifiable changes as perceived by their management respondents. Overall, in manufacturing, there was no noticeable shift towards international markets. UK manufacturing generally failed to invest in new machinery and R&D. During the 1980s, investment increased by only 2 per cent per year (whereas dividends jumped by 12 per cent per year), and in 1994 only 13 British companies appeared in the world's top 200 investors in R&D (Hutton, 1996). At the same time, however, companies faced increased competition: 'more establishments faced highly competitive markets in 1990 than did so in 1984' (Millward et al., 1992, p. 12). This was particularly the case for financial services, transportation, telecommunications and broadcasting as a result of domestic deregulation (Millward et al., 2000).

REFLECTIVE QUESTION

According to Bowen (1992, quoted in Needle, 2000, p. 54), 'you cannot pay for Japanese cars with British hairdressing'. What do you think of the argument that a healthy economy requires a healthy manufacturing sector?

Another major change in the British economy has been the marked shift away from public ownership. Privatization was a key component of Conservative government economic policy and has taken different forms. Most prominent has been the sale of public corporations, such as British Telecom (1984), British Gas (1986), British Airways (1987), British Steel (1988), water (1989), electricity distribution (1990), electricity generation (1991), British Coal (1994), British Rail (1996) and Her Majesty's Stationery Office (1996). The successive waves of privatization and contracting-out of a wide range of services substantially reduced employment in the public sector. Survey findings show that employment in state-owned corporations fell by 38 per cent, from 1.3 million to 0.8 million, between 1984 and 1990 (Millward et al., 1992; see also Beaumont, 1992), and by 1998 public sector industries accounted for less than one-third (32 per cent) of all employees covered by the survey (Cully et al., 1999). Another aspect of Conservative government economic policy directed management attention towards increasing 'flexibility' in the workplace and reducing labour costs. The other form of privatization has thus been private contracting and competitive tendering in, for example, the health care sector and city and central government. If events during the last years of public ownership are viewed as part of the preparation for privatization, the evidence suggests that privatization has had a negative impact on employment level (Pendleton, 1997a). Throughout the 1980s and 90s, then, privatization favoured an organizational strategy that reduced the business to its 'core' operations, and an HR strategy that promoted flexibility and reduced labour costs.

HRM WEB LINKS

Go to the following websites for more information on important economic trends and issues facing HRM: (www.statistics.gov.uk), (www.shrm.org), (www.ca.cch.com) and the 1998 Workplace Employee Relations Survey website www.dti.gov.uk/er/emar/1998wers.htm.

Changes in the labour market

The development of the UK economy along a trajectory of low investment in manufacturing, low levels of R&D, and privatization has led to many notable changes in the labour market. On the demand side, the aggregate unemployment rate in the final quarter of the 20th century indicates significant changes in the UK labour market. Figure 3.4 shows the path of unemployment in Britain since 1960, using the standard International Labour Organization (ILO) definition (that is, an unemployed person is someone without work who is actively searching for work and is available to take up a job). The graph shows that unemployment started to move gradually upwards in the late 1960s and early 1970s, surging upwards rapidly after 1979, falling rapidly in the late 1980s and increasing rapidly again after 1990. Since 1993, the unemployment level has fallen and in 2000, at a little over 5 per cent, reached its lowest level since the late 1970s.

A critical development on the demand side is the significant decline in employment in manufacturing in the final quarter of the 20th century, a trend that has occurred for half a century but accelerated over the past two decades. In 1950, 35 per cent of the total number in civil employment were employed in manufacturing; this had fallen to 26 per cent in mid-1984 and to 23 per cent in 1990 (Millward et al., 1992). During the same period, employment in the service sector increased from 47 per cent to 60 per cent of total employment, and within that, predominantly at the low end, in cleaning, fast food and retail serving. The share of employment in private sector services increased from 29 per cent in 1984 to 44 per cent in 1998 (Cully et al., 1999). Much of the growth in service employment has therefore been in what Thompson and McHugh (2002, p. 171) rather ingenuously refer to as 'no knowledge'

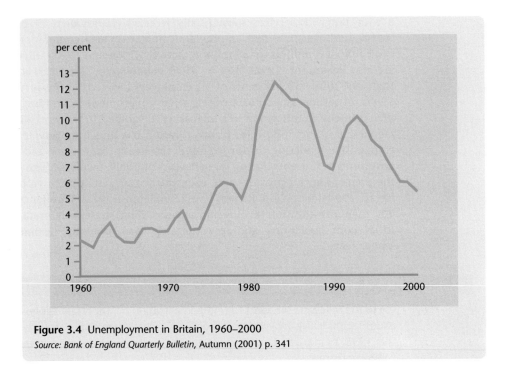

Figure 3.4 Unemployment in Britain, 1960–2000
Source: Bank of England Quarterly Bulletin, Autumn (2001) p. 341

work. High unemployment and, for millions of people, falling living standards marked the 1980s and early 1990s.

Another central theme of labour market analysis, which runs parallel to the globalization discourse, has been the use of non-standard employment contracts or contingency workers. New employment opportunities have increasingly been non-regular, that is, part-time, short-term and temporary agency work, and work for independent contractors. Some scholars refer to this phenomenon as 'labour market flexibility' (LMF), defined as 'a variety of functional techniques that organisations deploy to maximise the increased efficiency of the labour contribution to the strategic purpose of the organisation' (Williams, 1993, p. 1). A whole new vocabulary sprang up around the notion of flexible labour markets in the 1980s. Atkinson's (1985) flexibility model identifies three types of flexibility: functional, numerical and financial; it also categorizes the workforce into 'core' and 'peripheral' workers. Those workers on ongoing, full-time contracts constitute the core workforce; those on temporary or part-time contracts, and subcontracted and self-employed workers, constitute the numerical flexible or 'peripheral' workforce (Figure 3.5). Functional flexibility allows employees to be redeployed between activities and tasks, whereas, financial flexibility allows employers to pay according to individual and/or organizational performance (Chapter 9).

In 1993, 40 per cent of the UK workforce was employed in non-regular employment (Table 3.2). The 1998 Workplace Employee Relations Survey (WERS98) data show that the use of non-standard forms of employment has become 'commonplace' over the past two decades. The proportion of all employees working part time (defined as 30 hours or less per week) increased from 21 per cent in 1981 to 25 per cent in 1998 (Millward et al., 2000). The use of subcontract labour increased significantly in private and public sectors workplaces in Britain: in 1998, subcontracting was undertaken by 90 per cent of all workplaces (Cully et al., 1999). Many employers have cut labour costs and secured

Figure 3.5   One view of the labour market
Source: Vancouver Sun, BC, Canada, (1995) June 25

Table 3.2   Non-regular forms of employment, selected countries, 1973–93

	Self-employed (per cent of non-agricultural employees)		Part-time (per cent of total employment)		Temporary (per cent of total employment)		Total non-regular (per cent of total employment)	
	1973	1993	1973	1993	1983	1993	1973	1993
USA	6.7	7.7	15.6	17.5	–	–	(22.3)	(25.2)
Canada	6.2	8.6	9.7	17.2	7.5	8.3	23.4	34.1
Australia	9.5	12.9	11.9	23.9	15.6	22.4	(37.0)	(49.2)
Japan	14.0	10.3	13.9	21.1	10.3	10.8	38.2	42.2
Austria	11.7	6.3	6.4	10.1	–	–	–	–
Belgium	11.2	13.3	3.8	12.8	5.4	4.7	20.4	30.8
Denmark	9.3	7.0	(22.7)	23.3	12.5	10.7	(42.5)	44.0
Finland	6.5	9.5	6.7	8.6	(11.3)	13.5	(24.5)	31.6
France	11.4	8.8	5.9	13.7	3.3	10.2	20.6	32.7
Germany	9.1	7.9	10.1	15.1	9.9	10.2	29.1	33.2
Ireland	10.1	13.0	(5.1)	10.8	6.1	9.0	(21.3)	32.8
Italy	23.1	24.2	6.4	5.4	6.6	5.8	36.1	35.4
Netherlands	9.2	8.7	(16.6)	33.4	5.8	10.0	(31.6)	52.1
Norway	7.8	6.2	23.0	27.1	–	–	(30.8)	(33.3)
Portugal	12.7	18.2	(7.8)	7.4	(13.1)	8.6	(33.6)	(34.2)
Spain	16.3	18.7	–	6.6	15.6	32.0	(31.9)	57.3
Sweden	4.8	8.7	(23.6)	24.9	(12.0)	11.9	(40.4)	45.5
UK	7.3	11.9	16.0	23.3	5.5	5.7	28.8	40.9

Source: Standing (1997)

more flexible working practices by substituting full-time 'core' workers with part-time and temporary workers (Betcherman et al., 1994; Cully et al., 1999; Millward et al., 2000; Standing, 1997). Non-regular employment contracts facilitate 'a looser contractual relationship between manager and worker' (Atkinson, 1985, p. 17) – or, to put it more bluntly, employers can hire and fire workers as business circumstances change.

Atkinson's 'flexible firm' model is a variant of the dual labour market approach with the distinction between 'core' (primary) and 'peripheral (secondary) groups of workers. Critics of the flexible labour model have, however, challenged it on both ideological and empirical grounds, and argued that the notion of 'core' and 'periphery' is confused, circular and value laden (Hyman, 1988; Pollert, 1988; Williams, 1993).

REFLECTIVE QUESTION

Do you think there is a discrepancy between jobs associated with the so-called 'knowledge-based economy' and the types of job that many young workers actually do (for example 'McWork')?

On the supply side, one of the most important developments has been the growing convergence of the proportion of men and women in the labour force. Women's share of total employment increased from 34 per cent in 1959 to 42 per cent in 1980, reaching 47 per cent in 1998. The WERS98 data show that women's share of employment in workplaces (employing 25 or more workers) increased from 38 per cent in 1980 to 48 per cent in 1998, an increase 'almost exclusively driven by the expansion in part-time working among women' (Millward et al., 2000, p. 39). Table 3.3 shows that the proportion of all workplaces with a low concentration of female workers (fewer than 25 per cent) fell from 36 per cent to 27 per cent, and the proportion of all workplaces with a high proportion of female workers (75 per cent or more) increased from 22 per cent in 1980 to 29 per cent in 1998. Although the work done by the two sexes remains distinct, the majority of women workers being engaged in clerical, serving or cleaning work, WERS98 data suggest that, between 1980 and 1998, women in Britain made considerable inroads into middle and senior management (Millward et al., 2000). The WERS98 study also suggests that workplaces in Britain had, between 1980 and 1998, become more diversified; more employers were likely to employ at least some people from ethnic minorities. The number of those workplaces employing a more diversified workforce rose from 36 per cent in 1980 to 48 per cent in 1998. These supply-side trends are shown in Table 3.3.

Table 3.3 Composition of the UK workforce, 1980 and 1998

	1980 %	1998 %
Employees who are female		
Less than 25 per cent	36	27
75 per cent or more	22	29
Employees from ethnic minority groups	36	48

Source: Adapted from Millward et al. (2000), Table 2.6, p. 40

HRM WEB LINKS

Go to the following websites for more information on employment trends in Britain (www.statistics.gov.uk), Canada (www.statcan.ca/start.html and the Canadian Labour Force Development Board www.hrmguide.net/canada/), EU (www.eiro.eurofound.ie), USA (www.stats.gov and www.workindex.com/), South Africa (www.statssa.gov.za) and Australia (www.abs.gov.au).

HRM IN PRACTICE 3.3

IBM LABELS DIVERSITY A 'STRATEGIC IMPERATIVE'
Hiring women, gays and minorities is about more than doing the right thing

VIRGINIA GALT, *GLOBE AND MAIL*, 2002, JUNE 24, P. B3

Fishing is more fun, says IBM's 'dean of diversity,' but golf is the game of business – which is why, he explains, Big Blue has installed putting greens at some of its on-site day-care centers. Little girls should learn to play golf so they will not grow up to be 'competitively disadvantaged,' Ted Childs, global vice president of work force diversity at International Business Machines Corp., said during a recent visit to the company's Canadian headquarters.

Their mothers are getting golf lessons, too, as IBM drives its diversity initiative in a range of new directions as part of a sweeping corporate strategy aimed at increasing IBM's appeal in the marketplace. Right down to the games children play at the day-care centers, Mr. Childs is presiding over a cultural evolution at IBM – a company that was very white, very male, and very strait-laced when he joined as an affirmative-action hire in the USA 35 years ago.

> IBM should be a place where people feel comfortable being openly gay ...

IBM should be a place where people feel comfortable being openly gay and where women and people from minority group backgrounds have equal opportunity for promotion and advancement, said Mr. Childs, who is black. And anyone who has a problem with that need not apply to IBM, he added.

This is driven as much by market realities as it is by a desire to do the right thing, Mr. Childs said in an interview between meetings. IBM's effort to diversify the work force 'has moved from being a moral imperative to being a strategic imperative.'

IBM does business in 164 countries, it has operations in 73 countries and, even in its home base of the USA there are now more than 83 million people from visible minority backgrounds. 'This is a larger group than the individual country populations of Canada, Spain, France, Argentina, the United Kingdom, Italy, Egypt, South Africa ... Do we want to do business with those countries? The answer is yes. Do we want to do business with those 83 million? The answer is yes. We're going to see more companies owned by women or by ethnic minorities. If we get to them in their infancy and grow with them, that's how we'll grow. It's about opportunity, the opportunity for IBM to compete.'

Making international comparisons on economic variables, such as the rate of unemployment, income level and inequality, is problematic. One problem for researchers, for example, is how unemployment statistics are compiled. The number of times the UK method of compilation has altered since 1979 is a subject of political controversy. The Department of Employment states that there have been at least seven changes since 1979, which has reduced the number of 'unemployed' in the monthly count. Other commentators, more critical of government policies, argue that there have been at least 20 changes in the way in which the unemployment series has been calculated over the past 20 years. As one observer said: 'The definition of unemployment is a question more of semantics than of economics' (Johnson, 1988, p. 82). However, whatever the academic merits of the debate, the terms 'globalization' and 'employment flexibility' have real meaning for the men and women who live in the industrialized economies. In concrete terms, they mean that people are at risk of experiencing redundancy, long-term unemployment, immense upheaval and dislocation, poverty and despair, and employment insecurity.

REFLECTIVE QUESTION

Do you think that 'new technology' inevitably leads to higher productivity and an improvement in the quality of life? How many microprocessor-based pieces of equipment do you use (1) in your home, and (2) in your workplace? How does the diffusion of microprocessor-based technology affect HRM?

● The technology context

Over the past two decades, several developments relating to microprocessor-based technology have impacted directly upon the context within which HRM takes place. The terms 'new technology', 'microelectronic technology' and 'information technology' are all interrelated; indeed, these terms are frequently used interchangeably in everyday speech. The importance of 'information technology' arises from the integration between developments in microelectronics and telecommunications. At the end of the 1970s, observers were predicting a 'new industrial revolution' based not on steam but on microelectronics (see, for example, Jenkins & Sherman, 1979). It was judgements of this kind, together with intense media coverage, that prompted governments, industrialists and trade unions to wake up to the significance of microprocessor-based technology.

In the 1990s, developments in information technology have led some social observers to predict that 'thinking machines' will perform 'conceptual', 'managerial' and 'administrative' functions, thereby causing a further shift to 'a near-workerless, information society', the final stage of the 'Third Industrial Revolution' (Rifkin, 1996). When it has been reported that many workers in Britain and North America are actually working more hours each week in 2002 than they were two decades ago, it might be premature to speak of the 'end of work'; what we are more confident about, however, is the reconfiguring of the relationship of technology, globalization and work. Academics have identified at least three different forms of technological change that cause a reconfiguration of the relationship between technology and work (Millward & Stevens 1986). Using the example of microelectronic technology, there are:

1.　Advanced technical change: new plant, machinery or equipment that includes microelectronic technology (for example, computer-aided design).
2.　Conventional technical change: new plant, machinery or equipment not incorporating microelectronic technology (for example, containerization).
3.　Organizational change: substantial changes in work organization or job design not involving new plant, machinery or equipment (for example, self-managed teams).

Table 3.4 Diffusion of microtechnology in UK workplaces, 1984–98

	1984 %	1990 %	1998 %
Manufacturing microtechnology	44	66	87
Office microtechnology	25	62	90*
*Panel survey			

Source: Based on figures from Millward et al. (2000), pp. 37–8

Using two 'crude' indicators – the computerization of production and the computerization of office work – the WERS98 survey confirmed just how far microprocessor-based technology has become a feature of British workplaces across all sectors of employment (Table 3.4).

In 1984, a little over two-fifths (44 per cent) of manufacturing workplaces reported using microprocessor-based technology. The application of advanced technology increased substantially by 1998, when the proportion had risen to 87 per cent. Between 1984 and 1998, microprocessor-based technology was adopted more widely than before in smaller manufacturing workplaces. Among large manufacturing establishments (those employing more than 500 workers), the diffusion of microprocessor-based technology became almost universal, 94 per cent applying the technology. The uptake of microprocessor-based technology in the office (word processors) has been even more spectacular. Just a quarter of the workplaces surveyed in 1984 reported using computerized office equipment, whereas by 1998 the proportion was 90 per cent (Millward et al., 2000). Other research has shown the diffusion of microprocessor-based technology in different sectors of the economy. In financial services, for example, Wilson (1994) reports the adoption of computer-based technology, and in the UK clothing industry Lloyd (1997) describes the widespread diffusion of computer-aided design. The diffusion of microprocessor-based technology has been one of the 'most revolutionary developments' within British industry in the last quarter of the 20th century (Millward et al., 2000), a phenomenon that has affected both manual and non-manual workers.

Technological changes have provided the infrastructure for global free trade, as well as radically transforming the nature of work inside the organization for both blue-collar and white-collar employees. Research has been concerned with describing and interpreting the complex interplay between technical innovation, blue-collar and white-collar skills, and the reconfiguration of work structures and social relations, as well as trade union responses to technical change (Batstone et al., 1987; Bratton, 1992; Clark, 1993; Hogarth, 1993; McLoughlin & Clark, 1988). The analysis of technological change is not limited to Britain either. Studies on the impact of technological change have been conducted in Sweden (Bengtsson, 1992; Lowstedt, 1988), Finland (Penn et al., 1992), Denmark (Clausen & Lorentzen, 1993) and North America (Drache, 1995; Wells, 1993; Womack et al., 1990). Much of this research was initially stimulated by Braverman's publication *Labor and Monopoly Capital* (1974) and the upsurge of interest in the labour process debate that followed in its wake (Thompson, 1989).

Running parallel with the diffusion of microprocessor-based technology, however, is organizational change. The proportion of workplaces experiencing a substantial change in work organization or working practices affecting manual employees

HRM IN PRACTICE 3.4

E-MAIL DOESN'T SAVE TIME; IT WASTES IT, STUDY SAYS

VIRGINIA GALT, *GLOBE AND MAIL*, 2002, JUNE 26, P. B3

For all its early promise as a time saver, e-mail is more of a productivity drain than a benefit, according to new research by the University of Western Ontario.

Most organizations have succeeded in blocking 'hard-core spam' such as unsolicited pornography and ads that promise thinner thighs. But there has been an increase in internal e-mail and the inflow of so-called friendly spam – chatty notes from customers, suppliers, professional associates or, indeed, anyone 'you might have given your business card to,' said Christina Cavanagh, a professor of management communications at Western's Richard Ivey School of Business. 'E-mail is failing as a productivity tool in the workplace,' Prof. Cavanagh said in an interview yesterday.

Her research hit home with Alim Somani, who routinely grapples with 50 to 75 e-mails a day in his job managing the Toronto and New York operations of software company Infusion Development Corp. 'It's overwhelming, and its not the spam that's the problem; you can delete that,' Mr. Somani said in an interview. It's the little e-mail messages that pop up to say 'thx' after he has forwarded a requested file, or copies of e-mail messages that have also been scatter-gunned to several other colleagues, which cut into his productive work time.

> **For all its early promise as a time saver, e-mail is more of a productivity drain than a benefit, according to new research by the University of Western Ontario.**

E-mail addressed to five people often means that five people feel compelled to respond, 'where you only need one response,' said Mr. Somani. 'There is a tremendous amount of redundancy.' It's a sure sign of overload, Prof. Cavanagh said, when people read their e-mail while conducting a conversation, check their e-mail from home or take their laptops on vacation.

'Sadly, 60 per cent of respondents take time from their holidays to either dial up the Sunday before [their return to work] or periodically during the vacation period,' she wrote in her report, E-mail in the Workplace: A Productivity Study. She concluded that e-mail is a potentially great tool that is widely misused.

While her survey respondents cited real value in being able to communicate via e-mail with colleagues and customers in other time zones, they questioned the need for the person in the next cubicle or the manager down the hall to communicate by e-mail, Prof. Cavanagh said. 'Some respondents called this MBNWA – management by not walking around – or cited a laziness in not wishing to use other forms of communication,' she wrote.

increased from 23 per cent in 1984 to 35 per cent in 1998 (Cully et al., 1999; Millward et al., 1992). Of particular relevance here is the influence of Japanese 'lean production' concepts, such as 'just-in-time', total quality management, teamworking and business process re-engineering (Chapter 4). Business process re-engineering involves the radical redesign of business processes to create simultaneous changes in organizational design, culture, working practices and performance improvements. A number of researchers have documented shifts in work reorganization from traditional job designs based on Taylorist principles and rule-bound procedures towards flexibility and commitment. The Massachusetts Institute of Technology study by Womack et al. (1990), *The Machine that Changed the World*, identifies a work configuration labelled 'lean production' that incorporates Japanese-style manufacturing practices, including flexible work teams. This study has been particularly influential among academics and practitioners, but it has been criticized, not least because of its 'reliance upon an idealised mode of lean production' (Elger & Smith, 1994, p. 3). The logic of this line of argument is that flexible specialization requires a good 'fit' between technology and organization.

Although there is a considerable variation in the way in which managers conceptualize 'teamworking', and survey data on the spread of such work practices may therefore exaggerate the use of teams, the WERS98 study found teamworking to be a 'central element' of new work designs. About one third (35 per cent) of all establishments operated semi-autonomous work teams (Cully et al., 1999). In UK manufacturing the changes in work organization were introduced mostly for business reasons – improvements in productivity, quality, flexibility and cost-efficiency – rather than to benefit workers' job satisfaction or skills (Psoinos & Smithson, 2002).

HRM WEB LINKS

Go to the websites for the Centre for the Study of Work Teams (www.workteams.unt.edu) for more information on organizational design. The International Sociological Association's Research Committee on Economy and Society conducts research into economic activity at regional, national, and international levels, and provides information on the development of work (see www.ucm.es/OTROS/isa/rc02.htm).

● The political context

> History is never neutral. *Pierre Elliott Trudeau*

The political context in our model is the most complex and the most difficult to analyse, both because of its power to shape the nature of the employment relationship and because of its effects on the other contexts. Moreover, the influence of governments and their agencies – or what is referred to as 'the State' – permeates every aspect of business and people's work experiences and is in addition a major participant in the construction of context.

The State has three roles:

- First and foremost, the State is responsible for economic policy that partly influences labour markets and shapes the economic context within which employees and management interact.
- Second, the State establishes the legal context of employment relations through legislation and third-party intervention. Employment rights, pay equity, occupational health and safety, union–management relations and pension laws all impinge on HRM activities.
- Third, it is an employer in its own right.

The focus here is on the first two roles. Most HRM textbooks devote little attention to the role of the State, instead confining their coverage to the description of employment law. We think it is important not only to be aware of *what* employment laws have been enacted (see Table 3.5 below), but also to understand the political ideology underpinning State intervention: the '*why*' behind State involvement in constructing context.

The State and neoliberalism

In the final quarter of the 20th century, we witnessed a fundamental shift in political ideology and, subsequently, the role played by central governments in the Western hemisphere. Indeed, some have argued that the past two decades have comprised the most distinctive political era in recent history (Millward et al., 2000). To appreciate this distinctiveness, we need briefly to describe different types of State intervention in advanced capitalist economies. Drawing on Needle (2000) and Kuttner (2000), we can identify four:

- facilitative
- supportive
- directive
- neoliberalist (Chomsky, 1999).

During the first three decades of the 20th century, governments '*facilitated*' the smooth operation of the markets, largely through taxation and currency protection, shipping and trade production, and law and order. The economic crisis of the 1920s, the Second World War and the threat of communism ultimately led to the state adopting a more '*supportive*' role towards economic activities. State intervention in the economy was strongly influenced by the Keynesian economic doctrine that believed the free market is myopic and inclined periodically to 'self-destruct' (Kuttner, 2000). Supportive economic state policies were challenged by the rise of free global trade and inflation.

In the 1960s, Conservative and Labour governments engaged in '*directive*' policies, cooperating with employers' associations, for example the Confederation of British Industry (CBI), and the trade unions, such as the Trades Union Congress (TUC), in order to restructure British business and control inflation. The 1974–79 Labour government's 'social contract' is an example of this collaborative attempt at central planning. A lack of consensus among the trade unions, culminating in public sector strikes – the so-called 'Winter of Discontent' – ultimately defeated the Labour government and, with it, support for directive economic policies. The intervening 18 years (1979–97) of Conservative governments, led by Margaret Thatcher and her successor John Major, constituted a period of '*neoliberalism*' or 'New Right' economic doctrine.

Successive Conservative governments in Britain rejected Keynesian post-war economic orthodoxy and adopted 'supply-side economics'. Advocates of supply-side economics posited the theory that economic growth and employment creation are best achieved by governments withdrawing from economic intervention policies, by dismantling the administrative arrangements for regulating the labour market and by adopting a policy of 'tough love' towards the business sector. The 'love' is for business as a creator of wealth and jobs. The 'toughness' is for business with regard to non-protection and support. According to one management guru, 'Governments, with few exceptions, now realize that protecting business enterprises creates bloated companies unable to compete in global markets' (Champy, 1996, p. 18). Not only was neoliberalism preached and practised in the UK, but the economic doctrine was also pursued by the Mulroney government in Canada, the Kohl government in Germany and the Reagan administration in the USA.

The New Right regarded the neoliberalist doctrine as the optimal way in which to organize a modern economy. This economic path includes, above all (Kuttner, 2000, pp. 149–50):

> the dismantling of barriers to free commerce and free flows of financial capital. To the extent that there is remnant regulatory role, it is to protect property, both tangible and intellectual; to assure open, non-discriminatory access; to allow any investor to purchase or sell any asset or repatriate any profit anywhere in the world; to remove and prevent subsidies and other distortions of the *laissez-faire* pricing system; to dismantle what remains of government-industry alliances.

In other words, the role of the State is to assist this laissez-faire agenda. It is much better, argues the New Right, to limit government economic power and allow a 'free' market to enhance both the economic well-being of the individual and his or her individual liberty. Proponents of the neoliberalist economic orthodoxy argue that the market and zero deficits will remove impediments to investment, thereby creating jobs. Furthermore, post-war welfare systems were depicted as a major source of non-wage costs and labour market rigidity (Standing, 1997). Another feature of neoliberalism is the dismantling of the public sector, with criticisms that the public sector 'crowds out' private investment and employment. Moreover, the ideology of supply-side economics provides the theoretical justification for reducing the role and size of government and the privatization of utilities.

The State and the employment relationship

Over the past 40 years, 27 key UK Acts of Parliament have helped to shape the legal relationship between employers and employees, as well as between employers and employees' collective organizations – the trade unions (Table 3.5). The Conservative government, led by Margaret Thatcher and her successor John Major, systematically eroded, using a 'step-by-step approach', both the rights of employees and the collective rights of trade unions. The principal aim was to promote private enterprise, individualism, greater flexibility in the labour market and managers' 'right to manage'. The individual employment legislation, or 'floor of rights', established in the 1970s was increasingly being viewed by the government as a constraint on enterprise and an obstacle to efficiency and job creation. The Employment Acts of 1980, 1982, 1988, 1989 and 1990, the Trade Union Act of 1984, and the Trade Union Reform and Employment Rights Act 1993 aimed on the one hand to undermine individual employment protection and support for union organization and collective bargaining. On the other hand, however, their purpose was to increase the legal regulation of industrial action and trade union government. This body of legislation, affecting both individual and collective rights, was part of the Conservative government's agenda to reform the *context* in order to allow national-level neoliberalism to operate.

In terms of *individual employment rights*, amendments to the Employment Protection (Consolidation) Act 1978 reduced the provision for unfair dismissal. Extending the service qualification needed to make a claim for unfair dismissal from 6 months to 2 years reduced the number eligible to apply to the industrial tribunals. In the period 1987–88, there were only 34,233 applications to industrial tribunals compared with 41,244 in 1979 (McIlroy, 1991). A critical study of the law of unfair dismissal indicates that few applications for unfair dismissal were successful at an industrial

Table 3.5 Key UK employment legislation, 1961–2002

Year	Act
1961	Factories Act (Safety)
1963/72	Contract of Employment Act
1965	Industrial Training Act
1968	Race Relations Act
1970	Equal Pay Act
1971	Industrial Relations Act
1973	Employment and Training Act
1974	Health and Safety at Work etc. Act
1974/76	Trade Union and Labour Relations Act
1975/86	Sex Discrimination Act
1975	Employment Protection Act
1978	Employment Protection (Consolidation) Act
1980	Employment Act
1982	Employment Act
1984	Trade Union Act
1986	Wages Act
1988	Employment Act
1989	Employment Act
1990	Employment Act
1992	Trade Union and Labour Relations (Consolidation) Act
1993	Trade Union Reform and Employment Rights Act
1996	Employment Rights Act
1996	Employment Tribunals Act
1998	Employment Rights (Disputes Resolution) Act
1998	National Minimum Wage Act
1999	Employment Relations Act
2002	Employment Act

tribunal, that those applicants who were successful were rarely offered reinstatement or re-engagement, and that the level of compensation was low (Denham, 1990). In 1986–87, for example, 10,067 cases were heard at tribunals; of these, there were only 103 cases of reinstatement or re-engagement, and the median compensation was £1,805 (34.6 per cent of the awards not exceeding £999). Denham argues that unfair dismissal law, as it stands, has given employees a very limited degree of protection, and employers can often obtain the dismissals they want.

The purpose of the Employment Act 1989 was further to remove many regulatory restrictions, particularly for small businesses employing fewer than 20 employees. Section 15, for example, amended the 1978 Employment Protection (Consolidation) Act to increase from 6 months to 2 years the qualifying period of continuous employment after which employees were entitled to be given, on request, a written statement of the reasons for their dismissal. Protection for low-paid employees was further limited by Section 35 of the Trade Union Reform and Employment Rights Act 1993, which in effect abolished Wages Councils by the repeal of Part II of the Wages Act 1986. For those workers who are in good health, not pregnant and in a secure job, the changes in individual employment rights might seem to be of little consequence, but for those workers in the enlarged peripheral labour market, who are primarily female, curtailment of employment protection is not inconsequential and has adverse implications for employment security.

The Conservative government's *industrial relations legislation* sought to regulate the activities of trade unions throughout their 18-year period of office. The process began by repealing provisions for the statutory recognition of unions and by narrowing the definition of a trade disputes in which industrial action is lawful. The phrase 'in contemplation or furtherance of a trade dispute' no longer fulfilled the same function as it did prior to the 1982 Employment Act and, as argued at the time, 'It now denies legitimacy to many disputes which are clearly about industrial relations issues' (Simpson, 1986, p. 192). The policy objective of the statutes was designed to deter strikes and to limit their scale, as well as to regulate the unions' membership, discipline and recruitment policies. According to one industrial relations academic, the legislation marked 'a radical shift from the consensus underlying "public policy" on industrial relations during most of the past century' (Hyman, 1987, p. 93). According to the Secretary of State for Employment, the Employment Act 1988 sought to give 'new rights to trade union members', notably protection from 'unjustified' discipline on the part of union members and officials. The government justified the statute in the belief that, in recent years, some British trade unions had meted out harsh treatment to non-striking union members (Gennard et al., 1989). The purpose of the Employment Act 1988 was further to discourage industrial action and reduce the likelihood of 'militant' union leadership (McKendrick, 1988).

The Employment Act 1990 dealt with rights to union membership, the closed shop, unofficial industrial action, the dismissal of strikers and limits of secondary action. The 1990 Act gave those refused employment, on the grounds that they were not, or refused to become, a member of a union, the right to take the union to an industrial tribunal. Furthermore, the Act removed immunity from all forms of secondary industrial action. Thus, the complicated provisions of Section 17 of the Employment Act 1980, which made some form of secondary action lawful, were removed. The Trade Union Reform and Employment Rights Act 1993 had two main purposes, first, to further restrict trade union organization and activity, and second, to enact employment rights arising from EU directives and case law. Sections 1–7 of the 1993 Act related to internal union governance, such as the election of union officials. Sections 13–16 related to union membership, Section 13, for example, permitting employers to provide inducements to employees to opt out of collective bargaining or leave the union. These provisions were included following the decision of the Court of Appeal in two cases: *Wilson* v. *Associated Newspapers Ltd* [1993] and *Palmer* v. *Associated British Ports* [1993].

These changes in industrial relations law were used to tilt the balance of power in an industrial dispute towards the employer (Brown et al., 1997). By the middle of the 1990s, it was unlawful for industrial action to involve secondary action, secondary picketing, action in defence of the closed shop and action in support of union recognition by a third party. It was, however, lawful for an employer to dismiss on a selective basis individuals taking part in industrial action that the union had not authorized. In a scathing critique of the Conservative government's labour policies, Standing (1997, p. 14) argues that:

> nobody should be misled into thinking that the rolling back of protective and pro-collective regulations constitutes 'deregulation'. What supply-siders have promoted is pro-individualistic (anti-collective) regulations, coupled with some repressive regula-

tions and greater use of promotional and fiscal regulations, intended to prevent people from making particular choices or to encourage, facilitate or promote other types of behaviour.

The Conservative government's employment legislation has not, however, gone unchallenged. In the context of a strategically weakened trade union movement, the EU emerged as a countervailing influence on matters affecting the employment relationship. In 1989, the EU Social Charter (Appendix A), adopted by all Member States except the UK, introduced protection in such areas as improvements in the working environment to protect workers' health and safety, communications and employee involvement, and employment equity. The UK's rejection of the Maastricht Accord was, insists Towers (1992), the product of opportunism and belief that the Social Charter provisions would impose higher labour costs, leading to bankruptcies and job losses.

During the 18 years of Conservative government, the influence of EU law increased steadily (Brown et al., 1997). Although not a comprehensive body of employment legislation, EU employment law does draw on the west European tradition in which the rights of employees are laid down in constitutional texts and legal codes. Part II of the Trade Union Reform and Employment Rights Act 1993 enacts certain individual employment rights as a result of EU directives and case law. To comply with the European Union Pregnant Workers' Directive, for example, Sections 23–25 amended maternity rights. Sections 26–27 extended the right of employees to receive from their employer a written statement of principal employment details, and Section 28 protects employees against being victimized by their employer for taking specified industrial action related to health and safety.

HRM WEB LINKS

Go to the following websites to compare employment related legislation in the UK (www.hmso.gov.uk/acts.htm and www.venables.co.uk), Canada (www.labour-travail.hrdc-drhc.gc.ca//index.cfm/doc/english and www.law-lib.utoronto.ca/) and South Africa (www.acts.co.za).

'New Labour'

With the election of 'New Labour' in 1997, UK employers have had to accept new labour law initiatives in the areas of rewards, the Social Charter and union representation, which have ramifications for HRM. Shortly after being elected, the Labour government announced that a minimum wage would be imposed in the UK. The 1998 National Minimum Wage Act sets out the procedures for ensuring and enforcing a national minimum wage for all workers. The UK's self-exclusion from the Social Charter in the Maastricht Treaty limited the development of 'social dialogue' or discussion between employers and employee representatives at transnational level. The year 1999, described by the government itself as its 'year of delivery', was one during which the notions of 'partnership' were developed and the Employment Relations Act received the Royal Assent. Despite the UK opt-out, 53 of the very largest UK-based companies including ICI, GKN, British Steel, Pilkington Glass and Nat West, and 151 overseas-based enterprises operating in Britain had already negotiated 'Article 13' agreements that allowed for voluntary European Works Councils (Chapter 11) arrangements to be established before 1999. Cressey's (1998) case study of the Nat West Group and Nat West Staff Association voluntary agreement found that the voluntary route provided benefits for both employers and employees. The Labour government's decision to sign up for the Social Charter accelerated the diffusion of European Works Councils.

In 1997, the Labour government restored trade union rights to General Communication Headquarters workers, denied since 1984, and asked the TUC and the CBI to explore areas of agreement on union recognition. In broad terms, the 1999 Employment Relations Act offered an extension of individual employment rights and a number of measures to facilitate trade union recognition and organization, including a procedure to achieve recognition when opposed by employers (see Smith & Morton, 2001, for further details). The TUC reported 74 new recognition agreements, covering 21,000 workers, more than 50 per cent arising from employers directly approaching unions in the first 10 months of 1999 (Brown, 2000). The wide-ranging Employment Act, which received Royal Assent on 8 July 2002, supports the Labour government's commitment to improving organizational performance through 'fairness and partnership' at work. The Act includes provisions to implement the EU Directive on Fixed Term Work, the right to equal treatment on pay and pensions, a new right to time off for union learning representatives and a requirement for employers to use statutory minimum-dispute resolution procedures relating to dismissal, discipline and employee grievances.

HRM WEB LINKS

Go to the following website for more information on the 2002 Employment Act: http://www.dti.gov.uk/er/employ/index.htm.

Critics of New Labour argue that the government has simply continued the agenda of market discipline, deregulation and privatization. The New Labour government has enthusiastically embraced most of the public sector management changes introduced by the Conservative governments, and with the New Labour government placing more emphasis on performance management and linking public expenditure to 'sometimes incompatible targets', critics argue that it has reinforced a process of work intensification observed in the early 1990s (Bach, 2002, p. 325). Furthermore, it is alleged that New Labour has refused to challenge the hegemony of neoliberalism: 'New labour deals with globalisation as if it is a self-regulating, implacable Force of Nature, like the weather' (Hall, 1998, p. 11, quoted by Needle, 2000, p. 60).

Others, however, take a more sanguine view. Hutton and Giddens (2000, p. 214) argue that the open global economy offers 'opportunity, creativity and wealth' and that, in the absence of viable alternatives, the role of democratic governments is to improve the current global economy. These authors further develop the notion of the 'International Third Way', the establishment of global institutions to create the conditions that alleviate poverty in the Third World and inequality in the First World. Similarly, Joseph Stiglitz, (2002, p. 223), Chair of US President Bill Clinton's Council of Economic Advisers, has argued that 'systems of global governance are essential'. The notion of the International Third Way and the need to develop a global system of economic governance comprises arguably the most powerful discourse on economic management at this point in our history.

● The social context

Changes in the proportion of the population participating in the labour market and changing demographics determine the size and composition of the workforce. In addition, people entering the workplace bring with them different attitudes and values relating to work, parenthood, leisure, notions of 'fairness' and organizational loyalty. It is these human elements which make up the social context of HRM.

Demographic changes provide a starting point for analysing the social context. During the past three decades, the general pattern that has emerged is one of an ageing population as life expectancy for older people has risen at an unprecedented rate. At the same time, those older people have been starting their retirement earlier, some as early as 50 years old (Figure 3.6). Since 1951, the number of Britons of pensionable age has risen by over 40 per cent, from 5.5 million to over 9 million in 2000, or from just under 14 per cent to approximately 18 per cent of the population. The phrase 'population ageing' is, however, often misunderstood. It does not mean that senior citizens are about to become the dominant group in society: demographic data show that the real era of 'grey power' will be 2018.

Demographic projections are based on the most basic demographic fact: every year each person gets a year older. Analysing human behaviour according to age offers insights into socioeconomic variables. A 30-year-old, for example, is more likely to be married than a 20-year-old. A 55-year-old probably views work differently from a 25-year-old. The ability to forecast behaviour according to age has the advantage of allowing organizations to know more about the composition of the workforce and their needs. A 55-year-old employee with a teenage family is less likely to be interested in child care provision than a 25-year-old worker. Demographic data are an important source of information that can help managers in such areas as recruitment and selection, training and rewards management.[5]

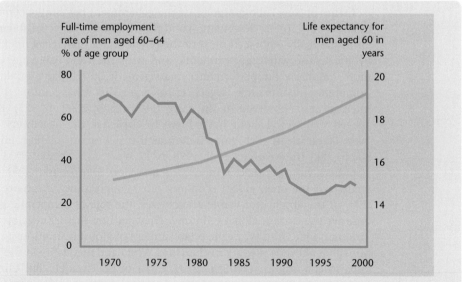

Figure 3.6 An ageing population working less

Source: Government Actuaries Department Institute for Fiscal Studies, reproduced in *The Economist* (2002) March 23, p. 53

HRM IN PRACTICE 3.5

MANDATORY RETIREMENT ATTACKED

RICHARD MACKIE, *GLOBE AND MAIL*, 2002, JUNE 14, P. A11

Governments should ban mandatory retirement at age 65 because it discriminates against people who are capable of working and who often need the money, Ontario Human Rights Commissioner Keith Norton said yesterday.

'Mandatory retirement, where age is used to determine the person's employment status, [is] unacceptable from a human-rights perspective,' Mr. Norton told a Queen's Park news conference. He predicted that governments would come under increasing political pressure to protect those who want to continue working after 65 as the number of older people in the population increases.

Demographic predictions indicate that by 2030, about one in four Canadians will be over age 65. This means 14 million people will be over the mandatory retirement age, from 3.7 million now. Of the 3.7 million, only about 6 per cent continued to work after 65, according to figures for 1996 compiled by Statistics Canada. 'As a political force, those older Ontarians are increasing in their political clout, and a political party that ignores that fact does so at their political peril,' Mr. Norton said.

'Governments should ban mandatory retirement at age 65 ...'

Lillian Morgenthau, founder and president of the Canadian Association of Retired Persons, which has 400,000 members across Canada, endorsed his arguments. She noted that 35 per cent of those over 65 live in poverty, and stressed that people often need to work to pay for food, housing, health care and transportation. Ms. Morgenthau's organization has 230,000 members in Ontario alone. The calls for an end to mandatory retirement were made as Ontario's Human Rights Commission announced a policy to counter discrimination against older people. Mr. Norton said that while human rights usually relate to protecting people from discrimination on the basis of race, religion, sex, sexual orientation or physical disability, increasingly there are problems with discrimination on the basis of age.

'Age discrimination does not invoke the same sense of moral outrage as other forms of discriminations, even though it can be as harmful in terms of its social, economic and psychological consequences as other forms of discrimination,' he said. The Supreme Court of Canada has accepted the discrimination implicit in mandatory retirement.

REFLECTIVE QUESTION

Is mandatory retirement an abuse of human rights or just 'common sense'?

Changes in the labour force – the number of people in the civilian working population – derive not only from changes in the size and age distribution of the population, but also from the variations in labour force participation rates. The participation rate represents the labour force expressed as a percentage of the working age population that actually participates in the labour force. In the 12 EU countries, the participation rate for all adults fell from 67.5 per cent to 65.7 per cent from 1973 to 1993 (Standing, 1997). In contrast, the participation rate among women increased from around 45 per cent to 56 per cent over this period (see also Cully et al., 1999; Millward et al., 2000).

HRM WEB LINKS

Go to the following websites for more information on demographic changes and participation rates in Britain (www.statistics.gov.uk), Canada (www.statcan.ca/start.html and the Canadian Labour Force Development Board, www.clfdb.ca), EU (www.eiro.eurofound.ie), USA (www.bls.gov and www.workindex.com/), South Africa (www.statssa.gov.za) and Australia (www.cibs.gov.au). The Centre for Studies for Aging at the University of Toronto conducts research on ageing (www.library.utoronto.ca/aging/dethome.html).

Whether people seek employment will often depend upon cultural values. Culture is a concept that can mean all things to all people, but Abercrombie and Warde (1988) use the term 'culture' to delineate the symbolic aspects of human society, which include beliefs, customs, conventions and values. Europe and North America are culturally diverse; within their borders lie many cultures and subcultures formed from divisions such as social class, ethnicity and gender, these cultures and subcultures in turn all being locally differentiated. Changing cultural values have an impact on HRM activities. Changes in traditional gender roles and new lifestyles, for example, change participation rates and the way in which workers are motivated and managed in the workplace. Whereas affluent working women have difficulty balancing work and home, poorer women on the minimum wage have the most difficult balancing act to perform (see Hochschild, 2000). Platt's (1997) study of employees at the American company Hewlett-Packard showed that professional men and women both spend about the same number of hours – about 50 – at work each week, but Hewlett-Packard women spend an average of 33 hours a week on housework or child care, compared with about 19 hours for men. On average, therefore, professional women have about 2 hours a day *less* leisure time than men. This dual-role syndrome can have detrimental consequences for women's health, psychological well-being and family life (Burchell et al., 1999; Felstead et al., 2002; see also Chapter 5). The notion of

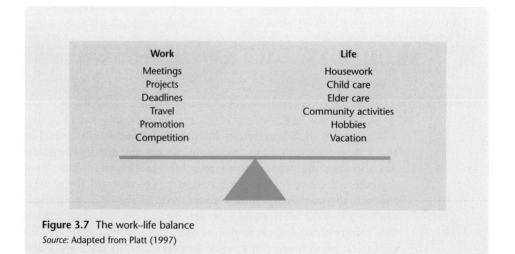

Figure 3.7 The work–life balance
Source: Adapted from Platt (1997)

work–life balance' for employees – the need to balance work and leisure/family activities – is said to impact on the way in which people are managed (Figure 3.7).

The concept of work–life balance is inherent to Western capitalist economies because paid work is constituted as a realm separate from that of non-paid domestic work. Felstead et al. (2002, p. 56) define work–life balance as 'the relationship between the institutional and cultural times and spaces of work and non-work in societies where income is predominantly generated and distributed through labour markets'. Although it is suggested that work–life balance is particularly relevant to women in the workforce, men are increasingly concerned as well. However, given the evidence of growing employment insecurity for many low-paid workers and the lack of provision for child care in the UK and North America, the probability of achieving the goal of a work–life balance seems remote for many people.

In addition, in the union–management relations arena, the 'consumer culture' promoting individualism may erode working-class customs and solidarity, which will undermine the collectivist culture of trade unions. In addition, it has been argued that whereas the 1980s saw the politicization of 'green' issues, one challenge facing organizations in this decade is the reassertion of underlying value systems. Chapman (1990, p. 29) asserts 'This implies that organizations will need to develop and communicate corporate cultures with which their staff can identify and to which they are willing to ally themselves.' Diversity in the workforce, changes in demographics and social values all, to a varying degree, make the management of people more complex and challenging.

● Change and human resource management

Analysing the context is important because, in various ways, conditions external to the organization present particular opportunities and constraints related to the management of work processes and people. Looking back, we can see how the context, and consequently the nature of, employment relations in the UK has undergone major alterations. In the 1960s, changing public policies covering labour markets, productivity and employment law extended the HRM function (Sisson, 1989). Different HR strategies and practices arose as the result of changes in the political economy. Farnham (1990, p. 25) argues that, 'As British industrial capitalism has developed, largely in response to changes in its market, technological and politico-economic contexts, so too have personnel management practices.' In the 18 years between 1979 and 1997, the context of British HRM has been profoundly influenced by the political environment: four consecutive Conservative governments dedicated to bolstering employers' 'right to manage', and the emergence of the EU as a political force on the employment front (Millward et al., 1992, 2000).

Over the past two decades or so, most work organizations, albeit not precisely at the same time or to the same degree, have faced the effects of free global trade, deregulation of the markets, privatization and, simultaneously, the need to improve productivity, quality and cost-efficiencies. The implications of globalization, international and national neoliberalism economic policies, new technology, different political doctrines and social changes are readily apparent. As we discussed in Chapter 2, depending on which strategic option is chosen – for example, cost minimization or 'differentiation' – globalization and national economic policies will ultimately determine the HR strategy taken by management and the subsequent HRM outcomes (see

Figures 2.3 and 3.2). If the company selects to compete through product and service innovation and high quality, the HRM contribution flows from the need to create a highly skilled and committed workforce. Such a business strategy will involve the need for flexible workers able quickly to cross over between job boundaries, the creation and maintenance of the required knowledge base, and the creation of an appropriate corporate culture, which encourages commitment to organizational goals. A cost minimization strategy, on the other hand, involves a different approach to labour management, which would exploit employment insecurity. High levels of unemployment and structural changes shift the balance of power in individual or collective contract negotiations towards the employer: employees and union representatives become more tractable in order to preserve jobs, and managers find that they are more able to introduce unilateral changes in working practices. In other words, each HR strategy aims to mesh strategic needs with operational requirements (Williams, 1993). More directly, international companies relocating to different parts of Europe bring to the host country their own management philosophy and practices, the result of which is not only a greater diversity of HR practices, but also pressure on indigenous management to adopt similar 'best practices' (Blyton & Turnbull, 1998).

The changes imposed by globalization have led some writers to take a more pessimistic view. Globalization will potentially force a *downward* harmonization of employment, health and safety, and environmental standards (Hutton, 1996). Underpinning the analysis of the UK labour market, for example, is the notion that the traditional employment contracts are anachronistic and no longer appropriate for competing in the new economic order. According to Champy (1996), a business process re-engineering guru, the 'new' business model is 'customer-driven' and flexible, and requires a different approach to managing labour. Thus, the neoliberalist economic model extols the flexibility and lack of regulations in the Asian labour markets (see also Wong, 2001). Critics of neoliberalism persuasively argue that the 'contract culture' has induced fear about job insecurity as firms downsize or threaten to relocate to low-wage developing countries (Hutton, 1996, 1997). Moreover, the neoliberalist doctrine is predicated upon fear and avarice. 'There needs to be fear and greed in the system in order to make it tick' (Hutton, 1996, p. 173), the former to encourage flexibility and the latter to stimulate private enterprise and risk-taking. In the early 1980s, one union leader summed up the effect of high unemployment when he declared 'we've got 3 million on the dole, and another 23 million scared to death' (Bratton, 1992, p. 70). Furthermore, 'unfettered' markets have caused 'inequalities and insecurities' in global labour markets (Faux & Mishel, 2000) and, simultaneously, existing collective trade union rights have been eroded, particularly in the USA, Britain and New Zealand (Standing, 1997).

Increased global competition and a reliance on 'fear' and contingency workers form a paradox. In general, part-time or contingency workers receive less training and pay, and have a low attachment to the organization. Thus, globalization itself may be the best reason for investing in people and giving all workers greater protection (Sukert, 2000). The dialectic of flexibility and cooperation, yet conflict, between employers and workers is key to understanding the renaissance of interest in the 'human' element in production. Interest and support for the new HRM paradigm represent a conviction that HRM has a strategic role to play in gaining competitive advantage, and concomitantly that HRM innovations have an important role to play in creating an organizational culture that builds trust, flexibility, cooperation and a commitment to organizational goals. In the long term, HRM practices and the relative standing of

HRM professions in organizations generally are strongly influenced by the prevailing economic and legal contexts that shape employment relationships.

The ramifications of new communication technologies for HRM are also apparent. Microtechnology potentially allows multinational corporations to operate in real time or in chosen time. Increasingly, multinational companies can readily transfer the production of all or parts of production to wherever the mix of materials, infrastructure, skilled workers, labour costs and regulatory requirements offers the greatest potential to maximize return on investment. Thus, large business organizations are able to supply their operations with components from around the plant, 'in an endlessly variable geometry of value searching. This implies bypassing economically valueless or devalued territories and people' (Castells, 2000, p. 53).

From an HRM perspective, major technological development involves changes in the way in which work is organized and workers are motivated and governed. These changes can take many forms including, flattened hierarchies, decentralized decision-making and flexible work teams. The recipients of these changes will in turn undergo almost constant 'skill disruption' as they switch from one obsolete skill set to enter another, new, set (Wallace, 1989). The workplace in the 'new economy' would, therefore, logically give workplace learning a high priority. This transformation presents opportunities for cooperation between managers and workers (and their unions), but such change also has the potential to exacerbate conflict between the parties. Where HRM professionals have played a prominent role in workplace technological change, their inclusion had a positive impact: 'their involvement was associated with a stronger level of workers' support for the change' (Daniel & Millward, 1993, p. 69). The rationale for different HR strategies can be explained by the labour exigencies of a particular international business strategy.

Taking the globalization of markets and competition together, what are the implications of these economic and technological changes for the recipients of HRM? Using the language of economists, it depends upon whether the recipient is a 'core' or a 'peripheral' employee. As Legge (1998, p. 20) argues: 'if you are a core knowledge worker with skills which are scarce and highly in demand, life may be good – empowerment, high rewards and some element of job security ... For the bulk of the workforce, though, things are not so rosy.' Williams (1993) estimates that, in America, only approximately 20 per cent of the national population is engaged in creation of 'new value-added production'; for the other 80 per cent, employment insecurity will therefore be a permanent feature of work. One of the problems of current shareholder-value-driven global capitalism is its inherent drive for profit, fostering a 'race to the bottom' in which employment standards tend towards worst rather than best practice. The case for the European regulation of employment standards and corporate governance through EU institutions is powerful.

Chapter summary

- We have attempted to cover a wide range of complex issues in this chapter. In essence, we have emphasized that the key to understanding managerial behaviour, such as HRM, lies within its context. The external domain influences the structure and functioning of a work organization, and organization decision-makers in turn influence wider society. Guest (1987) argues that interest in HRM in Britain and North America arose as a result of the search for competitive advantage, the decline in trade union power, and changes in the workforce and the nature of work.

● We have emphasized that to understand structural changes in the national economy, it is important to understand the global forces that have acted upon it and which UK capitalism has itself helped to shape. The global economy has become more integrated. For managers, the continuing restructuring of business operations is having a profound effect on competition and thereby on such HR activities such as HR planning, selection and development.

● New technology and processes such as 'lean' production methods and business process re-engineering impact in complex ways on people and their work, as well as on the HRM function. The Fombrun, Tichy and Devanna HRM model (see Figure 1.4) illustrates the link between external contexts and the search for competitive advantage through employee performance and HRM activities.

● As far as employment law is concerned, the Labour government's support for the EU Social Charter (Appendix B) is beginning to encourage senior management to have more regard for HRM. The UK Employment Act, which received Royal Assent in July 2002, supports the Labour government's commitment to improving organizational performance through 'fairness and partnership' at work. Furthermore, European studies show that HRM is not intrinsically anti-union (Brewster et al., 2000). In addition to union–management relations legislation, age discrimination is going to be banned from 2006 under a EU directive (*The Economist*, 2002, March 23, p. 53).

● The general indication is that the changing social context of HRM will continue to place more pressure on employers to pay more attention to the issues associated with a diverse workforce – in particular to be more sensitive to the issues and challenges related to an ageing workforce, women, ethnic minorities and the disabled.

Key concepts

● Culture   ● Political context

● Demographics   ● Social Charter

● Economic context   ● Technological change

● Globalization   ● Work–life balance

Chapter review questions

1. How does the notion of an 'open system' organization help our understanding of the HRM function?

2. Describe the major economic challenges facing HR managers.

3. How have political developments since 1997 affected HRM?

4. How will the 1994 European Works Council Directive impact on managers and HRM?

5. What are some of the likely consequences of an 'ageing' population for HRM?

6. How realistic is it to expect employees to achieve the goal of a work–life balance?

Further reading

Brown, W., Deakin, S., & Ryan, P. (1997). The effects of British industrial relations legislation, 1979–97. *National Institute Economic Review*, (161): 69–83.

Chomsky, N. (1999). *Profit over people*. New York: Seven Stories Press.

Felstead, A., Jewson, N., Phizacklea, A., & Walters, S. (2002). Opportunities to work at home in the context of work-life balance. *Human Resource Management Journal*, **12**(1), 54–76.

Hertz, N. (2002). *The silent takeover: Global capitalism and the death of democracy*. London: Arrow.

Hirst, P., & Thompson, G. (2000). Globalization in one country? The peculiarities of the British. *Economy and Society*, **29**(3), 335–56.

Hutton, W., & Giddens, A. (2000). *On the edge: Living with global capitalism*. London: Jonathan Cape.

Stiglitz, J. E. (2002). *Globalization and its discontents*. New York: Norton.

Wong, M. L. (2001). The strategic use of contingent workers in Hong Kong's economic upheaval. *Human Resource Management Journal*, **11**(4), 22–37.

Practising human resource management

Searching the web

On an individual basis, or working in a small group, visit each of the websites listed in the chapter. In addition, there are a number of online business periodicals available that can provide information on the external context of business. Some examples include *Financial Post* (www.nationalpost.com), *Fortune* (www.fortune.com), *Business Week* (www.businessweek.com) and *The Economist* (www.economist. com). Describe the current external challenges that are forcing work organizations to change the way in which people are managed in the workplace. Bring this information to class, and present your findings and recommendation in an oral report. Discuss any challenges the groups hold in common. Are any of the challenges unique to your country?

HRM group project

Form a group of three or four students. The purpose of this group assignment is to allow you to apply your knowledge of context to a business organization, and to consider the implications for HRM. Specifically, students will: (1) carry out research of secondary and primary sources related to the contextual elements discussed in the chapter, (2) apply key principles and theories to a case, and (3) demonstrate academic writing skills. Each group member should take responsibility for researching the various aspects of the assignment.

Select an organization of your choice, and familiarize yourself with the company's current products, services and global operations. Using one of the popular search engines, such as Yahoo! or Excite, search the World Wide Web for other timely information about the company. After you have completed your search, make a list of the issues affecting the organization in its external environment. Organize your list into the different context elements of one of the HRM models presented in Chapter 1. How would you characterize the nature of the external environment facing the organization (for example stable or unstable, certain or uncertain)? A team member(s) should interview at least one manager in an organization in the same sector as your case study. Based upon your research, the interviewer(s) should probe the nature of the organization's external environment: How do external factors – economic, political or demographic – affect the organization? How do these external factors impact on organizational strategy? How do they affect the HR strategy? Write your findings up in the form of a report.

Chapter case study

OIL TOOL INCORPORATED PLC

Oil Tool Engineering plc. was established in West Yorkshire in 1950 and 4 years later became part of Oil Tool International, an American multinational company engaged in the design, manufacture and marketing of machinery used at the well-head when drilling for oil and gas, both onshore and offshore. The company, whose corporate headquarters are in Houston, Texas, USA, has other manufacturing establishments in Scotland, Germany, France and Mexico, and employs 4500 people throughout the world.

Oil Tool Incorporated dominated the oil extraction industry for nearly 40 years. After a long period of growth and continual profits, things started to go wrong in 1995. Low productivity, rising production costs, a decline in oil field exploration and new competitors entering the industry culminated in a £76 million loss for the West Yorkshire plant. At this point, the senior management decided to bring in an outside consultancy firm, Mercury Engineers Inc.

Bill Dorfman, the plant manager, called a meeting with his senior management team and the consultants. Dorfman started the discussion: 'We all know that we have considerable auton-omy from the corporate management in Texas. That means we have the task of turning this plant around. If we fail, the plant will close. This is the company's biggest manufacturing operation in the world. But it would only be a question of months before another operation could be bigger. Headquarters have mothballed several of our operations, and the French and German plants could be 'geared-up' to our size within 12 months. What has gone wrong, and how do we turn this plant around?

Yvonne Turner, the marketing manager, began, 'Our sales have fallen in the Middle East because our customers want equipment that is lighter and more mobile. The design and the materials of our block-tree valve haven't changed for 10 years.' She went on, 'The Japanese are engineering equipment that is made with alloy metals and is lighter, stronger and has a microprocessor-based control system.'

Doug Meyer, the manufacturing manager, then jumped in: 'Don't blame us. If the market is changing out there, it's marketing's job to tell us and keep us informed. It's not just our manufacturing practices; we all know our prices are higher because of sterling's high exchange rate. And besides,' he said angrily, 'we lost that last Middle East order because the government refused to give us an export license. Whether there is a war or not, if we don't sell them the machinery, you can be damn sure somebody else will. We ought to get the local MP to have a word with the bureaucrats in the Board of Trade.'

At this point, Wendy Seely, the HR manager, intervened in the discussion, 'Well, I don't know whether we can blame everything on the tension in the Middle East or government in London. I do know, however, that EU Directives on pay equity and court decisions on retirement and pensions will push our labour costs up. We must find ways to reduce labour costs and improve quality standards,' she said. We can't achieve high-quality standards,' retorted Doug Miller, 'because your department stopped train-

ing apprentices and we can't find the quality we need using subcontractors.'

Feeling defensive, Wendy Seely argued, 'We ended the training programme for apprentices because the local college closed the first-year apprentice course as part of its own cost-saving measures. You can't blame my department for that.' Bill Dorfman decided to bring the meeting to a close. 'Would each department address the issues discussed this morning? We shall meet in 7 days and see whether there is a consensus on the way forward. Remember that we have to be competitive to survive. We have to quit whining and save this plant,' he said.

Source: Adapted from The drilling machine company: Japanization in small-batch production in J. Bratton (1992), *Japanization at Work*. London: Macmillan – now Palgrave Macmillan.

Discussion questions

Assume that you are a member of the consultancy team. Prepare a report outlining the contextual changes affecting Oil Tool Engineering.

1. What factors from the chapter can help to explain what happened to this company?

2. What information does this case give companies about the importance of scanning the external environment?

3. How can HRM help to solve some of the problems?

HR-related skill development

Most organizations face external contexts that are complex, dynamic and increasingly global. This makes the context increasingly difficult to interpret. To cope with often incomplete and ambiguous contextual data, and to increase their understanding of the general external context, organizations engage in a process called 'external environmental analysis'. All managers, including HR managers, need to be aware of the importance of scanning the external context in a systematic way. You can develop this management skill by going to our website, (www.palgrave.com/business/brattonandgold) and clicking on 'External environmental analysis exercise'.

Notes

1. Will Hutton and Antony Giddens, (2000). *On the edge*. London: Jonathan Cape, p. vii.
2. Alan Greenspan, US Federal Reserve Board chairman, reporting to the US Senate Banking Committee, 2002, July 16, and quoted in the *Globe and Mail* (2002, July 17), p. B1.
3. Noreena Hertz, (2002) *The silent takeover*, p. 275.
4. *Globe and Mail*, Will Bush bring big business to account? (2002, July 9), p. A12.
5. For a more in-depth examination of how demographics impacts on business and society, see David Foot and Daniel Stoffman (1996) *Boom, bust and echo*. Toronto: Macfarlane Walter & Ross.

Chapter four

Work and work organization

John Bratton

Work refers to physical and mental activity that is carried out at a particular place and time, according to instructions, in return for money. Differing forms of work organization generate and reflect tension, contradiction and change.

'Assembly line workers, once told to "check your brains at the door," are now prized for their ability to think and act independently, as automation, cross-training and new management styles are leading to greater productivity. A spokesman for DaimlerChrysler Corp. agrees there has been a shift. "A trend has been to give more responsibility to the [plant] floor and to cascade that responsibility down to empower our people … workers are organized in teams of 10, to learn the jobs of other team members so they can step right in when one of them is absent." The 2000 hourly workers in the plant are urged to think in terms of making continuous improvements.'[1]

'Mary Newell has worked at the Royal Bank of Canada for 25 years but only recently carved out a niche for herself that meets her own needs, as well as the bank's. Since April 1999, she has worked full time from home, selling credit-card services and debit machines to small and medium-sized businesses.'[2]

'A handful of companies … Forced to choose between sure failure and radical change, opted for the latter. They began to re-engineer. They ripped apart their old ways of doing things and started over with clean sheets of paper.'[3]

'The summer jobs in retail or the service sector – jobs that provide students with little more than pocket change – are no longer a stepping-stone along the career path to the "dream job" in McWorld. They are quickly becoming dead-end careers.'[4]

Chapter outline

Chapter objectives

After studying this chapter, you should be able to:

1. Explain the meaning of the term 'work'

2. Define job design and describe specific job design strategies

3. Understand the theoretical arguments underpinning current organizational and work design practices

4. Explain how the nature of work and different organizational designs affect human resource management (HRM) activities

The study of work and organizational forms has a long history. In the 18th century, traditional work rhythms and practices of pre-industrial society gave way to the division of labour and the discipline of the factory system of work organization. At the turn of the 20th century, the essence of the scientific management movement was the opportunity it afforded for increasing the control and coordination of workers' effort. In the 1960s, concern about declining productivity, increasing industrial disputes and worker dissatisfaction led to new work structures that emphasized worker autonomy and participation, and a variety of functional tasks through 'job enrichment'. Technological change and the processes of globalization produced 'new' systems of work organization in the 1990s. The managerial mantra of the 1990s was flexibility, and studies of organizational innovations such as flexible specialization, cellular production, lean production, team-based horizontal work structures, re-engineering and virtual organizations are now well established in the literature. Much of the rationale for new job designs and work structures was initially developed in the context of the USA and then generalized across North America and European economies. Hammer and Champy (1993), for example, inform us that 're-engineering' is necessary because the world is a different place. To respond more rapidly to global changes, to make organizations compete more aggressively in global markets, to have a workforce that is more flexible and attuned to the needs of customers, senior managers have to fundamentally restructure business processes.

Work can be studied from two broad academic perspectives: sociological and psychological. A *sociological* perspective of work is concerned with the broader contextual and structural factors affecting people's experience of work. An important theme for sociologists is that of the division of labour, which refers to the way in which people in society can specialize in doing particular types of work. At the level of the organization, the internal division of labour is a basis for efficiency and the control of workers. At a societal level, the division of labour has produced occupational structure: professional, management, clerical, skilled and unskilled manual occupations. Another important topic within the sociology of work is that of work-based inequalities and, within this, the gendered substructure of organizations, the pervasiveness of sexuality in organizations, and the interrelations between gender, sexuality and power in organizational life (Hearn et al., 1989; Littler & Salaman, 1984; Mills & Tancred, 1992; Thompson, 1989).

A *psychological* study of people at work attempts to understand individual behaviour, a large body of literature covering the academic field of 'organizational behaviour', concerned with managerial problems of motivation, job satisfaction, work stress, job design and any other factor relevant to working conditions that could impede efficient work performance. An early theory of individual work behaviour attempted to explain the nature of motivation in terms of the types of need that people experience (Maslow, 1954). Subsequent theoretical contributions from behavioural scientists, such as McGregor's Theory X and Y (1960), Herzberg's motivation–hygiene theory (1966) and Vroom's expectancy motivation theory (1964), have practical implications for the way in which organization controllers design work structures and rewards. A well-established model seeks to diagnose the interrelations between the core characteristics of work and the critical psychological processes acting on individuals and their immediate work groups (Hackman & Oldham, 1980).

The nature of the work and how managers organize work is a critical internal contingency affecting human resources (HR) activities (see Figure 1.3). The use of work teams, job enrichment tasks and inverting the shape of organizational hierarchies (Felstead & Ashton, 2000; Quinn et al., 1996) affects the recruitment and selection criteria for new employees. The new skills associated with work teams and decentralized, decision-making organizational structures influence the kind of workplace learning and training that people need. In addition, new ways of organizing work influence the design of reward systems.

The discourse on 'post-bureaucratic' work organizations – those using a system of work designed to invert bureaucratic principles by adopting decentralized decision-making, fewer managerial levels and flexible work practices – has emphasized competing claims over whether new forms of work organization lead to an 'enrichment of work' or the 'degradation of work'. On the one hand, optimists argue that new work structures 'empower' employees and celebrate the fact that managerial behaviour has shifted from the 'management of control' to the 'management of commitment' (Walton, 1985). On the other hand, others argue that some new work arrangements constitute 'electronic sweatshops' (Sewell, 1998) and that employee-empowering work regimes are basically 'a euphemism for work intensification' (Hyman & Mason, 1995). To capture the new realities of the modern workplace, critics often use the term 'McWorld', meaning that a vast amount of work experience, especially for young people, women and workers of colour, involves menial tasks, part-time contracts, the close monitoring of performance and entrenched job insecurity.

Some empirically based literature also offers a context-sensitive understanding of the processes of work reconfiguration (Bratton, 1992; Edwards et al., 2001; Geary & Dobbins, 2001). The 'context-sensitive' view makes the point that new work structures do not have a uniform outcome but are likely to be contingent on a number of variables, such as business strategy, union involvement in the change process and the extent to which 'bundles' of HR practices support the new work regime. Geary and Dobbins (2001), for example, argue persuasively that the introduction of work teams brought with it 'a mix of benefits and costs'. In sum, the identification of potential benefits and costs for employees as a result of organizational innovations provides a more complex picture, one that strongly supports the hypothesis that changes in the organization of work can strengthen or threaten the 'psychological contract' (Emmott & Hutchinson, 1998).

In this chapter we explain job design strategies and emerging organizational forms, as seen by sociologists and industrial psychologists researching the links between motivation, job satisfaction and work design. We examine the meaning of work in contemporary Western society. The broader context of work should be seen as providing essential background knowledge for managers and HR practitioners concerned with current job design techniques and emerging organizational paradigms. We critically evaluate alternative job design strategies, including Taylorism, post-Fordism, flexible specialization, Japanese work designs, re-engineering and learning organizations, and examine the implication of different work structures for managing the employment relationship.

REFLECTIVE QUESTION

Look at the quotes on the nature of work at the beginning of this chapter: what is your own experience of work? Have you or your friends had jobs in which you were expected to 'check your brains at the door'? Have you experienced work in a team?

How do you feel about working at home? What are the implications of new ways of working for (1) young people, women and workers of colour, and (2) HRM?

The nature of work

Filling in the forms to apply for a student grant is not seen as work, but filling in forms is part of a clerical worker's job. Similarly, when a mature student looks after her or his own child, this is not seen as work, but if she or he employs a child-minder, it is, for the minder, paid work. We can see from these examples that work cannot be defined simply by the content of the activity. So when we refer to the term work, what do we mean? We can begin to get a sense of what this question relates to and how society views work by exploring the following definition of work:

> Work refers to physical and mental activity that is carried out at a particular place and time, according to instructions, in return for money.

This definition draws attention to some central features of work. First, the notion of 'physical and mental' obviously suggests that the activities of a construction worker or a computer systems analyst are deemed to be work. Second, the tendency for the activity to take place away from our home and at set time periods of the day or night – 'place and time' – locates work within a social context. Third, the social context also includes the social relations within which the activity is performed. When a mother or father cooks the dinner for the family, the actual content of the activity is similar to that performed by a hospital cook employed to prepare meals for patients, but the social relations within which the activity occurs are quite distinct. Hospital cooks have more in common with factory workers or office workers because their activities are governed by rules and regulations – 'instructions' from the employer or employer's agent. Clearly, then, it is not the nature of the activity that determines whether it is considered 'work' but instead the social relations in which the activity is embedded (Pahl, 1988). Fourth, in return for physical effort and/or mental application, fatigue and loss of personal autonomy, the worker receives a mix of rewards, including 'money', status and intrinsic satisfaction. Watson (1986) refers to this mix of inputs (physical and mental activities, and so on) and outputs (rewards) as the 'implicit contract' between the employer and the employee.

Although this definition helps us to identify key features of the employment relationship, it is too narrow and restrictive. First, consider all the activities, both physical and mental, that do not bring in money. Such activities can be exhilarating or exhausting; they may involve voluntary work for the Citizen's Advice Bureau or encompass the most demanding work outside paid employment – child care. Again, the same activities – advising people on their legal rights and being paid for it or being employed in a nursery – would all count as 'work' because of the social relations and the monetary reward. Second, it is clear that the rewards, satisfaction and hazards of work are highly unequally distributed. Contemporary society rewards employees according to the kind of people they are and the kind of work they do; historically, women receive less money than men in similar work. Work can also be dangerous and unhealthy, but the hazards are not distributed evenly. Despite the publicity surrounding managerial stress, for example, the realities of the distribution of work-related hazards show that they are most prevalent among manual workers. Furthermore, it has been argued that this unequal distribution of work-related accidents represents the systematic outcome of values and economic pressures (Littler & Salaman, 1984).

There is no doubt that the nature and experience of work is changing. As part of the wider process of globalization and the implementation of new managerial strategies, there is an ongoing shift of paid work into the service sector, an increase in information technology and an increasing number of women being drawn into the waged labour force. Contemporary forms of waged work, particularly in the less developed industrialized economies, are dependent on the integration between work and the family (Moore, 1995). The nature of work in turn affects HRM activities. For example, the pay that an employee receives is related to social attitudes and traditions rather than the actual content of the activity; pay determination requires an understanding of the social division of labour, especially gender divisions of labour (Pahl, 1988). Management decides how the tasks are divided into various jobs and how they relate to other tasks and other jobs, contingent upon different modes of production and technology. Decisions are also made about control systems, the ratio of supervisors to subordinates, the training of workers and the nature of the reward system. HRM is thus both affected by and profoundly affects an individual's experience of work. Clearly, the way in which work is designed impacts on both the effectiveness of the organization and the experience and motivation of the individual and work group. It is this process of job design which we will now consider.

Job design

The need to harness human resources in innovatory ways to give organizations a competitive advantage has focused attention on the question of job design. This is defined as:

> The process of combining tasks and responsibilities to form complete job and the relationships of jobs in the organization.

Early developments

Innovations in how work is designed have interested academics and managers for centuries. For example, Adam Smith (1723–90), the founder of modern economics, studied the newly emerging industrial division of labour in 18th-century England. For Smith, the separation of manual tasks was central to his theory of economic growth. Smith argued that this division of labour leads to an improvement of economic growth in three ways:

1. output per worker increases because of enhanced dexterity
2. work preparation and changeover time is reduced
3. specialization stimulates the invention of new machinery.

In his book, *The Wealth of Nations* (1982 [1776]), Smith described the manufacture of pins and gave an early example of job design:

Man draws out the wire; another straightens it; a third cuts it; a fourth points it; a fifth grinds it at the top for receiving the head … the important business of making a pin is, in this manner, divided into eighteen distinct operations. (p. 109)

In the 19th century, Charles Babbage also pointed out that the division of labour gave the employer a further advantage: by simplifying tasks and allocating fragmented tasks to unskilled workers, the employer could pay a lower wage: 'in a society based upon the purchase and sale of labour power, dividing the craft cheapens its individual parts' (Braverman, 1974, p. 80).

The emergence of industrial division of labour gave rise to more radical studies of job design. Karl Marx (1818–83) argued that the new work patterns constituted a form of systematic exploitation and that workers were alienated from the product of their labour because of capitalist employment relations and the loss of autonomy at work: 'factory work does away with the many-sided play of the muscles, and confiscates every atom of freedom, both in bodily and intellectual activity' (quoted in Nichols, 1980, p. 69).

Since the beginning of the 20th century, interest in job design has intensified because of the writings of Frederick Taylor on 'scientific management'. Between 1908 and 1929, Henry Ford developed the principles of Taylorism but went further and developed new work structures based on the flow-line principle of assembly work. The human relations movement emerged in the 1920s and drew attention to the effect of work groups on output. Then, in the late 1960s, concern about declining productivity and the disadvantages of scientific management techniques led to the job redesign movement. Current interest and discourse on job design centres around Japanese management, which deals with more than job design as it emphasizes, for example, management style, skill and values, and aims to incorporate job design into an organization's employment strategy. We will now consider each of these approaches in more detail.

Scientific management

The American Frederick W. Taylor (1856–1915), pioneered the scientific management movement. This approach to job design, referred to as Taylorism was also influenced by Henry L. Gantt (1861–1919) and Frank B. Gilbreth (1868–1924). Taylor developed his ideas on employee motivation and job design techniques at the Midvale Steel Company in Pennsylvania, USA, where he rose to the position of shop superintendent. Littler (1982, p. 51) has argued that 'Taylorism was both a system of ideological assertions and a set of management practices'. Taylor was appalled by what he regarded as inefficient working practices and the tendency of workers not to put in a full day's work, what Taylor called 'natural soldering'. He saw workers who did manual work to be motivated by money – the 'greedy robot' – and to be too stupid to develop the 'one best way' of doing a task. The role of management was to analyse scientifically all the tasks to be undertaken and then to design jobs to eliminate time and motion waste.

Taylor's approach to job design was based on five main principles:

1. Maximum job fragmentation
2. The divorce of planning and doing
3. The divorce of 'direct' and 'indirect' labour
4. The minimization of skill requirements and job-learning time
5. The reduction of material handling to a minimum.

Thus, the centrepiece of scientific management was the separation of tasks into their simplest constituent elements (first principle). Most manual workers were viewed as sinful and stupid, and therefore all decision-making functions had to be removed from their hands (second principle). All preparation and servicing tasks should be taken away from the skilled worker (direct labour), and performed by unskilled and cheaper labour (indirect labour in the third principle); according to Littler, this is the Taylorist equivalent of Babbage's principle and is an essential element of more work intensification (1982). Minimizing skill requirements to perform a task reduces labour's control over the labour process (fourth principle), and finally, management should ensure that the configuration of machines minimizes the movement of people and materials to shorten the time taken (fifth principle). Taylor's approach to job designs, argues Littler, embodies 'a dynamic of deskilling' and offers to organizations 'new structures of control' (1982, p. 52).

Some writers argue that Taylorism was a relatively short-lived phenomenon, which died in the economic depression of the 1930s. Rose suggests that scientific management did not appeal to most employers – 'Some Taylorians invested a great effort to gain its acceptance among American employers but largely failed' (1988, p. 56) – but this view underestimates the diffusion and influence of Taylor's principles on job designers. In contrast to Rose, Braverman (1974, pp. 86–7) believes that, 'the popular notion that Taylorism has been "superseded" by later schools of "human relations", that it "failed" … represents a woeful misreading of the actual dynamics of the development of management'. Similarly, Littler and Salaman (1984, p. 73) have argued that, 'In general the direct and indirect influence of Taylorism on factory jobs has been extensive, so that in Britain job design and technology design have become imbued with neo-Taylorism.'

REFLECTIVE QUESTION

Can you think of jobs in the retail and service sector that would support the charge that work systems in the modern workplace continue to be imbued with neo-Taylorism?

Fordism

Henry Ford applied the major principles of Taylorism but also installed specialized machines and perfected the flow-line principle of assembly work; this kind of job design has, not surprisingly, come to be called Fordism. The classical assembly line principle should be examined as a technology of the control of employees and as a job design to increase labour productivity, both job fragmentation and short task-cycle times being accelerated. Fordism is also characterized by two other essential features:

- the introduction of an interlinking system of conveyor lines that feed components to different work stations to be worked on
- the standardization of commodities to gain economies of scale.

Fordism established the long-term principle of the mass production of standardized commodities at a reduced cost (Coriat, 1980).

Speed of work on the assembly line is determined by the technology itself rather than by a series of instructions. Management's control of the work process was also enhanced by a detailed time and motion study inaugurated by Taylor. Work-study engineers attempted to discover the shortest possible task-cycle time. Ford's concept of people management was simple: 'The idea is that man … must have every second necessary but not a single unnecessary second' (Ford, 1922, quoted in Beynon, 1984, p. 33). Recording job times meant that managers could monitor more closely subordinate's effort levels and performance. Task measurement therefore acted as the basis of a new structure of control (Littler, 1982).

Ford's production system was, however, not without its problems. Workers found the repetitive work boring and unchallenging, job dissatisfaction being expressed in high rates of absenteeism and turnover. In 1913, for example, Ford required about 13,500 workers to operate his factories at any one time, and in that year alone the turnover was more than 50,000 workers (Beynon, 1984). The management techniques developed by Ford in response to these HR problems serve further to differentiate Fordism from Taylorism (Littler & Salaman, 1984). Ford introduced the 'five dollar day' – double the pay and shorter hours for those who qualified. Benefits depended on a factory worker's lifestyle being deemed satisfactory, which included abstaining from alcohol. Ford's style of paternalism attempted to inculcate new social habits, as well as new labour habits, that would facilitate job performance. Taylorism and Fordism became the predominant approach to job design in vehicle and electrical engineering – the large-batch production industries – in the USA, Canada and Britain.

As a job design and labour management strategy, scientific management and Fordist principles had limitations even when the workforce accepted them. First, work simplification led to boredom and dissatisfaction, and tended to encourage an adversarial industrial relations climate. Second, Taylor-style job design techniques carry control and coordination costs. With extended specialization, indirect labour costs thus increase as the organization employs an increasing number of production planners, controllers, supervisors and inspectors. The economies of the extended division of labour tend to be offset by the dis-economies of management control structures. Third, there are what might be called cooperation costs. Taylorism increases management's control over the quantity and quality of workers' performance, but, as a result, there are increased frustration and dissatisfaction, leading to a withdrawal of commitment on the part of the worker. Quality control can then become a major problem for management. The relationship between controller and controlled can deteriorate so much as to result in a further increase in management control. The principles of Taylorism and Fordism thus reveal a basic paradox, 'that the tighter the control of labour power, the more control is needed' (Littler & Salaman, 1984, pp. 36–7; see also Huczynski & Buchanan, 2001). The adverse reactions to the extreme division of labour led to the development of new approaches to job design that attempted to address these problems, starting with the human relations movement.

Human relations movement

The human relations movement, which began to shift managers' attention to the perceived needs of workers, emphasized the fact that job design had to consider the psychological and social aspects of work. This movement grew out of the Hawthorne experiments conducted by Elto Mayo in the 1920s.

Mayo set up an experiment in the relay assembly room at the Hawthorne Works in Chicago, USA, that was designed to test the effects on productivity of variations in working conditions (lighting, temperature and ventilation). The Hawthorne research team found no clear relationship between any of these factors and productivity. The researchers then developed, after the fact, concepts that might explain the factors affecting worker motivation, concluding that more than just economic incentives and the work environment motivated workers: recognition and social cohesion were important too. The message for management was also quite clear: rather than depending on management controls and financial incentives, it needed to influence the work group by cultivating a climate that met the social needs of workers. The human relations movement advocated various techniques such as worker participation and non-authoritarian first-line supervisors, which would, it was thought, promote a climate of good human relations in which the quantity and quality needs of management could be met.

Criticism of the human relations approach to job design were made by numerous writers. Human relations detractors charged managerial bias and the fact that the human relations movement tended to play down the basic economic conflict of interest between the employer and employee. Critics also pointed out that when the techniques were tested, it became apparent that workers did not inevitably respond as predicted. Finally, the human relations approach has been criticized because it neglects wider socioeconomic factors (Thompson, 1989). Despite these criticisms, however, the human relations approach to job design began to have some impact on management practices in the post-Second World War environment of full employment. Running parallel with the human relations school of thought, though, came newer ideas about work that led to the emergence of a job redesign movement.

● Job redesign movement

During the 1960s and early 1970s, job design was guided by what Rose (1988) refers to as the neo-human relations school (Herzberg, 1966; McGregor, 1960; Maslow, 1954) and the wider-based quality of working life (QWL) movement. The neo-human relations approach to job design emphasized the fulfilment of social needs by recomposing fragmented jobs. The QWL movement can, in its turn, be traced back to the publication of two reports: the 'Work in America' report and the British report 'On the quality of working life' (Wilson, 1973).

Littler and Salaman (1984) put forward five principles of 'good' job design that typify the QWL movement's challenge to the principles of scientific management:

1. There is the principle of closure, whereby the scope of the job is such that it includes all the tasks to complete a product or process, thus satisfying the social need of achievement.
2. A good design incorporates control and monitoring tasks, whereby the individual or group assumes responsibility for quality control.
3. There is task variety, whereby the worker acquires a range of different skills so that job flexibility is possible.
4. Fourth is self-regulation of the speed of work.
5. The design encompasses a job structure that permits some social interaction and a degree of cooperation among workers.

In the late 1970s, competitive pressures compelled an increasing number of Western companies to reassess their job design strategies. Although several writers (for example, Kelly, 1985) have pointed out that the recent developments in job design cannot all be grouped together, it is possible to identify three broad types:

- job enrichment
- reorganization of assembly lines
- Japanese-style work design.

The following sections consider each of these in turn.

Job enrichment

The term job enrichment refers to a number of different processes of rotating, enlarging and aggregating tasks. An early example of this process was the use of job rotation, which involves the periodic shifting of a worker from one work-simplified task to another (Figure 4.1). The advantage of job rotation is, it was argued, that it reduces the boredom and monotony of doing one simplified task by diversifying a worker's activities (Robbins, 1989).

An alternative approach to job redesign was the horizontal expansion of tasks, referred to as job enlargement (Figure 4.2). Instead of only grilling hamburgers, for example, a griller's job could be enlarged to include mixing the meat for the burger or preparing a side salad to accompany the order. With a larger number of tasks per worker, the time cycle of work increases, thus reducing repetition and monotony.

A later and more sophisticated effort to address the limits of Taylorism and Fordism was the vertical expansion of jobs, often referred to in organizational behaviour text-

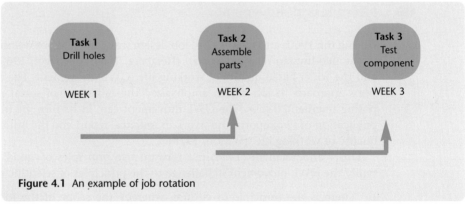

Figure 4.1 An example of job rotation

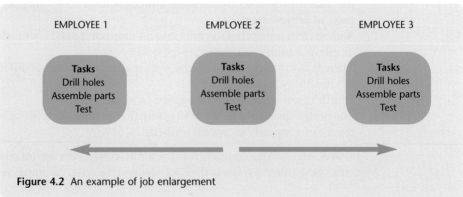

Figure 4.2 An example of job enlargement

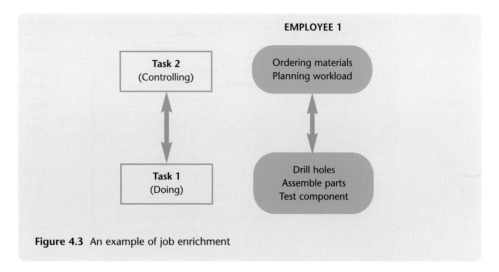

Figure 4.3 An example of job enrichment

books as job enrichment. This approach takes some authority from the supervisors and adds it to the job (Figure 4.3). Increased vertical scope gives the worker additional responsibilities, including planning and quality control. For example, the fast-food worker from our previous example might be expected not only to grill the burgers and prepare the salad, but also to order the produce from the wholesaler and inspect the food on delivery for its quality.

Hackman and Oldham's (1980) model of job enrichment – the job characteristic model – is an influential approach to job design. This model suggests that five core job characteristics result in the worker experiencing three favourable psychological states, which in turn lead to positive outcomes (Figure 4.4). The five core job characteristics are:

1. Skill variety: the degree to which the job requires a variety of different activities in carrying out the work, requiring the use of a number of the worker's skills and talents.
2. Task identity: the degree to which the job requires the completion of a 'whole' and identifiable piece of work.
3. Task significance: the degree to which the job has a substantial impact on the lives or work of other people.
4. Autonomy: the degree to which the job provides the worker with substantial freedom, independence and discretion in terms of scheduling the work and determining the procedures to be used when carrying it out.
5. Feedback: the degree to which the worker possesses information of the actual results of her or his performance.

The chef/manager of a small restaurant would, for example, have a job high on skill variety (requiring all the skills of cooking plus the business skills of keeping accounts, and so on), high on task identity (starting with raw ingredients and ending with appetizing meals), high on task significance (feeling that the meals have brought pleasure to the customers), high on autonomy (deciding the suppliers and the menus) and high on feedback (visiting the customers after they have finished their meals). In contrast, a person working for a fast-food chain grilling hamburgers would probably have a job low on skill variety (doing nothing but grilling hamburgers throughout the

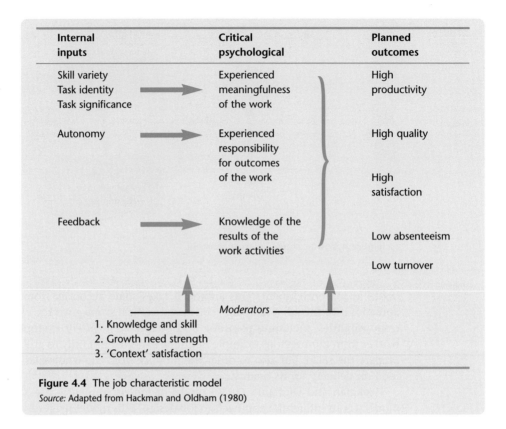

Figure 4.4 The job characteristic model
Source: Adapted from Hackman and Oldham (1980)

shift), low on task identity (simply grilling burgers and seldom preparing other food), low on task significance (not feeling that the cooking makes much of a difference when the burger is to be covered in tomato ketchup anyway), low on autonomy (grilling the burgers according to a routine, highly specified procedure) and low on feedback (receiving few comments from either co-workers or customers).

The model suggests that the more a job possesses the five core job characteristics, the greater its motivating potential. The existence of 'moderators' – knowledge and skill, growth need strength and context satisfactions – explains why jobs theoretically high in motivating potential will not automatically generate a high level of motivation and satisfaction for all workers. This means that employees with a low growth need are less likely to experience a positive outcome when their job is enriched. The job characteristic model has been tested by theorists and, according to Robbins, 'most of the evidence supports the theory' (1989, p. 210).

Some theorists have offered a more critical and ideological evaluation of job enrichment. Bosquet, for example, argues that modern management is being forced by labour problems to question the wisdom of the extreme division of labour and factory 'despotism'. Job enrichment (Bosquet, 1980, p. 378) 'spells the end of authority and despotic power for bosses great and small'; this should in turn lead workers liberated from boring jobs to demand total emancipation. An influential study by Friedman (1977) argues that although job enrichment techniques may increase job satisfaction and commitment, the key focus remains managerial control. He maintains that job design strategies such as job enrichment result in individuals or groups of workers being given a wider measure of discretion over their work with a minimum of supervision, and that this 'responsible autonomy' strategy is a means of maintaining and augmenting managerial authority over workers (Friedman, 1977) or is a 'tool of self-discipline' (Coriat, 1980, p. 40) for workers.

Thompson (1989) offers one of the most penetrating critiques of job redesign techniques. Drawing upon the contributions of various theorists and the empirical evidence, he argues that many job enrichment schemes 'offer little or nothing that is new, and are often disguised forms of intensified [managerial] control' (1989, p. 141). With the growth of call centres over the past decade, critical research has drawn attention to 'new' forms of managerial control. It is alleged that sophisticated electronic communication and employee-monitoring systems, electronic eavesdropping on sales–client conversations, and peer group scrutiny, have created 'electronic sweatshops' or a form of 'electronic Taylorism' (see Callaghan & Thompson, 2001; Sewell, 1998).

HRM IN PRACTICE 4.1

WORKERS TURN OFF AUTOPILOT AND TAKE CHARGE ON ASSEMBLY LINES OF THE 21ST CENTURY

SHERWOOD ROSS, *GLOBE AND MAIL*, 2001, SEPTEMBER 3, P. B12

Assembly line workers, once told to 'check your brains at the door,' are now prized for their ability to think and act independently, as automation, cross-training and new management styles are leading to greater worker involvement and greater productivity. 'Workers will tell you that things have changed from the early 1990s,' says Aleda Roth, an authority on manufacturing who has visited hundreds of assembly lines all over the world. 'You see a much more productive environment as managers get assembly line workers involved in process improvement and using the new technologies,' says Ms. Roth.

It wasn't always so. Command and control policies, Mr. Donkin says, 'produced results, but it was a wasteful system, wasting most of the human ingenuity residing in the workforce.' A spokesman for DaimlerChrysler Corporation, agrees there has been a

shift. 'A trend has been to give more responsibility to the [plant] floor and to cascade that responsibility down to empower our people,' says Trevor Hale. 'Nobody knows that job better than the person doing the job.'

'Never tell people how to do things. Tell them what to do and they will surprise you with their ingenuity.'

At Daimler's Toledo North assembly plant, 'We have a lot of job rotation built in' so that assembly line workers 'understand the big picture of operations in different areas,' Mr. Hales says. There, workers are organized in teams of 10, to learn the jobs of other team members so they can step right in when one of them is absent. Rotating job assignments also help to prevent repetitive motion injuries.

The 2,000 hourly workers in the plant are urged to think in terms of making continuous improvements. 'The change never stops,' Mr. Hale says. 'We encourage change in terms of improving quality.'

Manager Vick Crawley says: 'We have moved away from assembly lines where one person would add one piece. Today, people have multiple tasks that they do.' He says the new 'manufacturing cells' system requires more employee training and development than the traditional assembly line arrangement. 'We have *kaizen* [the Japanese term for continuous improvement] and employees get involved in designing their own cells.' Self-directed work initiatives have been around for some time, of course. As Second World War US General George Patton once wrote: 'Never tell people how to do things. Tell them what to do and they will surprise you with their ingenuity.'

Reorganizing assembly lines: beyond Fordism

According to Cloke and Goldsmith (2002, p. 138), 'In the new organizational paradigm, the fundamental unit of structure is not the isolated individual but the collaborative self-managing team.' In the UK, for example, the Workplace Employee Relations Survey of 1998 reported an increased adoption of work-teams both in production and as a method for upward communications (Cully et al., 1999; Millward et al., 2000). Such new organizational configurations that depart from the 'rational' Fordist model are the focus here and in the next section (see also Chapter 11 for 'upward' communication methods).

Before we examine some of the alternative work structures designed by managers, it is, however, important to note an analytical caution. Much of the organizational theory literature on newly emerging organizational forms simplifies the analysis to a polar comparison between 'traditional' Fordist and new or 'post-Fordist' work and organizational characteristics (Jaffee, 2001; Vallas, 1999). An example of binary comparisons between two approaches to work design is shown in Figure 4.5. As Jaffee (2001, p. 129) correctly argues, however, the enumeration of lists of binary opposite features 'conform more to conceptual elegance than empirical reality'. Organizational redesign is not a smooth transition from one ideal-type model to another, and new organizational forms are most likely to resemble a hybrid configuration that weld elements from the old organizational design with parts of the new.

	Fordist	Post-Fordist
1. Technology	• fixed, dedicated machines • vertically integrated operation • mass production	• micro-electronically controlled multi-purpose machines • sub-contracting • batch production
2. Products	• for a mass consumer market • relatively cheap	• diverse production • high quality
3. Labour process	• fragmented • few tasks • little discretion • hierarchical authority and technical control	• many tasks for versatile workers • some autonomy • group control
4. Contracts	• collectively negotiated rate for the job • relatively secure	• payment by individual performance • dual market: secure core, highly insecure periphery

Figure 4.5 Ideal types of Fordist and post-Fordist production system
Source: Warde (1990)

REFLECTIVE QUESTION

You have probably experienced group working as part of your business programme. Have you enjoyed the experience? What are the advantages/disadvantages of group projects? Why have 'team' projects become common practice in many business schools?

If Ford had once been the model of mass production – captured by Henry Ford's famous marketing slogan 'You may have any colour you wish, so long as it's black' – Toyota became the model for reorganizing assembly lines.

The early discourse on the limitations of Fordism is well captured by Michael Piore and Charles Sabel in their book *The Second Industrial Divide* (1984); according to these US authors, the Fordist model is incapable of responding quickly in highly competitive consumer industries. The alternative to Fordism was *'flexible specialization'*, which presented a revival of the 'craft paradigm'. This neoromantic perspective on organizational change is described (Piore & Sabel, 1984, p. 17) as:

> a strategy of permanent innovation: accommodation to ceaseless change, rather than an effort to control it. [Based] on flexible – multi-use – equipment; skilled workers; and the creation, through politics, of an industrial community that restricts the forms of competition to those favoring innovation.

The flexible specialization model had the following features:

- small-scale production of a large variety of products for differentiated markets
- the utilization of highly skilled workers exercising considerable control and autonomy over the labour process
- the use of process and information technology
- strong networks of small producers that achieved flexibility and efficiency through collaboration (see Piore & Sabel, 1984; Appelbaum & Batt, 1994).

In this scheme, the *flexible firm* model developed by Atkinson (1984) provoked extensive attention from European policy-makers, management theorists and practitioners. The analysis surrounding the flexible firm model also became *de facto* British government policy in the late 1980s and 90s (Sisson & Storey, 2000). As we discussed in Chapter 3, the flexible firm model is a variant of the dual labour market approach, but it is important in the flexibility discourse because it gave theoretical legitimacy to flexible employment arrangements and thereby contributed to the growth of non-standard labour. The centrepiece of the flexible firm model is formed by three types of flexibility (Chapter 6):

1. functional
2. financial
3. numerical.

In Europe, particularly in the UK, the flexible firm model has been linked with the post-bureaucratic agenda of promoting 'fluidity' by creating 'looser organizational boundaries' that tolerate 'outsiders' coming in to the organization (see Felstead & Jewson, 1999).

Japanese-style work design

The 'Japanese threat' challenged traditional marketing and manufacturing strategies in the 1980s and in so doing set off a process of organizational restructuring and concomitant changes in managing the labour process (Bratton, 1992; Thompson & McHugh, 2002). In America, the principles underpinning Japanese job design strategies were later referred to as 'lean' production (Womack et al., 1990).

The Japanese approach to managing production and the employment relationship is worth considering in some detail because it has attracted considerable attention from academics and managers. Two important questions are raised by this:

1. relating to the *concept*: what are the major characteristics of the Japanese model of management?
2. relating to the *impact*: are these characteristics so unique as to constitute the basis of a new phase in job and organization design, and what are the implications of such management practices for HRM?

This section presents answers to these questions and subsequently reviews some of the literature on Japanese management.

In 1986, the British industrial relations theorist Peter Turnbull described a new production system at Lucas Electrical (UK), which management had introduced to shift labour productivity on to a higher growth path and improve product quality. According to Turnbull (1986), the introduction of a 'module' production system led to a new breed of 'super-craftsmen' who were proficient in a wide range of skills. Turnbull used the term Japanization to describe the organizational changes at Lucas Electrical (UK) because they were based on the production methods used by many large Japanese corporations.

In addressing our first question, we see that the Japanese production model has three notable elements:

- flexibility
- quality control
- minimum waste.

Flexibility is attained using module or cellular manufacturing. The system achieves flexibility in two ways: by arranging machinery in a group or 'cell' – cellular technology – and by using a flexible multiskilled workforce. Machines are arranged into a 'U-shaped' configuration to enable the workers to complete a whole component, similar to the group technology principle introduced in the European and US automobile industry in the early 1970s (Coriat, 1980; Littler & Salaman, 1984). The job design underpinning a cellular work structure is the opposite of that of 'Taylorism': a generalized, skilled machinist with flexible job boundaries is a substitute for the specialized machinist operating one machine in one particular workstation.

Quality control is the second component of the Japanese production system. The management philosophy of total quality control (TQC) attempts to build quality standards into the manufacturing process by making quality every operator's concern and responsibility. TQC results in job enlargement as cell members undertake new self-inspection tasks and participate in quality improvement activities. With TQC, there are savings on labour and raw materials: fewer quality control inspectors, fewer rework hours and less material wasted (Schonberger, 1982).

Minimum waste is the third component of the Japanese production model. Waste is eliminated, or at least minimized, by just-in-time (JIT) production. As the name suggests, this is a hand-to-mouth mode of manufacture that aims to produce the necessary components, in the necessary quantities, of the necessary quality and at the necessary time. It is a system in which stocks of components and raw materials are kept to a minimum, ideally being delivered a matter of days or even hours before their use in the manufacturing process. An important beneficial outcome of JIT production is the reduction in inventory and scrap (Schonberger, 1982).

On turning to our second question, a survey of the literature reveals major differences between academics over whether or not such job design and employment relations constitute a significant departure from existing job design principles, Taylorism and human relations (see, for example, Elger & Smith, 1994). To help in understanding the diverse components of the Japanese model and the debate surrounding them, we have developed a theoretical framework for examining the concept of Japanization. This model is based principally on two important contributions to the debate on Japanese-style management: Oliver and Wilkinson's (1988) theory of 'high-dependency relationships', and Guest's (1987) HRM model. As Figure 4.6 shows, the model has six major components, which we will examine in turn. These components are:

1. a set of manufacturing techniques
2. a set of dependency relationships
3. a set of HRM policies
4. a set of supplier policies
5. a managerial ideology
6. a series of outcomes.

The *set of manufacturing techniques* comprises cellular technology (CT), just-in-time manufacturing, and total quality control (TQC), the principles of which have been discussed above. Japanese manufacturing processes create, it is alleged, a complex web

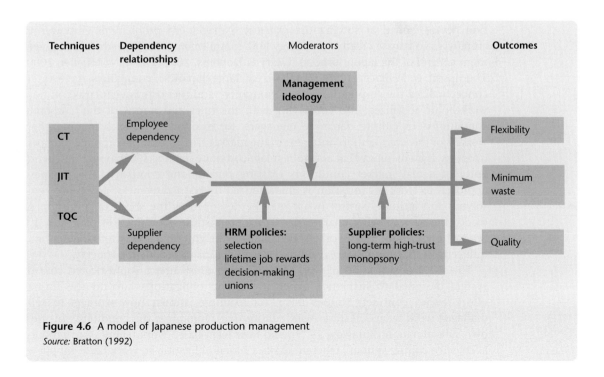

Figure 4.6 A model of Japanese production management
Source: Bratton (1992)

of *dependency relationships* that calls for adroit management. The cellular system implies a low level of substitutability of the workers and a heightened dependency on a multiskilled workforce. In addition, TQC heightens dependency when the safety net of the safety inspectors is removed. Furthermore, JIT is vulnerable to delays and stoppages. If the company is operating on a zero or minimum inventory, late delivery or stoppages resulting from strikes will quickly affect the manufacturing process. As Oliver and Wilkinson point out (1988, p. 135), 'A mere work-to-rule or overtime ban could be as disastrous for a company operating a JIT system as could a strike for a company not doing so.'

Implicit in our model is the need for a set of 'moderators' to counterbalance the company's dependency on its workforce and suppliers. The organization needs to develop social mechanisms aimed at exerting sufficient influence over employees' psychological contract to redress the imbalance in the employment relationship (see Chapter 1 for the importance of the psychological contract in HRM). A set of *HRM policies* and practices is designed to shape employee perceptions of expectations and obligations beyond the traditional form of employment relationship based on the cash nexus (Dore, 1973). Similarly, a unique set of *supplier policies* relating to the buyer aims to generate a reciprocal obligation between the buyer and the supplier (Oliver & Wilkinson, 1988). *Managerial ideology* and leadership behaviour also act as moderators. Finally, the *outcomes* or performance goals of the system are flexibility in terms of both workforce skills and tasks, minimum waste and the minimum number of quality defects arising from production.

This model illustrates three dimensions – technical (task flexibility), governance (delegated empowerment) and cultural (Findlay et al., 2000) – believed to underpin teamwork. The cultural or 'normative' dimension of Japanese-style teamworking draws attention to the social and psychological aspects of the employment relationship that aim to generate social cohesion and a 'moral commitment' to organizational objectives (Etzioni, 1988). From the cultural perspective, work teams are 'a socialization device' aimed at solving the classical management problem of empowering employees to release creativity, synergy and commitment without reducing management control of the labour process (Geary & Dobbins, 2001; Procter & Mueller, 2000; Thompson & Wallace, 1996). Analyses of large Japanese companies have often conceptualized the corporation as a 'community', and theorists have focused on how workers are socialized into complying with the rules and norms of the 'corporate community' or culture. Japanese managers, for example, constantly remind their workers of the 'competition' inherent in the market. The notion of corporate 'competitiveness' is an ideology that acts to regulate corporate members' behaviour independently of actual market conditions existing outside the company. The Japanese approach to work organization is characterized by cooperativeness, group problem-solving and attitude control (what may be described as the social organization of work), the system being characterized by a sophisticated production planning. JIT production itself modifies workers' behaviour by heightening a sense of 'urgency' and inducement to avoid mistakes and to discover defects in production quickly.

The social organization of work, critics argue, constitutes a sophisticated control system designed to influence expectations and obligations beyond the formal effort–reward contract. Studies have, for example, shown how workers in self-managed work teams create a work culture that reproduces the conditions of their own subordination (Burawoy, 1979), and how team-based work regimes can produce a 'coercive culture system', wherein exists a moral obligation to work hard, to 'put in a full day', because of peer-group pressure or 'clan' control (Bratton, 1991). In another study of work teams, the workers' discipline was more punitive than that of the managers: 'peer pressure in the groups was very important. [Team members] are tougher on [co-workers] than management' (Wells, 1993, p. 75).

Some may question the model of Japanese management outlined in Figure 4.6. Is it a description of what actually exists in Japan, or is it a set of manufacturing and employment practices that organizations should implement? Is it a theory or a helpful way of organizing a complex social phenomenon such as 'Japanese management'?

HRM WEB LINKS

Go to the following websites: the Centre for the Study of Work Teams (www.work-teams.unt.edu), DaimlerChrysler AG (www.daimlerchrysler.com), the Amalgamated Engineering and Electrical Union (www.aeeu.org.uk) and the Canadian Autoworkers Union (www.caw.ca). How do these different companies and unions view the introduction of work teams? Do teams improve performance? Are there any negative outcomes of teamworking for managers or workers?

A number of observers have acknowledged that models of Japanese manufacturing and employment practices may be based on myths. According to Whittaker (1990), there are 'multiple' challenges to Japanese-style employment: lifetime employment and the *nenko* payment system are, for example, undergoing reform in Japan. In addition, the pace of change has accelerated, spurred on by the economic downturn in the Japanese economy over the past decade. A Labour Ministry report has, for example, advocated that the practice of lifetime employment should be changed to mirror changing attitudes towards work and careers, and has applauded the growing trend in which mainly young Japanese citizens opt to change jobs, often frequently, rather than sign up for lifetime employment at a major corporation.[5] The fact that Japanese employment practices are changing in Japan should not, however, surprise us. A mature capitalist society is a highly complex and dynamic arrangement – perhaps the only thing that is constant is change itself. Moreover, notwithstanding the varied vocabulary that is used to capture organizational design, studies by Jurgens (1989) and Murakami (1995) of the US, British and German automobile industry, and case studies of *kaizen* and TQM techniques by Malloch (1997) and Jones (1997), serve to illustrate that Japanese-style teamworking is more than a 'passing fad' in management thinking.

In our view, the model shown in Figure 4.6 is a useful heuristic framework for organizing the complexities of a particular approach to job and organization design and management behaviour. It is best conceptualized as an 'ideal type'; as such, it does not necessarily follow that all elements of the model must, or indeed can, be applied to every workplace. The model maps out the 'systematic interlocking' (Thompson & McHugh, 2002) nature of self-managed work teams – technical, governance and cultural aspects – and the prerequisite 'bundle' of best HR practices needed to socialize the 'empowered' work regime. There is evidence that the transfer of Japanese industrial management into British and North American organizations has been highly selective (Jurgens, 1989). Furthermore, many British companies that have redesigned work around horizontal work teams do not fully appreciate the nature of high-dependency relationships (Oliver & Wilkinson, 1988) and have introduced these new organizational forms within a traditional adversarial union–management culture (Bratton, 1992).

Knowledge work and post-bureaucratic designs

Knowledge work

The final quarter of the 20th century was a period of transition for organizations, managers and workers, bridging the gap between traditional work and the emergence of 'knowledge work', in which work is no longer about the mass production of tangible commodities but is concerned with the organization's intangible assets – knowledge (Sveiby, 1997) – and in which knowledge is the principal asset of the corporation and indeed of countries (Drucker, 1993). The nature of 'knowledge work' is fundamentally different from what we have traditionally associated with the 'machine age' and mass production and marketing, the alleged differences between the natures of traditional work and knowledge work being illustrated in Table 4.1.

This shift from traditional to knowledge work has an important outcome for HRM because of the recognition that an organization's wealth and ability to compete exists 'principally in the heads of its employees, and, moreover, that it effectively "walks out the gates" every day' (Boud & Garrick, 1999, p. 48). Similarly, Quah argues that sustainable competitiveness depends not on 'having built the largest factory … [but] on knowing how to locate and juxtapose critical pieces of information, how to organize understanding into forms that others will understand' (1997, p. 4, quoted in Thompson & Warhurst, 1998, p. 1). This realization that knowledge work is fundamentally different has led managers to change strategies, patterns of interaction, HR practices and new organizational structures.

Table 4.1 The nature of traditional work and knowledge work

	Traditional work	**Knowledge work**
Locus of work	Around individuals	In groups and projects
Focus of work	Tasks, objectives, performance	Customers, problems, issues
Skill obsolescence	Gradual	Rapid
Skill/knowledge sets	Narrow and often functional	Specialized and deep, but often with diffuse peripheral focuses
Activity/feedback cycles	Primary and of an immediate nature	Lengthy from a business perspective
Performance measures	Task deliverables	Process effectiveness
	Little (as planned), but regular and dependable	Potentially great, but often erratic
Employee's loyalty	To organization and his or her career systems	To professions, networks and peers
Impact on company success	Many small contributions that support the master plan	A few major contributions of strategic and long-term importance

Source: Adapted from Despres and Hiltrop (1995) and Boud and Garrick (1999)

Post-bureaucratic work designs

Underpinning the debates on post-bureaucratic organizations, described below, are the implicit assumptions, first that the nature of work in the 'information age' has radically changed, and second, that organizations will experience superior performance if the typical bureaucratic pyramid model is reconfigured so that management structures are 'delayered' and decision-making is pushed down to the 'front line'. Some writers have described these anti-hierarchical characteristics in organizational design as a shift from 'modernist' to 'postmodernist' organizational practices (Clegg, 1990; Clegg & Hardy, 1999; Hassard & Parker, 1993; Heckscher & Donnelon, 1994).

Post-bureaucracy is part of an evolving series of 'conversions' associated with post-modern critiques coalesced around an antipathy to 'modernist' tendencies emphasizing functionalism, by which we mean an approach premised on assumptions concerning the unitary and orderly nature of work organizations, the notion of totality and grand narratives history. The bureaucratic features of 'modern' organizations are those of 'losing shape' and giving way to a flat, flexible and empowered 'postmodern' organizational form (Clegg & Hardy, 1999). Clegg (1990, quoted by Willmott, 1995, p. 90) outlines the main contrasting features of postmodernism thus:

> Where the modern organization was rigid, post-modern organization is flexible … Where modern organization was premised on technological determinism, postmodernism is premised on technological choices made possible through dedicated micro-electronic equipment. Where modernism organization and jobs were highly differentiated, demarcated and de-skilled, postmodernist organization and jobs are highly differentiated, demarcated and multi-skilled.

On the outside, the boundaries of the post-bureaucratic organization are blurred or 'fluid' as managers form temporary 'strategic alliances' with other independent firms that are linked by information technology – the 'network' structure or 'virtual' organization (Davidow & Malone, 1992). On the inside, these new organizational configurations offer, argue advocates, opportunities for 'flexible' work-related learning, more radical innovation and collaborative patterns of social interaction, allowing organizations to 'reinvent the future' (Hamel & Prahalad, 1994). The concepts of 'workplace learning' and 'organizational learning' are part of the conversation that fuels the postmodern debate on organizations based on the processing of knowledge and information (Huseman & Goodman, 1999; Jaffee, 2001). The notion that an organization 'learns' by processing information fits with the 'brain' metaphor of work organization (Morgan, 1997). The pursuit of flexibility and superior performance through designing a 'learning organization' is discussed in Chapters 2 and 10.

Five key features of Heckscher's (1994) ideal-type conceptualization of the post-bureaucratic organization provide an interesting insight into the internal practices and patterns of social interaction that we can expect to find in these emerging organizational forms. These features are:

1. organizational dialogue, persuasion and trust
2. information-sharing
3. behaviour based on principles
4. communication based on problem-solving
5. peer evaluation.

According to observers, management 'command and control' is replaced by *dialogue*, *persuasion* and *trust*, which allows a wide range of input to arise from the bottom and from across the organization rather than from the top of the hierarchy. The effectiveness of dialogue, persuasion and trust depends on access to and the *sharing of information* relating to the organization's operations. The behaviour and actions of managers and subordinates are dictated by general *principles* that allow greater flexibility, discretion and adaptation rather than by formal contractual rules and written procedures. Organizational communications and decision-making are driven by *problems* and projects rather than a hierarchical chain of command. In the post-bureaucratic organization, people's performance relies more on peer evaluation and negotiated standards of performance than on their immediate supervisor, seniority and formal credentials. Taken together, Heckscher's ideal-type features produce the 'master concept', 'an organization in which everyone takes responsibility for the success of the whole' (1994, p. 24). There appear to be few existing post-bureaucratic organizations, but Heckscher does cite the Shell-Sarnia chemical plant in Ontario, Canada, as being the 'most advanced exemplar' of this work regime.

A number of academics are critical of 'post-bureaucratic', 'postmodern' formulations (see, for example, Reed, 1993; Thompson, 1993; Thompson & McHugh, 2002). Thompson, for instance, accuses postmodern organizational theorists of having fallen victim to technological determinism and of mistaking the surface of work organizations for their substance. Thompson argues that the 'leaner' organization actually gives more power to a few: 'Removing some of the middle layers of organizations is not the same as altering the basic power structure ... By cutting out intermediary levels [of management] ... the power resources of those at the top can be increased' (1993, p. 192). One way of doing this is described in the next section.

HRM IN PRACTICE 4.2

COUNCIL MANAGEMENT FORCED TO SHED TIERS
Hackney Council is ridding itself of its 'historical baggage' as part of a radical management overhaul

STEPHEN OVERELL *PEOPLE MANAGEMENT*, 1997

London's Hackney Council will next week approve a radical organisational shake-up that will see tiers of management axed and top staff forced to reapply for their jobs.

Tony Elliston, Hackney's chief executive, has ambitious plans to see a total management overhaul completed by the beginning of 1998. This is intended to further his aim of pushing the troubled council to the top of Audit Commission league tables.

> **... units purchasing support services will be free to buy help from the private sector if in-house teams are not up to scratch.**

Under the new structure, units purchasing support services will be free to buy help from the private sector if in-house teams are not up to scratch. Personnel services and training, for example, will each operate as a trading unit, effectively as internal consultancies. There will also be a core central personnel function concerned with top-level recruitment and management and organisational development.

Elliston intends to scrap six

director posts and replace them with four new executive directors. These will have no budgets or staff, but will deal with corporate strategy.

The current tier of 15 assistant directors will be replaced with nine service directors responsible for targets and commissioning services. Delivery will be provided by units that will, in turn, buy support services such as legal, training or personnel from trading units operating in an internal market.

Asked about how top staff felt about reapplying for their jobs, Elliston replied: 'Huge changes are going to happen, not just a little here and a little there. If officers can't mirror that in their behaviours, they have got some life choices to make. New staff will be those most able to do the job.'

'... the only thing that matters is the community getting their services promptly, efficiently and professionally.'

Elliston said he was keen to avoid traditional titles such as director of education and director of housing. Instead, service directors will be responsible for areas such as learning and leisure, children and families and estate management and development.

'I do not want to see the creation of fiefdoms,' he said. 'It is only human to want to protect your patch, but they have got to be able to see that the only thing that matters is the community getting their services promptly, efficiently and professionally.'

The shake-up is expected to make initial savings of £5 million, which will be used to extend services or cut council tax bills. Hackney has already trimmed £58 off its bills this year, the largest cut in London. A parallel move towards devolution, with 'one-stop shops' for queries on, for example, housing and social services, is also under way.

HRM WEB LINKS

Go to the following website for Shell-Sarnia, Ontario, Canada (www.shell.ca) for more information.

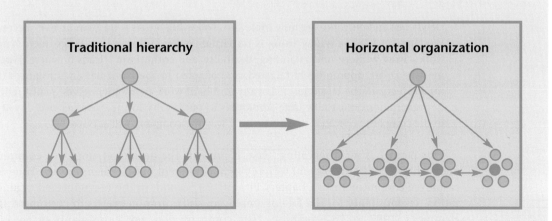

Figure 4.7 A traditional hierarchy versus horizontal (team-based) organization

STUDY TIP

You may wish to extend your understanding of 'postmodernism' and its implications for HRM by asking to what extent postmodernism represents a 'yearning for alternatives' or a 'distraction' from the critical analysis of current trends in organizations. Read John Hassard's chapter 'Postmodernism and organizational analysis: an overview' in Hassard and Parker (1993).

What do you think of the modern and postmodern discourse? Have the basic principles that originally defined capitalist work organizations (competition, technological change, a tendency to minimize costs, antagonistic employment relations over pay and effort levels) changed? How does your experience of work and organizations align with the popular management rhetoric?

Business process re-engineering

One major development in organizational design, which emphasizes process in a *horizontal* structure – the organization of work by self-managed teams (Figure 4.7) – is business process re-engineering (BPR), which falls within the post-bureaucratic genre. The BPR movement declares that organizational structures and the way in which work is structured have to be 'radically' changed so that the re-engineered company can become adaptable and orientated towards continuous change and renewal. According to the re-engineering guru James Champy, BPR is 'about changing our managerial work, the way we think about, organize, inspire, deploy, enable, measure, and reward the value-adding operational work. It is about changing management itself' (Champy, 1996, p. 3). Re-engineered organizations allegedly have a number of common characteristics (Table 4.2). Central to these organizational forms, argues Willmott (1995), is the 'reconceptualization of core employees' from being considered a variable cost to being represented as a valuable asset capable of serving the customer without the need for a 'command and control' leadership style. With the ascendancy of 'customer democracy', employees are encouraged to exercise initiative in creating value for customers and thereby profits for the company. According to Hammer (1997, pp. 158–9):

> Obedience and diligence are now irrelevant. Following orders is no guarantee of success. Working hard at the wrong thing is no virtue. When customers are kings, mere hard work – work without understanding, flexibility, and enthusiasm – leads nowhere. Work must be smart, appropriately targeted, and adapted to the particular circumstances of the process and the customer ... Loyalty and hard work are by themselves quaint relics ... organizations must now urge employees to put loyalty to the customer over loyalty to the company – because that is the only way the company will survive.

This passage is most revealing. First, it presents the debate on employee commitment, shared commitment and reciprocity in a different light. (We discuss the issue of employee commitment in Chapters 11 and 12.) Second, in the re-engineered organization, responsibility for the fate of employees shifts from managers to customers. In Hammer's (1997, p. 157) opinion, 'The company does not close plants or lay off workers – customers do, by their actions or inactions.'

Table 4.2 The re-engineered organization

Characteristic	Traditional model	Re-engineered model
Market	Domestic	Global
Competitive advantage	Cost	Speed and quality
Resources	Capital	Information
Quality	What is affordable	No compromise
Focal point	Profit	Customer
Structural design	Hierarchical	Flattened
Control	Centralized	De-centralized
Leadership	Autocratic	Shared
Labour	Homogeneous	Culturally diverse
Organization of work	Specialized and individual	Flexible and in teams
Communications	Vertical	Horizontal

Unlike earlier movements in work design, such as the QWL movement (see above), re-engineering is *market driven*. It focuses on the relationship between the buyer and seller of services or goods rather than between the employer and employee. Hammer and Champy (1993) emphasize that the 'three Cs' – customers, competition and change – and a shift in the national government policy of 'tough love' towards business have created the need for re-engineering business processes. For Champy (1996, p. 19), using a mixture of language discarded by the political 'old Left' and terminology of the 'new Right', 'a dictatorship of the customariat or ... a market democracy ... is the cause of a total revolution within the traditional, machine-like corporation'.

Practitioners and academics have, however, been critical of re-engineering. One management consultant has criticized the imprecise meaning of BPR and pointed out that senior managers have been using the term 'to legitimize other objectives' (quoted in *Management Today*, February, 1995). Grint and Willcocks (1995) offer a scathing review of BPR, arguing that it is not novel and pointing out that it is essentially political in its rhetorical and practical manifestations. Willmott (1995) is similarly scornful of BPR, emphasizing that re-engineering is 'heavily top-down' and pointing out that the re-engineered organization, using information technology, also, while creating less hierarchical structures produces 'a fist-full of dynamic processes ... notably, the primacy of hierarchical control and the continuing treatment of employees as cogs in the machine' (1995, p. 91). In his case study analysis of BPR in a hospital, Buchanan (1997) observes that the lack of clarity of BPR terminology and methodology offers 'considerable scope for political maneuvering' by politically motivated actors. A case study of BPR in the public sector found that conflict arose from 'very human needs to justify one's role in the new organization, or individual managers' needs to maintain their power bases within the organization' (Harrington et al., 1998, p. 50). Moreover, within the context of the employment relationship, BPR does not obviate the inherent conflict of interest between the two parties: the *employers* and *employees*. When examined in the context of employment relations, BPR can be interpreted 'as the latest wave in a series of initiatives ... to increase the cooperation/productivity/ adaptability of staff' (Willmott, 1995, p. 96).

HRM IN PRACTICE 4.3

WORKING PART-TIME NO BED OF ROSES: STUDY

VIRGINIA GALT, *GLOBE AND MAIL*, 2001, JULY 9, P. B4

Part-time work is not as idyllic as it may appear to envious full-timers, according to new Canadian research published in the *Harvard Business Review*. 'Professionals who work part-time must go to extreme lengths to make the arrangements acceptable to their employers and colleagues,' wrote academics Vivian Corwin, Thomas Lawrence and Peter Frost.

A common pitfall is the tendency to compress a full-time workload into part-time hours – for part-time pay, they found. Even with the compressed schedule, however, work still encroaches on what is supposed to be family time.

'It is not necessarily a panacea for a striking a balance between work and life,' the researchers wrote. The researchers interviewed a mother who confessed to sending an ill child to school in order to attend business meetings and prove her 'commitment'. They also interviewed a co-worker irked by a part-time colleague who would swan out of the office at noon on Wednesdays, wishing everyone else a good weekend. 'She didn't win many

> '**Professionals who work part-time must go to extreme lengths to make the arrangements acceptable to their employers and colleagues.**'

friends,' observed Ms. Corwin, a consultant in leadership development and human resource management and an associate faculty member at Royal Roads University in Victoria.

'Many part-timers are forced to work longer hours than they contracted for, and many suffer under the second-class status of part-time work,' the researchers found as part of a wide-ranging study on how employees in Canada and the USA balance the competing demands of work and home life. 'At the same time, part-time work makes organizations uncomfortable. It raises obvious questions about who will pick up the slack,' they wrote in their *Harvard Business Review* article.

Most part-timer arrangements are ad hoc, many professionals working part-time report that they are overlooked when bonuses are handed out, and may feel 'out of the loop' professionally. 'Most part-timers told us they accepted the consequences of their status as part of the deal. But they also said that sometimes their confidence was eroded, and they questioned whether the arrangement was worth the effort.'

HRM WEB LINKS

Go to www.bprc.warwick.ac.uk/bp-site.html, the website of the ESRC-funded Business Processes Resource Centre at Warwick University. It was created as a focal point in the UK for the dissemination of current knowledge and research, and to provide access to best practice thinking and application.

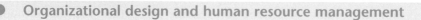

Organizational design and human resource management

The design of organizational structures and the way in which work is performed are critical features of new formulations of HRM. As Guest (1990) points out, underpinning the HRM model is the need to reconfigure organizational structures as the rhetoric is essentially 'anti-bureaucratic'. Guest further emphasizes the concomitant change in job design, believing that HRM takes as its starting point the view that organizations should be designed on the basis of the assumptions inherent in McGregor's (1960) Theory Y. According to McGregor, people work because they want to work rather than because they have to. Thus, Theory Y view of people assumes that when workers are given challenging assignments and autonomy over work assignments, they will respond with high motivation, high commitment and high performance.

Job and organizational design is related closely to all key HRM activities, including recruitment and selection, learning and development, rewards and employee relations; job design is basic to the recruitment and selection function. A company that produces small-batch, high value-added products using skilled labour within a team-based organizational arrangement will clearly have more rigorous recruitment and selection priorities than a company that specializes in large-batch production using dedicated machines operated by unskilled operators supervised in the usual pyramid-shaped organizational hierarchy. Job design affects workplace learning and employee training and development. As one of us as noted elsewhere, 'high quality workplace learning ... is contingent upon the quality of job design in the workplace' (Bratton, 1999, p. 491).

Several empirical studies have found a strong and consistent association between new forms of work organization, as well as higher levels of technical skills upgrading and training for their employees than are seen in those firms operating under 'traditional' work regimes (Adams & McQuillan, 2000; Felstead & Ashton, 2000; Osterman, 1995). Specifically, new forms of work organization require enhanced formal and informal learning in technical, decision-making and team-building skills. Compaq Canada, for example, sent its managers to a corporate 'wilderness' training centre to learn team-building skills. Success requires the team to learn to communicate with each other, cooperate and work together (Belcourt et al., 2000). If an organization chooses to introduce work teams, managers will have to consider such detail as the structure of teams, the actual rewards offered, whether these are contingent upon team or company performance, communication and input from team members (McClurg, 2001).

More recently, it has become fashionable to emphasize the contribution that reconfigured work structures have on the psychological contract. The nature of work and organizational structural features discussed in this chapter – the degree of formal rules and procedures, decision-making and governance processes – are critical factors in the formation and reformation of reciprocal expectations, aspirations and understandings. In their model of HRM, Beer et al. (1984), for example, envision job design broadening employee responsibilities and resulting in a 'substantial improvement in the 'four Cs' of commitment, competence, cost-effectiveness and congruence. In practice, however, there is much concern and debate over the rupture in the psychological contract resulting from restructuring, particularly 'delayering' and 'downsizing'. According to Edwards (2000, p. 290), downsizing is 'a planned, intentional reduction in personnel'. For those employees 'let go' there is the severing of the explicit employment contract, and for the survivors the psychological contract is adjusted in two ways. First, retained employees become distrustful of committing their energy to an organization that has displayed a lack of loyalty. Second, the survivors are frequently expected to undertake additional duties, with a corresponding increase in work intensification (Thomson & Millar, 2001). In a nutshell, job security has been the *quid pro quo* for employees' knowledge and skills, commitment and loyalty, and downsizing and the fundamental redesigning of work can result in less affective emotional attachment to their work organization, lower levels of commitment and loyalty, and the unilateral renegotiation of the psychological contract.

Important though the debate on the psychological contract is in highlighting the complexity of the employment relationship, it would be remiss in a textbook devoted to HRM tensions and paradoxes if it did not draw attention to the rich debate on how differing forms of work organization generate and reflect tension, contradiction and change.

Tension and paradox in job design

As we noted in Chapter 1, contradiction, tension and paradox underscore much of the critical analysis of HRM. Paradox is evident in work design, much of the contemporary literature on organizational and job design placing a great deal of emphasis on a number of paradoxes (Handy, 1994). There are a number of ways in which to think about and conceptualize paradox in work design. Here we use a simple model presented by Jaffee (2001) and illustrated in Figure 4.8. The model shows that paradox stems from what is called 'differentiation–integration tension'. This refers to the inherent tension between the management strategies for achieving a rational division of economic activities and, simultaneously, ensuring that these activities are coordinated and integrated. Differentiation and the division of labour are fundamental management principles that underscore organizational goals to control costs and the quality of their products or services. As organizations increase in size and complexity, integration becomes an issue. How do different workers, departments and managers coordinate and integrate their interdependent activities?

The tension between differentiation and integration within the organization can be illustrated by a familiar manufacturing strategy: management initially redesigns work involving a rigid division of labour and highly specialized tasks (for example Fordism). The *intended* consequence, however, is to rationalize and make the workers more effi-

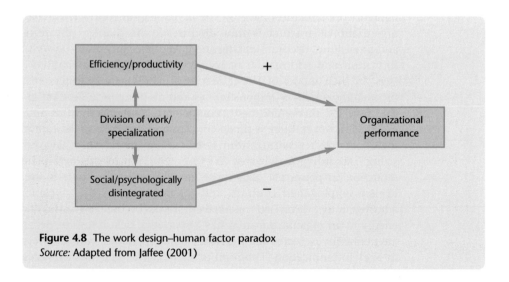

Figure 4.8 The work design–human factor paradox
Source: Adapted from Jaffee (2001)

cient and productive. The *unintended* consequence, however, is the creation of a socially disintegrated work experience that produces low levels of cross-communication, job satisfaction, motivation and commitment to the organization. In other words, the new work arrangement changes people's perceptions of management's commitment and expectations, thereby affecting the psychological contract. This, as we discussed earlier, can limit the positive contribution made by the specialization of labour. Existing views on the implications of JIT production further illustrate such tensions and contradictions. The effects of tighter logistical integration between firms can improve productivity, but a zero inventory can make a firm highly vulnerable to temporary stoppages (Bratton, 1992) and undermine the psychological contract resulting from the 'unrelenting' pressure to meet deadlines:

> The brinkmanship of just-in-time production creates *extraordinary pressures* on employees and work organization. Such pressures may drive out HR support activities ... needed to sustain employee motivation and morale. (Scarbrough, 2000, p. 16, emphasis added).

The crux of this problem is managerial 'control'. Management, as Geary and Dobbins (2001, p. 5) remind us, is not simply about controlling the labour process: it is also about enlisting workers' knowledge, creativity and discretionary efforts:

> Management remains caught between two opposing imperatives: attempts at regulating employees too tightly run the risk of endangering the employees' creativity and commitment to management goals, while empowering employees runs the risk of reducing management control.

This fundamental paradox at the heart of the employment relationship becomes even more acute when managers redesign organizational structures and arrangements that increase workers' participation and discretionary powers.

The notion of tension and paradox in work design is apparent in the debate on the affects of work teams. Many mainstream organizational scholars have argued that self-managed teams reverse Tayloristic deskilling tendencies. Piore and Sabel (1984), for example, posit that new 'flexible' work arrangements exemplify the re-emergence of the craft paradigm, but this interpretation of the Japanese model has its critics. Critical observers of changes in work structure have asserted that team-based work regimes are detrimental to workers' interests, arguing that limited 'empowerment' does not reverse the general deskilling trend but has a tendency to increase the intensity of work (Clarke, 1997; Rinehart et al., 1997; Sayer, 1986; Sennett, 1998; Tomaney, 1990; Turnbull, 1986) and offer management much 'tighter control' over the effort bargain (Malloch, 1997). Using Foucault's Panopticon metaphor (Chapter 1), a number of writers have produced pessimistic analyses of non-traditional job designs in which work teams function to 'reconstitute the individual as a productive subject' in order to enhance managerial control (Townley, 1994, p. 109).

As mentioned earlier in the chapter, others offer more optimistic analyses in which the outcomes of new work regimes are less deterministic (see for example, Geary & Dobbins, 2001; Thompson & McHugh, 2002). Whether non-traditional job designs results in the 'upskilling' or 'deskilling' of workers depends on, among other things, factors such as batch size, managerial choice and negotiation (Bratton, 1992). Although managerial techniques for monitoring work teams remain primitive, work

Table 4.3 Four approaches to job design

	Motivation assumptions	Critical techniques	Job classification	Issues
Scientific management	Motivation is based on the piecework incentive system of pay. The more pieces the worker produces, the higher the pay	Division of tasks and responsibilities Task analysis 'one best way' Training Rewards	Division of tasks and of 'doing' and 'control' leads to many job classifications	Criteria of motivation may be questioned No role for unions Cooperation costs Product inflexibility
Job enrichment	Motivation is based on social needs and the expectations of workers. To increase performance, focus on achievement, recognition and responsibility	Combine tasks Increase accountability Create natural work units Greater responsibility	Some supervisory tasks are undertaken by workers as the 'control' is shifted downwards	Criteria of motivation may be questioned Undefined union role
Japanese management	Motivation is based on teamwork or 'clan-like' norms and the organizational culture. Performance and motivation are social processes in which some workers try to influence others to work harder	Intensive socialization Lifetime employment Consensual decision-making Non-specialized career paths Seniority-based pay	Requires fewer job classifications because of flexibility and a degree of autonomy	Criteria of motivation may be culture-bound Collaborative union role Work intensification
Re-engineering	Motivation is based on the need to serve the customer. Performance and motivation are social processes in which strong leaders enthuse workers to work harder	Organizational norms and traditions are abandoned Networking Strong top-down leadership Workplace learning Information technology enables change Processes have multiple versions	Multidimensional jobs Workers are organized into process teams Workers are empowered to make decisions	Criteria of motivation may be questioned Market driven Undefined union role Work intensification

team autonomy has not eliminated worker resistance, and managerial control continues to be contested (McKinlay & Taylor, 1998). Similarly, the debate on BPR has focused on whether the empowerment of employees has resulted in work structures that are necessarily less restrictive or repressive than those designed following Taylorist principles. Willmott (1995, p. 96), for example, asserts that, with the assistance of microtechnology, re-engineering is an 'up-dating of Taylor's crusade against custom and practice in which the silicon chip plays an equivalent role in [re-engineering] to that performed by the stop watch in Scientific Management'. The benefits for managers and non-managers of jettisoning the old values and old ways of doing work appear to be mixed in terms of personal growth and empowerment.

When organizations adopt new work structures, the changes clearly impact on the nature of work, managers and non-managers, and place HRM centre-stage. The precise nature of the impact of these work design strategies is, however, subject to debate, as are the concepts associated with emerging organizational paradigms such as Japanization, BPR and the learning organization. For managers, HRM practitioners and employees, increasing attention has also focused on the implications of job redesign and organizational structure for the broader physical workplace environment and employees' health and safety (Chapter 5), the need for workplace learning (Chapter 10) and the need to synchronize bundles of HRM practices and labour relations to new work structures (Chapter 12).

Chapter summary

We started this chapter by examining the meaning of work in contemporary Western society and then proceeded to evaluate alternative job design strategies, including scientific management, job enrichment, Japanese work structures and re-engineering. These broad job design movements are summarized in Table 4.3.

- The review of the research reported here testifies that, in the early 21st century, flexibility is the management mantra on both sides of the Atlantic. Much of the literature on new organizational designs is couched in the language of 'empowerment' and 'postmodernism'. The postmodern organization has been characterized in the popular and academic management literature as flexible, enabling, innovative, creative, multiskilled and democratic. Despite, however, all the interest in self-managed teams, empirical evidence suggests that, in the vast majority of workplaces, the 'quality' of work does not match the rhetoric (Lowe, 2000) and 'non-educative work is systemic' (Bratton, 1999, p. 491).

- For Sewell, and Thompson and McHugh, contemporary work regimes embody neo-Taylorist principles and a technical mode of managerial control. The research on non-standard employment – including freelancers, home-workers and outworkers – and call centres, (see Millward et al., 2000) and the wider debate on the 'McDonaldization' of work and 'electronic sweatshops' suggest both change and continuation in the workplace.

- We have cautioned readers against the tendency to conceptualize new work structures as a smooth transition from one 'ideal-type' model to another. As others have pointed out, the widespread tendency to compress the specific into categories of general trends not only compresses variations in organizational design, but also attaches an apparent coherence to emerging organizational forms that is spurious (Salaman, 1981). The fact that Felstead and Ashton (2000, p. 18) found 'only three out of 10 employees currently work in "modern" organizations' exemplifies Littler's (1982) earlier argument that when it comes to new work designs, change is sporadic, intermittent and slow, and is subject to constant struggle and negotiation.

● The bedrock of emerging organizational forms – self-managed work teams – is a complex 'interlocking' arrangement of technical, government and cultural dimensions. The message of this chapter has been that, in the context of capitalist employment relationships, unintended consequences and tensions will arise with each new organizational form.

● We concluded our discussion on work and work organization by identifying some practical implications for managers and HR professionals. Organizational and job redesign affects both an organization's competitiveness and the experience and motivation of the individual and work group. New work structures typically impact directly on recruitment and selection criteria, performance appraisal, rewards, learning, training and development. Further studies indicate that work and organizational redesign can cause employees' perceptions of the psychological contract to change.

● The practical implication of changing the way in which work is organized is that managers and HR professionals have not only to develop new HR policies and practices, but also to cope with the tensions, contradictions and paradoxes associated with any new work structure. Finally, managers need to take steps to understand how new forms of work organization can change employees' perception of the content of the psychological contract and from this, when circumstances permit, shape a 'new contract' (Coyle-Shapiro & Kessler, 2000).

Key concepts

● Business process re-engineering   ● Job design

● Fordism   ● Job enlargement

● Human relations movement   ● Job enrichment

● Japanization   ● Scientific management

● Job characteristic model   ● Work

Chapter review questions

1. Why define 'work' by its social context rather than by the content of the activity?

2. Explain the limits of Taylorism as a job design strategy.

3. 'Job rotation, job enlargement and job enrichment are simply attempts by managers to control individuals at work.' Do you agree or disagree? Discuss.

4. Students often complain about doing group projects; why? Relate your answer to autonomous work teams. Would you want to be a member of such a work group? Discuss your reasons.

5. 'The notion of "Japanization" is a chaotic conception.' '"Japanization" is a useful framework for organizing the complexities of Japanese management practices.' Critically evaluate these two statements. Discuss your reasons.

6. 'McWork' is a symbolic term often used by critics of the 'new economy' to capture the realities of workplace life confronting young people today. What kind of jobs does 'McWork' refer to? How do the job design concepts discussed in this chapter help you to understand the term 'McWork'? Is it an accurate description of employment today?

Further reading

Geary, J., & Dobbins, A. (2001). Teamworking: A new dynamic in the pursuit of management control. *Human Resource Management*, **11**(1), 3–23.

Sparrow, P. (2000). New employee behaviours, work designs and forms of work organization: What is in store for future work? *Journal of Management Psychology*, **15**(3), 202–18.

Willmott, H. (1995). The odd couple? Re-engineering business processes: Managing human relations. *New Technology, Work and Employment*, **10**(2), 89–98.

Practising human resource management

Searching the web

Log on to the website for the Centre for the Study of Work Teams (www.workteams. unt.edu) and write a brief report explaining the stereotypical team-based organization, as you picture it. What main principles or practices can be identified as a source of efficiency? Can the team-based model be universally applied? What behavioural predictions would you make about people who work in 'post-bureaucratic' organizations? Find three companies that have introduced business process re-engineering but were disappointed with the results. What factors led to this disappointment?

HRM group project

Form a study group of three to five people, and go to the websites of Daimler-Chrysler AG, (www.daimlerchrysler.com), Motorola (www.motorola.ca), Johnson and Johnson (www.johnsonandjohnson.com), Union Carbide (www.unioncarbide. com), Harley-Davidson (www.harley-davidson.com/en/home.asp) or an alternative organization that interests members of the group.

Imagine that your group is a task force established by senior management to investigate the merits of work teams. Write a brief report addressing two aspects:

1. How are the following HRM activities – selection, training and rewards – affected when managers redesign the organization from being a traditional bureaucratic to becoming a team-based structure. One approach is to consider various companies or recruiters on the web (see examples in Chapter 7) and compare any differences between the job profiles listed by different organizations or

recruiters. Are any patterns visible between team-based and traditionally designed organizations?

2. How is a team-based structure likely to affect employees' psychological contract?

Present this report with the help of PowerPoint so that other members of the management team (class members) can understand the main arguments and reflect on the likely impact that teams would have on HRM.

Chapter case study

WOLDS INSURANCE PLC

Wolds Insurance plc is a large insurance company that employs 1850 people in its branches throughout the UK. The Underwriting Department at the Newcastle branch consists of 13 clerks, of whom one is a section head and another a head of department. The nature of the work in the department has fundamentally changed over the past 20 years from bookkeeping and an accounting process to clerical processing. There are various types of policy, the main difference being between 'commercial' and 'personal'. The vast majority of policies taken out are personal. Until late 1996, the underwriting department was divided into personal and commercial sections, but in January 1997 these were combined. Although clerks vary in the mix of commercial and personal policies they deal with, the variety in the work of each clerk is small.

Before 1993, the processing of policy issue at branch level was manual, the premium being calculated using manuals and charts. Details of the policy were then sent to the head office and issued from there. Head office had introduced a mainframe computer for this process in 1988, but the procedure at branch level remained much the same until mid-1993, when the VDTs were installed in the underwriting department.

At first, the department was not 'on-line', and premiums still had to be calculated manually. Policy details were, however, to be keyed in directly, and the VDT was used to check the details of any given policy. In 1994, the system went 'on-line', details of the policy being keyed in directly at branch level. In 1996, the computer was programmed to calculate premiums automatically. Management's aim was to computerize as many policies as possible through complex programming and standardization of the product. This reduced the processing time: for the majority of policies, it was necessary only to transfer details from form to screen and then use the right classification, as specified in the manual. Before on-line computerization, a clerk could deal with 35 policies a week, whereas afterwards 80 policies a week could be processed.

Clerical staff numbers were reduced to a third within 3 years, and the previously separate departments of commercial and personal were combined into one. The division of work in the branch was divided into four functions: underwriting, claims, cash and accounts. In addition, the clerks were divided into two types of employee: those knowledgeable on insurance, capable of answering enquiries and dealing with non-standard cases, and those who processed routine policies. In terms of the knowledge required, standardization had reduced the differences between the policies and had for some reduced the level of knowledge required. Many of the policies are now offered on a 'take it or leave it' basis, and the processing of the policy is routine and repetitive, requiring little knowledge of insurance. Details of the customer and cover required are keyed into the computer in the specified order, and the premium is calculated automatically. Some knowledge of insurance is, however, still required for dealing with enquiries.

The underwriting clerks are beginning to show signs of frustration as much of their working day is spent on routine processing. There is also tension between those clerks doing the routine processing and those working on the non-standard and more interesting cases. This is resulting in serious morale problems, high absenteeism and an increasing number of mistakes in the processing. The manager of the department and the HR manager realize that changes are needed, but they are unsure how to improve the situation.

(The case is based on 'Skill, deskilling and new technology in the non-manual labour process' by Heather Rolfe, in *New Technology, Work and Employment*, 1986, 1(1): 37–49.)

Discussion questions

You have recently been appointed HR assistant at Wold Insurance. June Cole, the HR manager, has asked you to consider ways of 'enriching' the work of the underwriting clerks. Prepare a written report focusing on the following questions:

1. What symptoms suggest that something is wrong in the underwriting department?

2. Using the job design concepts discussed in this chapter, suggest how to improve the clerical jobs in the underwriting department.

You may make any assumptions you feel are necessary, providing they are realistic and you make them explicit in your response.

HR-related skill development

Work team meetings are a vital part of the team-building and team performance process. Team meetings can be held for a variety of purposes: informing, collecting opinions and information, resolving conflict, problem-solving and decision-making. Such meetings can, unless properly managed by team leaders, be frustrating and a waste of time. As such, the ability to manage a team meetings well is a valuable HR-related skill. To understand what it means to be a designated leader of a work team, and to develop your team leadership skills, go to our website (www.palgrave.com/business/brattonandgold) and click on 'Team leadership skills'.

Notes

1. Sherwood Ross, Workers turn off autopilot and take charge on assembly lines of the 21st century, *Globe and Mail*, (2001, September 3), p. B12.
2. Patrica Chisholm, Redesigning work, *Maclean's*, (2001, March 5), p. 36.
3. Hammer, Michael, (1997) *Beyond reengineering*, New York: HarperCollins, p. xi.
4. Tony Clarke and Sarah Dopp, (2001) *Challenging McWorld*, Ottawa: Canadian Centre for Policy Alternatives, p. 64.
5. Annual labor report applauds job hopping and predicts fewer services for consumers, *Asahi Evening News*, Japan, (1992, July 1), p. 4.

Chapter five

Health and safety

John Bratton

Occupational health and safety is concerned with the identification
and control of hazards associated with the physical workplace environment.
These hazards, which range from technological, physical and chemical agents
to psychosocial disorders such as workplace stress, shape objective patterns of
interaction, behaviour and process and also subjective feelings about
the employment relationship.

'Long before you reach the Russian city, Norilsk announces itself with mounds of dirty blackened
snow on the fragile grass of the summer tundra. Then comes the hellish vision of the world's most
polluted Arctic metropolis. Looming at the end of the road is a horizon of massive smokestacks ...
and thousands of denuded trees as lifeless as blackened matchsticks. Inside malodorous smelters,
Russian workers wear respirators as they trudge through the hot suffocating air, heavy with
clouds of dust and gases. ... Pollutants from this factory have drifted as far as the Canadian
Arctic. Traces of heavy metals have been found in the breast milk of Inuit mothers.'[1]

'Businesses in Europe and North America lose $120 billion (US) a year because of stress,
depression and other mental disorders among employees. E-mail and voice mail are two of the
biggest sources of stress, because they erase the boundaries between work and home and
contribute to worker isolation in the office.'[2]

Chapter outline

Chapter objectives

After studying this chapter, you should be able to:

1. Explain the benefits of a healthy and safe workplace
2. Discuss some key developments in health and safety
3. Describe the major regulatory framework surrounding workplace health and safety
4. Describe some physical and psychosocial hazards in the modern workplace
5. Evaluate different management strategies for health and safety at work

Introduction

Most mornings, we turn the door-handle and set off to work in factories, steel mills, offices, banks, schools, hospitals, universities or some other workplace. Most of us assume that we will return home safely at the end of the working day, but many workers unfortunately will not. In 2000–01, 295 British workers lost their lives through a workplace fatality, and another 343,000 employees suffered a work-related injury serious enough to warrant having more than 3 days' absence from work (Health and Safety Statistics, 2000/01). In Canada, it is estimated that a workplace accident occurs every 9 seconds (Montgomery & Kelloway, 2002). The data underscore an important reality about work: that it can be a deadly and dangerous experience.

The World Health Organization (WHO) defines 'health' as 'a state of complete physical, mental and social well-being, not merely an absence of disease and infirmity'.[3] According to this definition, managers are immersed in one of society's greatest challenges – the design and maintenance of a work organization that is both effective in meeting business objectives, and healthy and safe for its employees. Occupational health and safety are concerned with the identification and control of hazards associated with the physical workplace environment, hazards ranging from technological, physical, biological and chemical agents to psychosocial disorders such as workplace stress. What is important to recognize, however, is that concerns about health and safety are no longer limited to areas of industrial work. In areas of knowledge work, office workers, managers and professionals are increasingly anxious about repetitive strain injury, sick building syndrome, work-related stress, workplace violence and second-hand smoke. Increasingly, all workers are demanding to work in a 'healthy organization'.

The decreasing tolerance for work-related hazards, the rising costs associated with workplace injuries and illnesses, and the growing recognition that health and safety forms an important subgroup of organizational contingencies affecting human resource management (HRM) (see Figure 5.2 below) underscore the need to understand how work and organizational design shape objective patterns of interaction and behaviour and subjective feelings about the employment relationship. In addition, the recent joint Health and Safety Commission/Department of the Environment, Transport and the Regions (HSC/DETR) strategy document reaffirms the importance of health and safety (James & Walters, 2002). In what follows, we begin considering the importance of health and safety in the HRM model and why a working knowledge of occupational health and safety is important for every manager. After giving a brief history of occupational health and safety, we review health and safety legislation in Britain and draw some comparisons with legislation elsewhere. The chapter then moves on to identify some contemporary hazards in the workplace before examining what managers can do to develop, promote and maintain a healthy and safe workplace. Finally, we seek to examine the paradoxes surrounding the issue of health and safety so that there can be a better understanding of the complexities of the employment relationship.

REFLECTIVE QUESTION

Read the chapter's opening quotation again. Who are the stakeholders in health and safety? What are the responsibilities of employers and government to ensure that work is conducted in a safe and healthy environment?

Consider an organization that you have worked in. Critically review its health and safety record and training.

Health and safety and human resource management

Although there has been a significant shift of mood among HRM researchers over the past decade (Sisson & Storey, 2000), reflected best perhaps by talk of a 'new agenda' (Sparrow & Marchington, 1998), it is unfortunately true that workplace health and safety is underresearched by HRM scholars and has been largely neglected in the HRM discourse. Moreover, the attitude of managers and employees towards accident and safety did not until relatively recently promote a healthy or safe workplace. The rising costs associated with workplace injuries and illnesses, 'psychological contract' issues, new health and safety laws, 'deregulatory' proposals and public opinion towards hazards are important reasons why more research should be devoted to workplace health and safety. But there is another important reason why HRM scholars and practitioners need to pay more attention to health and safety: if strategic HRM means anything, it must encompass the development and promotion of a set of health and safety policies to protect the organization's most valued asset, its employees.

The employer has a legal duty to maintain a healthy and safe workplace, the health and safety function being directly related to key HRM activities such as selection, appraisal, rewards and learning and development. Health and safety considerations and policy can affect the selection process in two ways. First, it is safe to assume that, during the recruitment process, potential applicants will be more attracted to an organization that has a reputation for offering a healthy and safe work environment for its employees. Second, the maintenance of a healthy and safe workplace can be facilitated in the selection process by choosing applicants with personality traits that decrease the likelihood of an accident. The appraisal of a manager's performance that incorporates the safety record of a department or section can also facilitate health and safety. Research suggests that safety management programmes are more effective when the accident rates of their sections are an important criterion of managerial performance. Safe work behaviour can be encouraged by a reward system that ties bonus payments to the safety record of a work group or section. Some organizations also provide prizes to their employees for safe work behaviour, a good safety record or suggestions for improving health and safety. Training and human resources (HR) development play a critical role in promoting health and safety awareness among employees, and indeed the Health and Safety at Work etc. Act (HASAWA) 1974 requires employers to provide instruction and training to ensure the health and safety of their employees. Studies indicate that safety training for new employees is particularly beneficial because accidents are highest during the early months on a new job.

On the question of the importance of occupational health and safety, although economic cost and HR considerations will always be predominant for the organization, the costs of ill-health and work-related accidents are not only borne by the victims, the families and their employers: the costs of occupational ill-health and accidents are also clearly borne by the taxpayer and public sector services. The health care sector, for example, bears the costs of workplace ill-health and accidents. Reliable estimates of the total cost of occupational ill-health and accidents are incomplete, which is perhaps symptomatic of the low priority given to this area of work. The Health and Safety Executive (HSE) has admitted that although occupational diseases kill more people in the UK each year than industrial accidents, there is only limited information on the former. A recent official survey put the cost to society for deaths and accidents (excluding occupational disease) in British workplaces at £10–15 billion, or 1.75–2.75% of the gross domestic product.[4] In Canada, compensation for victims of workplace accidents exceeds US $3 billion, this figure excluding the cost to the public health care system resulting from long-term work-related illnesses.

The changing approach to workplace health and safety

The traditional approach to safety in the workplace used the 'careless worker' model It was assumed by most employers, the courts and accident prevention bodies that most accidents resulted from an employee's failure to take safety seriously or to protect her- or himself. The implication of this is that work can be made safe simply by changing the behaviour of employees by poster campaigns and accident prevention training. In the past, the attitudes of trade unions often paralleled those of the employers and managers. Early trade union activity tended to focus on basic wage and job security issues rather than safety: trade union representatives used their negotiating skill to 'win' wage increases, and health and safety often came rather low down in their bargaining priorities. If union representatives did include health and safety as part of their activities, it was often so that they could negotiate the payment of 'danger' or 'dirt' money over and above the regular wage rate. According to Eva and Oswald (1981, p. 33), the tendency for union officials was 'to put the onus on to inspectors and government rather than to see health and safety as part of the everyday activity of local union representatives'. Among employees, dangerous and hazardous work systems were accepted as part of the risk of working. Lost fingers and deafness, for example, were viewed as a matter of 'luck' or the 'inevitable' outcome of work. In the early 1970s, a major investigation into occupational health and safety concluded that 'the most important single reason for accidents of work is apathy' (Robens, 1972, p. 1). So there is a paradox here. When there are major disasters on land, air or sea involving fatalities, society as a whole takes a keen interest, yet society's reaction towards the fact that hundreds of employees die and thousands receive serious injuries every year in the workplace tends to be muted.

In the 1960s, approximately one thousand employees were killed at work in the UK. Every year of that decade, about 500,000 employees suffered injuries of varying degrees of severity, and 23 million working days were lost annually on account of industrial injury and disease. Such statistics led investigators to argue that 'for both humanitarian and economic reasons, no society can accept with complacency that such levels of death, injury, disease and waste must be regarded as the inevitable price of meeting its needs for goods and services' (Robens, 1972, p. 1). Since the Robens report, there has been a growing interest in occupational health and safety. Moreover, it has been recognized that the 'careless worker' model does not explain occupational ill-health caused by toxic substances, noise, and badly designed and unsafe systems of work. Nor does this perspective highlight the importance of job stress, fatigue and a poor working environment in contributing to the cause of accidents. A new approach to occupational health and safety, the 'shared responsibility' model, assumes that the best way to reduce levels of occupational accidents and disease relies on the cooperation of both employers and employees, a 'self-generating effort' between 'those who create the risks and those who work with them' (Robens, 1972, p. 7).

Figure 5.1 A trade union view on workplace health and safety
Source: Eva and Oswald (1981)

In the late 1970s, the British Trades Union Congress (TUC) articulated a 'trade union approach' to health and safety emphasizing that the basic problem of accidents stems from the hazards and risks that are built into the workplace. The trade union approach argued that the way to improve occupational health and safety was through redesigning organizations and work systems in order to 'remove hazards and risks at source.'[5] An HSE document[6] would seem to support this approach, stating: Most accidents involve an element of failure in control – in other words failure in managerial skill … . A guiding principle when drawing up arrangements for securing health and safety should be that so far as possible work should be adapted to people and not vice versa. The trade unions' approach to health and safety, which draws attention to potential hazards in the labour process, is depicted in Figure 5.1.

The importance of health and safety

There are strong economic, legal, psychological and moral reasons why managers should take health and safety seriously.

Economic considerations

The recent HSC/DETR (2000) document made the 'business case' for health and safety in the workplace. In considering the economics of an unhealthy and unsafe workplace, it is necessary to distinguish between costs falling upon the organization and costs falling upon government-funded bodies such as hospitals. It is not difficult for an organization to calculate the economic costs of a work-related accident, an accident being defined as an unforeseen or unplanned event that results in an injury and

	£
1. *Cost of wages paid for the time spent by uninjured workpeople:*	
(a) assisting the injured person, or out of curiosity, sympathy and so on, or	
(b) who were unable to continue work because they relied on his aid or output	
In category (a) 6 employees lost on average 20 minutes	15.96
In category (b) 3 workers lost on average 60 minutes	24.00
2. *Cost of material or equipment damage:*	
In this instance the casing of a 5 hp electric motor was cracked beyond repair and replaced by a new motor	530.00
Installation cost	130.00
3. *Cost of injured worker's time lost:*	
Treatment for abrasion on leg. 2 hours lost at £7.59 per hour	15.18
4. *Supervisor's time spent assisting, investigating, reporting, assigning work, training or instructing a replacement and making other necessary adjustments:*	
One and a half hours at £12.95	19.43
5. *Wage cost of decreased output by injured worker after return to work:*	
4 days at 2 hours/day light work	74.00
6. *Medical cost to the company:*	
(A reduction in accidents does not necessarily mean lower expenses for running the works medical centre)	38.00
7. *Cost of time spent by administration staff and specialists on investigations or in the processing of compensation questions.* *HM Factory Inspector reports, insurance company and Department of Health and Social Security correspondence and so on:*	
Low in this case	66.00
TOTAL:	**912.57**

Additional Charges
Other cost elements not applicable to this accident but which must be considered in others include:
Overtime necessary to make up for lost production.
Cost of learning period of a replacement worker.
A wage cost for the time spent by supervisors or others in training the new worker.
Miscellaneous costs (includes the less typical costs, the validity of which will need to be clearly shown with respect to each accident):
– renting equipment
– loss of profit on orders cancelled or loss if the accident causes a net long-term reduction in sales
– cost of engaging new employees (if this is significant)
– cost of excess spoilage of work by new employees (if above normal)
– attendance at court hearings in contested cases.
Costs such as these are present in nearly every accident.

Figure 5.2 The estimated cost of a workplace accident
Source: Robens (1972, p. 189). The original figures have been adjusted for inflation. Used with permission

material damage or loss. The list of cost headings shown in Figure 5.2 demonstrates that designing and maintaining a safe work environment can improve productivity by reducing time lost because of work-related accidents as well as by avoiding the costs present in every work-related accident and illness.

There are also indirect costs associated with work-related accidents. In the example cited in Figure 5.2, the costs arising from an accident involving a fork-lift truck being driven too quickly round a factory gangway corner are calculated. The indirect costs can include: overtime payments necessary to make up for lost production; the cost of retaining a replacement employee; a wage cost for the time spent by managers and HRM personnel in recruiting, selecting and training the new employee; and, in less typical cases, the cost associated with loss of revenue on orders cancelled or lost if an accident causes a net long-term reduction on sales; and attendance at court hearings in contested cases.

The economic costs of work-related accidents, and the techniques for assessing them, require further research. A Canadian study suggests, however, that indirect costs of work-related accidents could range from 2 to 10 times the direct costs (Stone & Meltz, 1988). Studies conducted by the HSE (quoted in *Personnel Management Plus*, February 1993) indicate that the cost of industrial accidents can be as high as 37 per cent of the associated profits and 5 per cent of operating costs.

A healthy and safe work environment can reduce operating costs and improve organizational effectiveness. It has been long argued that managers must apply the same effort and creativity to designing and maintaining a healthy and safe workplace as they customarily apply to other facets of the business. As Robens (1972, p. 140) stated: 'accident prevention can be integrated into the overall economic activity of the firm'.

Legal considerations

With respect to workplace health and safety, the legal rights of employees can be categorized into two broad categories: individual and collective. The first source of individual rights evolves from common law. Every employer has a vicarious common law duty to provide a safe working environment for her or his employees. The primary source of individual rights arises from statute law; in Britain, an example is the HASAWA 1974. Within the European Union (EU), individual rights stemming from Directives under Article 189 of the Treaty of Rome are a second important source of legislated protection standards promoting safe working environments.

The main source of collective health and safety rights arises from the negotiated collective agreements between union and management. In current labour law, Canadian, American and New Zealand workers have legal rights to refuse to perform unsafe or unhealthy work (Pye et al., 2001). In 1974, a Royal Commission on the Health and Safety of Workers first articulated the three principal rights of Canadian workers: the right to refuse dangerous work without penalty, the right to participate in identifying and correcting health and safety problems, and the right to know about hazards in the workplace. These three fundamental rights continue to be enshrined in current Canadian legislation (Montgomery & Kelloway, 2002). In the European Union and the USA, failure to provide a safe working environment may result in the employer being prosecuted for corporate manslaughter. Health and safety legislation is discussed more fully in the next section.

HRM WEB LINKS

Visit the websites of the any of the following occupational health and safety organizations for detailed information on health and safety legislation: Britain (www.open. gov.uk/hse), Canada (www.hrdc.gc.ca), (www.canoshweb.org.en) and (www.ccohs. ca), Finland (www.occuphealth.fi), Australia (www.nohsc.gov.au), Hong Kong (www. hkosha.org.hk) and Europe (www.osha.eu.int).

Psychological considerations

Apart from economic and legal considerations, a healthy and safe work environment helps to facilitate employee commitment and improve industrial relations. In Beer et al.'s (1984) HRM model, it is recognized that, going beyond the legal requirement of 'due diligence', a healthy organization can have a strong positive affect on the 'psychological contract' by strengthening employee commitment, motivation and loyalty: 'there is some evidence to indicate that work system design may have effects on physical health, mental health, and longevity of life itself' (1984, p. 153). Similarly, at a 'collective level', it is argued that union–management relations are improved when employers satisfy their employees' health and safety needs. When employers take a greater responsibility for occupational health and safety it can change employee behaviour, and employees may take a less militant stance during wage bargaining if management pays attention to housekeeping.

Moral considerations

Do employers have a moral responsibility to provide employees and their dependants with a safe and healthy working environment? In this regard, Gewirth (1991) argues that those individuals who contribute to the causation of work-related diseases (for example asbestosis and lung cancer) and who do so knowingly can be held to be both causally and morally responsible for their action.

A major challenge to managers is clearly to provide a safe and healthy work environment for their employees. Economic and moral reasons dictate such a policy, but, as we have already stated, there is also a pervasive portfolio of legislation, regulations, codes of practice and guidance notes dealing with occupational health and safety, and, as with other employment law, the HR practitioner has taken on the role of advising managers on the content and legal obligations of this.

STUDY TIP

A growing number of 'normal' business activities are coming under scrutiny in Europe (and elsewhere) because of their doubtful ethical practices. As society's values are changing, certain practices are now being deemed controversial or unacceptable as far as meeting health and safety standards is concerned. Let us mention some of these. In Britain, in the cases of the ferry *Herald of Free Enterprise*, which sank with her bow doors open in 1987, and Great Western Trains, involving a major rail crash at Southall in 1997, the courts established that a charge of 'corporate manslaughter' could be brought against named individuals in the companies. In Canada, in the case of the Westray coalmine explosion, which killed 26 miners in 1992, an official inquiry established that politicians and senior managers had reopened the mine despite warnings that it was dangerous, with a long record of explosions and deaths.

Consider these three cases. How does a corporation, or its executives, balance the conflicting responsibilities of maximizing profit and providing a safe and healthy workplace? Think about all the pressures to meet shareholder expectations and the pressure to create jobs in an area of high unemployment. What would you have done in these cases? Do you think that health and safety concerns are overstated? What do you think of the merits of the argument that when a company's conduct is 'far below' what could reasonably be expected, named individuals can be charged with 'corporate manslaughter'? Go to www.ft.com (searching the global archives), www.pcaw.demon.co.uk and www.findlaw.com for more information.

● Health and safety legislation

The history of occupational safety legislation can be traced back to the Industrial Revolution in the 18th century. The conditions of employment in the new factories were appalling, as indicated by this 1833 testimony:

> I can bear witness that the factory system in Bradford has engendered a multitude of cripples, and that the effect of long continued labour upon the physique is apparent not only in actual deformity, but also, and much more generally, in stunted growth, relaxation of the muscles, and delicacy of the whole frame.[7]

The early conditions of employment have, however, to be related to their context before they can be evaluated historically. It must be remembered that employment standards were low before the process of industrialization began: comparisons of conditions of employment and health and safety provisions must begin from here rather than from late 20th-century standards. Many employment practices in the early factories were inherited from the preindustrial era, an example being child labour. In the new factories, children worked for their parents, collecting wastes and tying threads, as they had done at home. These children were necessarily involved in the same hours of work as the adults for whom they worked. Family labour was a bridge between the conditions of employment in the pre-factory world and the new factory system, and the early Factory Acts did not automatically abolish family labour.

HRM IN PRACTICE 5.1

BEATEN UP – JUST FOR DOING YOUR JOB

COLIN COTTELL, *GUARDIAN*, 2001, JULY 28

A commonly held view is that the public sector offers a quiet life, safe and secure, well away from the cut and thrust of business. Everyday reality can be rather different. 'Someone was banging on the window and giving a member of my staff racial abuse', says Jason Humphreys, a station supervisor on the East London line of London Underground. 'I told him, "Don't talk to my staff like that". He turned round, punched me in the stomach, and kicked me in the leg. Though it only lasted 20 seconds it seemed like it went on forever.' Mr Humphreys says that the attack, the fifth made on him in his 16 years on the

Underground, led him to reconsider his career. 'I did think of leaving. I had had enough. I thought, I can't do it any more. It was only the support of colleagues at work that convinced me to stay.'

David Cassells, a former nurse, has first-hand experience of the problem. 'There has always been a problem in the National Health Service, but in recent times it has become more serious. Now it's everywhere, not just one hospital, not just A&E, every ward, every department, even short stay wards', he says. ... Former social worker Christine Eales knows about abuse. She's had more than her fair share. 'During my seven years in the job, I was held hostage twice, shot at twice, and nearly stabbed' she says. 'I finally said "No, I have had enough" after a 14-year-old boy with a ball bearing gun shot at nine members of staff. You expect to be attacked in a client's house, or in the car park, but not sitting at your desk.'

'Nurses are by far the most vulnerable to attacks from members of the public ... '

Evidence of the threat to those delivering frontline public services is not just anecdotal. The TUC report *Violent Times*, found that: 'Nurses are by far the most vulnerable to attacks from members of the public; more than one in three had been physically attacked at work in the previous year. Other high risk jobs include care workers (21%), and those working in education and welfare (14%).'

'It puts people off coming into the profession. With unemployment so low, why be a nurse, with all that responsibility, a low salary, no back up and left so vulnerable, and to get abuse on top of all that? Not a good career move.' It's not just a question of more money, Cassells says. 'It's about bringing back control; having enough staff so they feel secure.'

Pioneering legislation

Up until the 1820s, the main pressure for imposing a minimum age and for limiting the hours of factory work came from humanitarians and some enlightened employers, such as the 'philanthropic Mr Owen of New Lanark' (Mathias, 1969). The *1802 Health and Morals of Apprentices Act* was designed to curb some of the abuses of child labour. This Act applied only to pauper apprentices in the factories; it restricted hours of work to 12, prohibited night work and provided for instruction in the 'three Rs'. Inspection was to be by a magistrate appointed by the local Justices of the Peace. Enforcement of the Act was ineffective, however, because the inspectors were 'generally well disposed to the mill-owner' (Gregg, 1973, p. 55).

The *1833 Factory Act* outlawed the employment of children under 9 years old, limited the hours of work of children aged between 9 and 13 to 8 per day and appointed four government factory inspectors to enforce the legal requirements. An Act of 1844 then imposed limited requirements for guarding dangerous machinery. The early safety legislation was confined to textile factories and affected only the conditions of employment of women and children. During the period 1850–1900, the Factory Acts were strengthened and extended to non-textile factories; this arose from a combination of factors, including social reformers, the inspectorate and, more significantly, campaigning by a growing and more militant trade union movement (Eva & Oswald, 1981).

The introduction of safety regulations was painfully slow, progress being hindered by consistent opposition from the majority of employers, who claimed that the Factory Acts would make British industry uncompetitive. In 1856, for example, employers succeeded in lowering the standards for guarding machinery where women and children worked. The *1867 Factory Act* extended safety laws beyond the textile mills and even began to abandon the myth that safety law's only purpose was to protect women and children: adult male employees had been considered, theoretically at least, capable of protecting themselves (Hobsbawm, 1968).

The *1901 Factories and Workshops Consolidation Act* introduced a more comprehensive health and safety code for industrial workplaces. This Act drew together five other statutes passed since 1878 and was followed in its turn by a large number of detailed regulations. It remained the governing Act until the Factories Act of 1937. The subsequent Acts of 1948 and 1959 added some new provisions but produced no fundamental changes in the scope and pattern of the legislation, leaving it to the Factories Act of 1961 to consolidate industrial safety law.

The Factories Act 1961

This Act defined a 'factory' as any premise in which two or more persons were employed in manual labour in any process for the purpose of economic gain. One aspect of the definition – that a place cannot be a factory unless it is one in which manual labour is performed – caused some litigation. The first Part of the Act is concerned with general provisions affecting the health of the factory employee. Thus, the Act establishes minimum standards in factories for cleanliness, space for employees to work in, temperature, ventilation and lighting. The Act laid down very specific standards: if, for example, there was less than 400 cubic feet for every employee in the workroom, a factory was deemed to be overcrowded. The basic rule for temperature was that after the first 30 minutes, the temperature should not be less than 60°F (15.5°C) in rooms where much of the work was done sitting and did not involve serious physical effort.

Part II of the Act laid down general requirements aimed at promoting the safety of factory employees. The Act, for example, governed the fencing of machinery in factories, Section 14(1) providing that 'Every dangerous part of any machinery ... shall be securely fenced.' There were further requirements relating to lifting equipment, floors and gangways, access to the workplace, ventilation and inflammable gas. The Act also contained general welfare provisions, such as the adequate supply and maintenance of washroom facilities, and a statutory reporting system for accidents and industrial diseases.

The Offices, Shops and Railway Premises Act 1963

The rise in employment in the service sector and the growth of white-collar trade unionism help to explain the extension of legal protection to office and retail employees. The Offices, Shops and Railway Premises Act allowed these premises protection similar to that provided for factories. The general provisions followed that of the Factories Act 1961, dealing with cleanliness, ventilation, lighting, temperatures and so on.

The Fire Precautions Act 1971

This Act listed designated premises for which a fire certificate was required, the list including premises being used as a place of work. Before issuing a fire certificate, a fire authority could impose requirements on the certificate holders, for example, relating to identifiable means of escape from the building in the event of a fire, fire-fighting training and limits on the number of people using the building.

The Robens report and the Health and Safety at Work etc. Act 1974

The Factories Act 1961, the Offices, Shops and Railway Premises Act 1963 and the Fire Precautions Act 1971 were the principal provisions on health and safety in place when occupational health and safety came under detailed scrutiny in the early 1970s from a government-appointed committee chaired by Lord Robens. In the 1960s, white-collar trade unions had pressed for health and safety legislation to be extended to employees in laboratories, education, hospitals and local government, who were not covered by any of the earlier statutes. In 1968, the Labour government thus set up the Robens Committee on Safety and Health at Work to review the whole field and make recommendations in the form of the Robens report. This wide-ranging document criticized attitudes and the existing state of health and safety law. Its findings can be summarized this:

● Despite a wide range of legal regulation, work was continuing to kill, maim and sicken tens of thousands of employees each year. The Committee considered that the most important reason for this unacceptable state of affairs was *apathy*.

● There was *too much law*. The Committee identified 11 major statutes, supported by nearly 500 supplementary statutory instruments. The Committee believed that the sheer volume of law had become counterproductive.

● Much of the law was *obscure, haphazard* and *out of date*, many laws regulating obsolete production processes. Furthermore, the law focused on physical safeguards rather than preventive measures such as training and joint consultation.

● The provision for *enforcement* of the existing legislation was fragmented and ineffective. The Committee felt that the pattern of control was one of 'bewildering complexity'.

● Existing health and safety law *ignored* a large number of employees: statutes prior to 1974 excluded over 8 million workers in communication, education, hospitals and local government.

The Committee made four main proposals to improve occupational health and safety:

1. That the law should be rationalized. A unified framework of legislation should be based upon the employment relationship (rather than on a factory or mine), and all employers involved with work or affected by work activities (except for domestic servants in private homes) would be covered by the new legislation.

2. That a self-regulating system involving employers, employees and union representatives should be created to encourage organizational decision-makers to design and maintain safe work systems and help employees to take more responsibility for health and safety. The basic concept was to be the employer's duty towards her or his employees – employers being bound to design and maintain safe and healthy systems of work – and the concomitant duty of the employees was to behave in a manner safeguarding their own health and that of their co-workers.

3. That a new unified statutory framework setting out general principles should be enacted.

4. That a new unified enforcement agency headed by a national body with overall responsibility should be established and should provide new, stronger powers of sanction.

In 1972, the Robens Committee published its report, and the Conservative Government introduced a new Bill in Parliament. Two years later, the Conservatives lost the general election, but in 1974 the reigning Labour Government reintroduced a similar Bill, which became the Health and Safety at Work etc. Act 1974 (HASWA), examined in more detail in the next section.

The Health and Safety at Work etc. Act 1974

This Act vested trade unions with significant powers related to workplace health and safety matters. As Nichols (1990, p. 366) points out, compared with the 1980s and 90s, the HASAWA was 'a product of a different politics and philosophy'. The complete coverage of this complex Act is outside the scope of this chapter, but we will highlight its salient features so that readers can become familiar with some important principles and terminology. The main duties on employers are contained within Section 2 of the Act (Figure 5.3).

General duties

2. (1) It shall be the duty of every employer to ensure, so far as is reasonably practicable, the health, safety and welfare at work of all his employees.

   (2) Without prejudice to the generality of an employer's duty under the preceding subsection, the matters to which that duty extends include in particular:

   (a) the provision and maintenance of plant and systems of work that are, so far as is reasonably practicable, safe and without risks to health;

   (b) arrangements for ensuring, so far as is reasonably practicable, safety and absence of risks to health in connection with the use, handling, storage and transport of articles and substances;

   (c) the provision of such information, instruction, training and supervision as is necessary to ensure, so far as is reasonably practicable, the health and safety at work of his employees;

   (d) so far as is reasonably practicable as regards any place of work under the employer's control, the maintenance of it in a condition that is safe and without risks to health and the provision and maintenance of means of access to and egress from it that are safe and without such risks;

   (e) the provision and maintenance of a working environment for his employees that is, so far as is reasonably practicable, safe, without risks to health, and adequate as regards facilities and arrangements for their welfare at work.

Figure 5.3 The Health and Safety at Work etc. Act 1974, Section 2: Duties on Employers

HRM WEB LINKS

Go to www.hmso.gov.uk/acts.htm for the full text of UK Acts of Parliament. For sites in other countries consult p. xxii of this book.

European Union health and safety legislation

In addition to health and safety legislation from their national governments, employers within EU Member countries have EU Directives to follow, which adds to the complexity of the situation. EU law affects the health and safety legislation of the UK since it overrides domestic law. The Social Charter (see Appendix A) gives added weight to occupational health and safety, stating that workers have the 'right to health protection and safety at the workplace'. EU Directives under Article 189 of the Treaty of Rome are also an important source of health and safety legislation. They cover a wide range of health and safety issues, such as the use of asbestos, the control of major industrial accident hazards, risk assessment, equipment regulations and the prevention of repetitive strain injuries. Directives are binding, although Member States can decide upon the means of giving them legal and administrative effect. In the UK, this is usually in the form of regulations, which are normally published with associated approved codes of practice and guidance notes. Teague and Grahl (1992, p. 136) optimistically argue that the new EU health and safety legislation will 'not be of the "lowest common denominator" type but "maximalist" in nature'.

HRM WEB LINKS

Visit the websites of any of the following occupational health and safety organizations: Australia (www.safetyline.wa.gov.au), Britain (www.open.gov.uk/hse), Finland (www.occuphealth.fi) and for other countries consult p. xxi of this book – for more information on how health and safety regulations impact on the design of work and the management of the employment relationship.

The UK's 'New Labour' Government has recently expressed a commitment to improving occupational health and safety. The *Revitalising Health and Safety* statement, launched by the Deputy Prime Minister and Chair of the HSC in June 2000, set national targets for improving health and safety performance:

● to reduce the number of working days lost from work-related injury by 30%
● to reduce work-related ill-health by 20%
● to reduce fatalities by 10% by 2010 (Health and Safety Statistics 2000/01).

Research on health and safety legislation in France and Germany demonstrates, however, the importance of joint safety committees for improving health and safety performance in the workplace (Reilly et al., 1995).

The implications of health and safety legislation for managers, HR professionals and health and safety specialists are formidable. The HSC has stated that 'Accidents and ill-health are never inevitable; they often arise from failures in control and organization. A central requirement in the regulations is for a risk assessment in order to help the employer decide what health and safety measures are needed.' If the ensuing debate on the Social Charter results in the EU adopting the 'maximalist' model, joint consultative health and safety committees will play a key role determining strategic approaches to workplace health and safety. As Legge (1995) points out, however, the track record of the EU in the area of health and safety has been 'modest', and, particularly during economic recession, employers, unions and governments tend to 'water down' Directives and fail to comply with health and safety regulations. Similarly, Bain (1997) provides a pessimistic analysis of trends in workplace health and safety. He

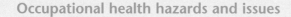

persuasively argues that, in Europe and the USA, powerful business lobbies and governments have mounted an offensive against health and safety legislation. The source of the current campaign for the 'deregulation' of health and safety safeguards is market driven and can be located in growing competitive pressures (Bain, 1997).

The perceptive reader will have noticed similarities between the argument opposing factory legislation in the 19th century and the 21st-century debate on the 1997 Kyoto Protocol, a pact for reducing greenhouse gas emissions linked to warming of the planet. Many Canadian and US corporations are opposed to the Kyoto Protocol because meeting the Kyoto targets would, they argue, make North American industry uncompetitive.

REFLECTIVE QUESTION

Henry Ford once said, 'History is bunk.' Consider the current debate on the 1997 Kyoto Protocol. Can the stakeholders – employers, employees, governments, communities – of today learn anything from the history of factory safety legislation in the 19th century? What are your views? What role, if any, should employers and governments play in meeting the Kyoto targets?

Occupational health hazards and issues

This section examines several health problems of special concern to today's HRM practitioners: sick building syndrome, workplace stress, alcohol abuse, smoking and acquired immune deficiency syndrome (AIDS).

Sick building syndrome

Interest in the physical aspects of the work building, as a factor affecting employee performance, goes back to at least the 1930s with the Hawthorne experiments in the USA (Chapter 4). In the 1980s, the construction of 'tight' office buildings with no openable windows in Europe and North America and building-related ill-health problems focused attention on the working conditions of office workers. In 1982, sick building syndrome (SBS) was recognized by the WHO as occurring where a cluster of work-related symptoms of unknown cause are significantly more prevalent among the occupants of certain buildings in comparison to others. Typical symptoms of SBS listed by WHO include: eye/nose/throat irritation; a sensation of dry mucous membranes and skin; a skin rash; mental fatigue; headaches; a high frequency of airway infection and cough; nausea; dizziness; hoarseness; and wheezing (Bain & Baldry, 1995). In 1992, the HSC calculated that the staff of 30–50 per cent of newly 'remodelled' buildings in Britain suffered a high incidence of illness. In Canada, it has been estimated that there are 1800 'sick' buildings affecting 250,000 workers. Based on such data, Bain and Baldry (1995, p. 21) argue that the problem of SBS has been 'severely underestimated'.

The causes of SBS have concentrated on possible structural or technical factors such as inadequate ventilation. The UK HSE suggests that SBS may be caused by a lack of fresh air supply, inadequate ventilation, unsuitable lighting, airborne pollutants and, at a more general level, low morale. Bain and Baldry propose, in the context of global price competition, recession and high energy costs, that SBS is related also to an emphasis on cost reduction and the intensification of office work. They conclude that 'Changes in the balance of power in the office environment have undoubtedly made it easier for management to gain employee acceptance of much more demanding practices and patterns of work' (1995, p. 30).

HRM IN PRACTICE 5.2

CAPITAL'S GLASS GLOBE FAILS GREEN TEST

DAVID HENCKE, *GUARDIAN*, 2001, JULY 30

London's new city hall – the glass globe designed by world-renowned architect Norman Foster – has been criticized in an official commissioned confidential report for falling 'well short' of 'an exemplar building' for the capital. The report warns that the building ... could leave the London authority's new employees open to absenteeism through sick building syndrome, glare and having to work in high humidity in summer and sudden chills in winter.

The report says the building fails to meet best energy use standards by setting carbon emissions of 70 kg per square metre per year. ... It claims the building 'has a standard that is 16% poorer than if a standard

> ' ... the building fails to meet best energy use standards ... '

naturally ventilated building had been chosen'. The report is critical of the use of air conditioning – even though it will use ecologically sound recycled water from boreholes – saying that naturally ventilated build-

ings have fewer instances of absenteeism by staff. 'Employees can lose more than a week per person per year through this problem' – known as sick building syndrome. Other criticisms cover the ... dangers of condensation and high humidity in the summer.

The official GLA [Greater London Assembly] website says the 50-metre-high building 'incorporates features designed to make the building as green as possible'. Victor Anderson, a Green party member of the GLA, said: 'The public website is propaganda.'

The growing incidence of SBS is a major challenge for the HR professional. SBS increases labour costs via 'absenteeism', which may in turn undermine the 'empowerment' approach associated with the 'soft' HRM model as managers resort to disciplinary measures to reduce time taken off work.

HRM WEB LINKS

Visit the website www.iea.cc/ergonomics for information on ergonomics, the study of relationships between the physical attributes of workers and their work environment.

Workplace stress

The term 'stress' in now part of the regular vocabulary of managers and employees. Although a certain degree of stress is normal in life, if stress is repeated or prolonged, individuals experience physical and psychological discomfort. The changing nature of work (Chapter 4), work experience and changes in society itself can lead to perceived stress in the workplace and are associated with ill-health (Smith, 2001). Stress at work can also impact negatively on job performance. Figure 5.4 illustrates some common symptoms of stress.

Tension and anxiety	Sleep problems
Anger and aggression	Digestive problems
High blood pressure	Chronic worry
Inability to relax	Irritability and boredom
Excessive alcohol and/or tobacco use	Uncooperative attitudes
Forgetfulness	Increased accidents
Increased absenteeism	Reduced job satisfaction

Figure 5.4 Typical symptoms of workplace stress

HRM WEB LINKS

Go to the websites www.stress.org.uk, www.hse.gov.uk, www.bham.ac.uk/IOH/, www.stress.org.uk/tuc.htm and www.hrreporter.com for more information on workplace stress.

Much research into job stress has tended to focus on 'executive burnout' and on individuals in the higher echelons of the organizational hierarchy, but stress can affect employees at lower levels too. One US study found that the two most stressful jobs were a manual labourer and a secretary. In another US study, researchers reported that the incidence of first heart attack was 2.5 times greater among skilled manual employees than among senior management grades, the rate in fact increasing the lower the occupational grade.[8] In a further report, a US health organization discovered that women in clerical occupations suffered twice the incidence rate of heart disease of all other female employees.[9] In addition to the physical and psychological disabilities it causes, occupational stress costs individuals and business considerable sums of money. The Conference Board of Canada has, for example, estimated that workplace stress costs the Canadian economy $12 billion annually (Montgomery & Kelloway, 2002).

HRM IN PRACTICE 5.3

WORKPLACE STRESS MORE PREVALENT THAN ILLNESS, INJURY

National survey finds Canadians more likely to suffer emotional, mental woes from jobs

JANE COUTTS, *GLOBE AND MAIL*, 1998, 8 APRIL

Toronto Workers are almost three times more likely to complain of health problems arising from workplace stress than from work-related illness or injuries, a Canadian survey shows.

The survey, conducted by Canada Health Monitor, found that 25 per cent of workers reported stress, mental or emotional health problems arising from work, compared with 9 per cent reporting workplace injury and another 9 per cent who said they suffered from work-related physical illness (such as headaches from bad air or noise).

'People aren't acknowledging workplace ill health as a major health issue, when it's a really big drag on healthcare budgets and productivity,' said Earl Berger, managing director of the Health Monitor, which is a national, semi-annual survey on health issues.

The tendency has been to focus on more tangible health problems than stress, an emphasis that is costing employers and employees a lot in the long run, Dr Berger said.

'People are staying away from work and they are staying away for long periods of time and somebody is paying for it,' Dr Berger said. While employees suffer from the stress they are feeling, employers lose productivity, insurance companies pay in disability claims and drug expenses, and the health system pays for care.

The research released to The *Globe and Mail*, based on random national telephone interviews of 1515 people done in 1996, was prepared for the Homewood Centre for Organizational Health, a new organization based in Guelph, Ontario, studying non-medical pressures on health.

'It's not necessarily change people have difficulty with, it's the uncertainty and loss associated with change.'

The research shows that while 20 per cent of white-collar workers report health problems because of workplace stress, compared with 25 per cent of blue-collar workers, it is blue-collar workers who are more likely to report being absent from work because of stress and who, when they are sick, stay off longer.

More than one-third of blue-collar workers said they stayed off work because of stress: 59 per cent of those who missed work were absent 13 days or more. In comparison, 24 per cent of white-collar workers with stress-related health problems stayed home from work: 35 per cent of them were absent more than 13 days.

Rick Lash, a consultant at the Hay Group in Toronto, which specializes in human resources issues, said in an interview that there are multiple messages for employers in the Health Monitor study.

'They have to deal with the culture they've created that's causing such a level of stress and anxiety for people on the job, right back to reassessing their strategy and looking at the impact of that strategy on workers,' he said.

Companies should also look at their managers' skills and their ability to help people handle change and manage their emotions on the job, he said. Employers also need to look for ways to support workers in times of change.

'It's not necessarily change people have difficulty with, it's the uncertainty and loss associated with change,' he said.

Today's unstable work environments are demanding from workers a flexibility many have not developed, coupled with increasing job expectations, Dr Lash said.

REFLECTIVE QUESTION

Think about a time when you felt under considerable stress. What were the causes of that stress? Could any of the work-related stressors be eliminated or reduced? If not, explain why.

Causes of workplace stress

Workplace stress occurs when some element of work has a negative impact on an employee's physical and mental well-being. Work overload and unrealistic time deadlines will, for example, put an employee under pressure, and stress may result. Workplace sexual harassment is another source of stress. In addition, occupational stress cannot be separated from personal life: illness in the family or divorce puts an employee under pressure and leads to stress. Factors that cause stress are numerous, and their relationships are complex, but researchers have identified two major types of stressor: work-related factors and individual factors.

Work-related factors

A variety of work-related factors – role ambiguity, frustration, conflict, job design, violence and harassment – can lead to stress.

Role ambiguity exists when the job is poorly defined, when uncertainty surrounds job expectations and when supervisory staff and their subordinates have different expectations of an employee's responsibilities. Individuals experiencing role ambiguity will be uncertain how their performance will be evaluated and will therefore experience stress.

Frustration, a result of a motivation being blocked to prevent an individual achieving a desired goal, has a major effect. A clerical employee trying to finish a major report before the end of the day is likely to become frustrated by repeated PC breakdowns that prevent the goal being reached. Huczynski and Buchanan (1991, p. 352) draw on Swedish research to illustrate the frustration of information technology:

> Office workers who used to wait happily for hours while folders were retrieved from filing cabinets now complain when their computer terminals do not give them instant information on request ... Stress arose mainly from computer breakdowns and telephone calls which interrupted their work. The employees never know how long these interruptions would last, and had to watch helplessly while their work piled up. So they worked rapidly in the mornings in case something stopped them later.

Conflicts, both interpersonal and inter-team, are another problem. When employees with different social experiences, personalities, needs and points of view interact with co-workers, disagreements may cause stress.

Job design is a further factor. Jobs that have a limited variety of tasks and low discretion, and do not activate employees' 'upper level needs' (see Figure 4.4), may cause stress. Huczynski and Buchanan (1991) report research showing that the most stressful jobs are those which combine high workload and low discretion. Craig (1981, p. 10) also identifies job design as a stressor for office workers:

> Countless office staff work in high bureaucracies which have been described as 'honeycombs of depression'. The work you're doing can make you sick: work under pressure of time, to keep up the production quotas or deadlines, work that 'drives you crazy' because it's so boring ... Office workers frequently keep tablets in their desks to get through the days, or take frequent days off. They then go to their doctor, where the problem is treated as a personal one, in isolation.

Workplace violence is a critical safety issue facing many organizations. There are three major types of workplace violence:

- *Type 1:* the perpetrator of the violence has no legitimate relationship with the targeted employee and enters the workplace to commit a criminal act (for example robbery). Retail and service industry employees and taxi drivers are those most exposed to this type of workplace violence.
- *Type 2:* the perpetrator is an employee or former employee of the organization,

typically a 'disgruntled employee' who commits a violent act against a co-worker or supervisor for what is perceived to be unfair treatment.

- *Type 3:* the perpetrator is a recipient of a service provided by the targeted employee. Social workers, health care providers and teachers are particularly vulnerable to this type of workplace violence (see HRM in practice 5.1).

Montgomery and Kelloway (2002) identify three groups of employee at particular risk of experiencing workplace violence:

1. those who interact with the public
2. those making decisions that influence other people's lives
3. those denying the public a request or a service.

The consequences of workplace violence go beyond immediate physical injury or death; research studies (see, for example, Montgomery & Kelloway, 2002) suggest that the trauma caused by the violence has negative results both for the individual employee (that is, impaired mental and physical health) and for the organization (that is, decreased commitment, retention and performance).

Harassment (racial and sexual) is another workplace stressor of increasing importance. Racial harassment can range from racist jokes or verbal abuse to racist graffiti in the workplace or physical attacks on black employees. No matter how subtle it is, racial harassment is extremely stressful; it can damage ethnic minority group employees' health and presents managers with a major challenge.

Sexual harassment can take two forms. The first is a hostile environment that involves behaviour that is unwelcome and undesirable or offensive. This kind of sexual harassment includes, for example, unwanted propositions and sexual innuendo. It can be difficult for an HR manager to convince employees and other managers to take this kind of sexual harassment seriously as it is often viewed as a 'joke', something to do with 'chatting up' attractive female co-workers or bottom-pinching. Evidence of behaviour that is sufficiently severe or pervasive as to cause changes in the conditions of employment can, however, lead to a legal case. The second form of sexual harassment is *quid pro quo* harassment, which is essentially a kind of sex-for-promotion blackmail. The alleged perpetrator is normally a superior, and the blackmail is either 'give in to my sexual desires and I'll give you promotion' or 'give in or your job prospects will suffer'. Both forms of sexual harassment relate to power relationships, harassment aimed at women by men who occupy positions of power. It is, as one writer put it, 'a new, formal title for an age-old predicament, the boss-man with anything from a lascivious line of chat, to wandering hands, to explicit demands for sex as a reward for giving you, the women, work'.[10]

Individual-related factors

Individual factors causing stress are equally varied and complex; they include financial worries, marital problems, pregnancy, problems with children and the death of spouse. A record number of mortgages, for example, were foreclosed in Britain in the early 1990s, doubtless causing considerable individual stress. A major personal factor that can cause stress among working women is the 'dual-role' syndrome – the additional burden of coping with two jobs: the paid job and the unwaged 'job' at home (cooking, housework, shopping, and so on) (Figure 5.5). As Craig (1981, p. 18) puts it:

Figure 5.5 Stress caused by the 'dual-role' syndrome
Source: Personnel Management Plus (1992, April)

> The pressures on working mothers are enormous. Feeling guilty because you're not an ideal stay-at-home mum ... get the breakfasts, get the shopping done, go to the launderette, fetch the kids from school, do the ironing, clean the house. A carefully worked out timetable can be upset and life thrown into chaos when your lunch hour is switched or you're required to do overtime without notice.

Research appears to support the 'dual-role' syndrome as an explanation of work-related stress. A Canadian study among bank employees reported that 22 per cent of the respondents said their stress was triggered by balancing family and work.[11]

Huczynski and Buchanan (2001) draw attention to research demonstrating a relationship between personality and stress. Individual factors include difficulty in coping with change, a lack of confidence and assertiveness in relationships and poor stress management. 'Type A' personalities – those individuals who are highly competitive, set high standards, place considerable emphasis on meeting deadlines and are 'workaholics' – tend to have a higher propensity to exhibit symptoms of stress (McShane, 2001).

In summary, Figure 5.6 illustrates examples of work-related and individual causes of stress.

Until recently, job stress was considered to be a personal problem, but it is now recognized that stress is a major health problem at work and that it is a responsibility of general management to provide the initiative to eliminate or reduce the causes of stress. At an organizational level, attention to basic job design principles can alleviate the conditions that may cause stress. At the individual level, HR professionals have conducted workshops on stress management to help individual employees to cope

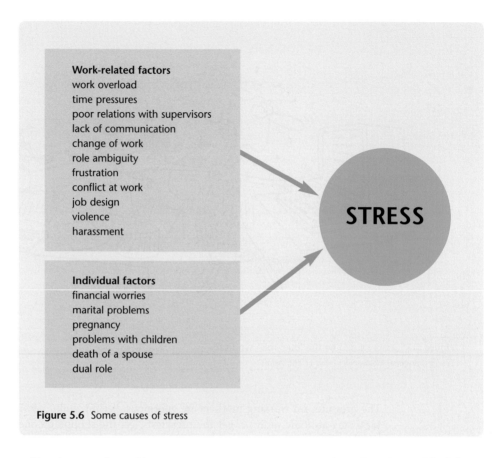

Figure 5.6 Some causes of stress

with stress and avoid an overexposure to stress-causing situations. Workshops designed to change 'lifestyles' by promoting healthy eating and fitness, while helping employees to relieve the strains caused by job stress, cannot eliminate the source of the problem. Like other occupational hazards, stress needs to be controlled at source; as discussed above, stress arises from a variety of sources, and it is important for HR managers to identify priorities and investigate ways of dealing with the problem. Management should look at the job design (Chapter 4) and organizational structure, and conduct detailed surveys to identify priorities for action. Table 5.1 shows some of the specific actions individuals and HR practitioners can take to alleviate occupational stress.

Table 5.1 Action to reduce workplace stress

Individual strategies	Organizational strategies
Physical exercise	Meeting with employees to discuss the extent of stress
Hobbies	Conduct a survey and inspect the workplace for stress-causing factors
Meditation	Improve job and organizational design
Group discussions	Improve communication
Assertiveness training	Develop a stress policy and monitor its effectiveness
	Train managers to be sensitive to the causes and early symptoms of stress

Alcohol and drug abuse

> A recent estimate indicates that in England and Wales there are approximately 3 million excessive drinkers and 850,000 problem and dependent drinkers. About one in 25 of the population in England and Wales, and possibly as high as one in ten in Scotland, may be personally affected by severe alcohol-related problems.[12]

The excessive consumption of alcohol is both a health problem and a job performance problem in every occupational category, be it manual, white-collar or managerial. In alcohol abuse, behavioural problems range from tardiness in the early stages to prolonged absenteeism in the later ones. A US study estimated that problem drinkers are absent from work for, on average, 22 days per year and are at least twice as likely as non-alcohol drinkers to have an accident.[13] The direct and indirect costs of alcohol abuse to employers include the costs of accidents, lower productivity, poor-quality work, bad decisions, absenteeism and managers' lost time in dealing with employees with an alcohol problem.

Employers have been advised to have a written statement of policy regarding alcohol abuse, which can be discussed and agreed with employees and, where applicable, union representatives. The policy should recognize that alcohol abuse is an illness, and it should be supportive, rather than punitive, or employees will hide their drink problem for as long as possible. The HSE, in the paper 'The problem drinker at work', advocates that a policy should encourage any employee who believes that she or he has a drink problem to seek help voluntarily, and should, subject to certain provisions, give the same protection of employment and pension rights as those granted to an employee with problems that are related to other forms of ill-health. Research in Scotland estimated that 20 per cent of employers had a policy to deal with the problem drinker. In addition to preparing a policy, management can devise a procedure for dealing with alcohol abuse; to encourage employees to seek advice, it is suggested that this procedure should be separate from the disciplinary procedure. Finally, the HRM department is advised to establish links with an external voluntary organization to obtain help and develop an employee assistance programme.

Smoking

It has been estimated that of the 600,000 deaths in the UK each year, 100,000 are caused by tobacco,[14] and 90 per cent of all those who die from lung cancer and chronic bronchitis are smokers. In addition, 40 per cent of heavy smokers (those smoking over 20 cigarettes a day) die before retirement age, compared with only 15 per cent of non-smokers.[15] The estimated cost associated with smoking in the workplace (that is, attributable to absenteeism, lost productivity and so on) is said to be approximately US $825 per employee per year (Montgomery & Kelloway, 2002). Figure 5.7 shows employers' costs associated with workplace smoking (money that 'goes up in smoke'). Recent research has highlighted the health risk of 'second-hand' or 'passive' smoking (inhaling other people's smoke). In 1997, the first second-hand smoke case against the USA tobacco industry, filed on behalf of thousands of US-based flight attendants in 1991,[16] resulted in a settlement of US $300 million.

In the past, employers have restricted employees' smoking in order to reduce fire risks or comply with hygiene standards. To reduce the risks and costs associated with smoking, to appease non-smokers and to deter possible legal action from employees

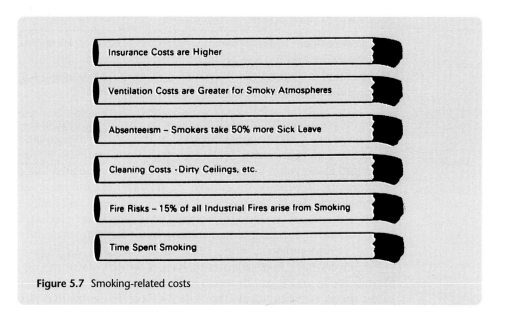

Figure 5.7 Smoking-related costs

suffering from polluted air caused by smoking, many organizations now have established policies on smoking at the workplace. The UK Civil Service, for example, restricted smoking in Inland Revenue offices. Management and union representatives at British Telecom agreed to ballot employees on their views on a smoking ban, the result being a 3 to 1 majority in favour of a smoking ban in common work stations. The company then set up a union/management working party to examine the details of implementation. Many employers believe that they would face hostility from employees if they implemented a non-smoking policy, but companies that have implemented non-smoking policies report an increased awareness of the health risks of smoking and little employee or union resistance. A government report found that '79% of smokers interviewed acknowledged the right of non-smokers to work in air that is free of tobacco smoke (and not surprisingly, 84% of non-smokers and 78% of ex-smokers also thought so)'.[17] HRM professionals agree that successful non-smoking policies require consultation with employees; in a unionized workplace, this requires a joint approach by management and union.

Acquired immune deficiency syndrome

I was not trained to manage fear, discrimination, and dying in the workplace.[18]

A textbook on human resource management for the next millennium would be incomplete if no reference were made to society's most recent menace – AIDS – caused by the human immunodeficiency virus (HIV), which attacks the body's immune system. In 2002, over 14 million people were estimated to be infected with AIDS in the three continents of Africa, Europe and the Americas. In South Africa, an estimated 4.7 million citizens were infected, equivalent to about one in four of the adult population.[19] Data from studies in Tanzania and Uganda show that between the ages of 25 and 35, four deaths in five are HIV related,[20] and in India, the WHO has estimated the number of people affected with AIDS to lie between 3 and 5 million.[21] In the USA,

AIDS was the leading cause of death among 25–44-year-olds between 1992 and 1996; to date 343,000 Americans have died of AIDS and another 900,000 are HIV-infected – about one in 250 people.[22]

In Canada, mandatory testing for AIDS is regarded as a serious intrusion on individual rights, and employers are prohibited from subjecting job applicants to any type of medical testing for the presence of the HIV virus. Furthermore, the employer is obligated to accommodate the needs of an employee with a disability such as AIDS by, for example, redefining work assignments. The fear of catching HIV can, however, create problems for human resource managers. Employees might refuse to work with a person with AIDS; as one North American human resource manager explained, 'No matter how sophisticated or educated you are, AIDS can trigger irrational things in people … There's a big potential for disruption. It could close a plant down.'[23] A North American chain store manager, one of whose employees developed AIDS and died, had to call in the Red Cross to explain to distraught employees that AIDS cannot be transmitted through normal contact in the workplace. Six months later, some employees were still refusing to use the drinking fountain or the toilet (see Chapter Case Study: Managing AIDS at Johnson Stores plc).

REFLECTIVE QUESTION

How does HIV impact on international HRM? (See also Chapter 2.)

Green (1998) reported that few US firms surveyed had a policy regarding AIDS and that larger firms were more likely to have HIV-specific policies, over 50 per cent of companies with more than 100 employees holding a specific AIDS policy. More worrying perhaps is the finding that there is, among employers, a 'declining interest' in AIDS education in the workplace. In 1997, 18 per cent of US companies surveyed provided HIV education for their employees, compared with 28 per cent in 1992 (Green, 1998). Companies that have encountered the problem of managing AIDS in the workplace have found that it is better to expect a problem and be proactive in educating employees on the issues raised by AIDS. As with any HRM policy, this requires a clear endorsement from top management down. The chairman of Levi Strauss, Robert Hass, confirms the need for senior management support: 'This [AIDS] is frequently viewed as something that the personnel department should take care of, but there has to be support from the top. You can't do it with one flyer.'[23] As attitudes and legal considerations change, AIDS has important implications for HRM policy and practices.

HRM WEB LINKS

Visit the following websites for information on AIDS and HRM: UK (www.tht.org.uk), Canada (www.cdnaids.ca), South Africa (www.aidslink.org.za), Australia (www. aidscouncil.org.au).

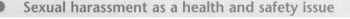

● **Sexual harassment as a health and safety issue**

Sexual harassment 'poisons the atmosphere in the workplace' (Keith, 2000, p. 287). It is a health and safety issue for two primary reasons: legal and economic. First, workplace sexual harassment is unlawful, and the courts have increasingly viewed its prevention as the responsibility of the employer. The legal concept of 'detriment' is important here. Sexual harassment is a 'detriment' per se; it can lead to an employment-related detriment to the female employee and, as such, has serious implications for management. In 1986, the European Parliament passed a resolution on violence against women, commissioning a report on the dignity of women at work, which led to the adoption of the EU code of practice (Figure 5.8).

In 1998, the allegations of sexual impropriety against US President Bill Clinton highlighted some difficult aspects raised by cases of sexual harassment in the workplace. The first issue is credibility because there is seldom a witness to support whether the conduct being complained about actually happened. There are, for example, no witnesses to the alleged conduct of Mr Clinton and the White House employee Monica Lewinsky. Credibility and circumstantial evidence are under scrutiny here. Who has more credibility? Is there indirect evidence that might support or dismiss the allegations? The Clinton case raises another issue that often applies to workplace investigations, the question of containment. In the Presidential investigation, the public prosecutor apparently had no interest in limiting the scope of the investigation, but for many HR professionals, in addition to what is legitimate and necessary in terms of conducting a sexual harassment complaint, containment is also an issue. The aim will be to contain the allegation and limit the knowledge about the complaint to those who need to know. HR professionals have to take appropriate action to prevent sexual harassment and to inform employees of the consequences of sexual harassment.[24]

Workplace sexual harassment is 'the most intimate manifestation of employment discrimination faced by women' (Curtin, 1984, quoted by Keith, 2000, p. 277), and legal protection against it is complex and sensitive. There is concern expressed by some authors about how women are treated in law (for example Debono, 2001), contending that women are disadvantaged because of a patriarchal or sexist jurisprudence. Debono (2001) found that there are sexist elements to the jurisprudence

This defines sexual harassment as 'unwanted conduct of a sexual nature' affecting 'the dignity of women and men at work'. It defines harassment as largely subjective, in that it is for the individual to decide whether the conduct is acceptable or offensive.

The code says that Member States should take action in the public sector and that employers should be encouraged to:

- issue a policy statement
- communicate it effectively to all employees
- designate someone to provide advice to employees subjected to harassment
- adopt a formal complaints procedure
- treat sexual harassment as a disciplinary offence.

Figure 5.8 The European Union code on sexual harassment

related to workplace sexual harassment decisions in the UK, USA, and New Zealand. Although the legislation is progressive, it is argued that, 'sexist attitudes still remain with those who have the power to use the legislation to compensate the victims' (Debono, 2001, p. 338).

Returning to the economic implications of workplace sexual harassment, research on consequences has identified a host of negative work outcomes, including a loss of commitment to work, decreased job satisfaction, increased absenteeism and decreased job performance (see, for example, Montgomery & Kelloway, 2002; Mueller et al., 2001), findings consistent with research on workplace violence. Less well researched are possible links between victimization and the 'psychological contract'. The stress caused by sexual harassment affects the expectations that employees and employers have of each other. It is highlighted because the victim's commitment and loyalty to the organization decreases and the intent to leave the organization increases. Thus, exposure to workplace sexual harassment is associated with impaired employee well-being and individual and organizational performance, and becomes a health and safety issue.

● Managing health and safety

Health and safety, perhaps more than any other HR activity, offers the manager an opportunity to be more proactive than reactive. It must be emphasized, however, that senior management's involvement in developing and implementing health and safety policies and programmes is essential. There are a number of strategies that can be used by organizations to ensure a healthy and safe workplace and ensure compliance with legal requirements. This section does not aim to be prescriptive, offering advice on what managers should be doing. Instead, the strategies summarized in Figure 5.9. are intended primarily to generate discussion on the implications of health and safety for management practices, and how health and safety measures can be reconciled with broader management objectives.

1.	Design	safe and healthy systems of work
2.	Exhibit	strong management commitment
3.	Inspect	the workplace for health and safety hazards
4.	Establish	procedures and controls for dealing with health and safety issues
5.	Promote	safe working behaviours
6.	Develop	training programmes
7.	Set up	health and safety committees
8.	Monitor	health and safety policies
9.	Draw up	an action plan and checklist

Figure 5.9 Strategies to improve workplace health and safety

Design safer systems of work

The most direct approach to ensuring a safe and healthy workplace is to design systems of work that are safe and without risk to health, which can often be done satisfactorily only at the design, planning and/or purchasing stage. It may be far more difficult to modify existing machinery or systems of work in order to eliminate or reduce hazards than it is to devise new ones at the investment stage. Thus, management must take cognizance of long-term organizational changes to control hazards. Simply trying to persuade employees, for example by poster campaigns, to adapt their behaviour to unsafe systems of work is unacceptable. The HSE maintains that the basic problem of accidents stems from hazards inherent in the workplace; as discussed above, 'Most accidents involve an element of failure in control – in other words *failure in managerial skill*. A guiding principle when drawing up arrangements for securing health and safety should be that so far as possible work would be adapted to people and not vice versa' (emphasis added).[6] As managers identify processes, machines and substances that are hazardous to the health and well-being of employees, they must modify the process to eliminate or reduce the hazard and risk 'at source'. In some cases, robots can perform hazardous tasks, such as paint-spraying and welding. The provision of protective equipment is the typical means used by organizations to reduce physical hazards, and this is also an employer responsibility.

Exhibit commitment

Senior management carries the prime responsibility under the HASAWA 1974 for ensuring a safe and healthy workplace. The Robens Committee believed that 'apathy' was a major cause of workplace accidents. No matter how much activity related to health and safety is initiated by HR professionals, health and safety should be an integral part of every manager's responsibility, from the chief executive officer down to the lowest-level supervisor. Anything less than total support from top management raises questions about the sincerity of the organization's commitment in the eyes of employees, government agencies and the public at large. To exhibit commitment, managers' salary and promotion might be tied to a satisfactory safety record and compliance. Larger organizations have also appointed specialists in the area, including health and safety officers, safety engineer and medical technicians. If safety officers are to be effective, they must be given adequate authority in the management hierarchy to make changes and implement changes.

Inspect the workplace

Another proactive approach to the management of health and safety is regular formal inspections of the workplace: regular monitoring of the work environment and regular physical examination of the employees. Construction sites and manufacturing plants, for example, require regular inspections to check the application of safety standards and relevant laws. In some manufacturing processes, frequent monitoring of air quality and levels of dust and noise is needed. Organizations may also monitor a wide range of matters relating to employees' health, from routine eye tests and chest X-rays to screening for breast/cervical cancer and the incidence of infertility and abnormal childbirths. A 'health' survey of employees can also help to identify hazardous and unhealthy processes.

We can identify three main types of formal inspection:

1. accident
2. special
3. general.

Accident inspections will follow an accident or dangerous incident (a 'near miss') in the workplace. *Special inspections* might concentrate on a particular work station, system of work or hazard. The safety committee might decide that it is necessary to examine the training of forklift truck operators or dust problems; this would be the first step in a plan of action. A comprehensive survey of the entire workplace is the purpose of *general inspections*. In a unionized workplace, these are frequently conducted jointly with the union safety representative. The Safety Representatives and Safety Committees (SRSC) *Guidance Notes*[25] recognize the advantage of formal general inspections being jointly conducted by the employer or manager and union safety representative:

> The safety representatives should coordinate their work to avoid unnecessary duplication. It will often be appropriate for the safety officer or specialist advisers to be available to give technical advice on health and safety matters that may arise during the course of the inspection.

Thorough preparation, including the design of a comprehensive set of checklists covering all aspects of the workplace, is essential if managers are to discover physical health hazards.

Establish procedures and controls

A health and safety policy is likely to fail unless effective procedures and controls are established. The procedures for handling health and safety problems need to meet some basic requirements:

- Allow employees' representatives to talk *directly* to the managers who can make decisions
- Operate without undue delay
- Be able to handle emergency problems
- Permit discussion about long-term decisions affecting health and safety.

Clearly, these recommendations have important implications for HR policy and action, so let us briefly examine these considerations. Problems might occur if line managers were expected by senior management to be responsible for safe working practices, but at the same time were denied the authority to make decisions and implement changes. In principle, organizational procedures should ensure that the authority of a particular level of management to make decisions matches the responsibility of each level of management for health and safety. The appointment of a safety officer may be a necessary prerequisite to establishing effective procedures and controls, but it is not sufficient. The position must be placed into the management hierarchy with clear lines of reporting and accountability, which will enable procedures for raising problems to operate, without undue delay, and avoid other managers absolving themselves from their responsibility.

It is recommended that the committee on health and safety include key departmental managers, employees and union representatives. At best, committees can be a vehicle for discussion and the strategic planning of health and safety. At worst, they can degenerate into a 'talking shop' that will draw scepticism from the rest of the workforce. Managers must perceive their rewards, or a significant proportion of them, as contingent upon the success of a health and safety programme. To evaluate that success, monthly, quarterly and annual statistics need to be reported directly to the senior management team.

Promote safe working behaviours

There are several safety-related behaviours that could improve safety performance in the workplace. The focus on behaviour is based on the observation that 70–95 per cent of workplace accidents resulting in an injury are caused by unsafe behaviours (Montgomery & Kelloway, 2002). This is not necessarily a replay of the old 'careless worker' philosophy but a recognition that managerial behaviour related to health and safety issues shapes the 'psychological contract'. An employee's perception of the 'safety climate' – the shared perceptions of the importance of health and safety in the workplace – affects employee safety behaviours. Thus, workers who perceive a positive safety climate in the organization are more likely to engage in safe working behaviours.

Develop training programmes

One way to obtain compliance with health and safety regulations is through enhancing employees' knowledge, understanding and commitment, which can be achieved through health and safety programmes. The purpose of safety training is generally the same as that of any other training programme: to improve job knowledge and skills, and to ensure optimum employee performance at the specified level. In health and safety training, specified performance standards include attention to safety rules and regulations regarding safe work behaviour. Like any other training, health and safety training should be developed systematically. First, problems or training needs will be identified by inspection, by accident reports and through discussion during health and safety committee meetings. Next, the planning, execution and evaluation of the training will take place (Chapter 10).

The HASAWA 1974 imposes a duty on employers to provide training to ensure a healthy and safe workplace. Research suggests that safety awareness training programmes only have a short-term effect on employees' behaviour, which suggests that after employees have completed their safety training at the orientation stage, management should organize regular refresher courses. Experience suggests that line managers, supervisors and safety representatives also need to be exposed to regular training. Top management support is a key ingredient in the availability and success of health and safety training, but studies indicate that the number of representatives attending TUC health and safety courses has fallen (Booth, 1985).

Set up health and safety committees

Health and safety is one area of working life in which there has been statutory support for employee representation for almost three decades. The 1998 Workplace Employee Relations Survey (WERS) found that 68 per cent of all workplaces reported the presence of at least one employee representative on health and safety matters (Millward et al., 2000). As already noted, joint health and safety committees may, under the EU

Social Charter, represent the future shape of European health and safety legislation (Reilly et al., 1995), and there is a substantial body of evidence to suggest that union health and safety representatives can make an important contribution to the improvement of health and safety at work (James & Walters, 2002). The HASAWA requires employers to establish safety committees where a safety representative requests this. If the union does not initiate such committees, organizations often have safety committees that involve employee members and are chaired by the safety or HR specialist. Making the committee effective lies mainly in the realm of management. A safety committee may develop into a 'talking shop' with ineffective decision-making; to avoid this, a senior member of the management team, with executive authority, should be a member of the committee.

HRM WEB LINKS

For more information on health and safety representation in Britain over the past two decades, go to the 1998 WERS website: www.dti.gov.uk/er/emar/1998WERS.htm.

The functions of the committees and their terms of reference depend on individual company policy, relevant safety legislation and the situation regarding employee–union relations. The SRSC *Guidance Notes* suggest the following terms of reference (Regulation 9, pp. 37–8):

(a) The study of accident and notifiable diseases statistics and trends, so that reports can be made to management on unsafe and unhealthy conditions and practices, together with recommendations for corrective action.
(b) Examination of safety audit reports on a similar basis.
(c) Consideration of reports and factual information provided by inspectors of the enforcing authority appointed under the Health and Safety at Work etc. Act.
(d) Consideration of reports which safety representatives may wish to submit.
(e) Assistance in the development of works safety rules and safe systems of work.
(f) A watch on the effectiveness of the safety content of employee training.
(g) A watch on the adequacy of safety and health communication and publicity in the workplace.
(h) The provision of a link with the appropriate inspectorates of the enforcing authority.

Employers or their representatives are primarily responsible for compliance with health and safety laws, but the existence of these committees does not diminish the employer's duty to ensure a healthy and safe workplace. The work of the safety committees should supplement management's arrangements for regular and effective monitoring for health and safety precautions – but it cannot be a substitute for management action. All forms of safety arrangement that encourage employee participation in workplace health and safety matters reduce the incidence of accidents. The studies by Reilly et al. (1995) and James and Walters (2002) show, however, strong support for union–management health and safety committees as an important variable for promoting a safer workplace. Reilly et al.'s study found that establishments with joint health and safety committees – and with all the employee representatives chosen by the union – have, 'on average, 5.7 fewer injuries per 1000 employees compared with establishments where management deals with health and safety matters without any form of worker consultation' (1995, p. 283).

Walters (1987) has undertaken a study of the implementation of the SRSC Regulations. The findings from his small sample of cases in the print industry suggest that the joint regulation of health and safety is based on the assumption of trade union organization and power in the workplace. With a hostile economic and political environment in the 1980s and much of the 1990s, this power diminished, and the SRSC Regulations have had a very limited direct effect on the joint regulation of health and safety in the workplace: 'It is only in the large workplaces that any significant application of the SRSC Regulations with regard to joint inspections, provision of information and time off for training seems to have been made' (Walters, 1987, p. 48). The authoritative study by Millward et al. (1992) indicates, however, that in spite of the hostile industrial relations climate of the 1980s, the propensity for joint health and safety committees to exist in the British workplace is still high.

Monitor policy

Safety specialists argue that the safety policy should reflect the employer's commitment to developing safe systems of work and pursuing a healthy work environment. Apart from giving details of the specialist safety services provided by the organization, the safety policy also outlines the safety responsibilities of all levels of management within the hierarchy. This part of the safety policy is particularly important for identifying which member of the management hierarchy should be involved when a health and safety problem arises in the workplace.

There is a growing awareness that many employers are, in practice, 'turning a blind eye' to new health and safety requirements. Furthermore, many safety policies are not that helpful in practice because of a failure to monitor their relevance to workplace arrangements, inadequate training, and supervisors and safety officers lacking authority to make decisions. The TUC (1986, p. 163) is critical of safety policies, arguing that 'many safety policies are just pious blueprints which look good but are either ignored or unworkable'. A proactive approach would involve managers regularly checking to ensure that safety policy, management procedures and arrangements work and are changed to suit new developments or work structures in the workplace.

Draw up action plan

Managers can be more proactive in the area of health and safety by developing an 'action plan' and checklist (Figure 5.10)

Paradox in workplace health and safety

The notion of paradox and tension that we have discussed in other areas of HRM is also apparent in occupational health and safety. The model in Figure 4.8 shows that paradox stems from the multiple consequences of a single management action, which seem to conflict with those of another. The abstraction presented in Figure 4.8 can be illuminated using a concrete health and safety case. Portable computers, cell phones and e-mail have enabled us all to be 'connected' to the Internet and the organization 7-days a week, 24-hours a day, improving, among other things, productivity. These high-tech instruments have, however, produced negative results, causing some observers to describe them as 'electronic versions of a ball and chain, keeping us in

HSE OHS checklist for employers
Preventing occupational ill health

Yes/No/Uncertain

- Do I know whether any of my operations involve a health risk?
  For example exposure to skin irritants such as solvents, poor working practices when using harmful materials, exposure to excessive noise, exposure to harmful dusts, fumes or gases, frequent heaving lifting or carrying
- Do I take account of any specific regulations or recommendations applying to these risks?
  For example specific regulations covering work with lead and asbestos
- Are all the risks that have been identified adequately controlled?
  For example through improved workplace design engineering controls or by using personal protection
- Is the effectiveness of controls being assessed and monitored?
  For example by regular environmental monitoring, possibly backed up with health checks

Placement and rehabilitation

Yes/No/Uncertain

- Do I know whether any of my operations carry specific health requirements?
  For example good eyesight or colour vision
- Do I know whether any of my operations present a hazard to people with a particular problem?
  For example dusty conditions may be unsuitable for some workers with chest problems
- Do I take these factors into consideration in a clear and fair way at recruitment and subsequently?
  For example by ensuring that the specific health requirements for a job are assessed and people are not turned down because of irrelevant health conditions
- Am I prepared to modify working arrangements where practicable to accommodate employees with health problems?
  For example by rearranging working hours, adjusting the height of work surfaces.

First aid and treatment

Yes/No/Uncertain

- Do my first aid procedures comply with the First Aid at Work Regulations?
  See HSE guidance booklet HS (R)11
- Have I considered my first aid needs for coping with illness at work, and made appropriate arrangements?
  For example emergency on call arrangements with a local doctor or nurse
- Have I considered whether any additional treatment services would be cost-effective in my operation and if so, made suitable arrangements?
  For example regular visits to the workplace by physiotherapists or dentists to avoid workers having to take time off for appointments

Health promotion

Yes/No/Uncertain

- Have I considered whether the benefits of health education, employee assistance or counselling programmes would justify their introduction, and have I introduced such programmes?
  For example programmes aimed at improving diet and reducing smoking and problem drinking. The workplace can be an ideal location in which to encourage employees towards healthier living
- Do I know whether screening tests are available that could improve the health of my staff by detecting treatable illness at an earlier stage, and if so, have I arranged for them to be carried out?
  For example arrangements with local health authorities or others for cervical smears to be carried out at the workplace

Information, instruction and training

Yes/No/Uncertain

- Do my employees understand any health risks involved in their work and how to minimise them?
- Have my employees received sufficient instruction and training in how to avoid ill health?
  For example hygiene procedures and correct use of personal protective equipment

If you answered NO or UNCERTAIN to any of these questions you need help.

Figure 5.10 Checklist for health and safety
Source: Health and Safety Executive

work mode around the clock' (Drohan, 2000, p. B15). The *intended* consequence of these high-tech instruments is improved productivity, but the unanticipated consequence of high-tech communications has yielded a major problem of stress and 'burnout' caused by the inability of individuals to maintain the boundary between work and home. This *unintended* consequence of the high-tech revolution can counteract the positive consequences.

Health and safety and organizational ecology form an important part of the HRM context, but it is not simply a technical issue, of, for example, supplying hard hats and goggles or ensuring adequate ventilation. Above all, workplace health and safety highlights the fact that the employment relationship involves an economic relationship, and health and safety focuses attention on economic costs and power relations within the organization. In terms of economics, since 'pure market' ideology panders to the shareholder and the consumer, 'profitability over safety' is favoured (Glasbeek, 1991, p. 196). With regard to power, Sass (1982, p. 52 quoted in Giles & Iain, 1989; emphasis added) has correctly emphasized that:

> In all technical questions pertaining to workplace health and safety there is the *social element*. That is, for example, the power relations in production: who tells whom to do what and how fast. After all, the machine does not go faster by itself; someone designed the machinery, organized the work, designed the job.

Most obviously, the economic cost of occupational health and safety to the organization is a double-edged sword. On the one hand, health and safety measures that protect individuals from physical or chemical hazards can conflict with management's objective of containing production costs. On the other, effective health and safety policies can improve the performance of employees and the organization by reducing the cost associated with accidents, disabilities, absenteeism and illness.

To manage the employment relationship effectively, it also needs to be recognized that the employer's perspective on health and safety issues can affect an individual's beliefs and levels of trust. Talk of a reciprocal commitment and a psychological contract has a hollow ring for many manual workers: more pressing may be malodorous processes and dangerous work systems. Critical, too, is the ability of large corporations to relocate to other parts of the world to avoid stringent health and safety laws and regulations. Creating a 'level playing field' in terms of health and safety legislation within major economic trading blocks may partly ameliorate this problem; since the passing of the Single European Act in 1987, for example, a company's health and safety policies have been influenced by EU Directives and the Social Charter.

Growing public awareness and concern about 'green' and environmental issues has had an effect on occupational health and safety. Organizations have had to become more sensitive to workers' health and general environmental concerns. Manufacturing, for example, 'environmentally friendly' products and services, and using ecologically sustainable processes, presents a continuing challenge to all managers in the early 21st century. Survey data also appear to confirm that managers in British workplaces are having to deal with health and safety issues unilaterally without consulting union health and safety representatives (Millward et al., 1992). Running parallel with these social developments is the growing demand from powerful business lobbies to 'deregulate' business operations, including dismantling health and safety legislation (Bain, 1997). Deregulation (Bain, 1997) and the growth of outsourcing (Mayhew & Quinlan, 1997) may operate to reduce protection of the organization's 'human assets'. If organizations adopt an HRM model that is 'union free', it might, given the research evidence (see, for example, James & Walters, 2002; Reilly et al., 1995), expose employees to greater workplace hazards, thereby offering a further paradox in the HRM paradigm.

In this chapter, we have placed occupational health and safety into the HRM context so that there can be a better understanding of managing the employment relationship. The discussion on paradox goes back to basics in reminding us of some of the complexities – economic, legal, social and psychological – and tensions inherent in the employment relationship. The key point is that health and safety policies and practices must, as with other aspects of the HR strategy, be properly integrated in the sense that they are both complementary to and compatible with business strategy.

● Chapter summary

● Employee health and safety should be an important aspect of managing the employment relationship. To follow the logic of the HRM model, organizations need to protect their investment in their human 'assets'. This chapter established the importance of workplace health and safety from an economic, legal, psychological and moral consideration.

● As in other aspects of the employment relationship, government legislation and health and safety regulations influence the management of health and safety. The HASAWA 1974, for example, requires employers to ensure the health, safety and welfare at work of all employees. Furthermore, in Britain, the HSC has overall responsibility for workplace health and safety.

● EU directives and the Social Charter are an important source of health and safety regulations and counter 'pure market' ideology. With such developments in the law, and a growing awareness of health and safety hazards, it is likely that HRM professionals will face challenges and greater responsibilities in this area during the foreseeable future.

● In this chapter, we have examined some contemporary health and safety issues, such as sick building syndrome, workplace stress, alcoholism, smoking, workplace violence and AIDS. We have identified sexual harassment as a workplace stressor, and therefore a health and safety issue, for two primary reasons: first, research suggests that the victim of sexual harassment experiences decreased commitment to the organization and work performance; second, the courts have increasingly viewed workplace sexual harassment as being the responsibility of the employer.

● Trade unions have attempted to secure improvements in health and safety at work through collective bargaining and have pressed for some stringent health and safety legislation. Under New Labour, the HSC/DETR strategy document gives support for the development of voluntaristic 'partnership' activity between employers and workers (James & Walters, 2002). See Chapter 12 for an extended discussion on 'partnerships' in the workplace.

● A broad array of policies and actions have been discussed to ensure a healthy and safe workplace and ensure compliance with legal requirements. It has been emphasized that senior management involvement is essential for developing and implementing health and safety policies and programmes.

Key concepts

- 'Careless worker' model
- Corporate manslaughter
- Health and Safety at Work etc. Act 1974
- Robens report
- Safety committee
- Safety policy
- 'so far as is reasonably practicable'
- World Health Organization (WHO)

Chapter review questions

1. Explain the 'careless worker' model. 'Spending money on health and safety measures is a luxury most small organizations cannot afford.' Build an argument to support this statement, and an argument to negate it.

2. Explain the role of an HRM specialist in providing a safe and healthy environment for employees.

3. Explain the symptoms and causes of job stress and what an organization can do to alleviate them.

4. 'Employers with poor safety records often have poor written safety policies.' Do you agree or disagree? Discuss.

5. Explain how training can improve occupational health and safety.

6. 'Stress on women both inside and outside the work organization is a huge challenge.' Discuss.

Further reading

Bain, P. (1997). Human resource malpractice: the deregulation of health and safety at work in the USA and Britain. *Industrial Relations Journal*, **28**(3), 176–91.

James, P., & Walters, D. (2002). Worker representation in health and safety: options for regulatory reform. *Industrial Relations Journal*, **33**(2), 141–56.

Mueller, C., De Coster, S., & Estes, S. (2001). Sexual harassment in the workplace. *Work and Occupations*, **28**(4), 411–46.

Montgomery, J., & Kelloway, K. (2002). *Management of occupational health and safety* (2nd edn). Scarborough, Ontario: Nelson Thomson Learning.

Smith, A. (2001). Perceptions of stress at work. *Human Resource Management Journal*, **11**(4), 74–86.

Practising human resource management

Searching the web

Government health and safety legislation provides for regulations to deal with various types of workplace health and safety hazard. A key element of these laws in Britain and Canada, for example, is the health and safety committee, which has a broad range of responsibilities. Go to the websites of the following occupational health and safety organizations: Australia (www.nohsc.gov.au), Britain (www.hse. gov.uk), Canada (www.hrdc-dhrc.gc.ca and www.ccohs.ca), Finland (www. occuphealth.fi), South Africa (www.asosh.org) or a country you are studying. Examine the relevant sections of the health and safety legislation that deal with health and safety committees. What information is given on the role of occupational health and safety committees? How can these committees help managers to provide a safer and healthier workplace?

HRM group project

Form a study group of three to five people, and visit the websites of any of the following organizations, one that a member has worked in or one that interests members of the group: Sainsbury's (www.sainsburys.co.uk), The Body Shop (www. bodyshop.co.uk), the Royal Bank of Canada (www.royalbank.com) or Lexus (USA) (www.lexususa.com). Critically review the organization's health and safety policies and training in terms of workplace violence and sexual harassment. Go also to the website of the American Institute of Stress (www.stress.org). Using other websites, define what a 'healthy organization' is. How do organizations go about achieving this status?

Chapter case study

MANAGING AIDS AT JOHNSON STORES PLC

Gwen Fine is the HRM manager at Johnson Stores plc, a large department store located in southeast England. One Monday morning in January, Norman Smith, a trainee manager in the hardware and electrical goods department, walked into Gwen's office, sat down and broke the news that he was terminally ill. But that was not all he said. He rambled on about a friend who had died of AIDS. Both Norman and Gwen knew what he was trying to say, but neither knew how to express it. Finally, Norman stopped and asked: 'You know what it is, don't you?' 'Yes, I do', replied Gwen. 'It's a terrible thing in our society.' Norman went on to tell her that he could expect to live for only 2 more years at best. Later that morning, Gwen reflected on the meeting with Norman and felt ashamed of her insensitive comment. She confided in a close co-worker her feelings: 'What a stupid, impersonal thing to say', she chided herself. 'The man is dying.'

Norman was on sick leave for 6 weeks following his meeting with Gwen in early January; a doctor's note described his illness as shingles. The staff in Norman's department were an understanding group and carried the extra work. In February, Norman phoned Gwen with good news: he was feeling better, and the store could expect to see him back at work the following Monday.

When Norman walked into the store, his co-workers were overwhelmed by the stark change in his appearance. 'My God, he looks terrible', Gwen thought when she met him later in the day. At 43, Norman was a handsome man, yet he had lost 30 lbs since Gwen had last seen him. Dark rings circled his eyes, and his cheeks were sunken. His tall frame seemed unsteady as he leaned on a walking stick he was now carrying. The illness had also caused unsightly skin eruptions and irritation on his legs.

Norman was confident, until returning to work, that he could keep his condition private. He had offered himself as a 'guinea pig' to a group of specialist doctors searching for an AIDS cure at the regional hospital, but the treatment demanded that Norman leave the store once a week. 'Why are you always going to the hospital?', his co-workers began asking. Rumours began to circulate in the store about Norman's illness, focusing on his sexuality and the possibility he had AIDS. Co-workers began behaving differently towards him. Staff in Norman's department avoided him and attempted to ostracize him. Employees in the store also refused to use the water fountain, cups in the canteen or the toilet. As another department manager stated, 'The linking of Norman's illness to AIDS triggered irrational things in people and Johnson's entire employees simply panicked. People are totally misinformed about AIDS.' The reaction from Norman's co-workers began to affect morale and cause disruption. In April, three long-serving employees in the hardware and electrical department requested a transfer. The sales in the department fell sharply in the first quarter of the year, and shortly after the release of the quarterly sales figures, Gwen received an e-mail message from her boss, Stan Beale, the store's general manager, requesting an urgent meeting to discuss Norman Smith.

(Note: the names of the characters and the company are fictitious, but the case is based on a true story taken from *Managing Aids: How one boss struggled to cope*, in *Business Week*, February 1993.)

Discussion questions

1. If you were in Gwen Fine's position, would you have handled the case differently? Explain.

2. Drawing on the concepts in this chapter, and your own research, what policy or procedural changes could be instituted at Johnson Stores plc to prevent such disruption in the future?

HR-related skill development

In recent years, many organizations have implemented 'stop-smoking' programmes. Research has documented that smokers are absent approximately 40 per cent more than non-smokers, providing employers with an economic incentive to introduce smoking cessation policies. For more information, go to our website www.palgrave.com/business/brattonandgold and click on 'Smoking cessation policies'. Choose an organization in your city. Using the information from our website as a guide, interview a manager responsible for health and safety; (ask, for example, whether the company has a policy on smoking). Using the information obtained from your interview, material from this chapter and Internet sources, write a report outlining the benefits and costs you would expect to see after implementing a smoking cessation programme.

Notes

1. Geoffrey York, Russian city ravaging Arctic land, *Globe and Mail*, (2001), July 25, p. A1.
2. Madelaine Drohan, Technology comes with a price: stress and depression, *Globe and Mail*, (2000), October 11, p. B15.
3. Quoted in Kinnersley (1987). *The hazards of work*, London: Pluto Press, p. 1.
4. Institute of Professional and Managerial Staffs, (1993). *Health and safety: keep it together*, pp. 5–6 and quoted by Bain (1997), p. 177.
5. TUC (1979). *The safety rep and union organization*, London: TUC Education, p. 10.
6. TUC (1989). *Workplace Health: A Trade Unionists' Guide*, London: Labour Research Department, p. 2.
7. Witness to the Factories' Inquiry Commission, 1833, and quoted in F. Engels (English edn) (1973), *The conditions of the working class in England*, London: Progress, p. 194.
8. See Fletcher, B. et al. (1979). Exploring the myth of executive stress, *Personnel Management*, May, and quoted in Craig B. M., *Office Survival Handbook*, London: BSSRS, p. 10.
9. Haynes, S. G., and Feinleils, M. (1980). Women, work and coronary heart disease, prospective findings from the Framingham Heart Study, in *American Journal of Public Health*, **70**, February, and quoted in BSSRS, p. 10.
10. Anna Raeburn (1980). *Cosmopolitan*, August, and quoted in Craig (1981), p. 19.
11. Ijeoma Ross and Gayle MacDonald, Scars from stress cut deep in workplace, *Globe and Mail*, (1997) October 9, p. B16.
12. Quoted in *Bargaining Report*, London: Labour Research Department, 1983.
13. Filipowicz, C. A. (1979), The troubled employee: whose responsibility?, *The Personnel Administrator*, June and quoted in T. H. Stone and N. M. Meltz (1988), *Human Resource Management in Canada* (2nd edn) Toronto: HRW, p. 529.
14. *Workplace Health*, p. 29.
15. From *Smoking – the Facts*, Health Education Council.
16. Tobacco firms agree to pay in secondhand-smoke case, *Globe and Mail*, 1997, October 11, p. A12.
17. From Smoking attitudes and behaviour, HMSO, quoted in *Smoking at Work* (1984), London: TUC, p. 62.
18. Lee Smith, a former executive of Levi Strauss & Co., quoted in Managing AIDS: How one boss struggled to cope, *Business Week* (1993), February 1, p. 48.
19. *Globe and Mail* (2002), April 8, p. A2.
20. Anonymous (1998). International: Serial killer at large, *The Economist*, February 7.
21. Anonymous (1998). India wakes up to AIDS, *The Economist*, December 20–January 2.
22. Jay Greene (1998). Employers learn to live with AIDS, *HR Magazine*, February.
23. *Business Week* (1993), February 1, pp. 53–4.
24. Malcolm MacKillop, How the Clinton case connects to work, *Globe and Mail*, (1998), January 29, p. B12.
25. SRSC *Guidance Notes*, paragraph 18.

Part Three

Human resource management practices

Chapter six

Human resource planning

Jeffrey Gold

Human resource planning is the process of systematically forecasting the future demand and supply for employees and the deployment of their skills within the strategic objectives of the organization.

'Most chief executives acknowledge that there is a link between HR practices and business performance.'[1]

'Retaining and motivating "knowledge workers" has become the primary aim ... When they leave, the business loses an essential element of intellectual capital.'[2]

'Sainsbury's has warned 100 store managers that their performance is unacceptable. It is understood to have employed headhunters to recruit replacements.'[3]

Chapter outline

Chapter objectives

After studying this chapter, you should be able to:

1. Understand the place of planning in human resource management (HRM)
2. Understand the different approaches to manpower planning
3. Explain the difference between manpower planning and human resource planning (HRP)
4. Understand key ideas in human resource accounting
5. Give details of developments in e-HR
6. Understand developments in the idea and practice of flexibility
7. Explain the importance of career management

At the start of the 21st century, there are increasing claims that the route to competitive advantage is achieved through people (Gratton, 2000). If identical non-people resources, in the form of finance, raw materials, plant, technology, hardware and software, are available to competing organizations, differences in economic performance between organizations must be attributed to differences in the performance of people.

For senior managers in an organization, whose task it is to plan a response to the pressures of continuous change, the attraction, recruitment, utilization, development and retention of people of the required quantity and quality for the present and future ought now to rival finance, marketing and production in the construction of strategic plans. Either explicitly or implicitly, all organizational strategies will contain human resources (HR) aspects. There is, however, the long-running issue of whether HR managers should have an input into the process of strategy-making. A crucial element in this is the degree to which a link exists between HR practices and performance of the business, or the so-called 'bottom line'. In recent years, there have thus been growing efforts to test for or establish a causal link between good HRM and business performance (Cooke, 2000). Furthermore, it might be argued that the management of people as a strategic asset provides an opportunity to embrace the high-performance paradigm of HRM activity based on high trust, high commitment and high productivity (Godard & Delaney, 2000).

Becoming more strategic represents something of a dilemma for the HR function. On the one hand, HR inputs might emphasize the importance of integrating policies and procedures with a business strategy in which people are seen as a factor of production who are required to make sure the business plan is implemented. The more business plans are based on figures and mathematical models, however, the greater is the need for information about people to be expressed in a similar fashion; the plan for people should 'fit' the plan for the business. The growth of what were called manpower planning techniques through the 1960s, which provided such information, and their incorporation into comprehensive computer models were a key factor in the personnel function's development.

By the 1980s, the 'hard' version of HRM (Legge, 1995) was part of a push to address the traditional weakness of personnel managers in making themselves more strategic. It can be contrasted with a 'soft' version that emphasizes people as assets who can be developed and through whose commitment and learning an organization might achieve competitive advantage. It is interesting that the two different orientations, although representing a contrast, are not always incompatible. Indeed, living with ambiguities and conflicting pressures is a common experience for many HR practitioners (Gold & Hamblett, 1999). Tamkin et al. (1997), in a study of UK organizations, showed that although there were many challenges to HR in becoming strategic, HR functions were adopting a variety of approaches to find a strategic role, both 'soft' and 'hard'. In some cases, this involved supporting business strategy by developing appropriate policies and procedures. Not all organizations, however, are as effective in developing strategy, and the HR function could develop policy to move the organization in an appropriate direction. In some cases, the HR function is able to be proactive and play a leading role in driving strategy.

The uncertainty and complexity of organization and business conditions in the 2000s has resulted in the employment of both 'hard' and 'soft' versions of HRM with concomitant approaches and methods relating to planning. For many years, theoretical development multiplied the number and sophistication of manpower planning techniques, but the activity slid in and out of favour at strategic levels. This was partly because the data and the computer models failed to live up to expectations, with the possibility that personnel departments were unable to make use of the theoretical advances. It was also because the 'people issue' fluctuated in importance. Thus, in times of relative full employment, people and their skills were important because of their scarcity. During the years of recession in the 1980s the manpower plan was used to slim down the workforce, whereas the demographic issues of the late 1980s appeared to make people important again. The recession in the first half of the 1990s, with the accompanying trends in 'downsizing' and 'delayering', paradoxically made the idea of detailed long-term planning less attractive (Tyson, 1995) while at the same time increasing the need for more complex and organization-specific approaches to planning the employment of HR (Parker & Caine, 1996). In the 2000s, there is growing evidence that progressive HR practices can enhance a company's sustainability and profitability if there is integration with business purpose although there is also evidence of a failure by many senior managers to recognize this (Caulkin, 2001).

This chapter will look at the transition from a traditional manpower planning approach, driven by top-down planning based on numeric techniques, towards HRP as a feature of HRM. The emphasis on quantities, flows and mathematical modelling, which appeared to be the main concern of manpower planning in the 1960s and 70s, is at least complemented by and integrated with a qualitative view of people whose performance lies at the core of business strategy. We have also shown that performance lies at the core of the HRM cycle composed of an arrangement of HR activities. HRP will therefore be concerned with the development and provision of a framework that allows an organization to integrate key HR activities so that it may meet the needs of employees, enhance their potential and meet the performance needs of business strategy.

● The genesis of human resource planning: manpower planning

Manpower planning owed its importance to the importance of business strategy and planning in many organizations. It is worth, just for a moment, paying attention to the process of planning at this level. A plan represents one of the outcomes of a process that seeks to find a solution to a defined problem. There have been many attempts to rationalize this process to provide a set of easy-to-follow linear steps so that efficient decisions can be made to formulate a plan from a choice of alternatives prior to implementation. Plans therefore represent the precise and unified articulation of an organization's strategy, produced as a result of a rational consideration of the various issues that affect an organization's future performance before making a choice of the action required. As explained in Chapter 2, senior managers will during this process conduct an appraisal of both internal and external situations using a range of techniques to assess the organization's strengths and weaknesses and the opportunities and threats affecting it – the so-called SWOT analysis. Formally, the emphasis will be on data that can be quantified, which is not surprising since the planning process itself is an organization's attempt to pre-empt and deal with identified problems and uncertainty, and numbers are certain, precise and simple to comprehend. This image of certainty and control is one that gives comfort to many senior managers, although,

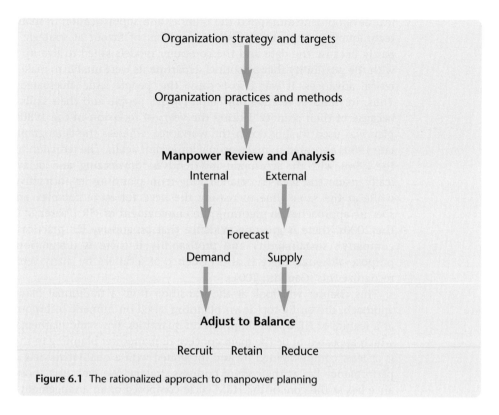

Figure 6.1 The rationalized approach to manpower planning

as argued by Mintzberg et al. (1998), the field of strategic management is filled with division and competing versions of how strategy actually works.

If business strategy and plans find their expression in measurable financial, marketing and production targets with an implicit or explicit demand for people, the manpower plan represents a response by the personnel function to ensure that the necessary supply of people is forthcoming to allow the targets to be met. The rationalized approach to manpower planning and its key stages are shown in Figure 6.1. The manpower plan could therefore be expressed in a way that matches or 'fits' the overall business strategy and plan. In theory at least, a manpower plan could show how the demand for people and their skills within an organization can be balanced by supply.

The rationalized approach leading to a balance of demand and supply can be found in some of the definitions and explanations of manpower planning posited over the past 30 years. In 1974, the Department of Employment defined manpower planning as:

> strategy for the acquisition, utilisation, improvement and preservation of an organisation's human resources.

This definition was broad and general enough to cover most aspects of personnel management work. Four stages of the planning process were outlined:

1. an evaluation or appreciation of the existing manpower resources
2. an estimation of the proportion of currently employed manpower resources that were likely to be within the firm by the forecast date
3. an assessment or forecast of labour requirements if the organization's overall objectives were to be achieved by the forecast date

4. measures to ensure that the necessary resources were available as and when required, that is, the manpower plan.

Stages 1 and 2 were linked in the 'supply aspect of manpower' with stage 1, being part of 'normal personnel practice' (Department of Employment, 1974). Stage 3 represents the 'demand aspect of manpower'. There were two main reasons for companies to use manpower planning: first, to develop their business objectives and manning levels; and second, to reduce the 'unknown' factor.

For Smith (1980, p. 7), manpower planning meant:

● demand work – analysing, reviewing and attempting to predict the numbers, by kind, of the manpower needed by the organization to achieve its objectives
● supply work – attempting to predict what action was and would be necessary to ensure that the manpower needed was available when required
● designing the interaction between demand and supply so that skills were utilized to the best possible advantage and the legitimate aspirations of the individual were taken into account.

We can see within such definitions and explanations the key influence of the language of labour economics. Thus, the notion of 'equilibrium' serves as an ideal, organizations being composed of a variety of supply and demand problems throughout their structure, which planning will need to bring into an overall balance at an optimum level. The movement towards equilibrium involves a variety of personnel activities such as recruitment, promotion, succession planning, training, reward management, retirement and redundancy.

The complexity of the interaction of these factors within the context of the aims of optimization and overall equilibrium made manpower planning a suitable area of interest for operational research and the application of statistical techniques (Bartholomew, 1971). In this process, organizations could be envisaged as a series of stocks and flows as part of an overall system of resource allocation. Models of behaviour could be formulated in relation to labour turnover, length of service, promotion flow and age distribution. These variables could be expressed as mathematical and statistical formulae and equations allowing the calculation of solutions to manpower decisions. With the growing use of computers, the techniques and models became more ambitious and probably beyond the comprehension of most managers (Parker & Caine, 1996). In large organizations, there was, however, a growth in the number of specialist manpower analysts who were capable of dealing with the complex processes involved.

HRM WEB LINKS

Go to www.informs-cs.org/wsc98papers/088.PDF where you will find a paper that applies Bayesian forecasting techniques and Markov chain methods to an 'employee scheduling problem' in manufacturing.

In the UK, the Institute of Manpower Studies,[4] based at Sussex University, was a principal advocate of manpower modelling. According to the Institute (Bennison, 1980, p. 2), the manpower planning process involved:

● Determining the manpower requirements; how many people;
● Establishing the supply of manpower;

● Developing policies to fill the gap between supply and demand.

The Institute favoured a flexible approach in which plans were developed based on an understanding of the whole manpower system. The first step in manpower analysis is to describe the current manpower system and set its expected objectives. The system can be drawn as a 'collection of boxes and flows representing the way that manpower behaves in the organisation' (Bennison, 1980, p. 5). Planners can then assess the critical 'decision points' for manpower policy. Decisions concerning the recruitment and promotion of managers can, for example, occur in a meaningful way using statistical planning techniques in which the 'practical limits of variation' (Bennison, 1980, p. 17) can be defined for factors such as level of labour turnover at particular points, the impact of developments in technology and forecasts of growth. If possible, the relationship of the factors to the decisions will be quantified, allowing the generation of promotion paths under different assumptions of demand and supply.

Emphasizing statistical models of the supply and demand of manpower at the expense of the reality of managing and interacting with people was bound to be greeted with suspicion, certainly by employees and their representatives, as well as by managers 'forced' to act on the results of the calculations. It can be argued that the manpower analysis is there to serve as an aid to decision-making, but the presentation of data and an inability to deal with the ever-increasing complexity of models were always likely to result in the manpower analysis being 'seen' as the plan. The domination of equations that mechanistically provide solutions for problems based on the behaviour of people may actually become divorced from the real world and possess a good chance of missing the real problems; hence manpower planning soon acquired a poor reputation. For example, Cowling and Walters (1990), reporting on a survey of personnel managers, found that few respondents attributed benefits of planning to increasing job satisfaction/motivation (33.5 per cent), reducing skills shortages (30.2 per cent) and reducing labour turnover (22.4 per cent). Of the respondents who used computers, 3.3 per cent reported a use for job design and 9 per cent one for job analysis. All of these were, and still are, vital areas of concern for any organization, areas that lie at the heart of proving the link between HRM activities and performance (Guest et al., 2000).

There were also a number of doubts about the connection between the business plan and the manpower plan. In a survey of US firms by Nkomo (1988), although 54 per cent of organizations reported the preparation of manpower plans, few reported a strong link between this activity and strategic business planning. Pearson (1991) reported the problem for manpower planners where business objectives might be absent or might not be communicated. Cowling and Walters found that 58.4 per cent of respondents faced a low priority given to planning compared with immediate management concerns; they concluded, 'Of comprehensive and systematic manpower planning fully integrated into strategic planning there exist few examples at the present time' (1990, p. 6).

During the 1980s, there were a number of attempts to make manpower planning techniques more 'user-friendly' to non-specialists. Thus, the fall-out from theoretical progress in manpower analysis was the application of techniques to help with particular problems in the workplace. Bell (1989) argued that personnel managers understood the concept of manpower planning even if line managers and corporate planners did not, and that they were able to use basic techniques.

Many personnel managers are able to use manpower planning techniques to help them understand and deal with 'real' manpower problems, for example, why one department in an organization seems to suffer from a dramatically higher labour turnover rate than others, or why graduate trainees are not retained in sufficient number. At a time when most people employed in most organizations were employed on permanent contracts with defined tasks to perform based on stable skill sets, personnel managers were able to build up a 'toolbag' of key manpower measures such as turnover, retention, stability and absenteeism. All could be relatively easily calculated either monthly or quarterly and expressed graphically to reveal trends and future paths.

Through the 1990s such techniques were incorporated into PC-based computerized personnel information systems (CPISs). As the software became more user-friendly, personnel departments were able to take advantage of this and make themselves more responsive to business needs. There are now many providers of HR software; we will explore such developments later in this chapter, but you may wish to examine some of the products and the claims made by the suppliers.

HRM WEB LINKS

Go to www.acas.org.uk/publications/pub_ab_absenceturnover.html, a booklet, published in the UK by the Advisory, Conciliation and Arbitration Service (ACAS). The book on absence and turnover provides assistance to organizations that have labour turnover and absenteeism problems. You will also find examples of formulae used to measure absenteeism and turnover.[5] Go also to www.softwaresource.co.uk/; this is a site established by the Chartered Institute of Personnel and Development, providing information and access to many HR software products and suppliers.

The use of manpower planning techniques within CPIS can be seen as part of a continuing search by the personnel function to find areas of expertise that would legitimize its position and prove its value by 'adding to the bottom line'. In this approach, manpower plans and policies serve as initiators of operations, and techniques are used to monitor the progress of operations and raise an awareness of problems as they arise. There is an attempt here to use manpower information as a way of understanding problems so that action can be taken as is appropriate. The disproportionate influence of the plan as a solution is replaced by an attention to planning as a continuous process of learning about HR problems. In this way, HR managers have been practising what Fyfe (1986, p. 66) referred to as 'the diagnostic approach to manpower planning'. This approach built on and broadened the rationalized approach in order to identify problem areas and understand why they were occurring. The theoretical idea of a balance of demand and supply, and equilibrium, can occur only on paper or on the computer screen; the more probable real-life situation is one of continuous imbalance as a result of the dynamic conditions facing any organization, the behaviour of people and the imperfections of manpower models. The diagnostic approach was based on the following thesis (Fyfe 1986, p. 66):

> before any manager seeks to bring about change, or reduce the degree of imbalance, he or she must be fully aware of the reasons behind the imbalance (or the manpower problem) in the first place. Unless managers understand more about the nature of manpower problems, their attempts to control events will suffer from the hit-and-miss syndrome.

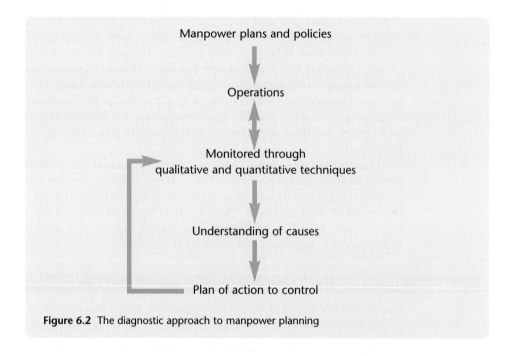

Figure 6.2 The diagnostic approach to manpower planning

Figure 6.2 shows the stages of this process.

In comparison with the rationalized approach, manpower problems using a diagnositic approach are to be identified and explored so that they can be understood, the data being used to help in this process and the speed of the computer providing support at an early stage. The rationalized approach will seek to minimize the time spent on such matters, preferring instead to focus on problems that can be easily defined or that most closely match ready-prepared solutions that may be difficult to challenge. In the rationalized approach, for example, organizational practices and methods – which include the division of labour, the design of work, the technology used, the relationships between departments and groups and the degree of management supervision – will precede the manpower review and be taken as a set of 'givens' in the ensuing calculations. Yet these may be the very factors that lie at the heart of manpower problems. Thus, a telephone sales organization that faces a problem of retaining staff may respond to this imbalance by stepping up recruitment and/or increasing pay. A diagnostic approach would, however, mean becoming aware of this problem by monitoring manpower statistics such as turnover[6] and stability, and obtaining qualitative data by interviewing staff. The interviews may reveal concerns with job satisfaction and the career paths open to staff, reflecting aspirations they hold that are not being met by current practices. Rather than express these aspirations openly for fear of conflict with management, many staff prefer to seek employment elsewhere. The loss of skilled labour has important cost implications and, in the face of a continuing shortage of skilled workers, a diagnostic approach to retention can provide a significant pay-off.

Bevan (1991) provides a guide to some of the reasons for high staff turnover. Significantly, but not unexpectedly, pay was not the only issue. Among the main factors identified were:

- the job not matching new employees' expectations
- a lack of attention from line managers and a lack of training
- a lack of autonomy, responsibility, challenge and variety within the work
- disappointment with the promotion and development opportunities
- standards of management, including unapproachable, uncaring and distant behaviour and a failure to consult.

These are all complex factors reflecting general areas of concern but requiring solutions that are specific to the context of each organization. In the case of the telephone sales example above, the organization could respond to the diagnosis in various ways. Management could, for example, accept the problem and do nothing except lower the quality of recruitment so that new staff would, hopefully, be less likely to have high career aspirations – hardly very progressive and not very complex, but certainly an option. The organization could, however, also attempt to improve the work environment and work practices in order to provide avenues for greater job satisfaction and personal growth. This might have implications for job design, departmental structure and management style, creating a tension that would have to be resolved.

In this way, manpower planning becomes integrated into the whole process of management of the employment relationship, which itself plays a proactive part in affecting organization, strategy, structure and practices. Importantly, manpower planning has a part to play in bridging the gap between the needs of the organization (as defined by senior management) and the needs of individual employees. This theme will be explored later in the chapter.

Although the diagnostic approach to manpower planning will have an incremental impact, the changes that it will bring will accumulate in the organization's value system and mould its response to significant human resource issues. A good example of this is provided by responses to the decline in the number of young people entering the UK workforce in the late 1980s. It had been predicted that such a decline would cause labour markets to tighten all over the UK, particularly in those areas and sectors in which organizations had already faced constraints on production posed by a shortage of skilled workers. Atkinson (1989, p. 22) outlined a range of responses to this problem based on three characteristics:

1. *Sequential:* 'introduced only slowly as the full seriousness of the shortage problem becomes apparent to firms'
2. *Hierarchical:* 'with more difficult/expensive responses deployed only when easier/cheaper ones have proved inadequate'
3. *Cumulative:* 'they will build on each other'.

Starting with tactical responses such as doing nothing or competing for the diminishing supply, an organization could progress to more strategic options such as identifying new and substitute supplies of labour and improving the use and performance of existing workers, the latter responses having important implications for the nature of the employment relationship and the approach to manpower planning.[7]

In the 2000s, losing staff is also seen as a loss of intellectual capital, and the replacement of 'knowledge workers' can be both expensive and time-consuming (Buckingham, 2000). As a response, an organization could attempt to engender high performance through the use of good HR activities. The intention to do so and its enactment can be referred to as human resource planning (HRP)

In the diagnostic approach to manpower planning, quantitative planning techniques are used in combination with qualitative techniques to identify and understand the causes of manpower problems. This information can then be used to generate solutions equal to the complexity of the problems. We have also seen that such an approach has the potential to affect organizational structure, job design and work practices. Organizations can also work out short-term tactics to deal with external manpower issues such as skills shortages and a decline in the number of young people in the labour market. In both the diagnostic approach and the rationalized approach, manpower plans are established with reference to a predetermined strategy. HRP, however, seeks to make the links between strategy, structure and people more explicit.

Throughout the 1990s and into the 2000s, the term 'human resource planning' has gradually replaced that of 'manpower planning' but its meaning and practice have been subjected to much discussion and variation. This can be seen to be as a consequence of the ongoing debate over what kind of approach to HRM should be adopted in order to provide superior performance at work. As we have indicated earlier (see also Chapter 2), there have been a number of efforts to explore the link between HRM practices and the bottom line. Although it is suggested that such efforts may lack consistency in methodology and provide different results, studies in general show that there is some benefit in adopting a 'high road' HRM strategy of high training, high involvement, high rewards and quality commitment (Cooke, 2000). In contrast 'low road' HRM is characterized by low pay, low job security and work intensification.

In addition to the general view of adopting a 'high road' HRM strategy, further research suggests the importance of introducing HR practices together in a 'bundle' so that they enhance and support each other (Cooke, 2000). Planning to introduce appraisal on its own will, for example, be far less effective without a consideration of training, reward, careers and the attitudes and styles of managers. It is also important to coordinate the implementation (Hoque, 1999), which highlights the importance of a more sophisticated view of HRP.

A 'high road' HRM strategy requires a belief by senior management that people represent the key source of competitive advantage because an organization's route to success is based on distinctive product and/or service quality as well as price. Furthermore, the continuing development of those people will be a vital feature of strategy in both its formation and its implementation. In this version, HRP builds on and develops the rationalized and diagnostic approaches to manpower planning that we have already identified in this chapter. It may certainly involve the use of manpower modelling, simulations and statistical techniques, but these will be set within an overall approach to planning that will underpin the bundle of interdependent policies and activities, with the emphasis on *human resource* management (Legge, 1995).

Although there is increasing evidence for a link between 'high road' HRM and business performance, such evidence may not always convince senior managers in their decision-making. Liff (2000) suggests that HRP implies a link to the resource-based view of firms in which market opportunities are considered against a firm's internal resources when setting strategy. Thus, a consideration of the distinctive expertise and skills of people is held to be a first-order element of making the strategy. There is, however, also significant evidence that many firms in the UK do not view people in this way, preferring to see HRM issues as a third-order issue (Coleman & Keep, 2001). Furthermore, when faced with difficulties, many organizations swiftly move towards the 'hard' version of HRM in which HR activities are designed to respond to strategy, people being viewed as a resource whose cost must be controlled. The emphasis is on human *resource management* (Legge, 1995). Taking the lead from strategy, HRP is in this version concerned more with the right number of people in the right place at the right time who can be utilized in the most cost-effective manner.

Consider, for example, the case of clearing banks in the UK. Whereas clearing banks in the UK could, for much of their history, take a generally reactive approach to a relatively stable environment, by the end of the 1980s and throughout the 1990s they faced an environment of continuous flux and change in the form of growing competition, deregulation in the markets for products and services and the introduction of new technology. In the past, clearing banks were considered to be places of employment where loyalty and commitment were rewarded with job security and continuous but slow career progression through a multitiered grading structure. These factors would make traditional banks ripe to adopt many 'soft' version HRM activities, but, at the same time, the banks were forced to adopt the 'hard' version, resulting in branch closures and the loss of many jobs (Storey et al., 1997).

This is a pattern that has been repeated across many organizations. HRP has been used to provide a framework to accommodate 'multifarious practices' of 'pragmatic and opportunistic' organizations (Storey, 1995a). Thus, at the same time as HRP can respond to the direction provided by changes in organizational structure and strategy to cut costs and staff numbers, a trend referred to as 'downsizing', it can also provide the means by which to achieve desirable HR outcomes such as commitment and high performance. You might be forgiven for thinking that HRP is no different from the use and reputation of manpower planning in this respect. Indeed, those involved in the formation and delivery of HR plans may sometimes feel the conflicts and pressures referred to earlier, requiring an interesting game of words to maintain the appearance of sense.

Another example can be found in the implementation of business process re-engineering (BPR) (Hammer & Champy, 1993) during the 1990s (see also Chapter 4). BPR is based on a radical change of business processes by applying information technology in order to integrate tasks to produce an output of value to the customer. As the change unfolds, unnecessary processes and layers of bureaucracy are identified and removed, and staff become more empowered to deliver high-quality service and products. HRP might focus on the need for skills and learning and other 'soft' HRM practices. Despite the efforts of advocates to disassociate BPR from 'downsizing' (Hammer & Stanton, 1995), BPR has, however, almost always been accompanied by unemployment (Grey & Mitev, 1995), a fact that an HRP plan may attempt, with difficulty, to disguise.

HRM WEB LINKS

Go to www.bprc.warwick.ac.uk/bp-site.html, the Economic and Social Research Council-funded Business Processes Resource Centre at Warwick University. This was set up as a focal point in the UK for the dissemination of current knowledge and best practice, and to provide access to best practice thinking and application.

BPR, along with other initiatives to restructure organizations, posed difficulties for HRP in the 1990s. Similarly, in the 2000s, many organizations respond to change and economic difficulties by cutting costs, which is usually translated into making staff redundant. In 2001, for example, following the 11 September attacks in the USA, there were a large number of job losses around the world in the airline industry, in addition to ongoing job losses in the face of world recession. Cooke (2000) points out that, in Britain, specific historical, social, political and institutional contextual features have provided a business environment that is incompatible with soft HRM. Thus, with pressure to sustain or increase profits, employees are more likely to be treated as a 'number' in the quest to reduce costs.

This stance has continued despite a realization that losing staff could have negative consequences for organizations as well as for those made unemployed. First, there is the loss of skill, knowledge and wisdom that employees accumulate over years of practice at work. The result of downsizing may thus be a loss of productivity.

HRM WEB LINKS

Go to www.pfdf.org/leaderbooks/l2l/spring98/pfeffer.html#box, an article by Jeffrey Pfeffer, a leading researcher who has shown that managing people using high-performance or high-commitment practices can produce enormous economic returns.

Second, there is the effect on those employees who remain at work after a period of downsizing. Where they respond sympathetically towards those made redundant, they may experience such effects of guilt, lower motivation and commitment, mistrust and insecurity (Thornhill et al., 1997); this is referred to as 'survivor syndrome'. A further effect, according to Appelbaum and Donna (2000), is that compromising productivity by downsizing is detrimental to the survivors. Third, redundancy is stressful for those made unemployed, possibly through the process of being made redundant itself and then through the experience of unemployment (Pickard, 2001).[8] The general difficulty that HR practitioners face in making people considerations an essential input for business strategy suggests that HRP needs to be considered less as a product, that is, a plan as a written document, and more as a process (Bin Idris & Eldridge, 1998). This echoes Mintzberg's criticisms of strategy as an explicit, rationally predetermined plan as incomplete; for Mintzberg, strategy is a 'pattern in a stream of decisions' (1978, p. 935). The source of such patterns may be formulations of conscious and rational processes expressed by senior managers as intended strategy, but may also comprise emergent, probably unintentional, learning and discoveries as a result of decisions made gradually over time. Included in this latter process of strategy formation will be the learning of and from employees through their interaction with the organization's structure, work processes and suppliers, clients or customers. Realized strategy will be the result of both intended and emergent processes. Thus, although plans in general suggest prediction, control and relationships that can be expressed in linear terms, it is doubtful whether the world works in this way, making ideas relating to chaos and complexity more attractive (Byrne, 1998).

HRM WEB LINKS

Go to www.brint.com/Systems.htm, which provides links to articles, papers, books and bibliographies on complexity and chaos.

Human resource accounting

We have seen how there has been an ongoing legitimacy problem for personnel and HR practitioners in that it is difficult to prove the special value of people in organizations, particularly in terms of finance and accountancy. The failure to make a connection between the specific contribution of people and the 'bottom line' has been a key factor in reducing the importance of decisions related to HR. The oft-quoted claims that 'people are our greatest asset' and that people and their knowledge and skills are the one distinctive resource that competitors cannot copy, has, however, led to various attempts to state the value of people in the language of accounting and to represent this value in an organization's financial statement. We refer to such efforts as human resource accounting (HRA), which we define as the process of identifying, quantifying, accounting and forecasting the value of human resources in order to facilitate effective HRM. We should, however, be aware that people in organizations differ from other assets in one important respect – unlike capital items and materials, they cannot be owned by an organization. People can be said to 'loan' their abilities to perform in return for rewards from the organization (Mayo, 2002). Organizations will seek to obtain the most from such a loan by combining the knowledge and skills of people with other resources to add value. Furthermore, such value-adding can increase over time through the knowledge and skills that people develop from performing their work and from specific activities such as training and development. An organization might therefore claim that it is important to include such value-adding capability on its balance sheet.

There have for many years been attempts to account for the value of people in organizations, the main focus having been how to develop models to measure the cost and values of people (Flamholz, 1985). One consequence of this was that there was a tendency to treat people in financial terms, 'the dominant image of HRA for many people' (Flamholz, 1985, p. 3) being putting 'people on the balance sheet'. Valid and reliable models of measurement were, however, lacking,[9] and HRA 'progressed at something less than a snail's pace' (Turner, 1996, p. 65). HRA found more favour in Sweden, where many organizations have used key ideas in decision-making, leading to a 'changed way of thinking' about the management of human resources (Gröjer & Johanson, 1998, p. 499). HRA was, for example, integrated into the management control process of three companies researched by Johanson and Nilson (1996). Managers were trained and information systems adjusted. Furthermore, HRA statements were included in the companies' annual reports. It was found that HRA techniques were useful as management tools, but management were also ambivalent towards HRA since the techniques could also be used to assess the efficiency of managers (Johanson, 1999).

HRM WEB LINKS

Go to www.fek.su.se/pei/indexe.html to explore the work of the Personnel Economics Institute at Stockholm University on human resource costing and accounting. You can also examine some performance indicators that could be used in HRA at www. sol.brunel.ac.uk/~jarvis/bola/personnel/assets.html.

As tools for management to control costs, HRA can be accused of contributing to a narrow view of people in organizations as being an expense to be minimized and cut when necessary. This view can significantly underrate the value of people in terms of the accumulation of knowledge and understanding as they learn at work, which makes them difficult to replace as well as difficult to copy. People therefore have a value that is greater than simply the cost of their employment. Although the value is difficult to capture in financial terms, knowledge and understanding in an organization form part of its intangible assets[10] or intellectual capital (Edvinsson & Malone, 1997). What is significant about intellectual capital is that as the knowledge economy advances, more organizations will need to invest in knowledge-creating activities (Chapter 10), in which the production of new knowledge is a vital differentiator between different organizations (Garvey & Williamson, 2002).

Edvinsson and Malone (1997) suggest that intellectual capital in an organization is composed of two factors. First, there is structural capital, such as hardware and software, trade and brand names and relationships with customers and suppliers – as Edvinsson and Malone (1997, p. 11) have written, 'everything left at the office when the employees go home'. Second, there is human capital, which is the knowledge and skills of employees at work as well as their values and culture. In combination, human capital plus structural capital equals intellectual capital.

REFLECTIVE QUESTION

What is the intellectual capital of your course? How is this intellectual capital valued?

The factors that comprise intellectual capital are clearly difficult to fit into traditional accounting frameworks. However, the difference between the financial value of the company (its book value) and its value in the capital markets (its market value) has increasingly been recognized as resulting from the assessment of a company's intellectual capital, especially its investment in HR. Such differences have led to a search to find a way of valuing intellectual capital in organizations. The Swedish company Skandia has, for example, developed a set of methods and tools to measure intellectual capital, these being referred to as the Skandia Navigator.[11] Mayo (2002, p. 38) suggests the use of a 'human capital monitor' to calculate the added value of people in an organization. The key idea is that added value, in the form of both financial and non-financial contributions, can be assessed by considering:

People as assets	– composed of employment costs, capability, potential, values alignment and contributions
+	
People's motivation/commitment	– affected by factors in the work environment such as leadership, practical support, reward and recognition, and learning and development.

Such considerations in HRA can be seen as part of a general move towards values in organizations, although there will still be many difficulties in gathering information to calculate each person's contribution (Mayo, 2002).

HRP, as both an intended and an emergent process, would need to manage knowledge as an input to decision-making and as an outcome, which would make it suitable for applying advances in the way in which information and communication technology (ICT) has been developed to support HRP activities via human resource information systems (HRISs). Indeed, capturing and disseminating organizational knowledge in all its manifestations have become a key feature of the emerging field of knowledge management (Chapter 10).

So what role does an HRIS have in the management of HR knowledge? According to Broderick and Boudreau (1992) there are three types of ICT application in HRM:

1. Transaction processing/reporting/tracking applications covering operational activities, for example payroll, record-keeping and performance monitoring
2. Expert systems to improve decision-making based on an analysis of decisions concerning such issues as sources of new recruits, salaries and training needs
3. Decision support systems to improve decision-making through the use of scenario modelling in areas where there are no clear answers, for example team formation and management development programmes.

Research by Kinnie and Arthurs (1996) found a widespread use of HRIS for transaction applications in operational areas such as employee records, payroll and absence control. There was, however, less use in expert systems and decision support applications, which represent more advanced uses of HRIS. Part of the explanation for the relatively unambiguous use of HRIS lies in the way in which HR departments prove their worth in organizations. A concentration on transactions applications provides a vital flow of data for others to make decisions. The use of HRIS for expert systems and decision support applications that reduce people to numbers might, however, be resisted by many HR practitioners as representing too much of a clash with people-orientated values (Kinnie & Arthurs, 1996). Therefore, it is argued, a 'half-way position' has been adopted that emphasizes the value of a limited use of HRIS but adds to cost-effectiveness when combined with the professional performance of HR tasks that cannot be performed by IT. Further research by Ball (2001) supports this position, most HRISs mainly being used for data administration and management rather than manipulation. Ball (2001, p. 690) concludes that 'HRM still seem to be the laggard in running its own systems' to support decision-making and strategy.

In the 2000s, many HR departments are using the Internet and related technologies to support their activities – a process referred to as e-HR (Trapp, 2001). HR departments are, for example, able to make use of many sources of information available on the Internet. Another approach is to allow staff to access information on personnel issues, for example how much holiday they have left for the year, via a company intranet. Furthermore, making such information available on the Internet as well, allows it to be accessed by staff from a PC anywhere in the world. One trend is to outsource many transactional services to outside HR service centres, with the claim that the transfer of administrative work will allow HR staff to concentrate more on strategic and high value-added work (Trapp, 2001). In addition, other ICT developments provide an opportunity for HR departments to work strategically with other functions. Many large and medium-sized organizations have, for example, attempted to integrate all information flows through enterprise resource planning (ERP) software. One supplier of ERP software claims that it contains tools to integrate resources, machinery, finance and human skills even where operations occur globally using different currencies, languages and legal requirements. HRM in practice 6.1 shows how one company used e-HR to reduce its HR budget.

HRM IN PRACTICE 6.1

C&W REVEALS PLAN TO SLASH HR OVERHEADS

STEVE CRABB, *PEOPLE MANAGEMENT*, 2001, 8 MARCH

A radical change programme, which will see 'significant' HR job losses and the 'e-enabling' of all HR processes, will propel Cable and Wireless into the top 2 per cent of leading-edge global companies.

This is the verdict of Rick Hutley of Cisco Systems, who sits on a council within C&W that is responsible for approving every 'e-initiative' in the company. Hutley was appointed to the council because of Cisco's reputation as a world leader in the e-business field.

Speaking at last month's HR Summit event in Montreux, Switzerland, Martin Reddington, C&W's e-HR transformation programme director, said that the company wanted to save £5.6 million from its global HR budget in the next financial year, and expected to see annual savings of up to £13 million by 2005. This would be achieved by a combination of increased efficiency, through 'e-enabled' HR processes, and job cuts.

'If anyone tells you that you can bring in e-HR functionality and retain your existing HR headcount ... there's something

wrong with the equation,' Reddington said.

C&W is consulting employee representatives over the scale of the job losses. It currently employs 400 HR practitioners, but plans to phase out all administrative and transactional roles, leaving a small core of 'more highly skilled HR professionals who can command senior management's attention', Reddington said.

> **'If anyone tells you that you can bring in e-HR functionality and retain your existing HR headcount ... there's something wrong with the equation.'**

He told *People Management* that the company was looking at the 'existing capability profile' of its HR staff, and would then match that against anticipated future needs to plan how to 'migrate the pool of talent'. The initial assessment should be completed by the end of this month.

Mark Withers, of the Mighty Waters consultancy, had been drafted in to handle the consultation process with affected employees, he added.

The changes will be underpinned by a new global IT system based on SAP's 4.6c technology. Until now, the firm has used a mixture of systems, including Oracle in the US, SAP in the UK and 'a patchwork quilt of systems in Europe'.

Every HR process will be 'e-enabled', including learning, recruitment, assessment, performance and reward management, induction and general administration. Global standards will be introduced across all 70 countries in which C&W operates, and exceptions will be made only if they are forced by local conditions.

According to Reddington, the company aims to run all of these processes on the 'pure' SAP architecture, with a minimum of add-ons, although he admitted that the learning, assessment and development and recruitment processes might require some extra technology.

HRM WEB LINKS

Find out about ERP's past, present and future at www.erpassist.com/browse.asp?c= ERPPeerPublishing&r=%2Fpub%2Ferp%5Foverview%2Ehtm. You can examine how 'optimal staffing' can be planned at the following web link: www.intentia.com/ w2000.nsf/pages/enm.

Whatever the claims of software suppliers, a crucial element in any HRIS is how information is used, especially in decisions concerning how people are employed at work. Liff (1997) outlines three perspectives on the use of an HRIS:

1. An HRIS may provide an objective view of an organization in which the information used is comprehensive and accurate, allowing the best decisions to be made.
2. The design of an HRIS, including the categories and classifications determining the information that should be collected, plays a vital role in constructing the reality of organization. Of vital importance here is the purpose of one category of data compared with another.
3. The way in which people relate to the information provided will depend on the 'maps' they hold concerning the organization, that is, the store of existing knowledge held by each person to make sense of what happens. Information will be used in making sense of what is going on and what needs to be done, and such information may be accepted or rejected on the basis of how far it accords with a person's 'map'. It is thus quite possible, since each person has a different view of life at work (a different 'map'), that the same information will be interpreted in different ways, leading to different decisions.

In three case studies, Liff (1997) found that each view could be used to explain managers' use of HRIS. Managers were thus attached to an objective view of an HRIS and the fact that the information it contained was neutral. That is, skills were defined from a 'rational reassessment of current labels' (Liff, 1997, p. 27). In addition, there was a belief that the HRIS categories could construct a new approach to managing staff and play a role in 'serving dominant business strategy'. The third view could, however, also be found, especially in the way in which apparent discrepancies in information produced by the system could be understood on the basis of existing knowledge of life at work.

Flexibility

Rapid advances in telecommunications and computing, and the pressure exerted to respond to global markets, are said to be having a significant effect on work pattern, work location and work times, although some survey evidence suggests such claims may be exaggerated (see Taylor, 2002 and below). In planning how to respond, many organizations invoke the idea of 'flexibility', a term given to a variety of different meanings, with a variety of implications for HRP (see also Chapter 3).

REFLECTIVE QUESTION

How many meanings for the idea of flexbility can you think of? As you consider these different meanings, examine the implications for skills, hours and location of work, type of contract and the overall motivation and satisfaction of people at work.

As a basis of our exploration of flexibility, we will first of all examine the theoretical framework of academics working in the fields of sociology and labour economics, referred to as 'labour market segmentation'. The framework attempts to classify and explain the ways in which organizations seek to employ different kinds of labour. For example, Loveridge (1983) developed a classification based on the following factors:

- the degree to which workers have flexible skills that are specific to an organization
- the degree to which work contains discretionary elements that provide stable earnings.

The classification shown in Figure 6.3 helps to explain how and why some organizations adopt different approaches to the management and planning of the employment relationship for different groups of employees. Thus, workers in the primary internal market include those with important and scarce skills that are specific to a particular organization; an organization would be anxious to retain such workers and develop their potential, and it would be such employees who would form the focus of application of the full range of HR activities. On the other hand, some workers operating in the secondary internal market will be deemed by management to be of less importance, except in terms of their availability at the times required by an organization. This group could include part-time, seasonal and temporary employees. Employers might wish to recruit and retain those employees deemed by management to be the kinds of worker who could be trained to the organization's requirements, but there would be less interest in applying the whole package of HR policies. Workers operating in the external markets would be considered to be someone else's concern.

Although the idea of labour market segmentation has been recognized for many

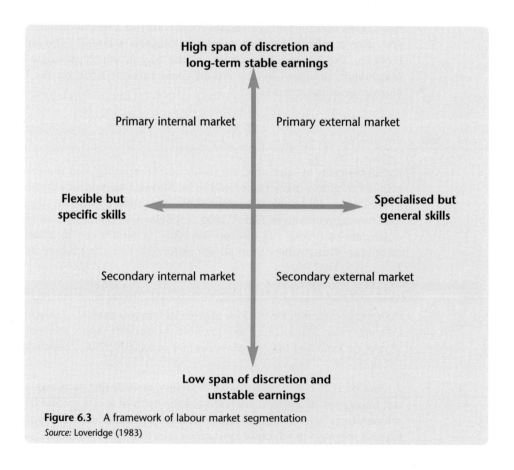

Figure 6.3   A framework of labour market segmentation
Source: Loveridge (1983)

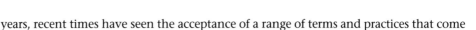

years, recent times have seen the acceptance of a range of terms and practices that come under the umbrella of the idea of 'flexibility', with all its definitions and implications.

HRM WEB LINKS

Go to www.flexibility.co.uk and use this site to explore different uses of the idea of flexibility.

The ambiguity of the idea of flexibility has allowed a number of interpretations to justify a variety of organizational activities (Chapter 4). Among these is the model of a 'flexible firm' (Atkinson and Meager, 1985, p. 2), which:

> draws into a simple framework the new elements in employers' manpower practices, bringing out the relationships between the various practices and their appropriateness for different companies and groups of workers.

This model identifies four types of flexibility (see also Chapter 4):

1. *functional:* 'a firm's ability to adjust and deploy the skills of its employees to match the tasks required by its changing workload, production methods and/or technology'
2. *numerical:* a firm's ability to adjust the level of labour inputs to meet fluctuations in output
3. *distancing strategies:* the replacement of internal workers with external subcontractors, that is, putting some work, such as running the firm's canteen, out to contract
4. *financial:* support for the achievement of flexibility through the pay and reward structure.

The flexible firm will achieve these flexibilities through a division of its employees into core and peripheral workforces. The core group is composed of those workers expected to deliver functional flexibility and includes those with firm specific skills and high discretionary elements in their work. The peripheral group is composed of a number of different workers. One category might be directly employed by a firm to perform work with a low discretionary element. Another category might be employed as required on a variety of contracts, for example part-time, temporary and casual workers; this category might also include highly specialized workers such as consultants. The final category comprises trainees, some of whom may be prepared for eventual transfer to the core group. It is important to remember, when considering the issue of flexibility, that organizations do have a choice about the type of flexibility that can be adopted.

The flexible firm model has been subjected to much debate. In the late 1980s, the model was criticized as being unsupported by the evidence and as presenting a self-fulfilling prediction of how such a firm should be created (Pollert, 1988). The evidence also showed a confused picture. At the time of the 1987 Employers' Labour Use Strategies Survey (Hakim, 1990), only a small minority of employers had a conscious core/periphery manpower strategy. An ACAS survey in the same year found, however, a growing range of flexible working practices (ACAS, 1988). This suggested that there were, in the late 1980s, many organizations adopting flexible working practices in an ad hoc, unplanned and – occasionally – opportunistic manner. Hakim praised the model of a flexible firm as a 'simplified synthesis' of key ideas whose achievement was to 'reveal the inner logic of existing labour strategies, to disclose the implicit structure of segmented labour markets' (1990, p. 180). Flexibility has, however, also been referred to as a 'panacea of restructuring' (Pollert, 1991, p. xx), as a way of conflating different changes in the organization of work such as multiskilling, job enlargement, labour intensification, cost control (Pollert, 1991) and self-managed teams (Wageman, 1997).

During much of the 1990s, it was difficult to discern whether the flexible firm remained as an ideal type providing managers with a new set of labels for old practices. During the difficult times of recession, when downsizing was adopted by many organizations to reduce costs and intensify the use of labour, flexibility could be presented more positively as way of dealing with change and responding more rapidly to customer requirements, thus securing the future survival of organizations and employment. Many organizations therefore adopted the language of flexibility, attempted to apply the practices but failed to consider the impact of changes in working practices and arrangements on the employment relationship. Research into the implications of 'lean systems of production', for example, found that multiskilling and more involvement in decision-making was offset by greater stress, higher workloads and feelings of blame and isolation (Institute of Personnel and Development, 1996).

In the late 1990s and into the 2000s, it has been argued that it is the 'hard' HRM approach, with its emphasis on people as numbers within a framework of cost control, that has held most sway in the talk and practice of flexibility (Richbell, 2001). Research by Guest et al. (1998) examined the overall stance of 40 policy-makers in a consortium of companies with an interest in career- and employment-related practices. It was found that there was very little evidence of a coherent policy towards flexible employment, the key factor instead being a desire to reduce and control costs, using short-term and temporary staff when required to circumvent cost constraints. Thus, Millward et al. (2000), drawing on data from 1998 Workplace Employee Relations Survey, indicated that, by 1998, 35 per cent of workplaces made use of short-term contracts and temporary working, compared with 19 per cent in 1980. There has also been a growth in the number of part-time workers, from 21 per cent in 1984 to 25 per cent in 1999, especially among women, who made up 80 per cent of part-time employees in 1999 (Department for Education and Employment, 2000) Significantly, from 1992 to 1999, years that saw a growth in overall employment in the UK, around 40 per cent of the increase in the number of employees was made up of part-time workers. There has also been an increase in the contracting out or outsourcing of services such as cleaning, security, transport and even HR and training, 90 per cent of workplaces with 25 or more employees outsourcing one or more service (Department for Education and Employment, 2000).

An important variation in working pattern has been the growth of teleworking and/or homeworking. Recent research (Huws, 1997) has identified five main types of teleworking:

1. *multi-site:* an alternation between working on an employer's premises and working elsewhere, usually at home but also in a telecottage or telecentre
2. *tele-homeworking:* work based at home, usually for a single employer and involving low-skilled work performed by people tied to their homes
3. *freelancing:* work for a variety of different clients
4. *mobile:* work carried out using communication technology such as mobile phones, fax machines, PC connections via the Internet, often by professional, commercial,

technical and managerial staff who work 'on the road'

5. *relocated back-functions* (call centres): specialist centres carrying out activities such as data entry, airline bookings, telephone banking, telephone sales and helpline services.

The number of people homeworking had, by 1998, increased in the UK to 680,000 or 2.5 per cent of the workforce (from 345,000 in 1981) as part of a general increase in the number of teleworkers and people engaging in e-work. It is, however, suggested that over a quarter of the UK workforce do some of their work at home. Over 200,000 people work in call centres (Department for Education and Employment, 2000). HRM in practice 6.2 indicates how the telecommunications company BT used home-working to improve the work–life balance of some of its employees.

HRM IN PRACTICE 6.2

FLEXIBLE WORKING POLICY RINGS IN REWARDS FOR BT

KAREN HIGGINBOTTOM, *PEOPLE MANAGEMENT*, 2001, 27 SEPTEMBER

The introduction of work–life balance policies at BT has reaped financial rewards and helped to improve staff loyalty, the telecoms group has revealed.

The company has enabled 4,000 employees to work from home since it introduced the policy in the 1980s. This has released £220 million of the group's real estate.

BT's homeworkers are supported by the company, which supplies them with the necessary furniture and IT equipment to work from home. Staff are also given mailbox addresses to protect their identities.

The company decided to widen its work–life balance policies in 1998, when the results of a staff survey revealed that 62 percent of its managers said their lives were skewed in favour of work. In addition, a third of that group said that they would not be prepared to accept promotion or greater responsibility because of the possible effect on their domestic lives.

> **'... you don't have to be bureaucratic to offer flexible working options.'**

The HR team decided to give staff the chance to arrange their own working patterns by piloting a year-long 'Freedom to work' programme in Cardiff. Eighteen employees in the software department were given the chance to decide their own working hours. The only stipulation was that business objectives had to be fulfilled.

'We sent questionnaires to the participants after the trial to test the success of the initiative,' Caroline Waters, director of employment policy, told *People Management*. 'We found that productivity had improved within the team and absenteeism had been reduced.'

The company then decided to roll out the initiative to 8,000 employees in the following year.

'This taught us that you don't have to be bureaucratic to offer flexible working options,' Waters said. 'One of the fears was that flexible working would lead to increased costs and bureaucracy, but this didn't happen'.

These forms of flexibility may well continue to develop as a feature of the general move towards e-commerce. In terms of the overall impact on business performance and the motivation and morale of people, there is, however, still very little evidence, and what evidence there is tends to reinforce the view that the strategic intention to engage in particular activities will have a crucial impact on HRP processes and the outcomes achieved from people. One view of the growth of call centres is, for example, that they provide an opportunity for job intensification. Thus, managers can tightly monitor and control staff performance (Stredwick & Ellis, 1998). One consequence of this is high rates of absenteeism and turnover, terms such as 'sweat shop' and 'slave labour' frequently being applied.

HRM WEB LINKS

Go to www.flexiblity.co.uk/flexwork/L_ecatt.htm, a site that provides the latest figures on the pattern of teleworking throughout Europe. www.tca.org.uk is the home page of the Telework Assocation; this provides advice to workers and managers, and includes an online magazine, job information and a teleworking handbook. Go also to www.successunlimited.co.uk/related/callcntr.htm, which examines the problem of bullying in call centres.

More generally, attempts to create the flexible job by removing demarcations and boundaries between areas of work can often mean a loss of valued features of work such as control over the pace of work. Furthermore, extending responsibilities within a job, but removing the prospects of promotion, often as a result of a flattened hierarchy, can easily engender feelings of job insecurity (Burchell et al., 1999). With a growing number of temporary and fixed-term contract workers, there has been some interest in the effect of employment status on motivation and commitment to work.

REFLECTIVE QUESTION

What do you think would be the effect of being given a fixed-term contract? How would it impact on your motivation and satisfaction at work?

Research by Guest et al. (1998) into the views of workers in a variety of different settings found that people on fixed-term contracts generally had a positive psychological contract. Reasons given for this was that employees on fixed contracts had more focused work to complete and did not have to engage in organizational politics or complete administrative duties. They might also face lower work demands than permanent staff, avoiding stress and taking less work home! Such employees perhaps benefit from a better work–life balance (Hogarth et al., 2001).

The work by Guest et al. (1998) highlights the key significance of the psychological contract, one of the most important findings beings that, irrespective of employment contract, the use of 'progressive' HR practices in combination with an opportunity to innovate within a role resulted in a positive psychological contract, with a positive outcome in terms of organizational commitment and motivation. The overall findings reinforce the view that, in planning to become more flexible, organizations are faced with a choice. Taking an ad hoc approach that is nevertheless driven by cost reduction associated with 'low road' HRM (see above) may produce improved short-term financial results but is likely to have a negative impact on motivation, innovation and commitment. Although the use of temporary and fixed-term contracts may have positive results in some contexts, a consistent finding in the research is, however, that 'high road' HR practices lead to a positive psychological contract and organizational outcomes. Organizations may be tempted by the 'wrong sort of flexibility' (Michie & Sheehan-Quinn, 2001, p. 302) which does not improve productivity or competitiveness. Sadly, it would seem that many organizations in the UK have given in to such a temptation.

Indeed, drawing on an in-depth survey of the attitudes of nearly 2500 employed people towards their jobs and life at work, Taylor (2002, p. 7) suggested that a significant degree of 'hyperbole' surrounded claims about flexibility and dynamic labour markets, with little evidence of a 'coherent human resource management agenda'. A key finding was that employees were less satisfied with their work and the number of hours worked. This finding applied to all levels of employee, including higher level professionals and managers as well as semi-skilled and unskilled manual workers. According to Taylor, 'The disgruntled manager has joined the disgruntled manual worker' in complaints about 'the long hours culture' (2002, p. 10). In addition, there were trends of a decline in organizational commitment and a sense of obligation to the firms that employed them. The survey casts doubts on many of the claims regarding flexible working in the UK. It was, for example, found that 92% of employees were permanently employed (rather than working part time or on temporary contracts), usually in a specific workplace (rather than home- or teleworking) and that there had been very little change in job tenure.

● Career management

One area of HRP that needs to be examined in the light of changes in the workplace is that of career management and development. In the past, the term 'career' was one that was usually applied to managerial and professional workers. Many organizations responded to the career aspirations of such employees through HRP policies and processes such as succession planning, secondment, 'fast-track' development for identified 'high-flyers' and a vast array of personal and management development activities. While organizations were structured into a number of hierarchical levels and grades, such employees could look forward to a path of promotion that signified the development of their careers. Along the way, of course, many employees encountered blocks to their careers, such as a lack of opportunities and support, and, for women, cultural and structural prejudices to career progress referred to as the 'glass ceiling' (Davidson & Cooper, 1992). Graduates too might find their aspirations unsatisfied as they experienced a gap between what they expected and what their organizations provided (Pickard, 1997). For many employees, however, it was indeed possible to embrace the idea of an organizational career that could be planned for the course of a working life, and theoretical models supported a view that careers could be planned and managed (Grzeda, 1999).

During the 1980s, with the growing influence of ideas relating to people-orientated HRM, many organizations began to see career development for a wider range of employees, the term 'career' being extended to apply not only to a movement through predefined stages such as those found in professional or organizational hierarchies, but also to personal growth and development through employees' interaction with their work environment. This view matched Hirsh's (1990, p. 18) 'developing potential' emergent model of succession planning in which, 'in a person based approach, posts can be considered as ephemeral and may be designed around people'. Furthermore, the responsibility for career management lay with the organization, to 'design and implement processes' that would 'optimize' organizational needs and individual preferences and abilities (Mayo, 1991, p. 69). Verlander (1985), for example, proposed a model of career management based on career counselling between employees and their line managers with support from the HR development department through training and coaching.

Through the 1990s and into the 2000s, there have been significant changes in the way in which careers are explained, understood and managed. Various tensions, such as competition, recession and short-term financial pressures, a breakdown in functional structures in favour of process structures and even the loss of bureaucratic personnel systems that planned career moves, have combined, in some companies, to 'dump the basic idea of the corporate career' (Hirsh & Jackson, 1997, p. 9), although many employees may still regard their job as a career step (Taylor, 2002).

Adamson et al. (1998) suggest there have been three changes in organizational career philosophy:

- an end to the long-term view of employer–employee relationship
- an end to hierarchical movement as being career progression
- an end to logical, ordered and sequential careers.

One of the manifestations of these changes is that fewer organizations would now claim to offer careers for life. If neither individuals nor organizations can plan for the long term, this suggests that the term 'career', with its implication of predictable progression, may have lost its commonly understood meaning. Arnold (1997, p. 16) provides a view of career in terms of how individuals view the world: a career is the 'sequence of employment-related positions, roles, activities and experiences encountered by a person'. Included in the sequence might be periods of leisure, education and domestic tasks. Over the course of a person's working life, an individual might expect to work for a variety of different organizations in a variety of positions, so each person will need a range of skills, learning new ones as required. This is referred to as the portfolio career (Templer & Cawsey, 1999). Another view, provided by Gibb (1998), is that careers and career development are better understood as chaotic systems, characterized by complexity and unpredictability.

Hirsh and Jackson (1997, p. 9) refer to a 'pendulum of ownership of career development', responsibility moving between the organization and the individual. Their case studies of UK organizations found that this pendulum had swung towards emphasizing individuals as driving the career and development processes, with the provision of career workshops, learning centres and personal development plans (Tamkin et al., 1995). At the same time, as many organizations began to engage in restructuring activities that led to 'delayering' and the removal of grades, the spread of career development initiatives could be seen as way of empowering and motivating staff who remained in place as part of a core workforce. Through HRP, an organization could aim to provide a framework for the integration of career management activities and processes. For many people, however, there has been a growing emphasis on accepting responsibility for their own career development through the skills of employability and lifelong learning (Verhaar & Smulders, 1999).

REFLECTIVE QUESTION

The notion of careers is subject to change and flux. Who do you think should be responsible for the development of people's working lives? How are you making yourself employable, and what are the skills of employability and lifelong learning?

Examine the HRM web link www.uea.ac.uk/ccen/employability/welcome.htm, a site typical of many university sites devoted to employability.

What seems to be emerging is a segmented pattern with a rhetoric of career development for everyone at work but with different patterns for different work groups:

- *Senior managers and 'high-potential' staff:* careers managed by the organization, not always for life, but with succession planning to fill senior positions
- *Highly skilled workers:* attempts to attract and keep key workers by offering career development paths
- *The wider workforce:* more limited development opportunities often caused by and resulting in uncertainty over career paths; there is an expectation that these workers should look after themselves.

It has been suggested that individuals and organizations can benefit from the development of career management skills. Ball (1997), for example, has provided such a model composed of four competencies[12] (Figure 6.4):

1. First is *optimizing the situation*, which involves creating circumstances to support career advances. This requires setting broad goals and anticipating future changes in organizations and one's life, as well as being in a position to respond. Within organizations, it involves spotting and using opportunities for development such as mentoring. Outside organizations, workers can build up a network that can provide them with assistance when required.
2. Second is the importance of the process of *career planning*. In the face of probable changes in work, individuals will need to learn how to review their skills and assess future learning requirements. This process will need to be completed several times throughout a working life.
3. By *engaging in personal development*, workers will become life-long learners. This aspect involves using development opportunities as they arise, crucial skills here being self-awareness (Stewart & Knowles, 1999) and a consideration of one's transferable skills. This will help in the identification of learning needs and in making plans to meet them.
4. Finally, there is the *balance between work and non-work*.

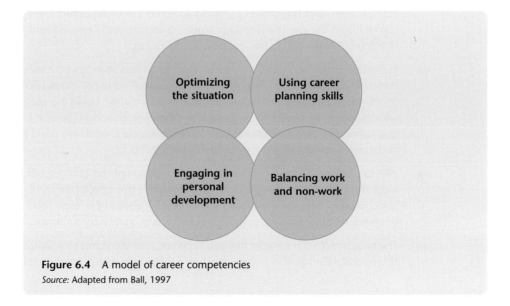

Figure 6.4 A model of career competencies
Source: Adapted from Ball, 1997

STUDY TIP

An important feature of HRP is that it can become both process and product orientated, embracing what Bardram (1997) refers to as the planning paradox. There is thus an acceptance that plans are fundamental in providing order and legitimacy to HR work, but they are not necessarily 'generative mechanisms' of the activities that occur. Instead, plans can be used 'to reflect on work, before or after' (Bardram, 1997, p. 2). Ongoing planning can occur in the course of the implementation of activities – referred to as situated planning – and this removes the false dichotomy between plan and action.

This view is a reflection of activity theory, one of a number of approaches to the consideration of action at work. Relationships between people and the activities in which they are engaged are set within an infrastructure that mediates what they do and how this is achieved. A key feature of this approach is the assumption of ongoing disturbances and inconsistencies that need to be dealt with. You can read more about the use of activity theory at www.edu.helsinki.fi/activity/. How could you use activity theory to study the planning paradox of HRP?

● Chapter summary

● This chapter has outlined the way in which early approaches to manpower planning were a response to the importance of business strategy and planning in order to ensure the availability of the necessary supply of people, in terms of both number and quality. A rationalized approach, based on the language of economics, was suggested, and the image of organizations as a series of stocks and flows allowed the application of advanced statistics in the construction of manpower models.

● This mechanistic approach, however, often missed the complexity of good manpower management, and manpower planning acquired a poor reputation, few benefits being claimed from the use of manpower planning techniques. There was also little evidence of a link between such plans and business planning.

● Personnel specialists were, however, able to utilize manpower measures of labour turnover, absenteeism and stability to diagnose and solve problems, increasingly aided by PC-based software packages. Manpower information could be used to initiate an understanding of problems such as low employee retention, with a follow-up using qualitative data before solutions were found. Manpower planning could play a vital role in the management of the employment relationship.

● HRP can be seen to be a continuation and extension of this process, which fully recognizes the potential of people and their needs in the development of strategies and plans. Studies have demonstrated the benefit of planning a 'high road' HRM strategy involving training, involvement, high rewards and quality commitment.

● The evidence of such benefits has not, however, convinced many organizations. We have shown that HRP has also become part of a rhetoric in which organizations have reconciled the dilemma of soft and hard versions of HRM. In many organizations, HRP uses sophisticated software packages to reduce the size of the workforce, or to 'downsize'.

- HRA has been advocated as presenting the value of people as assets, but there has been a lack of a valid and reliable model of measurement. Several organizations, especially in Sweden, have incorporated HRA methods into their management control processes, but research suggests some ambivalence of managers towards their use. Recent years have seen an attempt to value people as part of an organization's intellectual capital.

- HRP activities have recently been supported by HRIS, especially in transactions applications such as employment records, payroll and absence control. Such systems can also be provided over the Internet as a feature of e-HR. Through the use of ERP software, some organizations are attempting an integration of all information flows, but, as with all attempts to portray an organization through an information system, much depends on how the information is interpreted.

- In many organizations, the language of flexibility and a range of different practices have been employed, often without consideration for the effect on employment relations. There has been a growth in the number of part-time and homeworking employees, as well as in the outsourcing of services, but there is little evidence of the overall impact on business performance and people's motivation. Some research suggests growing job insecurity as valued features of work are lost, although other studies have found that a variation in contracts can be used to obtain a better work–life balance.

- Fewer organizations offer careers for life, and career planning has become more difficult. Each person will need a range of skills to develop a portfolio career, and there has been a growing emphasis on people accepting responsibility for developing their own careers and making themselves employable.

Key concepts

- Career management
- Core and peripheral workforces
- e-HR
- Employability
- Flexibility
- Human resource accounting
- Human resource planning (HRP)
- Labour market segmentation
- Manpower planning
- Planning techniques
- Teleworking
- The diagnostic approach

Chapter review questions

1. 'When an organization is mapping out its future needs, it is a serious mistake to think primarily in terms of number, flows and economic models.' Discuss.

2. How is HRP linked to corporate planning?

3. What would be your response to the publication of figures that showed an above-average turnover of students in a university/college department?

4. Should organizations faced with a shortage of skilled labour 'poach' these workers from other organizations by bidding up wages?

5. What is meant by the 'flexible firm'? Explain the implications of the flexible firm for the management of HR.

6. How can competencies help organizations to improve the management of careers in organizations?

Further reading

Hirsh, W., & Jackson, C. (1997). *Strategies for career development: Promise, practice and pretence*. Report No. 305. Brighton: Institute of Employment Studies.

Holbeche, L. (1998). *Aligning human resources and business strategy*. Oxford: Butterworth-Heinemann.

Liff, S. (2000). Manpower or human resource planning – what's in a name? In Stephen Bach & Keith Sisson (eds), *Personnel Management* (3rd edn), pp. 93–110. Oxford: Blackwell.

Mayo, A. (2001). *Human value of the enterprise: Valuing people as assets – monitoring, measuring, managing*. London: Nicholas Brealey.

Sennett, R. (1998). *The corrosion of character*. New York: Norton.

Stredwick, J., & Ellis, S. (1998). *Flexible working practices*. London: Institute of Personnel and Development.

Practising human resource management

Searching the web

Forming an HR plan requires a consideration of the requirements at both macro and micro levels. Although figures at the micro level will depend on the effectiveness of HRIS, you will at the macro level need a knowledge of figures and trends relating to different labour markets. Go to www.dfee.gov.uk/datasphere/, which links together three UK websites that hold information on HRP requirements at national, regional, local and sectoral levels. For the latest labour market trends, in the UK, go to www.statistics.gov.uk/statbase/Product.asp?vlnk=550&More=N. The UK government has also provided a site with information and research on the idea of work–life balance, see www.dti.gov.uk/work-lifebalance/. For HR stats elsewhere in the world: Europe (www.unece.org/stats/stats_h.htm), Australia (www.abs.gov.au), South Africa (www.statssa.gov.za) and USA (www.bls.gov)

HRM group activity

You have been requested to develop a plan for a call centre in the financial services industry that is seeking to move the work of employees to their homes; that is, they will become teleworkers at home.

- What are the HR implications of such a development?
- What difficulties might arise and how should they be overcome?

Try the following web links to begin your study: www.ukonlineforbusiness.gov.uk/advice/publications/teleworking/home.html, www.wfh.co.uk/wfh/index.htm and www.tca.org.uk.

CDX BANK

For many years, CDX Bank has been one of the UK's major clearing banks. Last year, following a period of intense negotiations amidst a realignment of global financial institutions, the board agreed to recommend a merger with the Singapore-based Eastern Banking Corporation (EBC). Essentially, the merger was a takeover of CDX by EBC, which was considered inevitable in light of the troubled position of CDX in global banking and declining profitability.

The troubles for CDX began in the early 1990s when the bank faced an environment that was increasingly competitive and fast moving. A series of bad financial decisions, combined with the need to reprocess operations, had led to declining profits and a growing crisis of confidence among shareholders, essentially the institutional investors and pension funds, who exerted pressure to maintain dividends. One result was a pressure on the cost base and a succession of voluntary and compulsory redundancy programmes. In 1992, there were 45,000 employees, but after 'downsizing', there are now around 25,000 staff, over 80% of them employed in the UK.

In the weeks leading up to the merger, staff at CDX became increasingly concerned about their future. Apart from the expectation that a further round of redundancies would be initiated, it was becoming clear that the merger would involve a restructuring and redefinition of roles, including a flattening of the grading structure. Furthermore, redundancy was this time likely to involve compulsion only. Many employees saw that their careers would become very unsettled and/or would 'plateau'. There were a number of key employees in CDX who were vital to the success of the merger, but many of these employees were beginning to seek work elsewhere, usually with other financial institutions.

Employee representatives within CDX had already expressed their concerns about these fears and the lack of information emerging from management discussions – 'communications about what is happening is a black hole; there seems to be no plan at all'. They also reminded management of earlier difficulties with employee morale among those who had remained following previous rounds of redundancy.

Senior managers from CDX and EBC eventually felt they had to respond: they could not afford to lose key employees to the opposition, and they wanted to plan to manage the change so that full information could be provided and employees treated with 'honesty and respect', whatever their fate. Management also wanted to make sure that all actions were based on good principles of HRM. They turned to the HR team for advice.

Discussion questions

1. What advice would you provide to managers on the 'good principles of HRM' during a merger or takeover?

2. What are the key HR problems in 'downsizing', and how can these be managed to maintain employee morale?

3. What are the key career issues in CDX, and what advice can you provide to remove or ameliorate employee concerns?

HR-related skill development

It is becoming increasingly evident that many of us will need to learn the skills of career management.

● What does the term 'career' mean to you, and who is responsible for the development of your career?

● What skills will you need to manage your career?

● What issues does the model of career competencies raise for managing your career?

Try the web link: www.adm.uwaterloo.ca/infocecs/CRC/manual/introduction.html, an online career development manual.

Notes

1. A finding from research carried out for the Chartered Institute of Personnel and Development on HR and business performance. Quoted in Guest, D. (2000). Piece by piece. *People Management*, **6**(15), 26–30.
2. Buckingham, G. (2000). Same indifference. *People Management*, **6**(4), 44–6.
3. Sarah Ryle, *Observer*, 2002, 13 January.
4. The Institute of Manpower Studies is now known as the Institute of Employment Studies; check their website at www.employment-studies.co.uk/.
5. ACAS is a good source of information with online publications on recruitment and starting work, employment policies and practices, working together for success, communications in the workplace, employment rights, problems between individuals and employers, relations between employers and employee representatives, and codes of practice.
6. You may also find labour turnover analysis referred to as 'wastage analysis'. Consider the source of such language.
7. It is interesting to note that fears concerning the 'demographic time bomb' proved to be largely unfounded in the UK as a consequence of the recession in the first half of the 1990s. Some organizations clearly did make efforts to respond: some supermarket chains, for example, adopted a policy of recruiting older workers. For many organizations, however, there were a number of new issues that had manpower implications requiring a strategic response.
8. Read Richard Sennett's *The corrosion of character* (1998) for an extensive consideration of the debilitating effects of downsizing and job insecurity.
9. The concepts of validity and reliability will be explored in more detail in Chapter 7.
10. Intangible assets may also include such features as brand names as well as knowledge and understanding. You may wish to consult Lev Baruch's home page at www.pages.stern.nyu.edu/~blev/ for details of how to measure intangible assets.
11. Further details can be found at www.skandia.com/en/sustainability/intellectualcapital.shtml.
12. Competencies will be explored further in Chapter 8.

Chapter seven

Recruitment and selection

Jeffrey Gold

Recruitment is the process of generating a pool of capable people to apply for employment to an organization. *Selection* is the process by which managers and others use specific instruments to choose from a pool of applicants a person or persons most likely to succeed in the job(s), given management goals and legal requirements.

'They do psychometric testing. I got in before all that mumbo-jumbo.'[1]

'HR Directors are largely dissatisfied with the quality of their employees ... they would re-hire less than 60% of current employees.'[2]

'Testing is a human interaction, and if you take this element away you'll soon lose the real customers: the candidates themselves.'[3]

Chapter outline

Chapter objectives

After studying this chapter, you should be able to:

1. Understand the place of recruitment and selection as a stage in the formation of the employment relationship
2. Understand the key legal requirements relating to recruitment and selection
3. Explain the nature of attraction in recruitment
4. Explain the effectiveness of the selection interview
5. Understand the value of psychometric testing

● Introduction

Recruitment and selection have always been critical processes for organizations. In recent years, there has been growing evidence that the formation of a positive psychological contract with employees provides the basis for a positive outcome in terms of organizational commitment and motivation (Guest et al., 1998). Recruitment and subsequent selection are vital stages in the formation of the expectations that form such a contract, on which, with an emphasis on a two-way flow of communication, employees select an organization and the work on offer as much as employers select employees. Thus, employers need to see the attraction and retention of employees as part of the evolving employment relationship, based on a mutual and reciprocal understanding of expectations, as well as an attempt to predict how a potential employee might behave in the future and make a contribution to the organization's requirements (Newell & Shackleton, 2000). Many approaches to recruitment and selection tend, however, to emphasize the power of employers. For example, traditional approaches attempt to attract a wide choice of candidates for vacancies before screening out those who do not match the criteria set in job descriptions and

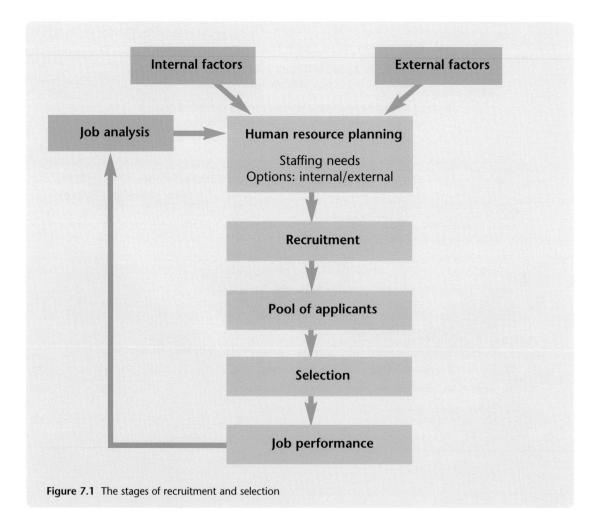

Figure 7.1 The stages of recruitment and selection

personnel specifications. Figure 7.1 shows an overall view of the stages of recruitment and selection, and the connection of these processes to human resource planning.

In the late 1980s and early 1990s, external factors such as skills shortages and the prospect of a significant decline in the number of young people (the so-called 'demographic time bomb') seemed to shift power to those with the skills to sell, and many organizations required a 'radical response' (Herriot, 1989, p. 35). Organizations were thus compelled to see the attraction and retention of employees as part of an evolving employment relationship, based on a mutual and reciprocal understanding of expectations. For a short time at least, a number of organizations did react to the impending shortages by adjusting and widening their recruitment criteria in order to increase the number of recruits. Many of the changes adopted could, however, be seen as tactical adjustments, most organizations being driven by the need to reduce costs and fill posts quickly and cheaply.

There are now wide variations in recruitment and selection practices, reflecting an organization's strategy and its philosophy towards the management of people. Employees seen as part of the *primary internal market* (Chapter 6) become the focus for the 'bundle' of human resources (HR) practices (Cooke, 2000) intended to bring about increased motivation, an increased acceptance of responsibility, deepened skills and greater commitment, providing the organization with a competitive edge. Such employees become part of an organization's core workforce, recruitment and selection representing the entry point activities. Seen in this way, emphasis may be placed on admitting only those applicants who are likely to behave, acquire skills and show 'attitudinal commitment' (Guest, 1989, p. 49) in line with the requirements of an organization's strategy. As we will explore below, many organizations have developed competency frameworks and used them to specify the skills and qualities required of potential employees (Roberts, 1997). Such frameworks have allowed organizations to adopt a range of sophisticated recruitment and selection techniques in order to identify and admit the 'right' people. In this way, as 'organizationally defined critical qualities' (Iles & Salaman, 1995, p. 204), a competency framework augments an organization's power. Once selected, employees may be able to progress and develop a career within that organization.

Approaches to the recruitment and selection of employees forming the *secondary internal market* could be subject to less screening at the point of entry, attention being paid mainly to possession of the required skills. Such employees might be recruited and selected by cheaper methods but still, perhaps, with a connection to organizational strategy via the specification of competencies. Given the findings relating to studies of workers on fixed-term contracts (Guest, 1998) and the emphasis given by some workers to work–life balance (Hogarth et al., 2001), it would seem, however, that the crucial feature of a positive psychological contract is the use of progressive HR practices whatever the employment contract, and this will include attention to effective recruitment and selection practices. Once again, employers do have a choice relating to the practices they adopt.

REFLECTIVE QUESTION

How would an employer prove to you that it was seeking a to develop a positive psychological contract? Go to the BP Career Centre at www.bpfutures.com/. Is BP a progressive human resource management (HRM) employer?

Variations in recruitment and selection practice are bound by the law of the land. Recruitment and selection have been notorious areas for demonstrating prejudice and subjective influence, which could well result in infringements under legislation dealing with discrimination. In the UK, the key legal provisions are contained in the Sex Discrimination Act 1975 (amended in 1986) and the Race Relations Act 1976 (amended in 2000), both acts disallowing discrimination. In general, there are three forms of discrimination that are against the law:

1. *Direct:* in which workers of a particular sex, race or ethnic group are treated less favourably than other workers, for example in a policy to recruit only men to management posts.
2. *Indirect:* in which a particular requirement apparently treats everyone equally but has a disproportionate effect on a particular group, the requirement not being shown to be justified. A job advert specifying that applicants should be 1.85 m tall might, for example, unjustifiably result in a low proportion of female applicants.
3. *Victimization:* in which individuals are discriminated against because they have exercised their rights under the law.

Since 1995, discrimination against part-time employees can be seen as indirect discrimination against women under the Sex Discrimination Act because most part-time employees are women. The Act is supported by the Equal Pay Act 1970, which sought to eliminate discrimination in pay between men and women. In 1983, this Act was amended to include work 'of equal value'. Under the Act, individuals can claim pay equal to that of a member of the opposite sex when they are doing:

- like work
- work rated as equivalent under a job evaluation scheme
- work of equal value, in terms of demands made under such headings as effort, skill and decision-making.

In certain circumstances, both the Sex Discrimination Act and the Race Relations Act allow for discrimination on grounds of genuine occupational qualification for a job. Under Section 7(2) of the Sex Discrimination Act, for example, it is possible to recruit a man only when:

> the essential nature of the job calls for a man for reasons of physiology (excluding physical strength or stamina) or, in dramatic performances or other entertainment, for reasons of authenticity, so that the essential nature of the job would be materially different if carried out by a woman.

In general, personnel departments have played a key role in bringing organizational practices relating to recruitment and selection in line with the provisions of the law, although indirect discrimination is more difficult to uncover and eliminate. One obvious process, allowed under the law, is to monitor employees' sex and ethnic origins in order to identify possible forms of hidden discrimination within procedures.

In addition to the above Acts, the Disability Discrimination Act 1996 makes it illegal to discriminate against disabled persons unless discrimination can be justified by the 'circumstances of the particular case'. The Act requires organizations employing more than 20 people to remove or make 'reasonable' adjustments to working conditions and procedures, that might disadvantage disabled persons, for example selection tests, working hours, the physical features of the premises and special equipment. The Act also widens the definition of disabled persons to include those registered as disabled and those discriminated against because of 'severe' disfigurements such as scars, skin disease and progressive conditions such as HIV and multiple sclerosis.

HRM WEB LINKS

A copy of the Disability Discrimination Act can be found at www.legislation.hmso. gov.uk/acts/acts1995/95050—b.htm. Visit also the disability page at www.disability. gov.uk/law.html.

In recent years, UK legislation has had to respond to directives from the European Union. Under the 1998 Data Protection Act, for example, individuals are allowed access to 'specified' information about them to ensure its accuracy. This will affect application forms and questions that can be asked relating to personal and health information. The Human Rights Act was incorporated into UK law on 1 October 2000 to implement the European Convention on Human Rights in the UK. Although it is not entirely certain what the impact of this Act will be, a person is guaranteed a right to privacy relating to family, beliefs and freedom of expression. Recruiters may thus need to avoid questions about sexual orientation, marital status or age unless these are relevant to the job.

The antidiscrimination legislation over the past 25 years provides the foundation for a growing interest in diversity at work, which, according to Schneider (2001, p. 27) is 'about creating a working culture that seeks, respects, values and harnesses difference'. It is suggested that diversity can provide an organization with a valuable resource in competing both globally and locally (HRM in practice 7.1).

HRM IN PRACTICE 7.1

SHELL LAUNCHES DIVERSITY SCHEME

KAREN HIGGINBOTTOM, *PEOPLE MANAGEMENT*, 2002, MARCH 7

Oil giant Shell is introducing a global diversity and inclusiveness standard in a bid to attract the best talent from around the world.

Under the standard, all areas of the company will be expected to report annually on diversity. This will involve the chair for each country that Shell operates in detailing how they will meet diversity targets. These findings will then be presented to Shell's committee of managing directors.

'The country chair will play an active part in ensuring that diversity action plans have meaning in the context of each country's legislation and culture. We have an interest in attracting the brightest talent and understanding our customer market better,' said Lesley Mays, Shell's head of diversity.

As part of its diversity targets, the company has identified a number of ways to measure progress within the organisation.

These include building a stronger talent 'pipeline' for local inhabitants and ensuring by 2003 that every country chair was filled by someone from that labour pool. It also plans to boost representation of women by having 20 per cent of senior executive posts filled with female staff by 2008.

'You have to look at the labour pools from around the world. We don't want to cut ourselves off from half of it,' Mays explained.

Shell expects to publish the results of its annual assurance plan by the end of the year. The report will outline the activities, plans and targets for each country.

HRM WEB LINKS

In the UK, you can find full details of antidiscrimination legislation, guidance, codes of practice and latest developments at the Commission for Racial Equality (www.cre.gov.uk/), the Equal Opportunities Commission (www.eoc.org.uk/) and the Disability Rights Commission (www.drc-gb.org/drc/default.asp). To find out about the latest developments in legislation, check *People Management*'s web pages at www.peoplemanagement.co.uk/law_home.asp.

In Canada, you can find details of human rights legislation, recent reports, guides and other material at the Canada Human Rights Commission site (www.chrc-ccdp.ca/). You can also obtain a copy of the *Guide to Screening and Selection in Employment* from here. Other human rights resources include the Canadian Human Rights Reporter (www.cdn-hr-reporter.ca/) and the Human Rights Research and Education Centre (Ottawa) (www.uottawa.ca/hrrec/). For sites in Australia, South Africa, Europe and the United Nations see p. xxii of this book.

Recruitment and attraction

If the HRM 'high road' (Chapter 6) is concerned with the development of an integrated 'bundle' of policies related to the management of people, recruitment and attraction represent vital stages in the determination of which employees will be able to benefit from such policies. Newell and Shackleton (2000, p. 113) refer to recruitment as the 'process of attracting people who might make a contribution to the particular organization'. Within this definition, we can highlight two crucial issues. First, there is a need to attract people, this implying that people *do* have a choice about which organizations they wish to work for. Second, the contribution that people will make to an organization is not totally predictable. Employees will potentially attempt to retain significant discretion with respect to the effort they are prepared to make and their commitment to the organization. Management will of course seek to influence this process to the advantage of the organization (Watson, 1994), but other parties involved may have different interests. Under different labour market conditions, power in this process will swing towards the buyers or sellers of labour – employers and employees respectively. It is therefore important to understand that the dimension of power will always be present in recruitment and selection, even in organizations that purport to have a 'soft' HRM orientation.

As the UK population becomes older, for example, many organizations will need to consider recruiting older employees and adjusting their policies towards them (Lyon & Glover, 1998). In addition, since the early 1990s, there have been more graduates entering the labour market, but the number of 'graduate' jobs has not kept pace, with a consequent reduction in the power of many new graduates to find employment on advantageous terms (Institute of Personnel and Development, 1997). It is also reported that many employers have reservations about employing graduates for 'non-graduate' jobs. Stewart and Knowles (2000) suggest, however, that small and medium enterprises are becoming a key source of graduate recruitment, and indeed such firms, which also have less formal and less bureaucratic recruitment practices (Barber et al., 1999), may be becoming more attractive to graduates.

Much will depend on the extent to which the overall management philosophy supports and reinforces an approach to HRM that focuses on the utilization and/or development of new employees once they have gained entry to an organization. Whereas HR policies will be designed to achieve particular organizational targets and goals, those policies will also provide an opportunity for individual needs to emerge and be satisfied. This view assumes that organizational targets and goals and individual needs can coincide, with mutual benefits to both sides of the employment relationship. Although many commentators would doubt that such mutuality could ever occur on the basis of equality, and that organizational needs, as determined by senior management, would always take precedence, we have already argued that, individual needs may, through HRM activities, influence the perception of the organization's needs. Recruitment and then selection processes will therefore aim to attract and admit those whom management view as the 'right' people for such an approach. But who are the 'right' people, and what do organizations expect of them?

One answer to these questions is based on organizations taking a strategic view of their recruitment requirements, the strategic plan representing the starting point. Research by Tyson (1995, p. 82) found that although there were many differences between organizations, HRM could help to shape the direction of change, influence culture and 'help bring about the mind set' that decided which strategic issues were considered. HR considerations, including the results of a review of the quantity and quality of people, should thus be integrated into the plan (Chapter 6). The goals, objectives and targets that emerge set the parameters for performance in an organization and for how work is organized into roles and jobs. A key role for HR is to align performance within roles with the strategy, so recruiting the 'right' people for a role depends on how it is defined in terms relating to performance to achieve the strategy (Holbeche, 1999). Such issues have traditionally been settled by the use of job analysis techniques, including a range of interviews, questionnaires and observation processes that provide information about work carried out, the environment in which it occurs and, vitally, the knowledge, skills and attitudes needed to perform well.

In recent years, information derived from the analysis of work performance has been utilized to create a taxonomy of either criterion-related behaviours or standards of performance referred to as competencies. Woodruffe (1992, p. 17) has defined competency as 'the set of behaviour patterns that the incumbent needs to bring to a position in order to perform its tasks and functions with competence'.[4] Competency frameworks are concerned with behaviour that is relevant to the job and the effective or competent performance of that job. Such frameworks are usually developed within organizations and are based on the understandings and meanings of behaviour that exist within an organization. According to research evidence (Coverdale Ltd, 1995), competency frameworks have a wide range of applications, including a more structured approach to training and development (Chapter 10), managing performance (Chapter 8) and the provision of a benchmark for rewards and promotion. It is claimed that competency frameworks 'lie at the heart of all' approaches to HRM (Boam & Sparrow, 1992, p. 13).

HRM WEB LINKS

SHL is one of the main suppliers of job assessment software that can be used to develop competencies. Details of their work profiling system (WPS) can be found at www.shlusa.com/selection/sel_workprofilingsys.html. They also provide a useful book on job analysis techniques at: www.shlgroup.com/uk/litigation/BestPractice/BestPractice_JobAnalysis.pdf.

Here is how a large financial services organization in the UK sets out its competencies:

- Self-control
- Self-development
- Personal organization
- Positive approach
- Delivering results
- Providing solutions
- Systemic thinking
- Attention to detail
- Creating customer service
- Delivering customer service
- Continuous improvement
- Developing people
- Working with others
- Influencing
- Leading
- Delivering the vision
- Change and creativity.

Each competency is defined and described by a range of indicators that enables assessment and measurement. The competency of 'creating customer service' is, for example, indicated by:

- anticipating emerging customer needs and planning accordingly
- identifying the customers who will be of value to the company
- recommending changes to current ways of working that will improve customer service
- arranging the collection of customer satisfaction data and acting on them.

The analysis and definition of competencies should allow the identification and isolation of dimensions of behaviour that are distinct and are associated with competent or effective performance. Competencies can therefore be used to provide, at least from an organization's point of view, the behaviours needed at work to achieve the business strategy. On this assumption, the assessment of competencies is one means of selecting employees, as will be discussed below. Competencies will enable organizations to form a model of the kinds of employee it wishes to attract through recruitment.

Whatever the model constructed, an organization's commitment to its HR processes will form part of its evolving value system and make it even more attractive to those seeking employment. Research into the success of Hewlett-Packard since 1992 (Gratton, 1997, p. 23) found, for example, the following features, which formed 'The HP Way':

> Values that place concern and respect for the individual at the centre
> A performance management process that links strategic and individual objectives
> Embedded people processes treated as important
> Measurement of people's needs, aspirations and commitment
> Management sensitivity to feelings of employees about their work

The HP Way is clearly designed to bring about increased motivation, an increased acceptance of responsibility, deepened skills and greater commitment from workers already employed within the organization. The research reported that 80 per cent of staff believed that they put in a great deal of effort and that the company had integrity. Although the main beneficiaries of the evolving philosophy will be those already employed, the enhanced focus on people will also increase the attraction of the organization among those external to the organization and form part of the image projected.

Projected images, values and information on espoused goals will interact with workers in the external labour markets, including both those employed and those unemployed. This interaction will determine the degree of attraction that potential recruits feel towards an organization.

REFLECTIVE QUESTION

Think about an organization you would like to work for. What images, values and information related to that organization come into your mind?

The image projected by an organization and the response from potential employees provide the basis for a compatible person–organization fit. Schneider (1987, p. 437), using a theory of interactional psychology, proposed an attraction–selection–attrition framework to explain the workings of this process and differences between organizations that are caused by the attraction of people to organizational goals, their interaction with the goals and the fact that 'if they don't fit, they leave'. The proposed framework is shown in Figure 7.2. Schneider uses the findings from vocational psychology to argue that people are attracted to an organization on the basis of their own interests and personality. Thus, people of a similar type will be attracted to the same place. Furthermore, the attraction of similar types will begin to determine the place. Following selection, people who do not fit, because of either error or a misunderstanding of the reality of an organization, will leave, resulting in an attrition from that organization.

At the heart of the framework lie organizational goals, originally stated by the founder and/or articulated by top managers, out of which emerge the structures and

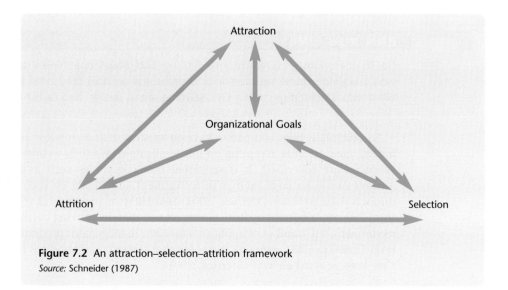

Figure 7.2 An attraction–selection–attrition framework
Source: Schneider (1987)

processes that will form the basis of attraction decisions. This framework has been supported by research conducted by Judge and Cable (1997), who found that job-seekers attempt to match their values with the reputation of an organization's culture. Furthermore, person–organization fit can be enhanced by an attention to socialization processes once new employees have been selected (Cable & Parsons, 2001).

The main approaches to attracting applicants can be summarized as follows:

- walk-ins
- employee referrals
- advertising
- websites
- professional associations
- educational associations
- professional agencies.

Advertising and other recruitment literature comprise a common means by which values, ethos and the desired image are made manifest, usually in the form of glossy brochures that are often aimed at graduates. In recent years, the undoubted expertise that exists within the UK advertising industry has been utilized in company recruitment. The utilitarian approach that focused on specifying job details, terms and conditions is increasingly being superseded by advertising that attempts to communicate a message about the company image. There has been a marked shift towards recruitment advertisements that are creative and reflect the skills normally used in product marketing. Recruitment advertising is now fully established within mainstream advertising.

In recent years, there has been a rapid growth in online recruitment, e-recruitment having become another facet of the rapid progression of e-HRM. Like many aspects of the dot.com revolution, e-recruitment has of course been subjected to rapid change with the arrival and departure of companies specializing in recruitment on the web. There are two types of operator on-line. First, there are general recruitment agents such as Monster and and StepStone. It is reported that there are over 300 on-line recruitment providers in the UK and 1400 across Europe, although such figures can never be certain in the flux and change of the dot.com world (Taylor, 2001).

HRM WEB LINKS

Go to the Monster (www.monster.co.uk) and StepStone (www.stepstone.com/workthing/index.htm) websites and examine the services they offer to job-seekers. What help is offered regarding CVs, learning about salaries and career development?

Second, many large companies have established their own websites for recruitment; indeed, most are only accepting on-line applications via their websites, where all their vacancies are advertised. It is suggested that companies such as BBC and British Airways can make large savings in recruitment advertising by such communication through their websites (Merrick, 2001) (see HRM in practice 7.2 for an example of this). One result noticed by British Airways was that, by moving to Internet and e-mail recruitment, the number of applicants for their management programme was reduced from 12,000 to 5000, although it was felt that the switch filtered out many who would have been rejected anyway (Merrick, 2001).

HRM IN PRACTICE 7.2

UNITED BISCUITS TO HALVE COSTS BY RECRUITING ONLINE

ZOË ROBERTS, *PEOPLE MANAGEMENT*, 2001, AUGUST 30

United Biscuits is to launch UBCareers.com – a comprehensive recruitment site expected to cut the company's resourcing costs by half. The company has already reduced the costs of its graduate recruitment process by 85 per cent after transferring it online two years ago.

'Between 1998 and 1999 we distributed 40,000 brochures, received about 4,000 applications and fielded hundreds of phone calls for a small number of graduate places,' said Aileen Roberts, development manager of organisational change at United Biscuits. 'With the launch of UBGraduate.com we

> **The company has already reduced the costs of its graduate recruitment process by 85 per cent after transferring it online two years ago.**

cut the number of final applications by 40 per cent through pre-screening. As all correspondence was done online, administrative work was reduced too.'

Expectations are high for UBCareers.com – which will go live next month. The firm predicts that implementation costs will be recouped 'in 10 hires'. Roberts says that to achieve the savings expected, the new system must be integrated into the wider decision-making process.

'To go online doesn't mean you have to do everything on the web,' she said. 'We will still use traditional media for many areas of recruitment. You need to mix and match your message in order to be competitive.'

REFLECTIVE QUESTION

Go to either the British Airways website at www.britishairwaysjobs.com/index.jsp or that of Merrill Lynch, an investment company, at www.ml.com. How do you think these websites filter out those who do and do not wish to work for British Airways or Merrill Lynch? Did you take the interactive challenges? Does on-line recruitment increase the power of employers in the graduate labour market?

Images presented in recruitment advertisements and brochures, as well as on-line, will form only part of the attraction. There is not a great deal of evidence that it is entirely effective; informal 'word-of-mouth' information about jobs is often more accurate and effective (Iles & Salaman, 1995). In any case, formal advertising can be expensive, and an organization will take account of a number of other factors in forming its recruitment plans and choice of media. These might include the following:

- the cost
- the time taken to recruit and select
- the labour market focus, for example skills, profession or occupation
- mobility of labour – geographic and occupational
- legislation on sex discrimination, race discrimination and disability.

A further manifestation of the image to which recruits will be attracted is a description of the actual work that potential employees will be required to do. The traditional way of providing such information is in the form of a job description, usually derived

```
                    JOB DESCRIPTION

                        Job title

                       Department

                     Responsible to:

                      Relationships

              Purpose of job/overall objectives

             Specific duties and responsibilities

                Physical/economic conditions
```

Figure 7.3 Job description format

from job analysis and describing the tasks and responsibilities that make up the job. Against each job description, there is normally a specification of the standards of performance. A typical format for a job description is given in Figure 7.3.

In addition to a description of a job, there is, in the form of a personnel specification, some attempt to profile the 'ideal' person to fill the job. It is accepted that the ideal person for the job may not actually exist and that the specification will be used only as a framework within which a number of candidates can be assessed. A common format for a personnel specification is the seven-point plan, based on the work of Rodger (1970), shown in Figure 7.4. An alternative to the seven-point plan is Munro-Fraser's five-fold grading system (1971), as in Figure 7.5. In both forms of personnel specification, it is usual to indicate the importance of different requirements. Thus, certain requirements might be expressed as essential and others as desirable.

Both job descriptions and personnel specifications have been key elements in the traditional repertoire of personnel managers. Over the years, various attempts have

```
                 PERSONNEL SPECIFICATION

                  Physical characteristics

                       Attainments

                   General intelligence

                    Specific aptitudes

                        Interests

                       Disposition

                      Circumstances
```

Figure 7.4 Seven-point plan

PERSONNEL SPECIFICATION

Impact on other people

Qualification and experience

Innate abilities

Motivation

Adjustment

Figure 7.5 Five-fold grading system

been made to develop and fine-tune techniques and practices. One such development has been the shift of emphasis in job descriptions away from specifying tasks and responsibilities towards the results to be achieved (Plachy, 1987). There has, however, been a growing awareness of the limitations and problems of such approaches. Watson (1994) noted that job analysis, used to produce job descriptions and personnel specifications, relied too much on the subjective judgement of the analyst to identify the key aspects of a job and derive the qualities that related to successful performance. In addition, the use of frameworks such as the seven-point plan may provide a 'cloak for improper discrimination' (Watson, 1994, p. 189).

The drive towards flexibility and changing work practices has seen the appearance of new forms of work description. Some organizations have, for example, begun to replace or complement job descriptions with *performance contracts*. These contain details of what a job-holder agrees to accomplish over a period of time, summarizing the purpose of a job, how that purpose will be met over the time specified and how the achievement of objectives will be assessed. This approach allows job requirements to be adjusted by agreement between the job-holder and his or her manager. It also allows a clear link to be established with other HR processes. Performance contracts signal to new recruits the expectation that their jobs will change and that they cannot rely on a job description as the definitive account of their work.

Competencies are, as we have already discussed, increasingly used to create a specification of the characteristics of those sought for particular positions (Roberts, 1997). It has been argued (Feltham, 1992) that the use of competencies allows organizations to free themselves from traditional stereotypes in order to attract applicants from a variety of sources. Stereotypes of the 'ideal' person may be contained within personnel specifications, and organizations may, despite warnings, be reinforcing the stereotype in their recruitment practices. Competencies appear to be more objective, have a variety of uses in attracting applicants and allow an organization to use more reliable and valid selection techniques.

The test of success of a recruitment process is whether it attracts a sufficient number of applicants of the desired quality within the budget set. Recruiters might reasonably expect a number of applicants per position available, referred to as the recruitment ratio, thus allowing a choice to be made. Changes to the recruitment process may affect this ratio. For example, as we have indicated above, e-recruitment via the

Internet may reduce the quantity, but not necessarily the quality, of applicants. Too many applicants may reduce the cost per applicant but add further costs in terms of the time taken to screen the applications. Too few applicants may be an indication of a tight labour market but may also be an indication that the values, ethos and image projected by the organization on to the market including information on the work, as provided by job descriptions and specifications, are poor attractors. Recruiters need to monitor the effect of such factors on the recruitment process. If there are insufficient applicants from particular ethnic groups or too few males or females, the recruitment process may indirectly discriminate and/or fail to meet legal requirements.

● Selection

As we have seen, it is usual for an organization that wishes to recruit new employees to define criteria against which it can measure and assess applicants. Increasingly, however, such criteria are set in the form of competencies composed of behavioural characteristics and attitudes, which cannot easily be measured. Rather than trust to luck, organizations are using more 'sophisticated' selection techniques. Organizations have become increasingly aware of making good selection decisions, since selection involves a number of costs:

- the cost of the selection process itself, including the use of various selection instruments
- the future costs of inducting and training new staff
- the cost of labour turnover if the selected staff are not retained.

It is also crucial to remember that decisions are being made by both employers and potential employees and that the establishment of mutually agreed expectations during selection forms part of a psychological contract (Chapter 1), which will strongly influence an employee's attitudes and feelings towards the organization (Herriot et al., 1997).

Underlying the process of selection and the choice of techniques are two key principles:

1. *Individual differences:* Attracting a wide choice of applicants will be of little use unless there is a way of measuring how people differ. People can vary in many ways, for example intelligence, attitudes, social skills, psychological and physical characteristics, experience and so on.
2. *Prediction:* A recognition of the way in which people differ must be extended to a prediction of performance in the workplace.

Selection techniques will, to a varying degree, meet these principles of measuring differences and predicting performance. Organizations may increasingly use a variety of techniques, and statistical theory is used to give credibility to techniques that attempt to measure people's attitudes, attributes, abilities and overall personality.

Some commentators would suggest that this credibility is 'pseudo-scientific' and that many limitations remain with selection techniques. Iles and Salaman (1995), for example, claim that this 'psychometric' model appears to value:

- *individualism:* in which individual characteristics are claimed to predict future performance

- *managerialism:* in which top managers define the criteria for performance
- *utility:* in which the costs and benefits, in money terms, of using different selection techniques are assessed.

REFLECTIVE QUESTION

What do you think are the implications and difficulties associated with individualist, managerialist and utilitarian values in selection?

We are reminded once again that power is an important consideration in decision-making on the employment of people. Selection instruments have an image of neutrality and objectivity, but the criteria built into such instruments, which allow the selection and rejection of applicants, make up a knowledge base that provides the organization and its agents with power.

Reliability and validity issues

Two statistical concepts – reliability and validity – are of particular importance in selection.

Reliability refers to the extent to which a selection technique achieves consistency in what it is measuring over repeated use. If, for example, you were being interviewed by two managers for a job in two separate interviews, you would hope that the interview technique would provide data such that the interviewers agreed with each other about you as an individual. Alternatively, if a number of candidates were given the same selection test, you would want to have some confidence that the test would provide consistent results concerning the individual differences between candidates. The statistical analysis of selection techniques normally provides a reliability coefficient, and the higher the coefficient (that is, the closer it is to 1.0), the more dependable the technique.

Validity refers to the extent to which a selection technique actually measures what it sets out to measure. There are different forms of validity, but the most important in selection is criterion validity, which measures the results of a technique against set criteria; this may be the present success of existing employees (concurrent validity) or the future performance of new ones (predictive validity).

Validation is in practice a complex process and would require studies involving a large number of candidates in order to allow a correlation coefficient to be calculated – in testing with criteria, this is referred to as a validity coefficient. If the coefficient is less than 1.0, an imperfect relationship between a test and criterion is indicated. Even if the coefficient indicates such a relationship, a selection technique may, however, still be worth using: that is, you would be better to use the instrument than not use it. In addition, different selection techniques can be assessed in relation to each other according to their validity coefficient results.

One difficulty is that it usually takes a long time to conduct validity studies, and by the time such studies were completed, it would be highly likely that the work from which some of the criteria were derived would have changed. Validity is also related to the particular environment in which performance is carried out and may have different values for different sexes and different ethnic groups. Such problems have not, however, stopped many organizations using tests and other selection techniques that have been validated elsewhere.[5]

Selection interviewing

Of all the techniques used in selection, the interview is the oldest and most widely used, along with application forms and letters of reference, referred to by Cook (1994, p. 15) as 'the classic trio'. Various attempts have been made to classify selection interviews, and it may be useful to point out some of the categories that have been developed:

● *Information elicited:* Interviews have a specific focus and require information at different levels:
  - An interview may focus on facts. The style of the interview will be direct, based on a question and answer session.
  - An interview may focus on subjective information once the factual information has been obtained.
  - There may also be a focus on underlying attitudes, requiring intensive probing techniques and usually involving qualified psychologists.
● *Structure:* Interviews may vary from the completely structured, based on planned questions and responses, to the unstructured, allowing complete spontaneity for the applicant and little control for the interviewer. A compromise between the two extremes is most likely, the interviewer maintaining control by the use of guide questions but allowing free expression on relevant topics.
● *Order and involvement:* The need to obtain different kinds of information may mean the involvement of more than one interviewer. Applicants may be interviewed serially or by a panel.

The selection interview has been the subject of much review and research over the past 50 years. During much of that time, the overall results on the validity and reliability of interviews have been disappointing. In 1949, Wagner carried out the first comprehensive review of research associated with the employment interview. Wagner noted that, in the 174 sets of ratings that were reported, the reliability ranged from a correlation coefficient (r) of 0.23 to one of 0.97, with a median of $r=0.57$. Validity, from the 222 results obtained, ranged from $r=0.09$ to $r=0.94$, with a median of $r=0.27$ (Wagner, 1949). Wagner considered such results to be unsatisfactory. This pattern of low-validity results continued in other research for the next four decades. In their review, for example, Ulrich and Trumbo (1965) agreed that the interview seemed deficient in terms of reliability and validity, and were forced to conclude that judgements about overall suitability for employment should be made by other techniques.

HRM WEB LINKS

Each type of employment test (performance, personality and knowledge tests) has a different purpose, and many tests have been validated on large populations. Check out www.queendom.com/tests.html and www.apa.org/science/test.html for more information on selection testing instruments. In the UK, tests should be endorsed by the British Psychological Society (www.bps.org.uk).

Table 7.1 Reasons for poor results from selection interviewing

Processing of information

Pre-interview	Use of application forms and photographs to reject on grounds of sex, scholastic standing or physical attractiveness
First impressions	Decisions made quickly leading to a search for the rest of the interview to support the decision. Negative information will be heavily weighted if the decision is rejection, but a positive early decision may lead to warm interviewer behaviour
Stereotypes	Interviewers may hold stereotyped images of a 'good' worker against which applicants are judged. Such images may be personal to each interviewer and potentially based on prejudice
Contrast	Interviewers are influenced by the order in which applicants are interviewed. An average applicant who follows below-average applicants may be rated as above average. Interviewers may compare applicants against each other rather than against objective criteria
Attraction	Interviewers may be biased towards applicants they 'like'. This attraction may develop where interviewers hold opinions and attitudes similar to those of the applicant

Skills of interviewing

Structure	Variations in interview structure affected reliability, low scores being gained for unstructured interviews
Questions	Interviewers may use multiple, leading, embarrassing and provocative questions
Listening	Interviewers may talk more than listen, especially if they view the applicant favourably. Interviewers may not be 'trained' to listen effectively
Retention and interpretation	Interviewers may have a poor recall of information unless guides are used and notes made. Interviewers have difficulty in interpreting information

There have been two lines of research to examine the reasons behind such poor results for the selection interview. The first focuses on the processing of information by interviewers that leads to a decision on acceptance or rejection. The second focuses on the skills of effective interviewing. Table 7.1 outlines a summary of this research.

By 1982, Arvey and Campion (1982) were able to report less pessimism about reliability and validity when interviews were conducted by boards (panels) and based on job analysis and job information. In particular, reference was made to the success of situational interviews (Latham et al., 1980) in which interview questions are derived from systematic job analysis based on a critical incident technique. Questions focus on descriptions of what an applicant would do in a series of situations. Responses are judged against benchmark answers that identify poor, average or excellent employees. In addition to situational interviews, Harris (1989) reported on other new developments in interview format that relied on job analysis. These included behaviour description interviews, which assess past behaviour in various situations, and comprehensive structured interviews, which contain different types of question, for example situational, job knowledge, job simulation and work requirements. Such developments have resulted in an enhanced effectiveness for the selection interview and improved scores for reliability and validity.

The use of questions about past behaviour combined with competencies in selection interviews has enhanced efffectiveness even further. Pulakos and Schmitt (1995) compared the validity results in selection of experienced-based (or behavioural) questions versus situational questions. The former are past-orientated questions and are based on the view that the best predictor of future performance is actual past performance in similar situations. Applicants are asked job-relevant questions about what they did in other situations. This contrasts with situational questions, in which applicants are asked what they would do in response to particular events in particular situations. Responses to both types of question can be scored on behaviour scales, but experience-based questions have shown better results with respect to predictions of job performance, that is, predictive validity. These results can be used by organizations with competency frameworks. An IT company has, for example, a competency relating to managing meetings. Interviewers could base questions around an applicant's past behaviour in managing meetings by asking the applicant to explain what she or he did in managing a specific meeting. Follow-up questions can used to reveal further features of the applicant's performance, which can then be assessed against the competency indicators. Research by Campion et al. (1997, p. 655) includes such questions as 'better questions' that enhance the effectiveness of the interview.

Barclay (1999) found a rapid increase in the use of structured techniques as part of a more comprehensive approach to selection. In particular, it was found that behavioural interviewing was being used systematically, especially in combination with a competency framework. Further research by Barclay (2001) found that behavioural interviewing was referred to in a variety of ways in organizations, for example competency-based interviewing, criterion-based interviewing, skills-based interviewing, life questioning and behavioural event interviewing. It was claimed that, however referred to, behavioural interviewing had improved the selection process and decisions made, a finding supported by Huffcutt et al. (2001) in their study of the use of interviews for positions of high complexity. However, as Barclay (2001) notes, behavioural interviewing still has some limitations. First, since behavioural questions are based on past behaviour, there is an assumption that behaviour is consistent over time, allowing prediction into the future. This assumption can be challenged on the basis that people do learn from their mistakes and can learn new ways of behaving. Furthermore, it might be suggested that people also tend to behave according to contingent factors such as time, place and especially the presence of others. A second assumption is that behavioural questions allow a fair comparison between different candidates; this might, however, disadvantage those candidates with more limited experience or a poor recall of their experience.

HRM WEB LINKS

Behavioural interviews, especially when linked to competency frameworks, can be quite daunting to candidates. To help you to prepare for such interviews, you might read the guide at www.finance.monster.co.uk/articles/guide/. Further details can be found at www.allaboutmedicalsales.com/competency.html.

It is interesting at this point to note that much of the progress in interviews as a selection technique has occurred where organizations have sought to identify behaviour and attitudes that match their models of the employees to be selected. This has required an investment in more sophisticated techniques of analysis. Although traditional job analysis techniques allow the production of models of jobs in terms of tasks and responsibilities, organizations faced with change and seeking to employ workers whose potential can be utilized and developed will increasingly turn to techniques of analysis that will produce inventories of characteristics and behaviours, such as competencies, associated with effective performance in the present and the future.

Psychometric testing

Selection based on competencies and attitudes has been one result of the increased attention given to personality factors and how such factors predict job performance. In particular, there has over the past 20 years been a growing interest in what has been referred to as the five factor model (FFM) as an explanation of the factors that determine a person's personality (Wiggins, 1996). The FFM[6] proposes that differences between people can be measured in terms of degrees of emotional stability (neuroticism), extroversion, openness to experience, agreeableness and conscientiousness.[7] Research by Salgado (1997), for example, sought to explore the predictive validity of the FFM in relation to job performance through a meta-analysis of 36 studies that related validity measures to personality factors. It was found that conscientiousness and emotional stability showed most validity for job performance, and that openness to experience was valid for training proficiency.

Personality research has lent support to the use of sophisticated selection techniques such as psychometric tests that have a good record of reliability and validity. Most people have some fears related to any test, and this has caused some confusion over the meaning, use and value of psychometric tests. The 1990s saw a rapid growth in the number of organizations using such tests, the result of more people, especially HR practitioners, being trained to administer tests, (McHenry 1997a).

We can make the following distinctions between different kinds of test:

● *Ability tests*. These focus on mental abilities such as verbal reasoning and numerical power but also include physical skills testing such as keyboard speeds. In such tests, there may be right/wrong answers or measurement that allows applicants for a position to be placed in ranked order.

● *Inventories*. These are usually self-report questionnaires that indicate traits, intelligence, values, interests, attitudes and preferences. There are no right/wrong answers but instead a range of choices between possible answers.

Both forms of test provide a set of norms, developed from the scores of a representative group of people (the 'norm' group) of a larger population, for example UK adult males or females in a sales role. Figures are then expressed in percentiles, which provides standardization. Thus, a raw score of 120 on a test or a section of a test might be placed in the 60th percentile, indicating that the applicant's result was higher than that of 60% of the norm group but less than the score obtained by 40%. If the test had good predictive validity, this would be a valuable indicator to allow a comparison to be made between different applicants. Inventories would also include some allowance for 'distortions' and 'fake' responses (Dalen et al., 2001) as such tests are generally thought to be less reliable than ability tests. An important issue here is the extent to which a test might discriminate against particular groups of people. Jackson

(1996, p. 2) reported that there have been a number of challenges in the US courts relating to unfairness in testing.

REFLECTIVE QUESTION

McHenry (1997a, p. 34) argued that work needed to be done to eliminate and correct tests that contained unfair items. He provided an example of a questionnaire on personality that contained the item, 'I think I would make a good leader.' This was answered 'true' by twice as many men as women, implying that men are twice as likely to become good leaders. What do you think of such an item and its implication?

HRM WEB LINKS

In recent years, there has been a growth in the availability of on-line psychometric tests via the Internet. You can find many tests to take yourself – without applying for a job; go, for example, to www.support4learning.org.uk/jobsearch/assess.htm for more information.

On-line testing is also being used for selection and other HR purposes – this being referred to as e-assessment. It is claimed that on-line testing provides organizations with the ability to test at any time and any place in the world with the added benefit of a quick processing of applicants. Furthermore, as tests are taken, the results can be accumulated and used to improve the validity of the tests. One difficulty, however, is that there is a loss of control over the administration of a test; thus, you can take a test at any time and in any place in the world – but also with anyone else to help.[8] Whatever developments occur in the use of e-assessment in recruitments, all tests need to conform to the requirements of discrimination laws. In the UK, tests should be endorsed by the British Psychological Society, who will check for any sexual and ethnic bias within the test. In addition to this endorsement, the impact of tests needs to be followed up and monitored to ensure that a test does not result in discrimination in practice against one sex or particular ethnic groups.

There is little doubt that the popularity of psychometric testing is set to continue, but there are doubts about an overreliance on tests with respect to their use in predicting future performance, especially in relation to complex tasks such as management. Within the FFM discussed above, for example, conscientiousness has been highlighted as a predictor of overall job performance. However, a study by Robertson et al. (2000) attempted to test the link between conscientiousness and the performance of 453 managers in five different companies. The results showed no overall statistical relationship, although there was a link with particular performance factors such as being organized and being quality driven. It was also found that there might be an inverse relationship between conscientiousness and promotability. This result supports the view that suitability for complex work cannot be assessed on the basis of a narrow measurement of psychological profile.

This situation also applies to the assessment of intelligence. Ceci and Williams (2000) suggest that the measurement of intelligence, although used in various ways with HR departments, does have drawbacks if such measurement is based on the assumption of intelligence as a fixed property of individuals. They argue that intelligent behaviour such as complex thinking is strongly connected to the setting, composed of the task, the location and the other people involved. Limitations on the value of intelligence, as measured by intelligence quotient (IQ) tests, as a predictor have lead to a growing interest in the assessment of another kind of intelligence based on feelings, sensing others' feelings and the ability to perform at one's best in relationship with others. This is referred to as emotional intelligence (Dulewicz & Higgs, 2000). There is, however, still limited research evidence relating to the value of emotional intelligence, especially in organizational contexts.

Assessment centres

Given the weakness of single measures, organizations are increasingly combining techniques and applying them together at events referred to as assessment centres. Such events may last for 1–3 days, during which a group of applicants for a post will undergo a variety of techniques. We can make a distinction here between development centres (Chapter 8), which yield information to help to identify development needs, and assessment centres, which are designed to yield information that can be used to make decisions concerning suitability for a job. It is argued that it is the combination of techniques, providing a fuller picture of an applicant's strengths and weaknesses, that makes an assessment centre so valuable. Although there may be no such thing as a 'typical' assessment centre (Spychalski et al., 1997), the general methods used are group discussions, role plays and simulations, interviews and tests. The following activities were, for example, used in the assessment centre to select customer service assistants for European Passengers Services Ltd (Mannion & Whittaker, 1996, p. 14):

- Perception Exercise
- Communication Exercise
- Structured Interview
- Personality Inventory
- Customer Service Questionnaire
- Tests for clear thinking and numerical estimation.

The objectives for using these methods were to generate information about:

- the ability to work under pressure
- characteristic behaviour when interacting with others
- preferred work styles
- the ability to think quickly
- the ability to make quick and accurate numerical estimates
- experience and aptitude for a customer service role.

The European Passengers Services assessment centre process was judged to be a success, underpinned by the objective and standardized decision-making of the assessors. Candidates attending an assessment centre will be observed by assessors who should be trained to judge candidates' performance against criteria contained within the competency framework used.

Have any of your colleagues applying for graduate training programmes been 'through' an assessment centre? What was their reaction to this process?

If your colleagues were to relay negative reactions to you about their experience of selection techniques with one organization, this might affect your image of it. *Face validity* is the reaction of applicants to selection techniques and, although not important in a technical sense, could be important in attracting good applicants to an organization. Techniques that may be effective from an organization's perspective may thus be seen as negative and unfair by applicants. In work carried out by Mabey and Iles (1991) on the reactions of MBA students to selection and assessment techniques, interviews were rated fair and useful, whereas tests left many feeling negative. The combination of techniques in an assessment centre was, however, seen as fair and useful in that the event allowed for the use of objective techniques and the opportunity for a dialogue between the applicant and the employer. The findings remind us of the dilemma that faced organizations in the 1990s. That is, although it is increasingly important to select the 'right' kinds of employee using a suitable range of techniques, there is also a danger that, in using such techniques, the organization may simultaneously manage to alienate the very candidates it wants to attract. Bauer et al. (2001) have sought to measure the reactions of applications for jobs using a selection procedural justice scale, in which procedural justice is concerned with the perceptions of applicants with reference to the fairness of selection procedures. Items in the scale include the job-relatedness of tests, the chance to demonstrate knowledge, skills and abilities, the provision of feedback and treatment with warmth and respect. The scale could be used by organizations to evaluate the fairness of their selection procedures and the correction of problems.

A consideration of procedural justice in selection goes some way towards Herriot and Fletcher's (1990, p. 34) idea of 'front-end' loading processes as a development of the social relationship between applicants and an organization. Both parties in the relationship are making decisions during recruitment and selection, and it is important for an organization to recognize that high-quality applicants, attracted by the image of an organization, could be lost at an early stage unless they were supplied with realistic organization and work information. Applicants have expectations about how the organization will treat them, and recruitment and selection represent an opportunity to clarify these. Realistic job previews (RJPs) provide a means of achieving this. RJPs can take the form of case studies of employees and their work, the chance to 'shadow' someone at work, job sampling and videos, the aim being to enable the expectations of applicants to become more realistic. Work by Premack and Wanous (1985) found that RJPs lower initial expectations about work and an organization, causing some applicants to de-select themselves, but also increase levels of organization commitment, job satisfaction, performance and job survival among applicants who continue into employment. Phillips (1998) highlights the role of RJPs both before job acceptance, to reduce attrition during recruitment, and afterwards, to improve performance, as part of socialization. Hom et al. (1999, p. 3) suggest that a key feature of RJPs is their promotion of accurate pre-employment expectations that serve to 'vaccinate' employees when faced with job demands once employed. They also serve to communicate an organization's honesty about such demands.

STUDY TIP

Most selection techniques are based on the idea that there is a relationship between particular variables such as personality or abilities and future job performance, but attempts to measure the strength of this relationship, the validity, do not show very convincing results. Some studies (for example Arthur et al., 2001) suggest that it is important to investigate non-linear relationships beween variables and performance. In addition, there is the problem that all performance at work takes place in a situation and that people develop ways of thinking and behaviour according to the situation; this is referred to as situated cognition and learning. Check the paper at www.exploratorium.edu/IFI/resources/museumeducation/situated.html.

There are also some doubts about the notion of validity as a real measure of the strength of a relationship. Instead, validity measures play a part in making the reality of the measurement. You can read more about the social construction of validity at www.ped.gu.se/biorn/phgraph/misc/constr/validity.html.

Chapter summary

- This chapter has examined the nature of recruitment and selection for organizations that are pursuing an HRM approach to the management of people. The attraction and retention of employees are crucial to an employment relationship, based on a mutual and reciprocal understanding of expectations. Employers have, however, significant power in recruitment and selection. The overall approach taken will reflect an organization's strategy and its philosophy towards the management of people.

- Recruitment and selection practices are bound by the law of the land, in particular with respect to sex, race and disability discrimination. Unless exempted by provisions of genuine occupational qualification, discrimination is against the law either directly, indirectly or by victimization. In recent years, discrimination legislation has been extended by directives from the European Union, especially the European Convention on Human Rights. There is also growing interest in diversity in the workplace.

- It is essential that organizations see that, whatever the state of the labour market and their power within it, contact with potential recruits is made through the projection of an image that will impact on and reinforce the expectations of potential recruits.

- Competency frameworks have been developed to link HR practices to the key requirements of an organization's strategy. Competencies can be used to form a model or image of the kinds of employee that an organization seeks to attract and recruit. The response to the image provides the basis for a compatible person–organization fit. Images will feature in recruitment literature and, increasingly, on the Internet via e-recruitment.

- Key documents in recruitment and selection are job descriptions and personnel specifications, although there is a growing awareness of the limitations of traditional approaches to their construction. Some organizations have switched to performance contracts, which can be adjusted over time. In addition, personnel specifications may be stated as competencies, which appear more objective.

● Selection techniques seek to measure differences between applicants and provide a prediction of future performance at work. Techniques are chosen on the basis of their consistency in measurement over time – reliability – and the extent to which they measure what they are supposed to measure – validity.

● The most common selection technique is the interview, which has been the subject of much research. Recent years have indicated that a structure and the use of behavioural interviewing based on competencies increase the effectiveness of interviews in selection. The use of competencies in selection is a reflection of the interest in assessing personality and abilities by the use of psychometric tests. Techniques of selection may be combined in assessment centres to provide a fuller picture of an applicant's strengths and weaknesses.

● There is growing interest in the perceptions of candidates with respect to the fairness of selection procedures. The use of RJPs can increase commitment and job satisfaction by clarifying expectations and communicating an organization's honesty.

Key concepts

● Assessment centres

● Attraction

● Competencies

● e-Assessment

● e-Recruitment

● Job description

● Personnel specification

● Psychological contract

● Psychometric tests

● Realistic job previews

● Recruitment

● Reliability

● Selection interviews

● Validity

Chapter review questions

1. How is an organization's strategy linked to recruitment and selection?

2. Decision-making in selection has become a two-way process. How can applicants' decisions be improved?

3. How can the predictive validity of the employment interview be improved?

4. Should job descriptions be abandoned?

5. 'Appeal to their guts instead of just their brains.' How far do you agree with this view of graduate recruitment?

6. Are assessment centres a fair and valid way of selecting employees?

● Further reading

Arthur, W., Woehr, D. J., & Graziano, W. G. (2001). Personality testing in employment settings. *Personnel Review*, **30**(6): 657–76.

Cook, M. (1998). *Personnel Selection* (3rd ed.). London: John Wiley.

Cooper, D., & Robertson, I. T. (2001). *Recruitment and selection*. London: Thomson Learning.

Newell, S., & Shackleton, V. (2000) Recruitment and selection. In S. Bach & K. Sisson (eds), *Personnel Management* (3rd ed.) (pp. 111–36). Blackwell: Oxford.

Roberts, G. (1997). *Recruitment and selection.* London: Institute of Personnel and Development.

Wood, R., & Payne, T. (1998). *Competency-based recruitment and selection*. London: John Wiley.

● Practising human resource management

Searching the web

The significant growth in the number of on-line recruiters has raised some concerns about standards of service. Go to the website of the Association of Online Recruiters at www.aolr.org/. The Association aims to establish best practice in on-line recruitment and to promote high professional standards throughout the sector. Check its code of practice. The Association is part of the Recruitment and Employment Confederation, established to provide a unified voice for those in the recruitment and employment industry; its website can be found at www.rec.uk.com/.

HRM group activity

You have been asked to carry out an independent assessment of the approach to on-line recruitment of different companies. Provide a report that covers the following: (1) an overall impression of the website and ease of navigation for applicants; (2) the image portrayed and the values presented; (3) key information; and (4) how the website attempts to set expectations related to the work. The following sites can be visited:

- Royal Bank of Scotland www.royalbankscot.co.uk/group_info/working/graduate/index.html

- Royal Bank of Canada www.royalbank.com

- KPMG www.kpmgcareers.co.uk/

- Sainsbury's www.sainsburys.co.uk/fresherthinking/html/home.htm

- Microsoft www.microsoft.com/uk/graduates

- Rolls Royce www.rolls-royce.com/careers/default.htm

- Lexus (USA) www.lexususa.com

MEISTER SOFTWARE UK

Meister Software UK is the British subsidiary branch of a German-owned worldwide network of software companies. Meister Software is the generic name for a range of software modules that provide a total information solution for manufacturing companies with a turnover of at least £50 million. The British branch is growing rapidly, and during the past year the number of employees has increased from 78 to 108. Most of the employees are graduates with sales, computer or finance backgrounds. The work is highly pressured and results focused, in return for which large reward packages are available.

Sales staff in particular need strong presentation and negotiation skills as the market is very competitive and contracts can be worth in excess of £0.5 million. Recently, however, the company has had enormous difficulty in selecting the right calibre of staff for the sales role, even though they are able to attract candidates in sufficient numbers. They recently commissioned an analysis of the role to help to provide a more successful model for the selection of salespeople at Meister. The model should allow the selection process to:

- identify differences between recruits that are important to the role
- carry out the identification of differences in a reliable and consistent manner
- make valid predictions about the future performance of recruits with confidence.

The findings revealed some interesting features of the sales role at Meister relating to the basic skills and attitudes of such a role, as well as indicating how the role was expected to be performed at the company. The first of these Meister factors concerned what was seen as 'professional-ism', suggested to be 'an ability to deal sensitively with prospective customers, being "human" rather than clinical'. References were made to a style of behaviour that was 'non-threatening' and 'non-arrogant' but also 'challenging' when required.

Complementing 'professionalism' was the need to 'make decisions in a complex manner'. This meant that salespeople were expected to be able to use large amounts of information, often simultaneously, to identify patterns and develop several possible alternative actions. Such skills were accompanied by a 'tolerance for ambiguity and a capacity to empathize' with prospective customers. In particular, reference was made to the need to be able 'to understand people and political issues as well as "facts"'.

It was expected that salespeople would 'show pride' in working for Meister and in the Meister product, but it was not expected that a salesperson would sell at all costs. Prospective customers had to be 'right' for Meister. This depended in part on how far sales staff could 'present information in a confident manner' and also in part on how far they could 'adapt their behaviour as they formed relationships with prospective customers'. The establishment of mutual expectations was seen at Meister as being a core value, and a salesperson had to be able to identify quickly if these could not be formed with a prospective customer. The salesperson's understanding of this would partly be formed by her or his interactions with others at Meister, which highlighted the need for 'peer respect and being a team player' rather than an individualist. It was, however, still expected that a salesperson would be 'self-motivating and be able to work alone'.

Discussion questions

Using the information about the sales role, you are required to investigate an appropriate selection strategy. You should consider:

1. The preparation of appropriate documentation

2. Which selection techniques could measure the attributes identified

3. How an assessment centre would operate for the selection of sales staff.

Include a justification of your results.

HR-related skill development

Choose an organization in your city. Using the information in this chapter as a guide, interview a manager responsible for recruitment (for example ask about their current recruitment methods and selection tests). Using the information obtained from your interview and material from this chapter, develop a comprehensive recruitment strategy for the organization based on the position of the person whom you interviewed. Prepare an advertisement, including the cost of advertising in appropriate media outlets. Identify appropriate employments instruments to be used and include the rationale behind your choice. Present your findings in the form of a business report or as an oral presentation to your class. You can also develop your interviewing skills by visiting our website (www.palgrave.com/business/brattonandgold) and clicking on 'Employment interviews'.

Notes

1. Quoted in the *Guardian* (2002) 4 February, p. 13.
2. Quoted in a 1999 survey of HR Directors for Development Dimensions International. www.ddiworld.com.
3. Robert McHenry in *People Management* (2001) 14 June, p. 37.
4. This definition, focusing on behaviour patterns, differs from the idea of competence used with National Vocational Qualifications, which concern the performance of activities within an occupation to a *prescribed standard*. You can read more about the development of National Vocational Qualifications at www.qca.org.uk/nq/framework.
5. For a further discussion on reliability and validity, the difference between them and some of the difficulties involved, try trochim.human.cornell.edu/tutorial/colosi/lcolosi2.htm. This is a page on Bill Trochim's Social Research Methods site (trochim.human.cornell.edu/), with some superb references to all aspects of social research.
6. You may see the FFM referred to as the 'big five' model of personality.
7. The key features of the FFM are:
   - *neuroticism:* adjustment versus anxiety, level of emotional stability, dependence versus independence
   - *extroversion:* sociable versus misanthropic, outgoing versus introverted, confident versus timid

- *openness to experience:* reflection of an enquiring intellect, flexibility versus conformity, rebelliousness versus subduedness
- *agreeableness:* friendliness versus indifference to others, a docile versus hostile nature, compliance versus hostile non-compliance
- *conscientiousness:* the most ambiguous factor, seen as educational achievement or as will or volition.

8. For a further discussion on the benefits and drawbacks of e-assessment, check *People Management* (2001) 14 June, pp. 26–37.

Chapter eight

Appraisal and performance management

Jeffrey Gold

Appraisal is a process that provides an analysis of a person's overall capabilities and potential, allowing informed decisions to be made for particular purposes. An important part of the process is assessment, whereby data on an individual's past and current work behaviour and performance are collected and reviewed.

'A "managerial witch-hunt and a general gripe and groan session about what I had or hadn't done over the last year".'[1]

'performance appraisal is, in practice, more of an organizational curse than a panacea.'[2]

'Assessment of performance has become a pervasive feature of modern life.'[3]

Chapter outline

Chapter objectives

After studying this chapter, you should be able to:

1. Explain the purpose and uses of assessment, appraisal and performance management

2. Understand contrasting approaches to assessment and appraisal

3. Explain the use of assessment and appraisal in employee development

4. Assess various approaches to understanding performance at work

5. Provide a model of performance management

6. Understand the use of different performance-rating techniques

Introduction

Of all the activities comprising human resource management (HRM), performance appraisal is arguably the most contentious and least popular among those who are involved. Managers do not seem to like doing it, employees see no point in it and, human resource managers, as guardians of an organization's appraisal policy and procedures, have to stand by and watch their work fall into disrepute. Remarkably, despite the poor record of appraisal within organizations, it is an accepted part of management orthodoxy that there should be some means by which performance can be measured, monitored and controlled (Barlow, 1989). Indeed, a failure to show that management is in control would be regarded as highly ineffective by those with an interest in the affairs of an organization. As a result, appraisal systems have for some time served to prove that the performance of employees is under control, or to give the appearance of being so. As Barlow (1989, p. 500) has stated:

> Institutionally elaborated systems of management appraisal and development are significant rhetorics in the apparatus of bureaucratic control.

It might be that the idea of control lies at the heart of the problem of appraisal in organizations.

In recent years, appraisal has become a key feature of an organization's drive towards competitive advantage through continuous performance improvement and change. This has in many organizations resulted in the development of integrated performance management systems (PMSs), often based on a competency framework. Indeed, survey evidence has found that discussing and appraising performance is one of the main uses of competencies (Strebler et al., 1997). Appraisal acts as an information-processing system, providing vital data for rational, objective and efficient decision-making related to improving performance, identifying training needs, managing careers and setting levels of reward. It is therefore essential to the idea of a 'high road' HRM strategy (Chapter 6) and lies at the centre of the 'bundle' of human resources (HR) practices (Cooke, 2000) that are required to achieve this. Furthermore, through the use of assessment metrics that connect to business objectives, appraisal and performance management provide the promise of matching HR practices with organizational strategy. In the public sector too, in a movement referred to as 'new managerialism' or 'new public management' (Pollitt, 2000), performance management has increasingly been seen as the way to ensure administrative accountability, the meeting of standards and the provision of value-added services.

This chapter will seek to explain why appraisal systems have, in the past, continuously failed to find respect among employers and employees alike. It will, however, also explore how, through performance management, appraisal has the potential to reverse past trends so that it is viewed less as a threat and a waste of time and more as the source of continuous dialogue within organizations between organizational members.

The purpose of appraisal and performance management

We will define appraisal here as a process that provides an analysis of a person's overall capabilities and potential, allowing informed decisions to be made for particular purposes. An important part of the process is assessment, whereby data on an individual's past and current work behaviour and performance are collected and reviewed.

The most usual rationalization and justification for appraisal is to improve individual performance, but there are also a variety of other declared purposes and desired benefits for appraisal, including:

- improving motivation and morale
- clarifying expectations and reducing ambiguity about performance
- determining rewards
- identifying training and development opportunities
- improving communication
- selecting people for promotion
- managing careers
- counselling
- discipline
- planning remedial actions
- setting goals and targets.

The potential list of purposes for appraisal has led to the view that appraisal is something of a 'panacea' in organizations (Taylor, 1998), although expectations and hopes are more often than not confounded.

REFLECTIVE QUESTION

Why do you think it is difficult to meet the hopes and expectations for appraisal systems at work?

In the 1990s, partly as a response to difficulties with appraisal as an isolated HR activity, there was a shift towards performance management and the need to link the requirements of business strategy to all employees. Walters (1995, p. x), for example, sees performance management as being concerned with 'directing and supporting

Table 8.1 The features of performance management

Feature	% Personnel practitioners reporting the feature
Objective-setting and review	85
Annual appraisal	83
Personal development plans	68
Self-appraisal	45
Performance-related pay	43
Coaching/mentoring	39
Career management	32
Competence assessment	31
Twice-yearly appraisal	24
Subordinate (180°) appraisal	20
Continuous assessment	17
Rolling appraisal	12
360° Appraisal	11
Peer appraisal	9
Balanced scorecard	5

Source: Armstrong and Baron (1998)

employees to work as effectively and efficiently as possible *in line with the needs of the organization'* (original emphasis). As Armstrong and Baron (1998) found in a survey of 562 personnel practitioners, the term 'performance management' can encompass a broad variety of features (Table 8.1). It is the strategic focus of some of these features that gives performance management its distinctive position in HRM; these will be examined in more detail later in the chapter.

Appraisal and control

In many organizations, appraisal takes place formally at predetermined intervals and involves a discussion or interview between a manager and individual employees. The purposes of such discussions can be broadly categorized into:

1. the making of administrative decisions concerning pay, promotions and careers, and work responsibilities – the *judgement* purpose
2. the improvement of performance through the discussion of development needs, identifying training opportunities and the planning of action – the *development* purpose.

Both categories require judgements to be made. In the first category, a manager may be required to make a decision about the value of an employee both in the present and in the future, and this may cause some discomfort. Several decades ago, McGregor (1957, p. 89) reported that a key reason why appraisal failed was that managers disliked 'playing God', which involved making judgements about the worth of employees. Levinson (1970) thought that managers experienced the appraisal of others as a hostile and aggressive act against employees that resulted in feelings of guilt related to being critical of employees. The tension between appraisal as a judgemental process and as a supportive development process has never been resolved and lies at the heart of most debates about the effectiveness of appraisal at work.

Making judgements about an employee's contribution, value, worth, capability and potential has to be considered as a vital dimension of a manager's relationship with employees. Although the occasion may be formally separated from the ongoing relationship, appraisal activities and decisions will be interpreted by an employee as feedback and will have a potentially strong impact on an employee's view of 'self', for example self-belief and self-esteem. What is particularly interesting is the way in which individuals respond to feedback, because there is no simple formula for how feedback can be used to motivate people, even though managers may be quite convinced, in their own minds, that there is. We do, however, know that feedback has a definite influence in terms of demotivation!

REFLECTIVE QUESTION

What motivates you to work? Make a list of these factors, and then make another list of what demotivates you. It is likely that the latter will be longer, covering a wide range of factors.

There is always a danger in any situation when a manager has to provide feedback to employees that the outcome will be demotivated employees. The seminal study

Table 8.2 Summary of findings from Meyer et al.'s (1965) study

- Criticism often has a negative effect on motivation and performance

- Praise has little effect – one way or another

- Performance improves with specific goals

- Participation by the employee in goal-setting helps to produce favourable results

- Interviews designed primarily to improve performance should not at the same time weigh salary or promotion in the balance

- Coaching by managers should be day to day rather than just once a year

that highlighted this was carried out by Meyer et al. (1965) at the General Electric Company. Although this work was carried out in the mid-1960s, it is remarkable how the lessons have been forgotten and how the mistakes uncovered at that time have been repeated many times over in many organizations.

The study looked at the appraisal process at a large plant where appraisal was judged to be good. There were 92 appraisees in the study who were appraised by their managers on two occasions over 2 weeks. The first interview discussed performance and salary, the second performance improvement. The reactions of the appraisees were gathered by interviews, questionnaires and observation. It was discovered that although interviews allowed for general praise, criticism was more specific and prompted defensive reactions. Defensiveness on the part of appraisees involved a denial of shortcomings and blaming others. On average, 13 criticisms were recorded per interview, and the more criticism received, the more defensive the reaction of the appraisee. The study revealed that the defensive behaviour was partly caused by most appraisees rating themselves above average before the interviews – 90 out of 92 appraisees in fact rated themselves as average or above. It was also found that, subsequent to the interviews, criticism had a negative effect on performance. A summary of some of the conclusions from this study is set out in Table 8.2.

Since this study, there has in many respects been a long search to find a way of appraising employees that mitigates the negative outcomes. There is still a tendency to associate feedback with criticism even though most people do their work well most of the time (Swinburne, 2001). In recent years, for example, there has been a growth in the process of multisource feedback (Kettley, 1997), during which individuals receive feedback from different sources, including peers, subordinate staff, customers and themselves. Where feedback is received from 'all round' a job, this is referred to as 360° appraisal or feedback.[4] The growth in such approaches is based on the view that feedback from different sources allows for more balance and objectivity than does the single view of a line manager (HRM in practice 8.1). We will examine multisource feedback and 360° appraisal in more detail later in this chapter.

Competencies have also been seen as a way of facilitating the review process, linking personal development plans (PDPs) to strategy and, increasingly despite many warnings, to pay (Sparrow, 1996).

HRM IN PRACTICE 8.1

PRET A MANGER TO DELIVER EXTRA ROUND OF APPRAISALS

ZOË ROBERTS, *PEOPLE MANAGEMENT*, 2001, SEPTEMBER 13

Employees at sandwich shop chain Pret a Manger are said to be clamouring for more appraisals after the company moved its review system online.

The new technology has also given HR staff time to cope with the extra demand.

'Our 360-degree appraisals for managers were always done on a paper-based system, which took about three months to complete,' Bruce Robertson, Pret's head of HR, told *PM*. 'But now we have halved the time it takes to do them and people have actually been asking for more appraisals.'

The company, known for its innovative approach to training and HR, found that the quality of the data became more direct and honest as managers and employees completing evaluations online felt more secure that their answers would remain confidential.

> ### 'Those that will survive are those that are innovative and care about the future of HR.'

'We can look to increase the number of 360-degree assessments now,' Robertson said. 'The appraisal and training process is a vital part of keeping the Pret work culture alive.'

Jac Peeris, chief executive of Skillvest, the training company that worked with Pret to provide the system, believes that businesses that invest in HR now are the future market leaders.

'In the present economic environment, companies must realise that their *only* asset is people. Those that will survive are those that are innovative and care about the future of HR,' she said.

HRM WEB LINKS

Because of the difficult nature of appraisal, there is a plethora of resources and training programmes available. If you want some basic advice on appraisal interviewing, check The A–Z of Work, produced by the Advisory, Conciliation and Arbitration Service (ACAS), at www.acas.org.uk/publications/pub_ah_employhandbook.html#2.

ACAS also publish a booklet on appraisal-related pay at www.acas.org.uk/publications/pub_ab_appraisalpay.html.

A problem-solving appraisal guide can be obtained from www.sol.brunel.ac.uk/~jarvis/bola/appraisal/practice.html.

The last conclusion in Table 8.2 emphasizes the role of managers as developers of their employees on a continuous basis. This role will be explored in more detail in Chapter 10, but it is worth stating here that assessing and appraising are likely to occur on both formal and informal occasions, and the latter will occur far more often than the former. Employees are able to accept criticism if it is useful and relevant to them and the work they are doing. Feedback provided in this way has a strong chance of improving performance and, crucially, provides an opportunity for a continuing dialogue between managers and employees out of which will emerge a joint understanding of individual development needs and aspirations. As many managers and employees have found, informal and continuous processes that are operating effectively will make the formal appraisal less isolated and less prone to negativity.

The extent to which employees are able to accept feedback will vary to a considerable extent between employees, and managers will need to be able to cope with such variations. That is, they will need to 'know' their people as individuals, and this itself will be a reflection of the development of managers. Recent work in understanding what makes people exert effort has shown that a variety of factors such as clarity of role, recognition, challenge, self-expression and contribution, contribute to this process. How these factors are combined cannot, however, be generalized, and each person will have his or her own perception of what is important. To understand this, managers are advised to 'get inside the head' of the employee (McHenry, 1997b, p. 29).

The shift towards a more developmental view of appraisal inevitably, however, comes into tension with management orthodoxy in which it is accepted that there should be some means by which performance can be measured, monitored and controlled (Barlow, 1989). Appraisal systems provide evidence that management is in control, and, as Randell (1994, p. 235) has pointed out, most appraisal schemes in the UK are underpinned by a 'performance control approach'. Figure 8.1 provides the key stages of this approach.

It is argued that the control approach is an outcome of the drive towards rationality and efficiency in our organizations. Such beliefs may certainly become part of a set of taken-for-granted assumptions that dominate life in organizations and may also be difficult to challenge. Organization leaders, managers and employees are often unaware of the ways in which such beliefs lie behind their actions. Morgan's *Images of Organization* (1997), for example, has provided an examination of the way in which metaphors lie at the foundation of our ideas and explanations about organizations. In this book, Morgan draws on literature highlighting the role of metaphor in explaining complex phenomena, such as organizations, by the crossing of images and language. An organization may thus be crossed with the image of a machine, and this may be very useful in understanding what does and what should happen in organizations. Metaphor, however, provides only a partial view rather than a complete view of a phenomenon: an organization may, for example, be compared with a machine or said to have machine-like qualities, but it is not and never will be a machine. A danger

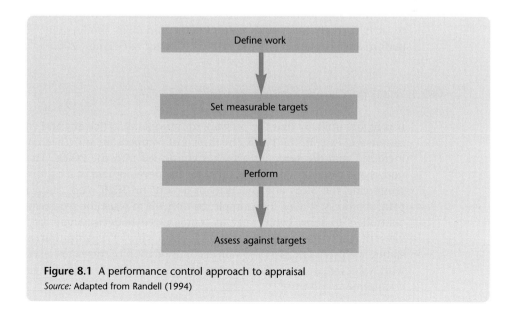

Figure 8.1 A performance control approach to appraisal
Source: Adapted from Randell (1994)

occurs, however, when the metaphor, in this case a machine, becomes a taken-for-granted assumption. The partial explanatory power of the metaphor may then be taken as a whole, and the organization may be seen literally as a machine. This is not as ridiculous as it sounds because much of the language of organizations, and many of the processes developed, can be related back to such an assumption. Mintzberg (1989, p. 339) argued that the form of structure called 'machine bureaucracy' has dominated thinking on how organizations should be constructed, and that terms such as 'getting organized', 'being rational' and 'achieving efficiency' represent evidence of this domination. As Mintzberg (1990, p. 340) wrote: 'I believe that to most people, what I am calling machine bureaucracy is not just a way to organize, it is the way to organize; it is not one form or structure, it is structure.'

We should not be surprised therefore to find an attachment by many managers to the idea of control in appraisal (Townley, 1994), and the perception by employees that they are being controlled by appraisal systems. Barlow (1989) took the argument further, pointing out that appraisal serves to make rational, simple and static a relationship between managers and employees that is ambiguous, complex and dynamic. Ambiguity, complexity and dynamism cannot be eliminated in reality, and therein lies the falseness of the experience of appraisal. For many employees, appraisal is just not seen as relevant. The following reflects the opinion of one manager about appraisal, gathered in a field study in a sector of the petrochemicals industry (Barlow, 1989, p. 505):

> If we were asked for a good man, we certainly wouldn't go hunting through appraisal forms. We'd do it by personal knowledge and I suppose, to some extent, by rule of thumb. Appraisal forms are no use. It's what's left out rather than what's put in that's important.

In this section, we have discussed how some of the research evidence has indicated that the reality of appraisal may be less than effective in the achievement of its purposes. The problem may be due to the way in which appraisal processes are formulated, based on an explicit or implicit performance control orientation. Organizational leaders and managers will need to ask themselves some fundamental questions on the purpose of appraisal and the nature of organizational control mechanisms if they are to achieve high trust, high commitment and high productivity within the high-performance paradigm of HRM activity (Godard & Delaney, 2000).

⬤　From control to development?

It is highly unlikely that the pressure for rationality, efficiency and control in organizations will ease. In the 1990s, the threats of competition and uncertainty, if anything, increased that pressure, and this has continued into the 2000s. The questioning of underlying principles that is required for the development of a culture supporting and reinforcing the ideas and practices of a 'soft' or 'high road' HRM model can be a painful process: it may, for example, be difficult to resist the requirements of financial controllers to show conformity to standardized budgets. There are, however, other views of reality that challenge the mechanistic view of organizations and its privileged status. Such views need to show an accommodation of the values of control combined with values that argue for the development of people and the gain of employee commitment and trust.

In a landmark paper, Walton (1985) wrote about disillusionment with the apparatus of control that assumed low employee commitment and mere obedience, reporting on a number of organizations that had attempted to move towards a workforce strategy based on commitment. Throughout the 1990s, the drive towards leaner and flatter organizational structures in response to the pressures of globalization, the advance of technology and the requirements of high-quality customer service meant the removal of layers of supervision and an investment, both psychologically and physically, in harnessing the potential of employees (Holbeche, 1998). The crucial contribution towards creating commitment, pride and trust is, however, management's devotion to nurturing a culture that supports the long-term development of people (Gratton, 1997). Assessment and appraisal can serve as the fulcrum of such a process, although considerable difficulties arise (Wilson & Western, 2000). The contrast between control approaches and commitment could not be greater for managers: the former involves a concentration on techniques, the latter a shift towards attitudes, values and beliefs. The skill for HRM practitioners is to acknowledge the importance of the former while arguing for a greater place for the latter.

REFLECTIVE QUESTION

What particular skills are needed by HRM practitioners to argue for two potentially conflicting points of view such as the need for control and the need for commitment?

A developmental approach to appraisal that attempts to harness potential would, for many organizations, mean a spread in the coverage of appraisal systems to all employees who form the primary internal labour market. For many years, discussions of potential and prospects for development have been confined to managers, providing a strong signal to the rest of the organization that only managers are worthy of such attention – with the implicit assumption that non-managers cannot develop. In the 1990s, however, more organizations attempted to harmonize conditions between different grades of employees and adopt HRM ideas and practices such as appraisal and performance management (Bach, 2000).

In shifting towards a more developmental approach, the suspicion that has surrounded control approaches may remain. Harper (1983) suggested dropping the word 'appraisal' because it put employees on the defensive. He recommended instead a shift towards future-orientated review and development that actively involved employees in continuously developing ways of improving performance in line with needs. The outcome could be a set of objectives to be achieved by individual employees. Such objectives might be concerned with immediate performance set against current tasks and standards, but they might also be concerned with a variety of work and personal changes, for example a change of standards, task, job or career. Once employees have been encouraged to pay attention to their progress at work, the organization must be able to respond to their medium- and long-term career aspirations (Chapter 6). The manager's role will be to resolve the inevitable tension that will result between individual goals and the manager's interpretation of organizational goals. But how can data about employees be gathered for such purposes? There needs, by necessity, to be a shift in attention towards the performance of work, and this provides a link to the shift from appraisal as an isolated HR activity to being performance management.

The performance of a work task can be presented as a relationship between means and ends (Ouchi, 1979). The means take the form of the attributes, skills, knowledge

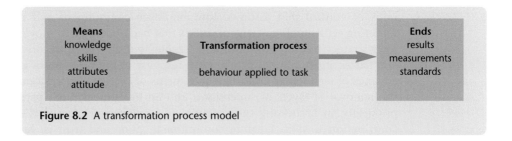

Figure 8.2 A transformation process model

and attitudes (competencies) of individual employees that are applied to a task in a specific situation. The ends are the outcomes, taking the form of results achieved, which may be measurable either quantitatively or qualitatively against an explicit or implicit standard or target. Between means and ends lies the behaviour of the individual in a transformation process, as shown in Figure 8.2.

Although all phases of this process can form the focus of appraisal, particular attention to behaviour in the transformation process will reveal how an individual has applied knowledge, skills and attitudes to a task, taking account of all aspects, including time and place, machinery and equipment, other employees and other circumstances, for example the presence of a manager or a customer. We must remember that all performance occurs in a context and that contextual factors can have a significant bearing on performance, these needing to be considered in the various processes of managing, measuring, assessing and rewarding performance (Armstrong & Baron, 1998). The attention paid to how an employee performs will provide rich data on current effectiveness and potential for further development.

If, for example, we assume that an employee has been trained to complete a basic task, attention to the transformation process will provide data on a number of issues. The first time she completes the task, an assessment of her behaviour will reveal nervousness until completion, when the results achieved can be compared against a standard. This nervousness can be corrected by adjustments to her skills and practice until confidence is gained. Further attention reveals that, once confidence has been gained, she performs with some sense of rhythm and flow that achieves a perfect result. Given static conditions and standards, this is as far as she can go in this task. She can continue to perform with confidence, but after some time this becomes too easy. This feeling prompts the employee to ask for some adjustment, possibly at first to the work targets and then to an extension of tasks within the job. The important point is that ease within the transformation process, assessed by the employee and others, leads to developmental adjustments. Continued attention to process may eventually result in a further range of adjustments, such as increased responsibility through job enlargement and job enrichment, and a reconsideration of the employee's future direction within the organization. On the way, the organization may benefit from rising efficiency and effectiveness, including better standards.

Through attention to the behaviour of an employee in the transformation process, data can thus be provided for a whole gamut of developmental decisions over time, starting with adjustments to reach minimum standards and then addressing career changes and progression. Figure 8.3 shows a representation of this development, starting at the centre with attention to immediate performance and extending outwards to career changes and progression. Individual employees are able to set targets, objectives and goals for each stage through appraisal.

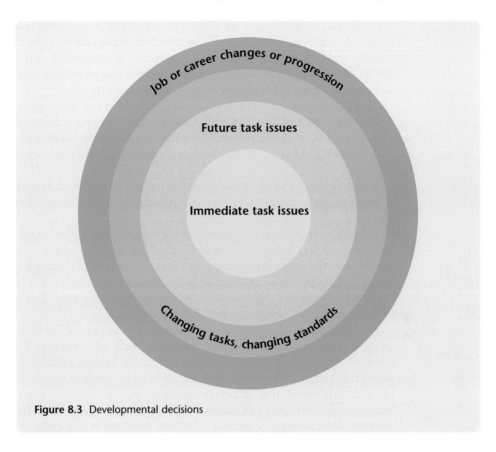

Figure 8.3 Developmental decisions

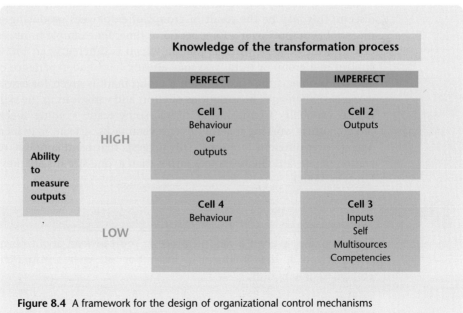

Figure 8.4 A framework for the design of organizational control mechanisms
Source: Adapted from Ouchi (1979)

A number of techniques have been developed that allow for the assessment and appraisal of the various stages of the transformation process. The ability to employ various techniques in appraisal will depend on a number of contingencies. Ouchi (1979) has provided a framework specifying these and allowing a choice of techniques to be made; Figure 8.4 has been adapted from his work.

This framework can be used to reconcile the dilemma that organizations may face in appraisal, that is, the dilemma between the desire to maintain control and the desire to foster a developmental emphasis. Bureaucratic forms of control depend (Ouchi 1979, p. 843) on the feasibility of measuring desired performance:

> the ability to measure either output or behaviour which is relevant to the desired performance is critical to the 'rational' application of ... bureaucratic forms of control.

In Ouchi's framework, if an organization either has the ability to measure outputs of behaviour or has a high understanding of the transformation process involved in production, the organization could opt for bureaucratic control and base appraisal on behaviour, output measurements or both. Thus, in cell 1, typical of traditional manufacturing and service organizations, where work process steps can be clearly stated, both behaviour and output techniques can be used.

In cell 2, only outputs can be successfully appraised, perhaps because work processes cannot be observed; this may occur with sales workers. The key issue here seems to be how such outputs are judged and the criteria utilized. Research by Pettijohn et al. (2001), for example, which sought to understand salespersons' perspectives of appraisal, found that although appraisal was a common practice within sales management, there was some dissatisfaction with the criteria used. In particular, salespersons preferred criteria such as customer satisfaction and product knowledge that lay within their control. The failure to include such criteria had implications for the use of appraisal to affect morale, turnover and overall performance.

In cell 4, employees' behaviour can be observed but outputs are more difficult to discern: this may be the result of groups of employees producing group outputs or measurable outputs over a long period of time, for example in research work. Particular difficulties occur when appraisal, which is inherently an individual process, is applied to a group or team; you may already have had experience of group-working and the problems that occur when a group mark is given for assessed work. In the workplace, there may be variations of effort and variations in the skill required. There is also variability in the life of teams, some teams coming together for a single project, others working together over several tasks. A team may increasingly have to operate over different locations. This suggests that team appraisal requires a consideration of relevant circumstances rather than a 'one-size fits all' prescription (Scott & Einstein, 2001).

HRM WEB LINKS

Team appraisal is often a difficult process. You can read about how the problems were tackled at the Smithsonian Institution at: www.si.edu/archives/archives/2rmapbackground.html.

In all the above cases, the logic of control may be extended to attach appraisal to some form of performance or merit-related pay system (Chapter 9). In cell 3, however, there is an imperfect knowledge of transformation and a low ability to measure output, making bureaucratic control virtually impossible. Ouchi refers to this cell as a 'clan' based on a ritualized, ceremonial or 'cultural' form of control arising from shared attitudes, values and beliefs. Cell 3 would include the work of most professionals, most managers and, increasingly forms of work organization in which higher levels of discretion and autonomy are granted to individual employees or teams. Behaviour, although difficult to observe formally, can be observed by those present at the point of production. A university can, for example, bureaucratically control who becomes a lecturer through its selection processes; hence it is possible to assess 'inputs' through qualifications and other attributes. Once the lecturer is in place though, his or her performance is much more difficult to assess and appraise. It can, however, be assessed and appraised by the lecturer personally through self-appraisal, and by others, for example students and/or peers. Such forms of appraisal are not without their problems, especially if organizations wish to exert bureaucratic control.

Consider further the work of professionals in the public sector in recent years, in which appraisal can be seen as part of shift towards mangerialist language and techniques. In response to deregulation and competition, often sponsored by central government, as part of the trend referred to as new managerialism or new public management (see above) (Pollitt, 2000), there have been various attempts to curtail the power of professionals within the public sector and remove or usurp their monopoly (Exworthy & Halford, 1999a). Research so far suggests the emergence of new relationships and a reordering of professions and management: head teachers, for example, require leadership skills, which include the assessment of their staff.[5] In the National Health Service, with over one million employees, many of whom are professionally qualified, appraisal (referred to as the individual performance review) was developed in the 1980s and has been seen as one of the tools necessary to bring a change in culture. Research by Redman et al. (2000) found that, after several years of experience, appraisal was generally valued, with particular strengths in setting objectives, personal development planning and, where they occurred, quarterly 'mini' reviews. There was, however, also evidence of 'patchy application' (Redman et al., 2000, p. 59). Others have found considerable resentment towards managerial processes in general (Exworthy & Halford, 1999b). The key issue, according to Flynn (1999, p. 26), is the 'concrete internal policies which control and limit professionals'.

Performance management

We have shown that there is considerable pressure on organizations to adopt performance control approaches to appraisal, and that even in organizations espousing an HRM orientation, beliefs that emphasize rationality and efficiency may become part of a set of taken-for-granted assumptions. An organization that desires to develop appraisal with a development focus will clearly need to challenge such assumptions as well as accommodate them. During the 1990s, the evident difficulties of assessment and appraisal as isolated activities resulted in a growing interest in PMSs to ensure that HRM could be seen as vital to an organization's concerns with performance improvement and competitive advantage. PMSs represent an attempt to show a strategic integration of HRM processes with assessment and appraisal central to a set of interrelated activities, which together can be linked to the goals and direction of an organization (see HRM in practice 8.2).

HRM IN PRACTICE 8.2

LEAP OF FAITH HELPS TESCO KEEP ITS COMPETITIVE EDGE

DOMINIQUE HAMMOND, *PEOPLE MANAGEMENT*, 2001, APRIL 19

Supermarket chain Tesco could have found itself in the same position as Marks and Spencer if it hadn't implemented a change programme three years ago, according to Alison Horner, the company's retail HR director.

Tesco's change programme, known as Futures, has put customer focus and the development of people centre stage and led to innovations in work design and customer service that have kept the retailer ahead of the competition, she said.

Speaking at a session on performance management, Horner said the success of the programme was evident in the continuing success of the company. Last week Tesco announced profits of £1 billion and total sales of almost £23 billion.

> **Tesco's change programme ... has put customer focus and the development of people centre stage.**

'It was a leap of faith, but not taking that leap of faith could have left us where Marks and Spencer is today,' she said.

The programme has seen 360-degree feedback introduced for all directors and managers. And managers now spend 40 per cent of their time developing staff. Customer service innovations include opening a new till when there are more than two people in a queue and a goal of greeting every customer and saying goodbye to them.

A recent innovation – employing runners to deliver food to shelf stackers – was introduced following a suggestion from a store worker in Worksop.

Tesco's results for the 12 months to 24 February 2001, released last week, showed international sales up 43 per cent to £2.9 billion. UK sales were up by 8.5 per cent to £19.9 billion, of which 4.8 per cent came from existing stores and 3.7 per cent from new stores.

Significant attention has been paid to setting organizational goals and directions to improve business performance and, importantly, to how such improvements can be measured. Based on the well-known dictum that 'if you cannot measure it, you cannot manage it', finding ways of measuring performance has become a major preoccupation in many organizations, in both the public and private sectors. There has, however, been a trend away from single financial measures, such as return on investment, towards the identification of value-drivers in organizations (Scott, 1998), although the inclusion of less tangible factors such as customer satisfaction and loyalty and intellectual capital may make these more difficult to develop.

HRM WEB LINKS

There are a variety of approaches and frameworks for setting performance measures. Try www.som.cranfield.ac.uk/som/cbp/, the home page of the Centre for Business Performance, which researches the design and implementation of performance measurement and management systems. The website of the Performance Management Association can be found at www.som.cranfield.ac.uk/som/cbp/pma/. One of the most popular frameworks for performance measurement is the balanced scorecard; you can find out more about this approach at www.balancedscorecard.org/. Another approach, derived from quality management, is the business excellence model, which can be examined at www.businessexcellence.co.uk/business-excellence-model.htm.

In the UK, new managerialism in the public sector has resulted in a customer-orientated approach to performance measurement (Mwita, 2000). In local government, for example, a Best Value framework was introduced in 1997. Indeed, Best Value now forms part of a statutory framework for performance management in local government and sets five dimensions of performance indicators:

1. *strategic objectives:* why the service exists and what it seeks to achieve
2. *cost/efficiency:* the resources committed to a service and the efficiency with which they are turned into outputs
3. *service delivery outcomes:* how well the service is being operated in order to achieve the strategic objectives
4. *quality:* the quality of the services delivered, explicitly reflecting users' experience of the services
5. *fair access:* ease and equality of access to services.

The overall aim of Best Value is to encourage a reorientation of service delivery towards citizens and customers and produce a quality-driven organization (Sheffield & Coleshill, 2001).[6]

Although the concern with performance measurement has certainly provided an impetus for the development of PMSs, there is still the crucial issue of how goals and targets are translated and incorporated into the various HRM processes. A key feature of a PMS is the attempt to provide a link between all levels of an organization through goals, critical success factors and performance measures. An organization's goals will thus be derived from business strategy and translated into sector goals, departmental goals, manager goals and employee and/or team goals respectively. At each stage, there will be an attempt to provide measurable performance indicators of the achievement of goals. Furthermore, in response to the dynamic conditions of globalization and technical change, there is a need to review and reset goals and targets through the year (Rose, 2000).

In addition to goals, which provide the direction for performance, PMSs will also provide a means of supporting performance through diagnosing development needs, providing ongoing feedback and review and coaching where required. As we have argued throughout this book, the crucial features of a 'high road' HRM strategy (Chapter 6) are the coordination of the implementation of HR practices (Hoque, 1999) and the belief by management that people represent the key source of competitive advantage. In a PMS, the attitudes of management are crucial because they are the key actors in the implementation of the various HR processes. The integrated nature of a PMS is outlined in the performance management cycle shown in Figure 8.5.

A PMS might incorporate, especially for managers, a development centre. Development centres are the same as assessment centres (Chapter 7) in that assessment tests and exercises are used to provide a report on individual strengths and limitations, but they differ in their emphasis on diagnosing development needs, leading to suggested development activities and a performance and development plan (PDP). Although a range of activities may be used, a development centre usually involves psychometrics and feedback from a qualified occupational psychologist, multisource feedback and a self-diagnosis against the organization's competency framework. A PDP also includes an attempt to link the overall business aim with key areas of responsibility, the competencies that are expected to be demonstrated in performing a role and goal setting with measurable objectives. Table 8.3 shows the inputs of a development centre held for managers at Yorkshire Water plc.

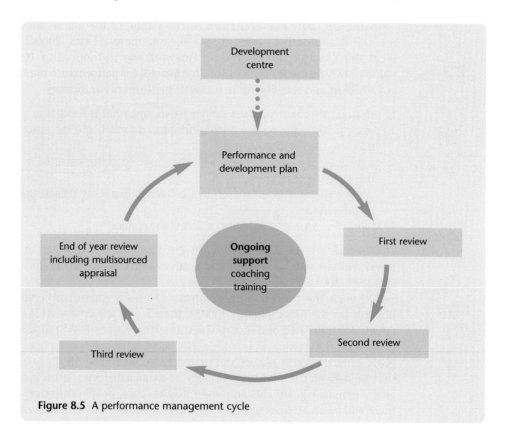

Figure 8.5 A performance management cycle

Although development centres are concerned with development needs, their similarity to assessment centres may make it difficult to escape the tension between judgement and development that is a feature of all processes concerned with assessing and appraising people at work. Carrick and Williams (1999) suggest that development

Table 8.3 The inputs of a development centre held for managers at Yorkshire Water plc

1. Participant and boss inputs	A 'strengths, weaknesses, opportunities and threats' analysis for the participant and a discussion of hopes for the future
2. Psychometric measures	– SHL OPQ, a personality questionnaire – FIRO-B, an interpersonal behaviour measure – A Myers–Briggs type indicator, a measure of psychological types – GMAA spatial relationships, a measure of the ability to make sense of complex data
3. Colleague survey	Feedback from 15 colleagues
4. Interview	A discussion of the results of tests and feedback
5. Self-assessment and performance development plan	

Source: Adapted from Davies (1996)

centres may for some participants result in the diagnosis of many development needs and have a demotivating influence. Because this may be the expected outcome for some potential participants, this may influence their decision to participate and their overall performance if they do. Overall, there is a need for considerably more research on the value of such centres.

Once a PDP has been established, according to the performance management cycle, work is carried out to meet the objectives set. There should also be ongoing coaching from the immediate manager and support for any training and development needs identified (Chapter 10). Objectives and performance are reviewed, perhaps every quarter or half year, to monitor progress and make any adjustments. During the course of the year, feedback might be obtained from different sources, being used to improve performance as well as being fed into the end-of-year review, at which an overall assessment and appraisal might also be carried out.

Referring back to our earlier analysis, we saw that a substantial record had been established to show the problems of appraisal. These stemmed mainly from the way in which systems were established as a way of superiors evaluating employees for a variety of purposes, for example improving performance, pay and promotion. Over the years, a large battery of techniques has been made available to organizations. Some of these techniques, for example psychometric tests and, more recently, assessments made based on competency frameworks carry validity and reliability scores suggesting greater 'objectivity'. What cannot be escaped, however, is that all employees have an opinion on how well they are performing, the rewards they desire and deserve, and the training they require. That is, whatever techniques of appraisal are employed, self-appraisal and self-rating will always be there too. When the emphasis of appraisal is on evaluation and performance control, it is only to be expected that differences will exist between an individual's self-appraisal and the appraisal of his or her superior. Campbell and Lee (1988) put forward a number of discrepancies between self- and supervisory appraisal:

- *Informational.* There is disagreement over work to be done, how it is done, and the standards to be used in judging the results.
- *Cognitive.* Behaviour and performance are complex, and appraisers attempt to simplify this complexity. Different perceptions will result in disagreement between appraisers and appraisees.
- *Affective.* The evaluative nature of performance control appraisal is threatening to appraisees and triggers defence mechanisms, leading to bias and distortions in interpreting information. Appraisers also may find appraisal threatening.

All this suggests that self-appraisal in an environment of evaluation and control is not effective, which is not surprising.

Campbell and Lee (1988, p. 307) have, however, suggested that:

> such pessimistic conclusions do not rule out the possibility that self appraisals can be used as important developmental and motivational tools for individuals.

We have already shown that employees are able to observe their own performance and obtain data for appraising strengths and weaknesses, and identifying future goals from the processes of working. We have also demonstrated that such observations may allow the organization to benefit from rising efficiency and effectiveness, including better standards. Allowing employees to appraise themselves for development purposes is an acceptance of the values of such a process for individuals and the organization. The extent to which employees are able to appraise themselves objectively becomes a question of how willing they are to seek and accept feedback from their work behaviour and the environment that they are in. Employees can learn to appraise themselves and will treat this as part of their own development if they can see its value for themselves rather than viewing it as a manipulative management tool.

REFLECTIVE QUESTION

How good are you at seeking feedback? What are the skills of effective feedback? The following website may help you: www.orgdct.com/feedback%20skills.htm.

Self-appraisal for development will not occur unless it is set in an environment that facilitates and encourages such a process. If a positive experience is gained from self-appraisal, employees may be willing to share their thoughts on the process with others. In recent years, many organizations have sought to increase the amount of feedback received and the number of sources of feedback. Kettley (1997) claims that the growing popularity of multisource feedback has arisen from a number of factors:

● It is a way of empowering employees and promoting teamwork by allowing employees to appraise their managers.
● It increases the reliability of appraisals and balance in flatter organizations.
● It reinforces good management behaviour by allowing people to see themselves as others see them.[7]

Most schemes appear to involve feedback to managers, although there are likely to be increased attempts to extend the process to all employees in the future. The various sources of feedback might include the immediate manager, subordinates (upward appraisal), peers, other parts of the organization (internal customers), external clients and customers, and self-rating. A scheme providing feedback from all or most of these sources – usually between 8 and 10 – is referred to as 360° appraisal or feedback.

As the number and range of multisource feedback schemes has grown, so too has interest in their impact. The crucial factor is the extent to which self-rating is supported by the ratings of others. What do you think the outcome would be if a manager had a positive perception of his or her performance but was rated less well by others, for example subordinate employees and internal customers? Yammarino and Atwater (1997) have provided a model of possible HRM outcomes based on the range of agreements between 'self-' and 'other' ratings (Table 8.4).

Table 8.4 Self–other rating agreement and human resource management (HRM)

Type	Ratings	HRM outcomes
Over-estimator	Self-ratings greater than other ratings	Very negative
In agreement/good	High self-ratings similar to other high ratings	Very positive
In agreement/poor	Low self-ratings similar to other ratings	Negative
Under-estimator	Self-ratings less than other ratings	Mixed

Source: Yammarino and Atwater (1997, p. 40)

There has been only limited evidence of the impact of multisource feedback. A study by Reilly et al. (1996) of the effect of upward appraisal on management performance showed an improvement where managers started from a low or moderate rating and the feedback process was sustained over time. There was less impact on managers who already had a high performance rating. The study found that the process created an awareness of the behaviours measured, leading to efforts by managers to improve against these measurements, especially in the early phases of the scheme. In addition, the scheme itself provided a powerful message to managers that performance would be assessed and improvement was expected. A further study by Atwater et al. (2000) found that where there were cynical attitudes among managers towards organizational change efforts, there was a low impact of feedback from subordinates on their behaviour. There was also a tendency to reinforce existing commitments to subordinates. Thus, high ratings from subordinates strengthened commitment whereas low ratings reduced it.

Other studies have shown that there are still dangers in feedback schemes that are used to judge employees and provide information for their development and performance improvement. Handy et al. (1996), in a survey of organizations using 360° feedback, found that whereas most were positive about its use and were confident that it was a stimulus for personal growth, there were also some problems. Individuals could be hurt by too much negative feedback, and there might be confusion over whether the process was for development or for judgement relating to pay or promotion.

Overall, there are apparently contradictory findings relating to the effect of 360° feedback on subsequent behaviour (McCarthy & Garavan, 2001), which raises important implications for how 360° feedback, and multisource feedback in general, are positioned in an organization and how support processes are established. In particular, organizations need to consider the preparation of employees to give and receive feedback and use the various rating techniques. Training programmes for such skills would be crucial before the implementation of multisource feedback schemes. It would also seem that such schemes have more value as development and performance improvement processes than as a judgement mechanism for pay and promotion (McCarthy & Garavan, 2001).

Approaches to performance rating

We can see that, throughout the performance management cycle (see Figure 8.5), there are a number of opportunities for performance rating to occur. The different approaches to rating can be classified as follows.

Inputs

This is a broad and potentially vague category that has traditionally been concerned with listing traits or personality attributes. Typical attributes are dependability, loyalty, decisiveness, resourcefulness and stability. Because such attributes may be difficult to define, there will be little agreement between the different users of lists of measures on their presence in employees. In Chapter 7 we referred to the issue of reliability. The use of personality attributes in assessment and appraisal can lack reliability, giving rise to charges of bias, subjectivity and unfairness. This is normally the case when managers attempt to measure their employees in appraisal interviews. As indicated above, many organizations now prefer to use reliable and valid psychometric instruments as a way of helping employees to diagnose strengths and weaknesses for a development plan.

Results and outcomes

The results and outcomes of work performance provide the most objective technique for collecting data for appraisal. When available, measurements can be taken at different points in time and comparisons made with objectives. Typical measurements might relate to production, sales, the number of satisfied customers or customer complaints. We can also include in this section the achievement of standards of competence as contained within, for example, National Vocational Qualifications (England and Wales) and Scottish Vocational Qualifications. Such standards attempt to describe what competent people in a particular occupation are expected to be able to do. Outcomes achieved can be assessed against performance criteria for each standard.[8]

It is not surprising that most measurements are quantifiable, although many organizations will attempt to modify quantification with qualitative measurements or comments. The attractiveness of results and outcomes as objective sources of data makes them a feature of many appraisal systems, but do such approaches reflect performance control or development approaches? Key questions will relate to how objectives, targets and goals are set, how managers and employees interact in work towards their achievement, and the use made by employees of measurements as feedback in order to develop further. As Pettijohn et al. (2001) found, it is important that the criteria used to judge performance are controllable by those being judged: a failure to be so affects morale and overall performance. During the 1960s, there was a growth in schemes of management by objectives, designed to control the performance of managers and stimulate them in terms of their development. If this could be achieved, the needs of managers and the organization could be integrated. Such schemes soon, however, came under attack, and many fell into disrepute. Levinson (1970, p. 134) attacked the practice of management by objectives as self-defeating because it was based on 'reward–punishment psychology', which put pressure on individuals without there being any real choice of objectives. Modern approaches to objective-setting, especially where they feature as part of a PMS, will face similar charges unless managers pay as much attention to the process by which objectives are set as to the content and quantification of objectives and the environment in which employees work towards their achievement.

Behaviour in performance

We have already examined how attention to the behaviour of employees in the transformation process will reveal how an individual has applied aptitudes, attitudes and competencies to the performance of work and will provide rich data on current effectiveness and potential for further development. Such attention can occur on a continuous basis, taking into account both subjective and objective data. Such an approach forms the foundation of PMSs concerned with the direction of performance and support for the continuing development of employees. Once these processes are established, employees may be more willing to accept more codified approaches to rating their behaviour. Frameworks of competencies associated with effective performance

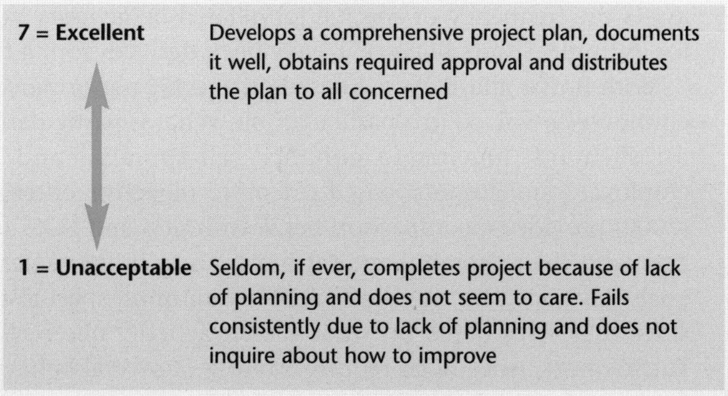

Figure 8.6 A planning behaviour-anchored rating scale
Source: Rarick and Baxter (1986)

can, for example, provide the integrating link within PMSs between the identification of key performance factors and setting objectives that can then be reviewed and rated, although there is evidence that the competencies identified are not always included in the appraisal process (Abraham et al., 2001).

In addition to competencies, and closely related, are behaviour-anchored rating scales (BARSs) which provide descriptions of important job behaviour 'anchored' alongside a rating scale. The scales are developed (Rarick & Baxter, 1986) by generating descriptions of effective and ineffective performance from people who know the job; these are then used to develop clusters of performance and scales. Each scale describes a dimension of performance that can be used in appraisal. An example from a scale developed for planning is shown as Figure 8.6. Between 'Excellent' and 'Unacceptable' would come the whole range of possible behaviours of varying degrees of effectiveness.

Table 8.5 Behavioural observation scales in a financial services company

Developing people

Gives praise where it is due to others in the team

1 Never	2	3	4	5 Always

Provides constructive feedback to colleagues

1 Never	2	3	4	5 Always

Shares best practice with others

1 Never	2	3	4	5 Always

An alternative to BARSs are behavioural observation scales (BOSs), on which raters assess the frequency of specific job-related behaviours that are observable. Table 8.5, for example, shows BOSs that have been derived from a financial services company.

Both BARSs and BOSs are based on specific performance and on the descriptions of employees involved in a particular job. What is particularly interesting is the potential for such instruments to enhance self-appraisal and allow a dialogue between employees and 'others' based on more objective criteria. Research by Tziner et al. (2000) provided a comparison between BARSs and BOSs with respect to ratee satisfaction with their appraisal and setting goals to improve performance. It was found that goals developed by the use of BOSs were more specific than those set using a BARS since they were based on what a rater actually observed rather than on evaluation. Furthermore, since BOSs require a rating of several behaviours rather than the identification of a single 'anchor', as in BARSs, this reduces bias and allows more specific feedback with the formation of clearer goals.

The recent trend towards PMSs has gone some way to reconciling the competing uses of assesssment and appraisal in organizations. The development of competency frameworks, along with other measurement devices, has improved the reliability and validity of feedback on employees' attitudes, aptitudes and performance. This still, however, does not remove the underlying control emphasis. Indeed, some (Townley, 1994) would claim that the use of the various techniques of appraisal serve to enhance the 'manageability' of employees. PMSs also place a great deal of faith in the support of the management team as the appraisers and facilitators of other people's development. There is no guarantee of either, and our understanding of what really happens in appraisals and in organizations generally is still limited. Importantly, so much of the literature concerning appraisal and performance management works from the neo-human relations assumption that all employees have an interest in achieving the objectives set or responding to measurements when they have participated in the process (Newton & Findlay, 1996). Employees do, of course, have an interest in what they do at work, but they also have many other interests with only a tangential connection to workplace performance, these possibly including many activities that work against management requirements for performance (Ackroyd & Thompson, 1999).

STUDY TIP

Assessment, appraisal and performance management are key HRM activities, but there have been many difficulties in providing effective explanations on how they should be carried out. Part of the reason for this is that there are different interpretations and different meanings relating to performance at work in each organization. Ethnographic research attempts to understand how such interpretations and meanings are made in particular social settings. Check the meaning of ethnography at www.ethnographic-research.com/research.html.

Because ethnographic research attempts to understand the customs, beliefs and behaviour of people, data are usually collected through fieldwork and may include the participation of the researcher. An explanation of ethnographic methods can be found at www.sas.upenn.edu/anthro/CPIA/METHODS/Ethnography.html. You can read a paper on an ethnographic study of virtual communities at www.ascusc.org/jcmc/vol3/issue1/paccagnella.html#s3.

Chapter summary

- This chapter has examined assessment, appraisal and performance management in organizations. It has been argued that although the use of appraisal has a poor record, it is an accepted part of management orthodoxy that performance at work should be measured, monitored and controlled. Within PMSs, appraisal allows the processing of information about performance that allows decisions to be made on setting goals to improve performance, identifying development needs and reward. As a key part of the 'bundle' of HR practices that contribute to a 'high road' HRM strategy, appraisal within PMSs becomes less isolated and more connected to organizational strategy.

- Appraisal and assessment have a variety of purposes in organizations that can be broadly categorized into a judgement purpose and a development purpose. Tension between these two purposes has made appraisal a difficult and unpopular activity, a particular difficulty being seen with the role of feedback and the response of people to judgements of their performance. Much research has demonstrated that appraisal often leads to lower motivation and morale if feedback is associated with criticism. In recent years, there has been an attempt to provide feedback from a variety of sources.

- Managers have a vital role to play in providing feedback, both formally during appraisal and informally as part of everyday work. The acceptance of feedback as valid will depend on its frequency as part of an ongoing relationship and on how well managers understand the perceptions of their staff.

- The performance control approach to appraisal is still seen as evidence of rationality and efficiency at work. Such beliefs often become taken-for-granted assumptions and difficult to challenge. Appraisal as control simplifies relationships but, in the process, makes it less relevant to people's experience of relationships at work and reduces its effectiveness.

- A more developmental approach to appraisal has been seen as a way of harnessing the employees' potential during times of rapid change. This has resulted in the adoption of appraisal and performance management for all employees in many organizations. More attention can be paid to performance at work that provides information on their effectiveness and the potential for further development.

- The contingent factors 'knowledge of the transformation process' and 'ability to measure outputs' need to be considered in approaches measuring performance at work. Whereas the measurement of behaviour and outputs may be suited to typical manufacturing or service work, other approaches increasingly need to be considered. Many professionals and others in the public sector have been subjected to mangerialist language and techniques as part of a trend referred to as new managerialism or new public management, although some research suggests considerable resentment towards this.

- Concern for measurement has led to an impetus in the development of PMSs, providing a link between organizational goals and targets and key HRM processes. There is growing use of development centres and PDPs, which attempt to link business aims with a person's key areas of responsibility, the competencies that are expected to be shown in performing a role and measurable objectives. There is some evidence, however, to suggest that development centres are not always successful in motivating people.

- PDPs might be reviewed using a variety of multisource feedback processes, including self-appraisal and feedback from managers, peers, subordinates and others as part of a 360° appraisal process. There is only limited evidence of the success of such activities. Cynical attitudes may lead to a low impact of feedback on managers. A key issue here is how people learn to give and receive feedback.

- Performance can be rated in different ways. Inputs in the form of personality attributes or traits may lack reliability and may be seen as subjective and unfair. Results and work outcomes allow quantifiable measurement and are therefore seen as more objective, but research suggests that the criteria used to judge performance need to be controllable by those being judged. Rating behaviour within performance allows the use of such techniques as BARSs and BOSs. Because these are based on people's specific performance at work, they can lead to a relevant dialogue about performance.

- Overall, appraisal and performance management tend to assume that all employees have an interest in achieving the objectives set or responding to measurements set by the organization, although there is much evidence to suggest that people have many other interests, not all of which match the requirements of the organization.

Key concepts

- 360° Appraisal or feedback
- Appraisal
- Assessment
- Best Value
- Bureaucratic control
- Development centre
- Goal setting

- Multisource feedback
- Performance and development plan
- Performance management systems
- Performance rating
- Self-appraisal
- Transformation process
- Upward appraisal

Chapter review questions

1. What should be the purpose of appraisal?

2. Is peformance management 'management by objectives' under another name? Will it suffer a similar fate?

3. Do PMSs enhance strategic integration in HRM?

4. How can employees learn to appraise themselves?

5. Do you think that students should have more say in appraising and assessing themselves and each other?

6. Do you think that appraisal and assessment techniques enhance the 'manageability' of employees?

Further reading

Bacal, R. (1998). *Performance management*. London: McGraw-Hill.

Halachmi, A. (2002). Performance measurement and government productivity. *Work Study*, **51**(2), 63–73.

Hartle, F. (1997). *Transforming the performance management process*. London: Kogan Page.

Hempel, P. S. (2001). Differences between Chinese and Western managerial views of performance. *Personnel Review*, **30**(2), 203–26.

Townley, B. (1999). Practical reason and performance appraisal. *Journal of Management Studies*. **36**(3), 287–306.

Walters, M. (ed.) (1995). *The performance management handbook*. London: Institute of Personnel and Development.

Practising human resource management

Searching the web

One of the most comprehensive resources for appraisal and performance management on the web is provided by the Zigon Performance Group at www.zigonperf.com/index.html, with links to on-line resources and articles. There are links to a variety of performance management websites at www.zigonperf.com/resources/links.html#Performance%20Management, including a performance management library at www.performaworks.com/performaworks/library/pmlibrary_newuser.asp. Information on a growing trend towards the use of software in appraisal can be found at www.hr-guide.com/data/209.htm. A variety of 'how to' articles, such as A Seven Step Process for Measuring the Results of Work Teams, can be found at www.zigonperf.com/resources/articles.html.

HRM group activity

During the 1990s, workers in the public sector were increasingly subjected to HRM processes such as appraisal and performance management. You have been asked to examine how these apply to schoolteachers.

First, find out the appraisal and performance management requirements for schoolteachers in England at www.hmso.gov.uk/si/si2001/20012855.htm and www.teachernet.gov.uk/performancemanagement.

Second, examine the view of the General Teaching Council at www.gtce. org.uk/. Use the search facility to find papers on performance management and appraisal.

Now find out the response of some of the teaching unions. The National Union of Teachers website is www.data.teachers.org.uk/nut/index.html, and the National Association of Schoolmasters and Union of Women Teachers is at www.nasuwt.org.uk/.

Chapter case study

INSIGHT COMMUNICATIONS

Insight Communications is a major telecommunications company. After a recent restructuring activity, the marketing and solutions department was reorganized into 12 virtual teams, each working in a different location across Europe. A key change was an increased focus on selling, in which teams had previously worked with sales units as consultants. The new role demanded that staff work in virtual cross-functional teams to deliver a complete solution to a customer, the idea being to reduce the need for customers to deal with different parts of the company.

Half way through the financial year, it was becoming evident that most teams were failing to achieve their targets. Of the 12 teams, 7 had low overall sales, 3 were significantly short of the expected achievement, and only 2 teams were meeting or ahead of the target. Furthermore, it was becoming increasingly difficult for the head of department to manage the performance of the teams, and, as the manager responsible for the achievement of an overall target, he was beginning to feel that the restructuring was a step too far. The monthly financial and performance reports showed an increasing variance against targets, and this made the head of department feel very uneasy about the future. The company was downsizing again, and this was a bad time to be failing to deliver.

In addition, team members were often expected to establish and lead the virtual cross-functional teams but had indicated that they often felt unable to meet this requirement and were disappointed about how their performance was judged. The large distances involved often resulted in isolation and a lack of communication.

Discussion questions

1. What are the key skills for a virtual cross-functional solutions sales team?

2. How can their performance be managed effectively?

3. What methods can be employed to achieve short-, medium- and long-term performance improvement?

4. What approaches to effective communication with virtual teams can be employed? What feedback skills are necessary?

HR-related skill development

Performance appraisal is, as we have discussed in this chapter, not a precise science but a subjective judgement. There are some guidelines that may, however, increase an employee's acceptance of the appraisal process and intention to improve performance in the future. Using the information in this chapter, and the following websites with sample performance assessment tools and guidelines – www. performancereview.com, www.works911.com/performance/index.htm and www. zigonperf.com/ PMNews/paradox_360.html – go to our website (www.palgrave.com/

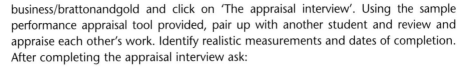

business/brattonandgold and click on 'The appraisal interview'. Using the sample performance appraisal tool provided, pair up with another student and review and appraise each other's work. Identify realistic measurements and dates of completion. After completing the appraisal interview ask:

- Is the appraisal process effective and fair?

- Did the activity illustrate the problems of appraisal?

- How might you suggest improving the appraisal process?

Notes

1. This is a comment from a manager on why he hated doing appraisals (Redman et al., 2000).
2. Taylor (1998, p. 185).
3. Bach (2000, p. 241).
4. You might consider other variations such as 180°, 270° and 540° feedback (see McCarthy & Garavan, 2001).
5. In the UK, the National College for School Leadership has been established with the aim of ensuring 'that school leaders have the skills, recognition, capacity and ambition to transform the school education system into the best in the world'. You can find further details on its website: www.ncsl.org.uk/. There has been a growing interest in the role of leadership in the public sector as a vital feature of meeting the challenges of the 21st century. Check the report from the Cabinet Office at www.cabinet-office.gov.uk/innovation/leadershipreport/default.htm and the Public Service Leaders Scheme at www.publicserviceleadersscheme.gov.uk/ index.htm.
6. You can find full details of the latest developments in Best Value at www.local-regions.detr.gov.uk/ bestvalue/bvindex.htm.
7. See Johnson (2001) for an example of how 360° feedback was used to develop multicultural management in a chemical company.
8. National Vocational Qualifications and Scottish Vocational Qualifications will be covered in more detail in Chapter 10, but you may wish to examine the websites at www.dfes.gov.uk/nvq/ index.shtml and www.sqa.org.uk/SVQ/.

Chapter nine

Reward management

John Bratton

> Reward refers to all of the monetary, non-monetary
> and psychological payments that an organization provides for
> its employees in exchange for the work they perform.

*'Although economic rewards play an important part in securing adherence to
organizational goals and management authority, they are limited in their effectiveness.
Organizations would be far less effective systems than they actually are if such rewards
were the only means, or even the principal means, of motivation available.'* [1]

*'There is no such thing as a good pay system; there is only a series of bad ones.
The trick is to choose the least bad one.'* [2]

Chapter outline

Chapter objectives

After studying this chapter, you should be able to:

1. Explain the key functions and role of reward management

2. Describe the notion of aligning business strategy with reward practices

3. Describe three key employee behaviours desired by organizations and the role that economic rewards play in shaping such behaviours

4. Define and evaluate different rewards options, including base pay, performance pay and indirect pay

5. Describe and evaluate reward techniques such as job analysis, job evaluation and appraisal

6. Explain how governments intervene in the pay-determination process

7. Explain the paradoxes and tensions in rewards systems in relation to managing the employment relationship

● Introduction

In the context of managing people, the reward system emphasizes a core facet of the employment relationship: it constitutes an economic exchange or relationship. That is, an employee undertakes a certain amount of physical and mental effort and accepts the instructions of others, in return receiving a level of payment or reward. Reward is one of the four human resource management (HRM) policy areas incorporated into Beer et al.'s (1984) and Fombrun et al.'s (1984) conceptual models and is identified as a key management 'lever' in Storey's model of HRM (Chapter 1). As the quotations at the head of the chapter attest, reward practices engender debate among academics and organizational leaders on the role that reward plays in achieving such substantive employee behaviours as task performance, flexibility, quality and commitment. According to Beer et al. (1984, p. 113), 'The design and management of reward systems constitute one of the most difficult HRM tasks for the general manager.'

Economic and social factors present challenges when designing and administering reward systems. Global forces at work today compel managers to improve labour productivity and the quality of their organization's products and services while controlling labour costs. Debates on 'high commitment – high performance' work systems link pay practices to employee attitudes and behaviour. Research interest here has focused on the role that reward, particularly performance-related pay, plays in controlling the workforce (Kessler, 2001). In addition, social and psychological factors impinge on reward management. Reward is critically important in forming an employee's notion of 'fairness', and the concept of the psychological contract (Chapter 1) suggests that any 'incongruence' of expectation concerning the rewards employees receive when they join the organization can lead to a perceived violation of the contract, resulting in decreased motivation and less trust in the employer (Morrison & Robinson, 1997; Rousseau & Ho, 2000). Managers seek to design reward systems that both facilitate the organization's strategic goals and meet the goals of individual employees. Given the complexity and the contextual pressures, it is, however, not surprising that Brown (1989, p. 25) states, 'The satisfactory management of employment requires the satisfactory management of remuneration as a necessary, if not a sufficient, precondition.'

Over the past decade, the way in which managers have managed rewards has undergone significant change, these changes often going hand in hand with new organizational and work configurations (Chapter 4). A growing number of organizations are rewarding their employees with different levels of pay based upon individual effort and achievement. Some writers have described these changes in pay practices as 'revolutionary' because they overthrow the old assumption that employees should be paid the same even though their contribution is different and because this philosophy is being transmitted down to all categories within the organization (Curnow, 1986). Other writers have been more critical and have interpreted these developments as an attempt to construct a more individually orientated (as opposed to union or collectively orientated) organizational culture (Bacon & Storey, 1993) driven by 'ideology' (Sisson & Storey, 2000), globalization and corporate downsizing (Sebbens, 2000).

Every work organization has to decide how to design a reward system. Regardless of any other rewards it offers to its employees, it must make three basic decisions about monetary reward: how much to pay, whether monetary rewards should be paid on an individual, group or collective basis, and how much emphasis to place on monetary reward as part of the total employment relationship. Decisions must be consistent with the organization's goals, with society's values on notions of fairness and with government legislation. The literature suggests that there is no single reward system that fits all organizations. To help in understanding this complex area, we provide a conceptual framework or model for studying reward management. This model identifies major reward concepts and processes and illustrates the various interrelationships: the link between business strategy and rewards, the objectives of reward systems, the reward options that are available to employers, the reward techniques used to establish internal equity, job analysis, job evaluation and appraisal. We also examine the role of government in reward management. On a more theoretical level, we conclude with a critical analysis of the position of rewards in the prescriptive HRM model, which reveals tensions, conflicts and contradictions.

The nature of reward management

In North America, the term 'compensation' is used as an alternative to the term 'reward'. Both of these terms are problematic, and we consider that 'reward management' best captures the current changes in management thinking on pay, with an emphasis on employee performance and flexibility (Armstrong, 1998). Managers typically define reward as the package of monetary rewards (wages, salaries and benefits), but employees generally define reward even more narrowly, as the wage or salary received from the employer for their work. To understand reward and comprehend its crucial role in managing the employment relationship, it is, however, necessary to conceptualize reward in its broadest sense.

An organization can provide two types of reward: *extrinsic* and *intrinsic*. Extrinsic rewards satisfy an employee's basic needs for survival, security and recognition, and derive from factors associated with the job *context*. This includes financial payments, working conditions and managerial behaviour. Intrinsic rewards refer to psychological 'enjoyment' and the satisfaction of 'challenge' (Bartol & Locke, 2000; Caruth & Handlogten, 2001), sometimes called 'psychic income', that a worker derives from her or his paid work, and satisfy 'higher-level' needs for self-esteem and personal development. These rewards derive from factors inherent in the way in which the work is designed, that is, the job *content*. This includes design features, such as the degree of variety of the work and the extent of autonomy, as well as the significance attributed to the work. Consequently, for our purposes, we will define reward in the following terms:

> **Reward refers to all of the monetary, non-monetary and psychological payments that an organization provides for its employees in exchange for the work they perform.**

The mix of extrinsic and intrinsic rewards provided by the employer is termed its *reward system*, the monetary or economic element of the reward system being called the *pay system*. A reward system also consists of the integrated policies, processes, practices and administrative procedures for implementing the system within the framework of the human resources (HR) strategy and the total organizational system. The management of rewards must meet numerous economic and behavioural objectives (Figure 9.1).

A pay strategy comprises an organization's plan and actions pertaining to the mix and total amount of direct pay (for example salary) and indirect monetary payments

- ■ Support the organization's strategy
- ■ Recruit qualified employees
- ■ Retain capable employees so that turnover is held to an acceptable level
- ■ Ensure internal and external equity
- ■ Be sustainable within the financial means of the organization
- ■ Motivate employees to perform to the maximum extent of their capabilities
- ■ Strengthen the psychological contract
- ■ Promote 'organizational citizenship'
- ■ Comply with legal regulations
- ■ Be efficiently administered

Figure 9.1 Objectives of the reward system

(benefits) paid to various categories of worker. In other words, the two key questions for pay strategy are 'How should monetary payments be paid?' and 'How much should be paid?'. The optimal choice relating to these two aspects of pay strategy ultimately depends on the organizational and reward system. At one extreme, the reward system may include direct pay only, at the other extreme no pay whatsoever. It is easy to think, 'Who works for nothing?', but many voluntary organizations, such as Oxfam and the Salvation Army, rely upon thousands of hours of unpaid labour. These examples illustrate the importance of intrinsic rewards derived from the work. The volunteers receive intrinsic rewards derived from the significance attributed to the work: they are not 'serving customers', they are 'feeding the destitute'. Similarly, highly qualified professionals may choose to work for organizations such as Médicins sans Frontières or Amnesty International, at a much lower salary than they could earn in a private hospital or law practice, because of the meaning attached to the work. The key point is that amount of pay needed to recruit and retain qualified workers will vary with the other rewards that the organization offers (Long, 2002).

To fully understand the conceptual analysis of the place of rewards within a HR strategy, it is first necessary to recall the nature of the employment relationship discussed in Chapter 1. We noted there that the way in which workers are rewarded for their work, as part of the wage–effort bargain, is central to the capitalist employment relationship. All pay systems contain two elements that are in contradiction with each other:

- ● First, *cooperation* between worker and employer or manager is an essential ingredient of the employment relationship if anything is to be produced and is fostered through the logic of financial gain for the worker.
- ● Second, *tensions and conflict* are engendered through the logic that makes the 'buying' of labour power the reward for one group and the cost for the other.

This fundamental tension underlying the employment relationship makes for an unstable contract between the two parties, which, in the context of global price competition and technological change, is constantly being adjusted. To increase market 'viability', for example, employers attempt to increase performance through pay incentives or pay cuts to reduce labour costs. Furthermore, 'effort' itself is 'a highly unstable phenomenon' and payment systems form part of an array of managerial strategies designed as 'effort controllers' (Baldamus, 1961).

The nature of the employment contract means that the employee and those responsible for reward management have different objectives when it comes to monetary rewards. For the individual employee, the pay cheque at the end of the month is typically the major source of personal income and hence a critical determinant of an individual's purchasing power. The absolute level of earnings determines the standard of living and social well-being of the recipient and will therefore be the most important consideration for most employees. Employees constantly seek to maximize their financial reward because of inflation and rising expectations. Furthermore, the axiom of 'a fair day's pay for a fair day's work' raises the question of relative income. In most cases, what is seen to be 'fair' will be a very rough personalized evaluation.

The organization, on the other hand, is interested in reward management for two important reasons. First, it is interested in the absolute cost of the financial rewards because of its bearing on profitability or cost-effectiveness. The importance of this varies with the type of organization and the relative cost of employees, so that in a refinery, labour costs are minimal, whereas in education or health they are substantial. Second, the organization views a reward system as a determinant of employees' work attitudes and behaviours. A reward system affects an individual's decision to join an organization, to work at her or his maximum potential, to undertake special behaviours beneficial to the organization that extend beyond contractual obligations – referred to as 'organizational citizenship behaviour' – to undertake training, to accept additional responsibilities and to remain with the organization. Employee dissatisfaction with the reward system may cause a variety of consequences, including high labour turnover, low task performance, low commitment and unionization of the workforce (HRM in practice 9.1).

HRM IN PRACTICE 9.1

SALARY SMARTS: LEARN WHAT YOU SHOULD EARN

SUZANNIE WINTROB, *GLOBE AND MAIL*, 2002, FEBRUARY 1

When Mark Schroeter saw the perfect position advertised on an on-line job board, he quickly sent in his resumé.

But with no salary mentioned, Mr. Schroeter wanted to be well-armed for an interview. So he scoured newspaper ads and the Web looking for similar job postings to determine salary expectations, and used com-

pensation information he'd gleaned from headhunters.

He was asked his salary during the first phone interview, and used what he called 'a direct and honest approach' to the issue. 'Some people sometimes are too shy or insecure to ask [about compensation] and, quite frankly, the worst that can happen is they'll say no', says Mr.

Schroeter. His research also came in handy when it was time to negotiate a benefits package, since it was his first time dealing with an employer directly instead of going through a placement agency. 'It almost behooved me to negotiate a little bit as opposed to taking the offer as what it was, just because the squeaky wheel gets the grease.'

Given the state of the economy and the aftermath of September 11, salaries aren't what they used to be. Levels have dropped off significantly in the last year. And with fewer jobs out there, more employees are staying put and 'relaxing their numbers,' says Keith McLean, president of PriceWaterhouse-Coopers' national executive search practice.

But that doesn't mean people shouldn't be paid what they deserve. Signing bonuses and piles of stock options may be temporarily out of reach, but there's still reason to figure out what compensation you can expect.

How to learn what you should earn? Probably the easiest way is to pore over help-wanted ads in newspapers and on the Web. Family, friends, neighbours, business associates, headhunters and others in your profession can also be great sources. Industry associations and publications

> **'Given the state of the economy and the aftermath of September 11, salaries aren't what they used to be.'**

can also be helpful. Don't forget to check out government surveys. On-line job boards also offer a range of resources, including tools for figuring out what you're worth. Monster.ca offers salary comparisons for IT jobs.

All of this information isn't the be all and end all, the experts warn. 'Surveys categorize companies and markets,' Mr. McLean says, 'If you have the wrong markets, you may be comparing apples and oranges.' Mr. Shedletsky of GSW Consultants says you have to consider the entire compensation package.

'The full package may be very different than just the salary. What are the benefits? What are the bonuses? Is there profit sharing? What other benefits accrue to the individual in terms of subsidization, parking? What's their policy around overtime? That will not all find its way into surveys. You have to negotiate it.'

REFLECTIVE QUESTION

Think about the reward system at your most recent job in terms of conflict and tension, workplace behaviour and equity. Did the reward system cause conflict or tension among the workforce? If so, why? What impact did the reward system have on your behaviour in the workplace? Do you believe that it was equitable?

Share your experience with members of your class. Of the reward systems described by class members, which appear to generate most conflict, which appear to be most effective or most equitable, and why?

A model of reward management

To help us examine the complexities of pay systems, we have developed a pay model that serves as both a framework for studying reward management and a guide for the chapter (Figure 9.2). The model contains five basic building blocks:

1. strategic perspective
2. reward objectives
3. reward options
4. reward techniques
5. reward competitiveness.

Our model shows first that reward management is linked to organizational strategy.

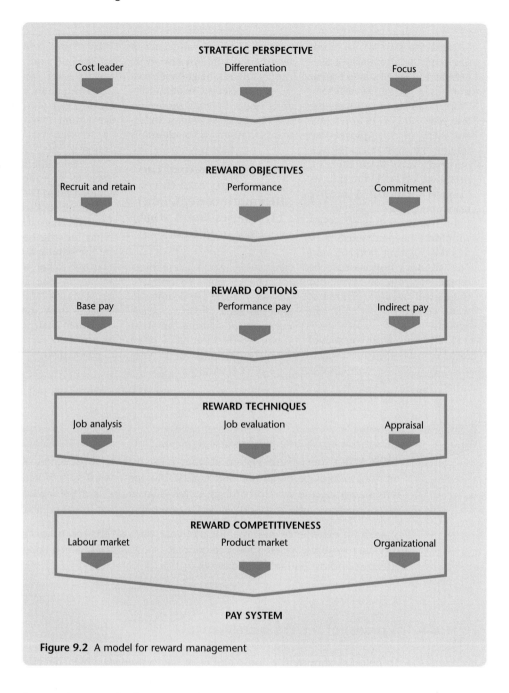

Figure 9.2 A model for reward management

A *strategic perspective* focuses on those reward choices which support the organization's strategic goals, the rationale being based on contingency theory. Going back to our discussion on business strategy (Chapter 2), this means that each business strategy – and in this example we used Porter's (1980) typology of cost leadership and differentiation – should be supported by a different HR strategy, including rewards. The underlying premise here is that the closer the alignment or 'fit' between the reward system and the strategic context, the more effective the organization.

The *reward objectives* emphasize the linkage between a reward system and human behaviour. There are three principal behaviours that are desired by management – membership behaviour, task behaviour and commitment behaviour – and the reward system can play a central role in eliciting all three behaviours (Long, 2002). The reward system is an important consideration when the organization is trying to attract suitable employees, and once workers are members of the organization, their task behaviour and levels of performance are influenced by the reward system. The employment relationship is more than an economic exchange: it embraces a social and a psychological relationship. Employees typically interact with other employees and managers. Acceptable and unacceptable workplace behaviour on the part of workers and notions of 'fairness' are inevitably partly socially determined. Commitment behaviour occurs when employees and managers alike voluntarily undertake behaviour beneficial to the organization that goes beyond the economic exchange and is linked to the notion of the psychological contract.

Every employer has *reward options*, shown in the third box of Figure 9.2. There are three broad reward components:

- *base pay,* the level of pay (wage or fixed salary) that constitutes the rate for the job, which is generally based on some unit of time: an hour, a week, a month or a year
- *performance pay*
- *indirect pay* or 'benefits' consisting of non-cash items or services (for example life insurance).

These and other alternative monetary rewards explained later in the chapter offer managers a choice of components and elements that can be included in the reward system that best fits their organization.

The fourth component of our reward model in Figure 9.2 shows *reward techniques.* Three techniques are examined:

- job analysis
- job evaluation
- appraisal.

Internal equity refers to the pay relationships between jobs within a single organization, this policy being translated into practice by reward techniques. The focus here is on comparing jobs and individuals in terms of their relative contributions to the organization's objectives. How, for example, does the work of the chef compare with the work of the receptionist or the waiter? Job evaluation is the most common method used to compare the relative values of different jobs inside the organization. Of course, not all of these reward techniques may be relevant to an organization, and in a unionized workplace there may be strong resistance to such techniques as appraisal.

Reward competitiveness is the fifth component of the model, referring to comparisons between the organization's pay and that of competitive organizations. Competitiveness is important if the organization is going to attract, retain and motivate its employees while achieving the other objectives of controlling labour costs and complying with pay legislation. Rewards that are perceived by prospective members to be inadequate or inequitable will thus make it difficult for the organization to attract the type of people necessary for success. There are also constraints that define the parameters within which reward choices can be made, including:

- labour market constraints

- product/service market constraints
- organizational constraints, including internal financial constraints and external legal constraints.

In terms of the latter, we should remind readers that the employment relationship involves a legal relationship, another objective of a reward system being compliance with employment legislation and regulations. We will now examine in more detail each of the five basic components of the reward management model.

HRM WEB LINKS

For the latest information on employment income in Britain, go to the National Statistics website at www.statistics.gov.uk. For information on employment income in North America, go to Statistics Canada's website at www.statcan.ca; for the USA go to the Bureau of Labor Statistics at www.bls.gov; for South Africa try www.statssa.gov. za and for Australia www.abs.gov.au. To obtain general information on reward management, go to www.rewardstrategies.com, www.employersinc.com/ seminars/altcomp. html, www.worldatwork.org and www.hrreporter.ca and click on 'Compensation'.

Strategic perspective

Contingency theory suggests that an organization's reward system should be dependent on its external and internal contexts. The external context is globalization, compelling business organizations to 'downsize' and become more cost-effective (Sebbens, 2000). The external environment also consists of the national context, which is strongly influenced by international developments. Some key national developments that affect the reward system include structural change in the labour market, restructuring in industry, shifts from traditional work to knowledge work, and social and political trends (Chapter 3). The significant internal context affecting reward management comprises organizational strategy, organizational restructuring, organizational culture and psychological contract issues.

Hill and Jones (2001, p. 3) define strategy as 'a specific pattern of decisions and actions that managers take to achieve an organization's goals'. As the hierarchy of established goals is translated from one level to the next, the reward for their satisfactory implementation constitutes critical elements of managerial control within the organization. A reward system is thus a key mechanism that can influence each step of the strategy process (Gerhart, 2000). In addition to its importance in influencing employee goal behaviours, a reward system influences at least two other important behaviours. The first is *membership behaviour*, which happens when qualified people join and remain with the organization. Thus, reward moulds the composition of the organization in terms of its competencies and intellectual capital. The second is *conflict behaviour*, which may derive from employee dissatisfaction with the reward system and is expressed through formal disputes, absenteeism or sabotage. This type of employee behaviour can undermine organizational strategy.

Taken together, current management literature suggest that a major determinant of success in business strategy implementation is an 'effective' reward system. By 'effective', it means that rewards fit or are aligned with the organizational strategy. In addition, the closer the alignment or 'fit' between the reward system and the strategic context, the more effective the organization (Gomez-Mejia & Balkin, 1992; Lawler, 1990; Mintzberg, 1998; Pfeffer, 1998). The notion of alignment is explained by Pfeffer (1998, p. 99) thus:

> The diagnostic framework is premised on the idea of alignment, that is, that an organization does specific things to manage the employment relationship and these practices need to be first, internally consistent or aligned with one another, and second, externally consistent, in the sense that the organization's procedures produce behaviors and competencies required for it to compete successfully given its chosen marketplace and way of differentiating itself in that marketplace.

Let us illustrate this contingency theory with an example of two business organizations with two different business strategies and completely different reward systems. Precision Engineering produces high-quality, customized machine tools for the aerospace industry. The manufacturing process is organized around self-managed work teams, and workers rotate through the various jobs within the teams that they are qualified to perform. Rather than pay an hourly wage rate to the skilled machine operators, which is the industry norm, the company pays a base salary, additional pay being awarded if the workers learn new skills. All employees receive an excellent benefits package and profit-sharing bonuses based on company profits. Labour costs at Precision Engineering are above the industry average. The culture at Precision Engineering encourages informal workplace learning, and, not surprisingly, labour turnover is extremely low. Seafresh Foods operates a plant that produces fish fingers. The work is organized around a conveyor belt with workers stationed along the assembly line performing each step in the process, from gutting the fish to packaging. The work requires little training and is monotonous. In contrast to Precision Engineering, workers at Seafresh Foods are paid an hourly wage rate that is 10% above the minimum wage, and there are no additional payments or benefits. Labour turnover exceeds 100 per cent a year.

REFLECTIVE QUESTION

Think about the business strategy and reward systems at these two companies. How can Precision Engineering compete when it pays above the industry average? And how can Seafresh Foods survive with such a high turnover? Go back to Chapter 2 and look again at the 'integrative model'.

The contingency approach would suggest that, despite the two completely different reward systems at Precision Engineering and Seafresh Foods, both are effective (Long, 2002). Going back to our discussion on business strategy (Chapter 2), each reward system is aligned with the firm's business strategy. Using Porter's (1980) typology – differentiation and cost leadership – Precision Engineering is following a differentiation competitive strategy, with a focus on high-quality machine tools. Owing to the complexity of the production process, high-skilled workers are employed and are given a considerable amount of autonomy. The reward system (salary, benefits and pay-for-knowledge) supports the 'high-commitment' HR strategy. But to answer the question we posed above – 'How can Precision Engineering compete when it pays above the industry average? – the firm competes with lower-paying competitors first because of higher productivity resulting from increased functional flexibility. Second, a highly skilled and flexible workforce reduces machine downtime and scrap rates. Third, the use of self-managed work teams eliminates the amount paid to supervisors and quality control inspectors; team members undertake these tasks. Finally, low turnover means that recruitment and training costs are reduced.

In contrast, Seafresh Foods depends on its survival by following a cost leadership strategy (in which low-cost production is essential). This competitive strategy requires low-skilled employees and little employee commitment because managers exert control using technology (the speed of the assembly line). Labour turnover is high, but unskilled workers are easy to recruit and training costs are low. At Seafresh Foods, the reward system (near-minimum wage only) supports a 'traditional low-commitment' HR strategy, (see HRM in practice 2.3 in Chapter 2 for a real-life example of business strategy and reward practice alignment).

At both macro and micro levels, the contingency approach has been used as an analytical tool for explaining developments and the factors influencing the choice of reward systems over time. The macro-economic exigencies of the past decade, for example deregulation, privatization and the need for flexibility and innovation, explain why managers chose a payment system based on a combination of individual performance, pay-for-knowledge and profit-sharing to meet the needs of a high-quality manufacturing strategy. The innovations seek to encourage entrepreneurial behaviour and encourage workers to take commercial risks in order to encourage employee flexibility and behavioural traits that promote both learning and quality, and also meet the perceived needs of 'post-Fordist' production models (Chapter 4).

Recent strategic management literature has emphasized the need for companies to adopt generic 'differentiation' or 'defender' strategies (Chapter 2) and to seek the alignment of business strategy, organizational design and reward practices, as illustrated in Table 9.1.

The debate concerns whether the current managerial drive to establish a close relationship between individual pay and individual performance constitutes a qualitative change from past management strategies. In other words, is the shift an ad hoc, reac-

Table 9.1 Alignment of business strategy, organizational design and reward practices

Traditional model rewards	Post-bureacratic model rewards
Base wage or salary	Variable pay
Based on cost of living and labour market	Based on business performance
Evenly distributed between employees	Differentiated
Correlated with seniority	Based on individual performance
Based on individual performance	Based on team (unit) and organizational performance
Viewed as a result of behaviour	Used as a means of communicating values

Source: Adapted from Pfeffer (1998a)

tive response to contextual changes, or do the reported changes surrounding reward systems represent a more proactive and strategic HRM approach (Kessler, 1995)? Management literature on the perennial managerial concern of motivation suggests that payment systems directly linking pay to individual or group performance is certainly not new. In the 1960s, it was advocated that an individual performance-based payment system – regulated through productivity bargaining – be adopted to increase labour productivity. The current trend towards variable or contingency pay arrangements can best be understood in terms of the dominant political ideology over the past two decades in many developed countries, particularly Britain and North America. A concerted ideological campaign against automatic annual pay increases and 'artificially inflated' public sector pay by the Thatcher government in the UK encouraged a movement towards linking pay to individual performance and local labour markets (Curnow, 1986; Pendleton, 1997b; Sisson & Storey, 2000).

Whether current pay practices conform to the historical pattern and can be judged as reactive, or as more proactive and strategic, is debatable. Recognizing the difficulty of identifying the strategic intent of managers, Kessler argues that there is insufficient evidence to support the hypothesis that the selection of payment systems is based upon the theoretical principle of 'fit' commonly cited in the literature. Furthermore, to depict recent developments in reward systems as evidence that pay is a 'key lever' in pursuit of the HRM goals of commitment, flexibility and quality is to ignore historical data. The alternative pay systems currently gaining popularity with managers indicate that they are selecting reward options to deal with new versions of traditional managerial problems. What might be qualitatively different and would indicate attempts to use reward in a strategic way, argues Kessler, is the use of variable pay systems to facilitate cultural change. As we discuss below, reward research indeed suggests that current reward practices aim to bring about a fundamental change in organizational culture. On the specific question of the concept of strategy–reward fit, however, there is evidence of an alignment between reward and business strategy (Rynes & Gerhart, 2000). Whether a fit between business strategy and pay influences organizational performance remains open to debate, but we shall leave this question until Chapter 13, turning now instead to the second component of the reward management model outlined in Figure 9.2 above.

Reward objectives

Any organizational reward system has three behavioural objectives:

1. membership behaviour to recruit and retain a sufficient number of qualified workers
2. task behaviour to motivate employees to perform to the fullest extent of their capabilities
3. compliance behaviour to encourage employees to follow workplace rules and undertake special behaviours beneficial to the organization without direct supervision or instructions.

Recruit and retain

The reward system enables an organization to attract and retain suitably qualified employees to perform the work of the organization. According to the neoclassical economic model, which is concerned with using demand and supply analysis, but incorporates psychological factors to explain human behaviour, people choose work organizations that maximize their utility, meaning that they consider not only pay, but also non-monetary factors such as job security, prestige, work environment and other aspects that matter to them. This hedonic theory of pay holds that jobs with less desirable non-monetary characteristics should command positive compensatory pay differentials, whereas jobs and organizations with more favourable characteristics should command a lower rate of pay. This market theory of pay is only partially true as there are many jobs that have undesirable non-monetary characteristics (for example dangerous and unhealthy work) but do not command positive compensatory pay differentials. Other 'post-institutional' economists (Rynes & Gerhart, 2000) point out that firms within an industry often have different enduring pay levels for the same occupations because of factors such as equity beliefs, ability to pay and HR strategy (Pfeffer, 1998a).

A reward system that is out of touch with what the market is paying for a particular job, or one that is inequitable may therefore demand constant recruitment just to secure the necessary workers. Furthermore, if employees, once recruited, perceive any internal inequity – for example, with another individual or group performing identical work – the organization may have difficulty retaining them for long. Constant recruitment and high turnover increase both recruitment and training costs. Caruth and Handlogten (2001, p. 4) suggest that 'Equitable pay, a sound benefits program, and a psychologically supportive organizational climate' may reduce employee turnover costs. Empirical research on how reward influences recruitment and retention is, however, limited and we have much to learn about how, why and when reward influences employees' attraction to and retention within an organization (Barber & Bretz, 2000).

Performance

Can money motivate people to work? This question has been a concern of employers and managers since the Industrial Revolution, the fact that the question is intensely debated being a reflection of its complexity (Bartol & Locke, 2000). Much of current management thinking on this question comes from theories of motivation. 'Needs' theories of motivation emphasize what motivates people rather than how they are motivated. The two most well-known needs theories are those of Maslow (1954) and Herzberg (1966). Maslow argued that higher-order needs become progressively more important once lower-order ones have been satisfied, whereas Herzberg demonstrated that pay takes on significance as a source of satisfaction when it is perceived as a form of recognition or reward. Monetary variables are a key component of the more recent 'process' theories of motivation, Vroom's (1964) expectancy theory, for example, granting a prominent role to rewards (see below).

As most prescriptive texts on employee behaviour affirm, understanding the nature of the relationship between pay, commitment and motivation is complex and requires, at the very least, a knowledge of both the individual and the context. From this perspective, it is not surprising therefore to find disagreement over the strength or effectiveness of the reward–commitment link. Locke et al. (1980, pp. 379–81) assert that 'Money is the crucial incentive because ... it is related to all of man's [sic] needs.' In contrast, Pfeffer (1998a, p. 112) argues, 'People do work for money – but they work even more for meaning in their lives.' Caruth and Handlogten (2001, p. 4) express the received wisdom on the pay–motivation link: 'A compensation system that rewards employees fairly according to efforts expended and results produced creates a motivating work environment.' In the debate on the rewards–motivation link, there is a tendency for writers to view workers through a management lens, at the expense of analysing management per se – what managers do and how well they do it. Blinder's (1990, quoted by Kessler, 1995, p. 261) insightful conclusion is particularly helpful in understanding the complexity of the reward–commitment link: 'Changing the way workers are treated may boost productivity more than changing the way they are paid.'

An increasing number of North American and British companies have adopted individual performance-related pay (IPRP; see below). A recent survey, for example, found, in a poll of 316 Canadian companies, that 74 per cent of employers offered performance-related pay arrangements, up 8 per cent from the 1996 figure.[3] The precise arrangements used vary widely from one firm to another: examples include piecework, commission and profit-sharing schemes. In 1998, for example, almost one-third – 30 per cent – of all workplaces in Britain operated a profit-sharing scheme for non-managerial employees (Cully et al., 1998). Smith (1992) suggests that variable or contingent reward systems are linked to the rhetoric of the 'enterprise culture', the enterprise culture in turn being the context for substituting performance-related pay for more traditional pay systems. Performance-related pay is said to underpin a more purposeful and 'objective-achieving' strategy for managing workers. As Smith (1992, p. 178) states, the apparent change to performance-related pay represents 'a move away from the traditional view of rewards as incentives aimed at generating short-term improvements in employee performance, and towards rewards or total pay systems aimed at improving organizational performance'.

Commitment

As we have noted, the employment relationship is more than just an economic exchange, embracing instead a psychological relationship. The new HRM practices imply a change in the commitment of parties to one another at the psychological level. Indeed, it is argued (Guest, 1998, p. 42) that the 'whole rationale for introducing HRM policies is to increase levels of commitment so that other positive outcomes can ensue'. Depending on the writer's perspective, the notion of commitment is discussed in terms of 'organizational citizenship behaviour' (Long, 2002) or of 'compliance' and 'control of meaning', psychosocial factors subject to management manipulation (Thompson & McHugh, 2002). The reward system aims to promote commitment behaviours, but employee commitment is an elusive construct because reward practices do not directly affect behaviour. Within the structured environment of the workplace, reward first affects employee attitudes, perceptions and perceived obligations rooted in the cultural environment in which paid work is performed, which in turn drives behaviour. These processes help to develop organizational commitment through a reference to shared goals and values, a sense of 'belonging', conformity and an intention to remain a member of the organization.

The fashionable argument that reward is one of the most noticeable HR practices through which the psychological contract can be 'created, fulfilled, changed, or violated' (Rousseau & Ho, 2000, p. 274) reflects the fact that financial reward lies at the heart of the employment relationship. A perceived breach involves perceptual and cognitive processes that convince the employee that the 'organization' has 'reneged' on the contract. So how does reward shape the psychological contract, and how does a breach of contract occur? According to Rousseau and Ho (2000), reward plays two important roles in shaping the psychological contract. The first is to signal to workers, through monetary incentives, the behaviour that the organization values. The second role is to promote a particular form of employment relationship 'based on what the compensation system signals, in conjunction with other human resource practices, regarding the attachment between workers and the firm' (Rousseau & Ho, 2000, p. 305). Violation refers to the feelings of anger and betrayal experienced when the employee perceives that a breach of contract has occurred. A violation may occur when communication on the nature of the contract turns out to be different (less favourable) from what the worker expected (Morrison & Robinson, 1997).

The perceptual and idiosyncratic nature of psychological contracts means that what others have received from the organization does matter: an employee may perceive a contract breach even if co-workers have received the *same* reward. Thus, the breach process is more complex than the process underlying equity judgements; it is 'a reciprocal relationship based on *perceived* obligations' between the employee and the organization (Morrison & Robinson, 1997, p. 242, emphasis added). In practice, every employee will put a somewhat different valuation on the rewards provided and on the value of their contribution, and may or may not perceive a contract breach depending on their individual traits and circumstances. The importance of a perceived breach of the psychological contract and subsequent employee behaviours will, however, vary for different organizations. Those practising a 'high-commitment' HR strategy and 'knowledge-based' organizations will find behaviour caused by perceived violation of the contract to be of particular importance, whereas those practising a 'traditional' HR strategy will be concerned primarily with measurable pay–task behaviour outcomes.

Reward options

Turning to the third heading in Figure 9.2, three reward options – base pay, performance pay and indirect pay – can be seen. The purpose of this section is to provide a foundation for answering the question 'What role should each of the three reward

Table 9.2 Types of employee reward

Type of reward	Examples	Type of behaviour
Individual rewards	Basic wage Overtime Piece rate Commission Bonuses Merit Paid leave Benefits	Time: maintaining work attendance Energy: performing tasks Competence: completing tasks without errors
Team rewards	Team bonuses Gain-sharing	Cooperation: with co-workers
Organizational rewards	Profit-sharing Share ownership Gain-sharing	Commitment to institutional goals

components play in the reward mix?' The mix of components to be included in the reward package will depend on the organizational and HR strategy and on reward objectives. Managers are particularly interested in effort-related behaviours, those behaviours which directly or indirectly influence the achievement of the organization's objectives. Table 9.2 classifies some of these behaviours into five groups: time, energy, competence, cooperation and commitment.

To be efficient, managers must ensure that employees turn up for work at the scheduled times; absenteeism and lateness must be minimized. In addition, employees must put into the job sufficient energy to complete their allotted tasks within set time limits. Job incumbents must also be competent so that the tasks are completed without error and above minimum performance standards (minimum acceptable levels of performance, typically set by management unless they are jointly negotiated). Changes in job design (Chapter 4) require employees to work cooperatively with co-workers to improve the organization's effectiveness.

REFLECTIVE QUESTION

Look again at HRM in practice 9.1. How many of the above types of reward did Mr Schroeter try to negotiate in his compensation package?

Three different types of reward – individual, team and organizational – are shown in Table 9.2.

- *Individual rewards* are paid directly to the individual employee and are based on a commitment of time, energy or a combination of both.
- *Team reward* systems have become more prevalent in Europe and North America as organizations have reconfigured work systems that emphasize self-managed teams.
- *Organizational rewards*, such as profit-sharing, have also grown in popularity as a way of motivating employees and to gain employee commitment to customer-driven work cultures (Pryce & Nicholson, 1988).

Let us now look at different types of pay in more detail in terms of the reward options headings in Figure 9.2.

HRM WEB LINKS

For information on team-based pay, go to www.ced.com.

Base pay

Base (or basic) pay is the irreducible minimum rate of pay for the job. It is calculated on time worked, rather than on the results achieved, and tends to reflect the value of the job itself as measured by some form of job evaluation. In many organizations, base pay is the basis on which earnings are built by the addition of one or more of the other types of reward. The base wage for a skilled machine operator, for example, may be $9.85 an hour for a 35-hour week, but operators may receive more because of additional incentive and overtime payment. Base pay can be selected for at least two important reasons:

- *simplicity:* it is easier to implement and administer than a performance-related system
- *psychological reasons:* it demonstrates a commitment on the part of the organization, thereby creating a greater likelihood of employee commitment to the organization (Long, 2002).

A distinction is often made between a salary and a wage. A *salary* is a fixed periodical payment to a non-manual employee; it is usually expressed in annual terms, and salaried staff typically do not receive overtime pay. A *wage*, however, is the payment made to manual workers, nearly always being calculated as an hourly rate. In North America and Britain, an increasing number of employers have lessened the divide between salaries and wages by introducing 'single-status' payment schemes. This type of reward system is designed to harmonize the terms and conditions of employment between manual and white-collar employees (for example so that manual and non-manual employees receive the same number of holidays, amount of sickness benefit and pensions).

Two main methods are used to establish the level of base pay. The first method – *market pricing* – may be based on the 'going industry rate' for a particular job and on traditional structures whose origins 'are shrouded in the mists of time' (Armstrong, 1998, p. 5). The second method – *job evaluation* – involves a systematic determination of the relative value or worth of all the jobs in the organization before correlating this system to the labour market. Both of these reward processes are discussed in detail later in the chapter.

Performance pay

Financial rewards added to base pay are related to certain work-related behaviours: performance, learning or experience. If these payments are not consolidated into base pay, they are known as 'performance pay,' 'variable pay,' 'contingency pay' or 'at-risk pay'. The main types of performance pay are as follows:

- *Performance-related pay* ties additional payments directly to performance, either of an individual or of a team of employees.
- *Incentive pay* is offered prior to setting actual performance targets.
- *Merit pay* is offered for outstanding past performance.
- *Commission* is a financial incentive typically offered to sales representatives on the basis of a percentage of the sales value they generate.
- *Knowledge-contingent* pay (also called skill-based or knowledge-based pay) varies according to the level and value of the skills and competencies achieved by the individual.
- *Team-based pay* provides rewards to employees based on their contribution to the work team.
- *Organization performance pay* provides additional income to employees based on the profitability of the firm.

IPRP is a system that directly ties pay to the level of performance rather than the fact of employment. The literature suggests that correctly designed IPRP systems have numerous advantages. First, they signal key task behaviours and provide information about current performance levels. Second, they reduce the need for other types of managerial control (for example direct supervision, technology or peer pressure) over the labour process. Third, the practice helps to change the culture of the organization and promote an 'entrepreneurial' type of behaviour. It is no coincidence, for example, that some of the most publicized IPRP programmes have been introduced in newly privatized public utilities. This has led some commentators to suggest that IPRP has been adopted in many organizations for largely 'ideological' reasons (Sisson & Storey, 2000).

The premise underpinning IPRP is the oversimplistic assumption that pay alone motivates workers. Psychological theory and empirical research suggest, however, that the link between incentives and individual motivation is a more complex process. One of the most widely accepted explanations of motivation is Vroom's (1964) expectancy theory, touched on earlier in the chapter. This approach to worker motivation argues that managers must have an understanding of their subordinates' goals and the link between effort and performance, between performance and rewards, and between the rewards and individual goal satisfaction. The theory recognizes that there is no universal principle for explaining everyone's motivation, which means that a successful link between performance and reward is difficult to accomplish in practice.

It is difficult to generalize about the limitations of IPRP systems because the types of system involved differ so widely (Long, 2002). IPRP systems can undermine teamwork, but, according to Pfeffer (1998a), the major problem with individual performance-related pay is the 'symbolic message' that variable pay sends to employees:

> A system ... rewarding myriad micro behaviors, sends the message that management believes people won't do what is necessary unless they are rewarded for every little thing. A system of micro-level behavioral and outcome incentives also tends to convey an absence of trust, implying that people must be measured and rewarded for everything or they won't do what is expected of them. (Pfeffer, 1998a, p. 223)

This upshot is that the more an organization emphasizes financial rewards above all else, the more intrinsic motivation diminishes. The extent to which an organization emphasizes performance pay will depend upon whether this type of reward supports the organization's strategy.

Before we leave this topic, we should note that much of the theory and research on reward–performance links and management reward practices is North American. In contrast, a cross-cultural study found that Chinese and American managers differed in the importance they attached to reward decisions. Chinese managers in the study, for example, placed more emphasis on work-based relationship needs and less emphasis on employee task performance when making a monetary recognition decision than did American managers (Zhou & Martocchio, 2001).

REFLECTIVE QUESTION

If you are an employer, paying employees only when the desired performance takes place sounds like 'common sense'. Can you think of any circumstances in which individual-based performance pay would be advantageous or disadvantageous for a particular organization?

The next three types of pay in the list above – *incentive pay, merit pay* and *commission* – need no further explanation.

Knowledge-contingent pay systems tie pay to work-related learning. From a management perspective, it is argued that, by encouraging functional flexibility, pay-for-knowledge systems reverse the trend towards increased specialization. From a trade union perspective, pay-for-knowledge arrangements individualize the employment relationship because they sever the link between increased pay and collective bargaining (Bacon & Storey, 1993).

Survey evidence indicates that many organizations are placing less emphasis on individual incentives and more on *team-based* and *organization-based performance rewards* (for example Long, 2002). This trend mirrors changes in organizational design and the current enthusiasm for work-based organizational structures. The oldest and best-known team performance systems are gain-sharing and the Scanlon programme:

- *Gain-sharing programmes* tie pay to performance by giving employees an additional payment when there has been an increase in profits or a decrease in costs to the firm. Incentives are based on a comparison of present profits or costs against historical cost-accounting data.
- *Scanlon programmes*, originally devised by Joseph Scanlon in the 1930s, are designed to lower labour costs and distribute the benefits of increased productivity using a financial formula based on labour costs and the sales value of production. Payments are typically fairly frequent (for example, monthly). The rationale is that psychological growth needs are fulfilled if the employee partici-

HRM IN PRACTICE 9.2

NORTEL NETWORKS CORP. SCRAPPING STOCK OPTIONS

PATRICK BRETHOUR AND GRAEME SMITH, *GLOBE AND MAIL*, 2001, JUNE 5

Nortel Networks Corp. is scrapping and replacing up to 111 million worthless stock options held by employees to shield them from the dramatic slump in the company's stock, raising the ire of investors and corporate governance experts.

The move, effectively a repricing, will see up to half of Nortel's workforce exchange options issued since November, 1999, a period that embraces the meteoric rise and decline of the Internet equipment maker's shares. Employees will get a reduced number of options at what will almost certainly be a lower exercise price. Some of the options being re-issued have an exercise price six times

greater than the company's current share price – and correspondingly little prospect of turning a profit for their owners in the near future.

> **'We've got to take steps to remain competitive.'**

Excluded from the plan are top executives, directors, workers who are laid off this year and employees in its optical components unit, who will shortly have a separate options plan. Because of the exclusion of directors and executives, there will be no shareholders' vote on the new program.

Company executives said the changes are necessary to attract and keep employees to fuel Nortel's future growth. 'We've got to take steps to remain competitive,' said Bill Donovan, senior vice-president of human resources, while acknowledging that this measure is 'extraordinary.' And he said the market for top talent is still tight, despite a tidal wave of layoffs at Nortel and its competitors. 'For good people, there still happens to be good opportunities.' Mr. Donovan said the group of 'critical' employees make up 10 to 20 per cent of Nortel's workforce, although about 50 per cent are eligible for the new options.

pates in organizational decision-making while being equitably compensated for participation. Bonuses in the Scanlon plan are paid monthly or quarterly on a plant-wide basis.

McClurg (2001) found that team-based reward systems are limited in number and often operate in a fashion similar to that of gain-sharing programmes.

Profit-related pay is a form of contingent performance pay that involves the employer paying current or deferred sums based on company profits in addition to established base pay. Payment can be in the form of current distribution (paid quarterly or annually), deferred plans (paid at retirement and/or upon disability) or combination plans. With encouragement from Conservative governments, profit-related pay became fairly widespread for some employees in Britain during the 1980s. The 1998 Workplace Employee Relations Survey found that 44 per cent of workplaces had some form of profit-related pay scheme in the late 1990s (Millward et al., 2000). Advocates of profit-sharing contend that it can increase performance, result in greater employment stability and form a 'win–win' situation for both employees and employers (Tyson, 1996). Profit-sharing is seen by managers as a way to increase organizational performance through employee involvement in decision-making (Pendleton, 1997b), and stronger employee identification with the business (Long, 2002).

An employee stock plan is any type of financial arrangement through which employees acquire shares in the company that employs them. Stock ownership, it is alleged, encourages employees 'to think like owners' (Long, 2002). At the time of writing (summer 2002) it is too early to assess how the high-profile collapse of Enron Corp., the US corporate giant, will diminish the popularity for employee stock plans in many industrialized countries but most notably in North America.

HRM WEB LINKS

Go to www.fed.org/resrclib/articles/create-ownership-culture.html for information on the role of employee stock options. For more information on profit-related pay and share-ownership schemes in Britain, go to the 1998 Workplace Employee Relations Survey website at (www.dti.gov.uk/er/emar/1998WERS.htm.

Indirect pay

Indirect pay (often known as 'employee benefits') refers to that part of the total reward package provided to employees in addition to base or performance pay. There are three main types of indirect pay:

1. health and life insurance
2. deferred income plans, often known as retirement or pension plans
3. miscellaneous benefits, which may range from the provision of a company car to the purchase of club memberships.

Figure 9.3 lists some of the various types of indirect pay or employee benefits.

One innovation is 'cafeteria' benefit programmes (CBP), which allow employees to select benefits that match their individual needs (HRM in practice 9.3). Employees are provided with a benefit account containing a specified payment, the types and prices of benefits being provided to each employee in the form of a print-out. This programme creates additional administrative costs, but advocates claim that employees, through

■ Private health care	■ Subsidized meals
■ Private dental and eye care	■ Car
■ Discounted insurance	■ Financial support for lifelong learning
■ Career breaks	■ Extra vacation days
■ Child care	■ Sports/entertainment vouchers
■ House purchase/moving expenses	■ Pension plans

Figure 9.3 Types of indirect pay or employee benefit

HRM IN PRACTICE 9.3

SAINSBURY'S TAILORS BENEFITS

PEOPLE MANAGEMENT, 2002, JULY 11

Sainsbury's is to survey its staff on pay and benefits, in a bid to target reward packages more effectively. In the next two months the company will carry out a 'forced ranking' survey. Staff have to choose which benefits they would take if they were only allowed one, such as pensions over holidays or bonuses over medical cover.

Glyn House, employment brand manager at Sainsbury's, said the results will help HR understand what staff want in their pay and reward packages. The results will be used to drive recruitment, retention and HR strategies. 'It may be that we will find younger staff would rather have a bonus scheme than a higher level of medical cover or the older staff will be more interested in pensions rather than increases to basic pay,' he said. 'This is a chance for HR to find out what staff want.'

participation, come to understand the value of benefits that the organization is offering. Young employees might, for example, select dental and medical benefits, whereas older employees might select a pension. Table 9.3 lists the most commonly cited advantages and disadvantages of cafeteria or flexible benefits schemes.

There is, however, some debate over employee benefits. Do they, for example, facilitate organizational performance? Do benefits impact on an organization's ability to attract, retain and motivate employees? Conventional wisdom says that employee benefits can affect recruitment and retention, but there is little research to support this

Table 9.3 Advantages and disadvantages of flexible benefits

Advantages	Disadvantages
Employees select benefits to match their individual needs	Poor selection creates unwanted costs
Benefits target the needs of a diverse workforce	Additional administrative costs arise
Maximizes the psychological value of benefits because paying only for most desired benefits	Encourages the cost of popular benefits to be marked up

conclusion (Milkovitch & Newman, 2002). Given the absence of empirical evidence on the relationship between employee benefits and performance, and the escalating cost of benefits, benefits are under constant scrutiny by managers.

HRM WEB LINKS

Go to www.ifebp.org, www.benefitslinks.com and www.benefits.org for information on benefits.

Reward techniques

Returning to Figure 9.2 above, let us consider the fourth reward management heading, that of reward techniques.

Internal equity refers to comparisons between jobs or skill levels inside the organization. Jobs and employees' skills and competencies are compared in terms of their relative contributions to the organization's goals (Milkovitch & Newman, 2002). Internal reward relationships affect employee behaviour in terms of staying with the organization, becoming more flexible by investing in more work-related learning or determining whether there is a breach in the psychological contract. Internal equity is established through three reward techniques:

1. job analysis
2. job evaluation
3. appraisal.

Job analysis

If financial reward is to be based on work performed, a technique is needed to identify the differences and similarities between different jobs in the organization. Knowledge on jobs and their requirements is collected through job analysis, which can be defined as:

The systematic process of collecting and evaluating information about the tasks, responsibilities and the context of a specific job.

Job analysis information informs the manager about the nature of a specific job, in particular the major tasks undertaken by the incumbent, the outcomes that are expected, the job's relationships to other jobs in the organizational hierarchy and job-holder characteristics. The basic premise underlying job analysis is that jobs are more likely to be described, differentiated and evaluated consistently if accurate information is available to reward managers (Milkovitch & Newman, 2002). Figure 9.4 shows that job analysis information is a prerequisite for preparing job descriptions and for job evaluation.

The process of job analysis consists of two main stages (Figure 9.5):

1. data collection
2. the application of data by the preparation of job descriptions, job specifications and job standards.

Collecting the information involves three tasks: identifying the jobs to be analysed,

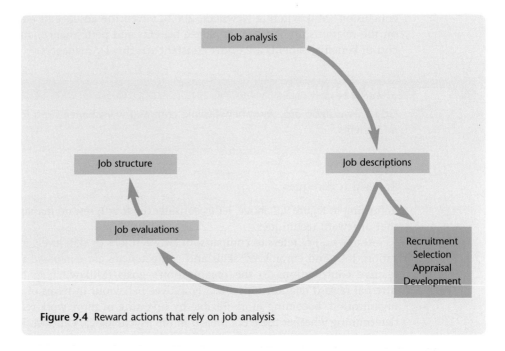

Figure 9.4 Reward actions that rely on job analysis

developing a job analysis questionnaire and collecting the data. In job identification, analysts first identify the jobs within the organization; in stable organizations, this can be accomplished by reading previous job analysis reports or the organization chart, or by interviewing workers. Questionnaires help analysts to gather information on the duties, responsibilities, human abilities and performance standards of the jobs investigated, but there is no one best way to collect the data as analysts need to make

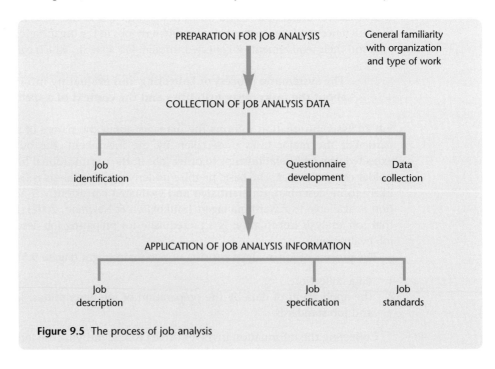

Figure 9.5 The process of job analysis

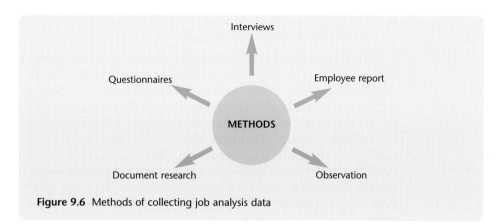

Figure 9.6 Methods of collecting job analysis data

trade-offs between accuracy, time and cost. Figure 9.6 illustrates five different methods of gathering job analysis data.

Job analysis information is then used to develop job descriptions, job specifications and job performance standards:

- A *job description* is a written statement that explains the purpose, scope, duties, and responsibilities of a specified job.
- A *job specification* is a detailed statement of the human characteristics involved in the job, including aptitudes, skills, knowledge, physical demands, mental demands and the experience required to perform the job.
- A *job performance standard* is a minimum acceptable level of performance.

Job evaluation

Job evaluation is a generic label for a variety of processes used to establish pay structures inside an organization. Formal job evaluation can be defined as:

> **A systematic process designed to determine the relative worth of jobs within a single work organization.**

The goal of job evaluation is to achieve internal equity by determining a hierarchy of jobs that is based on the relative contribution of each job to the organization. This hierarchy is then used to allocate rates of pay to jobs regardless of the incumbent. The importance of job evaluation to managers has increased because of equal pay legislation, which requires, either implicitly or explicitly, that gender-neutral job evaluation schemes be adopted and used to determine and compare the value of jobs within the organization.

Job evaluation is often misunderstood so the following three characteristics of all formal job evaluation methods need to be emphasized:

- First, the technique is systematic rather than scientific, the process depending on a series of subjective judgements.
- Second, the premise that job evaluation is based on the worth of the job rather than on the worth of its incumbent is fundamental (Risher, 1978; Welbourne & Trevor, 2000).

- Third, the validity of the job evaluation process, or how accurately the method assesses job worth, is suspect (Collins & Muchinsky, 1993).

Studies have suggested that formal job evaluation offers an opportunity for discretionary decision-making, 'departmental power' thus affecting the outcome (Welbourne & Trevor, 2000). A political perspective on job evaluation also emphasizes the fact that job evaluation ratings are often gender biased through the gender linkage of job titles. In one study, for example, evaluators assigned significantly lower ratings to jobs with a female-stereotyped title, such as 'secretary–accounting', than to the same job with a more gender-neutral title, for example 'assistant–accounting' (McShane, 1990). Furthermore, the presence of job evaluation might inhibit the development of a flexible 'high-involvement' workplace. The study by McNabb and Whitfield (2001) suggests that formal job evaluation may be incompatible with a 'commitment' HR strategy because the process adds 'rigidity' to the job and the pay structure and imparts a 'top-down' ethos to decision-making.

The job evaluation process itself comprises four steps:

1. gather the data
2. select compensable factors
3. evaluate the job
4. assign pay to the job.

Let us look at each of these in turn.

Gather the job analysis data

Information must be collected via a method of job analysis, and validity should be a guiding principle in this first step. The job analyser must accurately capture all of the job's content as ambiguous, incomplete or inaccurate job descriptions can result in jobs being incorrectly evaluated.

Select compensable factors

Compensable factors are the factors the organization chooses to reward through differential pay. The most typical compensable factors are skill, effort, knowledge, responsibility and working conditions.

Evaluate the job

There are four fundamental methods of job evaluation: ranking, job-grading, factor comparison and the point method, the latter being the most commonly used evaluation technique. For comparison purposes, we will provide brief descriptions of the other methods but will focus on the point method.

In *ranking* jobs are ordered from the least to the most valued in the organization, this rank order or hierarchy of jobs being based on a subjective evaluation of relative value. In a typical factory, we might finish up with the rank order shown in Table 9.4: in this example, the evaluators have agreed that the job of inspector is the most valued of the six jobs listed. Rates of pay will then reflect this simple hierarchy. This method has a number of advantages: it is simple, fast and inexpensive. The ranking method will be attractive for small organizations and for those with a limited number of jobs. Obvious disadvantages are that it is crude and entirely subjective; the results are therefore difficult to defend, and legal challenges might make the approach costly.

Job-grading, or job classification, works by placing jobs in a hierarchy or series of job grades. It is decided in advance how many grades of pay shall be created, the jobs

Table 9.4 Typical job-ranking

Job Title	Rank
	Most valued
1. Forklift driver	1. Inspector
2. Machinist	2. Machinist
3. Inspector	3. Secretary
4. Secretary	4. Forklift driver
5. File clerk	5. Labourer
6. Labourer	6. File clerk
	Least valued

falling into each grade based on the degree to which the jobs possess a set of compensable factors. The lowest grade will be defined as containing those jobs which require little skill and are closely supervised. With each successive grade, skills, knowledge and responsibilities increase. Grade A will, for example, include jobs that require no previous experience, are under immediate supervision and need no independent judgement. Grade F will contain jobs that require apprenticeship training under general supervision with some independent judgement. In our example in Table 9.4, the file clerk and the machinist might be slotted into grades A and F respectively. The advantage of this method is that it is relatively simple, quick and inexpensive. A disadvantage is that complex jobs are difficult to fit into the system, as a job may seem to have the characteristics of two or more grades.

Factor comparison is a quantitative method that evaluates jobs on the basis of a set of compensable factors. Jobs in the organization are compared with each other across several factors, such as skill, mental effort, responsibility, physical effort and working conditions. For each job, the compensable factors are ranked according to their relative importance in each job. Once each benchmark job has been ranked on each factor, the job evaluator(s) allocate a monetary value to each factor. This is done by deciding how much of the pay rate for each benchmark job is associated with skill requirement, how much with mental effort and so on across all the compensable factors. The main disadvantage of this approach is that it is complex, and translating factor comparison into actual pay rates is a cumbersome exercise. Because of its complexity, it is used less frequently than the other methods.

The *point method* is also a quantitative method and is the most frequently used of the four techniques. Like the factor comparison method, the point method develops separate scales for each compensable factor in order to establish a hierarchy of jobs, but instead of using monetary values, points are used. Each job's relative value, and hence its location in the pay structure, is determined by adding up the points assigned to each compensable factor.

The exercise starts with the allocation of a range of points to each compensable factor. Any number between 1 and 100 points might be assigned to each factor. Next, each of the factors is given a weighting, which is an assessment of how important one factor is in relation to another. In the case of the machinist, for example, if skill is felt to be twice as important as working conditions, it is assigned twice as many points (20 versus 10). The results of the evaluation might look like those displayed in Table 9.5.

Table 9.5 Point system matrixes

	Factor					
Job Title	Skill	Mental effort	Responsibility	Physical effort	Working conditions	Total
Forklift driver	10	10	10	10	5	45
Machinist	20	15	17	8	10	70
Inspector	20	20	40	5	5	90
Secretary	20	20	35	5	5	85
File clerk	10	5	5	5	5	30
Labourer	5	2	2	17	9	35

The point values allocated to each compensable factor are then added up across factors, allowing jobs to be placed in a hierarchy according to their total point value. In our example, this would mean that the machinist's wage rate would be twice that of the labourer. Such a differential might be unacceptable, but this difficulty can be overcome by tailoring the job evaluation scheme to the organization's pay policy and practical objectives.

The point system has the advantage that it is relatively stable over time and, because of its comprehensiveness, is more acceptable to interested parties. The shortcomings include the high administrative cost, which might be too high to justify its use in small organizations. A variation of the point system is the widely used 'Hay plan', which employs a standard points matrix applicable across organizational and national boundaries. Managers should, however, be aware that, as far as job evaluation is concerned, there is no perfect system because the process involves subjective judgement. Moreover, if women are employed, care needs to be taken to ensure that there is no gender bias in the job evaluation ratings, for example, by giving a higher weighting to physical demands and continuous service in the organization, which tend to favour men. Aspects of the Equal Pay Act are discussed later in this chapter, the focus here having been on job evaluation as a technique to achieve internal equity in pay within the organization.

Assign pay to the job

The end product of a job evaluation exercise is a hierarchy of jobs in terms of their relative value to the organization. Assigning pay to this hierarchy of jobs is referred to as pricing the pay structure, this practice requiring a policy decision on how the organization's pay levels relate to those of their competitors.

Appraisal

Performance appraisal is the process of evaluating individuals in terms of their job performance and is examined in detail in Chapter 8. The appraisal process has come under much critical scrutiny in recent years. It is argued, for example, that the technique is designed to make employees 'known' to the organizational controllers and to assist in the process of managerial control. As such, 'appraisal remains inextricably linked to the contested terrain of control and thus lies at the heart of the management of the employment relationship' (Newton & Findlay, 1996, p. 56). It is suggested that the growing use of performance appraisal is symbolic of the desire by managers to change their organizational culture to 'a system of shared meaning' (Robbins, 1990, p. 438). The appraisal process provides a 'disciplinary matrix' with which to communicate and reinforce organizational values and inculcate employee loyalty, commitment and dependency (Legge, 1995; Townley, 1989, 1994).

HRM IN PRACTICE 9.4

WORKERS SUE FORD FOR BIAS

N. SHIROUZU, *GLOBE AND MAIL*, 2001, FEBRUARY 15

A group of salaried workers at Ford Motor Co. has sued the auto maker, charging that it used an employee-evaluation system to weed out older workers.

The complaint comes against the backdrop of unease inside Ford about the new review policy, which marks a sharp change from the company's previous practices and is a highly visible symbol of chief executive officer Jacques Nasser's crusade to overhaul the 98-year-old company culture. The policy, a merit-based review system, was instituted at the beginning of last year. Under Mr. Nasser's evaluation system, which affects some 18,000 Ford salaried workers around the world, employees are graded A, B or C. Last year, 10 per cent of salaried workers received A grades, 80 per cent got Bs and

10 per cent received Cs.

The auto maker altered the system, analogous to the grading system on a curve used in school, for this year's evaluation so that only 5 per cent of the affected workers would receive Cs, and 85 per cent Bs

---

Ford is committed to becoming 'a diverse company ...'

---

and 10 per cent As. According to the company, those workers who receive Cs are not eligible for a pay raises or bonuses, and those who get a C ranking for two years straight may be asked to accept demotion or leave the company.

Ford spokesman Ed Miller declined to comment specifically on the age discrimination

case, but noted that the new evaluation system is not biased against older executives and engineers. 'This suit attacks diversity, but we see diversity as being race, gender, and age,' he said. Ford is committed to becoming 'a diverse company, racially, ethnically and along gender lines, age and sexual orientation.' The suit highlights the obstacles that corporations face when they use personnel policies to affect culture.

But lawyers for the plaintiffs in the age discrimination complaint say Ford is using the evaluation system to systematically pluck out older managers. 'We believe the new evaluation system was deliberately designed to reduce Ford's workforce based on age,' said Sue Eisenberg, one of the three principal lawyers for the plaintiffs.

Reward competitiveness

The final component of the reward management system in Figure 9.2 above is reward competitiveness, which refers to reward relationships external to the organization – comparisons with competitors (Milkovitch & Newman, 2002). How should an organization position its pay relative to what competitors are paying? The organization has three options: to be a pay leader, to match the market rate or to lag behind what competitive organizations are paying. The constraints defining the parameters within which reward choices can be made include those relating to:

- the labour market
- the product/service market
- the organizational.

Labour markets

Managers may typically be heard saying, 'Our pay levels are based upon the market.' Understanding markets requires an analysis of the demand for and supply of labour. The demand for people focuses on organizations' hiring behaviour and how much they are able and willing to pay their employees. The demand for human resources is a derived demand in that employers require people not for their own sake but because they can help to provide goods and services, the sale of which provides revenue. The supply of human resources focuses on many factors, including the wage rate for that particular occupation, its status, employees' qualifications and the preferences of people regarding paid work and leisure.

Economists inform us that in a perfectly 'free market', the pay level of a particular occupation in a certain geographic area is determined by the interaction of demand and supply. Most markets, including labour, are not free, however, but have what economists call 'imperfections' on both the demand (for example, discrimination) and the supply (for example, membership of a professional body) side. The labour market provides a context for reward management and can set limits within which it operates.

Product market

Competitive pressures, both national and global, are major factors affecting level of pay. An employer's ability to pay is constrained by her or his ability to compete, so the nature of the product market affects external competitiveness and the pay level that the organization sets. The degree of competition between producers and the level of the demand for products are the two key product market factors, both affecting the ability of the firm to change the prices of its products and services. If prices cannot be changed without suffering a loss of revenue from decreased sales, the ability of the organization to pay higher rates is constrained. The product market factors set the limits within which the pay level can be established.

Organizational

Conditions in the labour market and product market set the upper limits within which the pay level can be established. Within the European Union and in many industrialized countries, the floor, or minimum, is set by minimum wage legislation. The conditions in both the labour and product markets offer managers a choice; the pay level can be set within a range of possibilities. The concept of strategic choice emphasizes the role of managerial choice in determining the pay level to be established within an organization. A general model of the factors influencing the determination of external competitiveness and pay level is presented in Figure 9.7.

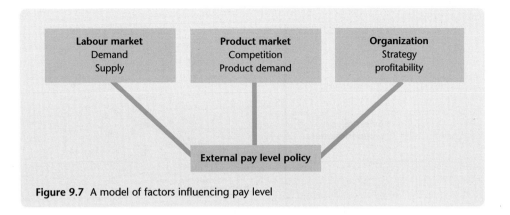

Figure 9.7 A model of factors influencing pay level

Establishing pay levels

Having considered each of the components of reward management, let us now look at how pay levels are established in practice.

The appropriate pay level for any job reflects its relative and absolute worth. A job's relative worth to the organization is determined by its ranking through the job evaluation process, whereas its absolute worth is influenced by what the labour market pays similar jobs. What is the 'going rate'? To answer this question, most organizations rely on pay surveys of key or 'benchmark' jobs; the data are used to anchor the organization's pay scale, other jobs then being slotted in on the basis of their relative worth to the organization.

HRM WEB LINKS

Go to www.statistics.gov.uk (UK New Earnings Survey), www.salariesreview.com/surveys/index.cfm, www.bls.gov, www.watsonwyatt.com, (KPMG) www.kpmg.com, www.haygroup.com (Hay Management Consultants USA), www.abs.gov.au (Australia) and www.kelly.co.za (South Africa) for published pay surveys.

Determining the right pay level means combining the results of the job analysis and evaluation process (internal equity criteria) and market pay data (external competitiveness criteria) on a graph, as depicted in Figure 9.8. The horizontal axis depicts an internally consistent job structure based on job evaluation, each grade being made up of a number of jobs (A–O) within the organization. The jobs in each category are considered equal for pay purposes – they have about the same number of points. Each grade has its own pay range defining the lower and upper limits of pay for jobs in that grade, and all the jobs within the grade have the same range. Jobs in grade 1 (that is, jobs A, B and C), for example, have lower points and pay range than jobs in grade 2 (D, E and F). The actual minimum and maximum pay rates paid by the organization's competitors are established by survey data.

Individual levels of pay within the range may reflect differences in performance or seniority. As depicted, organizations can structure their rate ranges to overlap a little with adjacent ranges so that an employee with experience or seniority might earn more than an entry-level person in the pay grade above.

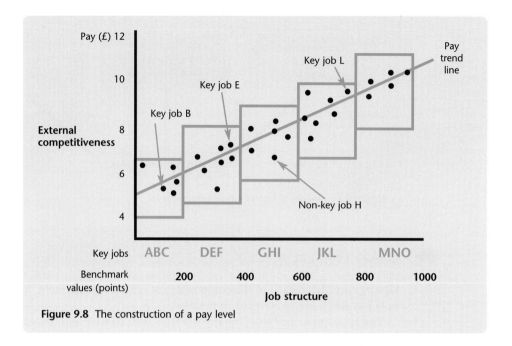

Figure 9.8 The construction of a pay level

Each black dot on the graph in Figure 9.8 represents the intersection of the going pay rate (the vertical axis), as determined by the pay survey, and the point value (horizontal axis) for a particular benchmark job. Key Jobs B, E and L are, for example, worth 100, 375 and 750 points respectively and are paid £5.50, £7.00, and £9.80 an hour. A pay-trend line is drawn through the dots, as close to as many points as possible, using a statistical technique called the 'least squares method'. The pay-trend line serves as a reference point around which pay structures and rates are established for non-benchmark jobs in the organization. There are two steps in this process. The first step is to locate the point value for the non-benchmark job on the horizontal axis; the second is to trace the line vertically to the pay-trend line and then horizontally to the pay scale. The amount on the vertical axis is then the appropriate pay rate for the non-benchmark job. Non-benchmark Job H is, for example, worth 500 points. By tracing a vertical line up to the pay-trend line and then horizontally to the vertical pay scale in Figure 9.8, it can be seen that the appropriate pay rate for job H is £8.00 per hour. Thus, both market survey information and job evaluation translate the concepts of external competitiveness and internal equity into pay practices.

Once a pay-trend line has been established, management has three choices – to lead the competition, to match what other organizations are paying or to lag behind what competitors are paying their employees – establishing a lag or lead policy by shifting the pay-trend line down or up. The least-risk approach is to set the pay level to match that of the competition, although some organizations may set different pay policies for different categories of employee with different skill sets. The company could, for example, adopt a 'lead' policy for critical skills, such as computer design engineers, a 'match' policy for less critical skill sets and a 'lag' policy for jobs that could be easily filled in the local labour market. Within organizations a variety of pay policies may thus exist. Although the pay levels within an organization reflect external competitiveness and internal equity considerations, the decision on the final pay level – the organization's pay policy – will be determined by many factors including, competitive strategy, HR strategy, reward objectives, organizational design and culture.

● Government and pay

In European states and North America, government has a profound impact, both directly and indirectly, on employees' reward. In the UK, the *direct* effect on pay occurs through legislation and pay control plans, the key UK legislation related to reward management being shown in Table 9.6.

HRM WEB LINKS

Go to the following websites to compare employment standards legislation relating to reward. www.hmso.gov.uk/acts.htm provides Acts of Parliament for the UK in full; www.labour-travail.hrdc-drhc.gc.ca/sfmc_fmcs/index.cfm?fuseaction=english gives information on Canadian employment standards and legislation. When there, click on the 'Employment law' button. For other countries, see a list of links on p. xxii of this book. Are there any major differences in the statutory provision provided by your jurisdiction and that of others?

Government can also directly affect reward management by introducing pay control programmes, which typically aim to maintain low inflation by limiting the size of pay increases. Pay controls can vary in the broadness of their application and

Table 9.6 Key UK legislation relating to reward management

Act	Date	Coverage
Equal Pay Act	1970	Male and female employees to receive equal pay for like work, equivalent work and work of equal value
Sex Discrimination Act	1986	Removal from the employer's pay structure, wage regulations, collective agreement, and so on, of any term that is discriminatory
Social Security and Contribution and Benefits Act	1992	Enforcement of statutory maternity pay for a maximum of 18 weeks Employer responsible for sick pay for the first 28 weeks of absence through sickness
Employment Rights Act	1996	Restricts unauthorized deductions and payments from the wages of employees Guaranteed payment for a whole day Right to an itemized pay statement Notice pay if the employer becomes insolvent
National Minimum Wage Act	1999	Enforcement of a statutory mimimum wage Written statement on wage calculations

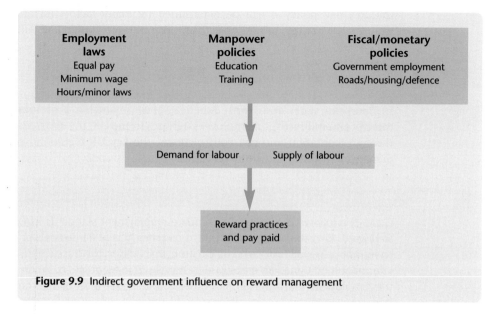

Figure 9.9 Indirect government influence on reward management

in the stringency of the standard applied. Broadness of application can include all employees, public and private, or focus on one particular group, for example the government's own employees. The standard for allowable pay increases can range from zero to increases equal to some change in the consumer price index or a measure of labour productivity. Over the past two decades, numerous governments have used a tight control of public sector pay to influence pay trends in their economies. In Britain, the Conservative government's approach to public sector pay was summarized in 1990 by Norman Lamont, then Chief Secretary to the Treasury, when he said that the government had used a 'combination of pressures' to 'reproduce the discipline which markets exert in the private sector'.[4]

In addition, government has an *indirect* influence on the pay-setting process, as depicted in Figure 9.9. Government actions affect both the demand and supply of labour and consequently pay levels. First, legislation can restrict the *supply* of labour in an occupation: a statute setting minimum age limits would, for example, restrict the supply of young people; second, government also affects the *demand* for labour. The government is a major employer and therefore a dominant force in determining pay levels in and beyond the public sector. Another indirect influence on pay levels, by affecting the markets and in turn pay, comprises government fiscal and monetary policies. Reward techniques (performance appraisal and job evaluation) and outcomes (pay levels and pay structures) must also comply with the laws passed by Parliament. This responsibility usually falls on the HR specialist. Given the importance of equal pay legislation for reward management, the next section examines the important issue of pay equity.

REFLECTIVE QUESTION

It has been pointed out by some that minimum wage regulations increase the cost of doing business and cause unemployment. What do you think of this argument? Go to www.fraserinstitute.ca and www.clc-ctc.ca for contrasting views on this issue.

Equal pay legislation

Discriminatory employment practices are a manifestation of prejudicial patterns of behaviour in society generally.[5]

Pay equity is important to all workers and thus has implications for satisfaction with the level of pay (Brown, 2001). The concept of pay equity is in conflict with the view that employees' pay should be dictated by the supply and demand of labour. Equal pay legislation has existed in the UK for three decades, but its origins can be traced back to 1919 when the International Labour Organization made the concept of equal pay for work of equal value one of its founding principles. Then, in 1951, the International Labour Organization passed Convention 100: 'Each member shall ... ensure the application to all workers of the principle of equal remuneration for men and women workers for work of equal value.' In 1972, the UK became bound to EEC Article of the Treaty of Rome, which stated that 'Each Member State shall ... maintain the application of the principle that men and women should receive equal pay for equal work.' The Equal Pay Act 1970 inserted into contracts of employment an implied term, the 'equality clause'. This enforced equal terms in the contract of employment for women in the same employment, requiring the elimination of less-favourable terms where men and women were employed on like work, and where a job evaluation assessor had rated the work as equivalent in the same employment.

Despite the existence of equal pay legislation in the UK since 1975, income disparity between men and women is widely acknowledged. In the UK, women working full time are still in receipt of only 81.5 per cent of the hourly earnings received by men (New Earnings Survey, 2001). Equal pay legislation has failed to address the problem of occupational segregation, that is, the gap between the types of job performed by men and those performed by women, which is acknowledged to be an important source of lower earnings for women relative to men. Research suggests that the percentage of women employed in an occupation is negatively associated with earnings: 'In sum, being a women has a negative effect on income', conclude Gattiker and Cohen (1997, p. 523). One commentator has also suggested that equal pay for women will not be guaranteed by legislation alone but will be secured 'only when its justice is adequately understood and practised by men' (Wedderburn, 1986, p. 503).

HRM WEB LINKS

Go to the following websites to compare male and female pay levels: www.statistics.gov.uk, www.ilo.org, www.clc.ca, www.tom.quack.net/wagegap.html, www.statssa.gov.za and www.abs.gov.au. How does pay for women compare to men in your jurisdiction?

In 1982, the European Court held that the UK's Equal Pay Act did not comply with Article 119 of the Treaty of Rome because equal pay was available for work of equal value only when the employer had chosen to conduct a job evaluation study, which a woman could in fact compel her employer to do. Consequently, the Equal Pay Act was amended by the 1983 Equal Pay (Amendment) Regulations, which meant that even where there is no 'like work' or non-discriminatory job evaluation, the equality clause entitles a woman to conditions corresponding to those of a man if their work is of 'equal value'. The new Regulations were first tested in the case of *Hayward* v. *Cammell Laird Shipbuilders Ltd* [1987], in which a cook – supported by her trade union and the

Equal Opportunities Commission – established her work as being of equal value to that of men working in the shipyard as insulation engineers, painters and joiners. Conway (1987) argues that 'The equal value concept recognizes that occupational segregation persists and that the concomitant under-valuation of "women's" work is responsible for a large part of the earning's gap.' The European Commission further expanded the provision for equal opportunities within the European Union with the Fourth Medium-Term Action Programme on Equal Opportunities, which came into operation on 1 January 1996 (see Singh, 1997).

All legislation requires, either implicitly or explicitly, that gender-neutral job evaluation schemes be adopted or developed and used to determine and compare the value of female-dominated and male-dominated jobs. Formal job evaluation can be seen as important in generating a feeling of equity in the workplace (McNabb & Whitfield, 2001) and thus constitutes the foundation of pay equity (Conway, 1987). It is critical that job evaluation schemes are designed and applied with the least possible amount of bias, particularly gender bias.

STUDY TIP

Managing the employment relationship means having a good appreciation of employment law. *Selwyn's Law of Employment* (Selwyn, 2000) offers a readable and comprehensive coverage of UK employment standard relating to reward management. Obtain a copy of the book and, using the index, list the statutes and any principal legal judgements that impact on reward management. Since an HR specialist is typically not a lawyer, what role does an HR specialist play in the area of employment standards legislation?

Paradox and reward

Let us finish our discussion of reward management by examining some of the fallacies and inconsistencies inherent in reward systems. First, attempts to foster worker commitment through variable pay arrangements might be undermined if reward to superior performers could not be paid because of the poor financial performance of the company. Disappointment resulting from unfulfilled expectations might be a source of dissatisfaction with the organization, leading to a breach of the psychological contract rather than increased commitment. Betcherman et al. (1994), for example, note that most variable reward systems fail to 'stick' for economic reasons: there are no profits or productivity gains to share. We should note Beer et al.'s (1984) and Pfeffer's (1998a) argument that IPRP creates tensions that can undermine workers' 'intrinsic motivation'. Furthermore, IPRP is prone to the 'twin vices of subjectivity and inconsistency' (Kessler, 1994) and might become discredited in the eyes of subordinates because of perceived 'procedural injustices' caused by subjective and inconsistent appraisals by managers. The literature would suggest that if this occurred, the psychological contract would be breached and employee commitment weakened.

The goal of flexibility through a pay-for-knowledge system might also not be achieved because of economic reasons, especially if the high cost of paying for additional skills, which is not directly relevant to increasing productivity, leads to the 'capping' of skill or knowledge acquisition. Again, in the context of raised employee expectations, disappointment is likely to impact negatively on the psychological contract and the commitment goal.

Finally, we should appreciate the relationship between the choice of payment system and managerial power. The selection of the reward system does not operate in a vacuum, reward practices being dictated by perceptions of power between labour and management. The implication is that we can predict that pay systems will change according to their effectiveness, vis-à-vis the relationship of effort to wages (Baldamus, 1961) and the balance of power (Nichols, 1980). In the context of a neutered, politically weak labour movement (for example Australia, Britain, New Zealand and the USA), it seems that managers' interests have focused on reward systems that link pay to individual performance. The balance of power between workers and management is a strategic factor that helps to explain the selection of pay arrangements within any HR strategy.

⬤ Chapter summary

- This chapter has emphasized that reward management is central to the effective management of the employment relationship. An effective compensation system is designed to satisfy employee needs consistent with organizational objectives. A reward system influences at least two important employee behaviours: membership behaviour and conflict behaviour, which may derive from employee dissatisfaction with the reward system.

- A reward system is a key mechanism that can influence each step of the strategy process. Current management literature suggest that a major determinant of success in business strategy implementation is an 'effective' reward system, 'effective' meaning that the reward system *fits* or is aligned with the organizational strategy. Thus, the closer the alignment or fit, the more effective the organization.

- We discussed in the chapter why no single best pay system exists. A pay structure or pay system is dynamic. A pay system that may seem highly appropriate in one period, with a particular organization and work design supporting a management strategy, can be highly inappropriate in the next, when the business strategy and organizational design has changed.

- Changes in reward systems reflect both organizational and ideological shifts in management thinking. Reward innovations are a response to changing business strategies that demand more flexibility and commitment from workers. The adoption of more IPRP systems is ideologically driven to encourage 'entrepreneurial' behaviour, but there is an apparent lack of consensus on the type of reward system that might encourage such attitudinal and behavioural change (Kessler, 2001).

- We have examined the complex argument that reward practices create, fulfil, change or violate the psychological contract, explaining how this phenomenon involves perceptual and cognitive processes that convince the employee that the 'organization' has 'reneged' on the contract. A violation may occur when communication on the nature of the contract turns out to be different (less favourable) from what the worker expected, and it may also occur if the organization unilaterally changes the contract.

● The pay model we have developed shows that reward is multidimensional, incorporating such aspects as pay structures, pay levels, incentives and benefits. It emphasizes two fundamental policy issues: internal equity and external competitiveness. Job evaluation, which seeks to ensure that the job structure is based on the content and relative contribution of the work, should ideally be seen as a technique to achieve internal fairness or equity in pay. Empirical evidence testifies, however, that job evaluation contains subjective elements. Organizations can use pay survey data to position their rewards in order to lead, match or lag behind their competitors depending upon external and internal pressures.

● We have also examined how government intervenes both directly and indirectly in the pay determination process. Keeping up to date and complying with pay legislation is a prime responsibility of HRM specialists.

● Finally, we have explored some of the ambiguities and inconsistencies in reward systems in relation to managing the employment relationship. Much of the literature suggests that the reward system is part of a diverse range of interlocking control techniques that contain internal tensions and inconsistencies, and form part of the rhetorical vision of the post-industrial work organization. Under the logic of political economy, pay systems – whether associated with 'hard' or 'soft' HRM models (Chapter 6) – cannot obviate the contradictory tensions that bedevil employment relations.

Key concepts

● External competitiveness   ● Job evaluation

● Government   ● Pay equity

● Internal equity   ● Pay model

● Job analysis   ● Point method

Chapter review questions

1. Explain the statement 'The design of reward systems is contingent upon the organizational context in which they must operate.'

2. How does reward affect and shape the psychological contract?

3. Is money the prime driver of employee performance?

4. What does job evaluation have to do with internal equity and efficiency?

5. 'Equal pay for women will be secure only when its justice is adequately understood and practised by men' (Wedderburn, 1986). Do you agree or disagree? Discuss.

● Further reading

Armstrong, M. (1998). *Employee reward.* London: Institute of Personnel and Development.

Caruth, D., & Handlogten, G. (2001). *Managing compensation: A handbook for the perplexed.* Westport, CT: Quorum.

Kessler, I. (2001). Reward system choices. In J. Storey (ed.), *Human resource management: A critical text* 2nd edn, pp. 206–31. London: Thomson Learning.

Kruse, D. (1996). Why do firms adopt profit-sharing and employee ownership plan? *British Journal of Industrial Relations,* **34**(4).

Morrison, E., & Robinson, S. (1997). When employees feel betrayed: a model of how psychological contract violation develops. *Academy of Management Review,* **22**(1), 226–56.

Rynes, S., & Gerhart, B. (eds) (2000). *Compensation in organizations: Current research and practice.* San Francisco: Jossey-Bass.

Singh, R. (1997). Equal opportunities for men and women in the EU: A commentary. *Industrial Relations Journal,* **28**(1).

● Practising human resource management

Searching the web

On an individual basis, or working in a small group, pick two or three on-line HR-related websites (e.g. www.rewardstrategies.com, www.evanomics.com, www.remuneration.org, www.shrm.org/hrlinks, www.compensationcanada.com, www.bizcenter.com/designing.htm, www.hkihrm.org, www.ahri.com.au and www.ipm.co.za) and explore 'Rewards/compensation and benefits'. Also enter the website of an organization you or the group are familiar with, or one you have studied (e.g. www.britishairways.com). From the information in this chapter and from your research, develop two or three reward objectives and decide what types of reward you would include in a reward system. Explain the reasons for your choice. Bring this information to class and present your findings and recommendation in an oral report.

HRM group project

Form a group of three or four students. The purpose of this group assignment is to allow you to apply your knowledge of reward theory to a business organization. Specifically, students will:

- carry out research on secondary and primary sources related to reward management
- apply key principles and theories to a case
- demonstrate academic writing skills.

Each group member should take responsibility for researching the various aspects of the assignment.

One team member(s) should interview at least one manager or an HR professional responsible for rewards. The interviewer(s) should probe the nature of the organization's reward strategy and system: What is the organization's reward strategy? How does the reward strategy relate to business strategy? In addition, ask about reward options: What is the mix between base, performance and indirect pay? What new reward systems have been introduced, and why?

CITY BANK

The past decade has been a watershed for the UK banking industry, particularly for City Bank, a medium-sized clearing bank. Following the deregulation of the financial sector in 1986, City Bank has faced increased competition from other financial institutions, for example building societies, an intense squeeze on profit margins and the need to make considerable provisions for bad debts. Under such pressure, City Bank introduced new technology, new financial products and a new reward system for bank managers and staff. Information and communication technologies enabled the bank to process much larger volumes of business and, just as importantly, these new technologies themselves facilitated the development of new, technically based, products and services (such as home banking, smart cards and debit cards) that City Bank started to market to its customers.

Running parallel with these technical changes was the dismantling of the paternalistic personnel management system. In essence, City Bank's bureaucratic culture and its associated belief system for managers and staff of appropriate behaviour being rewarded by steady promotion through the ranks was swept aside. The new culture in the fast-changing environment emphasized customer service and the importance of measuring and rewarding staff according to their performance. Other features of the new culture were the widening gulf between career and non-career staff, the segmentation of recruitment and training, growing occupational specialization and a declining employment level.

The new performance-related reward system was introduced at a senior management meeting in January 1996. Addressing the meeting, Elizabeth Mulberry, Director of Human Resources, said that the proposed reward system would be a key strategy to 'maintain our share of the high street business'. She went on to outline that the salary of bank managers would in future be tied to their 'leadership skills and the quality of customer service'. The Chief Executive Officer of City Bank explained the new direction like this:

> City Bank's culture has entered a new phase, and the climate is favourable for a shift in emphasis from management by paternalism to management by leadership. It is essential that bank managers ensure that the broad picture is known, understood and reflected in measurable personal objectives for those in their management team. Branch leadership also requires the ability to discriminate in the reward given to the exceptional compared with the standard performance.

Under the new reward system, the pay of each branch manager would be linked to her or his leadership skills and the quality of customer service. The reward system would link managers' pay to behaviour traits relating to leadership and customer service. Central to the drive for quality customer service, explained Elizabeth Mulberry, would be the way in which bank managers and their staff treated their customers. A questionnaire would be periodically sent out to a sample of the branch's customers, and the branch manager and staff would be evaluated for base salary on such variables as the length of time that customers queue for service, customer focus and the ability to communicate bank products and services. In turn, each bank manager would be rated on bank revenue variables (for example the number of new mortgages, employee development and leadership. According to the inter-office memorandum that was to be sent out to the 400 branch managers, variable pay for both managers and staff was to be based on what was accomplished: 'because customer service is central to City Bank's strategic plan, a three category rating system that involves "not meeting" customer expectations, "meeting" them or "far exceeding" them is the essence of the new reward system.'

As a research assistant for Right Consulting Services, a large consulting firm that specializes in management development in the finance and banking sector, you have been given the task of drafting a report to one of the firm's associates, Dr D. Perry.

Assignment

Your report to Dr Perry should:

1. outline the merits and limitations of City Bank's proposed reward system for the managers and staff

2. identify an alternative reward system for City Bank's employees congruent with their strategic plan.

HR-related skill development

The formal job evaluation process is concerned with assessing the relative worth of different jobs in an organization rather than the performance of the individual employee occupying the position. As we have emphasized in this chapter, the process is systematic rather than scientific, depending on the judgement of people. To give you experience of the job evaluation process using the point methods, we have devised a fairly realistic simulation of what would go on in a job evaluation committee. You can participate in the simulation and develop an important HR skill by going to our website, www.palgrave.com/business/brattonandgold and clicking on 'Job evaluation exercise'.

Notes

1. Herbert, S. (1991). Organizations and markets. *Journal of Economic Perspectives* **5**(33); quoted in Pfeffer (1998a, p. 215).
2. Richard Johnston, Human Resources Director of Flowpak Engineering, quoted by Bratton (1992, p. 171).
3. *Globe and Mail*, 1997, August 26, p. B12.
4. Quoted in Future uncertain for public sector pay. *Bargaining Report*, Labour Research Department, May 1991.
5. Smith, A., Craver, C., & Clark, L. (1982). *Employment discrimination law* (2nd edn, p. 1), quoted in Lord Wedderburn (1986, p. 447).

Chapter ten

Human resource development

Jeffrey Gold

Human resource development comprises the procedures and processes that purposely seek to provide learning activities to enhance the skills, knowledge and capabilities of people, teams and the organization so that there is a change in action to achieve the desired outcomes.

'A commitment to learning at work is as much a statement of values, an assertion of the kind of society that people want to live in, as an economic imperative. It implies a preference for a more inclusive society.'[1]

'Despite the fact that most employers appear to support the abstract concept of lifelong learning, it is also clear from the same study that the majority of employers were not enthusiastic about being encouraged or assisted in supporting greater other or general training.'[2]

'One of the greatest business challenges is to find some models for how a whole organization can learn.'[3]

Chapter outline

Chapter objectives

After studying this chapter, you should be able to:

1. Discuss the place of human resource development (HRD) within human resource management (HRM)
2. Understand the connections between HRD and strategy
3. Discuss the effectiveness of a national infrastructure for HRD
4. Explain how HRD may be implemented
5. Explain key ideas of workplace learning
6. Understand developments in knowledge management and e-learning

● Introduction

Human resource development (HRD), as an organization's investment in the learning of its people, acts as a powerful signal of its intentions. First, by replacing the words 'training cost' with 'investment', there is an indication that a longer-term view is being taken, particularly with respect to the outcomes of HRD. There is a significant contrast with the view of training as a short-term cost, which has persistently acted as a powerful break on many training strategies. HRD implies that learning will be a strategic consideration in an organization. Second, HRD acts as a triggering mechanism for the progression of other HRM policies that are aimed at recruiting, retaining and rewarding employees, who are recognized as the qualitative difference between organizations. The investment in employee learning is a way of creating a primary internal market, and policies aimed at progressively upgrading skills reduce an organization's dependency on external sources of skill. Third, if an organization is seeking to adopt a 'high-road' HRM strategy (Chapter 6; Cooke, 2000), engendering the conditions whereby loyalty and commitment towards an organization's aims can be encouraged, HRD carries the prospect of unleashing the potential that lies within all people, allowing employees to contribute to and indeed transform strategy.

In recent years, ideas and practices relating to HRD have moved beyond a narrow conception of training and development. Many organizations now attempt to take a holistic view that embraces the idea of learning at individual and organizational levels as a crucial source of competitive advantage. HRD has attempted to move out of training departments into every aspect of organizational life as many organizations claim attraction to the idea of a learning organization, with increasing moves towards finding ways to integrate work and learning. Technology, global markets, customer expectations and competition have all contributed to the view that organizations need to achieve 'high-performance working', leading to the generation of high value-added products and services for customers, and trust and commitment from enthusiastic employees (International Labour Organisation, 2000, p. 1). Key features of such an approach are the attention paid to learning throughout the organization and the fact that learning is the only strategy to cope with change. There is a growing emphasis on viewing an organization as a total learning system and finding its 'core competencies', which reveal its 'collective learning' (Prahalad & Hamel, 1990, p. 82). In addition, continuing advances in information technology have fostered an e-learning movement, and accelerating change has stimulated a growing interest in organization learning and knowledge management, the development of an organization's intellectual capital (Edvinsson & Malone, 1997) and the potential for learning between organizations.

These are indeed powerful notions that have made learning at work a 'hot topic' (Grey, 1998), feeding the message that learning is an obvious 'good thing'. One important consequence is a growing interest in the profession of HRD and its theoretical development. HRD practitioners, for example, form a significant section of the Chartered Institute of Personnel and Development (CIPD) in the UK,[4] where they are able to present themselves as the experts in the development of knowledge, skills and learning, and as proactive in their approach to change (Mankin, 2001). Accompanying this growth, there has been more focus on the theoretical basis of HRD (Woodall, 2001), new journals and conferences being devoted to HRD as a separate discipline rather than a subdiscipline of HRM.

As we will examine below, however, not all organizations have responded positively to the message of the virtues of HRD. In particular, in the UK, there continues to be a lack of investment in workforce learning, causing significant concern in government. Furthermore, some of the assumptions that underpin an organization's investment in people are questioned, especially if they are framed in terms of the mutual interest of employees and employers in the benefits of learning at work (Rainbird, 2000).

Strategy and human resource development

In most formulations of HRM, training, employee development and any other learning activities that form an organization's HRD provision represent significant if not pivotal components. Ashton and Felstead (1995, p. 235), for example, regard the investment by an organization in the skills of employees as a 'litmus test' for a change in the way in which they are managed. Of the 'bundle' of HR practices required for a 'high road' HRM strategy (Cooke, 2000, p. 5), HRD has a pivotal role in the integration of practices to create an internal labour market with links to organizational structure and strategy. A key image, as mentioned above, is that of high-performance working (International Labour Organisation, 2000), in which high-level skills and high discretion in the performance of work allow a decentralization of decision-making to those people closest to customers. Associated with such a view is the importance attached to learning, especially within self-managed teams; team members are able to define their own learning needs (Stern & Sommerlad, 1999).

It has, however, long been recognized that there are some key elements of organizational context that will limit and constrain the design of HRM policies and their implementation, what Guest (1989, p. 50) referred to as the 'cement' that binds the system to ensure a successful outcome to HRM policies. Included in the 'cement' are both the support of leaders and senior managers and a culture that reinforces HRM.

Two important implications arise from this view. First, employees are recruited for a skilled working role that will require learning and change, rather than for a job that might soon become obsolete. Employees are expected to retrain, and indeed many employees undertake courses of self-study in order to continue their learning and remain 'employable'. Employees are therefore carefully selected as much for their ability to learn as for their current repertoire of skills. Once recruited, employees become worth investing in, although the form of this investment may be subtler than simply possessing a large training budget. That is, learning becomes embedded into workplace practice as an ongoing process.

Second, line managers are fully involved in the development of their subordinates, to such an extent that the differentiation between learning and working becomes virtually impossible to discern (and include in a budget). There is an emphasis on informal learning and an appreciation of its value, which line managers regard as part of their job and a responsibility on which they will be assessed. It is the acceptance of this responsibility, more than any other within HRM, by line managers, that carries the potential to produce the outcomes of loyalty, flexibility, quality and commitment. Not least of these outcomes is that more formal HRD activities, such as training courses, are likely to prove their value, but the transfer of learning into the workplace can also alter the nature of work itself and the relationships between managers and employees. Thus, the processes linking performance, appraisal and development would be carried out effectively by line managers as part of their normal work, resulting in the assessment of the need for job improvement and career development.

REFLECTIVE QUESTION

Do you recognize the image of line managers portrayed above? What factors might prevent its realization?

McGoldrick and Stewart (1996) have identified leadership as a key variable in linking strategy, culture and the commitment of employees. The view of leadership employed draws upon Bass' (1985) idea of transformational leadership, made up of four components:

- charisma
- inspiration
- individualized consideration
- intellectual stimulation.

The International Labour Organisation (2000, p. 1) model of high-performance working also sees leadership as a 'starting point' for providing vision and a 'sense of momentum and direction'. Such views of leadership are particularly important when strategy is considered. Over the years, particularly in the West, managers in organizations and writers have viewed the process of planning strategy as deliberate and purposeful. This has been labelled by Mintzberg (1990) as the 'design school' model of strategic work. The key features of this approach are a prescription to assess external and internal situations, uncovering threats and opportunities, strengths and weaknesses and the declaration of an intent incorporating the values and visions of the strategy-makers. This is followed by an attempt to formulate strategies that simply and clearly reconcile the gap between perceptions of current reality and desires for the future.

It would thus seem that the extent to which HRD becomes a feature of strategy depends on the ability of senior managers to sense important environmental trends and signals in HRD terms, that is, learning for employees. Pettigrew et al. (1988), in a model of factors that trigger and drive training activity, identified the external forces that may begin the process. Technological and market changes may signal a skills gap, government requirements on health and safety may force training to be considered, or financial support from external agencies may become available. Crucially, Pettigrew et al.'s model recognized the importance of a positive culture for training and the existence of training 'champions' among leaders and senior managers who contribute to a company philosophy that supports training, at least in espoused terms. Although crucial, this view of strategy places a great reliance on the ability of senior managers to deliberate on the factors, which include HRD action through plans and policy.

This is, however, a top-down view of the process. Mintzberg (1987) provided a view of strategy-making that can foster learning within an organization if senior managers allow it. Strategies can emerge from the actions of employees, as exemplified by the following quotation (Mintzberg, 1987, p. 68):

> A salesman visits a customer. The product isn't quite right, and together they work out some modifications. The salesman returns to the company and puts the changes through; after two or three more rounds, they finally get it right. A new product emerges, which eventually opens up a new market. The company has changed strategic course.

Through employees' interaction with production processes, customers, suppliers and clients, both internal and external to their organization, employees can monitor, respond to and learn from evolving situations. If the information can flow to create knowledge, strategies can be formed by such interactions as well as be deliberately formulated. The whole process requires the reconciliation of emergent learning with deliberate control. Leaders and senior managers must be able to use the tension between the two processes of deliberate and emerging strategy-making, and resolve the dilemma, in order to craft a strategy for the real world. If they can see strategies only in deliberate planning terms, they not only run the risk of such strategies becoming unrealized, but also waste the learning that can emerge from their employees.

Integrating HRD into strategy therefore requires the development of the senior management team so that the dilemma to be resolved between control through planning and emergent learning becomes an acceptable form of their thinking. Recent years have seen increased attention being paid to the view of managers as strategic learners who are able to appreciate the complexity of the issues that impact on organizations and the groups and individuals within them. Managers are encouraged to debate and discuss the key issues that emerge, set them in a wider context and utilize the learning gained in order to bring competitive advantage (Grundy, 1994). This may also involve a greater degree of involvement and transparency in decision-making, as attempted by managers at Gucci in HRM in practice 10.1.

HRM IN PRACTICE 10.1

GUCCI UNVEILS ITS DESIGNS ON TRAINING STRATEGY

STEVE CRABB, *PEOPLE MANAGEMENT*, 2001, JUNE 14

Gucci, the luxury goods company, is involving the trade unions in determining its training strategy. This is unheard of in Italy, but is totally in keeping with the company's desire to be 'transparent', according to Gucci's corporate HR director, Renato Ricci.

The company has been growing dramatically since it went public in the mid 1990s. Revenue has risen from $263 million in 1994 to $2.26 billion last year (£1.64 billion), while profit has increased from £32.4 million to $408 million over the same period. This is partly down to the acquisition of other firms, including Yves Saint Laurent.

To help manage this change, Gucci plans to create a consensus-based culture, with a partnership environment and a new and powerful employer brand, Ricci told PM.

> **As part of the new approach, the company is building a new training centre in Florence ...**

The firm has developed a new 'contractual trade-off', involving switching from a focus on productivity to results. It also has a new management style ('from controlling to empowering'); a less antagonistic industrial relations climate; a new

relationship with the local communities in which it operates; and a new definition of talent.

As part of the new approach, the company is building a new training centre in Florence that will serve all the leather goods industry, rather than Gucci's employees alone.

Within the company's flatter hierarchy, pay rates for the 'modellers' who execute designs have been increased massively, and a 'Maestro' can now earn up to £65,000, which in Italy is equivalent to a senior manager's salary. This reflects the key role played by the modellers; in 1994 Gucci produced four collections a year, whereas today it has 20 collections.

Strategic human resource development

These deliberations on the making of organization strategy are mirrored in recent deliberations on strategic HRD. An orthodox view makes HRD entirely responsive to organizational strategy and most probably to the requirements of a broader HRM strategy. It is for others to define the needs relating the work to be carried out and the skills and knowledge necessary for implementation. HRD specialists respond by providing solutions (Garavan et al., 1999) through the development of a training system involving the identification of training needs by employees. This view is very much tied to the idea that skills are quantifiable and measurable, allowing tasks to be defined in terms of the skills and people assessed against such definitions (Thursfield, 2000). An extension of this view is to incorporate competencies, expressed as either criterion-related behaviours or standards of performance (Chapter 7). Organizational goals can be cascaded through to employees and expressed as performance expectations. Line managers work with employees to set performance targets and identify the competencies required for effectiveness. HRD is tied to the performance management system (Chapter 8), and its contribution will be judged on the benefits it brings in achieving performance targets.

Alternative versions of strategic HRD provide for a more reciprocal and proactive influence on organizational strategy. HRD specialists are able to play an important role by developing new ideas that both match strategy and take it forward. They also develop facilitating and change management skills (McCracken & Wallace, 2000), which they are able to do because managers themselves appreciate the emergent features of strategy-making and provide support for learning activities.

Gold and Smith (2003) highlight the various ways in which senior managers can respond to external pressures for change. One such response is to see learning as the way forward. That is, the need for change includes HRD as a principal component in the formation of a strategic plan. This is accompanied by managers acting as key advocates of HRD, recognizing that people are more likely to be productive when they feel that their work is personally meaningful and not simply a means to another end (Boud & Garrick, 1999). One important effect is that management become more accepting of ideas from others within the organization, a culture that supports learning thus being developed. Although such ideas can feature in any organization, they seem to have particular relevance to emerging knowledge-based organizations in which the production of new knowledge is a vital differentiator (Garvey & Williamson, 2002).

Generally, however, there is scant evidence that strategic HRD has made significant progress in the UK. As Coleman and Keep (2001) point out, even where strategic management is taken seriously, the focus in the UK is in most cases on profit maximization and cost minimization, which makes HRD and skills a fourth-order consideration. Training is seldom considered either as an input or a direct outcome of strategic considerations, and this confounds the drive towards high-performance working, learning organizations and 'high road' HRM. Indeed, Guest (2000) found, in a survey of over 1000 managers and chief executives, that although those who adopted 'high-commitment' HRM practices (Chapter 6) showed a link to business performance, most respondents (90%) did not put people issues as a top priority; marketing and financial matters had much greater importance. This highlights a key point about strategy-making: even when strategy is given full consideration, there are a number of possible paths that may be taken – for example cost, mergers, information technology, marketing – and using the skills and learning of the workforce is only one of them (Coleman & Keep, 2001). Choosing a path other than skills and learning lies at the core of a UK problem of low-priced and low-quality production and a low demand for skills. It is a problem with which governments have become increasingly concerned.

Establishing human resource development

A principal and underlying assumption within HRD is that, through the provision of learning activities in whatever form, employees are worth investing in, and there will be benefits for the individuals involved, the organization, the economy and society as whole. There are, however, different and usually competing ways of presenting the case for HRD, which carry significantly different implications for how HRD is provided, delivered and measured.

In the UK, decisions about HRD are taken principally by those in organizations in what is referred to as a voluntarist approach. The role of government in this approach is to encourage organizations to take responsibility for their own training and development and its finance. This can be contrasted with a more interventionist approach in which the government or its agents seek to influence decision-making in organizations and make decisions in the interests of the economy as a whole. There is in France, for example, a system of training levies supported by a range of other interventions that form a 'social partnership' (Noble, 1997, p. 9) between the government and organizations. The levy is an annual sum of money set by the government as a proportion of payroll, which is then used as a grant to organizations to fund training. If an organization does not provide training, it pays the levy but does not receive any grant. In the UK, however, the voluntarist approach relies heavily on market forces for skills, and in particular on the views of decision-makers in organizations.

One view, probably the dominant one, is that people are worth investing in as a form of capital. People's performance and the results achieved can then be considered as a return on investment and assessed in terms of costs and benefits. This view is referred to as human capital theory (Garrick, 1999). Although the theory may be dominant, it may also obscure key processes such as how management can ensure successful performance and how costs and benefits can be measured. Furthermore, it can present HRD in fairly narrow terms based on tangible and measurable benefits (Heyes, 2000), which may place a restriction on activities that have an uncertain pay-off over a longer time period. Investment can therefore become reduced to a cost.

Nowhere in the industrialized West is the restriction on development more in evidence than in the UK, where Taylorist–Fordist approaches to control (Chapter 4), through job design and the deskilling of jobs in order to reduce training costs, continue to hold sway in many organizations. In Chapter 8, we referred to the role of metaphor in understanding organizations and how the machine may come to be seen as the ideal way of organizing. Marsick and Watkins (1999) suggest that the machine metaphor[5] causes jobs to be seen as parts coordinated by a rational control system, in which performance can be measured as observable behaviour that is quantifiable and criterion referenced. A number of other implications can be drawn:

- Attitudes are important only insofar as they can be manipulated to reinforce desired performance.
- Each individual has a responsibility for his or her part, but no more, and has to work against a set standard.

- Learning is based on a deficit model, which assesses the gap between the behaviour of employees and the set standard.
- Training attempts to close the gap by bringing employees up to, but not beyond, the desired standard or competence.
- There is little place for a consideration of attitudes, feelings and personal development.

A further implication of the above ideal is a subservience of HRD to accounting procedures that measure the cause-and-effect relationships between programmes and output and profit in the short term. If a relationship cannot be shown, there will be pressure to provide the proof or cut the cost of the training. Even where organizations espouse an HRD approach, sufficient amounts of the machine ideal all too often remain in place, and hidden from view, to present an effective and powerful barrier to organization learning.

REFLECTIVE QUESTION

To what extent do the above features of the machine metaphor influence learning programmes in which you are involved?

Human capital theory (and the implied machine image) may be dominant in HRD but can be contrasted with a softer and more developmental view of people and their potential. Gold and Smith (2003), for example, found that some managers who were strong advocates of HRD took a developmental humanistic approach based on the personal empowerment of the workforce through learning. The achievement of results is still important, but the key argument there is that individuals are most productive when they feel that their work is personally meaningful rather than simply a means to an end. Furthermore, that learning provides a way of coping with change and fulfilling ambitions. HRD can therefore move beyond the technical limitations of training and embrace key notions of learning and development implied in such concepts as the learning organization and lifelong learning. The tensions between human capital theory and the developmental humanist view still, however, require those involved in HRD to present arguments in appropriate terms.

These views provide a background against which the case for HRD is made at the different levels of individuals, the organization and the economy/society. In recent years, there have been various attempts to do just this. At the individual level, for example, evidence is presented that there is a close relationship between learning in all its forms and job prospects, especially in terms of avoiding unemployment and increasing overall earnings (Campbell, 1999). Dearden et al. (2001), in an analysis of data from the Labour Force Survey in the UK, found that there were wage premiums with different vocational and academic qualifications. Thus, a first degree provides a premium of 28% for men and 25% for women. For training at work, there are difficulties in making precise measurements, but the effect of training is overall to provide a positive wage effect (Machin & Vignoles, 2001).

At the level of the organization, there have been many attempts to prove that HRD has an effect on performance, but, as Machin and Vignoles (2001) suggest, this is a difficult link to show. This is partly because research tends to examine the impact on intermediate factors such as labour turnover and productivity rather than on profitability. There is also the 'endogeneity problem' (Machin and Vignoles , 2001, p. 11).

That is, the direction of causality may be reversed: this means that instead of HRD being the cause of an improvement in production and profitability, it may instead be that more productive and profitable firms do more HRD. Others have, however, argued that HRD serves a variety of purposes other than profitability (Green, 1999), for example attracting good-quality staff, indicating the values of the firm and engendering commitment in times of change. Of course, HRD is, as we have argued above, a central feature of the bundle of HR practices that have been shown to impact on corporate performance.

At the level of the national economy and society as a whole, there are inevitable difficulties in separating out the linkages. At a most basic level, there is a connection between school enrolment, the proportion of the labour force in higher education and the size and rate of growth of a country's gross domestic product (Sianesi & Van Reenan, 2000). There is, however, a lack of systematic evidence to support a link between training and economic growth (Machin & Vignoles, 2001), although this has not prevented an identification of the importance of skills for national competitiveness and the negative phenomenon of social exclusion (Skills Task Force, 2000).

If these are the arguments used to support HRD, why is there continuing concern about skills levels and overall commitment to HRD in the UK? There has been a large effort to examine the causes of low commitment to HRD and significant responses by the government and others to create an infrastructure of support for HRD.

Skills and commitment

First, the examination of skills and the commitment to HRD have been long-standing issues in the UK. Recent concerns relating to global competition, change and the impact of information and communication technology (ICT) have, however, provided an impetus for a more strategic consideration, particularly in the context of a view that there is a transformation from industrial production to a knowledge-based society. The attention to skills and commitment to HRD can therefore be seen as part of a broader agenda pursued by UK governments during the 1990s, starting with the White Paper, *Education and Training for the 21st Century* (Department for Education and Employment, 1991) and moving on to the 1998 Green Paper *The Learning Age* (Department for Education and Employment, 1998a), with visions of a 'learning revolution' incorporating 'lifelong learning' and the 'learning society'.

HRM WEB LINKS

One consequence of the 'learning revolution' in the UK has been a very rapid development of web resources. Check the Department for Education and Skills (previously the Department for Education and Employment) website at www.dfes.gov.uk/ where you can find links to latest research commissioned by the UK government. The strategy with targets can be found at www.dfes.gov.uk/delivering-results/. www.lifelonglearning.co.uk/ provides access to a site established to promote the idea of lifelong learning, including Learning Towns and Cities at www.lifelonglearning.co.uk/learningcities/index.htm and Learning Partnerships at www.lifelonglearning.co.uk/llp/index.htm. The idea of a learning society was the focus of a research project set up in 1994 and completed in 1999; the website containing the findings can be found at www.staff.ncl.ac.uk/f.j.coffield/.

In relation to the general supply of skills to the economy, the Skills Task Force (STF) was set up in 1998 by the government to develop a National Skills Agenda to 'ensure that Britain has the skills needed to sustain high levels of employment, compete in the global marketplace and provide opportunity for all' (National Skills Task Force, 1998, p. 38). There then followed one of the most rigorous investigations of skills and commitment to HRD ever conducted, with 18 commissioned research reports, two major skills surveys to examine skill needs, shortages and recruitment difficulties, and an exploration of the link between business strategy and HRD. In addition, there have been detailed case studies from such key sectors as engineering, telecommunications and banking and finance. One of the key findings (National Skills Task Force, 2000) was that there was a mismatch between skill supply and demand, especially in technical jobs such as craft and professional work. Many employers seemed, however, to underestimate or not recognize their skills gaps, or not consider future needs. It was also found that training tended to be concentrated among managers and senior staff, while unskilled, 'flexible' workers and those in small organizations received very little – a finding confirmed in a survey by the CIPD (Cannell, 2002).[6] The Task Force established skill priorities (National Skills Task Force, 2000) relating to basic skills, generic skills, intermediate skills, ICT specialist skills and mathematics. There was also concern about the number of qualified adults in the workforce, especially when compared with countries such as France and Germany.

Overall, the research supported a pattern suggesting the continuation of the findings of Finegold and Soskice (1988), who presented the idea of a self-reinforcing cycle of low-quality products and low skills in the UK. They argued that, as a nation, the UK's failure to educate and train its workforce to the same level as its competitors was both a cause and a consequence of its relatively poor economic performance – a cause because the absence of a well-educated and trained workforce restrained the response of UK organizations to changing world economic conditions, and a consequence because the production techniques of UK organizations for many years signalled a demand for a low-skilled workforce. In the 1990s, it has been argued that employers, expecting low skills among their workforce, aimed to compete in low-skilled product and service markets (Keep, 1999). Furthermore, if a narrow human capital view is taken, employers will seek a return from training with a demonstration of a contribution to profits; if this cannot be shown, the investment may be curtailed and seen as a cost that can be cut. There are certainly many examples of organizations in the UK that do not take a restricted view, and attempts have been made to show the effect of HRD activities not just on the bottom line, but also on the climate of work and willingness to change (Johnson et al., 2000).[7] However, in many organizations within the voluntarist environment of the UK, that is, where employers have a choice about how much they can invest in HRD, many choose to minimize, leaving those outside organizations (government and its agents) with little option but to offer a range of supply-side measures and 'exhortation' to employers to provide more activities (Keep, 1999).

REFLECTIVE QUESTION

Not all countries follow a voluntarist approach to HRD. In France, for example, there is a system of training levies. What are the benefits of compulsory levies? What might the problems be?

HRM WEB LINKS

The work of the STF, including access to all reports and research, can be found at the following website: www.dfee.gov.uk/skillsforce/1.htm. Employers Skill Survey and Case Study reports can be found at: www.skillsbase.dfes.gov.uk/Reference/Reference. asp?sect=1&page=7.

Working on the basis of a voluntarist approach to HRD, successive governments in the UK have framed their policies on the idea of a market-led system for skills in which demand and supply determine the amount of training provided. In particular, the demand for skills must come from decision-makers in organizations, although, as we have already suggested above, there is a tendency to make HRD a fourth-order consideration strategically, and pressures to meet financial targets in the short term can lead to a low level of demand for HRD. This seems in particular to affect the large number of the workforce who have low or no qualifications, whereas those who are well qualified may receive an unequal share of HRD resources (Skills Task Force, 2000). For those outside work, low qualifications may prevent entry into the labour market and contribute to the emerging difficulties of social exclusion; as we will see, this issue has become a crucial feature of policy-making in recent years.

Given the difficulties above, the role of government and its agents within a market-led approach has been to improve the UK's training infrastructure and provide funding for interventions to support the smooth working of the system where markets fail. In addition, there have been efforts to stimulate the demand for skills within organizations. Important foundations in the infrastructure have been the establishment of a framework of vocational qualifications based on national standards, that is, National Vocational Qualifications (NVQs, in England and Wales) and Scottish Vocational Qualifications (SVQs), and a national network of regionally based institutions to coordinate national HRD initiatives aimed at improving the functioning of the markets.

NVQs and SVQs have been developed to provide a national framework of vocational qualifications in the UK. The framework, covering most occupations, provides qualifications based on the required outcomes expected from the performance of a task in a work role, expressed as performance standards with criteria. These describe what competent people in a particular occupation are expected to be able to do and are usually referred to as 'competences'. It is claimed that NVQs and SVQs are directly relevant to employers' needs since they are based on standards set by employer-led standards-setting bodies. There may be up to five levels of a qualification, each level being defined by the national framework (Table 10.1).

There has undoubtedly been an increase in the number of people gaining qualifications in the UK. According to the Qualifications and Curriculum Authority (QCA),[8] which is the agency acting as the guardian for all standards in education and training, 3,715,061 NVQ certificates were awarded up to 30 June 2002, an increase of 11% on the number awarded up to 2001. Competence-based NVQs and SVQs have not, however, been without their critics. There have been concerns over the meaning of competence, with its emphasis on the achievement of outcomes and assessment measured against standards in preference to an attention on knowledge and understanding. In addition, short-term political pressures have, throughout the history of NVQs, tended to influence and distort their development (Williams, 1999), and there are doubts whether NVQs and SVQs provide a more effective framework for training

Table 10.1 The national framework for National Vocational Qualifications/ Scottish Vocational Qualifications

Levels	Definitions
Level 1	Competence which involves the application of knowledge in the performance of a range of varied work activities, most of which may be routine and predictable
Level 2	Competence which involves the application of knowledge in a significant range of varied work activities, performed in a variety of contexts. Some of these activities are complex or non-routine and there is some individual responsibility or autonomy. Collaboration with others, perhaps through membership of a work group or team, may often be a requirement
Level 3	Competence which involves the application of knowledge in a broad range of varied work activities performed in a wide variety of contexts, most of which are complex and non-routine. There is considerable responsibility and autonomy and control or guidance of others is often required
Level 4	Competence which involves the application of knowledge in a broad range of complex, technical or professional work activities performed in a variety of contexts and with a substantial degree of personal responsibility and autonomy. Responsibility for the work of others and the allocation of resources is often present
Level 5	Competence which involves the application of a range of fundamental principles across a wide and often unpredictable variety of contexts. Very substantial personal autonomy and often significant responsibility for the work of others and for the allocation of substantial resources feature strongly, as do personal accountabilities for analysis, diagnosis, design, planning, execution and evaluation

Source: Department for Education and Skills at www.dfes.gov.uk/nvq/what.shtml

than other approaches (Hillier, 1997). Keep (1999) suggests that NVQs have added to the number of vocational qualifications on offer rather than rationalizing them: according to the QCA, for example, there were 743 NVQ titles in the framework at the end of September 2001, accessible via a national database. Despite the criticisms, however, NVQs and SVQs have become an important feature of the training infrastructure and are used by governments to set targets and by some organizations to build and implement training plans, as shown in HRM in practice 10.2.

In terms of institutions to support delivery of the government's strategy, this was from 1990 until 2001 principally the responsibility of locally based Training and Enterprise Councils (TECs) (Local Enterprise Companies, or LECs, in Scotland). TECs and LECs undertook a wide variety of activities, including the finance and administration of the various programmes designed to improve the position of young people in the training market and enhance their employability. Such programmes included

HRM IN PRACTICE 10.2

GETTING THE VALUE FROM NVQs AT THE NORTHERN SNOOKER CENTRE

JUNE WILLIAMSON, COMPANY SECRETARY

The Northern Snooker Centre Ltd (NSC) is a long established family business in Leeds. With over thirty-three staff, the company has developed from having 9 snooker tables to over 27 plus 16 pool tables and three bar and lounge areas which are open 24 hours a day and 365 days a year. The family owners have consistently worked towards developing a customer-focused culture and ethos based on staff training and development, teamwork and leadership. The company regards the 'team' as the whole workforce and has therefore sought to provide learning opportunities for everyone using NVQs as a key mechanism.

NVQs offer added value to NSC particularly through the training of employees as assessors. In-house assessment has provided bonding opportunities by allowing time to be set aside for training and discussion. Morale, communication and recognition have all been boosted. NVQs also offer convenience and flexibility. Staff have been able to set their own pace and most learning is at work.

> **Recent revisions of NVQs have been a breath of fresh air.**

Recent revisions of NVQs have been a breath of fresh air. Previously there was a lot of repetition in providing evidence against the performance criteria for each unit. This led to huge evidence portfolios which were monotonous to compile and assess. Now, we can use different kinds of evidence like taped discussions between student and assessor for a cross-section of units.

In NSC, NVQs have been confidence builders with no exams and no feeling inadequate in front of a class of people. Staff who have not studied for many years have felt a great sense of achievement in completing their NVQ work.

The company covers the cost and offers wage increases, with a celebratory night out on completion. NVQs benefit everyone – company and employees alike.

Youth Training (now called the New Deal) and Modern Apprenticeships, which aimed to improve the number qualified in technical, craft and junior management skills. Importantly, NVQs and SVQs were a required component of such schemes and were used by TECs and LECs to measure the success of programmes and to meet targets set by government.

A key strength of the TECs was that, as locally based institutions, they formed key links with local bodies such as local authorities, careers services, chambers of commerce and so on. However, whereas TECs could point to significant achievements in providing business support and increasing the number of qualifications, there were concerns about a variability in performance between TECs and the clarity of focus in achieving government objectives (Department for Education and Employment, 1998a). There were also difficulties relating to boundaries, many TECs focusing on narrowly defined business areas such as a city or a town (Coulson, 1999). During the late 1990s, UK government policy was increasingly influenced by what has been referred to as 'New Regionalism' (Webb & Collis, 2000). The basic idea here was that a region should form the basis of thinking and policy relating to development, competitiveness and growth. This could be augmented by the notion of a 'learning region' in which local knowledge and relationships across a region provide a context that supports learning between institutions.

In the UK, particularly in England,[9] these arguments were used to create Regional Development Agencies in 2000 in order to develop regional strategies and action plans and, from 2001, to replace TECs with a Learning and Skills Council (LSC) with delivery units set at a subregional level, for example West Yorkshire or North Yorkshire. The LSC oversees all post-16 years of age education and training. Forty-seven local LSCs replaced 82 TECs, a key difference being that the national LSC set the guidelines on the achievement of targets relating its vision as its website describes: 'by 2010, young people and adults in England will have the knowledge and productive skills matching the best in the world'. LSCs also provide contracts for the delivery of services to small businesses, usually called 'Business Links' (although officially called the Small Business Service).

HRM WEB LINKS

You can find up to date information about strategies, plans and services from the various websites. Try www.lsc.gov.uk/ for the LSC home page. Information about Modern Apprenticeships can be found at www.realworkrealpay.info. Go to www.local-regions.detr.gov.uk/rda/info/ for information about the formation of Regional Development Agencies. Other agencies forming the infrastructure include the Learning and Skills Development Agency at www.lsda.org.uk/home.asp, with a Learning and Skills Research Centre at www.lsrc.ac.uk/; Sector Skills Councils at www.ssda.org.uk/ssc/sscouncil.shtml and the Small Business Service at www.sbs.gov.uk/.

The demand for skills

It would appear that radical changes in the HRD infrastructure are being sought by the UK government in order to stimulate learning. As the Secretary of State's Foreword to the 1998 Green Paper (Department for Education and Employment, 1998a) describes, 'Learning is the key to prosperity ... Investment in human capital will be the foundation of success in the knowledge-based global economy of the twenty-first century'. For a market-led approach to operate to ensure a high demand for skills, action is, however, required principally from within organizations, and, as we have already indicated, many organizations may not regard HRD as being central to their requirements other than to keep production in shape. In such circumstances, it is not always clear whether HRD has a direct causal impact on improvements in organizational measurements such as profitability. As Green (1997) has reported, the benefit to employers of training is established through 'intermediate' variables such as labour turnover and organizational commitment, although evidence to support this is not robust. Most important is probably the definition of the firm-specific skills required for the specific production requirements of an organization. If tasks are designed as requiring a high level of skill, this will trigger a requirement for a highly trained workforce and for investment in that workforce if skilled labour is not available in the external market. Furthermore, the presence of skilled employees is likely to contribute to the interpretation by managers that any changes, particularly in technology, can be dealt with by their employees, so they are able to take advantage of any benefits that the changes may bring (Green & Ashton, 1992). The recognition of trade unions may also lead to more effective HRD strategies (Green et al., 1998).

Considering technological change specifically, it is possible to foresee two scenarios as a response to technological change. First, on the basis of pressures to meet short-term targets and a poor HRD infrastructure, investment in skills is considered too risky. The consequence is the use of new technology to deskill employees and reduce cost. Alternatively, on the basis of an established skill base that meets the situational requirements of production and belief and trust in the ability of employees to learn, any change is used to take advantage of human talents and 'up-skill' employees. It is important to understand that the second scenario may be part of an overall pattern in which the organization seeks to satisfy the expectations of a number of stakeholders, including employees, the community at large and financial bodies.

The second scenario is also one that has been supported by government policy through the Investors in People (IIP) initiative. Established in October 1991, IIP provides a set of standards for training and development requiring organizations to develop business plans that include schemes to develop all employees and evaluate the results. Until 2001, the initiative was managed by the TECs, but it is now delivered by local LSCs and Business Links, and is a feature of their targets in terms of both the number of organizations that commit to IIP and the number that achieve the standard. Although the processes involved proved for some organizations, even those committed to IIP, to be too difficult, or circumstances such as restructuring caused a delay in reaching the standard, the main result appears to be an improvement in training practice (Hillage & Moralee, 1996). Furthermore, a study examining organizations that had already gained IIP found that the main benefits of IIP came if it was used as a way to assess performance and implement continuous improvement (Alberga, 1997). It could, however, be argued that IIP represents something of a spurious means of stimulating the demand for HRD within an organization. Down and Smith (1998), for example, found that many organizations achieving IIP had least to change because they were already doing what was required to achieve the award. Alternatively, as Gold and Smith (2003) argue, IIP plays a special role in providing a rationale, a process and a positive language for HRD where managers are already convinced of its virtues.

In pursuance of its Lifelong Learning agenda, government has identified that 'driving up demand' for learning, of any kind, among individuals is a key goal (Department for Education and Employment, 1999, p. 55). The basic idea is that if individuals, particularly underqualified adults, seek to engage in learning activities, this will improve their employability and their openness to further learning within organizations, and become a source of competitive advantage. Once again, we can see the influence of human capital theory, although this has also been criticized by those who take a more humanistic approach (Field, 2000) and would challenge the simplistic link between the education and learning of individuals and economic advances. A number of initiatives have nevertheless been launched, including the University for Industry (UfI) and Learndirect.[10]

Another initiative was the idea of Individual Learning Accounts (ILAs), in which individuals could obtain up to £150 towards the cost of a programme of learning. ILAs were particularly targeted at people who wanted to improve their basic skills, up to NVQ level 2. However, although introduced in 1998, the scheme was suspended by 2001 owing to claims of fraud. A limited evaluation of ILAs revealed that they might simply have replaced individual or employer funding for learning with public funding; that is, some people would have done the learning without ILAs. There is, however, also evidence that a number of people who would not normally access courses were able to access them and enjoy learning (Payne, 2000). A further initiative has been the Union Learning Fund (ULF), which supports trade union projects for learning. Where unions were recognized within organizations for collective bargaining purposes, they could also appoint learning representatives (Rana, 2001).

HRM WEB LINKS

The home page of Investors in People is www.iipuk.co.uk/. You can find the University for Industry at www.ufiltd.co.uk (www.scottishufi.co.uk in Scotland) with access to Learndirect at www.learndirect.co.uk. Further information relating to the Union Learning Fund can be found at www.dfes.gov.uk/ulf/.

The learning movement

The concern over HRD in the UK has continued into the 21st century. After the work of the STF and others, a further contribution to the development of a strategic framework was provided by the Performance and Innovation Unit of the Cabinet Office. Seeking to 'join up' the thinking across various government departments, a workforce development project was established to explore both the economic problems of low productivity compared with other countries and the issue of social exclusion as consequence of low skill level (Performance and Innovation Unit, 2001). The project sought to consolidate on much of the previous work producing recommendations for government, employers and individuals. However, the problem of a weak demand for skills remained. No single answer was available: both radical and incremental measures were needed, with a particular emphasis on demand-led approaches. This once again raises the intractable problem of how decisions are made relating to skills in organizations and how HRD becomes a feature of organizational life.

Gold and Smith (2003) suggest that the recommendations, ideas and exhortations relating to HRD and learning at work, plus the structures to support these, are a feature of what they term the learning movement. The key point is that even though the learning movement provides the resources to support HRD, decision-makers still have a choice and can remain oblivious to pressures for more HRD, or sceptical about the benefits. Gold and Smith found that making a decision in favour of HRD was related to a recognition of the need to change and that this could be achieved through HRD. A further factor was, however, the background orientations of the decision-makers, which made them favourably disposed towards HRD; that is, the managers themselves had had positive experiences of HRD or espoused values of openness, trust and commitment, which they believed could be achieved through HRD. It was also found that, once a decision to pursue HRD had been made, it was usually then necessary to persuade others, which often required a great deal of discussion and action to keep HRD alive, especially where more sceptical views might block progress.

The implications here are clear. Pursuing a policy of HRD has to reflect the strategy of senior managers who are able to view their organizations in a variety of ways. Seeing people as being worth investing in means being able to ward off the competing pressures that might challenge this view while at the same time providing the support for a value system that we might call a learning environment. In such an environment, key participants are able to respond to calls for the spread of HRD activities throughout the workforce, and to ensure their success. Of particular importance are the actions of managers at all levels in supporting learning and turning an aversion to risk-taking into opportunity-spotting.

Although there are many recommendations to adopt a more strategic approach to HRD and make it more business driven, there remains the crucial factor of how HRD is implemented. A number of uncertainties and tensions arise here. Who, for example, should take responsibility for HRD? Should it be HRD specialists, with their sophisticated repertoire of interventions and techniques, or line managers, who are close to work performance and are able to influence the way in which people learn and develop, and the environment in which this occurs? How should needs be identified, and whose interest should they serve: that of employees seeking opportunity and reward for the sacrifice of their effort, or that of the organization in the pursuit of goals and targets? What activities should be used, and do the activities add value? How does HRD relate to business goals? Overall, there is insufficient evidence about what is happening inside organizations when HRD is considered, which is compounded when we consider both formal and informal approaches to learning at work. It is becoming clearer that, although formal aspects of HRD, such as plans, policies and activities, can have a crucial impact, informal features may be of even greater importance. In particular, we might consider the impact of work groups on learning or how line managers really inhibit or support HRD processes. These aspects of HRD are certainly significant, although they are also more difficult to examine and measure.

Formal models of implementation have shown a remarkable tendency to match the conventional wisdom of how organizations should be run. Depending on the resources committed to their activities, trainers have had to justify the commitment by an adherence to prescriptive approaches. Employees traditionally learnt their jobs by exposure to experienced workers who would show them what to do ('sitting by Nellie'). Much learning undoubtedly did occur in this way, but as a learning system it was haphazard and lengthy, and bad habits as well as good could be passed on. In some cases, reinforced by employers' tendencies to deskill work, employees were unwilling to give away their 'secrets' for fear of losing their jobs. Most importantly, line managers did not see it as their responsibility to become involved in training, thus adding to forces that served to prohibit any consideration of valuing employee potential.

A systematic training model

The preferred routine is to adopt a systematic training model, an approach that emerged during the 1960s under the encouragement of the Industrial Training Boards.[11] The approach was based on a four-stage process shown in Figure 10.1 and was widely adopted, becoming ingrained in the thinking of most training practitioners.

This model neatly matches the conception of what most organizations would regard as rationality and efficiency, a consistent theme in many HRM processes (Chapters 6–8). There is an emphasis on cost-effectiveness throughout: training needs are identified so that wasteful expenditure can be avoided, objectives involving standards are set, programmes are designed and implemented based on the objectives, and outcomes are evaluated, or more precisely validated, to ensure that the programme meets the objectives originally specified and the organizational criteria. There is a preference for off-the-job learning, partly because of the weaknesses identified in the 'sitting by Nellie' approach, and partly to formalize training so that it is standardized, measurable and undertaken by specialist trainers. The trainer can focus on the provi-

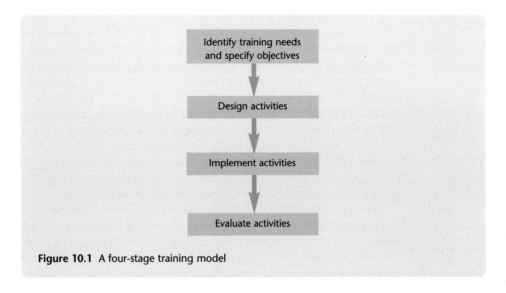

Figure 10.1 A four-stage training model

sion of separate training activities that avoid the complexity of day-to-day work activities and make evaluation all the easier.

In this systematic model, training needs assessment and analysis is concerned with identifying gaps between work performance and standards of work or performance criteria that have a training solution. Once these have been identified, clear and specific objectives can be established that can be used to design learning events and evaluate the outcomes. Training needs can exist and be identified throughout an organization. Boydell (1976) identified three possible levels; organization, job or occupation, and individual. Needs are in theory identified at corporate or organizational levels and fed through to the individual level. The approach reflects a mechanistic view of organizations and the people within them. In particular, there is an emphasis on the flow of information down the hierarchy to individuals, whose training needs are assessed against standards defined by others. Each person has a responsibility to perform against the standard and to receive appropriate training if they are unable to meet the standard. Emerging from a consideration of needs will be plans for development activities. These may take the form of on-the-job or work-based opportunities supported by line managers and others, or off-the-job courses run by specialists and, increasingly, open and distance learning or e-learning (see below) activities. Evaluation occurs as the last stage of the model. Although a number of writers have pointed out the value of evaluation at each stage (Donnelly, 1987), the image of evaluation encompassed by many trainers is that of a final stage added on at the end of a training course. In such cases, evaluation serves to provide feedback to trainers, so that small adjustments and improvements may be made to activities, or to provide data to prove that the training meets the objectives set, so that expenditure on training may be justified.

REFLECTIVE QUESTION

The four-stage model may be rational and efficient, but is it a model of HRD?

Over the years, the basic elements of the four-stage training model have remained, and most organizations that claim to have a systematic and planned approach to training would have some representation of it. There have also been a number of refinements by advocates of a more realistic and more sophisticated model. Donnelly (1987) has argued that senior management may, in reality, abdicate responsibility for training policy to training departments, with a consequent potential for widening the gap between training and organizational requirements. Essential prerequisites for any effort to implement a training model are a consideration of budgets, attitudes, abilities and culture or climate. A key requirement of training activity is that it should be relevant and 'reflect the real world'. We can, however, easily see how training could become either isolated from organization strategy or reactive to it. Garavan et al. (1999, p. 171) suggest that a 'jug and mug' metaphor may be suited to the trainer role here, with a very passive involvement of learners at any stage.

Bramley (1989) argued that the training subsystem may become independent of the organizational context. He advocated turning the four stages into a cycle that is open to the context by involving managers in analysing work situations to identify desirable changes, and designing and delivering the training to bring the changes about. Evaluation occurs throughout the process, with an emphasis on managers taking responsibility for encouraging the transfer of learning that occurs during training into workplace performance. In this way, the model is made effective rather than mechanistically efficient.

Refinements to the basic form of the systematic model imply that a more sophisticated view of training is taken. This essentially involves taking account of reality and organizational context. Implicit in such a view are the inherent limitations of organizational reality, which may prevent the basic model operating or may maintain training activity at a low level. The reality may thus be little consideration for training in relation to organizational strategy and a culture that emphasizes short-term results against set standards. Managers may refuse to accept responsibility for identifying staff training needs and supporting the transfer of learning where training is undertaken. These are all features of an organization's learning climate, a consideration of which is essential for the implementation of an HRD approach.

Taylor (1991) argued that it is possible to present two views of why systematic training models may not match organizational reality. In the first, referred to as the rehabilitative critique, it is argued that the systematic model's concepts are sound and can be used as an approximation to reality, serving to highlight the problems to be overcome at each stage by refining techniques. In identifying training needs, for example, trainers may not have access to the 'real' learning needs of the organization because of a lack of access to information and low credibility with senior managers. The refinement would be for trainers to raise the profile of training. However, the second view – the radical critique – argues that the systematic model is based on flawed assumptions and is merely a 'legitimising myth' (Taylor, 1991, p. 270) to establish the role of the trainer and allow management's right to define skill within the employment relationship. It is often assumed, for example, that training is in everyone's best interest. In times of rapid change, however, the definition of skill and the redesign of work, which determines and is determined by employee learning, may lead to a divergence of interest between employees and management and unbalance the employment relationship between them.

Taylor (1991) concluded that while systematic models may have helped to professionalize the training activity and provide a simple and easily understood explanation of training procedures, such models were incomplete and really only suitable for organizations operating in stable environments where goals could be clearly set, outcomes measured and mere compliance obtained from employees. According to Taylor (1991, p. 273), however:

> Continued adherence towards what is still essentially a mechanistic procedure may well prevent trainers tapping into the more nebulous but powerful organizational forces such as mission, creativity, culture and values.

An integrated approach

In contrast to the mechanistic view of training implied by the systematic approach above, many organizations, especially those facing uncertain environments and the expectation of rapid and continuous change, have sought a more integrated approach in recent years. It is an approach that highlights key interdependencies within organizations, such as the link to strategy, the role of line managers and perhaps the emergent features of learning. It is therefore an approach to which the label 'human resource development' seems more suited.

Because change may occur frequently, it is important the people are able and prepared to move beyond their existing skills, knowledge and abilities. In Chapter 6, we highlighted that there were significant tensions in the idea of making workers more flexible and multiskilled; one possible path, however, is that the developmental potential of people is brought to the fore, and this allows HRD specialists to play a more proactive role.

As we have already indicated, the development of competency frameworks (Chapter 7) seeks to link business objectives and employee performance. As we explained in Chapter 8, competencies can be utilized within a performance management system to provide a performance and development plan that will include an identification of training needs and a plan to meet such needs. Instead of being driven by trainers, training needs are demand-led (Chiu et al., 1999) relating to business needs, the requirement for change or the results of self-assessment. Research into the use of competencies has found that the main uses are discussion and rating of job performance, and identifying training needs (Strebler et al., 1997). It is interesting to note that overall satisfaction with competencies depended on the way in which they were introduced and the provision of training for those who would be required to use them. It was, however, also found that where competencies were used in performance review, identifying training and development needs might actually be detrimental to confidence when using competencies. It seemed that some respondents were sceptical that actions agreed in performance reviews would actually be carried out. As one manager observed: 'I am convinced that unless the system is undertaken professionally, it has negative value and becomes a cynics' charter. It is therefore all or nothing' (quoted in Strebler et al., 1997, p. 76). This difficulty highlights the importance of the line manager's role in the assessment and development of others.

HRM WEB LINKS

There are many HRD resources available on the web. For a closer look at needs analysis, try www.trainingneedsanalysis.co.uk/index.htm. This is the site of a company specializing in needs assessment, but they provide a great deal of information about various processes and the selection of different methods.

If you are looking for activities, try www.trainingzone.co.uk/. You will have to join the site, but once you are logged on, it is an amazing collection of resources and news, as is www.trainersnetwork.org/. Other HRD training sites are www.labour.gov.za (South Africa) and www.anta.gov.au (Australia).

www.mapnp.org/library/trng_dev/trng_dev.htm is the training and development page of the Free Management Library. If you are prepared to explore a little, you will find links to many HRD resources.

Whatever the quality of the assessment of needs and the HRD activities undertaken, the context in which these occur has a vital impact on their value. A policy of HRD has to be translated into the structures, systems and processes that might be called a learning climate. The learning climate in an organization is composed of subjectively perceived physical and psychosocial variables that will fashion an employee's effectiveness in realizing learning potential (Temporal, 1978). Such variables may also act as a block to learning. Physical variables cover the jobs and tasks that an employee is asked to undertake, the structure within which these are set, and factors such as noise and the amount of working space. Of particular significance is the extent to which the work carried out can be adjusted in line with employee learning, for example following the completion of an HRD activity. Psychosocial variables may be more powerful; these include norms, attitudes, processes, systems and procedures operating in the workplace. They appear within the relationships in which an employee is involved, for example with managers, work colleagues, customers and suppliers.

At the heart of the learning climate lies the line manager–employee relationship. HRD requires the integration of the various activities, the key to achieving this lying in the thoughts, feelings and actions of line managers. Some organizations have recognized this and have included 'developing others' within their competency frameworks for managers (Industrial Relations Services, 2001). A number of roles have been associated with managers to support the fusion, including coaching and mentoring.

Coaching was, of course, originally a development within the sporting field aimed at improving performance (Evered & Selman, 1989), but during the 1970s and 80s it was adapted as a management activity to enhance the development of employees, with particular emphasis on the transfer of learning from formal training courses into workplace activity. Coaching is now one of a range of activities within organizations concerned with helping both managers and staff, but the particular focus of attention in coaching is combining performance improvement with HRD (Megginson & Pedler, 1992). This focus is not, however, without tension, and the quandary of being accountable for performance and HRD could lead to a regression into stereotyped management behaviour (Phillips, 1995). That is, managers may find it difficult to develop their staff when there is need to meet performance targets, the latter usually taking precedence. Recent times have nevertheless seen the emergence of coaching in a variety of contexts, including executive coaching for managers working at more senior levels within organizations (Carter, 2001).

Mentoring in organizations can be understood as help by one person given to another to find new meanings in work and/or life (Megginson & Clutterbuck, 1995). The distinctive feature of mentoring, and in contrast to coaching, is the focus on longer-term learning and development. To ensure that the focus is maintained, mentoring is therefore more likely to be carried out by a more senior or experienced

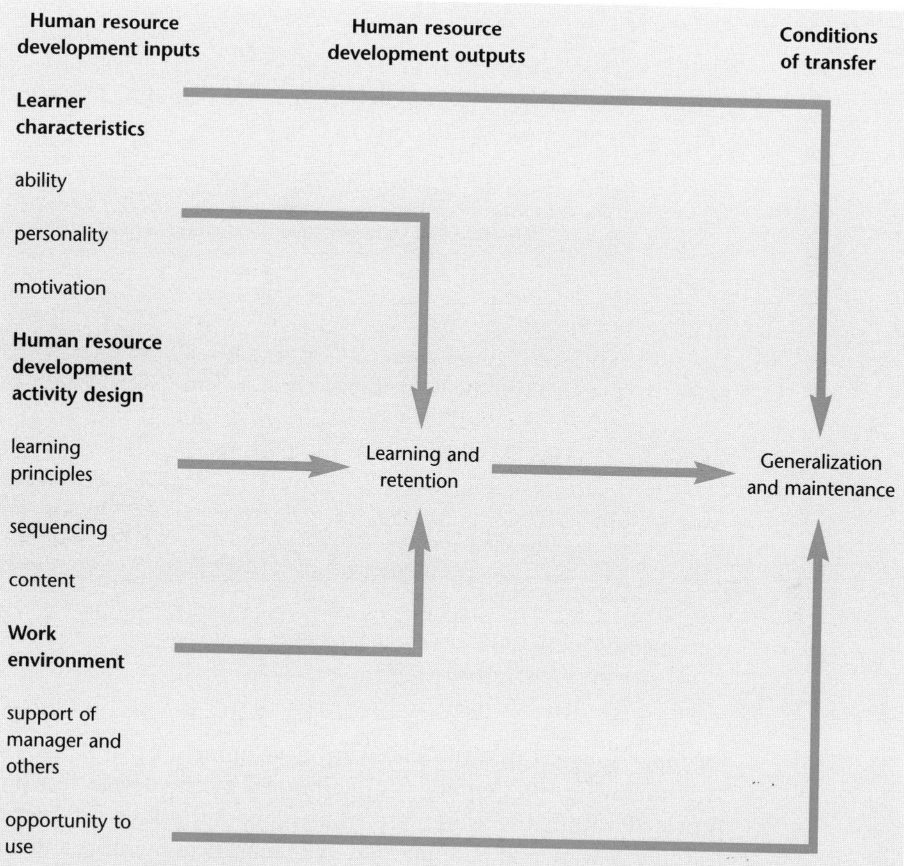

Figure 10.2 A model of the transfer within human resource development
Source: Adapted from Baldwin and Ford (1988)

manager who is not the line manager, although the line manager may fulfil this role in some organizations. Over the past 20 years, there has been a great deal of interest in mentoring. Recent attention has examined the matching of mentor and mentee (Hale, 2000), the delivery of mentoring, including tele-mentoring (Stokes 2001), and mentoring change managers during projects of change (Rix & Gold, 2000). However, because mentoring is a process usually involving conversations between two or more people held in private, there remain gaps in understanding related to what happens, the experience of the participants and the value gained (Megginson, 2000).

Coaching and mentoring are both processes that feature HRD as a management responsibility. In particular, they are processes that can provide a link between HRD activities, transfer to work and evaluation. Figure 10.2 shows a model of the transfer within HRD adapted from the work of Baldwin and Ford (1988, p. 65). The model specifies six crucial linkages, indicated by arrows in Figure 10.2. We can, for example, see that new skills can be learnt and retained, but support and opportunity to use the learning must be provided in the work environment. Key support activities comprise coaching and mentoring by managers to include goal-setting, reinforcement activities, encouragement to attend and modelling of behaviours. Billett (2001, p. 213), for

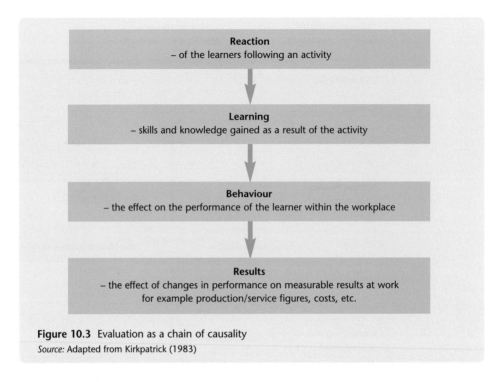

Figure 10.3 Evaluation as a chain of causality

Source: Adapted from Kirkpatrick (1983)

example, suggests that the successful development of workplace knowledge, particularly following HRD inputs, is underpinned by the degree to which 'affordances' are provided within the workplace, that is, opportunities for learners to engage with learning at work and be supported by managers as mentors and coaches.

The activities of managers to support transfer within HRD are a key feature of the evaluation of HRD. As we indicated above, within the mechanistic view of training, evaluation appears as final stage. The key purpose of evaluation is to show how training input leads to particular outputs and outcomes. In a well-known model of evaluation (Kirkpatrick, 1983), for example, measurements could be taken at four stages to show a chain of causality in order to prove a result. Figure 10.3 shows the stages.

This view of evaluation matched the mechanistic view of training and became the orthodoxy for many years, with a number of adaptations to improve its working. There have, however, been persistent doubts about its efficacy and value when applied to many training and development activities (Guba & Lincoln, 1989), especially the idea that the outcomes of training can be quantified and measured as though in a chain of causality. As we have indicated above, there are key factors in the organizational context, such as the support of others and opportunities for application, that affect the ability to use new skills and knowledge and affect overall work performance. Thus, whereas the mechanistic view of training will seek to use evaluation to prove the worth of training, ultimately to the organization in terms of cost savings and profit improvement, an HRD approach will seek to use evaluation to improve the quality of HRD activities and enhance the learning of participants in activities. It will do this by providing data for feedback and review discussions, especially between participants and their managers or peers so that opportunities for application and continued learning can be identified. In this way, evaluation can play a key role in workplace learning (see below).

HRM WEB LINKS

If you would like more information about mentoring, visit the European Mentoring Centre at www.mentoringcentre.org/. This includes access to research about mentoring from its annual conference. Further material can found at the National Mentoring Network at www.nmn.org.uk/ and at www.mentoring-australia.com. More information about coaching can be found at www.coachingnetwork.org.uk/ResourceCentre/WhatAreCoachingAndMentoring.htm.

If you would like to explore an organization's learning climate, an on-line questionnaire can be found at www.psych.rochester.edu/SDT/measures/auton_learn.html. Go to www.orau.gov/pbm/training.html for a set of links on evaluation and the impact of training, but if you wish to explore the technique of reviewing in learning, try www.reviewing.co.uk/. This site also has a section on evaluation and transfer at reviewing.co.uk/reviews/evaluation-transfer.htm. For a broad view of evaluation and the latest ideas for practice, www.evaluation.org.uk/ is the site of the UK Evaluation Society.

The move from mechanistic training towards an HRD approach is not without its difficulties and problems. Chief among these, especially where there is an explicit link with organizational strategy, is that an organization can be understood as a single and unified entity in which the voice of management is dominant. As Garavan et al. (1999) argue, most comments about HRD tend to make such an assumption and adopt a top-down perspective. Typical of such a view is the idea that competency frameworks, working as a link between strategy and performance, provide descriptions of a 'one best way' approach to fulfil work tasks; they also work prescriptively to state corporate values for everyone (Industrial Relations Services, 2001). There is, however, also the potential of such frameworks to restrict creativity and retreat to narrow and mechanistic training activities that serve short-term needs (Garavan & McGuire, 2001). Further difficulties arise from the generalized and abstracted presentation of a skill as a combination of different competencies. As Holman (2000) argues, the root problem is the belief that there are definitive meanings of skill. Instead, skill is often dependent on the situation and context, which are highly varied.

A further manifestation of the unified view is the notion of learning as a 'good thing', but such an assumption should also beg the question, good for whom? It is increasingly being recognized that, rather than seeing organizations as single, unified and stable entities, a more pluralist and dynamic view needs to be adopted composed of a set of ongoing activities and processes. It is within such activities and processes that people make sense of what they do and how work should occur, including what should and should not be learnt. As Bratton (2001) argues, where management presents HRD to pursue policies of 'lean' production, employees may be reluctant to learn new skills. In the context of a change to the employment relationship during restructuring, an employee may be required to learn but may also become aware that such learning has a cost and could undermine her or his collective relations with other employees. Employees may realize that the learning agenda belongs to management and that talk of corporate values, strategy and competencies are not neutral but rest on a dominant management ideology.

Based on the contested possibilities of HRD, Gold and Smith (2003)[12] have presented an image of how learning activities may or may not become accepted features of ongoing life at work. This is shown as Figure 10.4.

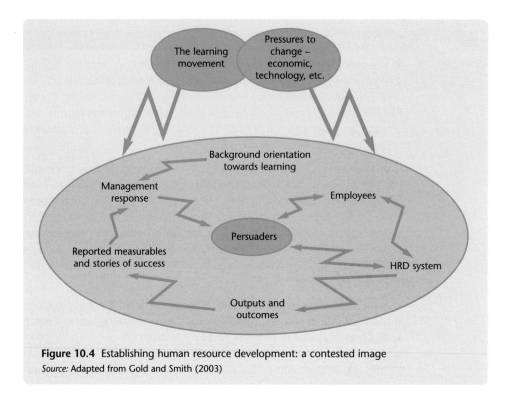

Figure 10.4 Establishing human resource development: a contested image
Source: Adapted from Gold and Smith (2003)

A number of features of this image have already been referred to above, for example the idea of the learning movement as the recommendations, ideas and exhortations relating to HRD and learning at work plus the structures to support these, as well as the strategic management responses to change and the learning movement based on background orientations that made them favourably disposed towards HRD. A significant feature of the image is the jagged arrows; these indicate that HRD does not proceed in a linear or unproblematic manner but on the basis of meanings that have to be made between different people. There may thus be an HRD plan developed to respond to changes in the market, but how such a plan is implemented will depend on the interests of various individuals and groups. The image suggests that such people may need to be persuaded of the value of HRD and convinced to engage in various activities. A key group to be convinced might, for example, be the managers who would need to coach others and support their learning. Persuading other employees may not always be as easy.

Given that some employees may undertake HRD activities, the image indicates that particular outputs and outcomes may be achieved, but these may not always be attributable to the activities even where systematic evaluation is undertaken. Precise cause-and-effect 'bottom-line' pay-offs from HRD may be difficult to show (Johnson et al., 2000). Given the need for some evidence of effectiveness of HRD for further decisions, what may, however, be provided is indirect measurable outcomes and anecdotal evidence in the form of people telling stories to each other about their experiences. The latter are a particularly interesting form of evidence, and stories are an important source of making sense of work, allowing people to explain HRD events in a meaningful and memorable way (Gabriel, 2000).

REFLECTIVE QUESTION

Do you think the image above helps to explain why HRD becomes more established in some organizations than others? Have you told stories to explain the value of any learning you have done?

The image goes some way towards explaining the variegated establishment of HRD and movement beyond the notion of mechanistic and linear training. It brings out the inherent uncertainty and the importance of talk and persuasion at work to make HRD happen. There are, however, still some important issues to consider, such as the importance of informal learning, especially the learning that occurs within working practice, and how learning can become organizational. We will consider such issues in the next section.

Workplace learning

If there is a single theme that has in recent years widened and transformed the idea of HRD, from a subset of HRM into a matter of strategic concern, and is central to organizational progress and survival, it is the theme of learning. Learning in the workplace is seen as the crucial contributor to dealing with change, coping with uncertainty and complexity in the environment and creating opportunities for sustainable competitive advantage. Workplace learning has therefore become a key idea in recent years. First, it casts a whole organization as a unit of learning, allowing managers to take a strategic view and others to think in terms of how their learning impacts on the wider context. Second, it is an idea that unifies an increasingly diverse set of influences and disciplines within HRD (McCormack, 2000), such as training and organization development, and information systems. Some writers have extended the influences further. Swanson (2001), for example, talks about HRD as an octopus that draws on a variety of different influences – anthropology, sociology, speech communications, music, philosophy and, in the future, chaos theory. McGoldrick et al. (2001, p. 346), accepting the multidisciplinary character of HRD, argue that there is 'no single lens for viewing HRD research', that a variety of perspectives are being employed and that this is leading to increasing sophistication in theorizing about and understanding learning at work. Third, workplace learning highlights the significance of HRD practitioners as people with specialist knowledge and skills, and contributes to the advancement of their professional status (Gold et al., 2002). Key ideas for application include, for example, the learning organization and organization learning, knowledge management and production and e-learning. We will first of all consider the idea of the learning organization.

Many organizations have been attracted by the idea of becoming a learning organization (sometimes referred to as a learning company). This was an idea that had a significant impact during the 1990s, a large number of conferences, books and journals being devoted to it. Although there has been significant ambiguity surrounding the meaning of the term, there is little doubt about its impact – it became the vision of many organizational leaders and managers. A survey in 1996 of chief executives (KPMG, 1996) found that respondents believed that:

- learning and adaptation must be accelerated through innovative and creative means

● learning must at least keep pace with the change in their organization's environment
● learning and innovation are the key to their organization's survival and success
● building a learning organization is a way of challenging and moving away from their current culture.

In the UK, the idea of the learning organization was developed by Pedler et al.'s (1988) learning company project report, which provided the following definition: an organization which facilitates the learning of all its members and continuously transforms itself. Pedler et al. went on to provide a list of dimensions of a learning company that could be used to differentiate it from a non-learning company. Among these were a learning approach to strategy, participative policy-making, 'informating' (that is, the use of information technology to inform and empower people), reward flexibility and self-development opportunities for all (Pedler et al., 1991). Another source of encouragement for the learning organizations was Senge's (1990) idea of five disciplines that were required as a foundation:

● personal mastery
● a shared vision
● team learning
● mental models
● systems thinking.

What became clear was that such models represented an ideal of a learning organization but became difficult to implement. The KPMG survey (1996, p. 2), for example, found that even where managers were in favour of learning organizations, they often faced difficulties in finding support for the idea: 'I have been trying to foster the learning concept for some time but with little success as the resistance to change is too great.'

REFLECTIVE QUESTION

Why do you think the learning organization idea has been difficult to implement?

Part of the difficulty, as explained by Garavan (1997), has been the idea that a learning organization was an ideal rather than a reality that could be achieved. In recent years, the idea has been compared to a journey, possibly one that is never completed. This has not of course prevented many organizations trying, but it may be the case that the various models of learning organizations are too distant from organizational reality. Learning organizations have nevertheless retained some of their persuasive appeal as an influence on thinking about workplace learning.

Understanding learning

A further difficulty may relate to how we understand and explain learning in organizations. Throughout the 20th century, there have been many ideas concerning learning. A distinction is usually made between 'associative learning' (or behaviourism) and 'cognitive learning', the main differences between the two traditions being summarized in Table 10.2.

We can see how the nature of the work that employees are required to perform will

Table 10.2 Traditions of learning

Associative learning or behaviourism	Cognitive learning
Learning in terms of responses to stimuli: 'automatic' learning	Insightful learning
Classical conditioning (Pavlov's dogs)	Thinking, discovering, understanding, seeing relationships and meaning
Operant or instrumental conditioning	New arrangements of previously learned concepts and principles

lead to the acceptance of a particular view of learning. It will also underpin much of a manager's understanding of human behaviour and motivation. The reduction of work into low-skilled and repetitive tasks will therefore favour associative and behaviourist views of learning even where, in the initial phases of learning, knowledge and understanding are required. The main thrust of the learning is to produce behaviour that can be repeated time after time in relatively unchanging conditions. More complex work favours the need for knowledge, understanding and higher-order cognitive skills, underpinned by cognitive learning theories. However, the acquisition of knowledge and understanding also requires an outlet for action through behaviour in the workplace.

Some theories of learning contain elements of both associative and cognitive learning but most importantly emphasize the process of learning and its continuity. This has resulted in a great deal of attraction to such theories in organizations pursuing HRD policies. Kolb (1984), for example, provided an integrated theory of experiential learning in which learning is prompted through the interaction of a learner and her or his environment. The theory stresses the central role of individual needs and goals in determining the type of experience sought and the extent to which all stages of learning are completed. For learning to occur, all stages of a learning cycle should be completed. Individual learners will, however, have an established pattern of assumptions, attitudes and aptitudes that will determine effectiveness in learning.[13] Kolb's learning cycle is shown as Figure 10.5.

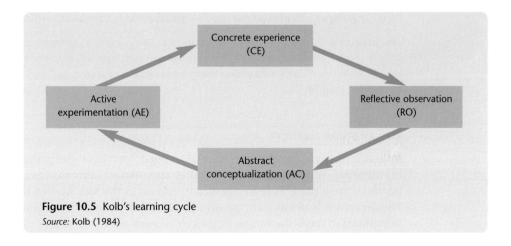

Figure 10.5 Kolb's learning cycle
Source: Kolb (1984)

According to Kolb, learning occurs through grasping an experience and transforming it. The transformation of the impact of experience on the senses (CE), through internal reflection (RO), allows the emergence of ideas (AC) that can be extended into the external world through new actions (AE). Unless the process can be completed in full, learning does not occur, and individuals may not begin the journey to qualitatively finer and higher forms of awareness, which may be called development.

Kolb's model has been very influential for many HRD practitioners. There has been a growing critique and reassessment of the model (Holman et al., 1997), but it has heightened awareness of the factors that contribute to learning or prevent learning at work. Learning activities at work could thus be designed on the basis of individual and group learning preferences. Learners might also attempt to overcome their blocks to learning. Individuals might, for example, lack the belief that they can take action in certain situations or believe that certain activities should not be carried out because this would cause offence to their values. The important point about such blocks is that they are based on personal meanings, feelings and emotions towards learning, and this connects with other models of learning. Neurolinguistic programming, for example, examines the way in which learners represent the world in their brains and order their thoughts by language to produce largely automatic actions (Dowlen, 1996). Learners can examine how such processes occur and how they can model themselves on the processes of others whom they see as more effective. Harri-Augstein and Webb (1995) presented an approach to learning based on uncovering personal meanings and myths that produce 'robot-like' performance and appear very difficult to change. It is suggested that, through critical awareness, learners can begin to experiment and change. Such views of learning link to a growing interest in adult learning and development and the importance of reflection to examine behaviour, and assumptions and premises about learning (Mezirow, 1991).

HRM WEB LINKS

If you want to explore around 50 theories of learning, www.tip.psychology.org/ provides access to a database. www.anlp.org/ is the home page of the Association of Neuro-linguistic Programming, but if you want to read a critical examination, try www.easyweb.easynet.co.uk/~dylanwad/morganic/art_nlp.htm.

A key writer in adult learning has been Stephen Brookfield. If you want to read more about his views, go to www.nlu.nl.edu/ace/Resources/Documents/AdultLearning. html. This paper includes a coverage of self-directed learning and critical reflection.

The idea that learners construct meanings as they learn is referred to as constructivism; you can find more about this view and its implications at www.exploratorium. edu/ifi/resources/constructivistlearning.html and www.stemnet.nf.ca/~elmurphy/ emurphy/cle.html.

Organization learning

Although many organizations have attempted to pursue the vision of a learning organization, which by necessity requires attention to individual and group or team learning, there has also been significant interest in the idea of organization learning. The difference between learning organization and organization learning is subtle but important: whereas the former is concerned with ideas and practices to enhance the learning of groups and individuals so that the organization can benefit, organization learning is an attempt to use the ideas of learning at an organizational level, that is, it relates to how learning occurs organizationally. Much of the interest in organization learning has occurred in academic circles, and it now constitutes a field of interest in its own right, with journals and conferences, along with an emerging and diverse body of knowledge, devoted to it (Easterby-Smith et al., 1999). It is not just, however, academics who have an interest: organization learning is also invoked as a response to cope with the challenges of global competition and technological change.

The key idea is that if current ways of working (the organization's routines) are insufficient, the organization must learn new ways of doing things (Easterby-Smith et al., 1998). As we have indicated above, however, this immediately raises questions about the status and view of the term 'organization'. Much of the organization learning literature works from the assumpion that an organization is a single and unified entity with the ability to learn. The difficulty here is that learning is clearly a human attribute whereas the term 'organization' is used to understand a set of activities and processes carried out by people working with other resources. As pointed out by Weick and Westley (1996), organizations cannot be directly perceived, so explaining learning at an organizational level requires the invocation of particular metaphors, which is not equal to direct experience. A biological metaphor of organization might, for example, suggest that organizations learn very much like humans – hence Dixon (1994) turns Kolb's learning cycle, an explanation of individual learning, into an organizational learning cycle. A computer metaphor might explain learning for individuals and organization as information-processing in which data are taken in, made sensible, stored in memory to be called upon as required and corrected for errors if these are found. Whatever the metaphor employed, there still remains the problem of how learning by individuals and groups becomes a property of the organization.

One view of organization learning that has gained popularity in recent years is the cultural view (Yanow, 2000). The importance of this view is that it focuses attention on what groups practise and on the values, beliefs and norms that are shared through talk, rituals, myths and stories between members of a group. Thus, in any place we refer to as an organization, there will be a variety of groups, all practising or 'organizing' according to the meanings they have made within the group. Organization learning therefore is concerned with what people do in their local situation. This also means that organization learning is not only concerned with change, innovation or finding new ways to compete. Because organization learning is based on the meanings made within groups, it can also be concerned with sustaining the group and its practices – which those outside the group may call 'resistance' to change and learning. Furthermore, most collective learning takes place informally within relationships that are to be found in the 'dark side' of organizations (Pedler & Aspinall, 1996). This is difficult territory for researchers to access.

The cultural view supports some of the research that has been carried out indicating that organization learning is mostly informal and improvisational, 'situated' in a particular context, and is a function of the activity that occurs at a local level (Lave & Wenger, 1991) within communities of practice (CoPs). Furthermore, learning within CoPs is likely to be at variance from what is supposed to happen, at least in the eyes of managers, who will have formed and espoused abstract versions of what should be learnt but miss vital details in the process. Brown and Duguid (1991) used the ideas of CoPs and situated learning to make a distinction between canonical practice and non-canonical practice, the former referring to what is supposed to be learnt and the latter to what is actually learnt and practised in the working context. Learning is strongly related to becoming a practitioner within a CoP, with its own norms, stories and views about what is effective. This makes the task of achieving the benefits of organization learning even more complex. It also explains how so much insight and understanding remains hidden in organizations and how the downsizing trends of the early 1990s often resulted in the break up of CoPs and the loss of core knowledge. Brown and Duguid (1991, p. 53) argued that an organization needs to be conceived as a 'community-of-communities' and 'see beyond its canonical abstractions of practice to the rich, full-bloodied activities themselves'. Recent years have seen some attempt to harness the creative potential of CoPs. Thus, although they are informal and self-organizing around the demands of the situation (Wenger & Snyder, 2000), it is argued that managers can identify potential CoPs and provide an infrastructure of support so that they can be made 'a central part of their companies' success' (Wenger & Snyder, 2000, p. 145).

REFLECTIVE QUESTION

How far are students members of a CoP? Do they practice 'non-canonically'? What difficulties does this cause?

Given the essentially informal nature of CoPs, it is interesting how they have become recognized as contributors to company success; this might be understood as the human capital version of informal learning (Garrick 1998). We would, however, suggest that the ongoing and everyday processes that make up life within CoPs are not amenable to easy control by managers.

● Knowledge management

In recent years, the interest in organization learning and indeed informal learning within CoPs has been stimulated by the view that the economy has become knowledge based (Organisation for Economic Co-operation and Development, 1996), the basic idea being that knowledge becomes the key ingredient of products and services. Differences between organizations and nations will therefore depend on the extent to which information can be obtained, turned into knowledge and applied to production. The emphasis on knowledge has resulted in a plethora of new concepts, such as knowledge workers, knowledge-intensive organizations, knowledge networks and knowledge societies. There is also an emphasis on the skills of employees who are recast as knowledge workers. They are the owners of intellectual capital since it is people who are able to construct, manipulate and apply new knowledge, adding value to what is produced. Human capital accumulation has therefore become one of the new reasons for an investment in HRD (Garavan et al., 2001) and a contrast to the previous narrow conceptions implied by human capital theory.

The key reason for such developments has of course been the advances made in the application of ICT, especially in combination with the Internet. ICT can be used to store, retrieve, analyse and communicate information involving a convergence of microtechnologies, computing, telecommunications, broadcasting and optical electronics in a revolutionary way (Castells, 1996). An important characteristic of the revolution is how knowledge is applied to knowledge-generating and information-processing/communication devices with a feedback loop that enables knowledge and information to be viably accumulated and transferred. Not all knowledge can, however, be captured by ICT, and this highlights the never-ending value of people.

In considering knowledge, it is common to distinguish between '*knowing-that*' and '*knowing-how*'. The former is concerned with knowledge about facts and explanations for facts that are explicit and communicable, and the latter refers to the ability to do something in a particular situation. Knowing-that is based on knowledge that has been codified, for example written into books, journals or papers on the Internet, and therefore becomes communicable. It is this knowledge which lies at the heart of the digital revolution.

Knowing-how is, however, particularly important in the performance of skilled work. Whereas performance may require knowing-that, dealing with the particulars of a situation, especially a new or unexpected situation, 'cannot be accomplished by procedural knowledge alone or by following a manual' (Eraut, 2000 p. 128). Such knowledge is personal, based on the requirements of the situation and the understanding of the person carrying out the performance. This is referred to as tacit knowledge; it is the ability to deal with different situations, known and unknown, often responding spontaneously to surprise through improvisation and without thought (Schön, 1983). To work out the difference between codified and tacit knowledge, think about riding a bike. Could you codify the explanation into a manual for riding bikes? It is more likely that it will be very difficult to explain the skill of riding a bike because the understanding is tacit. Tacit knowledge is needed to maximize the benefit accrued from the rapid accumulation of codified knowledge generated by advances in ICT. It is also crucial to the development of new knowledge.

One of the most well-known knowledge-based approaches to organization learning is Nonaka and Takeuchi's (1995) knowledge-creating model. According to this model, organization learning and the creation of knowledge have to start with an individual's tacit knowledge. First, this has to be expressed to the individual using diagrams, metaphors, drawings. Because it is tacit, the knowledge is difficult to codify in words. Second, there is an attempt to express the knowledge to others. Third, this knowledge is combined with that of other members of the group. In the final stage, the knowledge becomes tacit again but in a new form. It is accepted by the group and becomes part of their accepted behaviour. And so the process begins again. One limitation of the model is that it is based on a number of case studies and presents a rather idealized version of the processes. Making tacit knowledge explicit is, however, also a feature of other versions of organization learning. Crossan's (1999) framework is, for example, composed of the four subprocesses of intuiting, interpreting, integrating and institionalizing. Nevertheless, as Crossan acknowledges, the subprocesses are unlikely to flow without inhibition. Factors that may prevent flow include institutionalized features such as reward systems, planning systems and structures; there is also an influence from group dynamics and other relationships between people.

There may be difficulties in applying models of organization learning and knowledge-creating, particularly with reference to tacit knowledge, but this has not prevented the rapid growth of attempts to capture the knowledge that is generated by learning. This is one of the key factors that is driving the interest in knowledge management, which Mayo (1998, p. 36) defines as:

> the management of the information, knowledge and experience available to an organization – its creation, capture, storage, availability and utilization – in order that organizational activities build on what is already known and extend it further.

Many organizations have attempted to introduce knowledge management, including the appointment of managers as learning officers or knowledge officers and installing networked software to accentuate the process (Lank, 2002). Other roles include company librarians, webmasters and designers, and information consultants. The basic argument is that if knowledge is, in the knowledge economy, the source of competitive advantage, its capture and storage will form an essential resource; it is the organization's intellectual capital. In some respects, following a point made by Scarborough and Swan (2001), knowledge management superseded the learning organization phenomenon from the late 1990s, although there has increasingly been more attention paid to the systems and technologies of knowledge management than to learning within the workplace, thereby 'glossing over the complex and intangible aspects of human behaviour' (Scarbrough and Swan, 2001, p. 8).

HRM WEB LINKS

Go to www.brint.com/km/; this site provides access to many resources relating to knowledge management, including The Online Book on Knowledge Management, at www.kmbook.com. The knowledge management server at the University of Texas has links to resources and publications on knowledge management at www.bus. utexas.edu/kman/. See also (Europe) www.emeraldinsight.com/jkm.htm; (Australia) www.knowledge.standards.com.au; (South Africa) www.kmssa.org.za/html.

One attempt to restore the link with learning has been the work of Kessels (1996, 2001) and others on knowledge productivity. According to Garvey and Williamson (2002), successful knowledge-productive organizations are proactive in learning new ways of doing things. They do this by going beyond formal knowledge management systems and attempting to work also with informal and tacit knowledge. This means creating a climate of trust whereby people can share ideas informally. There is an acceptance that learning is a social activity, and this may not always be productive. Managers and others therefore have to work very hard to enrich the working lives of employees. As argued by Kessels (1996, p. 4), 'Personal enrichment is thus less of an employee privilege than a condition of good performance.'

e-Learning

One area in which the technology revolution is having a massive impact in HRD is the provision of e-learning. Until very recently, the term 'e-learning' would have been covered by a range of different activities involving the delivery of HRD activities, including computer-based training, web-based training and on-line learning. Preceding these terms were those of 'distance learning' and 'flexible learning'. Through the rapid investment in web facilities, all these terms have now been incorporated under the heading 'e-learning'.[14] It is difficult to define e-learning precisely, and any attempt to pin it down is likely to be superseded by events. The CIPD, however, uses the following (Sloman & Reynolds, 2002, p. 3):

> Learning that is delivered, enabled or mediated by electronic technology for the explicit purpose of training in organizations. It does not include stand-alone technology-based training such as the use of CD-ROMs in isolation.

The distinction between e-learning and other technologically based delivery lies in the use of networked ICT and the Internet. This includes the delivery of learning materials via the web in a way very similar to that of flexible learning packages. In addition, supported learning can be provided over the Internet within 'virtual communities'. There are also many ways to support learning informally across the Internet, for example Microsoft Communities (www.communities.msn.co.uk) or Community Zero (www.communityzero.com/).

Research has suggested a number of benefits of e-learning (Pollard & Hillage, 2001), including the ability to learn 'just in time' at the learner's pace and convenience, the provision of updatable materials and a reduction in delivery costs. HRM in practice 10.3 shows an attempt by ScottishPower to provide training for employees at home. There is also the possibility of collaborative working, sometimes with learners spread over large distances, with tutor support. Most computer-mediated conferencing systems enable a moderator to track participation and adjust provision as required. On the downside, a learner clearly needs access to ICT with an Internet or network connection. This can be expensive to set up and requires collaboration between information technology and HRD/learning specialists. Furthermore, the material has to be digital, and this is far from the only way to deliver learning.

HRM IN PRACTICE 10.3

SCOTTISHPOWER TAKES IT TRAINING DIRECT TO EMPLOYEES' HOMES

PEOPLE MANAGEMENT, 2001, MAY 3

ScottishPower employees could soon be accessing IT training from home if a pilot study proves successful.

Selected staff can already log on to an IT training web site that offers more than 800 courses, together with support services such as online mentoring, advice and coaching.

The scheme is an extension of an existing £1 million-a-year

ScottishPower employees could soon be accessing IT training from home ...

training initiative based on a network of community learning

centres that are open to staff and local people. The centres have already cut the amount of conventional IT training, but Paul McKelvie, director of ScottishPower Learning, said that the firm was interested in developing home learning, because this could be more convenient for some employees.

Several larger organizations have attempted to use e-learning to recast central HRD provision through the creation of corporate universities. The University for Lloyds TSB, for example, provides computer-based facilities for all its staff and access to learning materials as well as career information. They claim more than 2000 computers in branches and departments to complement the existing facilities at the group's central and local training centres, and there is also a call centre facility to provide support (Source: www.lloydstsb.com/about_us/community/supporting_our_staff/0,999,general,00.html). Cunningham et al. (2000) suggest that most corporate universities are simply re-badged training departments, but that they may over time develop into significant suppliers of HRD activites, going beyond the boundaries of their initiating organizations. There are also likely to be growing links between corporate universities and more traditional universities in a variety of strategic alliances (Clarke & Hermens, 2001).

HRM WEB LINKS

The e-learning centre provides links to articles and resources relating to e-learning; you can find it at www.e-learningcentre.co.uk/. The eLearning Network acts as a source of information and best practice at www.elearningnetwork.org/frameset.htm. www.unext.com/about.htm shows an attempt between leading universities to provide on-line programmes. www.smartforce.com/corp/marketing/ is the website for Smartforce, one of the larger e-learning companies. www.capellauniversity.net/ capella_university.htm provides access to Cappella University, which offers 500 on-line undergraduate and postgraduate courses. If you are interested in speculations on the effect of technology on the future, you can read the work of BT's futurologist at www.innovate.bt.com/ideas/futurology.

There are clearly more developments to come in e-learning, and technological developments, including improved access possibilities, will certainly continue apace. The role of HRD specialists will inescapably be affected as learners move from being present in training rooms to being members of virtual communities. There will be many opportunities for knowledge-sharing through a variety of modes of contact and timing of interactions. Much will, however, depend, as we indicated earlier, on the nature of the demand for skills within organizations, which will have a knock-on effect on the supply of e-learning materials and activities. As recent research on training in the knowledge economy shows, many barriers to learning at work still exist, and these have a negative impact on willingness to learn (Schramm, 2002). Learners can, however, increasingly bypass organizational barriers by joining informal learning communities on-line.

STUDY TIP

HRD is, as has been shown in this chapter, a wide-ranging concept that has not yet established a distinctive position in organizations or the academic world. A key issue concerns the purpose of HRD, and it would be easy to respond in a relatively instrumental fashion – that it is to improve and enhance an individual's, organization's or nation's productive capability. This would, however, represent too narrow a view. In this chapter, we have argued that, by adopting a pluralist view of organizations, there are bound to be different views on the purpose of HRD and the way in which learning is valued. One approach to studying different perspectives in HRD and projects of learning has been to use learning histories, in which, through access to events and documents, a researcher attempts to understand what is happening and facilitate individual and organizational reflection. You can read about learning histories at www.ccs.mit.edu/LH/. Within a learning history, different values can be studied through the use of narratives and story-telling, which allow people to express their versions of events, incorporating what they value and how they feel. Data from story-telling can then be used in narrative analysis. You can read more about this in Riesman (1993).

Chapter summary

- This chapter has examined the idea and practice of HRD as investment in people's learning at work. The idea incorporates traditional views of training and development but seeks to extend attention to learning throughout an organization as a strategy to cope with change. The message of learning at work has become an obvious 'good thing', and this has led to growing interest in HRD as a profession and its theoretical development, although there are continuing debates about the meaning of HRD.

- For HRD to become a feature of organizational strategy requires senior managers to incorporate the need for learning within their consideration of trends and signals in the environment, such as changes in markets and technology. A strategy for HRD can often respond to organizational strategy by the use of competencies to set performance expectations and targets. Strategic HRD can also influence organizational strategy through the development of new ideas, especially where senior managers appreciate that learning is a way of responding to external pressures for change.

- In the UK, there is little evidence that HRD is a key consideration in strategic management. People are not usually a top priority, marketing and financial matters having greater importance.

- There is, broadly speaking, a 'voluntarist' approach to HRD in the UK, contrasted with a more 'interventionist' approach in some other countries. Decision-makers in organizations determine the demand for skills, taking a broadly human capital view that may lead to a restricted approach to HRD. In contrast, some organizations adopt a developmental humanist approach, which can lead to a greater focus on the potential of people for learning.

- There is evidence to suggest that learning has an impact on an individuals' earning power and employment prospects. For organizations, HRD is a key element of the bundle of HR practices that impact on performance. For nations, investment in skills has implications for competitiveness and social inclusion. The UK government has given significant attention to supporting progress towards a learning society. Low skill levels among many workers remain a problem in the UK, but there have been developments to improve the HRD infrastructure through a national framework of qualifications and new institutions to administer national programmes.

- A systematic approach to training is still the preference in many organizations; this emphasizes the need for cost-effective provision. Recent years have seen attempts to develop a more integrated approach that recognizes interdependencies with organizations and the importance of line managers in HRD. This often involves the use of competency frameworks and performance management systems.

- The learning climate in an organization greatly influences the effectiveness of HRD policies, especially the relationships between managers and employees. To support HRD, managers have been encouraged to become mentors and coaches. Both roles can provide a link between HRD activities, evaluation and the transfer of learning.

- HRD makes a unitarist assumption about organizations, leading to top-down approaches. Competency frameworks describe a 'one best way' to perform work, which may restrict creativiy. There is likely to be a variety of views on work and learning.

- Workplace learning is a more recent notion that takes a broad organizational perspective on learning and allows a range of influences on HRD, including ideas relating to the learning organization. The importance of learning at work has increased attention to learning theories, especially experiential learning and models that examine personal meanings and encourage reflection.

- Organization learning has become a key field of interest. Some explanations assume that organizations learn like people, but there are also attempts to provide different explanations by focusing on the culture of groups and how learning occurs in the context of their practice with CoPs.

- Advances in ICT have resulted in a greater interest in knowledge production and knowledge management. Knowledge can be concerned with facts and explanations that can be codified and easily communicated. There is also knowledge that is tacit, more indeterminate, difficult to express and concerned with responding to difficult problems.

- Technology is creating an e-learning revolution, leading to a new alliance between providers, new methods of delivery and the formation of virtual communities of learners. HRD specialists are learning new skills to support e-learning provision.

Key concepts

- Coaching and mentoring
- Developmental humanistic approach
- e-Learning
- Evaluation
- Human capital theory
- Human resource development
- Interventionist approach
- Knowledge management

- Learning climate
- Learning organization
- Organization learning
- Strategic HRD
- The learning movement
- Transfer of learning
- Voluntarist approach
- Workplace learning

Chapter review questions

1. What is meant by strategic HRD and how is it connected with organization strategy?

2. What should be the role of government in HRD?

3. How can graduate skills be better employed by organizations?

4. Learning is a 'good thing' for everyone. Discuss.

5. What should be the role of managers in the learning organization?

6. Can organizations gain benefits from the work of CoPs?

Further reading

Ashton, D., & Felstead, A. (2001). From training to lifelong learning: the birth of the knowledge society. In J. Storey (ed.) *Human resource management*, pp. 165–89. London: Thomson Learning.

Garvey, B., & Williamson, B. (2002). *Beyond knowledge management*. Harlow: Pearson Education.

Keep, E., & Rainbird, H. (2000). Towards the learning organization? In S. Bach & K. Sisson (eds) *Personnel management* (pp. 173–94). Oxford: Blackwell.

Stewart, J., McGoldrick, J., & Watson, S. (eds) (2002). *Researching human resource development*. London: Routledge.

Walton, J. (1999). *Strategic human resource development*. London: Prentice-Hall.

Wenger, E., McDermott, R. A., & Snyder, W. (2002). *Cultivating communities of practice*. Boston: Harvard Business School Press.

Practising human resource management

Searching the web

HRD is increasingly being seen as a separate discipline in its own right rather than a subdiscipline of HRM. As a consequence, more attention is being paid to HRD research by academics, and more interest has arisen in the results of research by HRD professionals. You can find more details about the 'academic' study of HRD at the following websites:

- www.ahrd.org/, the site of the Academy of HRD in the USA
- www.b.shuttle.de/wifo/ehrd/=portal.htm, the European HRD portal, providing research-based information on HRD in Europe
- www.lums.lancs.ac.uk/ufhrd/, the site of the university forum for HRD in the UK.

For other HRD sites, see p. xxi of this book.

HRM group activity

You are the HRD manager of a large consultancy that employs a wide range of professionally qualified staff and have been tasked with developing a continuous professional development (CPD) policy for different professional groups employed. Visit the Professional Associations Research Network at www.parn.org.uk/parn.cfm?sct=100&content=homepage2.cfm. This has a CPD centre providing access to case studies, guides and publications on CPD.

A key group within the consultancy are the engineers. www.iie.org.uk/devcareer/index.asp?page=8 provides access to the professional development page of the Institution of Incorporated Engineers, and www.iee.org/OnComms/pn/ provides information on professional networks for electrical engineers.

There are also qualified surveyors (CPD information at www.rics.org/careers/cpd/), chartered accountants (see www.icaew.co.uk/) and architects (visit www.site.yahoo.net/riba-cpd/).

Make a presentation on the key features of a CPD policy and the specific requirements for the different professional groups.

ATKINSON GENERATION

Atkinson Generation (AG) is a leading distributor of engines and equipment. The company has main dealer status with Watson Engines, the UK's principal producer of power engines. There are 35 staff based at its location in Banbury.

After several years of profitable trading, the company has, for the past 2 years, been faced with a significant loss. There is a sense of 'lack of direction' and a need to change quickly and dramatically in order to survive. A recent meeting with Watson Engines has presented AG with a stark choice: it has to 'shape up or ship out'. Since the dealer status with Watson Engines accounted for 80% of its business, managers at AG realized that radical changes were needed. A shared purpose and vision, combined with training that met a nationally recognized benchmark, was required.

The four AG managers attended a series of workshops organized by the local chamber of commerce, where they could share experiences and learn from other companies. They were then able to produce a strategic plan incorporating key performance indicators and a breakdown of the skills necessary for its delivery. More important would be the style of managing change and the provision of learning opportunities for all staff to meet their desires. As indicated by the Managing Director, John Atkinson: 'I fundamentally believe that everyone at AG should be able to identify what they need to learn and get on and do it.'

The following were considered to be key elements:

- A learning and development-oriented appraisal system needs to be established for everyone in the company so that individual needs can be identified.

- All managers must become 'learning managers' so that they can coach and support others.

- Communication needs to provide full information on company results and the budget as well as allow feedback from staff.

- The company should seek support from its local business advisory service regarding a national benchmark for training and development, qualifications and financial support.

1. How can appraisal be utilized to identify individual learning needs, and how can the company ensure that such needs link to the strategic plan and key performance indicators?

2. What are the skills required by 'learning managers'? What training do such managers need?

3. What are the requirements for effective two-way communication?

4. What help can be provided for this small company regarding benchmarking, qualifications for its workforce and finance for its training?

HR-related skill development

HRD is an important HRM function in terms of both implementing organizational strategy and facilitating organizational effectiveness. After learning needs have been determined and learning objectives set, formal learning programmes must be designed. Designing a formal learning session or workshop involves a number of critical activities and decisions, including those related to content, learning methods, materials and equipment, and site. All managers should be effective coaches and teachers. To help you to develop teaching and coaching skills, we have developed an activity that requires you to design and deliver a segment of a learning module. To gain knowledge of the 10 steps of programme design and be able to identify the skills of effective trainers, go to our website www.palgrave.com/business/brattonandgold and click on 'Coaching'.

Notes

1. Stern and Sommerlad (1999, p. xiv).
2. Keep (1999, p. 5).
3. Edgar Schein talking about learning organizations in an interview featured in *Harvard Business Review*, March 2002.
4. In 2001, the CIPD's annual membership questionnaire totalled 101,634 members, of whom 39,393 members (38.75%) stated key responsibilities involved training and 12,248 (12.05%) of whom stated a key responsibility as management development (Source: CIPD Membership Secretary).
5. You might be interested to consider the implications of other metaphors referred to by Marsick and Watkins, that is, open systems, brain, chaos and complexity.
6. This is not to suggest that there have been no concerns about management and leadership development in the UK. In April 2000, the Council for Excellence in Management and Leadership was appointed to develop a strategy ensuring that the UK had the managers and leaders of the future to match the best in the world. A report was published in May 2002. The Council's website is www.managementandleadershipcouncil.org/index.htm.
7. In the UK, the National Training Awards have been established since 1987 as annual awards for organizations, groups and individuals who demonstrate that an investment in HRD brings about value-added benefits, to identify excellence in HRD and to celebrate and promote exemplars. The objectives have more recently been extended to encompass the broadened scope of government policy. Thus, current objectives include the encouragement of a greater commitment to lifelong learning, training and self-development, and the identification and promotion of the contribution of performance improvements by various learning routes. More details can be obtained from the website at www.nationaltrainingawards.com/.
8. In Scotland, this function is performed by the Scottish Qualifications Authority.
9. The focus of attention moved from the UK to England following the devolution of powers to the Scottish Parliament and the Welsh Assembly.
10. The Ufl was set up in 1998 to provide a learning service for adult learners aged over 16, with the aim of increasing the number of adults participating in structured learning and skills levels to world class. Learndirect supports Ufl with an on-line learning service.
11. Industrial Training Boards were set up under the Industrial Training Act of 1964 to administer the collection of a training levy and the distribution of training grants within particular sectors of the economy, for example construction and engineering. As a highly interventionist approach, most

were eventually abolished during the 1980s, but they left a significant legacy in their propagation of training ideas. The Industrial Training Boards that still exist operate under strict regulations – see www.dfes.gov.uk/ria/archive.shtml.

12. The image works with what is referred as the sociology of translation, drawn from actor network theory. Further understanding can be gained from the Actor Network resource at www.comp.lancs.ac.uk/sociology/antres.html. You might also like to consult John Law's home page at www.comp.lancs.ac.uk/sociology/jlaw.html.

13. Kolb's experiential learning model is one of a number that have led to the popularity of assessing our approach to learning through learning-style questionnaires. If you would like to examine your style of learning, try www.cdtl.nus.edu.sg/success/sl8.htm, which includes links to various on-line instruments. You could also try www.support4learning.org.uk/education/lstyles.htm#Mainly.

14. On Wednesday 22 May 2002, a search for 'e-learning' on Google returned 952,000 hits.

Chapter eleven

Employee relations

John Bratton

Employee relations are a set of human resource practices that
seek to secure commitment and compliance with organizational goals and
standards through the involvement of employees in decision-making
and by managerial disciplinary action.

'Historically, managers hoarded information, controlling its release
to bolster their power. Those days are over forever.'[1]

'If you're trying to create a high-trust organization, an organization where
people are all-for-one and one-for-all, you can't have secrets.'[2]

'The pressures leading firms to explore the introduction of employment involvement
practices have a great deal to do with productivity, flexibility, and
competition – management's agenda – and less relationship to workers'
desire for a stronger voice in the operations of the worksite.'[3]

Chapter outline

Chapter objectives

After studying this chapter, you should be able to:

1. Explain why managers might want to increase employee involvement (EI) and participation

2. Describe the different dimensions of EI

3. Appreciate the importance of organizational communications in the human resource management (HRM) paradigm

4. Explain different approaches to organizational communications

5. Understand the structure and role of consultation committees, including works councils

6. Explain the concepts, values and legal framework that underline the disciplinary process in employment

The title of this chapter – 'Employee relations' – needs a brief explanation. Over the past decade, various labels to cover the multiple aspects of the employment relationship have fallen in and out of fashion. As we noted in Chapter 1, some authors use the terms 'personnel management' and 'human resource management', and for one particular aspect of employment relations, the terms 'industrial relations', 'labour relations' and 'employee relations' are used interchangeably by some authors. Each of these terms has its own particular set of meanings among the academic community. 'Industrial relations' and 'labour relations' have, for example, been associated with industrial trade unions, collective bargaining and strikes. The term 'employee relations' became popular among some British academics during the 1980s and was used to reflect the emergence of a 'new industrial order' (see Blyton & Turnbull, 1998). However, as Mabey et al. (1998, p. 278) comment, each label has 'its own connotations [and] none of them succeeds entirely in capturing the essence of the numerous unfolding types of relations associated with work'. Although we are concerned to include 'traditional' union workers in our analysis of HRM, we use the label 'employee relations' in a restricted manner as a way of addressing some individual and collective aspects of employment relations at work. Within this perspective, 'employee relations' denotes an assortment of employer initiatives for improving workplace communications, for engaging employees either directly or indirectly in decision-making and for securing employee compliance with management rules through disciplinary action. We will seek to demonstrate that these selected employee relations practices constitute important social technologies that aim to improve employee commitment and productivity. In Chapter 12, we will examine the collective aspects of relations between unionized workers and employers or their agents – managers – using the term 'union–management relations'.

Over the past decade, interest in EI has grown considerably in Europe and North America (Marchington, 2001; Mayrhofer et al., 2000; Verma & Taras, 2001). EI is regarded as playing a central role in the development of a high performance work systems (Marchington, 2001). In Britain, successive Workplace Employee Relations Surveys (WERSs) documented the growth of EI initiatives (Cully et al., 1999; Daniel & Millward, 1983; Millward et al., 1992, 2000). The **European Works Council** Directive of 1994 (see later in the chapter for a description of European Works Councils, or EWCs) also stimulated academics and practitioners to examine in even greater depth the participation and communications debate (Mayrhofer et al., 2000). The call for greater worker involvement in decision-making and work itself has a long history (Brannen et al., 1976), but the current unprecedented interest appears to be associated with globalization, the exigencies of knowledge-based work and the need for managers to share information and decision-making in order to achieve a competitive advantage. Much of the academic literature characterizes employee involvement and two-way communications by being 'management rather than union driven' (Marchington & Wilkinson, 2000; Sisson & Storey, 2000) and part of a 'management agenda' (Verma & Taras, 2001). EI is therefore closely associated with a high-trust, high-commitment HR strategy (Chapter 2).

There are three aspects to the contemporary debate on EI. First, from a managerialist perspective, it is argued that EI initiatives fundamentally transform the climate of employment relations because they lead to long-term changes in workers' attitudes and commitment; as such, EI shapes 'organizational citizenship' (HRM in practice 11.1). A violation of an employee's psychological contract (Chapter 1) may be prevented by communication (Guest & Conway, 2002; Morrison & Robinson, 1997). As Morrison and Robinson (1997, p. 237) argue, 'Communication ... will help to minimize the "false consensus effect," whereby people assume that they share the same perceptions.'

Second, it is suggested that communications – the least empowering form of EI – plays a critical role in constructing and maintaining a 'strong' organizational culture, and, as a feature of the leadership process, 'communication style' is seen as being critical

HRM IN PRACTICE 11.1

PARTNERSHIP EQUALS PROFITS

JENNIE WALSH, *PEOPLE MANAGEMENT*, 1998, MARCH 19

Companies that continue to resist any form of employee participation risk losing business advantage, according to a report due to be published by the Involvement and Participation Association.

More than 65 per cent of organisations that allow their workforce full involvement in all business activities, including long-range planning and product development, believe they are gaining a competitive edge.

The study, Benchmarking the Partnership Company, is based on a survey to benchmark key principles at work in firms committed to partnership, and includes case studies from Rover, Remploy, ScottishPower, the John Lewis Partnership and HP Bulmer.

The report concludes that successful partnership operates within a set of mutual commitments and obligations between an organisation and its people. These include commitment to business goals, job security and direct employee participation in training, development and job design.

Although 70 per cent of companies in the survey were unionised, partnership operated in the same organisations on both a representative level (using formal bargaining structures) and through individual participation (such as self-managed teams).

The report's authors, David Guest, professor of occupational psychology at Birkbeck College, and Riccardo Peccei, lecturer in industrial relations at the London School of Economics, admitted to being surprised by the survey results.

> 'By opening the books and involving everyone in the business it is now possible for everyone to see how business decisions impact on us all.'

'The most striking thing is that partnership pays off,' Guest said. 'Organizations have a better psychological contract, there is greater trust between employees and employers and performance is higher.'

To ensure that these positive results were not simply employer propaganda, the survey cross-matched managers' responses with those of employee representatives – and achieved the same results.

But although employee involvement is clearly beneficial to 'partnership' companies, the practice is not widespread.

'Some organizations still have relatively low trust in their em-

ployees and in employee bodies such as trade unions,' Guest said. 'But, according to the evidence, this view is misplaced. Organizations that are prepared to take risks are reaping the benefits.'

According to Guest, the principles of shared obligations that underpin the benchmarks are important in making them an accepted part of the overall culture of the organisation. The most successful examples are companies, such as Rover, where the partnership culture continues to exist despite changes in the leadership of the company and the unions.

Stephen Dunn, head of group HR at ScottishPower, admitted that partnership is not an easy option for companies facing shrinking profits and increased competition. But he believes that partnership arrangements between ScottishPower and its three trade unions has forced all parties to think in new ways and to work for business advantage.

'It is about looking for solutions to things that, in the past, may have led to conflict,' he said. 'By opening the books and involving everyone in the business it is now possible for everyone to see how business decisions impact on us all.'

to 'transformational' leadership (Trethewey, 1997). The link to leadership and change, which comes from interpersonal communications theory, emphasizes the different ways in which managers communicate the content of a message and how those ways affect manager–subordinate relationships. Witherspoon (1997, p. x), a specialist in leadership and communication, argues that, 'leadership is to a great extent a communication process', and in our three-dimensional model of management (Figure 1.3), communication is part of the process of influence by which managers accomplish their work.

The third aspect of the EI debate is, from a critical perspective, the argument that EI initiatives, by promoting the individual employee rather than employees' collective bodies, deliberately undermine the role of the trade unions (Wells, 1993). Moreover, EI increases managerial control over the labour process (Thompson & McHugh, 2002). In terms of public policy, recent interest in EI and 'partnerships' deals between unions and management has been encouraged by UK and European Union (EU) legislation, in particular, the 1994 EWC Directive.

When EI practices fail to create, or reinforce, desirable employee behaviours, managers may resort to disciplinary action to encourage compliance with organizational rules and standards. Discipline at work is the regulation of human activity to produce predictable and effective performance (Torrington, 1998). It ranges from the threat of being dismissed to the subtle persuasions of mentoring. Maintaining discipline is one of managers' central activities. A framework of legal rules and procedures surround the disciplinary process to provide a fair and consistent method of dealing with alleged inappropriate or unacceptable behaviour.

In this chapter, we discuss the issues of governance and employee rights in the workplace. First, we clarify the terms and the various forms of EI before presenting a theory of EI. The chapter then goes on to explain key issues related to communications in the workplace. Indirect employee participation, in the form of joint consultative committees and EWCs, is also examined, along with some paradoxes associated with EI. We conclude the chapter with an overview of process and rules governing disciplinary action.

REFLECTIVE QUESTION

On first impressions, do you think that EI in the decision-making process leads to higher quality decisions?

The nature of employee involvement

A review of the literature reveals that the terms 'employee participation' and 'employee involvement' have different meanings. In essence, *employee participation* involves workers exerting a countervailing and upward pressure on management control, which need not imply unity of purpose between managers and non-managers. *Employee involvement* is, in contrast, perceived to be a 'softer' form of participation, implying a commonality of interest between employees and management, and stressing that involvement should be directed at the workforce as a whole rather than being restricted to trade union channels. As Guest (1986, p. 687) states: 'involvement is considered to be more flexible and better geared to the goal of securing commitment and shared interest'. When people talk about participation or involvement, they are reflecting their own attitudes and work experiences, as well as their own hopes for the future. Managers tend to talk about participation when they in fact mean consultation. In this context, consultation, which is explored more fully later in the chapter, usually means a structure for improving communications, either 'top-down', or 'upward' in the form of problem-solving communications. When offered consultation, employees, and in unionized workplaces union representatives, tend to believe, however, that they are about to be given participation. Differing expectations among employees will affect their attitude, their propensity to participate and ultimately the success of participation techniques in the organization. A vital first step, if there is to be any meeting of minds, is therefore to create a common language and conceptual model.

Definitions of EI or participation do not always reflect the range of possibilities – from having some say over how work is designed and executed to exerting a significant influence over strategic decisions. Strauss maintains that meaningful employee participation in decision-making requires that workers are able to exert influence over their working environment. He defines participation as 'a process which allows employees to exert some influence over their work and the conditions under which they work' (Strauss, 1998, p. 15). If we take the literal meaning of the term 'employee participation', the process should provide workers or their representatives with the opportunity to take part in and influence decisions that affect their working lives. As such, an employee participation environment creates an alternative network to traditional hierarchical patterns (Stohl & Cheney, 2001).

There are two types of participation:

- direct
- indirect.

Direct participation refers to those forms of participation in which individual employees, albeit often in a very limited way, are involved in decision-making processes that affect their everyday work routines. Examples of direct EI include briefing groups, quality circles, problem-solving teams, self-managed teams (see Chapter 4 for a discussion on work teams) and financial involvement. As a direct form of EI, financial involvement, which includes profit-related rewards, aims to improve competitiveness by educating employees on the operation of the business. Financial participation initiatives are therefore predicated on the belief that workers with a financial stake in the enterprise are more likely to be better 'corporate citizens' and work more productively for the company (Marchington, 2001). For a discussion on profit-related rewards, see Chapter 9.

Indirect participation refers to those forms of participation in which representatives or delegates of the main body of employees participate in the decision-making process. Examples of indirect participation include joint consultation committees (JCCs), EWCs and 'worker directors', all forms that are associated with the broader notion of 'industrial democracy' (Bullock, 1977). It is clear from the WERS data that indirect EI has become less extensive in the period between 1980 and 1998 (Cully et al., 1999; Millward et al., 2000).

Management theorists have provided conceptual models of employee involvement (see Daft, 2001; Salamon, 1987). Figure 11.1 depicts an adaptation of such models and shows the relationship between three constituent elements:

1. the forms of involvement, direct and indirect
2. the level of involvement in the organizational hierarchy
3. the degree of involvement.

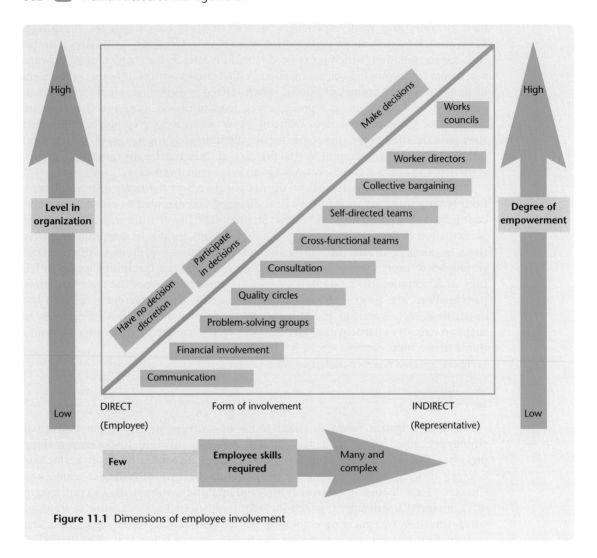

Figure 11.1 Dimensions of employee involvement

The diagram shows a continuum of employee involvement from a situation in which employees have no autonomy (for example, a traditionally designed assembly line) to full involvement, where workers participate in strategic decision-making. Current methods of EI fall along this continuum. Those methods are based on involvement through the communication of information, financial involvement, upward problem-solving, quality circles, extended consultation, cross-functional teams, self-directed teams, collective bargaining, worker directors and works councils.

STUDY TIP

These different forms of EI need to be understood as part of a human resources (HR) strategy. Before reading on, go back and look at Figure 2.8, re-reading that section of the text. Thinking about the different HR strategies and their rationale, what is the connection between business strategy, HR strategy, EI and two-way communications?

These different forms of EI are evident in North America and Europe. As we discussed in Chapter 4, many US and Canadian companies have introduced quality circles, briefing groups and various forms of work teams; in Chapter 9, we examined the growth of financial participation schemes, such as profit-sharing and stock options (see HRM in practice 9.2). In the EU, EWCs are a common feature of the corporate governance landscape, although it is outside the scope of this chapter to examine the wider debate on works councils, worker directors and European-style industrial democracy. Similarly, EI through the process of collective bargaining is examined in Chapter 12. Before examining EI techniques in detail, however, let us address the question, 'Why the enthusiasm for EI?'

HRM WEB LINKS

For general information on EI schemes, go to www.acas.org.uk (Britain), www.hrdc-drhc.gc.ca (Canada), www.clc-ctc.ca (Canada), www.workindex.com/(USA) and www.eia.com (international).

A general theory of employee involvement

Management has continually to address two interlinked problems – those of control and commitment – with regard to managing the employment relationship. Fox (1985) argues that, faced with the management problem of securing employee compliance, identification and commitment, management has adopted a range of employment strategies including EI. The current enthusiasm for improved EI needs to be viewed within the context of changing business and concomitant HR strategies in which the purpose of the latter is to secure EI support and commitment to high-performance work systems. EI aims to support management's goals either directly through performance improvements, or indirectly through organizational commitment (Marchington, 2001). The commitment–performance link is predicated on a number of assumptions, first that giving workers more autonomy over work tasks will strengthen organizational citizenship. Moreover, it will increase workers' commitment to the organization's goals, which will in turn result in enhanced individual and organizational performance. The involvement–commitment cycle is depicted in Figure 11.2 and is the reverse of the vicious circle of control discussed by Clegg and Dunkerley (1980) and Huczynski and Buchanan (1991). Lubricating the whole commitment–performance process is a communication style that attempts to build an internal culture encouraging initiative, learning, creativity and greater employee identification with the organization.

REFLECTIVE QUESTION

What do you think of the assumptions underpinning the involvement–commitment cycle? Can the growth of EI be explained by employer 'needs', or are there other forces determining this employee relations practice?

Management theorists have put forward three main reasons why senior management introduces EI schemes (Verma, 1995):

- moral
- economic
- behavioural.

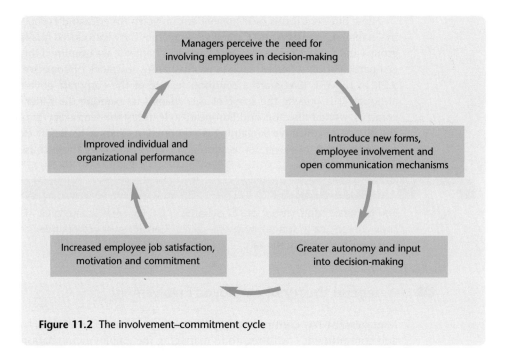

Figure 11.2 The involvement–commitment cycle

The first reason for introducing EI is derived from an ethical, political and moral base, the argument being that, in a democratic society, workers should be involved in the decision-making process when the outcomes of those decisions impact on their lives. EI therefore presents a socially acceptable management style. The development of EI and communications will be encouraged because companies generally desire to project 'a socially responsible stance on such issues' (Marchington & Wilding, 1983, p. 32).

The second reason for introducing EI, championed by the 'model of excellence' school in North America, derives from the utilitarian principle that EI improves the quality of decision-making and productivity. Marchington (1982) argues that EI potentially improves the quality of a decision and its chances of successful implementation on the factory floor. Similarly, it is asserted that EI improves productivity and energizes workers (Verma & Taras, 2001), as well as increasing employees' trust in management (Mabey et al., 1998) and reducing work stress (Mackie et al., 2001). Research on the EI–firm performance link suggests that giving employees a 'voice' on a range of organizational decisions yield benefits to both the organization and the workforce (Heller et al., 1998).

The third justification for EI derives from the perennial managerial problems associated with perceived dysfunctional behaviour: resistance to change, strikes, absenteeism and other forms of conflict (Beer et al., 1984; Guest, 1986). EI is seen as a solution to these dysfunctional human behaviours. According to Beer et al. (1984, p. 53) by introducing EI schemes:

> Employers hope that participative mechanisms will create a greater coincidence of interests between employers and employees, thereby increasing trust, reducing the potential for conflict, and increasing the potential for an effective mutual influence process.

Surveys of managers have shown that EI is typically management initiated with the objective of enhancing employee commitment to organizational goals (see Delbridge & Whitfield, 2001; Marchington, 1995, 2001; Marchington et al., 1992). The most frequently cited reason for introducing financial participation (for example profit-sharing schemes) was, for example, to promote worker identification and commitment (Marchington, 1995, 2001). In addition, EI arrangements might be introduced in order to avert union organization. As Beer et al. (1984, p. 153) posit, 'Some companies introduce participative methods at the shop floor in the hope that a greater congruence of interest will make it less likely that workers will organize.' Thus, EI practices might go hand in hand with changes in an organization's culture away from a collective trade union focus and towards an individual-orientated focus. By promoting a direct relationship between worker and management (Batstone & Gourlay, 1986). EI practices can also, according to Townley (1994), be used to 'educate' and 'reconstitute the individual', thereby making workers' behaviour and performance more manageable.

HRM WEB LINKS

For more examples of companies introducing EI practices, go to the websites of the following companies: General Electric (www.ge.com), Wal-Mart (www.walmart.com), IBM (www.ibm.com), ICI (www.ici.com) or a company you are studying. Once there, go to 'Employee participation' or/and 'Communications' and follow the prompts.

● Organizational communication

Downward communication patterns from managers to non-managers need to be explored within the wider context of  organizational communications theory. The exchange of information and the transmission of meaning is the very essence of organizational lives. Information about the organization – its production, its products and services, its external environment and its people – is a prerequisite for effective employee involvement in decision-making. A strong advocate of high-performance work systems, Pfeffer (1998a, p. 93), not surprisingly, argues that 'the sharing of information on such things as financial performance, strategy, and operational measures conveys to the organization's people that they are trusted' Organizational communications can be simply viewed as the process by which information is exchanged between a sender and a receiver, but the communication process is complicated by organizational characteristics such as hierarchy and power relations, and by the fact that managers and non-managers all have idiosyncrasies, abilities and biases.

We need to begin with a notion of what is meant by organizational communication. One simple definition focuses on information *disclosure*: 'The systematic provision of information to employees concerning all aspects of their employment and the wider issues relating to the organization in which they work' (Advisory, Conciliation and Arbitration Service [ACAS], 1987, p. 3). Meaning is a core concept in communication, and researchers in this field of study define their discipline in complex behavioural and contextual terms. Byers, in her book *Organizational Communication: Theory and Behaviour*, brings together three notions associated with communications – behaviour, meaning and context – and defines organizational communications as 'both behaviours and symbols, generated either intentionally or unintentionally, occurring

- Communicating is the fundamental process of organizing

- Understanding communication provides insights into management strategies

- Senior management should be committed to open communication

- Communication skills are the basis for effective leadership

- Management should take the initiative in devising and maintaining the communication system

- Messages should occur in a form that can be readily understood

- Information should be perceived to be relevant to employees

- Efficacy – desired effect or effectiveness of written versus face-to-face channels of communication

- Messages should be consistent with actions

- Male and female managers communicate differently in the workplace

- Cross-cultural communication is an increasing feature of a diverse work organization

- Training in communication skills increases the effectiveness of the system

- Communication systems should be monitored and evaluated

Figure 11.3 Key issues related to communications in the workplace

between and among people who assign meaning to them, within an organizational setting' (1997, p. 4). Communication is *symbolic*, which means that the words managers and workers speak or the gestures they make have no inherent meaning. Symbolic meanings, conveyed both verbally and non-verbally, only 'gain their significance from an agreed-upon meaning' (Martin & Nakayama, 2000, p. 61). To make it more complicated, people communicate differently depending on the context in which communication occurs, each message may have multiple layers of meaning, and culture influences communication, by which the perception of reality is created, sustained and transformed: 'All communities in all places at all times manifest their own view of reality in what they do. The entire culture reflects the contemporary model of reality' (Burke, 1985, quoted in Martin & Nakayama, 2000, p. 62).

The role of organizational communication can be seen in studies of managers and their work. Writers (for example Mintzberg, 1973) have found that managers spend a vast proportion of their working time on interpersonal communications, indeed, the business of managers is communications. In our discussion of management, communication is an important skill for 'getting things done' (Figure 1.2), but our model of management also suggests that various contingencies, for example the internal characteristics of an organization, such as structure, impact on the communication process. The size of the organization will generally affect how sophisticated the communication system is. In small organizations, the system might be informal and subject to frequent management intervention. In large organizations, on the other hand, specialists may serve as employee communications managers. Most organizations use a mixture of formal and informal ad hoc arrangements to communicate to their employees. Furthermore, communications will be determined by the organization's business and HR strategy: for example, the more the company's manufacturing and HRM strategies empower people and are knowledge and innovative orientated, the more important communications become.

Communication scholars have emphasized that, to be effective, organizational communication must take place regularly, it must be a two-way process to give employees the opportunity to participate, and it should involve all members of the management team, including first-line supervisors. Researchers, academics and practitioners have also stressed some key issues related to communications in the workplace (Figure 11.3).

Approaches to studying communications

Before examining some of these key issues related to organizational communications, we should be aware that, as in other disciplines, research and writing on organizational communication reflect different theoretical perspectives. This section briefly discusses three major perspectives for understanding organizational communication:

1. functionalist
2. interpretivist
3. critical.

Functionalist approach

The functionalist approach is the dominant perspective and studies communication as intended or unintended action. The work organization is viewed as an entity, different communication acts being variables that shape and determine the operations of that entity (Neher, 1997). The functionalist approach views communication as a metaphorical pipeline through which information is transmitted between a sender and receiver (see Figure 11.4 below). Functionalists categorize behaviours or messages in terms of accomplishing goals and objectives (Neher, 1997).

Interpretivist approach

The interpretivist approach is a reaction against the functionalist perspective (Neher, 1997), attempting to understand the process of human communication rather than the role that communication plays in managing the organization. Interpretivists argue that human beings do not behave as predictably as is suggested by the functionalist school. We may thus be able to predict that most organizational members, or some members, will react to a certain message in a certain way, but we cannot make the prediction for all members. Some members will do one thing and some another when presented with identical information. Interpretivist scholars argue that because people are so complex in their behaviours and exhibit a *choice* in responding to stimuli, functionalist explanations of organizational behaviour are inappropriate.

Critical approach

The critical approach derives from the critical theory school, which seeks to expose the often hidden but pervasive power that post-industrial organizations wield over individuals. Whereas the functionalist approach is concerned with making the organization more efficient, the critical theorist is more concerned with examining communication, such as myths, metaphors and stories, as a source of power and, moreover, understanding why organizational practices that maintain strong controls over workers are considered legitimate and are hence not resisted (Alvesson, 1996; Eisenberg & Goodall, 1997). Thompson and McHugh, for example, citing various sources, assert that organizational communication is often 'a tool of ideological influence' and seeks to exert influence over people (2002, p. 264). Organizational communication is thus studied in terms of hidden exercises of power and managerial hegemony.

⬤ A communications model

The communications model depicted in Figure 11.4 is an example of the functionalist approach to communications, depicting interpersonal communication as a process by which information is exchanged between a sender and a receiver. Organizational people have three basic methods of transmitting information:

- verbal
- non-verbal
- written.

Verbal communication ranges from a casual conversation between two employees to a formal speech by the managing director. In face-to-face meetings, the meaning of the information being conveyed by the sender can be expressed through gesture or facial expressions, which is referred to as non-verbal communication. *Written* communication ranges from a casual note to a co-worker to an annual report. Electronically mediated methods of communication, such as e-mail and video-conferencing systems (VCSs), are an increasingly popular form of communication within and across organizations and have revolutionized written and verbal business communications (although not without some cost, see Chapter 5). The content of any message consists of *what* is being communicated; the *way* in which content is communicated – through the various channels – describes the sender's communication style. And different communication styles affect the perception of a message or set of messages.

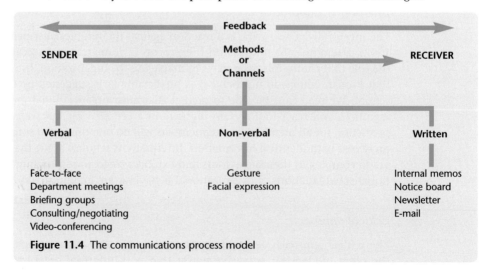

Figure 11.4 The communications process model

This interpersonal communications model has its limitations in that it characterizes communication as a linear process and ignores different cultures and subcultures and organizational hierarchies and power relationships (Rees, 1998; Tan, 1998; Thompson & McHugh, 2002). It is argued, therefore, that this contextually impoverished model of organizational communication needs to be augmented by a sensitivity to cross-cultural norms, as well as to the overall organizational contexts that give rise to the shared meanings, which allow interpersonal communication to occur.

HRM WEB LINKS

For more information on electronic business communication, go to www.idm. internet.com/ix/, www.intrack.com/intranet/ and www.internetjournal.earth.

Developing a communication system

Communication theorists adopting a functionalist perspective have identified a number of challenges that must be taken into account when managers try to devise a communication system that will enable the organization to run more efficiently.

Disparate geographical locations

In a large organization, for example a hospital, university or electricity company, there might be multiple sites or plants that create a problem of contact and consistency in the communication system. Video-conferencing technology may be used to communicate between worksites when dealing with routine, non-controversial information and simple issues. Panteli and Dawson's (2001) study on the use of video-conferencing questioned the appropriateness of VCS to all forms of multisite workplace meeting. Contrary to earlier research, they found that VCSs are not a rich communication medium and are not appropriate for meetings requiring complex decision-making activities or 'more creative discussions'.

Large variety of skill groups

A large public organization such as a local government is responsible for different types of employee: refuse collectors, fire-fighters, librarians, social workers, environmental officers. This might mean that there is no community of interest and no common corporate objective, which normally binds employees together. Considerable time and effort may have to be spent on identifying relevant information for each of the skill groups and in disseminating this to them. It also indicates that there are challenges in centralizing and coordinating the communication system in such organizations.

Cross-cultural communications

In a globalized economy and culturally diverse organizations, there is growing recognition that managers should, in order to communicate effectively, understand the importance of culturally sensitive communications (Blum, 1997; Tan, 1998). Culture can be defined as a community's shared attitudes, values, behaviour and acts of communicating or 'mental programmes' that are passed from one generation to the next (Hofsted, 1980). Therefore, communication both outside and inside the workplace is a culture-bound activity (Martin & Nakayama, 2000; Tan, 1998).

According to cross-cultural studies, managers in different cultures place more or less emphasis on written rather than oral communication and can be more or less direct when communicating perceived good or neutral news. Researchers have, for example, observed that Japanese managers prefer oral communication to written communication and can be more indirect and circular; they can therefore go off at a tangent when discussing an issue. In contrast, North American managers display the opposite communication traits; they tend to prefer written communications and expect messages to be explicit and to the point. Although we should be cautious of the dangers of stereotyping cultural or national characteristics, the literature suggests that misunderstanding and conflicts may arise when managers from an Asian culture interact with those from a Western culture as the former may consider the direct approach to communicating preferred by the other party to be offensive (Tan, 1998). One practical application of the insights obtained from studies on the West–East cultural divide is cultural diversity training (Chapter 2).

Gendered communications

If communication is culture-bound, there is evidence to suggest that it is also gender-bound. Gender can be defined as the characteristics associated with being a man or a woman, which are shaped by culture notions and have to be learned. A number of academics have written about the gender differences between the way in which men and women communicate in work organizations. Current psychological research on leadership and team dynamics suggests that men and women exhibit different inter-personal communication styles (Crawford, 1995; Tannen, 1993; Winter et al., 2001). Studies suggest that male managers tend to be loud, direct, dominant and aggressive. Women, on the other hand, tend to be more open, self-revealing and polite when they speak (Aries, 1996), are superior at decoding non-verbal communication and possess 'softer', more 'feminine' skills of communication, which are valued in post-bureaucratic organizations (Hawkins, 1995; Helgesen, 1995; Wajcman, 1998). In other words, communication is a context-bound exchange of meaning between organizational people and is a gender-bound activity.

Employment arrangements

The growing tendency to employ part-time workers creates challenges in ensuring that face-to-face communication takes place with all employees. Added to this is the fact that certain groups of employees, for example sales representatives, can spend a large proportion of their time away from their office.

Financial constraints

In a highly cost-conscious business environment, managers may face a challenge in justifying the cost of practising effective communication, for example an employee news bulletin. In a study conducted by one of the authors, a respondent said that 'communications is underfunded and undervalued' (quoted in Bratton & Sinclair, 1987, p. 10).

REFLECTIVE QUESTION

Thinking about your own work experience or the experience of a friend, relative or family member, can you cite a situation in which you have perceived differences in communication style between men and women? How important is it to recognize that communication is 'culture-bound'?

Two-way communication

The functionalist literature on communication provides guidance on what constitutes 'good practice'. It is emphasized that communication can flow in three directions – downwards, upwards, and horizontally – as depicted in Figure 11.5. Communication that flows from one level of the organization to a lower level is a *downward* communication. When we think of managers communicating with subordinates, the downward pattern is the one we usually think of. *Upward* communication flows to a higher level in the organization; it keeps managers aware of how employees feel about their jobs and the organization in general. Communication that flows between employees at the same level in the organization is a *horizontal* communication. This type of communication includes communication between co-workers in different departments or divisions of the organization, and between co-workers in the same team.

This formal communication follows the organization's chain of command or hierarchy, but the organization's informal communication network, the grapevine, is

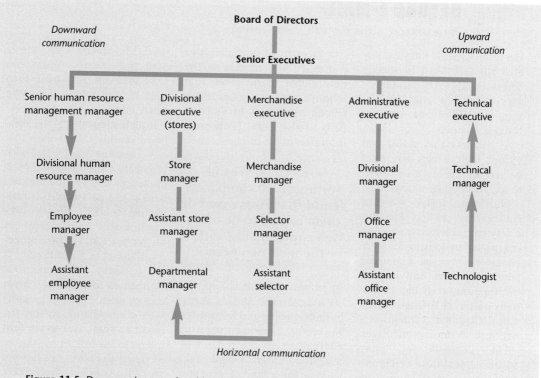

Figure 11.5 Downward, upward and horizontal communication in a retail store

based not on hierarchy but on social relationships. The grapevine is an important means through which employees fulfil their need to know about the organization. New employees generally digest more information about the company informally from their co-workers than they do from formal orientation programmes, and 75 per cent of employees claim that the grapevine is their first source of important information in the workplace (McShane, 2001).

It is also emphasized that communication is a two-way process, with upward and downward communication flows. The most common forms of two-way communication are 'suggestion schemes', attitude surveys and employee appraisals. Two-way communication should not, however, be confused with consultation. The aim of the two-way communication process is often only to ensure that employees have understood the message; it does not necessarily imply that employees' reactions, feelings and criticisms will have any effect upon the decision-making process. In 'post-bureaucratic' organizations (see Chapter 4 for a discussion on bureaucracy and organizational design), in which employee participation is essential, there will be other structures and processes that enable employees to be involved more directly in decision-making. Thus, information disclosure and two-way communication are essential prerequisites given the rise of 'knowledge work' and job redesign that puts a premium on work-related learning, flexibility and commitment.

HRM IN PRACTICE 11.2

BEYOND E-MAIL

KEVIN MARRON, *GLOBE AND MAIL*, 2000, FEBRUARY 25

Electronic mail – long considered the last word in speedy communications – suddenly seems too slow and cumbersome for the instant world of Internet business.

As business goes global and virtual, basic e-mail may soon be left in the dust of cyberspace, replaced by a new set of sophisticated tools for real-time collaboration on-line. 'E-mail is a very critical business tool, but companies are looking for more effective ways of managing what they have and making information available to the right people at the right time,' says Claudine Simard, a national technology manager.

The demand for more advanced real-time collaboration tools is being spurred by the growth of 'collaborative commerce' – a creature of the new global marketplace that requires close cooperation among companies in different parts of the world (sometimes in different industries), their

> **A recent survey of Fortune 1000 companies found that 70 per cent of them expect to be using Web conferencing within the next two years.**

employees, customers, suppliers and partners. Already, many business people and knowledge workers are experimenting with alternatives to the tedium of telephone and e-mail tag, looking for a way of avoiding

what Ms. Simard calls 'the e-mail hot potato, where you send someone an e-mail, then wait all day to see if they've acted on it or to get a reply.'

Instant messaging – the Web-based on-line chat system that has become popular with teenagers around the world – is finding its place in the business world. And so are Web conferencing tools, such as Net-Meeting that helps people set up live voice and video communications over the Internet. A recent survey of Fortune 1000 companies found that 70 per cent of them expect to be using Web conferencing within the next two years, and 46 per cent intend to use instant messaging. Many of the tools can be, and are being, used effectively today.

REFLECTIVE QUESTION

Do you think that web-based on-line chat systems will improve cross-cultural communication? How does this new communications technology impact on international HRM?

Survey evidence indicates that managers use a variety of arrangements for communicating with their subordinates, including regular meetings, suggestion schemes, newsletters, management chain and opinion surveys (Cully et al., 1999; Millward et al., 1992, 2000). Table 11.1 lists six frequently discussed direct communication methods and shows the proportion of workplaces operating such schemes. The survey data offer support to the argument that organizations are using combinations or 'clusters' of certain EI practices associated with new organizational designs, such as team briefings. Designated work teams were reported in 65 per cent of workplaces. This 'conjunction of management practices' might be construed as a model of direct employee participation in decision-making (Cully et al., 1999). One important observable change between 1984 and 1998 was the use of briefing groups, up from 36 per cent to 65 per cent. Team briefings are considered to be an effective way of passing information downwards and upwards through the hierarchy – that is, of increasing the two-way communication flow. Other changes include workforce attitude surveys or ballots, up from 12 per cent to 45 per cent. Not indicated in Table 11.1 is the considerable variation in the application of communication methods across sectors of the British economy – manufacturing, service and public sector – employment size and the type of trade union present. Small establishments were, for example, least likely to use any of the specified EI schemes. Trade union opposition to team briefings stems from the perceived threat to the shop stewards' leadership role within the workplace; in North America, for example, team briefing has been used as part of a union avoidance strategy (Chapter 12).

HRM WEB LINKS

Further details on the research methods used and outcome of the surveys, including information on how managers communicate with their subordinates, can be found at the website of WERS 98: see www.dti.gov.uk/er/emar/1998WERS.htm and www. data-archive.ac.uk.

Table 11.1 Use of communication methods, 1984–98 (percentages)

| | % of all workplaces | | |
	1984	1990	1998
Briefing groups	36	48	65
Problem-solving groups (for example quality circles)	–	35	49
Regular meetings between management and workforce	34	41	48
Surveys or ballots	12	17	45
Regular newsletters	34	41	–
Suggestion schemes	25	28	–

Source: Culley et al. (1999); Millward et al. (1992, 2000)

Information disclosed by management

What type of information is communicated through the various communication activities? The two issues that are the subject of most communications are terms and conditions of employment and major changes in working methods or work organization, investment plans being least commonly reported as the subject of a large volume of communication. Managers in organizations with recognized unions give more information on all topics than do managers in organizations without recognized trade unions (Millward & Stevens, 1986). Another interesting finding from survey studies is that UK-owned establishments are less likely than their foreign-owned counterparts to disclose information to their employees: around 50 per cent of UK-owned establishments gave their workforce information, compared with 60 per cent of foreign-owned establishments.

● Indirect employee participation

Let us turn to another dimension of EI, consultation and indirect employee participation. In its simplest form, consultation may take the form of an informal exchange of views between a group of workers and their manager on an incoming piece of machinery or a reorganization of the office. However, where the size of the organization makes access for workers to management difficult and there is a trade union present, a more formal and indirect employee participation network needs to be established. Such a body is a joint or 'labour–management' committee (LMC):

> Involving employees through their representatives in discussion and consideration of relevant matters which affect or concern those they represent, thereby allowing employees to influence the proposals *before* the final management decision is made (Institute of Personnel Management, 1981, emphasis added).

LMCs are voluntary workplace institutions negotiated between management and employee representatives. Consultation through an LMC differs from joint regulation or collective bargaining because the latter forms of indirect participation utilize the processes of negotiation and agreement between representatives from management and employees. We can develop the difference between joint consultation and collective bargaining further. The difference between them rests on the notion that both conflict and a common interest are inherent elements of the employment relationship that need to be handled in different ways. Consultation is viewed as a means of promoting action when there are no obvious conflicts of interest, whereas collective bargaining is a means of reconciling divergent interests, but we should, however, stress that every aspect of the employment relationship has the potential for conflict. The distinction between the two approaches to participation is concerned with the 'formal identification of those aspects of the employment relationship in which this conflict should be legitimized and subject to joint agreement by inclusion within the process of collective bargaining' (Salamon, 1987, p. 259).

The balance between joint consultation and collective bargaining will depend upon the power of trade unions. Daniel and Millward (1983, p. 135) found that the existence of LMCs or JCCs was closely allied to the relative bargaining power of the unions:

> consultative committees may tend to become an adjunct to the institutes of collective

bargaining where workplace trade union organization is well established, but provide an alternative channel of representation where it is weak.

Models of joint consultation

Academics have put forward two different models of consultation. The *revitalization model* suggests that recent support for consultation has coincided with the increased use of direct EI approaches by employers. This, it is argued, has the effect, whether planned or not, of undermining collective bargaining and consequently weakening workplace trade unionism (Batstone, 1984; Edwards, 1985). In contrast, the *marginality model* suggests an increased trivialization and marginalization of joint consultation in the early 1980s, particularly in organizations confronted by deteriorating economic conditions (MacInnes, 1987).

Marchington (1987) has challenged the conceptualization of these two models, arguing that the two consultative models do not describe the full range of processes that may take place in the consultative arena. Instead, Marchington proposed a third model, the *complementary model*, in which joint consultation complements rather than competes with joint regulation or collective bargaining. The argument is that 'consultation acts as an adjunct to the bargaining machinery' (Marchington, 1987, p. 340). With this model, collective bargaining is used to determine pay and conditions of employment, whereas joint consultation focuses on issues of an integrative nature and helps to lubricate employment relationships; both processes can provide benefits for employees and the organization. Millward and Stevens' (1986) study found support for Marchington's complementary model, reporting that 'complex consultative structures co-exist with complex collective bargaining arrangements in the public sector in particular' (Millward & Stevens, 1986, p. 143).

Extent of joint consultation

Evidence has been collected from a number of surveys on the extent of joint consultation since the early 1970s (ACAS, 1987; Brown, 1981; Cully, et al., 1998; Millward & Stevens, 1986; Millward et al., 1992). The 1998 WERS of private sector, multinational companies in the UK found that the overall proportion of the workplaces with LMCs fell between 1984 and 1998 from 34 per cent to 28 per cent. Data for EWCs, which represent another type of indirect employee participation, are also shown in Table 11.2. In private manufacturing, some of the decline in the incidence of LMCs came about as a result of employment shrinkage in the sector. LMCs were still more

Table 11.2 Incidence of European Works Councils and consultative committees, 1984–98

	% of all workplaces		
	1984	1990	1998
Consultative committee	34	29	29
European Works Councils	–	–	19

Source: Adapted from Culley et al. (1999) and Millward et al. (2000)

HRM IN PRACTICE 11.3

MOTOROLA CLOSURE REVIVES DEBATE OVER CONSULTATION

CHRIS TAYLOR, *PEOPLE MANAGEMENT*, 2001, MAY 3

The argument over workplace consultation has flared up again following Motorola's decision to close its manufacturing plant in Bathgate, West Lothian, with the loss of 3,200 jobs.

The redundancies at the mobile phone factory, along with Ericsson's decision to axe 12,000 jobs globally, have prompted renewed calls for firms to be compelled to discuss with employees such decisions before they are finalised.

The Transport and General Workers' Union (T&G) claimed that, because the UK had refused to implement EU rules on worker consultation, companies favoured closures in Britain as a way of dealing with European or global problems.

> ‘We are seeing a multi-national sweeping away thousands of jobs with a stroke of a pen.’

‘We are seeing a multi-national sweeping away thousands of jobs with a stroke of a pen’ said Jimmy Elsby, T&G assistant general secretary. ‘The government could do some-thing with a stroke of its pen and sign up to the information and consultation directive to give us some say in the decisions of these companies.’

But Dominic Johnson, CBI head of employee relations, said that Britain's situation differed ‘only at the margins’ from that of its European neighbours.

‘The EU's collective redundancies directive (already in force) places onerous requirements on management to consult on the implementation of redundancies and the fundamental decisions on which they are based,’ Johnson said.

common in larger establishments than smaller ones and were more frequently reported in public sector workplaces. This finding is significant because, given the antipathy towards trade unions throughout the 1980s and early 1990s, British management might have been expected to substitute joint consultation for joint regulation (Sisson, 1993).

In total, some 67 per cent of UK workers and managers are in workplaces with joint consultative arrangements, either in the workplace or a higher level in the organization (Cully et al., 1998). Although we have always to be careful when making international comparison – as, for example, researchers define HR practices differently – survey studies show that, across Western Europe between 1997 and 2000, EI practices and downward and upward communication have increased by an average of 52 per cent (Mayrhofer et al., 2000). In Canada, 43 per cent of workplaces reported some form of EI in decision-making (Verma & Taras, 2001). These findings need to be contrasted with more critical studies suggesting that EI in decision-making has not shown any sign of substantive improvement (Thompson & McHugh, 2002).

Main issues discussed by joint consultative committees

With regard to the issues dealt with by JCCs, surveys have found that where consultative machinery and collective bargaining machinery exist together, there is an overlap between consultation and bargaining or joint regulation arrangements (Millward et al., 1992). The separation of joint consultation from collective bargaining is often attempted by simply excluding from the bargaining table any item that normally is the subject of joint regulation. The result can be the creation of the 'canteen, car park, toilet paper syndrome' and has prompted some observers to characterize the subject matter of JCCs as a 'diet of anodyne trivia and old hat' (MacInnes, 1985, pp. 103–4). However, Millward, et al. (1992) found that, in manufacturing, more substantive issues were being discussed, including production matters (18 per cent of respondents reported this issue as being the most important item that the committee discussed), employment issues (12 per cent) and government legislation or regulations (9 per cent).

The structure and operation of JCCs

When choosing a joint consultative structure or developing an existing one, it is necessary for managers to make a number of decisions guided by its aims, philosophy and strategy. Joint consultation requires a high-trust relationship and regular information disclosure to all participating parties. Managers have to decide how much information will be disclosed, by whom and how. Management's role in a consultative structure is generally to communicate information and be fully involved in the process; anything less than this will result in decisions being made or agreed upon without their knowledge or support. Managers may adopt either of two broad approaches: they can integrate the two processes of consultation and negotiation within the collective bargaining machinery, or they can agree to maintain a separate machinery of joint consultation and regulation.

Three main reasons have been identified for the *integration* of consultative and negotiating machinery:

1. Communicating, consulting and negotiating are integrally linked together in the handling of employee relations.
2. Union representatives need to be fully involved in the consultative process, if only as a prelude to negotiations.
3. As the scope of collective bargaining expands, the issues left are otherwise allocated to what may be viewed as an irrelevant process.

On the other hand, substantive reasons have been cited for establishing *separate* consultative and collective bargaining structures:

1. Separation may help to overcome organizational complexity.
2. The fact that collective bargaining deals with substantive or procedural matters, and consultation addresses other matters of common interest, forces the two structures apart.
3. Regular JCC or LMC meetings and the publication of minutes ensure that joint consultation is accorded a proper place in the organizational system and confirms management's commitment and responsibility to consultation with its employees.

An example of joint consultation and collective bargaining structure in the public sector is shown in Figure 11.6.

When there are two sets of arrangements, the terms of reference of the LMC need to be specified by defining both its subject matter and the nature of its authority. The subject matter may be defined in terms of:

● excluding from its deliberation anything which is subject to joint regulation, that is, substantive (for example pay and vacation time) and procedural (for example discipline and grievance processes) matters

- enumerating the items that are to be regarded as matters for joint consultation (for example, a corporate plan, HR trends, education and training)
- items chosen on an ad hoc basis, deciding whether or not an issue should be dealt with in the joint regulation machinery.

HRM WEB LINKS

For more information on JCCs, go to the websites of ACAS (www.acas.org.uk) and the Trades Union Congress (www.tuc.org.uk). See also www.ccma.org.za (S. Africa) and www.airc.gov.au (Australia).

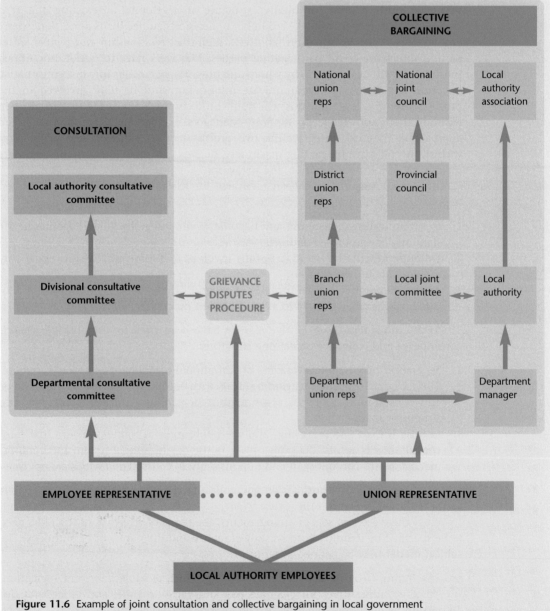

Figure 11.6 Example of joint consultation and collective bargaining in local government

European Works Councils

EWCs have been part of the German industrial relations landscape since the end of the Second World War. Much of the early research on works councils was focused on German 'codetermination' (*Mitbestimmung*) and worker participation in decision-making, manifested in the Works Constitution Act. EWCs are not the same as LMCs or JCCs: whereas LMCs are voluntary committees, the term 'European Works Council' is used to describe only *mandatory* consultative committees. Accordingly, works councils can be defined as 'Institutionalized bodies of collective worker participation at the workplace level, with specific informatory, consultative and codetermination rights in personnel, social and economic affairs' (Frege, 2002, p. 223).

Works councils are legally independent of trade unions, and their members are elected in a ballot of all employees rather than just union members. The key functions of EWCs are:

- establishing two-way communication between employees and management *and* union and management
- maintaining peaceful and cooperative employment relations (as EWCs are not allowed to initiate a stoppage of work)
- providing training for representatives.

Since the early 1990s, UK managers, trade unions and academics have become more interested in the EWC model, this renewed interest having come about for three principal reasons. First, EU legislation has focused attention on EWCs. As mentioned earlier, the 1994 EWC Directive required organizations employing more than 1000 employees in the EU (excluding the UK) and at least two establishments in different Member States, with at least 150 employees (again excluding the UK) to set up works councils. The EWC Directive's principal objective is to induce organizations across the EU to set up an EWC system for the purpose of informing and consulting employees. In December 1999, the 1994 EWC Directive became law in the UK. To date, agreements between management and unions to establish EWCs have been concluded in over 600 European companies (Gilman & Marginson, 2002). The new EU Directive on Information and Consultation (2001) is likely to provoke further interest and academic research, especially in Member States without a strong EWC tradition (for example, Britain and Ireland).

Second, the decline of union membership in Britain and bargaining power over the past two decades has induced trade union leaders to explore the extension of union and workers' rights outside the traditional collective bargaining arena, under the umbrella of EU employee governance law. Third, the introduction of mandatory EWCs in 'transitional economies' in Central Europe has evoked a debate about the conditions for a successful implementation of EWC (Frege, 2002). Although the EWC system is still in its infancy, at least in the UK, EWCs are 'the most prominent, widespread and powerful form of industrial democracy in contemporary capitalist societies' (Frege, 2002, p. 221).

The 1998 WERS of private sector, multinational companies in the UK found that 19 per cent of the workplaces operated an EWC (Cully et al., 1998). EWCs have differing degrees of power (Mayrhofer et al., 2000): in Germany, for example, where EWCs have been a feature of the workplace for decades, employee representatives can resort to the courts to prevent or delay managerial decisions in areas such as changing working practices and dismissals. The range of issues discussed and the degree of legislative support for EWC would, comment Mayrhofer et al. (2000, p. 226), 'shock US managers brought up on the theories of "manager's right to manage"'. The study by Frege (2002) concluded that there is a lack of research on the determinants of different employment relations, how EWCs work in practice and the specific relation between unions and works councils. Evaluating the existing literature, Frege (2002, p. 241) concludes, 'we know much about the ontology of works councils (what is a works council, what does it do) but much less about the determinants, outcomes and underlying causal relations'. In terms of EWC–organization performance links, Addison et al. (2000) have also made a contribution to the debate. Using economic data from Germany and Britain, they argue that mandatory EWCs might be a policy to be considered in strong union work regimes with decentralized 'distributive bargaining'. Mandatory indirect participation in decision-making would appear to be associated with higher productivity in workplaces with more than 100 workers and in economies with centralized pay bargaining (for example Germany).

Obstacles to employee involvement

Two major impediments to the introduction of EI have been identified in the literature: the attitude of trade unions and the attitude of management to the consultative procedure.

Trade union attitudes

Trade unions traditionally prefer bargaining to consultation and have characterized consultative processes as a potential managerial strategy for 'incorporating' union representatives into management forms of control or as a union avoidance strategy (Clarke, 1977; Gilson & Wager, 2000). As two trade union researchers state: 'Joint consultation came to be seen as at best an inadequate expedient, at worst a positive menace, preventing unions from defending their members as resolutely as they might' (Coates & Topham 1980, p. 238). Moreover, one industrial relations theorist has asserted that 'increasing the involvement only of employees ... appears to be part of a strategy aimed at reducing the role and influence of stewards' (Batstone, 1984, pp. 264–5). More recently, the dominance of US thinking on HRM, the use of non-union organizations as 'exemplars of good practice' and the individualization of organizational communication have partly explained union hostility to innovations in EI (Mayrhofer et al., 2000). According to Brewster et al. (1999), however, the non-union implications of HRM and EI regimes sit uncomfortably with the history and circumstances of employee relations in Western Europe.

Even in a 'collectivist communication' regime, union representatives face the potential problems of role conflict, loss of contact with the membership and lack of knowledge and expertise. When the shop steward is confronted by divergent role expectations, the result is role conflict. In one case, for example, it was found that the stewards were consistently more keen on EI than were their constituents. Providing the union representatives did not neglect the 'protective' aspects of their responsibilities, the stewards were, however, free to become more involved in the decision-making process (Marchington, 1980). Whether the unions were aware of it or not, Gilson and Wager's analysis (2000, p. 178) shows that some of them participating in LMCs engaged in 'a trade-off between concessions (for example agreeing to greater flexibility) and strategic input'. Consultative procedures are more likely to succeed if managers are aware of the fears and potential problems that may confront union representatives sitting on participative bodies. It would be counterproductive to an organization committed to greater employee participation were workplace union representatives to become resentful of a perceived managerial intention to alienate them (Marchington, 1982).

Management attitudes

The other major obstacle to consultation comprises managerial philosophy and HR strategy. Managers seek to construct an organizational culture that reflects their own ideologies and styles of management and will reinforce their strategies and control (Gospel & Palmer, 1993). It is therefore not surprising to find evidence that the major obstacle to EI is resistance to change by middle and junior management (see, for example, Marchington, 1980; West, 1980). EI, by its very nature, might be expected to pose a threat to the more autocratic manager. It is, argues Rendall (1986, p. 42), 'the unspoken refusal of a hard core of managers and supervisors to implement change that prevents companies from evolving from authoritarian to participative'.

What is clearly apparent in the debate is that EI activities are a critical component of the 'high performance–high commitment' work system. EI is characterized by a high-trust employment relationship, one of operating by consent rather than coercion. Moreover, 're-engineering' the organization involves EI, as discussed in Chapter 4, and requires managers to 'let go' (Champy, 1996). Evidence suggests, however, that many managers tend to resist participation because 'it's contrary to their habit-formed ways of thinking and behaving' (Rendall, 1986, p. 42). As is the case with all HR policies, the effective implementation of EI necessitates commitment at the most senior level of the organization: anything less might mean indirect and direct EI arrangements being 'squeezed out' because of pressure of work. As one industrial relations commentator put it (quoted in Bratton & Sinclair, 1987, p. 39):

> Time is probably a big problem, time and pressure of work ... making time to do it ... that's why most things go by the board because everybody is busy ... Also, it's not just a question of going into meetings ... need to prepare the brief, think about what you are going to say ... it's as much time again.

What is apparent from the studies is that the attitudinal aspects of EI are much more crucial than the 'mechanics' of the various structural configurations of EI schemes. Provided organizations are aware of these attitudinal problems among managers, they may be ameliorated through training, not just in conventional communication skills, but also in the process and dynamics of 'living with EI'.

● Employee involvement and paradox

The types of EI scheme initiated by management to improve organizational performance contain contradictions and paradoxes. Stohl and Cheney (2001) analyse four main types of EI paradox:

- structure
- agency
- identity
- power.

They posit that paradox is inherent in EI processes and that these paradoxes 'set limits' that constrain the effectiveness of EI networks.

Organizational *structures* are created to govern EI, but most organizations eliminate workers from the most influential network: the executive. Strauss (1998) explains this potential paradox. Most EI initiatives involve direct participation (for example briefing groups), but this form of EI can make only limited changes to the way in which work is designed because 'really important decisions', for example investment in new technology, are made by senior management. It is not surprising, then, that although EI is 'often intended to enhance productivity by empowering workers to make decisions, the system's very design prevents workers having a say in how they might become more involved' (Stohl & Cheney, 2001, p. 362). Put another way, workers should be learning, innovating and voicing their opinions in the way we, the managers, have planned!

The notion of *agency* relates to an individual's sense of being and a feeling that she or he can or does make a difference (Giddens, 1984). EI is rooted in the belief that workers can have an effect and that their knowledge and skills are fundamental to organizational success. The notion of agency helps us to examine the psychological contract within a frame of interpretation that calls for substantial individual expression and contribution. One paradox of agency references the tensions and contradictions present in work teams in which self-managed work teams may rely on the active subordination of team members to the will of the team. Thus, 'Do things our way but in a way that is still distinctively your own!' Not surprisingly, workers may become ambivalent and hesitant about participating in such a regime.

The paradox of *identity* addresses issues of boundaries, space and the divide between the in-group and the out-group (Stohl & Cheney, 2001). The paradox of identity is linked to the notion of employee commitment. At one level, EI implies commitment to the processes of learning and discussion, and to diversity and difference. At another level, however, 'commitment is expected to equal agreement' (Stohl & Cheney, 2001, p. 380). Within the context of EI and work-based learning networks, voicing an alternative view is interpreted by managers and non-managers alike as a means of resistance, as lack of commitment or even as evidence of 'sabotage' (Zorn et al., 1999). In a so-called 'learning organization', the paradox of identity may be expressed as 'Be a *self*-directed learner to meet *organizational* priorities.'

The fourth paradox is the paradox of *power*, which centres on issues of leadership, access to resources, opportunities for voice and the shaping of employee behaviour. The popular EI literature emphasizes the importance of 'strong leaders' to facilitate and lead participatory efforts. Stohl and Cheney (2001, p. 388) provide persuasive evidence of EI regimes 'getting workers to make decisions that management would have made themselves'. In other words, 'Be an independent thinker, just as I have commanded you!' These examples suggest that paradox is an integral part of the EI paradigm and partly account for the continued scepticism towards EI on the part of some observers (see, for example, Thompson & McHugh, 2002). As discussed in Chapter 1, the challenge for managers is whether creativity and innovation can emerge from these paradoxes (Handy, 1994).

Discipline at work

So far, we have looked at management-initiated EI and communication practices and the mandatory works councils that seek a diversity of voices in organizational decision-making. To complete the discussion on employee relations, we must examine a third set of practices and processes: those of discipline. When EI 'voice' mechanisms fail to create or reinforce desirable employee attitudes and behaviours, managers may resort to disciplinary action. Indeed, there is evidence that there has been an increased use of formal disciplinary measures since EI practices were introduced. Bratton's (1992, p. 197) analysis of work teams, for example, showed that when a payment-by-results scheme was withdrawn, it 'increased the propensity of management to invoke formal disciplinary procedures'. Similarly, Mabey et al. (1998) found a disjuncture between the rhetoric of empowerment and the practical reality of total quality management. Their study found that workers had 'negative perceptions' of total quality management because of a culture incorporating the 'excessive use of disciplinary actions against individuals' (Mabey et al., 1998, p. 66). In recent years, rates of disciplinary sanctions and dismissals have increased, providing further evidence of the general UK movement from *collective* relations towards *individualization* of the employment relationship (Knight & Latreille, 2000).

The modern workplace is pervaded by rules established by management to regulate the behaviour of workers. Indeed, it is argued that obedience underscores the relationship between the employer and employee: 'There is certainly nothing more essential to the contractual relation between master and servant than the duty of obedience' (Cairns, 1974, quoted in Wedderburn, 1986, p. 187). Disciplinary practices, ranging from oral warnings to termination of the employment relationship, aim to make workers' behaviour predictable. As discussed elsewhere in this text, the employment relationship involves a legal relationship, and for those employers and managers who share a less-than-sophisticated management style known as 'my way or the highway', there is a framework of legal rights regulating the disciplinary process. The purpose of these laws and standards is to provide a fair and consistent method of dealing with alleged inappropriate or unacceptable work behaviour, but they vary widely between national legal systems. In addition to legal rules, collective agreements in unionized workplaces generally grant management the power to 'institute rules of behaviour and to mete out punishment, subject to the employees' right to grieve' (Giles & Starkman, 2001, p. 308). The purpose of this section is modest; it is to provide an overview of the disciplinary concepts, practices, procedures and statutory rights found in the workplace. UK students and practitioners requiring a detailed knowledge of employment law relating to discipline and dismissal are advised to refer to *Selwyn's Law of Employment* (2000) or a similar text.

HRM WEB LINKS

Go to the following websites to compare employment standards legislation relating to discipline at work: www.hmso.gov.uk/acts.htm, which provides full texts of UK Acts of Parliament; www.labour-travail.hrdc-drhc.gc.ca//index.cfm/doc/english for a comparative study of Canadian employment standards. See also p. xxii of this book.

Disciplinary concepts

Discipline can be defined as the process maintaining compliance with the rules that regulate employment in order to produce a controlled and effective performance. The purpose of discipline is:

- *improvement:* the disciplinary process is seen as one of counselling the disobedient employee back to acceptable behaviour
- *punishment:* the disciplinary process is seen as being about imposing penalties
- *deterrent:* the process is seen as educational to deter others.

Corrective discipline refers to management action that follows the infraction of a rule. In North America, the 'hot-stove rule' is used to guide correct discipline. This states that disciplinary action (for example warnings or suspension from work) should have the same characteristics as the penalty an individual receives from touching a hot stove. These characteristics are that discipline should be with warning, immediate, consistent and impersonal. Most modern workplaces apply a policy of *progressive discipline*, which means that the employer notifies employees of unacceptable conduct and provides them with an adequate opportunity to correct their behaviour.

Disciplinary rules and procedures are necessary for promoting orderly employment relations as well as fairness and consistency in the treatment of individuals. *Rules* set standards of conduct and performance in the workplace, whereas *procedures* help to ensure that the standards are adhered to and also provide a fair method of dealing with alleged failures to observe them. A disciplinary process should incorporate the requirements of natural justice, which means that employees should be informed in advance of any disciplinary hearing of the alleged misconduct, be given the right to challenge the alleged evidence, have the right to representation and to have witnesses and be given the right to appeal against any decisions taken by management (Selwyn, 2000).

Rules of behaviour

Every organization has rules, for example rules about time-keeping, quality standards, safety and personal hygiene. Rules of behaviour in the workplace should be clear, readily understood and no more than are sufficient to cover all obvious and usual disciplinary matters. The UK Employment Rights Act 1996 requires employers to provide written information for their employees about certain aspects of their disciplinary rules and procedures. In particular, employees should be given a clear indication of the type of conduct, often referred to as 'gross misconduct', that may warrant summary dismissal, that is, dismissal without notice (Selwyn, 2000). Workplace rules

- Theft, fraud and deliberate falsification of records
- Physical violence
- Serious bullying or harassment
- Deliberate damage to property
- Serious insubordination
- Bringing the employer into serious disrepute
- Serious incapability while on duty brought on by alcohol or illegal drugs
- Serious negligence which causes damage or injury

Figure 11.7 Typical 'gross misconduct' in the workplace
Source: Selwyn (2000)

will be shaped by national cultures and subcultures. Behaviours considered acts of 'gross misconduct' are shown in Figure 11.7.

Penalties

The employer can impose a number of penalties for infractions, such as:

- rebuke
- warnings
- transfer or demotion
- suspension
- dismissal.

A rebuke may be, for example, a simple 'Don't do that.' For most employees, the rebuke may be sufficient to change behaviour. Formal warnings should not be given lightly because the manager is making some sort of commitment to action if the behaviour is repeated. Furthermore, the legislation on dismissal in Western countries has made the system of warnings an integral part of disciplinary practice, which has to be followed if the employer is to succeed in defending a dismissal decision. All written warnings should be dated, signed and kept on record for a period agreed by rules known to both sides. Disciplinary transfer or demotion is a penalty that is substantial but falls short of dismissal. Suspension involves a penalty that is serious but avoids the disadvantage of being longlasting. If all other penalties fail to modify the employee's behaviour, the employee may be dismissed with 'just cause'. There is an array of legal statute and precedent intended to safeguard the individual employee against unreasonable dismissal, the point of legal intervention varying from one country to another (Torrington, 1998).

Procedures in discipline

Across Britain, formal disciplinary procedures are the norm even in the smallest workplaces. Survey data have revealed that among those workplaces with 25–49 employees, 88 per cent operated a formal disciplinary procedure (Cully et al., 1998). The way discipline is managed in the workplace will tend to vary depending on the seriousness of the infraction and the management style. In larger workplaces with an HR department, its role is often to advise managers of the legal rules and company policy, and to ensure consistency within the legal and company guidelines. A formal procedure provides a framework that avoids the risk of inconsistent ad hoc decisions. Torrington (1998) identifies four key features of a disciplinary procedure:

1. fairness
2. facilities for representation
3. procedural steps
4. management rules.

The disciplinary process must be conducted in a fair manner, *fairness* being best ensured by even-handedness in the disciplinary hearing. The employee should be entitled to know the nature of the charge in sufficient detail to enable her or him to prepare a case (*Hutchins* v. *British Railways Board* [1974]). Employees should always be given an opportunity to state their case (*Tesco (Holdings) Ltd* v. *Hill* [1977]) no matter what the circumstances are. Fairness will also be enhanced if there is an appeal stage.

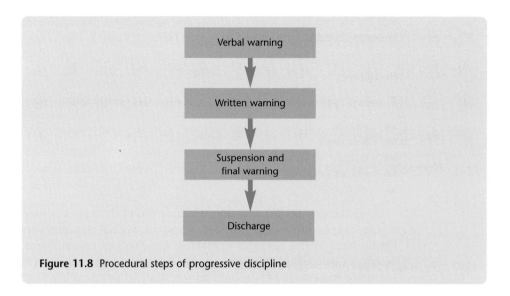

Figure 11.8 Procedural steps of progressive discipline

Due process should allow for the employee to be informed of her or his right to appeal to a higher level of management that has not previously been involved in the disciplinary decision or to an independent arbitrator (Selwyn, 2000).

To help the errant employee explain her or his case, the disciplinary procedure should allow *facilities for representation*, which means that another employee or representative should be allowed to accompany the employee (*Rank Xerox (UK) Ltd* v *Goodchild* [1979]). In the UK, Section 10 of the Employment Relations Act 1999 creates a new right for a worker, when invited by the employer to attend a disciplinary hearing, to make a reasonable request to be accompanied by a single companion. The representative can be either an official of an independent trade union or a co-worker. (Selwyn, 2000).

Procedural steps should be limited so that there are sufficient for justice to be done but not so many that matters become long and drawn-out. The steps are typically associated with progressive discipline, which means that the employer notifies the employee of unacceptable conduct and provide her or him with an adequate opportunity to correct the behaviour. A typical progressive discipline procedure is shown in Figure 11.8.

An employee who has committed an infraction is verbally warned and informed that if the same infraction is repeated (within some specified time period), the degree of disciplinary action will be increased. If the employee commits the same or a similar violation (or possibly an unrelated infraction) within the specified period, the employee will then be given a written warning, which will be placed in her or his personnel file. An employee who again transgresses in the misconduct, will be suspended from employment for a period of time without pay and will be given a final warning. This warning will normally specify termination of the employment contract as a result of another such infraction. If the employee is again guilty of misconduct, the employee may be discharged for 'just cause'. The legal notion of just cause means that there is a factual basis to warrant the dismissal, and/or the nature of the penalty was justified, taking into account all the relevant circumstances (Centre for Labour–Management Development, 2001).

Management rules pervade every workplace. Rules underscore management's prerog-

'Good' disciplinary procedures should:

- Be in writing

- Specify to whom they apply

- Be non-discriminatory

- Provide for matters to be dealt with without undue delay

- Provide for proceedings, witness statements and records to be kept confidential

- Indicate the disciplinary actions which may be taken

- Specify the levels of management which have the authority to take the various forms of disciplinary action

- Provide for workers to be informed of the complaints against them and where possible all relevant evidence before any hearing

- Provide workers with an opportunity to state their case before decisions are reached

- Provide workers with the right to be accompanied [by a co-worker or trade union official]

- Ensure that, except for gross misconduct, no employee is dismissed for a first breach of discipline

- Ensure that disciplinary action is not taken until the case has been carefully investigated

- Ensure that workers are given an explanation for any penalty imposed

- Provide a right of appeal – normally to a more senior manager – and specify the procedure to be followed

Figure 11.9 Advisory, Conciliation and Arbitration Service guide to disciplinary action
Source: Selwyn (2000)

ative to design work, to make decisions and to take actions to manage the workplace. Management rules typically cover six aspects of workplace activity and behaviour: insubordination, negligence, safety, theft, unacceptable behaviour at work (for example, the harassment of co-workers or fighting) and unreliability. Management rules provide guidelines on employee behaviour as long as the rules are clear, understood and supervised.

The UK ACAS code of practice on disciplinary and grievance procedures (Figure 11.9) provides a practical guidance on how employers and managers should deal with disciplinary issues in the workplace.

STUDY TIP

Most medium and large organizations have a disciplinary framework within which managers administer rules and conduct disciplinary interviewing, and to protect employee rights, most jurisdictions have a framework of law to administer the disciplinary process. In order to avoid unfair dismissal charges or grievances, a manager should have an understanding of the law relating to discipline and dismissal. Obtain a copy of *Selwyn's Law of Employment* (2000) and, using the index, list the statutes and any principal legal judgements that impact on discipline and dismissal. Here are some questions you may wish to seek the answers to:

- What is meant by the term 'rules of natural justice'?
- What is meant by 'just cause'?
- Who has the burden of proof in discipline cases?
- When is dismissal appropriate for a first offence?

REFLECTIVE QUESTION

What do you think of the ACAS guidelines in Figure 11.9? How important is it for an organization's disciplinary process to be seen to be 'equitable'?

● Chapter summary

- EI occurs when employees take an active role in the decision-making process within the organization. EI may be formal or informal, direct or indirect, voluntary or legislated; it may range from a manager exchanging information with an employee or an employee representative on a specific issue, to complete participation in a major investment decision.

- Greater participation has been identified with high-performance work systems and the 'commitment HR strategy'. As many companies attempt to draw upon their employees' skills and knowledge more fully, EI and two-way communication can be seen to be a logical development in employee relations to enlist employees' skills and cooperation.

- The terms 'employee participation', 'employee involvement' and 'employee empowerment' have different meanings. Differing expectations among employees and union representatives therefore tend to affect the attitudes of the key players in the industrial relations system, the propensity to participate and ultimately the success of any experiments in EI. Hence, a vital first step, if there is to be any meeting of minds, is to create a common language and conceptual framework.

- Communicating is the fundamental process of organizing and leading in the workplace. It includes written, verbal and non-verbal communication, each of which encompasses several methods of transmitting information. Communication flows downwards, upwards, and horizontally in organizations. From a functionalist perspective, the role of the HRM department is to ensure that there are no deviations or blockages in that flow that can cause communication problems.

- The fewer obstacles that occur in communication, the more goals, feedback and other management messages to employees will be received as they were intended. Organizational communications can also be interpreted as a strategy to build a strong corporate culture in order to exert more control over the workforce.

- Data available from WERS studies provide evidence that British managers are adopting EI techniques. There is, however, a deep scepticism that EI schemes might be used by managers to circumvent established collective bargaining machinery, marginalize the role of the workplace union representatives and strengthen 'individualism' in the management of the employment relationship. We also noted that the 1994 EWC Directive and the 2001 EU Directive on Information and Consultation are likely to provoke further interest in and research on indirect EI, especially in Member States without a strong EWC tradition, such as Britain.

- Organizational communication and EI innovations are more likely to succeed if management is aware of the concerns and potential problems confronting union representatives.

- Discipline is a key feature of employee relations in the workplace. Disciplinary practices vary between national legal systems, but, to command support among the workforce and avoid violations of the psychological contract, managers should design and apply disciplinary practices with due regard to the requirements of natural justice.

Key concepts

- Briefing groups
- Critical approach
- Employee involvement
- Employee participation
- European Works Councils
- Functionalist approach

- Grapevine
- Interpretivist approach
- Joint consultation
- Non-verbal communication
- Organizational communications

Chapter review questions

1. What are the links between HR strategies and EI and communication practices?

2. Describe the communication process, identifying its key components. Give an example of how this process operates with written, verbal and non-verbal messages.

3. Identify and discuss different schemes that the HR department manages in order to improve organizational communications.

4. 'EI is a central component of high-performance work systems.' Do you agree or disagree? Discuss.

5. Explain the difference between joint consultation and collective bargaining.

6. What is the difference between participation and involvement in the workplace?

Further reading

Frege, C. (2002). A critical assessment of the theoretical and empirical research on works councils. *British Journal of Industrial Relations*, **40**(2), 221–48.

Marchington, M. (2001). Employee involvement at work. In John Storey (ed.), *Human resource management: A critical text* (2nd edn), (pp. 232–52). London: Routledge.

Neher, W. (1997). *Organizational communication*. London: Allyn & Bacon.

Verma, A., & Taras, D. (2001). Employee involvement in the workplace. In M. Gunderson, A. Ponak & D. Taras (eds), *Union–Management relations in Canada*, 4th edn, Don Mills, Ontario: Addison-Wesley.

Practising human resource management

Searching the web

On an individual basis, or working in a small group, pick two or three on-line HR-related websites (e.g. www.jiscmail.ac.uk/lists/industrial-relations-research.html, www.shrm.org/hrlinks, www.labour-travail.hrdc-drhc.gc.ca//index.cfm/doc/english or www.fdmmag.com/articles/03aco.htm) and the Employee Involvement Association (www.eia.com), and explore 'Employee involvement'. Enter the website of an organization you or the group are familiar with, or one you have studied (e.g. www.rolls-royce.com, www.microsoft.com, www.thebodyshop.com or www.royalbankscot.co.uk/). From the information in this chapter and from your research, select a cluster of EI-type practices and explain the reasons for your choice. (Hint: make some assumptions about your business and HR strategies.) Bring this information to class, and present your findings and recommendation in an oral report.

HRM group project

Form a group of three or four students. The purpose of this group assignment is to allow you to apply your knowledge of EI and information disclosure in the workplace to an organization. Specifically:

1. Carry out web-based research of the law relating to EI and the disclosure of corporate information in at least two countries, for example Australia, Britain, Canada or the USA, and other EU Member States.
2. Compare the laws and write a brief management report on the major provisions covering EI and information disclosure.

How are the laws similar and different? A team member(s) should interview at least one manager or HR professional. The interviewer(s) should probe the nature of the organization's EI arrangements: What EI arrangements does the organization use? How does the EI system relate to the business strategy? What EI initiatives have been introduced and why? Each group member should take responsibility for researching the various aspects of the assignment.

COMMUNICATIONS AT FORRESTER COMPUTER SERVICES

In this age of 'flatter' management structures, Forrest Computer Services (FCS) must have one of the flattest. Last year, it reduced its management hierarchy to almost pancake proportions when it introduced self-managed teams and abolished all but the most senior management jobs.

FCS has a business team of 14 senior managers reporting to the three people who make up the Board. Below this are a host of client teams, each with about 15 members, operating as separate commercial units without a manager. Teams have to be able to provide a full client support service and draw on all the technical, financial and administrative skills that this requires. Within this framework, employees can decide whom they want to team up with, and teams can elect whether or not they want a leader. Those which have opted for a team leader have not necessarily chosen the person most senior under the older organization. This was a radical reorganization brought about by necessity. The decision followed a massive deficit of £72 million on a turnover of £726.5 million in 2001; this shocked the company, which had been growing steadily. Initially, this meant slashing costs and therefore staff, so the workforce shrank from 750 to fewer than 500 employees.

But FCS senior management knew they had to do more than cut costs: they had to improve productivity and competitiveness if the company were to remain in an ever-tightening market. 'We introduced self-managed teams to build up our client service because that is where we must have the edge', said Forrest's HR director, Carolyn Oliver. 'Every software house can provide the software and systems the clients want: it is the efficiency with which the client is handled that makes the difference and that comes down to the way we are organized', she said.

Reorganization put a tremendous burden on the HR department, the way in which it had to work and the communication system. On top of the reorganization, working practices – recruitment processes, reward strategies, training and development, and employee participation – were completely reassessed. On the one hand, this created a free-flowing organization with the flexibility and motivation to react to changes in the market. On the other hand, it bolstered the need for watertight HR systems to keep this motivated mass from running out of control. Oliver said that the implementation of the plan proved to be a massive employee participation exercise, and in the early weeks, there was much misleading and irrelevant information being communicated through the grapevine.

'Top management wanted the ideas to come from the shop floor. So we brought together 20 people from all levels of the organization bar the most senior, put them into two teams and sent them away for the weekend to thrash out their own ideas of how the company should be organized', explained Oliver. This was, however, only the beginning of the consultation process. The next step involved setting up employee task forces to look at the different issues implied by reorganization. FCS's senior managers disseminated information from the two working parties around the company and asked people to apply for one of the 70 places available on the ten task forces. About 200 people applied from the spectrum of jobs and locations in the company.

Six weeks later, the task forces presented their findings to the Board. 'They ranged from one extreme to the other. Some liked the way things were and simply wanted to stay put. Others wanted to do away with all senior managers right to the top', remarked Oliver. FCS opted for something in the middle – a senior business team with many client teams reporting in. The HR department had to make the system work. Carolyn Oliver admitted frankly that she had underestimated the reaction of managers to their sudden loss of power. 'They felt threatened and believed that their services would no longer be required by the company', she said. It was a 'hard slog' convincing them that the new-style FCS was for them too, Oliver said. 'You cannot reassure managers by writing to them or making promises in a company newsletter', she went on to explain.

As all the teams were essentially operating in the same computer services market, there was a danger that they would all end up competing against each other instead of against company competitors. Oliver admitted there has to be a tight coordination of client service teams, a close control of the standards they work to and effective organizational communication. Introducing multiskilled, self-managed teams also highlighted demands from employees for a more permanent system of employee participation in the company.

Discussion questions

1. What methods could the company have adopted to convince the managers that they had a future at FCS?

2. Should managers try to eliminate the organizational grapevine?

3. Discuss the alternative channels of communication that FCS could have used to disseminate information from the first two working parties to employees.

4. What recommendations would you make for establishing a permanent system of employee participation at FCS? Justify your case.

HR-related skill development

The formal disciplinary process is concerned with regulating employee behaviour to produce controlled and effective behaviour. The disciplinary interview is a central part of the disciplinary process, but most managers use the formal disciplinary interview as the last resort. Many managers also lack the basic knowledge and skills to conduct such a legally bound activity. To help you develop this important management skill and to give you experience of the disciplinary process, we have devised a disciplinary case with supporting information. You can participate, at either an individual or a group level, in the simulation and develop an important HR skill by going to www.palgrave.com/business/brattonandgold and clicking on 'Disciplinary interview exercise'.

● Notes

1. Champy (1996, p. 146).
2. John MacKey, CEO, quoted in Pfeffer (1998a, p. 93).
3. Anvil Verma and Daphne Taras (2001, p. 454).

Chapter twelve

Union–management relations

John Bratton

Union–management relations address the collective aspects of the employment relationship and focus on the relations between organized employees (represented by a union) and management, and on the processes within which a union and an employer interact to regulate the employment contract.

'The increasingly powerful "new economy" seems to offer little role or place for trade unions.'[1]

'Pay, the principal component of any employment contract, is now fixed by formal collective bargaining for no more than one-third of the employed population.'[2]

'"New record high for employers recognizing unions in 2001." This report confirms that unions are very much back in business and that employers want to do business with them. Sensible employers understand that today's unions seek partnership and good working relationships. They can be good for business, as well as good for staff.'[3]

'Any extension of union recognition is not likely to be employer-led.'[4]

Chapter outline

Chapter objectives

After studying this chapter, you should be able to:

1. Describe contemporary trends in union–management relations
2. Explain and critically evaluate different types of union–management strategy
3. Explain the pattern of trade union membership and union structure
4. Understand the nature and importance of collective bargaining
5. Describe the core legal principles relating to union–management relations
6. Critically evaluate the importance of 'new unionism' and 'partnership' for union–management relations

The previous chapter examined a variety of employee relations policies and practices, seeking to identify their role and significance in managing the employment relationship. Whereas, as explained in Chapter 11, 'employee relations' potentially contain 'collectivist' notions, it primarily addresses individual aspects of relations between employees and management. Union–management relations, on the other hand, address the *collective* aspects of employment relations. The quotations opening this chapter were chosen to illustrate the coverage of union–management relations – management, unions and collective bargaining – and, as a field of study, its relevance in the post-industrial economy. There is considerable controversy among academics over the definition of the terms 'industrial relations' and 'union–management relations' (see Wajcman, 2000; Wood, 2000), but in this chapter we use the terms interchangeably. It should also be noted that some employment policies – pay and benefits, employee involvement schemes and joint consultation – can result from employee relations policies, union–management policies or both, and in the workplace the policies may be virtually indistinguishable in either union or non-union settings (Gunderson et al., 2001).

Over the past two decades British union–management relations have been substantially modified by a combination of economic, political and social factors. Indeed, the new economic and legal climate has changed the landscape of union–management relations so much as to cause one industrial relations scholar to state: 'It is difficult to believe that such a world existed less than twenty years ago' (Hyman, 1997b, p. 317). In Chapter 3, we provided a survey of these economic and political developments and discussed the beginning of a process of change and adaptation on the part of management and labour. With the election of the Conservative government in 1979, many observers consider the period 1983–87 to be a 'watershed' in British union–management relations. In addition, although the history of British union–management relations can cite a number of watersheds, what is not in doubt is that the past two decades have witnessed major contextual changes, including the shift from manufacturing to service employment, hostile union legislation, a sharp diminution of union membership and the contraction of collective bargaining (Cully et al., 1999; Marginson & Wood, 2000; Millward et al., 2000).

The experience of fundamental change in the context, institutions and processes of union–management relations was not unique to the UK. In the rest of the European Union (EU), the traditional pattern of union–management relations also underwent profound modifications. Throughout Europe, the drive for competitive advantage has been pursued consistently and universally, and employers and managers have demonstrated initiative and determination in remodelling their national industrial relations systems. European employers have, for example, increasingly exercised their prerogative over key business decisions and enhanced management legitimacy, with government help, by popularizing the ideological argument for the veneration of the 'marketplace'. European trade unions have been weakened both numerically and politically, and have been forced, in general, to retreat. The trade unions' participation in the collective bargaining process has similarly been marked by retreat and action to defend living standards, working conditions and rules governing the use of human resources (Baglioni & Crouch, 1991). The response to intensified global competition has not, however, been the same in every EU Member State (Morley et al., 2000). Thus, in some respects, the pattern of European industrial relations systems remains sharply diversified, as it was in the 1970s. In other respects, however, comparative analysis reveals similarities between European Member States, pointing to what writers refer to as a 'transnational convergence' (Baglioni & Crouch, 1991; Morley et al., 2000; Streeck & Visser, 1997).

In North America, global competition over the past two decades has resulted in changes in the USA that have prompted some writers to describe the 'transformation of American industrial relations' (Kochan et al., 1986). Although the transformation thesis might be an exaggeration of the perceived changes in that country, and although the thesis is not universally accepted in the USA, US companies have, with government indulgence, persuaded or compelled a weakened trade union movement to accept significant changes in collective agreements and working practices. Furthermore, US companies have increasingly turned to a union-free environment, what is referred to as a 'union replacement' strategy. This management response to unions includes either relocating the business to a rural region where unionization is less well developed (for example, southern states such as Kentucky) and/or using consultants to run employee programmes to induce the workforce to consider withdrawing from their union. Industrial relations in different parts of North America have not, however, all followed identical routes. As numerous Canadian scholars have pointed out, Canadian unions have, in terms of legal support for unions, membership trends and bargaining strength, enjoyed relative success compared with unions in the USA and Britain (Murray, 2001).

Running parallel with (and not unrelated to) these contextual and union management changes has, of course, been the ascendancy of the human resource management (HRM) model. Much of the critical literature presents the HRM model as being inconsistent with traditional union management relations and collective bargaining, albeit for very different reasons (Godard, 1991; Guest, 1995; Wells, 1993). Critics argue not only that HRM policies and practices shift the mode of regulating the employment contract from the collective towards the individual, but also the HRM paradigm is designed with the object of weakening or avoiding union presence in the workplace (Godard, 1994).

Others, however, have argued that independent trade unions and variants of the HRM model can not only coexist, but are even necessary to its successful implementation and development. They argue that trade unions should become proactive or change 'champions', actively promoting the more positive elements of the 'soft' HRM model (Chapter 1; Betcherman et al., 1994; Guest, 1994; Verma, 1995). As part of this discourse is the notion of **social partnership**, which has recently moved to the centre stage of British union–management relations (Bacon & Storey, 2000). The social partnership model is conceptualized in terms of 'mutual gains' for both unions and the organization. For the unions, partnership offers union representatives 'a place at the table' and the potential opportunity to revitalize union influence and membership in the workplace (Coupar & Stevens, 1998). For the employer, partnership can offer flexible working, employee commitment and the opportunity to undertake major restructuring with union support (Heery, 2002). Not surprisingly, the notion of social partnership and its potential benefits to the stakeholders is subject to considerable debate in the HRM/industrial relations literature.

The HRM/industrial relations discourse poses some interesting questions for academics and practitioners. Can, for example, a worker be simultaneously committed to the goals of both the organization and the trade union? How does the HRM concept of 'high worker commitment' present a threat to unions? Is 'dual commitment' possible? Can HRM-inspired initiatives, such as work teams, coexist with seniority and 'job control' unionism? In terms of the individualization of the employment relationship, can the HRM model function alongside traditional collective bargaining? Is the social partnership model compatible with the traditional role of unions, which is to defend their members' interests? Some industrial relations scholars suggest that trade unions face strategic choices: they can either simply oppose the changes or opt for a proactive interventionist strategy that will embrace the more positive elements of the HRM model. Others, on the other hand, cogently argue that HRM and strong unions are incompatible.

This chapter examines these interrelated questions by providing an analysis of management and union strategies. After defining union–management relations and the scope of this interdisciplinary field of study, we deal with a number of strategic decisions that management must take with regards to trade unions. The chapter then proceeds to discuss trends in union membership and structure, collective bargaining and the legal context of union–management relations. Finally, the chapter turns to the issue of social partnership, 'worker commitment' and an assessment of the unions' response to the HRM model and union contraction.

REFLECTIVE QUESTION

Look again at the quotations at the start of this chapter. Do you think that unions have a role to play the new 'knowledge-based' economy?

Union–management relations

As we mention above, there is controversy among the academic community over the precise meaning and relevance of 'industrial relations'. Much of the debate concerns reappraising the significance of industrial relations in the light of declining union membership, the contraction of collective bargaining and the apparent marginalization of traditional industrial relations, in the research and academic community as well as in the workplace. As Wood (2000, p. 1) suggests, the 'lifeblood' of industrial relations – unions and collective bargaining – 'once so central … seem to have ceased to be of such consuming interest'. It has therefore become widely accepted that union–management or industrial relations must be reconceptualized and extend its focus beyond unions, collective bargaining and strikes to a broader concern with the employment relationship (Taras et al., 2001; Wood, 2000). Furthermore, it is acknowledged that any reconceptualization of modern union–management relations must focus sufficient attention on the fact that these principal institutions and processes are not gender-neutral but reflect 'masculine priorities and privilege' in work organizations (Wajcman, 2000, p. 183).

In a non-unionized workplace, managers have flexibility in designing work, selecting, promoting and training people, determining rewards and other HRM practices, but much of this can change when workers join a union. After recognizing the union, representatives from union and management negotiate a collective agreement that spells out details of the employment relationship that will be *jointly* determined. This can typically include establishing some control on each of the four key HR policies and practices of the HRM model shown in Figure 1.4. First and foremost, unions seek to control *rewards* and attempt to maximize the pay side of the wage–effort contract. In the area of *recruitment and selection*, unions have, in some industries at least (for example construction, film and theatre), had some control over external recruiting. Unions also take an active interest in work-related learning and *employee development*; they try to ensure that training opportunities are distributed equitably and that the employer adheres to the principle of maintained earnings during training. Perhaps most controversially, the whole practice of *employee appraisal* poses challenges to the unions. The central tenet of traditional unionism has been the collectivist culture, namely the insistence on rewards according to the same definite standard and its application in the workplace. Such collectivist goals have resulted in unions strongly resisting all forms of performance appraisal based on individual performance.

HRM IN PRACTICE 12.1

CAW ABANDONS FIGHT FOR UNION AT ONTARIO WAL-MART

MARINA STRAUSS, *GLOBE AND MAIL*, 2000, APRIL 20

The Canadian Auto Workers Union has walked away from Wal-Mart's Windsor, Ontario, store – the only unionized outlet in the company's North American operations – ending a bitter four year battle that put the spotlight on labour relations at the world's largest retailer.

The CAW's Retail Wholesale Canada division dropped its rights to represent about 140 of the 250 employees of Wal-Mart Canada Inc.'s store in Windsor. Observers suggested the cost of its legal battles were mounting in the face of persistent employer opposition to the union.

The decision is a victory for US-based Wal-Mart Stores Inc., which has vigorously fought unionization efforts, observers said. The dispute came in stark contrast to the image that Wal-Mart projects to the world as a big, happy family, reinforced by morale-building slogans and a company cheer – repeated every morning by employees in every store.

Wal-Mart's culture has been cited as a key factor in the company's remarkable growth since it was started 38 years ago by Sam Walton in Arkansas. The discount chain operates more than 3,500 stores around the world. Last year, it posted sales of $165-billion (US) and a profit of $5.5-billion. It has 166 outlets in Canada, where it set down roots in 1994.

> ... good employee morale is critical to a happy and productive workplace.

Wal-Mart Canada spokesperson Andrew Pelletier acknowledged that sales productivity at the Windsor store has probably suffered from the labour tensions over the years. But he said it will be 'business as usual' now that the union has abandoned the cause. He said good employee morale is critical to a happy and productive workplace.

He also said the anti-union employees conducted their campaign independently of the company.

'Not to put too fine a point on it: The situation was fraught with legal and labour relations problems,' the ruling said. Moreover, 'the union and company faced complex, lengthy and costly legal proceedings to resolve contentious issues', the ruling said.

Marlene Needle, one of the anti-union employees, said in a telephone interview that she was 'ecstatic' about the resolution. 'It's been a long four years,' said Ms Needle, 40, a 'support manager' at the store who earns $10 an hour and said she has no problems with her working conditions. 'It's what we wanted.'

George King, lawyer for the anti-union employees, said he charged them a reduced fee – the equivalent of their union dues. They never actually paid dues to the union because of the dispute.

These examples illustrate that 'control over work relations' (Hyman, 1975, p. 31) is a central feature of union–management relations. Union–management relations, for current purposes, refers to:

● the relations between organized employees (represented by a union) and management
● the processes that regulate the employment contract
● the context within which a union and an employer interact.

Let us briefly expand on the components of this definition. The *'relations'* between the workforce and management are both economic and social: it is an economic relation because employers buy employees' physical and mental abilities, and it is a social relation because when employees enter into a contract they agree to comply with the employer's standards and rules. These relationships between the workforce and management may be played out in different arenas – at the workplace level, at the industry level and at the national level – where union, employer and government representatives participate in a social dialogue on economic and employment-related issues.

The term *'processes'* refers to collective bargaining, by which unions represent their members' interests through formal negotiations with management representatives. *'Context'* refers to the economic, legal and political conditions and constraints within which union–management relations take place. Our definition of union–management relations recognizes the fluidity of contexts and the processes of control over the employment relationship. This dynamic mix means that, in a unionized environment, managing the interactions between union and management representatives can be a significant area of HRM activity.

HRM WEB LINKS

Go to www.eiro.eurofound.ie/ for information on economic, political and collective bargaining developments in the EU. For information on industrial relations in North America, go to the website at Cornell University (www.workindex.com/) and click on 'Labour relations'. See also www.ir-net.co.za (S. Africa) and also p. xxii of this book.

 ## Management strategies

Management plays a predominant role in constructing collective relations in the workplace, managers shaping the options and largely determining the outcomes (Hyman, 1997), and employees and their unions generally reacting to management initiatives. Over the past two decades, British scholars have shown a much greater interest in the study of management and management strategy, and there is a large body of literature that examines the links between 'new' management organizational practices (Chapter 4) and management behaviour. A number of empirical studies have investigated how British managers have reorganized the conduct of workplace union–management relations (see, for example, Cully et al., 1999; Gollan, 2002; Guest, 1995; Millward & Stevens, 1986; Millward et al., 1992, 2000).

The management of an organization involves choices and constraints. On the one hand, management may seek to maintain unilateral control of the organization by retaining or extending its managerial prerogative or the right to management. Alternatively, management may accept the legitimacy of trade unions in the decision-making process – management by agreement. In the 1970s, public policy and managers were strongly influenced by the recommendations of the 1968 Donovan Commission. In the 1980s, and for most of the 1990s, employers changed and shifted more towards individualistic approaches to managing the employment relationship. In essence, the early debates on HRM/industrial relations centred on the belief that management introduced new initiatives, found new confidence and changed the emphasis in its union–management relations policies (Sisson, 1994). Recent survey and case study data suggest, however, this trend has again shifted somewhat to embrace the 'social partnership' model (Bacon & Storey, 2000; Heery, 2002; Sparrow & Marchington, 1998). To examine management's strategic decisions and actions towards trade unions, we need to examine industrial relations strategies.

Strategies towards unions

An industrial relations strategy refers to the plans and policies used by management to deal with its trade unions (Gospel & Littler, 1983). The notion of alternative industrial relations strategies is closely linked to the concept of 'business strategy' and 'human resource (HR) strategy' (Chapter 2). Even when an organization has a simple business strategy, its HR and industrial relations strategies may be very complex and often suggest different and contradictory directions (Anderson et al., 1989). The choice of a strategy towards unions involves managers in considering a number of complex factors: labour market conditions, legal and political conditions, the history of the organization, management philosophy or values, and the union and bargaining structures facing the management (Anderson et al., 1989; Cappelli, 1984; Thompson, 2001).

The relationship between the business strategy, the economic environment and the union–management strategy is perhaps the easiest to establish. The outcome of union–management pay bargaining will have a direct impact on the organization's ability to implement the business strategy. Under the EU monetary system, for example, British managers have to ensure that local pay and productivity movements correspond with those of other EU competitors. It is therefore much less likely in 2003 than in 1973 that the industrial relations manager will enter the negotiations with a 'do your best' mandate from senior management. The following quotation, taken from a case study, illustrates the constraints: 'Previously we would have a management meeting. I would then do the negotiating. If at the end of the day I had to go two or three per cent more than we intended, that would be it ... Now, if I want to go outside the budget I have to get permission from head office.'[5] These internal constraints at the bargaining table reflect external constraints caused by competition. Global price competition and privatization has thus caused organizations to search for alternative business strategies and, at the same time, re-evaluate their relationships with trade unions.

Although it is simplifying a complex phenomenon, the various strategic alternatives can, for analytical purposes, be classified into three broad industrial relations strategies (Anderson et al., 1989; Thompson, 2001):

- union acceptance
- union replacement
- union avoidance.

The *union acceptance strategy* is defined here as a decision by top managers to accept the legitimacy of the union role and, in turn, of collective bargaining as a process for regulating the employment relationship to support their corporate strategy. The reform and restructuring of workplace bargaining arrangements during the 1960s and 70s have been characterized as an industrial relations strategy designed to engender 'a degree of order, regulation and control' (Nichols & Beynon, 1977, p. 129). Survey evidence indicates that, even in the inimical environment of the 1980s, a number of important Japanese companies chose a union acceptance strategy, albeit in a modified form, to achieve their employment objectives (Bassett, 1987; Wickens, 1987). In Britain, between 1984 and 1998, 1998 Workplace Employee Relations Survey (WERS98) data indicate a sharp decline in the adoption of a union acceptance strategy. In the private sector, for example, the proportion of workplaces adopting a union acceptance/recognition strategy fell from 48 per cent to 25 per cent (Millward et al., 2000).

The *union replacement strategy* means that top management have decided to achieve their strategic goals, whether this involves introducing new technology, relocating to another part of the UK or European Community or subcontracting out work, without any consultation or agreement with trade unions. De-recognition refers to a decision by senior management to withdraw from collective bargaining in favour of unilateral arrangements for the governance of employment relations. Douglas Smith, chair of the Advisory, Conciliation and Arbitration Service (ACAS), said in his 1987 address to the Institute of Personnel Management conference that 'across the spectrum there were now managements whose intention was increasingly to marginalise trade unions'. Several studies over the past two decades provide convincing evidence of de-recognition practices in Britain (Claydon, 1989; Smith & Morton, 1993). Similarly, US corporations in the 1980s adopted a union replacement strategy, and an increasing number of top management decided to decertify (de-recognize) the existing unions (Cappelli & Chalykoff, 1985). Opposition to unions is said to be so intense in US business organizations that 'American employers are willing to engage in almost any form of legal or *illegal* action to create and maintain a union-free environment' (Deery, 1995, p. 538, emphasis added). Among North American industrial relations theorists there is a popular view that Canadian employers are less willing to oppose unionization than are their US counterparts. Bentham's (2002, p. 181) recent study suggests, however, that this may be a misconception because the vast majority of Canadian workplaces studied 'engaged in actions that can only be characterized as overt and active resistance' to unions.

HRM WEB LINKS

For information on how union–management strategies in Britain have changed over the past two decades, go to the WERS98 website: www.dti.gov.uk/er/emar/1998WERS.htm.

De-recognition continued in UK workplaces during the 1990s. The WERS98 results show that 6 per cent of all established workplaces de-recognized unions between 1990 and 1998 (Millward et al., 2000). Bacon and Storey's (2000) analysis of management action reveals a 'disjuncture between unions and "new" corporate thinking'. One manager expressed the 'new' management thinking towards unions like this:

Collectivism via trade unions is something we want to remove ... We are not anti-union, it is just that they are incompatible with our current direction. I think we can win by edict in the current climate and drive through changes against any opposition and hope that in the end people will see there is no choice. (quoted in Bacon & Storey, 2000, p. 412)

One interesting aspect of Bacon and Storey's study is the evidence suggesting that British management did not take full advantage of its power. Two reasons are given for this. First, the 'heavy threats' to the unions contributed to higher levels of employee apprehension, dissatisfaction and mistrust of management. This observation can be linked to the importance of the 'psychological contract' discussed in Chapter 1. It is highlighted here because it would appear that the adoption of a union replacement strategy, particularly in a period of major organizational restructuring and potential 'downsizing', can rupture the contract, with subsequent decreases in employee loyalty and commitment. With this in mind, Bacon and Storey's (2000, p. 423) comment that managers were 'reluctant to sacrifice employee trust' is important. The second reason managers did not use their power and push through with de-recognizing the unions was because the very threat of such action alone 'allowed managers to introduce many of the changes they had wanted to drive through' in the workplace (Bacon & Storey, 2000, pp. 413–14). Overall, then, although most managers have an enduring preference for non-union relations (what is referred to as 'unitarism'), pragmatic considerations in these cases deterred the adoption of a union replacement strategy.

The *union avoidance strategy* is defined here as a decision to maintain the status quo of a non-union workforce by pursuing HR policies such as non-union grievance and discipline procedures, employee participation schemes, work teams and the active countering of union recruitment campaigns. Given that the majority of business organizations are not unionized, we can assume that the union avoidance strategy is the most prevalent industrial relations strategy in Britain and North America, although, as Gollan (2002) has recently stated, research on management strategies towards non-union employee representation is limited. Researchers argue that employee involvement schemes increase employees' motivation and commitment to organizational goals and therefore reduce the need for a trade union (Chapter 11). Management also establishes consultative councils to give non-union employees a 'voice', and 'independent' staff associations as a substitute for unions in determining pay to keep the worksite 'union free'. In addition, the selection process can be used to screen out applicants likely to be prone to joining a union, and training can be used to build commitment to the organization. The retail giant Marks & Spencer exemplifies the union avoidance strategy: the company's chairman and chief executive put it like this:[6]

Human relations in industry should cover the problems of the individual at work ... the contribution people can make, given encouragement – these are the foundations of an effective policy and a major contribution to a successful operation.

The choice of an industrial relations strategy for a particular organization will depend upon the interrelationship between constraints and strategic choices and between managerial objectives, as delineated by the business strategy, HR strategy and alternative management styles. Whatever industrial relations strategy is selected, it must also be evaluated in order to identify where objectives have been achieved and where they have not. Comparative measures of industrial conflict, cooperation and grievance rates can, for example, be used to evaluate an industrial relations strategy. A recent study by Gollan (2002) of the union avoidance strategy at News International Newspapers (UK) evaluated the effectiveness of the company's non-union Employee Consultative Council and News International Staff Association. The results revealed 'widespread dissatisfaction with management' and a 'perceived lack of effective voice' among employees (Gollan, 2002, p. 329). Moreover, the benefits to the company of a union avoidance strategy were 'questionable': the management's strategy 'could result in greater indirect union influence in workplace issues and greater employee dissatisfaction at the workplace' (Gollan, 2000, p. 330).

Finally, it is also important to recognize that no single strategy is adopted by employers and managers: management can choose from a variety of strategies, empirical evidence suggesting that union avoidance tactics often appear to be used alongside union acceptance and union replacement tactics (Anderson et al., 1989). As Gospel and Littler (1983, p. 12) conclude, 'The combination of strategies has been highly complex, and employers have searched in a zig-zag backwards and forwards movement between them'.

In Britain, since the election of the 'New Labour' government in 1997, political and legal contexts have encouraged both management and unions to reassess their strategies. Evidence of this is the growing interest in the notion of 'partnership' and the small number of partnership agreements that have been negotiated at, for example, Barclays Bank, ScottishPower, Tesco and Hyder (previously Welsh Water) with some of the 'super-unions', such as the General, Municipal Boilermakers' Union (GMB), UNISON and AMICUS. The notion of social partnership is part of a broader management strategy to improve organizational performance and has received support from Prime Minister Tony Blair. These valedictory words from Blair's address to the 1999 Trades Union Congress (TUC) conference sent a strong signal to organizations that they should reassess their union management strategies:

> I see trade unions as a force for good, an essential part of our democracy, but as more than that, potentially, as a force for economic success. They are part of the solution to achieving business success and not an obstacle to it (quoted in Brown, 2000, p. 305).

We examine the notion of 'partnership' in more detail below, but at this point we should also note examples of workplace partnership outside the EU. In post-apartheid South Africa, for example, trade unions have shifted from confrontation with employers to participation in newly created 'tripartite forums' in order to encourage private investment and further the economic interests of working people (Barrett, 1996). In Canada, Betcherman et al. (1994) note some interest in tripartite collaboration between management, labour and government to create 'high-performance' workplaces (see also Streeck, 1996; Terry, 1995).

HRM WEB LINKS

Go to www.ipa-involve.com and www.acas.org.uk for information on how many work organizations have negotiated 'partnership' agreements in the UK.

The significance of this debate on union–management strategies is this: the HRM model is *not* restricted to a 'union exclusion' environment. Guest (1995) analyses the strategic union–management relations options available to management, the 'new realism' option appearing to illustrate the case of HRM and union–management relations operating in tandem. With support from New Labour and EU legislation on European Works Councils (Chapter 11), British managers are beginning to take a more proactive approach towards union involvement in decision-making, workplace partnerships and the more positive developmental elements of the HRM model. With the current enthusiasm for partnership, it is easy to forget that management strategies can and do change depending on the economic and political climate, and that different strategies can be applied to different firms within the same industrial sector and to different groups of employees within the same organization. With this caveat in mind, the implications of the growing globalization of corporate structures will compel top management to make strategic choices about their business processes and how they will arrange related aspects of HR practices and union–management relations.

STUDY TIP

The importance of business strategy to the development and implementation of union–management strategy cannot be overstated. In order to understand alternative union–management strategies, one must first understand business strategy. Before reading on, go back to Chapter 2 and reread the section containing Figure 2.8. If you are writing an assignment on union–management strategies, you may wish also to obtain a copy of Gospel's (1994) book *Markets, Firms and the Management of Labour in Modern Britain*. Thinking about the different business strategies, how are business strategies and union–management strategies related? Can we predict that one type of business strategy will be more likely to encourage the adoption of a workplace 'partnership'?

Trade unions

In the 1970s, British trade unions were considered to be powerful social institutions that merited close study. Indeed, one scholar referred to trade unions as 'one of the most powerful forces shaping our society' (Clegg, 1976, p. 1). Between 1968 and 1979, trade union membership increased by 3.2 million to 13.2 million, and union density (the proportion of the workforce belonging to a union) exceeded 50 per cent. The sheer scale of union organization represented a 'decade of exceptional union growth' (Bain & Price, 1983, p. 6). In contrast, between 1979 and 2000 union membership in Britain dropped sharply: in 1979, 53 per cent of workers were union members; by 2000, this had fallen to 29 per cent. The 1980s were referred to as the 'decade of non-unionism' (Bassett, 1987). This section examines trends in union membership over the past two decades and goes on to examine trade union structure and bargaining power, in the belief that a knowledge of these developments is important for understanding the debate on HRM and unions.

Union membership

The decline in aggregate membership of British trade unions is well documented and is shown in Table 12.1. In 1979, when Margaret Thatcher was first elected Prime Minister of Britain, union membership was over 12 million. Since then, however,

Table 12.1 Union membership in the UK, 1971–2000

	Members (000s)	% of employed
5 year annual average		
1971–75	11,548 (+1.5)	50.0
1976–80	12,916 (+1.5)	55.9
1981–85	11,350 (–3.5)	49.1
1986–90	10,299 (–1.7)	44.6
1991–95	8,740 (–4.0)	37.8
1996–2000	7,910 (–9.5)	34.2
Annual		
1989	10,158 (–2.1)	44.2
1990	9,947 (–2.1)	43.9
1991	9,585 (–3.6)	43.8
1992	9,048 (–5.6)	42.3
1993	8,700 (–3.8)	40.2
1994	8,278 (–4.9)	38.1
1995	8,089 (–2.3)	35.0
1996	8,008 (–1.0)	34.7
1997	7,918 (–1.1)	34.2
1998	7,916 (–0.0)	34.2
1999	8,021 (+1.3)	34.7
2000	8,085 (+0.8)	35.0

Source: Sneade, A. (2001) Trade union membership 1999–2000: an analysis of data from the certification officer; and The Labour Force Survey, *Labour Market Trends*, September, 433–41. London: Department of Trade and Industry

membership has fallen by over 4 million, or 37 per cent. From the peak years of 1976–80, union density fell from 55 per cent, to 34 per cent in 1996–2000. Although union membership appears to be relatively stable in a few North European countries and Canada, union decline is a worldwide phenomenon (Verma et al., 2002).

Table 12.2 Union presence by broad sector, 1980–98

	Percentages			
	1980	1984	1990	1998
All establishments	73	73	64	54
Broad sector				
Private manufacturing	77	67	58	42
Private services	50	53	46	35
Public sector	99	100	99	97

Source: Adapted from Millward et al. (2000, p. 85). Used with permission

Table 12.2 describes the pattern of union decline across major sectors of the British economy from 1980 to 1998. Drawing on WERS98 data, union presence at workplace level remained stable in the early 1980s at 73 per cent but then fell sharply to 64 per cent in 1990, and continued to fall to 54 per cent in 1998 (Millward et al., 2000). The survey also showed that union presence differed significantly across the broad sectors of the economy. The decline in union presence was most marked in private manufacturing – down from 77 per cent in 1980 to 42 per cent of workplaces in 1998. Although trade union presence in the public sector remained almost ubiquitous over the two decades, it fell from 50 per cent of establishments in 1980 to 35 per cent in 1998. Furthermore, in both private manufacturing and services, the decline was 'more substantial in small workplaces' and among traditionally 'male-dominated' worksites (Millward et al., 2000, p. 86).

It is helpful to situate Britain's trade union experience in an international perspective (Table 12.3). In the EU and North America, trade union density in the 1990s was highly variable. In four of the EU Member States – Spain, the Netherlands, Germany and France – trade union density in 2000 represented less than 30 per cent of the workforce. In the three EU Member States of Sweden, Finland and Denmark, union density in 2000 came close to 80 per cent of the workforce. In North America, trade

Table 12.3 Union membership in selected countries as a percentage of all employees, 1970–2000

Country	1970	1980	1990	1995	2000
Australia	50	48	40	33	35
Belgium	45	56	51	53	69
Canada	31	36	36	34	32[a]
Denmark	60	76	71	82	80
Finland	51	70	72	81	79
France	22	17	10	9	9
Germany	33	36	33	29[b]	29[b]
Ireland	53	57	50	38	44
Italy	36	49	39	38	35[c]
Japan	35	31	25	24	22
The Netherlands	38	35	25	26	27
New Zealand	41	56	45	22	24
Norway	51	57	56	56	56
Portugal	61	61	32	32	30
Spain	27	25	11	15	15
Sweden	68	80	82	83	79
UK	45	50	39	32	29
USA	23	22	16	15	14

NB. Unweighted European Union average = 30.4%

a 1999 figure

b Post-East–West unification figure

c 1999 figure

Source: Brown et al. (1997), Organisation for Economic Co-operation and Development, International Labour Organization and the EIRO website

union density in Canada stood at 32 per cent, and in the USA at 14 per cent, in 2000. There are difficulties in interpreting absolute differences in union membership between countries, but the trend is clear: many have experienced a substantial decline in union membership over the past two decades (Brown et al., 1997).

REFLECTIVE QUESTION

Can you think of any environmental factors (for example new legislation) that may lead workers to join unions? What internal factors (for example perceived violation of the employment contract) may affect unionization?

HRM WEB LINKS

For further information on union presence in the workplace in different countries, go to the International Labour Organization website (www.ilo.org), and for the figure for EU Member States go to www.eiro.eurofound.ie. See also p. xxii of this book.

Interpreting union decline

Although the general pattern clearly indicates that union membership and density have fallen sharply and continually since 1979, there is a debate over the precise scale of the trend, its cause and likely duration. Part of the problem is measurement. Estimates of the decline in union density range from as few as 8.3 percentage points to as many as 12.1. These strikingly different estimates occur because the key statistic of union density can be measured in nine different ways depending on which of three different data series for potential membership and trade union membership are used (see Kelly & Bailey, 1989).

One influential explanation of variations in the rate of unionization over time categorizes the determinants under the following headings (Bain & Price, 1983):

- business cycle
- public policy
- work and organizational design
- industrial restructuring
- employer policies
- union leadership.

Although Bain and Price's approach is comprehensive, it is difficult to 'disentangle' the relative importance of each of the six determinants in interpreting aggregate union decline in the UK since 1979. Within the *business cycle* framework, Disney (1990) suggests that the downturn in union density in the 1980s was caused by 'macroeconomic' factors. Trade unions' traditional difficulties in recruiting and gaining recognition in the private services sector, smaller establishments, foreign-owned plants and newly established 'green-field' sites have intensified. Proponents of the business cycle explanation also assume that high levels of unemployment have eroded the constituencies of manual workers, from which unions have traditionally recruited (Waddington, 1992).

Following the election of a Conservative government in 1979, *public policy* towards trade unions shifted away from a positive encouragement of trade union recognition.

The suggested determinant, government action, clearly can affect unionization. Public policies that create a favourable environment for union recognition will initiate a virtuous circle of recognition and increase in membership, a circle that can be put into reverse by adverse policies and government 'example-setting' or role model (Towers, 1989). Freeman and Pelletier (1990), using a quantitative analysis of changes in union density, estimate that the Thatcher government's industrial relations laws reduced British trade union density by 1–1.7 percentage points per year from 1980 to 1986. This type of analysis is, however, fraught with problems: it is very difficult to disentangle cause and effect when dealing with trade union law (Disney, 1990).

Others argue that employers have used the fear of unemployment and a hostile trade union to redesign the nature of work and organizations, which has impacted negatively on union–management relations. The studies by Millward et al. (1992, 2000) offer several explanations for the pervasive decrease in union density between 1980 and 1998. The variation is explained by *work and organizational design* characteristics, such as changes in establishment size and the age of the workplace: 'older workplaces have higher densities', argue Millward et al. (1992, p. 63). Similarly, Machin (2000, pp. 631–4) has identified the negative association of unionization in the workplace with the age of the establishment: the sharp fall was 'driven by the failure to organize in the newer workplaces' – defined as those less than 10 years old at the time of the survey. Comparing the WERS98 results with those of earlier workplace surveys, Cully et al. (1999, p. 110) point to 'a relatively marginal role for unions'.

The continual *industrial restructuring* from manufacturing to service employment also affects union membership. Millward et al. (2000) conclude that a union presence continues to be widespread in the public sector and concentrated in large workplaces in the private sector. There is, however, evidence of 'a general withering of enthusiasm' for union representation within continuing workplaces, especially in the private sector and 'a lack of recruitment among new workplaces in both private and public sectors' (Millward et al. 2000, p. 136). Another significant development is the collapse of compulsory unionism – the 'closed shop' – among non-manual workers in highly unionized British companies (Wright, 1996).

The restructuring of British industry and labour market factors are clearly critical in determining whether workers decide to become and remain union members, but *employer policies* and behaviour will significantly influence workers' support for unionization. If managers are openly hostile or less supportive of unions in their workplace, workers will be more likely to perceive union membership to be an act of 'disloyalty' to the organization and, more importantly, jeopardizing their employment prospects. As we noted when we discussed union–management strategies, the 'strategic de-recognition' of unions is a small but growing trend (Bassett, 1988; Brown et al., 1997), and this trend has been associated with the growing adoption of the HRM model. Undy et al. (1981) have argued that *union leadership* has a positive effect on union growth as leaders act as catalysts in union recruitment campaigns. Isolating and measuring the independent effect of union leadership on union growth from the other variables is, however, problematic for researchers (Bain & Price, 1983). As has already been mentioned, the inclusion of the union 'voice' in workplace governance was not part of the management mantra during the 1980s and 90s.

With the defeat of the Conservative government in 1997 and the passage of the Employment Relations Act in 1999, the climate for union recognition became more favourable. In broad terms, this Act offers a number of measures, including a procedure to achieve recognition in the face of employer opposition, to encourage union membership and recognition (Wood & Godard, 1999; Wood et al., 2002). Moreover, the whole rhetoric of New Labour towards the trade unions, and social partnership in particular, encourages employers and workers to reassess the benefits of unionization. The widely referenced WERS98 results have not captured the most recent trend in recognition agreements and increases in union membership attributed to the 1999 Employment Relations Act. The TUC's annual survey, *Focus on Recognition* (TUC, 2000), revealed that unions won 470 new recognition agreements with employers in 2001, compared with 159 in 2000. As a result, the TUC is referring to a 'union renaissance', claiming that over 120,000 additional workers are now represented by a union (TUC, 2002). The analysis of trade union development over the past two decades emphasizes the interplay between long-term economic developments, the shift towards the service sector, the increasing number of peripheral workers, the adverse political and legal environments and the growing number of firms adopting a union exclusion strategy.

HRM WEB LINKS

For further information on the union renaissance report and the latest figures for union recognition agreements, go to the TUC website at www.tuc.org.uk and follow the headings to 'Organization and recruitment'.

Union structure

The word 'structure' in relation to trade unions denotes the 'external shape' of trade unions (Hyman, 1975) or job territories, the areas of the labour market from which the union aims to recruit. A union's internal structure, the relationship between its parts, is referred to as 'trade union government'. There are many variants of union structure within countries, traditionally expressed in terms of the four classic 'ideal types' within British union structures: craft, industrial, general and white-collar unions. In practice, however, most of these classical union structures have never existed in their true forms (Ebbinghaus & Waddington, 2000). The British union movement is associated with multi-unionism as craft and general unions cross the boundaries of workplaces and industries (Visser & Waddington, 1996). Technological change has both undermined the traditional craft unions and created new occupations, thus blurring the distinction between manual and non-manual. The wave of union mergers over the past two decades reflects the 'deep crisis' in unionization and has resulted in the formation of 'super-unions' (Ebbinghaus & Waddington, 2000).

Table 12.4 describes the wave of mergers and amalgamations in the British union system since 1979. It reveals that the number of trade unions affiliated to the TUC has fallen from 109 to 69, almost entirely as a result of mergers. Over the period 1986–95, there were 99 mergers, and the overall number of British unions fell by 142 (Willman, 1996). Table 12.4 also reveals a philosophy of 'big is best' to encourage 'natural growth' and an 'industrial logic' (Waddington, 1988) in order to avoid the duplication of administrative costs. In 1992, for example, the formation of the Graphical, Paper and Media Union (GPMU) united the craft tradition in printing, represented by the National Graphical Association (NGA), with the primarily non-craft Society of Graphical and Allied Trades (SOGAT). In January 2002, the formation of AMICUS joined the largely manual Amalgamated Engineering and Electrical Union (AEEU) with the white-collar and blue-collar Manufacturing, Science and Finance (MSF)

Table 12.4 Largest Trades Union Congress (TUC) affiliated unions, 1979–2001

Ranking (size)	Union	Affiliated membership		Per cent change	Website
		Membership (000s)			
		1979	2001	1979–2001	(www)
1.	UNISON [a]	1,697	1,272	(–)25.0	unison.org.uk
2.	AMICUS [b]	2,196	1,132	(–)48.5	aeeu.org.uk and msf.org.uk
3.	Transport and General Workers' Union (TGWU)	2,862	858	(–)70.0	tgwu.org.uk
4.	General, Municipal Boilermakers' Union (GMB)	967	692	(–)28.4	gmb.org.uk
5.	Union of Shop, Distributive and Allied Workers (USDAW)	470	310	(–)34.0	usdaw.org.uk
6.	Communication Workers Union [c] (CWU)	197	284	(+)44.2	cwu.org.uk
7.	Public and Commercial Services Union (PCS)	n.a.	267	–	pcs.org.uk
8.	Graphical, Paper and Media Union [d] (GPMU)	313	200	(–)36.1	gpmu.org.uk
9.	National Union of Teachers (NUT)	291	206	(–)29.2	teachers.org.uk
10.	National Association of Schoolmasters and Union of Women Teachers (NASUWT)	124	183	(+)47.6	nasuwt.org.uk
Total TUC membership		12,175	6,721	(–)44.8	tuc.org.uk
Number of TUC unions		109	69	(–)36.7	

a Merger in 1992 of NALGO, NUPE and COHSE.
b Merger in 2002 of the Amalgamated Engineering and Electrical Union (AEEU) and the Manufacturing, Science and Finance Union (MSF).
c Growth is caused by merger activity within the communications industry.
d Merger in 1992 of the Society of Graphical and Allied Trades (SOGAT) and the National Graphical Association (NGA).

Source: TUC Research Department (2002)

Union. In explaining merger activity, formal union links to the British Labour Party, what is called a 'political logic', are also influential (Waddington & Whitston, 1994).

The structure of British trade unions is recognized to be complex, diverse and 'chaotic' (Hyman, 1997b), and the competitive scramble to seek membership anywhere has created trade union structures that are even more bewildering and incomprehensible. The membership distribution between individual trade unions is skewed. At one extreme, there is a relatively small number of trade unions with a disproportionate share of the total union membership, whereas at the other, there is a large number of unions with very small memberships. As the data in Table 12.4 show, the 10 largest TUC-affiliated unions have a total membership of over 5 million, 80 per cent of all TUC membership. The major structural characteristic of British trade unions in 2003 is the predominance of horizontal or 'conglomerate' unions, that is, large individual unions whose members are distributed over a wide range of different industries. In the past decade, parallel trends of restructuring have become evident among trade unions in other developed capitalist economies (see, for example, Ebbinghaus & Waddington, 2000; Streeck & Visser, 1997; Visser & Waddington, 1996).

HRM WEB LINKS

For further information on union membership, governance, services and policies go to any of the websites listed in Table 12.4 or p. xxii of this book for other starting points.

Union bargaining power

There has been considerable debate over the effects of the decline in union membership and density on unions' bargaining power. The contraction of employment in the unionized manufacturing sector is widely assumed to undermine union bargaining strength. One indicator of union bargaining power is the propensity of strike activity, and the most noticeable feature of Figure 12.1 is the substantial fall in the number of officially recorded stoppages over the last quarter of the 20th century. In the period 1960–79, with both Conservative and Labour administrations, the number of stoppages each year never fell below 2000, whereas throughout the 1990s the number of reported stoppages never rose above 500.

Although any comparison involving the number of strikes must be made with caution because of the exclusion of some of the smallest stoppages from the statistics, the trend is nonetheless unequivocally downward, and the strike has virtually disappeared as a union tactic. Between 1990 and 1998, the incidence of both strike and non-strike industrial action declined sharply, from 13 per cent to just 2 per cent of workplaces. In addition, strike action affected only 2 per cent of unionized workplaces in 1998, compared with 16 per cent in 1990 (Millward et al., 2000). In 1999, official statistics show 205 strikes, the second lowest total since records began in 1891 (Broughton & Gilman, 2001). As Cully and his colleagues observe (1999, p. 245),

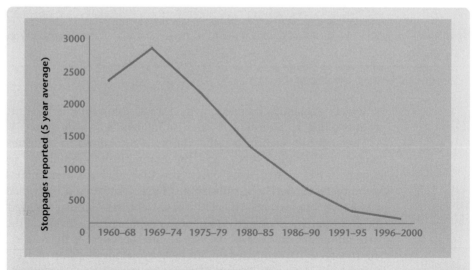

Figure 12.1 Britain's changing strike pattern, 1960–2000
Source: Data from *Employment Gazette Labour Market Trends*

'Collective action of any kind has thus virtually disappeared from British workplaces.' The reasons for this are numerous and their exploration lies beyond the scope of this chapter. Kelly (1988), for example, points to draconian fines meted out to the print unions as a reason for the low propensity of British workers to strike, and several studies identify new industrial relations law, the pre-strike ballot provisions of the Trade Union Act 1984 (Bassett, 1987; Brown et al., 1997).

All earlier evidence suggests that the strike pattern is strongly cyclical: the propensity to strike rises during an economic boom and falls during a recession. Furthermore, the decline in strike activity over the past two decades occurred in all Organization for Economic Co-operation and Development countries (Kessler & Bayliss, 1995). Moreover, strike patterns cannot be used as an unambiguous index of union power, and nor does it mean that strikes are a thing of the past (Kelly, 1988).

Collective bargaining

The previous sections have examined the principal 'actors' in industrial relations: management and the unions. We now focus our attention on an important industrial relations process that regulates employment relations, that of collective bargaining. We define collective bargaining as an institutional system of negotiation in which the making, interpretation and administration of rules, as well as the application of statutory controls affecting the employment relationship, are decided within union–management negotiating committees. Several important points arise from this definition:

1. Collective bargaining is a process through which representatives of the union and management jointly determine some rules appertaining to the employment contract.
2. There are two types of rule: substantive and procedural. Substantive rules establish terms and conditions of employment, such as pay, working hours and holidays, whereas procedural rules regulate the way in which substantive rules are made and interpreted, and indicate how workplace conflicts are to be resolved.
3. The parties that negotiate the collective agreement also enforce the agreement. The British system of collective bargaining is perhaps most noted for its lack of legal regulation. Collective agreements are, with a few exceptions, not regarded as contracts of legal enforcement between the parties.[7]

Collective bargaining structure

The structure of collective bargaining is the framework within which negotiations take place and defines the scope of employers and employees covered by the collective agreement. There is in Britain no single uniform structure of collective bargaining, the major structural characteristic of the system being wide variety. Thus, collective bargaining is conducted at several levels: at the workplace, corporate or industry level. The term 'multiemployer bargaining' refers to an arrangement whereby a number of employers reach a central collective agreement on pay and conditions with a trade union(s). The multiemployer agreement therefore covers all those companies which are signatories to the agreement. Single-employer bargaining, particularly in large multiplant businesses (for example the motor industry), can be either centralized or decentralized. Where a holding company covers a group of companies, bargaining can be conducted at the level of the subsidiary companies or below – at the divisional level or at the level of the individual plant. Some multiplant companies have a single-company agreement applying to all their plants, whereas other similar companies have a separate agreement at each plant.

In practice, survey evidence shows that collective bargaining structures are closely linked with business structures and 'profit centres'. Union recognition and the coverage of collective bargaining are mutually dependent, and both have been contracting. This is best charted by considering bargaining over rewards (Brown et al., 2000). Table 12.5 reveals the changes in the pattern of pay determination since 1984. Based upon WERS98 data, the table shows that the proportion of British workplaces (with 25 or more employees) in which collective bargaining was the dominant method of pay determination fell from 60 per cent in 1984 to 29 per cent in 1998.

The WERS98 survey results also revealed changes in the level at which the pay bargaining occurs in Britain. There has been a marked decline in the influence of national or industry-wide collective agreements. In 1984, multiemployer agreements featured in 41 per cent of workplaces, whereas by 1998 multiemployer arrangements had contracted by around two-thirds, to 13 per cent. Table 12.5 also indicates that bargaining over pay is no longer the norm in Britain: the proportion of all workplaces in which pay was not subject to negotiation increased from 40 per cent in 1984 to 71 per cent in 1998, although the aggregate data mask variations in pay bargaining. The proportion of workers covered by collective agreements broadly reflects the pattern of union density, workers employed in the public sector and in workplaces employing 25 or more individuals being more likely to have their pay determined by collective bargaining (Brown et al., 2000; Cully et al., 1999). It should be noted that the fall in the proportion of workers covered by collective bargaining over the past 20 years also occurred in Australia, Japan and the USA (Brown et al., 1997).

Bargaining over pay, effort level and the control of work is the *raison d'être* of trade unionism, but the WERS98 descriptive statistics underscore how little involved union shop stewards (elected representatives of union members in the workplace where they are themselves employed) are in pay bargaining and how shop steward influence over work organization issues is 'minimal'. In workplaces where shop stewards were reported to be involved in pay bargaining, over one-third of the managers engaged in the process indicated that the 'negotiations' amounted to 'no more than consultation' (Brown et al., 2000, p. 616). Brown et al.'s (2000) analysis of the WERS98 data suggests

Table 12.5 Basis for pay determination in Britain, 1984–98

	Percentages		
	1984	1990	1998
Collective bargaining	60	42	29
Level of negotiations			
Multi-employer bargaining	41	23	13
Single-employer, multisite	12	14	12
Workplace/establishment	5	4	3
Not the result of collective bargaining	40	58	71

Source: Millward et al. (2000), p. 186. Used with permission

that, in many instances, the term 'bargaining' is an inappropriate choice of language for the way in which pay decisions are reached because the essential ingredients of bargaining, that is, discussion and agreement, may both be absent.

Demonstrating any change in bargaining is more problematic because of inconsistencies in the questions posed by researchers, so only a 'crude' indicator is gained by comparing earlier studies. Whereas, in 1966, for example, it was reported that in 46 per cent of workplaces shop stewards exercised influence over recruitment and selection, union influence in this key area of HR activity had by 1998 'collapsed'. In addition, apart from the handling of grievances, union influence in the regulation of work design aspects of the employment contract had, overall, 'very substantially' declined (Brown et al., 2000, p. 617). In summary, union influence over pay and work organization aspects of the employment contract is not the norm in the modern workplace.

HRM WEB LINKS

The WERS98 survey *First Findings* is available at www.dti.gov.uk/er/emar/1998wers.htm.

The collective agreement

The outcome of union–management negotiations is a collective agreement (in North America also referred to as a 'contract'). The collective agreement provides for the terms and conditions of employment of those covered by the agreement, also specifying the procedure that will govern the relationship between the signatories. In Britain, the terms of the collective agreement are binding in law on the parties *if* they are incorporated into the individual contract of employment (see Selwyn, 2000, for a legal discussion on incorporation). The content of the collective agreements varies widely. Generally speaking, the greater the level of aggregation (for example industry-based agreements), the fewer the subjects that can be covered in detail. The following provisions are typically found in a collective agreement: pay rates, benefits, hours of work, working arrangements and workload (referred to as 'substantives rules'), and guidelines dealing with discipline, grievances, technological change and redundancy (referred to as 'procedural rules').

Trade unions and human resource management

The literature presents the HRM model as being inconsistent with traditional stereotype union–management relations in North America and Britain. As Adams (1995) points out, the adversarial traditions of Anglo-Saxon industrial relations systems elicit 'low trust' and non-cooperation between labour and management rather than a propensity towards 'high trust' and cooperation. Guest (1987, 1990) suggests there is a prima facie case that the 'collectivist' traditions of trade unions must be at odds with the 'individualistic' goal in the normative HRM model: 'there is no recognition of any broader concept of pluralism within society giving rise to solidaristic collective orientation' (Guest, 1987, p. 519). The HRM model poses a threat to trade unions in at least four ways:

1. the individualization of the employment contract
2. the demise of union representation
3. the intensification of work
4. the undermining of union solidarity through organizational commitment.

First, the 'web of rules' that regulates the modern employment relationship is being increasingly established, argue management critics, unilaterally by employers rather than through bilateral – union–management negotiations – processes. Although appraisal has been characterized as being an explicit HRM technique to 'control' workers' activity (Townley, 1994), it also, when used to determine reward for individual performance, undermines the *raison d'être* of unions: bargaining the effort–wage contract. As Bacon and Storey (1993, pp. 9–10) correctly argue, 'Performance-related pay individualizes the employment relationship because it isolates employees and personalizes issues such as design and evaluation of work'. Moreover, by reducing the role of unions in pay determination, performance appraisal severs the link between increased rewards and collective action. In effect, the HRM reward system offers formal and psychological contracts for hourly workers that have been the norm for many managers (Guest, 1989). Individual performance-related pay and pay-for-knowledge are the paradigm individualistic HRM techniques that symbolize attempts by management to move towards an 'individually orientated' rather than union-orientated organizational culture (Bacon & Storey, 1993).

Second, the collective logic of trade union representation is challenged by other HRM high-commitment practices. HRM advocates call for the 'socialization of the workforce' (Champy, 1996, p. 155). Work-based learning programmes that potentially strengthen support for corporate culture and 'socialize' workers to accept the hegemony of managerial authority can undermine workplace unionism (Bratton, 2001). At the company Xerox, for example, Wells (1993, p. 67) argues that training attempted 'to shape the workers' attitudes to management as well as to provide job skills'. Promotion based on individual performance and 'competencies', rather than seniority, inevitably removes an area of the internal labour market from union influence. The HRM practice of communicating directly to the workforce information on quality and business operations can weaken the position and authority of union stewards. Furthermore, team-based work regimes, closely associated with the new HRM model, can undermine collective union consciousness. Team practices try to engender a new corporate culture in which workers identify with the symbols and values that managers communicate directly to them (Bacon & Storey, 1993), in which deviant behaviour is managed by the workers themselves (Bratton, 1992; Wells, 1993) and in which team members create a culture that reproduces the conditions of their own subordination, a new organizational culture (Burawoy, 1979).

Third, critical writers on the labour process have plausibly argued that new HRM work structures are a sophisticated form of labour intensification and therefore have largely negative implications for workers (Sayer, 1986; Thompson & McHugh, 2002; Tomaney, 1990). If we accept the tenor of this research, we can plausibly argue that new HRM-inspired work initiatives will fulfil a historic role of creating working conditions that *encourage* rather than weaken workplace unionism. The ability of work teams to mortally weaken workplace unionism is contingent upon the context in which they are utilized and upon the union strategies adopted. Management's goal of labour flexibility and adaptability is akin to management demands for the removal of 'restrictive working practices' in the 1960s. On this issue, the unions demonstrate a willingness, and have the capacity, to bargain.

Fourth, the HRM goal of worker commitment is potentially the 'main challenge to the union' (Guest, 1989, p. 43). The importance of 'commitment' to the development and implementation of HR strategy has been stressed in recent years, but the notion of worker commitment is complex. It implies a social psychological state of deep identification with a work organization and an acceptance of its goals and values (Guest, 1995). One variant of the HRM model explicitly contrasts the relative advantages of two approaches to workplace control systems: compliance and commitment (Figure 1.5). Compliance demands a control system based on formally established rules and procedures; it is 'bureaucratic control' (Edwards, 1979). Bureaucratic control generates 'reactive' behaviour patterns such as working to contract. In contrast, the HRM model seeks to elicit high commitment from workers and thereby cultivate 'proactive' behaviour with committed workers expending their effort 'beyond contract' for the enterprise (Guest, 1995, p. 113). The notion of worker commitment as a powerful, cost-effective mechanism of control is a common theme in critical industrial sociology literature (see, for example, Burawoy, 1979; Edwards, 1979; Friedman, 1977). The rationale behind the goal of worker commitment is explained by the tensions inherent in the capitalist employment relationship: the need to achieve both the control *and* the consent of workers in order to maximize profits. As Lincoln and Kalleberg (1992, pp. 23–4) put it:

> The problem of control in organizations is in large measure solved when the commitment of its members is high. Committed workers are self-directed and motivated actors whose inducement to participation and compliance is their moral bond to the organization.

The case for eliciting the commitment of workers seems plausible, but literature on the topic suggests that the commitment concept is problematic. As Guest (1987) argues, the first issue is 'commitment to what?' Writers taking a managerial perspective are interested in commitment to values that drive business strategy, but Guest (1987, 1995) points out that workers can have multiple and perhaps competing commitments to a profession, a career, a craft, a union and a family. Arguably, the higher the level of commitment to a particular set of skills or professional standards, the greater the likelihood of resistance to multiskilling and flexible job designs. The goal of commitment might thus contradict the goal of flexibility.

Closely associated with the debate on HRM and union–management relations is the related notion of 'dual commitment'. Theorists and practitioners have posed the question of whether workers can be simultaneously committed to the goals and values of both the work organization and their trade union. The argument goes something like this. If US-style HRM models underscore 'individualism' and commitment, this approach to managing people must be incompatible with the core ideologies of workplace trade unionism – 'collectivism' and representation. Using a simple matrix model, Guest (1995) argues that, logically, if commitment to company and union are caused by the same variable, they operate from competing ends of the same continuum and dual commitment is not possible. On the other hand, if they are caused by different variables, dual commitment is possible because a change in a variable affecting company commitment need not influence union commitment. Murphy and Olthuis (1995) found support for the notion of dual commitment. Their Canadian study reported that 'many workers are attached to *both* the union and the company and have a type of "dual commitment" [and] attachment to the company does not necessarily lessen attachment to the union, and vice versa' (Murphy & Olthuis, 1995, p. 77). This, and the body of research that Guest (1995) reviewed, appears to support the hypothesis that dual commitment is possible where the union–management relations climate is characterized as being cooperative and non-adversarial.

The logic of the HRM model is (at least in theory) that workplace unionism will eventually 'wither and die'. This interpretation of HRM is expressed by trade union leaders thus: 'In the wrong hands HRM becomes both a sharp weapon to prise workers apart from their union, and a blunt instrument to bully employees' (Monks, 1998, p. xiii). The new corporate culture certainly aims to encourage workers to identify with their company's ideals and their work team rather than with the union collective. The argument that unions and HRM cannot coexist does not, however, appear to be consistent with the empirical evidence (Wood, 1995).

● Union strategies: partnership and paradox?

The debate on trade unions and HRM provides the backcloth to examining union strategies. The actual formulation of a strategy depends to a large extent on the external conditions facing the union, employers' HR actions and the internal politics of the union. As with management strategies, trade unions have adopted different strategic responses to environmental and organizational change; several reasons can explain this diversity of responses. Trade unions are complex organizations that have developed with different ideologies and associated strategies. 'Business unionism' – dealing with 'bread and butter' issues – is, for example, the dominant ideology in the USA and has also played a large part in union development in Britain, Canada and Japan (Adams, 1995). The unions' response will also be partly conditioned by their experience of management-initiated HRM policies. Furthermore, the response will be different depending on whether the union perceives management to be adopting 'hard' or 'soft' versions of the HRM model (Legge, 1995). Several industrial relations theorists have sought to clarify the types of response made by European, Canadian and US unions (Beaumont, 1991; Martinez Lucio & Weston, 1992). It would be misleading to develop a typology of union strategies – one with mutually exclusive categories – but, for our purposes, we have identified two dominant strategic approaches for the renewal of British trade unions:

- organizing strategy
- partnership strategy.

Organizing strategy

The organizing strategy, also referred to as 'new unionism', is internally focused and places a renewed emphasis on the recruitment and organization of new union members. The union 'organization model' developed in North America has informed the strategy, which embraces a number of basic principles and union tactics: a change in union priorities, strengthening workplace union organization, 'targeted' recruitment campaigns, person-to-person recruitment and 'issue-based' organizing, for example focusing on 'justice, dignity and respect' issues in the workplace (Heery, 2002). The purpose of this strategy is, despite the novelty of the language, rather traditional: it is to establish an effective workplace union organization that can be self-sustaining in terms of recruitment and service to members. Union recruitment drives will be supported by the statutory union recognition procedure introduced by the UK Labour government in 2000. The Employment Relations Act 1999 union recognition procedure is, however, likely to help union recruitment campaigns only in sectors of the economy 'where unions already have a presence' (Wood et al., 2002, p. 233). In analysing the nature of this union strategy, Heery (2002, pp. 27–8) has noted that it focuses on the 'qualitative interests' of workers and is built on the assumption of 'opposed interests' between workers and the organization.

To be successful, the organizing strategy for union renewal requires five broad conditions to be present in the workplace (Kelly, 1998):

- a perceived sense of injustice or violation of the contract
- attribution of the injustice to managerial behaviour
- the presence of effective workplace unionism through which the collective action can occur
- confidence that collective action will have the desired effect, that is, it will remove the injustice
- charismatic union leaders who can mobilize the membership and legitimize collective action.

Of these five influences on non-union employees to unionize, perceived union 'instrumentality' – a belief that a union will improve working conditions – apparently has the greatest effect (Charlwood, 2002). According to Heery (2002), an analysis of WERS98 data suggests that these five conditions for renewal are currently absent. Although survey evidence reveals a wide variation across the workforce, a sense of injustice and discontent, workplace unionization, union efficacy and an effective cadre of union leaders are relatively absent, making the organizing strategy difficult to develop and implement. Any study of the trade union strategic response to HRM and change has to be cognizant of the possible difference between trade union rhetoric and labour's actual response in the workplace.

HRM IN PRACTICE 12.2

HONDA FACES CAC BALLOT

GREGOR GALL, *PEOPLE MANAGEMENT*, 2001, OCTOBER 25

More than 3000 workers at Honda are due to vote later this year on union recognition. The announcement follows a prolonged campaign by the Amalgamated Engineering and Electrical Union (AEEU) to secure recognition at the carmaker's Swindon plant.

The AEEU applied to the Central Arbitration Committee (CAC) on 9 October for statutory union recognition after repeated requests to the company for voluntary discus-

sions. If the workforce votes in favour, it will be the biggest ballot by the CAC and the biggest statutory union award to date. But the AEEU could use the application to solicit a voluntary deal from the company. The union can meet the 10 per cent membership threshold demanded by the CAC for an application to be accepted, having increased its membership over the past two years to a total of 1600.

'We want to work in partner-

ship with Honda and our members to make this company stable, secure and successful,' said Sir Ken Jackson, general secretary of the AEEU. 'We are confident that employees at Honda will see the clear advantages of AEEU representation and vote "yes" to recognition.'

Honda has not recognized any union since it opened its Swindon site in 1985. It is the only non-unionized car manufacturer in the UK. The company had previously told the AEEU its 'associates' – employees – were happy without union recognition. The company instead runs an 'associate representative council', which this year, for the first time, negotiated employees' annual pay rise.

Mike McEnaney, Honda's director of business information, said: 'We already have very good relations and communications channels with our employees. If they feel that union representation would add further benefits, then Honda will of course respect their wishes.'

Partnership strategy

The second dominant strategy for the renewal of unions is the 'social partnership' strategy. This strategy is externally focused, with its emphasis on union–management relations, and seeks to develop a new form of workplace governance around the notion of partnership. The theoretical basis of the approach can be traced back to North American literature on 'strategic partnerships', 'mutual gains' and 'win–win' rewards coming to labour by cooperating with employers to develop high-performance work systems (Betcherman et al., 1994; Guest, 1995; Kochan et al., 1986; Verma, 1995). In the early 1990s, it was argued that, rather than viewing the 'soft' HRM model as a threat, 'unions should champion it, becoming more enthusiastic than management' (Guest, 1995, p. 134). The premise here is that the policies and practices inherent in the 'soft' HRM model include many to which trade unions could subscribe. With the election of New Labour in the UK in 1997, and the 1999 Employment Relations Act, union leaders and managers were challenged to reappraise collective relations in the workplace (Bacon & Storey, 2000). In 1999, the TUC published *Partners for Progress: New Unionism at the Workplace*, which advocated workplace partnership between local union representatives and managers. In the context of a continuing contraction of members and collective bargaining coverage, the unions presented themselves to potential members and employers alike as 'facilitators of cooperative collective relationships' that would have mutual economic benefits (Brown, 2000, p. 303).

The term 'partnership' is used in a variety of ways. At the European level, it can refer to union involvement in the European Social Dialogue. At national level, partnership can be applied to tripartite discussions between employer and union representatives and the government, for example between the Confederation of British Industry, the TUC and the UK government. At workplace level, partnership is the term applied to agreements to promote flexibility in working practices in exchange for employee involvement mechanisms. Partnership agreements seek to give unions a place at the 'strategy table' by portraying themselves as an authoritative partner in economic and business management, hence:

> Partnership provides a clear workplace philosophy based on employer and union working together to achieve common goals such as fairness and competitiveness, and recognizing that although they have different constituencies, and at times different interests, these can best be served by making common cause wherever possible (Industrial Relations Services, 1998, p. 12, quoted in Munro & Rainbird, 2000, p. 225).

By embracing partnership, the trade unions seek to improve union influence and membership by building long-term partnerships with employers. The TUC document *Partners for Progress: New Unionism at the Workplace* outlined six principles of workplace partnerships (Figure 12.2).

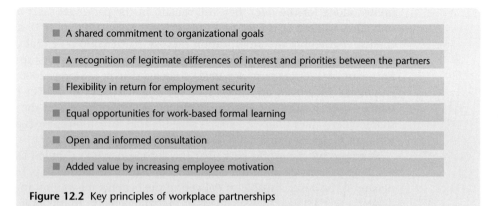

- A shared commitment to organizational goals

- A recognition of legitimate differences of interest and priorities between the partners

- Flexibility in return for employment security

- Equal opportunities for work-based formal learning

- Open and informed consultation

- Added value by increasing employee motivation

Figure 12.2 Key principles of workplace partnerships

HRM WEB LINKS

For further information on the TUC's position on workplace partnership, go to the TUC website at www.tuc.org.uk.

More than fifty partnership agreements, for example between the Co-operative Bank and the union BIFU, Tesco and the Union of Shop, Distributive and Allied Workers, and Legal and General and AMICUS–MSF, have been negotiated. Partnership agreements typically provide a commitment to employment security in exchange for flexible working. Other features address 'dignity' at work, employee 'voice' and work-related learning and employee development issues. UNISON's 'Return to Learn' partnerships, for example, are restricted to workplace learning and 'represent both continuity and change in relation to traditional collectivist approaches to servicing members' needs' (Munro & Rainbird, 2000, p. 227). The majority of the recent partnership agreements have been negotiated in 'mature' establishments undergoing major organizational 'restructuring' following privatization, for example Hyder (Heery, 2002). From an employer's perspective, partnership can facilitate major restructuring with the support of the union, de-emphasize costly distributive collective bargaining over innovation and change, reduce costs, improve customer service standards, improve quality and strengthen employee commitment to organizational goals (Thomas & Wallis, 1998).

REFLECTIVE QUESTION

What do you think of workplace partnerships? How does the partnership strategy reframe employment relations? What are the advantages and disadvantages of partnership?

Partnership agreements also have their detractors (for example Bacon & Storey, 2000; Clayton, 1998; Kelly, 1996). Clayton (1998), for example, remains sceptical about the likelihood of workplace partnership developing as a vehicle for reconstituting trade union power in response to long-term decline. To paraphrase Guest (2001), UK management is currently driving the bus, and although the unions may be invited along for the ride, they will remain in the passenger seats to offer guidance only; they will not be trusted to do any driving. Kelly (1996, p. 101) argues that, rather than strengthening the unionization process, partnership potentially can 'weaken or inhibit the growth of workplace union organization', and partnership agreements may form part of 'a longer term *non-union* strategy' (Bacon & Storey, 2000, p. 410, original emphasis). Moreover, an analysis of the characteristics of British corporate governance – a preference for short-term financial performance and the maintenance of shareholder values (Purcell, 1995) – suggests that British business is an infertile environment for social partnership (Heery, 2002).

Statutory provisions, in particular the European Works Council Directive of 1994, will help to override potential employer opposition to partnership, but whether partnership is, however, capable of delivering the benefits for unions and employers will depend upon a balanced assessment of the arrangement. In the long run, partnership is likely to be sustained if it holds the promise of real benefits for employer, employees and unions. The interests of employers and labour are not identical so an effective approach to partnership must involve acceptable trade-offs, the trade-offs associated with the partnership model being shown in Table 12.6. It is hard to disentangle the effects of partnership; with this in mind, the challenge for trade unions is to transcend the polarized positions of outright opposition to partnership and cooperation, and focus on a strategy to extract the potential from partnership without eschewing traditional union building activities. The outcome is indeterminate and will depend upon the ongoing interaction between union and management, and, as Heery (2002) concludes, upon whether the 'qualitative' gains (for example 'voice', dignity and respect) are not heavily outweighed by 'quantitative' losses (for example job loss, work intensification and lower income growth).

We should note the apparent contradiction between the two union strategic alternatives. The organizing strategy is predicated on the assumption that workers' and employers' interests are different; whereas partnership assumes the reverse. This seemingly contradictory mix of union positions may be justified because of a growing divergence in business and HR strategies within national economies. Just as an HR strategy is contingent upon the business strategy, the argument is that union strategies differentiate between 'good' and 'bad' employers. Partnership can thrive and deliver the benefits for all stakeholders where 'acceptance of unions remains high and there is a commitment to value-added competition' (Heery, 2002, p. 31). Elsewhere, however, a traditional organizing strategy might be required. This perspective recognizes the links between business, HR and union strategies, as well as the role of power in organization decision-making; as such, it brings a certain 'realism' to the study of HRM and union–management relations that is frequently lost in the rhetoric and in the prescriptive HRM texts.

Finally, several writers have noted the relatively small number of partnership agreements in British workplaces. If the partnership strategy has not been extensively adopted, there are at least three possible explanations:

- Employers might be too preoccupied with 'downsizing' rather than introducing the relatively costly partnership alternative.
- The investment cost associated with the partnership is high, as are the risks, given that any social partnership arrangement will experience the underlying conflicts inherent in employment relations.
- Employers might also be reluctant to invest in partnership because the effect on the 'bottom line' is unclear (Chapter 13).

Table 12.6 The benefits and costs of a partnership strategy

	Benefits	Costs
For organizations	■ Efficiency gains ■ Lower absenteeism/turnover ■ Better union–management relations ■ Potential for improved performance	■ Greater investment in work-related learning and other human resource programmes ■ Having to share information ■ Having to share decision-making
For workers	■ Access to work-related learning ■ Potential increased skills ■ Discretion over the work process	■ A need for greater commitment to the firm ■ Job loss and lower income growth ■ Greater work intensification and job-related stress
For unions	■ Participation in decision-making ■ Affirmation of an independent 'voice' for workers ■ Access to information ■ Improved status	■ A move away from job control unionism ■ Isolation from union members ■ Union 'polices' work changes ■ Leaders challenge

Source: Adapted from Betcherman et al. (1994)

Legal context of union–management relations

Management and union strategies, collective bargaining processes and outcomes (for example pay levels, labour productivity and industrial disputes) are influenced by economic, political and legal factors. The state, which is normally thought of as comprising the executive, Parliament, the judiciary, the civil service and the police and armed forces, has considerable influence on union–management relations in two major areas: through legislation and through third-party intervention.

Collective labour law is an aspect of union–management relations that interacts with the institutions, processes and behaviour of the key 'actors' in the system. Union organization and governance, relations between different unions, union recognition by employers, collective bargaining and manifestations of collective workplace conflict, such as strikes, are the main concerns. Whereas individual labour law governs the relation between individual employees and their employer, collective labour law governs the collective aspects of the employment relationship. The Employment Relations Act 1999, for example, provides a statutory framework for union organization and governance and collective bargaining, including statutory union recognition provision, changed balloting procedures and increased protection for union members when participating in official industrial action (see Chapter 3 for a discussion of industrial relations legislation over the past 20 years, and Wood & Godard, 1999, and Wood et al., 2002, for an analysis of the Employment Relations Act 1999). Some of the key UK legislative provisions related to unions and union–management relations are shown in Table 12.7.

Table 12.7 Main UK legislative provisions related to union–management relations, 1980–99

Act	Date	Coverage
Employment Act	1980	Public funds for union ballots (since repealed) Provision for codes on picketing and closed shop
Employment Act	1982	New definition of a 'trade dispute'
Trade Union Act	1984	Compulsory secret ballots for union positions and before industrial action, otherwise no immunity
Employment Act	1988	Greater control to members of union governance
Employment Act	1990	Abolished the closed shop and immunity in respect of secondary industrial action
Trade Union and Labour Relations (Consolidation) Act	1992	Consolidated all relevant law on unions and labour relations Together with Advisory, Conciliation and Arbitration Service Code provides for disclosure of information to unions for collective bargaining purposes
Trade Union Reform and Employment Rights Act	1993	Independent scrutineer of union elections given more powers Voting fully postal
Employment Relations Act	1999	New statutory framework for collective bargaining, including statutory union recognition provision, changed balloting procedures and increased protection for union members when participating in official industrial action

HRM WEB LINKS

Go to the following websites to compare collective labour law relating to unions and union–management relations: www.hmso.gov.uk/acts.htm provides the full text of UK Acts of Parliament, www.labour-travail.hrdc-drhc.gc.ca//index.cfm/doc/english and www.law-lib.utoronto.ca/ give information on Canadian laws, and www.laborlink.org and www.dol.gov/elaws/aud_gen_emp.asp outline the US information.

The UK third-party intervention institution, ACAS, was established in 1974 in order to promote orderly union–management relations and to intervene in those industrial disputes the government viewed as particularly damaging to the national economy. ACAS is a state mechanism and is funded by the government. In 1993, legislation removed ACAS's responsibility for the promotion of collective bargaining. The role of ACAS as an arbitrator and mediator is less significant today given the decline in official industrial stoppages, but ACAS figures for 2000 reveal that requests for individual conciliation are increasing each year.

HRM WEB LINKS

For information on ACAS, go to www.acas.org.uk. See also p. xxii of this book.

⬭ **Chapter summary**

- This chapter has examined three alternative union–management strategies; union acceptance, union replacement and union avoidance. Research on management strategies indicates that a union avoidance strategy is the one most frequently adopted by UK and US companies. We have emphasized that the selection of an industrial relations strategy involves managers considering a number of complex economic, political, legal and historical factors. Given the different conditions facing each organization, culture and leadership philosophy and styles, each union management strategy is likely to be unique and display contradictory practices.

- We have also examined union membership, structure, collective bargaining and union strategies. What is the significance of all the data on trade union membership and strike activity to HRM? In a nutshell, the dramatic reduction in union membership, the significant decline in the number of strikes and the trajectory of decentralized bargaining has led to a shift in power towards management. Where the preferences of management and unions differ, as they often do, the party with the perceived power will dictate the outcome nearer to their preferences. The argument here is that this shift in bargaining power makes it more likely that employers will be tempted to take a short-term view and choose traditional cost-cutting HR measures that can potentially violate the psychological contract.

- Although long-term economic forces played a part in such developments, the politics of the 'New Right' of Thatcher in Britain and Reagan in the USA in the 1980s and much of the 1990s played a critical role in management resurgence, the decline of unionization and power, and the demise in multiemployer collective bargaining. In Britain, the politics of New Labour appear to be encouraging a resurgence of union growth and influence in the workplace.

- Analysing four fundamental factors influencing union–management – the state of the labour market, management's strategic capacity, labour's strategic capacity and the legal and political context of union–management relations – we can say that the jury is 'still out' on whether New Labour's policies will reverse industrial relations trends in the foreseeable future.

- This chapter examined two dominant union strategies: organizing strategy and partnership strategy. We noted that the long-term success of the partnership strategy will depend upon ongoing union–management relations and on whether or not the 'qualitative' gains are heavily outweighed by 'quantitative' losses. We also emphasized the apparent contradiction in the two union strategic alternatives. Drawing upon the recent work of Heery (2002), we concluded that partnership can thrive and deliver the benefits for employers, employees and unions where a union acceptance strategy is the norm and there is a commitment to value-added competition. In other worksites, an organizing strategy might be required.

Key concepts

- Collective agreement
- Collective bargaining
- Management strategy
- New unionism

- Social partnership
- Third-party intervention
- Union density
- Union structure

Chapter review questions

1. What is meant by the term 'union–management relations'?

2. Why are union–management strategies said to be the result of strategic choices?

3. To what extent, and why, can some variants of the HRM model be viewed as a union exclusion strategy?

4. How can contextual factors explain the development of British trade unions?

5. To what extent is collective bargaining in Britain too fragmented to function effectively in an enlarged European market?

6. What contradictions might be found in the twin goals of new unionism and social partnership?

Further reading

Brown, W., Deakin, S., Nash, D., & Oxenbridge, S. (2000). The employment contract: from collective procedures to individual rights. *British Journal of Industrial Relations*, **38**(4), 611–29.

Charlwood, A. (2002). Why do non-union employees want to unionize? Evidence from Britain. *British Journal of Industrial Relations*, **40**(3), 463–91.

Gollan, P. J. (2002). So what's new? Management strategies towards non-union employee representation at News International. *Industrial Relations Journal*, **33**(4), 316–31.

Guest, D. (2001). Industrial Relations and Human Resource Management. In John Storey (ed.), *Human Resource Management: A Critical Text* (2nd edn) (pp. 96–113). London: Thomson Learning.

Heery, E. (2002). Partnership versus organizing: alternative futures for British trade unionism. *Industrial Relations Journal*, **33**(1), 20–35.

Roche, W., & Geary, J. (2002). Advocates, critics and union involvement in workplace partnerships: Irish airports. *British Journal of Industrial Relations*, **40**(4), 659–88.

Wood, S., Moore, S., & Willman, P. (2002). Third time lucky for statutory recognition in the UK. *Industrial Relations Journal*, **33**(3), 215–33.

Practising human resource management

Searching the web

On an individual basis, or working in a small group, pick two or three on-line union-related websites, (for example www.tuc.org.uk (UK), www.ilo.org (the International Labour Organization in Geneva), www.clc-cta.ca (Canada) or www.aflcio.org/

home.htm (USA). What are some of the major issues affecting workers around the world? What identifiable strategies have the unions developed, and how do they compare with the union approaches discussed in this chapter? Bring this information to class and present your findings in an oral report.

HRM group project

Form a group of three or four students. The purpose of this group assignment is to allow you to apply your knowledge of union–management strategies in the workplace. Specifically, your task is to examine how two selected organizations have formulated and implemented a union–management strategy.

First, enter the websites of two organizations, for example Barclays Bank (www.barclays.co.uk/) or Tesco (www.tesco.co.uk/). Then compare the partnership agreements negotiated between the different management and unions.

How are the agreements similar and different? Do the partnership agreements contain the TUC's six principles (see Figure 12.2 also)? What kinds of change or external business pressures did the organizations face, and how does a partnership help the organizations to manage change? Given the nature of your selected organizations' business strategy and structure, is conflict a likely obstacle to change in the organizations? How does the union–management strategy relate to business strategy? Is there any evidence that union–management relations facilitate or hinder change? How well do you think managers have managed union–management relations in these organizations? What other changes do you think that the organizations should make to their HR/IR strategy and why?

Each group member should take responsibility for researching the various aspects of the assignment. Present your findings in a written report.

Chapter case study

EAST YORKSHIRE CITY COUNCIL

Rose Peller, the newly appointed Chief Executive of East Yorkshire City Council, had a mandate to restructure the City's local government. One of her first tasks was to set up a quality committee of senior managers to transform the Council's culture, employee attitudes and performance, her objective being to introduce total quality management throughout the Council's administration. Workshops on total quality management started with the senior management team and department managers, some of the workshops on leadership aiming to turn old-fashioned local government managers into 'active leaders', trying to enthuse instead of dictate.

The proposed changes are both physical and cultural. Part of the restructuring is to introduce open-plan working areas throughout the Council's buildings, in terms of both dismantling the counters between staff and customers and getting managers out of their offices. It is envisaged that the manager's role will become one of facilitator, and employees, after they have been organized into quality teams, will have greater autonomy and no longer hand problem-solving automatically to managers. In addition, Ms Peller, with support from the Conservative-controlled Council, is planning to introduce performance-related pay, which will be linked to personal goals rather than office targets. Together with total quality management, it is expected that this will contribute to the new culture in local government. At a planning meeting, Rose Peller expressed her views in a forceful manner: 'Since the department managers will be working in teams, they should know more about the people they are working with, which should make the appraisal system fairer. The more people work together and get rid of these hierarchical barriers the better', she said.

East Yorkshire City Council employs 620 manual and non-manual employees, and 85 per cent of the Council's workforce are in UNISON, the recently created public sector union.

Assignment

As an assistant HR officer at East Yorkshire City Council, you have been asked to produce a report for the planning committee on the industrial relations and negotiating issues associated with the introduction of total quality management and performance-related pay. Your report should include the anticipated reaction of the trade union UNISON and the union's objectives in future negotiations between senior management and the union.

HR-related skill development

The grievance process is an integral part of administering the collective agreement, a grievance being a formal dispute between an employee (or the union) and management involving the interpretation, application or alleged violation of the collective agreement. The union files most grievances, and once they have been filed, management should seek to resolve them fairly and quickly. Handling a grievance is a key skill for managers in a unionized (and non-unionized, if there is a grievance process in place) workplace, but many lack the basic knowledge and skills to conduct a formal grievance investigation and interview.

To help you to develop grievance management skills and to give you experience of the grievance process, we have devised a grievance case with supporting information. You can participate, either at individual or group level, in the simulation and develop an important HR skill by going to www.palgrave.com/business/brattonandgold and clicking on 'Handling grievances'.

Notes

1. Machin (2000, p. 643).
2. Brown et al. (2000, p. 616).
3. John Monks, TUC General Secretary, commenting on the new annual TUC survey on union recognition, www.tuc.org.uk, January 2002.
4. Wood et al. (2002, pp. 215–33).
5. Richard Johnson, Personnel Manager, Flowpak Engineering, quoted in Bratton (1992, p. 162).
6. Lord Sieff (1981), Chairman and Chief Executive of Marks & Spencer, and quoted by Purcell and Sisson (1983) Strategies and practice in the management of industrial relations, in G. Bain (ed.), *Industrial relations in Britain*, p. 114, Oxford: Blackwell.
7. See *Ford Motor Co. v. Amalgamated Union of Engineering and Foundry Workers* (1969). For a discussion of this important judgment, see Davies, P., & Freedland, M. (1984) *Labour law: text and materials*, p. 779, London: Weidenfeld & Nicolson.

Part Four

The evaluation context

Chapter thirteen

Evaluating human resource management

John Bratton

Human resource management evaluation refers to the procedures and processes that measure, evaluate and communicate the value added of human resource management practices to the organization.

'HR measurement – a practice that is central to the future growth and success of our profession.'[1]

'HR used to be the feel-good department. Now the focus is on value added. We are in the midst of a fundamental shift from being a cost item on the balance sheet to being, if not a profit centre, then to at least being able to justify return on investment.'[2]

'HR must become bottom-line valid. It must demonstrate its validity to the business, its ability to accomplish business objectives and its ability to speak of accomplishments in business language. The HR function must perform in a measurable and accountable way for the business to reach its objectives.'[3]

Chapter outline

Chapter objectives

After studying this chapter, you should be able to:

1. Explain the importance of measuring the human resource management (HRM) contribution

2. Describe some variables used to measure the value added of HRM

3. Understand some techniques for evaluating the HRM function

4. Critically evaluate research on the HRM–performance link

During the past two decades, the human resource (HR) function has undergone an unprecedented change in its role, status and influence (Cully et al., 1999; Fitz-enz & Davison, 2002; Millward et al., 2000; Phillips, 1996). Commentators have pointed to the 'balkanization of the personnel role', which refers to the trend of outsourcing HR functions and the marginalization of HR specialists in organizational decision-making (Tyson, 1987). More recently, commentators have emphasized the change of focus of the HR specialist from that of an 'employee advocate' to being a 'member of the management team' (Schuler, 1990), or from an HR 'partner' to 'player' (Beatty & Schneier, 1996; Ulrich & Beatty, 2001). The message is that the HR specialist is involved in both operational – recruitment and selection, rewards, training and development, and employee relations – and strategic dimensions of the business. The quotations opening this chapter reveal details of the emerging role of the HR professional. It is against this development that HR professionals have become increasingly concerned with demonstrating the financial contribution – the 'value added', the 'bottom-line contribution', the 'return on investment' (ROI) – that the HR function makes to the organization's performance. Pfeffer (1994) found that one of the 16 'best practices' in 'successful' companies was 'measurement of the practices' and noted that 'organizations seriously committed to achieving competitive advantage through people make measurement of their efforts a critical component of the overall process' (Pfeffer, 1994, p. 56).

As we first mentioned in Chapter 2, demonstrating the HR contribution to organizational performance has become *the* dominant research issue in HR, so what types of performance data are available to measure the HRM–performance link? What types of HR practice and programme produce superior performance results? Do 'high-commitment-type' HR systems lead to above-average results compared with 'control-type' systems? Do organizations with a better 'fit' between HR and business strategies have a superior performance? How does the HR function contribute to the organization's financial 'bottom line'? To answer such questions, HR professionals have to be able to measure, evaluate and communicate the value added of HR practices. As Ulrich and Beatty (2001, p. 306) argue, 'The objective of HR professionals is to ensure that HR adds value to strategic planning and business results of the organization'. When, however, only 23 per cent of workplaces with 25 or more employees have HR specialists (Millward et al., 2000), our focus here on the value-added approach to HRM must be directed to all managers.

In this chapter, our objective is important but modest: it is to review the literature advocating the need for a value-added approach to HRM. The first section draws upon Phillips' (1996) work and identifies management trends that connect organizational performance and the HR function's role in the process. As a preliminary step towards understanding the impact of HR activities on organizational performance, the chapter discusses a variety of fundamental concepts and issues before focusing on specific ways by which to evaluate the HR contribution; it includes a discussion of statistical evaluation, and HR accounting and auditing. The final section reviews studies that seek to demonstrate a link between HR strategy and organizational performance (for example Arthur, 1994; Becker & Gerhart, 1996; Betcherman et al., 1994; Buyens & De Vos, 2001; Delaney & Huselid, 1996; Frege, 2002; Huselid, 1995; Hutchinson et al., 2000; Ichniowski et al., 1996; Pfeffer, 1998a; Youndt et al., 1996).

● Rationale for human resource management evaluation

The notion that the HR function should move beyond its administrative and controlling roles and add value has been popular in US management texts for over a decade. Drucker, the American management guru, suggested, for example, that the HR department should behave differently and demonstrate its strategic capabilities, needing to 'redirect itself away from concern with the cost of employees to concern with their *yield*' (emphasis added).[4] Developments in the role of HRM derive from changing business demands and trends (Fitz-enz, 2000; Fitz-enz & Davison, 2002; Nutley, 2000; Phillips, 1996; Ulrich & Beatty, 2001; Vedd, 2001), most of which we have examined throughout this text. According to Phillips (1996), there are seven compelling trends in management thinking and practices that have changed the role of HR (Figure 13.1):

- organizational change
- flexibility and productivity improvements
- the adoption of HR strategies
- the increased importance of human capital
- increased accountability
- partnership relationships and
- the growing use of HR information systems.

One development that we discussed in Chapter 4 is *organizational change* and restructuring, which includes teamworking, total quality management and 're-engineering'. Alongside these structural changes are increased employee involvement and employee 'voice' arrangements. The role of HR in this change process is to become an 'enabler', a 'change agent', and be consultative rather than administrative. The second trend – increasing labour *flexibility* and productivity – envisions the role of HR as that of an initiator, enabler and evaluator of these work restructuring regimes. The adoption of *HR strategies* by work organizations underscores the importance of measuring the contribution of individual, team and organizational variables towards organizational performance (see HRM in practice 13.1). The resource-based model of

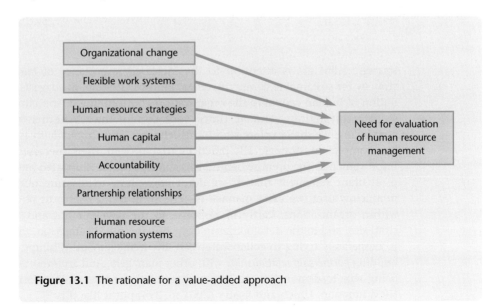

Figure 13.1 The rationale for a value-added approach

HRM IN PRACTICE 13.1

HR FOCUSING ON HOW IT CAN ADD VALUE

TERRENCE BELFORD, *GLOBE AND MAIL*, 2002, MARCH 25

Human resources professionals are in the midst of reinventing themselves – changing what they do for the companies that employ them and how they relate to those on the operations side. Their goal is to shoot for the corporate gold – a seat around the senior management table right alongside decision makers like the chief operating, information and finance officers.

The single most important tool they have in their uphill struggle is the intellectual capital held within any corporation. In the past, the profession has focused on winning the hearts of employees. Today their aim is to quantify and harness their minds. 'HR used to be the feel-good department,' says Michael Ford, president of the Human Resources Institute of Alberta. 'Now the focus is on value added. We are in the midst of a fundamental

shift from being a cost item on the balance sheet to being, if not a profit centre, then to at least being able to justify return on investment.'

> **Success and a seat at the senior management table will depend on HR professionals looking beyond their traditional playing field.**

Granted, such a fundamental shift takes time and brings with it a certain measure of confusion. 'The main problem right now is figuring out just what HR is going to do within a corporation,' says Paul Juniper, president of the HR Professionals Association of Ontario. 'Historically we have performed administrative functions like payroll, pensions and benefits administration. 'We were the personnel

department. We hired, we fired, and we took care of the details. We never added a lot of value to the company.'

That role changed with the advent of the technological age. In the past decade, many employers found that they could first automate most of those traditional functions and then become more effective by outsourcing them to third parties. For HR professionals, what seemed like a threat to their livelihood may actually have been a blessing. 'Suddenly, we were relieved of these humdrum tasks ... That left the HR department free to devote its time to developing a new role, one that could help the company reach its strategic objectives.'

Success and a seat at the senior management table will depend on HR professionals looking beyond their traditional playing field, Mr. Juniper adds.

strategic HRM draws attention to the increased importance of *human capital* as a strategy for sustainable competitiveness. Phillips (1996, p. 6) suggests that the contribution of human capital to the organization's bottom line is 'sometimes subtle, occasionally mysterious, and at times very convincing'. Whether the evidence is convincing, we shall explore later in this chapter. The *accountability* issue is illustrated by examples of strategic HR practices that present their successes in measurable improvements. The premise behind this concept can be illustrated by Fitz-enz's (2000, p. 4) blunt statement that 'if we don't know how to measure our primary value-producing asset, we can't manage it'. The sixth trend relates to power and politics within organizations. Partly in response to the development and adoption of HR strategies, and to the development of outsourcing the HR function, the HR profession is 'desperately trying to collaborate with line management' (Phillips, 1996, p. 20) by building *partnership relationships* with other managers. And an important part of this is being able to demonstrate to line management the bottom-line contribution of the HRM function. Ulrich and Beatty (2001, p. 294) put it like this:

HR professionals must be more than partners; they must be players. Players contribute. They are engaged. They add value. They are in the game, not at the game. They deliver results. They do things that make a difference.

The seventh important development encouraging accountability in the HRM function is the growing use of *HR information systems*. The capability of IT systems allows greater amounts of data to be collected, analysed and reported, and potentially leads to more accurate measures of the economic value of worker performance. These seven changes are closely integrated and relate to greater demands for accountability and value-added HR practices and systems.

REFLECTIVE QUESTION

According to Peter Drucker, 'You can't manage what you can't measure.' At a time when so many people are engaged in so-called 'knowledge work', how valid is this maxim when strictly applied to managing people?

Human resource management–performance model

For HR measurement, demonstrating the link between HRM strategy and organizational performance requires the measurement of some set of variables. The method-

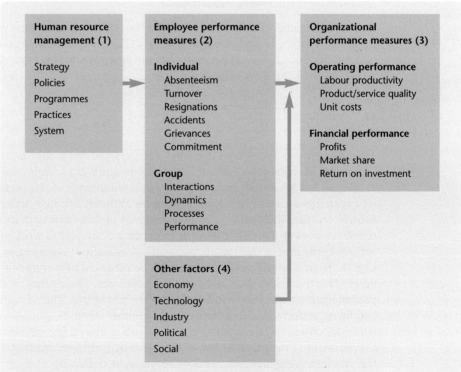

Figure 13.2 Human resource management–organization performance model
Source: Adapted from Phillips (1996)

ology for ensuring high internal validity would ideally permit a calculation of how different HRM strategies or individual practices affect economic performance while controlling the other factors that might influence those performance outcomes. High internal validity refers to the extent to which the results can be generalized to infer the likely impacts of HRM practices were they to be introduced elsewhere. Figure 13.2 presents a basic model showing the relationship between HRM practices and organizational performance. The HRM added-value model indicates the overall relationship between three major elements:

- HRM
- HR performance measures, at both individual employee and work team levels
- organizational performance measures.

Human resource management

The HRM (1) element in Figure 13.2 includes the HR strategy, policies, programmes, practices and system that exist in work organizations and have an impact on employee and group performance, which in turn affects individual and organizational performance. Much of the recent research has focused on how 'innovative' bundles of HRM practices, such as selection, training and learning, appraisal and rewards, impact on employee performance. It is worth emphasizing Fitz-enz's (2000, p. xii) point that 'people are the only element with the inherent power to generate value'.

Employee performance measures

The second element in Figure 13.2 depicts the performance effects of HRM, estimated in part by employee performance measures (2). Researchers and practitioners have a number of options when it comes to measuring individual employees and teams. Saks (2000) outlines three measurements:

- traits
- behaviours
- outcomes.

The research can focus on evaluating the personal *traits* that are considered to be important in employees. A particular HR practice may thus result in employees exhibiting key attributes, such as loyalty or commitment to the organization. Despite its popularity, making trait assessments is difficult because traits are not clearly defined entities. In contrast, the measurement of *behaviour* data focuses on what an employee does or does not do in the workplace. Examples of work-related behaviours include being absent from work, poor time-keeping and resigning from employment. Unlike traits, work-related behaviour can be observed and recorded with some reliability. The third approach is to measure *outcomes*, the things produced or accomplished during a specific period of time in the workplace. The advantage of measuring employee performance in terms of the 'number of units completed', the 'accident level' or 'customer complaints' is the apparent objectivity involved. Whether it is commitment to the organization or absenteeism, turnover, accident or grievance rates, the problem of deficiency and reliability must be dealt with.

As we discussed in Chapter 4, teamworking has become more common in British and North American organizations, as has interest in measuring team performance. Drawing on the work of Hackman and Oldham (1980; see Figure 4.4), research suggests that team performance is strongly influenced by four *input* variables – team structure, team norms, team composition and team leadership – and by *process* variables – teamworking and team learning – which affect team performance outcomes. The measurement of these input and process factors is not, however, well developed (Saks, 2000).

Team process refers to the behaviours that take place in the team (across individuals and across time). Although a review of all team process theory is outside the scope of this chapter, we should highlight two important concepts that help to clarify potential process indicators of team effectiveness. There seems to be ample evidence that how the team approaches the job to be done has important consequences for ultimate team performance, this being referred to as 'work team strategies' (Kline, 1999). The second concept is that of team learning, as the amount of informal learning that takes place within a team appears to affect team outcomes (Kasl et al., 1997).

When defining team performance, researchers and practitioners are usually thinking in terms of how well the team has been able to accomplish certain team *outcomes*. In work organizations, team performance is conceptualized in terms of efficiency, that is, accomplishment relative to the resources utilized, efficiency thus being an output to input ratio. Banker et al. (1996), for example, studied the impact of work teams on labour productivity, which was measured as a ratio of the number of units produced to the total number of production hours. Their results indicated that labour productivity improved following the formation of work teams. Finally, when undertaking research on work team performance, or when team data are to be analysed, it is important to remember that the unit of analysis is the team, the sample size therefore being the number of teams involved in the investigation (Saks, 2000).

Organizational performance measures

Individual employee and work team measures affect organizational performance, the third element in the model shown in Figure 13.2. Researchers and practitioners have used a number of organizational performance measures (3), including labour productivity ratios, product and service quality, unit cost ratios, revenue productivity and ROI. Saks (2000) also points out that researchers frequently tend to rely on single indicators of performance, ignore the relationships between 'multiple measures', tend to ignore the fact that some measures of organizational performance, for example change in market share, take longer to materialize than, say, a change in employee behaviour, and use performance indicators across dissimilar workplaces with no regard for their appropriateness, thus rendering comparisons meaningless.

Given that work organizations exist in order to accomplish a goal(s), researchers have often conceptualized organizational performance in terms of goal attainment, four specific indicators reflecting this approach:

● profit-related indices
● productivity
● quality
● perceptual measures of goal attainment.

Profit-related indices or financial variables include percentage ROI. Labour *productivity*, a popular indicator, is usually defined as the quantity or volume of the major product or service that the organization provides and is expressed as a rate, that is, productivity per worker or per unit of time. Huselid (1995), for example, measured productivity in terms of sales per employee. Another indicator is *quality*, which usually refers to the attributes of the primary service or product provided by the firm. Bratton (1992) reported improvements in quality as a result of teamworking measured in terms of fewer complaints of unit defects from other teams. The airline industry conducts random surveys of passengers to obtain data on perceptions of quality of in-flight service. The monitoring of performance data can of course be used as a surveillance tool – 'a modern-day Panoptican' (Cully et al., 1999, p. 114). Finally, although 'hard' financial data are often used to measure organizational outcomes, researchers also use *perceptual measures* to quantify performance. Cully et al. (1999), for example, measured perceived workplace economic performance by asking managers to compare their own organizations in a particular area (for example productivity) relative to other organizations in the same industry, using a subjective scale ranging from 'a lot above average' to 'a lot below average'.

The organizational outcome measures discussed here are important for at least three reasons. First, these are employee-related outcomes and as such they are most directly influenced by HR practices. Different rewards and training programmes are, for example, likely to have some influence on most, if not all, of the outcomes. Second, these outcomes (for example productivity, quality and employee unit cost) can influence the organization's financial operational goals. Third, the outcomes can influence the individual psychological contract (Chapter 1) as well as aspects of individual behaviour and/or outputs.

Other factors

Disentangling the HRM–organizational performance equation is complicated by the fact that employee performance measures are only one set of variables that impact organizational performance. Other variables (4), such as changes in the economy, technology, industry, government policies and social trends, the fourth element in Figure 13.2, also affect organizational performance. A company that exports its products can, for example, experience a substantial rise or fall in revenue productivity as a result of a sustained strengthening or weakening of a nation's currency. Further support for the 'other factors' caveat is the financial implosion of many companies following the 11 September 2001 attack on the World Trade Center in New York: the financial performance and subsequent collapse of Canada's second largest airline, Canada 3000, was, for example, the result of the sharp fall in passenger traffic after the attack rather than of HRM practices or employee performance.

HRM WEB LINKS

Go to www.bbk.ac.uk/manop/man/mgesrc.htm for information on carrying out research on the relationship between HRM and organizational performance.

Measurement issues

Measurement is central to the HRM–organization performance model, but there are a number of challenges in selecting and using measurement. First, do the measurements accurately describe the phenomena they claim to measure? Income statements, often regarded as objective and accurate reflections of an organization's financial performance, can be based on measures that are inaccurate and in some cases fraudulently misleading. The wave of corporate accounting scandals that implicated top US executives at Enron, Adelphia Communications and WorldCom in 2002 has, for example, severely shaken the trust of investors, employees and market-watchers in reported financial statements. In June 2002, for instance, WorldCom Inc. revealed one of the largest accounting scandals in management history, admitting that it had overstated its profits by US $3.85 billion. Accurate measurement of the HRM contribution to the organization's financial 'bottom line' obviously becomes entirely misleading with such fraudulent accounting practices.

The second challenge facing researchers and practitioners when using measurements, and one not unrelated to the first challenge, is that research on the outcomes of new HR strategy requires management participation and, moreover, a disclosure of commercially sensitive information on performance indicators that many managers are unwilling or unable to provide to an independent researcher. The researcher therefore has to use 'intermediate' performance indicators such as accident, absenteeism and grievance rates. One set of performance indicators in Betcherman et al.'s (1994) survey of Canadian workplaces included voluntary resignations, lay-offs, accidents/injuries and formal grievances and complaints.

A third challenge is that a key element in the HRM–organizational performance equation, 'HRM practices', is based on subjective judgements. Researchers and respondents might, for example, define a 'self-managed team' in different ways, with or without a 'supervisor' or team 'leader', or define an 'employee involvement' practice as employee 'participation' or as 'involvement' in corporate governance – the proverbial 'apples and oranges'. Subjective judgements of HR practice may be especially problematic when comparing multiple workplaces or work units within a single company. If the respondents to a questionnaire share a different meaning and definition of an 'HR practice', estimates of the effects of the new strategic HR practices will be biased.

A fourth challenge is how to isolate external variables. Exchange rates can, for example, significantly affect the financial 'bottom line', which makes it difficult to measure accurately the impact of HRM practices. Guest (1997, p. 268) recognizes this problem when he states, 'We also need a theory about how much of the variance can be explained by the human factor.' Even if relevant indicators are made available to the researcher and the external variables are isolated, the problem of identifying the causal links remains a challenge. Do certain HRM practices lead to better-performing firms, or do better-performing firms adopt certain HRM practices? Given the current state of affairs, it appears that there is no single conceptual model of organizational performance – but there is no shortage of possibilities either. In short, the implications of HR strategic choices for organizational performance are difficult to measure with complete confidence. With this in mind, Ichniowski et al. (1996, p. 312) argue that, 'The key to credible results is creating a collage of studies that use different designs with their own particular strengths and limitations'.

Overall, these measurement challenges may raise questions concerning the appropriateness of HR and organizational measures, questions that underscore the importance of the statistical concepts of reliability and validity. When evaluating the HRM contribution to the organization's performance, all measures, whatever the level of measurement (individual, team or organization), must be of high quality; that is, they must be reliable and valid. *Reliability* refers to the degree to which a measure results in the same values when it is repeated. *Validity* refers to the appropriateness of the inferences we draw from a test score. In using employment tests (for example ability tests; Chapter 7) to make selection decisions, we are, for example, making an inference from a test score about an applicant's future job performance. If the measures have poor reliability and validity, the results of the HRM–organizational performance research will therefore at best be difficult to interpret, and at worst lack credibility (Saks, 2000). The various measurement options described here reflect a mixture of objective and subjective data. Each has its own strengths and weaknesses with regard to reliability and validity.

REFLECTIVE QUESTION

What do you think of these measurement issues? Can the measurement of the HRM contribution be truly objective?

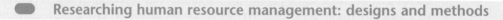

● Researching human resource management: designs and methods

Both the academic researcher and the HR professional must make choices about how to handle the most important HR variables and how to study them; these choices demand an overall research design. According to Palys (1997, pp. 76–7, emphasis added), 'research design involves stating a game plan through which one can gather information that addresses one's research purpose in a simple, elegant, and systematic way'. The 'game plan' through which researchers gather information on the contribution of HRM strategy usually takes the form of one of the following four research designs:

- survey
- case studies
- experimental
- meta-analysis.

Here we offer a brief summary of each design.

Survey research

Of all the data-gathering techniques available to the academic and the practitioner, the survey, either written or oral, is used most extensively. In its most basic form, a survey elicits information on people's opinions of or attitudes towards a certain topic by asking people specific questions. The large-scale surveys of changing employment relations in Britain between 1980 and 1998 conducted by Cully et al. (1999) and Millward et al. (2000) are good examples of this type of research design. Surveys have been used to gather information on employment relations since the beginning of large-scale industrial capitalism. In 1880, a survey of French workers to study employer pay practices (Bottomore & Rubel, 1956, quoted in Gray & Guppy, 1999, p. 4) asked:

> (1) Does your employer or his [sic] representative resort to trickery in order to defraud you of part of your earnings? And; (2) If you are paid piece rates, is the quality of the article made a pretext for fraudulent deductions from your wages?

In this case, the researcher using a survey to elicit information was Karl Marx.

Survey research is most appropriate when the researcher wants to learn about the relationship between variables and to be able to predict the level of one variable with knowledge of another, for example 'What makes women (or men) managers prefer one style of workplace leader over another?' Survey research designs are also used for assessing the impact of change (Kraut, 1996), such as the impact of introducing a specific recruitment and selection practice on long-term team cohesiveness and performance. HR practitioners use employee attitude surveys to evaluate the effectiveness of their HR department (Phillips, 1996).

HRM WEB LINKS

Go to any of the following websites for information on the purpose of the survey: www.lpsos-reid.com (the Angus Reid Group), www.gallup.com (the Gallup Poll) and www.norc.org (the National Opinion Research Centre).

Qualitative case study research

Qualitative research refers to the gathering and sorting of information through a variety of techniques, including interviews, focus groups, observations and the use of archival data in organizational files, records or reports. A case study is an intensive description and analysis of a phenomenon or workplace unit such as an employee, team or organization. The case study researcher seeks holistic description and interpretation, and uses a wide range of qualitative research techniques.

In an attempt to differentiate between quantitative and qualitative approaches to serious inquiry, Berg (1998) explains that 'quantity' is an amount of something whereas 'quality' refers to the what, how, when and where of a thing. *Qualitative research* thus refers 'to the meanings, concepts, definitions, characteristics, metaphors, symbols, and descriptions of things' (Berg, 1998, p. 3). Qualitative inquiry is a process that locates the researcher in the workplace, studying 'things in their natural settings, attempting to make sense of, or to interpret, phenomenon in terms of the meanings people bring to them' (Denzin & Lincoln, 2000, p. 3). *Quantitative research*, however, emphasizes the measurement and analysis of causal relationships between variables rather than of processes – that is, *how* things happen.

Qualitative researchers stress the socially constructed nature of the workplace and employment relations, and the situational constraints that shape the research (Denzin & Lincoln, 2000). Qualitative case study research is most useful when the researcher wants to obtain a rich, in-depth description of some event or process. Qualitative data obtained from interviewing employees and/or managers, coupled with actual results on a work-related issue, create a very convincing case study (Phillips, 1996).

Experimental research

The origin of experimental research can be traced back to the work of John Stuart Mill's treatise entitled *A System of Logic*, first published in 1873. Mill proposed a number of principles, in the form of canons or laws, which he argued were a requirement for establishing order among controlled events. One law, the method of difference (quoted in Merriam & Simpson, 1995, p. 52), stated:

If an instance in which the phenomenon under investigation occurs, and an instance in which it does not occur have every circumstances in common save one, that one occurring only in the former, the circumstances in which alone the two instances differ is the effect, or the cause, or an indispensable part of the cause of the phenomenon.

Merriam and Simpson (1995) interpret Mill's law as meaning that if two sets of events are alike and something is either added to or taken from the event, causing a difference between those two events, the difference can be attributed to what was added or withdrawn. Isolating and observing single variables in this way is common in the natural sciences but less useful in the social sciences because of the multivariate nature of human activity.

Although the conditions required for true 'classical' experimental designs are lacking, the approach is, however, used to conduct research in the workplace. Experimental research designs are used to provide evidence regarding cause-and-effect relationships with as much control as possible. An experimental design can, for example, test the effects of a HR practice such as a training workshop or a pay system on employee attitudes and behaviours.

Take the training workshop. Two work teams are given training on problem-solving and team leadership skills, some measure of achievement (for example quality or productivity) then being administered at the end of the month. The measurement of achievement for those teams exposed to the training is compared with that of another similar team deprived of the training. Experimental research therefore incorporates two important features: an *experimental group* and a *control group*. The experimental group is exposed to, or deprived of, some particular HR intervention (manipulation), whereas the control group is part of the research study but does not receive the HR intervention (Figure 13.3). The pre and post measures for the control group are the same as those collected from the experimental group. By comparing and contrasting the scores on these measures, the expectation is that there will be an increase or improvement in scores (from pre-test to post-test) for those in the experimental group who received the HR intervention but not for participants in the control group.

Although 'true' experimental research designs provide the means of testing the causal effects of HR interventions in the workplace, there are a number of ethical concerns facing the researcher who conducts experimental research, the most important of which are participants' freedom of choice to participate, the right to receive beneficial interventions and the deception of participants (Saks, 2000).

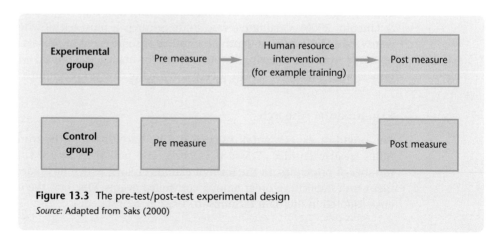

Figure 13.3 The pre-test/post-test experimental design
Source: Adapted from Saks (2000)

Existing research and meta-analysis

In recent years, a new technique called meta-analysis has been used to study the impact of HR practices. This technique allows the researcher or HRM professional to combine the results of existing research in a particular area and to calculate the overall effect of an HR intervention. Meta-analyses of selection tests, for example, provide information on the usefulness of the various tests for predicting job performance. The results of a meta-analysis can be particularly useful to small organizations that do not have the ability to conduct the large-scale research studies that are often required to test the validity of a selection test or the impact of a particular HR practice (Saks, 2000).

The defining feature of meta-analysis is the statistical analysis of the results of many empirical studies. Drawing upon the work of Saks (2000), the meta-analysis review process is depicted in Figure 13.4. The meta-analysis review process begins with a compilation of all the relevant empirical studies on the HRM topic under investigation. After reading the papers, the researcher formulates hypotheses about the potential study characteristics that might affect the relationship between the variables being investigated. The results of meta-analyses in HRM can help HR professionals to decide whether an HR intervention will add value. An organization can, for example, use meta-analysis to measure the value added of a training programme (see, for example, Alliger et al., 1997).

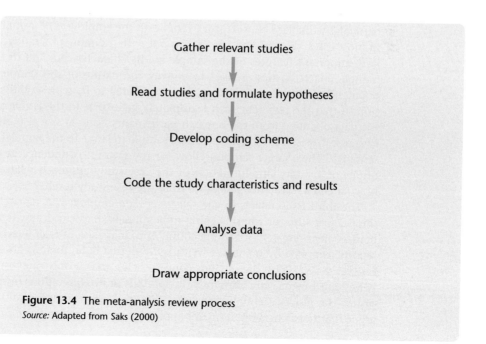

Figure 13.4 The meta-analysis review process
Source: Adapted from Saks (2000)

Research design issues

Whichever of the research designs discussed above we choose to adopt, a number of common issues cut across them all.

When academics conduct research in the workplace, at issue is the question of how knowledge is constructed. The study of knowledge and the justification of belief (Dancy, 1985) is referred to as epistemology, and at the heart of epistemology lie such questions as, 'Which beliefs are justified and which are not?', 'What is the relationship between seeing and knowing?', and, in management studies, 'Whose knowledge is produced in the research interview?' This has practical implications in terms of:

- the research context
- the nature and size of the sample
- the sources of data employed.

First – considering the *research context* – the investigator has to decide how important it is for the purposes of the research to conduct the inquiry in an actual organization. This might involve one organization, such as in an experiment to test the effects of an HR practice, or several, allowing the researcher to study differences between particular HR strategies. The issue of research context is illustrated by the academic debate on quantitative survey versus qualitative case study. It is argued, for example, that workplace surveys generate a vast number of quantitative data that can test theories and permit a statistical analysis of HRM practices and performance. Critics of this research design point out, however, that the researcher is 'outside looking in', and, given the nature of the research instrument, a mail questionnaire, the results cannot hope to provide an accurate picture of the subtleties and intricacy of the way in which work is structured and *actually* performed, and of the dynamics of the employment relationship. Case studies, on the other hand, involve the researcher being 'inside', and qualitative methods can provide rich data on workplace HR activities.

The second issue relates to the *nature and size of the sample* under investigation. There will be occasions on which the researcher may wish to study all the people in a particular workplace context (for example all the employees of a small company), but in most cases, research may be carried out with a sample of employees. Two particularly important features of the sample are its characteristics and its size. The phrase 'sample characteristics' is used to convey the nature of the sample relative to the population of interest. The sample is constructed to be representative of the population so that the researcher can legitimately generalize to the whole population from the data obtained from the research participants. Sample size also affects representativeness; that is, it is harder for a small sample (relative to the population) to be representative. Thus, larger samples allow for the greatest confidence in generalizing the results of a study. One limitation of the case study approach relates to sample size: how far can a researcher generalize from the case study results?

The third issue relates to the *sources of data* employed. A research design usually implies just who (or what) is going to be measured, assessed, tested or monitored. In management research, it is quite common to make use of mail questionnaires or self-reports compiled by managers. With self-reported data, there is always the potential for bias (Saks, 2000), the obvious concern being that if only one response is received per establishment, 'any idiosyncratic opinions or interpretations of the questions can distort the results' (Ichniowski et al., 1996, p. 309). Thompson and McHugh (2002) argue that researchers often do not appreciate important limitations of self-completed questionnaires. In particular, they point out potential problems when investigators rely on managerial informants for data on HR interventions and their effects when the informants themselves have a role or stake in the practice. The data are less than accurate because such informants may, rather than reporting the reality (what *is*), fall into a normative (what *ought to be*) mode (Guest, 1999; Thompson & McHugh, 2002).

In other words, self-completed mail questionnaires have the potential to induce 'socially desirable responses', responses that are intended to make the respondent look good in the eyes of the investigator or society at large (Saks, 2000). Thus, asking a manager in a survey if she or he 'values employee voice' is likely to produce an affirmative answer; most people will reason that they will look unreasonable if they do not answer 'Yes' to this question. The investigator can check on the possibility of distortion in self-reports by surveying the views of relevant others. The value of talking to both managers and workers is emphasized by Nichols (1986, quoted in Bratton, 1992, p. 14):

> a study which systematically samples both managers and workers is always likely to provide at least some snippets of information that rarely surface in other accounts and to suggest different lines of interpretation.

There is another issue related to data collection that we should also note: the notion that we can ever have an objective account of the phenomenon under investigation, because all such accounts are 'linguistic reconstructions'. This is called the 'constructivist model'. A constructivist or formative approach recognizes that the researcher and those being researched create the data and ensuing analysis through an interactive process. The researcher's data do not *discover* social reality; rather, what is 'discovered' arises from the interactive process and its political, cultural and structural contexts (Charmaz, 2000). The interview is traditionally viewed as an opportunity for knowledge to be transmitted between, for example, a manager and a researcher, yet, through the interactional process, the viewed and the viewer are active makers of meaning, assembling and modifying their questions and answers in response to the dynamics of the interview. The researcher is not simply a conduit for information but is instead deeply implicated in the production of knowledge (Schneider, 1999).

The constructivist approach suggests that what the manager and the situation actually are is a consequence of various accounts and interpretations. From this perspective, managers act as 'practical authors' of their own identities (Shotter, 1993). This does not mean that knowledge is impossible: 'No one *does* know, because no one *can* know' (Dancy, 1985, p. 7, original emphasis). It does mean, however, that the knowledge that is produced on what managers and HR specialists allegedly do cannot be an objective narrative about their workplace activities, and we must maintain a healthy scepticism as we journey through the HRM discourse (Grint, 1995).

The key point arising from this overview of research design is that research in HRM is in a state of flux, and new research methods have developed for seeing and doing. Moreover, there is no 'one best way' to do HR research, each research practice making the workplace and HR practices transparent in a different way. Of course, we all have our biases, but our intention in this chapter is not to privilege one methodological practice over another – quantitative survey research versus qualitative case study research, for example.

PRODUCTIVITY IS A TIME BOMB

HENRY MINTZBERG, *GLOBE AND MAIL*, 2002, JUNE 13

Some economists have been issuing dire warnings about the Canadian economy recently. 'Economists are concerned that Canadian companies have been adding too many workers – and therefore expenses – without showing a corresponding increase in output,' wrote a reporter in the *Globe and Mail* recently. The implication, almost in so many words, is that these foolish Canadian managers are running around hiring people they don't need. These economists know better: they have statistics.

Since I am not an economist, and am suspicious of statistics in any event, but work in the world of managers and organizations, let me venture another hypothesis: Productivity is killing the American economy. What is productivity, exactly? In fact nothing exactly. You take some measure of output, some gross product or other, and divide it by the number of declared hours of work and the like. The result, I assure you, is gross. It represents what can be measured and ignores all sorts of interesting things that cannot.

Ideas are outputs too, but they don't figure because they can't be measured, even if they may show up much later in the form of better products and processes. So if a company emasculates its new product development activity, or closes research laboratories that looks good to the economists because the hours of declared work go down while the measured output remains the same.

Hours worked show up as long as they can be counted – a worker who spends 37.5 paid hours on the job, for example, even his or her 2.1 hours paid overtime. But what about the manager on a monthly salary who now works 60 hours instead of 50? That doesn't count in these statistics – burning out doesn't count.

> **But as workers and managers depart, out goes commitment, out goes respect, out goes the social glue that binds people together in a healthy social system.**

I received an e-mail recently from someone I had been working with in the US. He said, 'Henry, you won't believe what's going on here. More cost cutting. We have hardly anyone left to make things work.' A sizeable portion of American business is now rotting from within, while the economy becomes astonishingly more productive. Well, maybe it is not all that astonishing.

Thanks to 'shareholder val-ue' – no human values in this, just an obsession with short-term stock price – workers and managers get 'downsized' regularly so that those who are left have to do that much more. And often they have to do it with less, because of the enhanced bargaining power of their employers. This too, drives up productivity, alongside the living standards of those who own the stock, for a while at least.

But as workers and managers depart, out goes commitment, out goes respect, out goes the social glue that binds people together in a healthy social system. Indeed, out goes the database of the company, which is in the heads of the managers more than in the computers. And with the managers goes much of the potential for innovation, because that comes from the grounded initiatives of middle managers far more than the ethereal 'strategies' of senior executives. America does have one great hope. That is to convince its major trading partners to imitate this nonsense. 'Shareholder value' is sweeping across this so-called globe, although the Germans, Japanese, and some others remain a bit reticent. The Canadians, too, apparently. But economists are working on that.

Approaches to evaluating human resource strategy

Previous sections of this chapter have described the measurement of individual, team and organizational variables, as well as the different approaches to researching HR practices. Once the data have been collected, the emphasis shifts to evaluation – the ways in which the data are used and analysed to interpret the HRM–organizational performance link. Evaluating the effects of labour practices and economic performance is well established in the field of industrial relations: numerous empirical studies have, for example, monitored the impact of unions on wages and productivity. Although the 1960s and 70s saw research on the effects of such management initiatives as employee involvement schemes on various outcomes (attitudes, job satisfaction and productivity), Purcell (1989, pp. 72–3) suggested that if it were possible to prove that 'enlightened or progressive' HRM was invariably associated with higher productivity and lower costs, 'life for the ... HRM executive would be easier. As it is, there is little conclusive evidence.' Similarly, Legge (1995, p. 196) makes the point that there are 'few, if any, systematic evaluations' of 'high-commitment' management practices on organizational performance.

With regard to the HRM–performance link, there are still gaps in our knowledge, but there have over the past two decades been 'considerable advancements' in the evaluation of HR strategy on organization performance (Phillips, 1996). Much of this research has been spurred on by debates surrounding the relative merits of high-performance work systems and the new HRM paradigm. There are a number of ways of evaluating HRM practices and the HRM system, three of which will be described here:

- statistical evaluation
- financial evaluation
- system evaluation.

Statistical evaluation of the human resource strategy

The statistical evaluation of HR strategy includes basic descriptive indices, such as measures of central tendency, as well as statistics that allow us to make statements about the relationship or correlation between HR practices and outcome variables. It is outside the scope of this chapter to cover statistical analysis, but Tables 13.1 and 13.2 illustrate how descriptive statistics and regression analysis are used to present research findings. Table 13.1 compares the arithmetic mean differences found in Betcherman et al.'s (1994) study of Canadian HR strategies. The study reported a statistically significant association between 'participation-based' HR practices and employee behaviour and operating outcomes, and a less significant association for financial outcomes.

Regression analysis is a statistical method for evaluating the relationships between variables. A manager wanting to know how likely it is that employees will resign can use the information to help to demonstrate a positive link between a 'participative' HR strategy and performance outcomes. Predictions of the likelihood of an employee resigning, and the resultant associated costs, can then be made on the basis of different HR strategies – 'traditional' and 'participative'. In Betcherman et al.'s (1994) study (Table 13.2), regression analysis pointed to the positive and statistically significant impact of a participation-based HR strategy on two out of three behaviour outcomes. That is, workplaces with that HR strategy had approximately a 10 per cent higher probability of experiencing improved resignation, lay-off and accident trends than workplaces with the same organizational characteristics but operating under a traditional HR strategy. Turning to other areas, the results of the regression analysis were statistically significant only in the case of unit costs.

Table 13.1 Proportion of establishments reporting improvements in performance outcomes, by human resource strategy, 1988–93

	Human resource strategy	
Performance outcome	Traditional	Participative
Behaviour outcomes		
Resignations	42.0	55.0
Accidents	37.0	46.0
Grievances	33.0	40.0
Operating outcomes		
Labour productivity	79.0	85.0
Unit costs	35.0	49.0
Product/service quality	95.0	94.0
Financial outcomes		
Profits	47.0	52.0
Sales	63.0	66.0
Market share	66.0	71.0

Source: Adapted from Betcherman et al. (1994, p. 66)

Table 13.2 Estimated impact of choice of human resource strategy on the probability of reporting improved behaviour outcomes (relative to traditional human resource strategy)

	Human resource strategy	
Performance outcome	Traditional	Participative
Behaviour outcomes		
Resignations	10.0	11.0
Accidents	+	11.0
Grievances	+	+

Source: Adapted from Betcherman et al. (1994, p. 68)

HRM WEB LINKS

Go to the 1998 Workplace Employee Relations Survey website www.dti.gov.uk/er/emar/1998WERS.htm for more examples of statistical techniques used to compute the mean differences and measures of association between variables.

Financial evaluation of the human resource strategy

In recent years, HR professionals have had to demonstrate the value added of their programmes and departments. They have also had to develop the skill to communicate with other managers, in the language of business, the HR contribution to the financial 'bottom line' (Fitz-enz, 2000; Pfeffer, 1994; Phillips, 1996). As Pfeffer (1994, p. 57) argues, 'In a world in which financial results are measured, a failure to measure human resource policy and practice implementation dooms this to second-class status, oversight, neglect, and potential failure'. It has thus become apparent that HR specialists need to be able to evaluate in financial terms the costs and benefits of different HR strategies and individual HRM practices. A production manager, for example, proposes investing in new technology and incorporates into the proposal projected increases in productivity and resultant decreases in unit production cost. With this in mind, HR professionals must compete for scarce organizational resources in the same language as their colleagues and present credible information on the relative costs and benefits of HR interventions. This section describes one approach to evaluating HR strategies in financial terms: return on investment.

The basic approach here is to calculate the cost of a HR intervention, such as training or an employee participation arrangement, and to determine the benefit in monetary terms of results such as improved productivity or a reduction in absenteeism, accidents and grievances. For example, a food-processing plant was considering implementing a training programme to improve the quality of the meat-cutting and house-keeping, and the number of preventable accidents. The cost of the training intervention was calculated in terms of direct costs, indirect costs, development costs, overhead costs and pay, the total cost of the training intervention being calculated to be £18,475. The benefits of the training intervention were calculated in terms of the improvement in the quality of the meat packaging and the reduction in the number of accidents. After training, there were 330 fewer meat portions rejected per shift, which was calculated as saving £74,250 per year. They also reported a decrease of nine accidents per year, at a cost saving of £8,213 per year (see Figure 5.2 for information on typical accident costs). The total saving to the organization was thus £82,463.

To calculate the ROI of an HR intervention programme, the manager needs to calculate the total costs and benefits of the programme using the following formula (Saks, 2000):

$$\text{ROI} = \frac{\text{Net benefits}}{\text{Intervention costs}}$$

The return on the investment for the training programme in the above example is therefore £82,463/£18,475 = 4.5 (45 per cent), or £63,988 per year (£82,463–£18,475). The method of calculating the ROI involves estimating the costs and benefits of an HR intervention, but in reality it can be more difficult to calculate the *full* benefits. This is because 'soft' measures such as communication, learning, interpersonal skills and so on are much more difficult to quantify in monetary terms than are 'hard' measures such as absenteeism, productivity and labour productivity. Although the calculation of ROI in the evaluation of HR practices is a powerful way to demonstrate the value added of HR intervention, very few organizations actually use the technique in practice (Saks, 2000). For more detailed and complex examples of calculating the ROI of HR practices, the reader should refer to readings devoted to these topics (Fitz-enz, 1995, 2000; Phillips, 1996).

Evaluating human resource management systems

Statistical and financial evaluations of the HR contribution are best suited to evaluating particular HR practices or programmes. When evaluating an entire HRM system, managers have used two methods in recent years (Nutley, 2000; Saks, 2000; Vedd, 2001):

- HRM auditing
- HRM benchmarking

HRM auditing

The term 'HRM audit' can be interpreted in different ways, but, as in a financial audit, there are a number of generally accepted elements of audit practice (Nutley, 2000, p. 22):

- independence from the subject being audited
- technical work in the form of a systematic gathering and analysis of data
- an evaluation of HR activities, policies and systems based on the evidence
- a clearly defined object of the process
- action in response to audit findings.

In other words, an HRM audit is a process of evaluating the effectiveness of the entire HR function (Phillips, 1996). According to Phillips (1996), the use of HR audits has been increasing in North American workplaces. A number of benefits result from an HR audit (Figure 13. 5).

The HR audit process consists of a number of sequential steps. Step one involves the HRM auditor determining the scope of the audit. The audit may be comprehensive and focus on the entire HR function, or programmatic and focus on a specific HR practice. Step two requires the HRM auditor to decide how to conduct the audit. During this phase, the auditor will need to gather information on state-of-the art practices in each area of HRM and on ratios or measures for absenteeism, turnover, grievances and workplace accidents. Step three requires the audit team to collect the information through a variety of methods, including interviews, surveys and organizational data, the survey being the commonly preferred method (Phillips, 1996). Step four involves the team analysing the data and comparing statistics, noting discrepancies and corrective actions. Step five, the final stage of the HRM audit process, involves the audit team writing a report on the results of the audit. The report typically provides a summary of the strengths and weaknesses of the HRM function, explains the deficiencies and provides suggestions for corrective action to address these deficiencies. According to Phillips (1996), the HR audit is an important exercise that can help to

- Provides verifiable data on the human resource management function
- Clarifies the human resource function's duties and responsibilities
- Identifies critical human resource problems
- Helps to align human resource strategy with organizational strategy
- Improves the status of human resource function
- Helps to reduce human resource costs
- Helps to review and improve the human resource management information system

Figure 13.5 Benefits of a human resource audit

improve the efficiency of the HR function, but it falls short of a valid approach to measuring the HRM contribution to the organization's bottom-line performance.

HRM benchmarking

Benchmarking, which was first used as part of the US quality movement, involves managers and non-managers learning and adopting so-called 'best practices' by comparing their HRM practices with those of other (more successful) organizations (Phillips, 1996). It is thus a form of auditing. Benchmarking HRM practices serves a number of important purposes. First, organizations can gauge their own practices against those in 'excellent' organizations and can get an idea of how they compare and how well they are doing. Second, benchmarking enables managers to learn from other organizations about effective HR strategies. Third, benchmarking can help to create and initiate the need for change because it identifies what an organization needs to do to improve relative to the HR strategy in excellent companies.

The benchmarking process for HRM evaluation purposes consists of seven key phases (Phillips, 1996), shown in Figure 13.6:

1. Identify exactly which HR practice managers wish to benchmark. An organization might, for example, wish to benchmark HR training, HRM performance measures

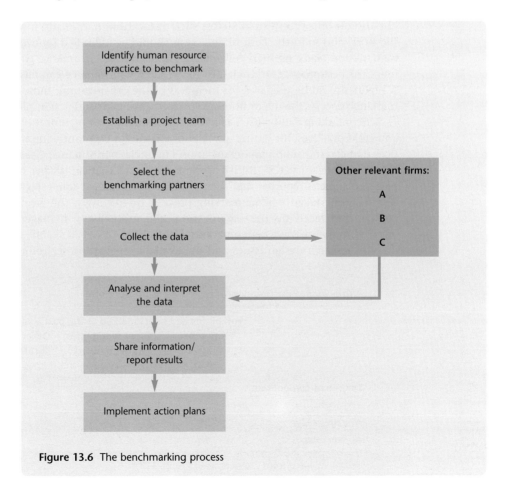

Figure 13.6 The benchmarking process

or HR reward systems. Factors that are chosen for benchmarking should be those considered to be most important and critical for an organization's success and overall effectiveness.

2. Establish a project team because of the amount of work required to conduct a benchmarking evaluation.
3. Identify the benchmark partners. These partners should be those prepared to participate in the exercise and with so-called 'best practices'. They may include internal units, competitors and non-competitors in the same industry, organizations or international organizations.
4. Collect data from each of the benchmarking partners (for example firms A, B and C).
5. Analyse and interpret the data.
6. Following the analysis of the data, prepare the major findings from the benchmarking partners in the form of a written report.
7. Develop action plans to improve HR strategy and practices.

This final step in the benchmarking process involves calculating performance gaps between the way things are and the desired or 'best practice', the 'best practices' that are most important for a particular organization depending on its business strategy and technology. As Pfeffer (1994, p. 65) argues, 'The specific implementation of the practices, and the form they may take, are obviously contingent not only on strategy but also on other contextual factors such as location, nature and interdependence of the work, and so forth.' Performance gaps should be identified for every benchmarked item. Action plans are then developed to address the performance gaps and to implement the best practices in each area for which a performance gap has been identified. A report should be prepared for members of the organization, indicating the benchmarking process, the major findings, performance gaps and action plans.

Benchmarking can be used as a tool for evaluating an organization's HRM strategy and HRM practices, for setting new standards and for constantly improving HRM practices that can impact on an organization's financial performance (Saks, 2000). Cully et al.'s large-scale survey of British workplaces found that, in 48 per cent of all workplaces, managers reported that their establishment had, at some stage during the past 5 years, undertaken a benchmarking process. Interestingly, the greater the degree of competition faced by the organization, the more likely managers were to have engaged in competitive benchmarking (Table 13.3).

With research design issues and the available evaluation techniques in mind, the

Table 13.3 Benchmarking, by degree of competition

	Workplaces had benchmarked in the past 5 years against:		
	Any other workplaces (%)	Other workplaces within industry (%)	Other workplaces located overseas (%)
Degree of competition			
Very high	57	48	11
Average or low	39	36	3
All workplaces	**48**	**42**	**7**

Source: Adapted from Culley et al. (1999, p. 118)

rest of the chapter focuses on selected studies that have explored the association between HR strategy and organizational performance.

REFLECTIVE QUESTION

Identifying 'best practices' is a critical issue in HRM benchmarking. If you were involved in an HRM benchmarking exercise, how would you define or identify what constitutes 'best practices'?

Demonstrating the human resource strategy–organization performance link

In the late 1990s, demonstrating that there was indeed a positive link between HRM and performance became *the* dominant research issue in the HRM field (Guest, 1997). Academics have been interested in understanding the effect of specific HRM practices for a long time. For example, the famous 'Hawthorne' studies in the mid-1920s (Chapter 4) identified job design practices that could affect worker performance, and 50 years later, Hackman and Oldham (1980) showed that redesigned work configurations could increase worker motivation. What is different in the renewed interest in understanding the link between HRM practices and performance, however, is that current research focuses on the impact, if any, of specific HRM practices or HR strategies on organization-level 'bottom-line' outcomes (Bamberger & Meshoulam, 2000; Phillips, 1996). Within this genre, debate has focused largely on the competing merits of 'best HR practice' (universalistic prescriptions) models and the 'best fit' (contingency) models (Storey, 2001). The review of studies informed by the universalistic thesis was undertaken in 1996 by Ichniowski and his colleagues and suggested there were potentially 'large pay-offs' when 'bundles' of best HR practices were adopted. Furthermore, the research by Betcherman and his Canadian colleagues (1994) provides new evidence on the subject. In this section, we review key studies to gain an understanding of the nature of the HRM–organization performance link and to assess the degree to which HR strategy may predict economic performance.

In an early study of coherent 'bundles' of HR practices or HR strategies, Arthur (1994) investigated the performance effects of two labour management taxonomies: 'control' (traditional personnel management) and 'commitment' (new HRM) in US mini-steel mills. His statistical regression results indicated that, at least in the context of a high-tech mass production plant, commitment-type HRM practices were associated with both lower scrap rates (an indicator of production quality) and a significantly lower number of labour hours per ton of steel (an indicator of labour efficiency) than control-type HRM practices (Arthur, 1994). In addition, Arthur found that *integrated*, and sets of, 'best' HRM practices had a greater impact than individual HRM practices. Arthur acknowledged that the HRM–performance linkage might be contingent on other contextual factors, such as the business strategy and technology, but concluded that HR strategy was associated with variations in organizational performance. Arthur's research, however, left major questions unanswered: What is the magnitude of the effect of HR strategy on economic outcomes? And how generalizable are the findings?

MacDuffie (1995) conducted a similar study with a large sample of multinational motor car assembly plants, suggesting that Arthur's (1994) findings could be generalizable at least to other manufacturing workplaces. MacDuffie's study provided an

HRM IN PRACTICE 13.3

HR 'CAN LOWER NHS DEATH RATES'

ZOË ROBERTS, *PEOPLE MANAGEMENT*, 2001, OCTOBER 11

There is a direct link between the quality of HR practices and patient mortality in the health service according to a startling research report, *Organisation, Management and Effectiveness in NHS Trusts*.

The research, which is completed but not yet published, found that the quality of HR initiatives had a significant impact on the level of patient care and mortality in hospitals.

'Our analysis found a strong relationship between aspects of HR management and death rates,' said Carol Borrill, researcher at the Aston Centre for Health Services Organisation Research, who carried out the report with colleague Michael West. 'The higher the levels of staff teamworking, training, development and appraisals, the lower the patient mortality.'

Andrew Foster, HR director for the NHS Executive, flagged up the importance of the results when he spoke at the AHHRM conference.

'Until now there has been no research that links current HR practices with a bottom-line output like patient mortality,' he told *PM*. 'The overall challenge for anyone involved in HR is to convince general man-

---

'We were pleased to find that ... staff working in teams experienced higher levels of innovation and lower levels of stress.'

---

agement of the value of people management. This study shows a demonstrable link between HR and output in the NHS and I consider it to be the strongest weapon in my locker.'

Foster is compiling a five-year plan for HR in the NHS that will have a high-profile launch

next year on the 54th anniversary of the service.

'The plan will have a significant section that relates to evidence-based cases for HR in the boardroom – so research into HR and patient mortality will be included in this,' Foster said. 'With a fixed budget you need an evidence-based case for investment in people issues.'

Despite research linking people management and productivity, the range of outputs from the NHS has proved hard to measure. The researchers surveyed 81 hospitals over a period of two years and gathered information on the quality of HR initiatives and on performance data.

'We were pleased to find that the results were consistent with an earlier teamwork survey, which found that staff working in teams experienced higher levels of innovation and lower levels of stress,' Borrill said.

---

insight into the 'internal fit' or contingency theory, that is, how bundles of work and HR practices support, or fail to support, one another. Although a specific HR practice may be associated with increased organizational performance, the largest effects are obtained when complementary HR practices and technology are grouped into internally consistent clusters. In a later publication, Frits and MacDuffie (1996) provided further support for the 'internal fit' perspective, suggesting that when teamworking and complementary HR practices are introduced simultaneously, 'not only does new work practice induce an incremental improvement in performance, but so do the complementary practices' (Frits & MacDuffie, 1996, p. 428). This is shown in Figure 13.7.

When a new work practice, such as the self-managed work team, is introduced, the greatest impact on performance over a period of time will occur when a complementary bundle of HR practices accompanies the new work regime (line B). If, however, no complementary HR practices have been established, the only improvement in performance is caused by the new work practice per se (line A). Various complementary HR practices have been associated with teamworking, including the hiring of 'team

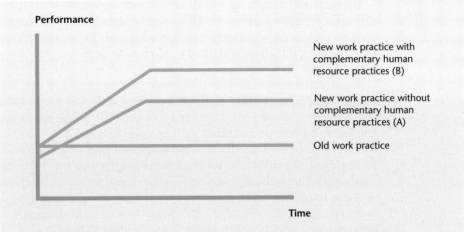

Figure 13.7 Performance implications of complementary human resource practices
Source: Adapted from Frits & MacDuffie (1996, p. 428)

players', extensive formal training, rewards systems and a leadership style that encourages cooperation and informal work-related learning. Despite these important findings, the studies by MacDuffie (1995) and Frits and MacDuffie (1996) were limited in that they focused on 'intermediate' variables such as productivity and quality, rather than on overall financial outcomes, and were unable to measure the magnitude of the effect of HR strategy on the organization's financial bottom line (Bamberger & Meshoulam, 2000).

Huselid's (1995) study responded to these limitations and attempted to estimate how greatly the HR strategy impacted on the organization's financial bottom-line outcome. In his study, Huselid (1995) determined that so-called 'high-performance' HR practices had two major dimensions. The first dimension referred to worker skills, which included various practices to enhance workers' knowledge, skills and abilities (for example formal and informal learning). The second dimension referred to worker motivation, which included practices recognizing and reinforcing desirable worker workplace behaviours (Table 13.4).

Table 13.4 The two dimensions of high-performance human resource practices

Worker skills and internal processes	Employee motivation
Information-sharing	Performance appraisals to determine pay
Job analysis	Performance to determine promotion
Internal hiring	Qualified applicants per positions
Regular attitude surveys	
Quality of work–life programs	
Participation teams	
Profit-sharing	
Training	
Formal grievance procedures	
Employment tests for hiring	

Source: Huselid (1995)

Drawing data from a sample of nearly 1000 establishments, Huselid found strong support for the positive effects of 'commitment' or 'high-performance' HR practices on both intermediate individual worker outcomes (for example turnover and productivity) and organizational financial outcomes. In particular, HR practices were significantly related to lower employee turnover and higher productivity and corporate financial performance. In practical terms, Huselid indicated that a 1 standard deviation increase in each HRM subsystem practice scale was found to raise net sales per employee in a single period by nearly 16 per cent of the mean sales generated per employee. With respect to financial outcomes, a similar 1 standard deviation increase was found to be associated with a per-employee gain in annual accounting profits of $3,814. Huselid's study also provides some insight into the 'fit' perspective. His findings suggest that although *internal* fit – the degree to which complementary HR practices are implemented as a cluster – does have a significant and positive effect on financial outcomes, *external* fit – the degree to which HR strategy is aligned with business strategy – does not (Bamberger & Meshoulam, 2000).

Since Huselid's research, an increasing number of studies have investigated the relationship between clusters of HR practices and organizational performance. Delery and Doty (1996), for example, identified seven strategic HR practices that have been linked to organizational performance: internal career opportunities, training, results-orientated appraisals, profit-sharing, employment security, participation and job descriptions. They found that 'differences in HR practices are associated with rather large differences in financial performance' (Delery & Doty, 1996, p. 825). In another study of the HR strategy–organization performance among manufacturing businesses, Youndt et al. (1996) measured what they considered to be the most recognized areas of HRM: staffing practices, training practices, performance appraisals and compensation systems. When these HR practices were combined into two indexes – labelled the administrative HR system and the human-capital-enhancing HR system – they found that HR practices impacted positively on organizational performance when the HR practices were aligned with the organization's business strategy.

Delaney and Huselid (1996) studied the impact of HRM practices on perceptions of organizational performance. Their findings suggest that, 'progressive HRM practices, including selectivity in staffing, training, and incentive compensation, are positively related to perceptual measures of organizational performance' (Delaney & Huselid, 1996, p. 965).

Reviewing US research on the HRM–organization performance link, Ichniowski et al. (1996) concluded that the empirical evidence of intra-industry studies, on steel-making, automobile assembly, apparel manufacture and metal-working, showed that high-performance work configurations and complementary bundles of HRM practices gave rise to superior output and quality performances, and that the magnitude of these performance effects was 'large'.

Betcherman et al.'s (1994) analysis, using data generated from Canadian companies, is consistent with the conclusion drawn by Ichniowski and his colleagues. The Canadian study found a statistically significant association between the new HRM approach and unit costs, regression analysis confirming that organizations operating under more strategic and participation-based HRM models experienced outcome trends that were superior to those seen in organizations operating a traditional employment model (see Table 13.2 and Figure 13.5 above). This survey-based study provided evidence that new HRM practices operate best in certain workplace 'environments'. The more intangible corporate 'ideology' variables – 'progressive decision-making' and 'social responsibility' – appear to be having a more significant impact on performance outcomes than are team-based programmes or incentive-pay plans. The results suggest that, 'innovative [HRM] practices and programs on their own are not enough to substantially improve performance. What seems more important is that they be introduced into a supportive work environment' (Betcherman et al., 1994, p. 72). This conclusion is consistent with Ichniowski et al.'s (1996, p. 322, emphasis added) main hypothesis that:

> There are no one or two 'magic bullets' that are *the* work practices that will stimulate worker and business performance. Work teams or quality circles alone are not enough. Rather, *whole systems* need to be changed.

HRM WEB LINKS

Go to www.pfdf.org/leaderbooks/121/index.htm1#spring98 for an article by Jeffrey Pfeffer which demonstrates that a 'high-commitment' HR strategy results in positive economic returns.

Looking to European studies, Cully et al.'s (1999) national survey measured *perceived* workplace performance but did not quantify the impact of HR strategy on organizational outcomes. Addison et al. (2000) demonstrated that employee involvement (EI) could be effective in increasing labour productivity and a firm's profits. Using data from Britain and Germany, Addison et al. examined the effects of different EI vehicles on organizational performance, as well as investigating the mediating influence of trade unions. The primary measure of profits is the organization's subjectively assessed relative financial performance, and that of organizational surplus is labour productivity. Addison et al.'s (2000) findings suggest that, in unionized workplaces, the level of EI will be negotiated between the management and unions, and profits will be lower than the maximum. Furthermore, the link between EI and financial performance in unionized workplaces is likely to be less clear-cut because EI arrangements reflect union power rather than a competitive response to external factors. Addison et al.'s report also predicts that EI in non-union regimes in Britain will 'work' and show positive economic results for the firm, but the union–EI nexus is associated with negative outcomes. Finally, the German evidence indicated that mandatory EI is associated with higher productivity in larger organizations (employing more than 100 workers) and lower productivity gains in smaller workplaces.

Despite these interesting findings, Addison et al.'s study has limited value in demonstrating the link between HR strategy and performance because it examined only one HR practice and did not quantify the effect of coherent clusters of HR practices on overall organizational performance. The results therefore need to be read with some caution. As Huselid (1995, p. 641) noted, to the extent that any single HR practice reflects an organization's wider propensity to invest in such HR practices, 'any estimates of the firm-level impact of the particular practice will be upwardly biased'. In other words, the sum of these individual measures may significantly overstate their contribution to the financial bottom line. Furthermore, as with all studies, the footnotes should be read. The British dataset is the 1990 Workplace Industrial Relations Survey (Millward et al., 1992), and the German data were collected using a survey of over 1000 establishments and selected interviews in 1994. In addition, as with earlier studies, no 'hard' financial data were collected – profit being measured subjectively – to allow a comparison of HR practices and economic performance. Also, others have noted (Cully et al., 1999) that the concepts of labour productivity and value added have meaning, but there are no standardized measures that allow a comparison of operating performance indicators. This problem of non-standardized measures of labour productivity makes international comparison at best problematic. In addition, perceptual measures of firm performance often result in respondents overstating the performance of their workplace (Cully et al., 1999). Finally, the study was unable to control for response bias; in simple terms, the researchers were unable to deal with the possibility that more successful establishments were systematically more likely to adopt EI strategies.

Buyens and De Vos (2001) conducted a qualitative study to measure the added value of the HR function as perceived by managers in Belgian organizations. The objective of the study was to investigate how the value of the HR function was perceived by three groups of managers – top managers, HR managers and line managers – within the sample of 256 organizations. Qualitative data were gathered through interviews, focus groups and a questionnaire. The researchers asked the different groups of managers to describe how they saw the value added of HR practices. Buyens and De Vos (2001) found that, for 'top managers', the HR function added value through its change programmes following restructuring and 'downsizing'. HR managers, on the other hand, most frequently mentioned 'management of the employee' as the area in which the HR function delivered value to the organization. The findings suggested that line managers had 'a rather traditional view of the HR function' (Buyens and De Vos, 2001, p. 81) because a majority most frequently mentioned functional HR activities such as selection and training as the domain in which the HR function added value. Buyens and De Vos concluded (2001, p. 81) that: 'the HR function can deliver value within different areas, ranging from administration to strategy formulation'. The researchers acknowledged that the data were 'highly subjective in nature' and that the findings might be contingent on other factors such as size or industry. Moreover, the study was unable to quantify the magnitude of the value added of the HR function.

STUDY TIP

Evaluating the value added of different HR strategies means having a good appreciation of research designs, HR measurements and the approaches to evaluating HR practices. Obtain a copy of Buyens and De Vos's (2001) article. What research design do the authors use? How do they seek to measure the value added of HR? Drawing on the material in this chapter, what are the strengths and weaknesses of the study?

An examination of the more recent empirical research reveals that the measurement of the value added of HR strategy and individual HR practices across studies is not consistent. This is a serious problem, and the development of reliable and valid measures of HR strategic practices is needed to advance research (Ichniowski et al., 1996). Moreover, the notion of what constitutes 'superior performance' needs to be disaggregated, and, in order to gain a meaningful insight into what 'performance' means, the researcher and practitioner need to be able 'compare and contrast performance measures at a variety of individual and organizational levels' (Truss, 2001, p. 1146). With these limitations in mind, recent studies, especially in the US literature, have consistently pointed to the positive effects of HRM practices. The upshot is that organizations implementing a package of internally consistent and mutually rein- forcing HRM practices experience significant improvements in performance. This suggests, however, an apparent paradox. If the pursuit of identifiable 'soft' HRM prac- tices leads to improved organizational performance, one would, from the perspective of 'economic rationality', expect such practices to be more widely used. This apparent paradox may result from the long-term investment costs associated with the resource- based approach to strategic HRM and the pressure on individual managers to achieve short-term financial results.

REFLECTIVE QUESTION

What do you think of this line of argument? If, indeed, 'high-commitment' HR strate- gies significantly improve overall company performance, why does a relatively small proportion of workplaces adopt such an HR strategy?

● ## Theorizing the human resource management–performance link

Although most HRM models provide no clear focus for any test of the HRM– performance link, it is commonly assumed that an alignment of organizational strategy and HRM strategy will improve organizational performance and competitive- ness. How, therefore, can the positive association between HR strategy and organiz- ational performance be explained? The resource-based strategic HRM model assumes a simple causal chain of 'soft' HRM policies of empowerment and learning–employee commitment–synergy–improved organizational performance (Guest, 1997, 2000). This 'involvement–commitment cycle' is the reverse of the vicious circle of control organizational theorists discussed in the early 1980s.

A core assumption of this approach is that committed workers are more productive. Thus, according to Beer et al. (1984, p. 19): 'Increased commitment can result not only in more loyalty and better performance for the organization, but also in self-worth, dignity, psychological involvement, and identity for the individual.' Arthur (1994, p. 673) justified his results on the HRM–performance link by drawing upon behavioural-control theory, and argued that by:

> Setting up a formal participation mechanism, and providing the proper training and rewards, a commitment system can lead to a highly motivated and empowered work force whose goals are closely aligned with those of management. Thus the resources required to monitor employee compliance … can be reduced. In addition, employees under these conditions are thought to be more likely to engage in organizational citi- zenship behaviors, non-role, unrewarded behaviors that are believed to be, nonetheless, critical to organizational success.

Strategic HRM theorists have argued that the HRM contribution to organizational outcomes is a function of three interrelated processes. First, HR strategy, through poli- cies, programmes and practices, shapes the human capital base. Second, HR strategy influences the degree to which the organization is able 'to exploit this human capital base' in terms of worker motivation to maximize the full potential of human capital.

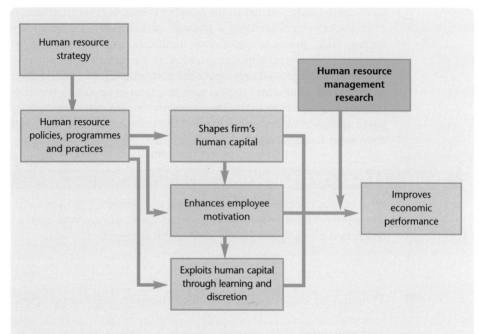

Figure 13.8 A general theory of the human resource management–organization performance link

Third, HR strategy enhances organizational performance by influencing the degree to which motivated and gifted workers are provided with the opportunity and the means to contribute to operational decision-making (Bamberger & Meshoulam, 2000). These three interrelated processes are shown in Figure 13.8.

As we discussed in Chapter 2, strategic HRM theorists have argued that underlying the assumed HRM strategy–performance processes are a number of well-grounded organizational behaviour theories (Bamberger & Meshoulam, 2000). Organizational behaviour theory (Wright & McMahan, 1992) explains the effects of HR strategy on human capital in that it posits that intellectual assets may be enhanced through HRM workplace learning strategies. Furthermore, agency theory (Eisenhardt, 1989) explains the effects of HR strategy on worker motivation by arguing that HR practices may be used to align better the interests of workers with those of management. In addition, control theory (Snell, 1992) explains the effect of HR strategy on the opportunities for worker contribution to decision-making in that certain HR practices (for example teamworking, quality circles and joint consultation arrangements) provide for greater EI in organizational governance. One empirical study, for example, found that EI arrangements increased the economic performance of firms because of the 'creativity' of labour–management discussions (Freeman & Lazear, 1995). Figure 13.8 also demonstrates the critical role of research in the development, implementation and evaluation of effective HR strategy and individual HR practices. Central to the model is the notion that HRM research is required to monitor and evaluate the effectiveness of HR strategy in order to ensure its contribution and value added to the organization. Despite advances in empirical research, our understanding of the nature of the HRM–organizational performance link is still, however, limited (Truss, 2001).

Chapter summary

- We began this chapter by offering some quotes from HRM practitioners and by reviewing some of the literature which argues that the HRM function is going through a transition, one in which the evaluation of HRM is being recognized as both fundamental and necessary.

- We have suggested that, in an increasingly competitive environment and with HR specialists playing a role in the strategic planning process, those in charge of organizations are demanding accountability on the part of all functional areas, including the HR department. Identifying the extent of the alignment of organizational and HR strategies and developing HR practices to improve 'fit' requires the measurement and evaluation of HR practices.

- The issue is whether HR professionals are capable of demonstrating their contribution and value added to other members of the management team in a quantifiable way and of providing useful data and information that clearly indicate the outcomes of HR strategy in a meaningful manner comparable with those of other organizational departments. This of course requires that sound, ongoing evaluation be carried out, the results being reported and communicated throughout the organization.

- We have examined different ways of demonstrating the value added of HRM in terms of level of measurement, different research designs and evaluation techniques. Although these topics have been discussed separately, they are of course closely connected. We have also discussed the limitations of the research. For Legge (2001, p. 31), for example, much of the research on the HR high-commitment–firm performance link 'is at best confused and, at worst, conceptually and methodologically deeply flawed'. Our intent is to help the reader make sense of research, and to critique and evaluate published research in the strategic HRM genre.

- The chapter examined the possibility of measuring individual, team and organization-level variables. Major research designs for investigating HR strategy–performance links include surveys, case studies, experimental studies and meta-analysis. Turning to evaluation, we examined statistical evaluation, financial evaluation and the use of HR audits and benchmarking when evaluating HR systems.

- Despite the methodological challenges associated with demonstrating the HR strategy and the organization–performance link, the different research designs, both quantitative and qualitative, and the limitations of the research, there is now a substantive body of literature demonstrating that HR strategy and practices can and do make a positive impact on a variety of organizational outcomes.

- A major challenge for HRM researchers is to continue not only to examine the value added of different HR strategies, but also to predict the magnitude of the value added of the HRM function for organizational outcomes more accurately and to make their research results meaningful to HR practitioners.

Key concepts

- Epistemology
- Experimental research
- HRM auditing
- HRM benchmarking

- HR measurement
- Qualitative research
- Research design
- Return on investment

Chapter review questions

1. What forces are driving the added value movement in the field of HRM?

2. To what extent do you agree or disagree with the statement that 'The least important HR practices are measurable, while the most important HR practices are not.' Discuss.

3. Explain the statement that 'all evaluation methods require the measurement of some set of variables'.

4. What are the strengths and weaknesses of (a) the survey approach and (b) the case study approach to HRM research?

5. How effective is the HR audit for measuring an HR strategy's contribution to the financial 'bottom line' of a company?

6. How can the effect of HR strategy on organizational performance be explained?

Further reading

Buyens, D., & De Vos, A. (2001). Perceptions of the value of the HR function. *Human Resource Management Journal*, **11**(2) 2, 70–89.

Fitz-enz, J., & Davison, B. (2002). *How to measure human resources management* (3rd edn). New York: McGraw-Hill.

Legge, K. (2001). Silver bullet or spent round? Assessing the meaning of the 'high commitment management'/performance relationship. In J. Storey (ed.), *Human resource management: A critical text* (pp. 21–36). London: Thomson Learning.

Nutley, S. (2000). Beyond systems: HRM audits in the public sector. *Human Resource Management Journal*, **10**(2), 21–38.

Truss, C. (2001). Complexities and controversies in linking HRM with organizational outcomes. *Journal of Management Studies*, **38**(8), 1121–49.

Practising human resource management

Searching the web

On an individual basis, or working in a small group, pick two or three on-line HR-related websites (e.g. www.jiscmail.ac.uk/lists/industrial-relations-research.html, www.shrm.org/hrlinks, www.labour-travail.hrdc-drhc.gc.ca//index.cfm/doc/english, www.fdmmag.com/articles/03aco.htm, www.hrreporter.com or www.peoplemanagement.

co.uk). Search for articles on evaluating HRM and the HRM–performance link. Based on your search:

1. list the research methods used, for example survey or case study, and the use of financial evaluation measures (for example ROI)
2. list the HR practices investigated
3. identify and discuss the factors that are encouraging the movement towards a value-added approach to HRM.

Bring this information to class and present your findings in an oral report.

HRM group project

Form a group of three or four students. The purpose of this group assignment is to gain a better understanding of the HR audit and/or the benchmarking process. Specifically:

1. Contact the HR department of one organization that conducts HR audits or HR benchmarking and is willing to discuss its auditing or benchmarking process with members of the group.
2. Design a series of questions to learn about the auditing or benchmarking process. In particular, be sure to gather information concerning each of the steps in the two processes outlined in the chapter. For example, describe the scope of the audit and identify what to benchmark (see Figure 13.4).
3. Analyse the results of your interviews. What conclusions can you make about the auditing or benchmarking process, and what conclusions can you make about the organization's HR department?

Each group member should take responsibility for researching the various aspects of the assignment. Present your findings to your class. For further information on benchmarking and 'best practices', go to www.human-resources.org.

Chapter case study

ALPHA HOTEL

Alpha Hotel is an exclusive all-season resort located in the Canadian Rockies, 90 minutes' drive west of Calgary. The hotel employs over 1100 employees during the winter skiing season and during the peak summer months. The HR department does its own recruitment and selection, administration of pay and benefits, customer-service training, supervisory leadership training programmes and relations with the trade union covering the non-managers.

Andrew Bellamy, the newly appointed hotel manager, has received a mandate to ensure that Alpha Hotel remains a destination of choice for Japanese and European tourists, and to reduce operating costs without jeopardizing the hotel's strategic goal. After attending an executive management workshop on 'Accountability in human resource management', Andrew Bellamy added this item to the agenda for the next management meeting. The following table showing indices of HRM effectiveness in North American major hotels was attached to the agenda.

Table 1 Indices of human resource management effectiveness in North American hotels

Index	Hotels (n=2400)
Customer satisfaction	4.39
Overall productivity	3.99
Employee commitment	2.35
Employee satisfaction	4.01
Grievance rate	2.01
Absenteeism	4.20
Turnover	5.09

Note: All items are measured on a scale of 1 = very low; 6 = very high

At the monthly senior management meeting, individual reaction to Andrew's contribution included the following. Amy Finley, the assistant general manager, made a strong case for outsourcing the work of the HR department. Her final comment to the management team was: 'It's HR's job to demonstrate that it can do the work better and more cheaply than any other source. If it can't, then we should outsource the HR function.'

Rowena Phillips, the front-desk manager, did not argue strongly for outsourcing the HR function but asked a number of questions: 'Does HR follow "best practices"?' 'How do their programmes help to reduce our operating expenses?' 'How does our HR function compare with that of our main competitors?'

Ron Levine, the food services manager, was neutral but commented that the 'Wine appreciation course' for restaurant servers delivered in November by HR staff had been 'a great success', adding 'the wine sales increased substantially in the following 3 months over the Christmas period because the servers were able to "up-sell" the wine.' Ron went on to give some details on the design and delivery of the three 1-day wine appreciation workshops. The total direct cost for the three workshops was $6,000. The indirect cost included the wages paid to the 60 servers (servers being paid $9 per hour) to attend the training. Wine sales increased by $23,000 per month in the high season between December and February.

Jean Marlow, the HR manager, agreed that it would be helpful to know the value added of her department but went on to say that 'Evaluating the contribution of HR programmes to the hotel's financial bottom line is too difficult and too time-consuming.'

Assignment

As corporate vice president of HR for Alpha Hotels Inc., you must persuade Jean Marlow of the merits of measuring the HR contribution and demonstrate the value of the HR function to the Alpha Hotel management team. Describe some of the things you would do to demonstrate the value added of the HRM department and its work to the organization, making sure that its accomplishments are presented in language that is convincing to the other managers. State whether you would suggest conducting an HR audit or benchmarking to demonstrate the value added of the HRM department to the hotel. Be sure to justify your recommendations.

HR-related skill development

A work-based learning intervention programme presents an overview of the learning activity that the manager or HR specialist is proposing to undertake. It should tell the reader why the work-based learning intervention is necessary, what costs are involved and how it will benefit the organization. In essence, the work-based learning intervention proposal underscores the whole notion of accountability in HRM.

Many managers, however, lack the basic knowledge and skills to craft such a proposal. To help you to develop this important management skill and to give you the experience of writing a work-based learning intervention proposal, we have devised a realistic case study that requires you to demonstrate your understanding of ROI. You can participate, at either individual or group level, in the exercise and develop an important HR skill by going to www.palgrave.com/business/brattonandgold and clicking on 'Learning intervention proposal'.

Notes

1. Paul Juniper, President, HRP Associate of Ontario, Canada, 'President's Message'. *HR Professional*, February/March, 2003, p. 9.
2. Michael Ford, President of the HR Institute of Alberta, quoted by Terrence Belford, HR focusing on how it can add value, *Globe and Mail*, 2002, March 25, p. B11.
3. Tim Epps, Vice President, People Systems for Saturn Corp., quoted by J. Phillips (1996). *Accountability in human resource management*, Houston, TX: Gulf Publishing.
4. Peter Drucker, How to measure white-collar productivity, *Wall Street Journal*, 1985, November 26, p. 28 and quoted by Phillips (1996, p. 5).

Chapter fourteen

Conclusion: Whither HRM?

John Bratton and Jeffrey Gold

'Instead of accepting the "superior wisdom" of experts, patients/customers/clients increasingly look upon those experts with a critical eye.'[1]

'International bureaucrats – the faceless symbols of the world economic order – are under attack everywhere.'[2]

'The idea of the "knowledge economy" appears to place the fundamentals of human resource management onto an entirely new footing.'[3]

'The use of global HR networks is becoming critical.'[4]

Chapter outline

Chapter objectives

After studying this chapter, you should be able to:

1. Describe the different ways in which the preceding chapters relate to one another

2. Explain the professional standing of those practising human resource management (HRM)

3. Assess how HRM practice and theory is regarded by others

4. Understand some possible scenarios for the future of HRM

Introduction

For nearly 20 years, the term 'human resource management' has been used to conceptualize a particular approach to managing the employment relationship and, frequently, as a contrast to 'personnel management'. We started this journey into HRM by examining its evolution and examined some of the theoretical models used in its study. It was acknowledged that all activity involving the management of the employment relationship, whether termed HRM or personnel management, involved ambiguity, tension, uncertainty and possible contradiction and paradox. In Part One of the book, we emphasized that HRM views the workforce as the most important asset for generating value, which gives organizations a potential, sustainable competitive advantage. We pointed out that, starting from this premise, HRM decisions and practices impact on strategic goals and need to be integrated into the organization's strategy. We also emphasized in Part Two that there is a range of external and internal contextual factors that impact and shape HR strategy and practices, organizational form and work experience. In Part Three, we endeavoured to describe and evaluate a range of HR practices used to motivate, develop and maximize the inherent potential of the workforce. Finally, we examined the pressure to evaluate the contribution of HRM and the growing body of research that seeks to measure the HRM–organizational performance link. The purpose of this chapter is to reflect on the major landmarks visited along the journey and attempt to draw general conclusions about HRM, and its current and future status, against the background trends in European and global capitalism.

The complexities, interdependencies and particularities of national experiences and organizational needs make the task of predicting the future an heroic, some may say foolhardy, challenge. The evidence gathered in the preceding chapters points, however, to a number of developments during the 1980s and 90s and into the 2000s that have affected the practice of HRM and are likely to continue. We will begin by assessing the current status of HRM, with particular reference to the notion that HRM and those engaged in its practice have secured a recognized professional status, especially within British management. We will also consider whether such a status is concomitant with particular approaches to policy and practice, that is, whether HRM professionals are recognized as being sufficiently expert by others in the workplace to influence organizational life in a particular way. For example, what status do other managers give to HRM, and what is the voice of the recipients of HRM activity? We will then consider some of the current trends and suggest a number of future possibilities for managers and HR specialists.

Professional status

Professional recognition is highly valued in Western orientation, and throughout the 20th century, the number of people engaged in professional work has steadily increased. In the UK, for example, the National Skills Task Force (2000) suggested a 50 per cent increase in the number of professional workers from 1981 to 1998, with a forecast of a further 20 per cent up to 2009. Not all professionals are, however, the same, some clearly being more powerful than others or making claims in support of a powerful influence. For practitioners in a field of professional work institutions, the professional associations usually advance such claims, the strength of which symbolize the status and power of the particular profession. In HRM (and personnel),

Table 14.1 An ideal type of professionalism

Friedson's ideal type of professionalism criteria	Human resource management (HRM) in the UK
Specialized work that is grounded in a body of theoretically based, discretionary knowledge and skill that is given special status	Cross-disciplinary theoretical underpinning for all human resource (HR) activities and ongoing attempts to improve practice. Dissemination of developments in knowledge via journals, conferences, electronic media and so on. No unified HRM theory, debates existing over whether such a theory can ever be formed. Generally low status at strategic levels of decision-making. Emerging evidence of high commitment/performance from HR activities, and the trend towards knowledge production and management could enhance status
Exclusive jurisdiction created and controlled by occupational negotiation	Continuing debates regarding who practises HRM – HR function or line manager responsibility? Specialized practice of some techniques. Considerable growth of the Chartered Institute of Personnel and Development (CIPD)[5] with chartered status since 2000. However, exclusivity not yet achieved; there is no regulation of a licence to practise
A sheltered position with labour markets based on the qualifying credentials of the occupation	CIPD does not regulate the point of entry for HR practitioners. Movement into HR may frequently occur through internal promotion. Growing requirement for CIPD qualifications, and the professional journal, *People Management*, is a key location for HR recruitment. Variegated character of HRM prevents total sheltering
A formal training programme to provide qualifying credentials	CIPD Professional Qualification Scheme delivered throughout the UK. National standards regulate overall content at three levels – support, practitioner and advanced practitioner. Growing number of Masters degree programmes in HRM and related areas, usually delivered by academic HRM departments
An ideology that asserts a commitment to doing good-quality work	CIPD code of professional conduct for members with internal disciplinary procedures for malpractice. Expulsion from the CIPD is possible, but this could not prevent a continuation of practice

2000 saw the creation of the Chartered Institute of Personnel and Development (CIPD), following an earlier merger between the Institute of Training and Development and the Institute of Personnel Management (IPM). Although the new title suggests something of a compromise, the merger did reflect an attempt to enhance the status of practitioners and espouse an approach to practise that we would call HRM.

In Chapter 1, we discussed the change from 'personnel' to 'HRM'. To some, this change represented the use of a new label and emphasized the limited and piecemeal diffusion of the HRM style, with only islands of innovation in HRM. The sustainability of the HRM paradigm was also questioned. One set of perspectives therefore emphasizes the superficial nature and continuities of managing the employment relationship. For others, the changes represented a transformation of how people could and should be managed at work. This set of perspectives emphasized the differences between the stereotyped personnel and human resources (HR) models. Whereas personnel management evoked images of 'welfare' professionals interfering with and hindering the line manager, of reactive 'fire-fighting' management and of submitting to militant shop stewards, HRM emphasized strategic integration and the HR professional as a member of the senior management team, strategic planning and proactive management. It is the latter image that the CIPD seeks to promote, but what are the key elements of professional work and status, and how do HR professionals match such requirements?

According to Dietrich and Roberts (1997, p. 16), the starting point for professional work is the existence of clients facing complex issues and problems related to decision-making complexity where such clients are 'incapable of pre-thinking all the issues involved with a decision because of the complexities involved'. This provides for the 'economic basis' of professionalism. Through their possession of specialist knowledge and skills, which is based on a particular kind of education and training, professionals make claims that they will help their clients to tackle and solve the problems they face. Continuing and successful practice allows a profession to acquire certain privileges that enhance its status and power. So how does HRM stack up? If we consider Freidson's (2001) notion of an ideal type of professionalism, a brief assessment can be made (Table 14.1).

In terms of representing a profession, HRM and its professional association, the CIPD, have clearly made significant advances in both the extent of influence of some of the main ideas and the size of the CIPD's membership. There remain, however, some interesting questions to consider. First, at the level of practice, do those with 'human resources' in their job title do anything different from personnel managers that might be considered an enhancement or a progression? Second, is there anything emerging that might help HR or personnel managers to improve their status in strategic discussions? Third, what is the response of those on the receiving end of HRM, that is, the employees and managers who are selected, rewarded, appraised, trained, and so on?

Human resource management: does it work?

To start to answer these questions, let us first consider the use of different job titles.

The growth in the number of organizations using 'human resources' within a job title of a specialist practitioner was one of the noticeable features of the 1998 Workplace Employee Relations Survey. Hoque and Noon (2001) drew on these survey data to evaluate differences between those companies which used 'personnel' in their job titles and those which used 'HR'. The findings suggested that HR specialists were more qualified and that employee development was more likely to feature in strategic plans, suggesting that they had a greater involvement in the design of plans. Of particular importance were the sophisticated practices associated with HRM, such as personality testing, the use of attitude surveys and off-the-job training; these were more likely to be found in organizations with an HR specialist. In conclusion, the authors suggested that the difference between 'HR' and 'personnel' did matter and that HR specialists were likely to be perceived as 'more credible professionals' (Hoque & Noon, 2001).

Moving to the second question above, that part of the credibility for HR professionalism might be concerned with an involvement in strategic planning will hearten many advocates of an HRM approach. Indeed, since its first appearance in the US in the 1980s, the importance of a strategic connection and integration of key HR activities with strategy has been the distinguishing feature of HRM compared with personnel management (Purcell, 2001). Since that time, the ongoing research we examined in Chapter 13 appears to demonstrate that such a connection pays off. Such work is important in two ways with respect to the stature of HRM professionalism:

1. The research that demonstrates a positive association between strategic HRM and organizational performance adds to a body of theoretical knowledge that provides the foundation for professional status.
2. Such knowledge forms a repertoire of ideas and activities that serve to persuade others of the legitimacy of HRM.

Thus, HRM professionals are able to make claims about the efficacy of their involvement in strategic work on the basis of their expertise of a particular body of knowledge, and from such expertise flows authority and status (Middlehurst & Kennie 1997). In recent years, such claims have been strongly associated with a link between HRM (especially the 'high road' version; Chapter 1) and high-commitment/performance work and, if there is such a link, how this occurs. The 'breakthrough' studies reviewed by Ichniowski and his colleagues in the US and the work of Guest and others in the UK have been very important in this respect.

HRM WEB LINKS

Check the workplace reorganization, HRM and corporate performance website at www.bbk.ac.uk/manop/man/mgesrc.htm, from which you will be able to download various papers.

Some doubts, however, remain. First, if there has been a 'breakthrough' in terms of providing the evidence, any knowledge of the HRM–commitment/performance link seems to have fallen on deaf ears, as indicated by the surveys of Taylor (2002) and even Guest (2000). Particularly galling was the finding by Taylor (2002, p. 7) of little evidence of a 'coherent human resource management agenda'. It would seem that, in the UK, there is still some way to go before HRM professionals are able to make claims that have a persuasive appeal equal to that of marketing and finance.

Second, a number of writers (for example, Legge, 2001; Thompson & McHugh, 2002) continue to express doubts about the claims themselves. As we emphasized in Chapter 13, there are problems with measuring performance at work when worker outcomes need to be included. Furthermore, even when some link is made between HRM activities and outcomes, there can be no certainty of the direction of causality. A cluster of HRM practices may thus be introduced as the result of favourable profits or overall organizational performance. Legge (2001) goes on to highlight the complexity of any attempt to link HRM processes with organizational performance – however this is measured. Each organization has, for example, its own history, culture and experience, all of which influence in a unique way the choices and decisions that will be made. The accounting scandals in some prominent US corporations in 2002 further illustrate the difficulty of using valid and reliable organizational performance measurements.

Third, there are also a variety of views from those on the receiving end of HRM practices, covering job insecurity, work intensification and job-related stress. Mabey et al. (1998), in a collection of case studies, argue that the voice of such recipients has been underrepresented. They report workplace accounts of HRM interventions, providing compelling insights into employment relations and help us move away from the somewhat moribund academic debate on 'soft' versus 'hard' HRM models. The case studies affirm that significant changes have taken place at work under the guise of HRM. However, on the question of the delivery of HRM goals such as greater commitment and unified culture, Mabey et al. (1998, p. 237) conclude that, 'many of [HRM's] prized goals ... remain unproven at best, and unfulfilled at worst'. But not all is 'doom and gloom', the data also providing evidence that, in terms of benefits arising from HRM innovations, the benefits for the 'majority of participants' seem to 'outweigh the costs to the minority' (Mabey et al., 1998, p. 240).

Guest (1999) has also sought to evaluate employees' experiences of HRM, partly in response to criticisms from writers such as Legge.[6] In addition, he wanted to examine the particular influence of high-commitment/performance practices, which he felt was lacking in Mabey et al.'s (1998) study. Using data from an annual survey of a stratified random sample of 1000 workers in the UK, conducted by the CIPD to examine the state of the employment relationship, Guest (1999) found that progressive HR practices were consistent with positive outcomes such as feelings of fair treatment, security and satisfaction with the job and motivation. Guest's conclusion is that a 'large proportion of the UK workforce' seems to 'like' HR practices (Guest, 1999, p. 22), although he does acknowledge some of the limitations of the survey and the lack of evidence on strategic integration of the practices. As Nichols et al. (2002) observe, however, employee satisfaction surveys, claiming to reveal either positive or negative views of the work situation, are rating not simply management practices but also how workers perceive their own work situation relative to their local economic position, constraints and opportunities: everything cannot be reduced to management techniques. Furthermore, it is doubtful that the methodological difficulties outlined by Legge (2001) will have been satisfied.

At this point, we need to review what we have said about the nature of the employment relationship and address a number of issues that will help us to speculate on the future of HRM, while at the same time providing the reader with some analytical 'tools' for studying the HRM literature. Although change is a defining feature of the 'New Economy', the core characteristic of the *capitalist employment relationship* has not changed. As we first discussed in Chapter 1, a set of tensions revolves around the buying and selling of human resources and the indeterminate nature of workers' physical or intellectual 'efforts' in the labour process. In other words, the 'pay–effort bargain' is inherently conflict-prone because workers still predominantly seek to 'maximize' and employers to 'minimize' pay. The leverage of human knowledge and skill to generate value is in turn mediated by antagonistic employment relations and technological and organizational change, whereas the accumulation of profit is mediated by product markets and global competition. These sets of complex relationships create patterns of conflict, accommodation and cooperation and engender persistence in employment relations; they also cause minor and fundamental change.

Another feature of the employment relationship emphasized throughout this text relates to the notion of *paradox*. We do not wish to rehearse all the arguments in the previous chapters but instead to cite a few examples: selection instruments designed to identify individuals possessing 'team' traits while espousing the need for 'independent' and critical thinkers; work regimes that call for critical reflection, creativity and experimentation while insisting that workers maintain a 'zero defects' record; employee participation schemes to enhance productivity but exclude from any influential position the very people whom the formal participatory structure is supposed to empower; learning organizations claiming to emancipate workers but maintaining an electronic surveillance of operating procedures – computer-controlled autonomy (Bratton, 1992); reward systems that link pay and promotion to individual performance yet expect people to collaborate and share their knowledge and information with co-workers (ask your professor how this paradox may occur in a university setting). Managers often appear to be caught between two contradictory imperatives: regulating human endeavours too tightly undermines workers' leverage potential, whereas empowering workers undermines management control. We have assumed that paradox is inherent in HRM practices and organizational structures. By illustrating and explaining how various paradoxes in HRM are produced and reproduced, we hope to encourage a greater understanding of and sensitivity towards managing the employment relationship in the future.

In addition, we wish to draw attention to the need for an understanding of *historical trajectories* in our study of HRM.[7] The foregoing chapters have emphasized the historical development of HRM and its current practices, which reaffirm Storey's (2001, p. 6) argument that HRM emerged in the 1980s as 'a historically-situated phenomenon'. Whatever the claims of academics and practitioners to apparently 'new' HRM practices, most have deep historical roots: whether it is the 'discovery' of the importance of informal learning in the discourse on competitive advantage (recognized in the apprenticeship system of the Middle Ages); the 'discovery' that contract workers are less committed to the organization than permanent workers (well understood and documented by Niccolò Machiavelli in his book *The Prince*, written in 1513); the 'discovery' of the 'virtual' organization without face-to-face human activity with people working at home and connected through electronic networks (resembling key structural elements of the preindustrial 'putting-out' system); or the 'discovery' that 'social partnerships' are advantageous to management faced with uncertainty in product markets and global competition (as researched by the Committee of Inquiry on Industrial Democracy, chaired by Lord Bullock in 1977). Thus, most of the important practices that make up the 'new' HRM phenomenon are not all that new, and HRM is therefore a product of a set of complex forces at a particular point in the history of Western capitalism. In a field of management so variable and divergent, HRM cannot be understood in the context of simplistic linear models that expunge old practices and substitute new ones. Developments in HRM over the past decade may thus be seen as 'innovative' and as evidence of change, but at the same time, when viewed through a historical lens, there is a realization of déjà vu.

We also need to emphasize one of the main features of our treatment of HRM throughout the book, first discussed in Chapter 1: the need to understand the importance of differing '*standpoints*' in management theory. The two standpoints we have presented in this book are mainstream on the one hand, and critical on the other. An understanding that all aspects of managing the employment relationship can be investigated and interpreted from these different standpoints is an important analytical 'tool' for evaluating the diverse range of HRM literature and how differing standpoints produce contradictory claims and conclusions related to HRM. In this context, it will be legitimate to examine the recent growth of call centres from either the 'New Economy' or 'electronic sweatshop' perspective. A sensitivity to differing theoretical approaches to researching HRM therefore contributes to our ability to identify and understand the roots of apparent tensions, contradictions and paradoxes that pervade much of the literature on and experiences relating to HRM practices.

The three dimensional model of management we introduced in Chapter 1 (Figure 1.3) provides a framework for speculating on possible future directions for HRM. It shows that a complex set of external and internal factors, or 'contingencies', affect managerial behaviour. The external contingencies include the environment, strategy and the organization. The major external pressures affecting British business include globalization – the removal of barriers to free trade and the closer integration of national economies – national macroeconomic conditions, environmental standards and controls, technological change, national public policy changes such as employment legislation, and cultural changes. Two of the best-known, and most widely accepted, explanations of social change in terms of a dominant factor are the economic theory and the technological theory of change (Cohen, 1968). The economic theory of social change rests on the assumption that changes in product and labour markets, the 'infrastructure' of society, are the prime movers of change.

Some of the recent changes in the UK, Europe and the global economy we have documented in this book can be regarded as a 'transformation' (Millward et al., 2000). We expect many of these changes to continue for the foreseeable future. In spite of the fact that financial markets are massively destabilizing, inequality of income and wealth, both within countries and between the developed and developing world, has increased, a growing number of people around the world are rejecting a system whose logic either ignores or undervalues their humanity, and the risks facing the global environment are on a scale that is unprecedented, globalization is here to stay. The issue seems now to be how we can better manage globalization (Hutton & Giddens, 2000; Stiglitz, 2002).

There appears to be a growing consensus that globalization is not working for the stability of the world economy, for sustainable development (meeting the needs of the current generation without compromising the prospects for future ones) and for most developing countries and the world's poor (Stiglitz, 2002). This concern over the dysfunctional aspects of globalization is likely to continue to fuel the debate for greater government intervention in order to tackle societal problems of unemployment, inequality and pollution. The European Union (EU) is likely to play a pivotal role in reshaping globalization and international economic architecture (the International Monetary Fund, the World Trade Organization and the World Bank) on the international stage, and in Europe through European macroeconomic and regulatory policies. We consider that the prospect is for the EU to pursue economic stabilization and sustainable growth through an active macroeconomic policy. To avoid the 'race to the bottom' in employment and environmental standards, the EU will probably regulate the more self-destructive tendencies of markets, give more governance rights to trade unions and, given the ratification of the Kyoto Protocol, strengthen environmental standards, a role once undertaken by each nation-state (Kuttner, 2000). The EU will therefore come under increasing pressure to create a pan-European system of economic governance to temper globalization's extremes and make European capitalism economically efficient, equitable, ecologically sustainable and socially acceptable: globalization with a human face.

In the UK, the Labour government has continued to promote the discipline of the market to encourage the efficient allocation of goods and services – 'flexibility' in the employment relation – and has not sought to reverse the privatization of key sectors of the economy. In the wake of corporate corruption threatening financial markets and pension funds, the initiative for 'reinventing government' may, however, receive wider public support. The apparent renewed interest in the role of government makes economic models based on unfettered markets and privatization alone an unpalatable solution. Indeed, in Europe, North America and elsewhere, debate has fundamentally shifted because of the need to address issues of public transport, safe drinking water, pollution, unemployment and low-cost housing. The introduction of a statutory minimum wage, the European Works Council Directive and the Employment Relations Act 2002 in Britain will help to reverse the decline in union membership and will likely give unions more 'voice' in the workplace as well as in the public arena, where we expect these community issues will be vigorously debated.

The technological theory of social change is widely used to speculate on future changes in work organizations and society. Technology, especially information and communication technology (ICT), acts, it is argued, as a catalyst for change in organizations leading to new organizational forms, work and skill requirements. As we pointed out in Chapter 4, new organizational forms such as alliances, cross-organizational networks and multiemployer sites are emerging, with inevitable consequences for the employment relationship (Rubery et al., 2000). Furthermore, as the information age develops and the number of knowledge workers grows, what has been referred to as the 'post-bureaucratic organization' will continue to develop. Cyberspace will remove physical space requirements for meetings and decision-making. A new domain will open up for organizational activity, allowing for interaction with physical objects and human processes but possibly also bypassing them (Pearson, 1999, p. 415). Such changes will create new opportunities for complex decision-making with regard to the employment of people at work, which will impact on the employment relationship.

Developments in ICT may also strengthen and enhance the status of HR specialists, but there is nothing inevitable about this. Such technological change might threaten the position of HR specialists to act as specialist mediators of information who have the knowledge of how to access the right information and transform it into the knowledge that is required. Like all professionals, HR specialists rely on a mix of knowledge and skills that can be codified and recorded in abstract terms and also on knowledge that comes through application in complex situations. The latter is difficult to copy by non-specialists and relatively indeterminate. The former, however, can, through its codification, be made available to non-specialists. Thus, administrative HR work can be outsourced, and artificial intelligence expert systems can emulate expert problem-solving behaviour. If HR specialists are to preserve and develop their status, they will need to retain and develop their indeterminacy; expertise will not be enough.

ICT, of course, widens access to knowledge on a global scale and is also impacting on the composition and mobility of labour. Remote collaboration will need to be facilitated, international careers managed and performance controlled. Rather than concentrating on traditional administrative activities, which can be automated and outsourced, HR specialists in global firms can, however, step up and work more strategically. A recent survey of CIPD members in major international organizations found that, although 33 per cent of respondents were working in international transactions, and were therefore at risk of outsourced e-HR, two-thirds were working in capability and business development, often involving the creation of global HR networks, and usually at board level (Brewster et al., 2002).

Developments in ICT are also significant in the emergence of new fields of activity such as biotechnology and nanotechnology.[8] In both of these areas, knowledge and practice are rapidly expanding and will be leading industries over the next 10–20 years. They will produce new products and new ways of working across disciplines. As a study by Foresight (2000) suggested, much of the work will involve 'multi-disciplinary teams', which will require an ability to 'understand each other's "language", and future business and education strategies need to take account of the need to develop these teams' (Foresight, 2000, p. 4). HR professionals will need to consider their position in relation to emerging 'hybrid' professionals and the part they can play in cross-disciplinary teams.

Whatever the technological developments, HR professionals, like all other professionals, are faced with readjustments of personal and social values. There is a growing expectation of what experts can provide and deliver, accompanied by increased cynicism and a distrust of authority figures (Scase, 1999). Increased access to information will challenge the role of all professionals in assisting complex decision-making. However, the growth in knowledge-intensive organizations and the continued decline in low-skilled blue-collar employment are bound to create new challenges for the management of the employment relationship and therefore sufficient room for manoeuvre for those in HRM. We will now consider some of the possibilities.

It should be readily apparent from our discussion throughout this book that the issue of knowledge has become a pre-eminent consideration in any talk about the future. Managers look towards the achievement of knowledge-based organizations and have become increasingly attracted to the idea of knowledge management. We have already indicated in Chapter 10 how knowledge management, principally through the arguments of information systems professionals, superseded the idea of the learning organization – an HRM and human resources development notion. Over the next few years, what Scarbrough and Swan (2001, p. 8) refer to as the 'complex and intangible aspects of human behaviour' will need to be reconsidered in relation to the systems and technologies of knowledge management, and this will provide a considerable opportunity for HR specialists. For example, any idea concerned with the management of knowledge carries with it an assumption of the existence of knowledge and, in the context of changing circumstances, the production or making of new knowledge. We have identified that this is not without its difficulties, but it does highlight the importance of human beings as 'knowledge workers'[9] and emphasizes the value they bring to an organization. If, however, as suggested by Storey and Quintas (2001), it is assumed that knowledge workers will be more highly qualified and have an expectation for work that is autonomous and challenging, the knowledge they produce will be less easily captured and codified, a basic requirement for knowledge management systems.

REFLECTIVE QUESTION

You are likely to become a 'knowledge worker'. What are your expectations of how the knowledge you produce will be valued? How do you want to be managed?

The production of knowledge adds value to individuals and groups if it can be shared, and to organizations if it can be captured and utilized. Sharing is a primary process (Veng Seng et al., 2002). This requires certain physical structures, for example intranets and collaborative knowledge networks, and new roles such as that of 'chief learning and knowledge management officer' (Veng Seng et al., 2002,

p. 146) but just as important is the environment of support and trust for learning at work. An optimistic scenario is that of organizations in the future building learning into the ethos of practice, however dispersed, networked or fragmented the physical structure. In such a scenario, there is an inclusive approach to human resources development, technology and e-learning being used as vehicles to achieve learning (Gold et al., 2002).

The need for some kind of strategic HRM presence should be implied by our comments so far. Indeed, if there is to be a progression of knowledge management through learning that adds to the stock of 'intellectual capital', this provides too good an opportunity to miss with respect to developing meanings and measures of people's added value at work (Mayo, 2002). However, the automation of transaction work in HRM, its outsourcing and/or its devolution to line managers all provide some degree of threat to HRM specialists. Evidence presented by Truss et al. (2002) shows that, even if HR does not play a role in strategic management, people can still be managed strategically by others not in an HR role, in that they are recruited, deployed, motivated and managed with some link to a business plan. One scenario would see the threats as an opportunity for HR specialists to become more strategic and indeed encourage the removal of transaction work from its area of responsibility (Cunningham & Hyman, 1999).

Apart from a presence on the board or in the senior management team, how can HRM become strategic? Working with the 10 schools of strategy outlined by Mintzberg et al. (1998),[10] Purcell (2001) suggests that HRM would have most to gain by working with the configuration school, which sees strategy-making as a process of transformation in which an organization, according to the situation, adopts plans or positions to work with the existing configuration but also recognizes the need to transform, when appropriate, to reach a new configuration. For example, a life-cycle view of an organization can be taken, with a corresponding variation of strategy, and HR practices can be adapted to fit with circumstances. In this way, as patterns of configuration emerge over time, HR specialists need to work in coalition with others to achieve integration. Whatever strategic decisions need to be made, HRM is seen to be a necessary feature of implementation (Purcell, 2001).

Strategies to change or transform an organization from one configuration state to another highlight another opportunity for HRM: as that of change agent. This is not a particularly new role in HRM or personnel, but the pace of change in recent years, and unpredictable events such as the attacks on the US on 11 September 2001, serve to give it more prominence. Ulrich (1997, p. 31) sees competence in change management as 'the most important for success' for HRM professionals, and Caldwell (2001, p. 50) suggests that, as leaders of HR change, they can 'make a potentially decisive contribution to business success'. We would, however, go further. In recent years, there have been many attempts to transform organizations, for example culture change, business process re-engineering, manufacturing resource planning, enterprise resource planning and total quality management. All have left their mark on the organizational landscape, and all tend to fail to live up to their potential. In the UK, change often occurs in reaction to events with opportunistic implementation. Most models of change work with an image of the need to counteract resistance and use force to move from one state to another. Such models reflect the thinking of the past, based on machine-like images of organizational dynamics. In the 21st century, however, there are new versions of how change occurs in organizations, reflecting the influence of developments in such fields as chaos and complexity theory, postmodernism and critical management studies (see the HRM-related web links at the end of the chapter). Such developments often highlight the importance of people and their interests in the context of change and present the HRM professional with new and distinctive skills to master.

Profound and constant transformations have been characteristic of the world for over 200 years, especially during the second half of the 20th century (Hobsbawm, 1997), and we know that innovation and change impact on organizational strategy and have far-reaching implications for HRM. What concerns us in this final section, however, is why one HR strategy is favoured over another: why should firm A adopt a 'commitment HR strategy' and firm B adopt a 'traditional HR strategy' when both are in the same sector? This cannot be explained solely in terms of a lack of information on the relative merits of a learning-and-commitment-focused-strategy versus a cost-and-control-focused-strategy. There is an accumulation of empirical evidence confirming that investment in HR improves the financial 'bottom line', yet relatively few organizations have adopted a commitment HR strategy. This apparent disjuncture between knowledge and management practice, what others have referred to as a 'conundrum', is partly explained by Pfeffer's 'one-eighth rule'. First, 50 per cent of managers do not really believe that there is a connection between a commitment HR strategy and superior performance. The 50 per cent who do recognize a connection will, however, make only single changes rather than adopting a systemic strategic approach. And of the organizations that make comprehensive strategic changes, only 50 per cent will persist with the new strategy because of pressure for short-term results. Thus, 'since one-half times one-half times one-half equals one-eighth, at best a small fraction of organizations will actually do what is required to build profits by putting people first' (Pfeffer, 1998a, p. 29). In addition, however, we need to understand that HR strategies are context-bound and mediated by product markets, technological innovation and profit-making.

External contextual pressures affect organizations differently, and, as a result, organizations develop different business strategies across sectors, these in turn giving rise to different HR strategies. In some of the early literature on HRM, it was assumed that managers would automatically possess a bias towards innovation, but this assumption seems to be false. Capitalist enterprise has a bias only towards profitability. And, what is clear is that, in the area of HRM, there is a 'high road' to productive efficiency (high wages and high investment in people) as well as a 'low road' (low wages and low investment in people). In a capitalist economy, managers generally transform employment relations only if greater productive efficiency is to be gained using the new way than otherwise.

With globalization, areas of the world that regulate the labour market and have relatively high wages and healthy working conditions become vulnerable to the discipline of the global market in a general race to the bottom. A good example of this is the transfer of jobs from Canada and the US to Mexico, and from Mexico to China. Since the negotiation of the North American Free Trade Agreement, continuing pressure has been placed on high-wage manufacturing workers in Canada and the USA as companies have moved or threatened to relocate their operations further south. As a result, Mexico's manufacturing base has expanded, and the manufacturing wage level has increased to around CDN$1.50, considerably lower than the Canadian and US manufacturing wage level of around CDN$18 an hour. There is, however, evidence that American companies, some of whom are champions of HRM, are closing down their Mexican operations and moving to 'greener – that is, cheaper – pastures' in

China where the manufacturing wage level is 20–25 cents an hour (Greider, 2002, p. 30). As Kuttner (2000) correctly argues, global laissez-faire pulls business organizations into areas of the globe where there are people prepared to work for low wages and there are fewer regulations. This reality, of course, fuels the contrasting interpretations of trends in the New Economy: the 'knowledge thesis' (Albert & Bradley, 1997) versus the 'insecurity thesis' (Heery & Salmon, 2000).

In our analysis of strategic HRM, we emphasized that whether managers adopt a high-commitment HR strategy or a cost control HR strategy will depend upon the relative advantages of each vis-à-vis the 'master' strategy, and whether inherently political regulations and pressure from organized workers encourage a 'high road' approach to competitiveness. It follows logically from this premise that, when it comes to HR strategy, there is no 'universal' or 'one-best way', and the prediction that one HR strategy, generally assumed to be the 'high-commitment' HR strategy, would be widely adopted by organizations across the economy seems theoretically unsound given the complex dynamics operating in the global market. Put another way, if long-term profitability depends on the mobilization of human capital, and workers are seen as part of the solution rather than the problem, employers and managers are more likely to adopt a high-commitment HR strategy. On the other hand, the so-called New Economy still contains scores of industries in which the business plan relies heavily on a low-paid, low-skilled and tightly controlled workforce: 'McWork'. In such enterprises, employers and managers tend to view workers as part of the problem rather than the solution.

In reviewing the evidence, we consider that the prospect is for the continued diversity of HR strategies. Some organizations will adopt the 'high road' to economic competitiveness using human capital and a high-commitment HR strategy, whereas others will continue to use a 'low road' and a traditional HR strategy, and still more will use a combination of the various strategies for different occupational groups depending on the problems and opportunities confronting management. Thus, diversity of HRM has been the defining feature of UK organizations in the past, and this will probably continue in the future. The gains made by HR professionals during the 1990s cannot be guaranteed; professional power is not a naturally occurring feature of our world and should be regarded as contingent and ephemeral. Professional power and the influence of HR specialists will rise and fall depending on how well they predict and respond to changing external and internal forces that influence and shape organizational strategies, as well as on how competent they are at demonstrating the value added of HRM to their colleagues.

Our final point concerns the problem of shareholder value-driven capitalism and corporate leadership and rewards. Although some have suggested that the greatest challenge facing HRM professionals is an internal issue – identifying and using credible evaluation methods, and convincing senior and middle management that HR activities do contribute significantly to organizational goals – we would also agree with those observers who suggest that internal issues revolving around the use of stock options for chief executives, and rewards contingent upon meeting 'hard' short-term financial targets, serve to undermine HRM (Armstrong, 1989; Legge, 1995; Sisson & Storey, 2000; Storey, 1995a, 2001). In the aftermath of recent accounting-related scandals in some US companies, stock option abuses, self-obsessed chief executive officers and other nefarious activities, this issue is even more pressing. A high-skilled, learning-orientated, high-performance workplace is a long-term investment strategy. As long as chief executives are either unable or unwilling to invest in people because they have to meet short-term financial targets or wish to maximize their own inflated rewards from share options, the development and diffusion of long-term commitment HR strategies in UK workplaces, and with it the ability to leverage human knowledge, will continue to remain limited.

Final comment

Your journey through some theories and practices of HRM is now drawing to a close. Throughout this book we have emphasized diversity in both the theory and the practices, endeavoured to make the field more transparent and relevant through vignettes, web-based sources and case studies, and, through the use of discussion questions, study tips and reflective questions, encouraged independent thinking and critical inquiry. The time has now come to reflect on what you have learned from this journey.

Adult education scholars emphasize the need for reflectivity as a critical component of the learning process; reflection is like using a mirror to help us to look back on our actions and thought processes; reflective learning occurs where we have experiences and then step back from them to evaluate the learning we have experienced. There are several ways of carrying out reflection. One approach is systematically to go back through all that you have learned so far. Another approach, however, is to look at the additional reading listed at the end of each chapter. Other sources of information, particularly material that tends to differ with the approach taken in this textbook, provide mirrors for us and allow us to look at topics from another perspective. Furthermore, other people – friends, relatives and co-workers – provide mirrors for us, allowing us to understand HRM from another perspective, so talk to other people about the topics covered in *Human Resource Management: Theory and Practice*.

Finally, your own experience of work is excellent material for reflection and can provide insightful information on and understanding of HRM theory and practice. To help you start the reflection process, go back to the beginning of each chapter and consider whether you have personally achieved the major learning objectives.

Notes

1. Matzdorf et al. (1999, p. 94).
2. Joseph Stiglitz (2002, p. 3).
3. Storey and Quintas (2001, p. 345).
4. Brewster et al. (2002, p. 34).
5. The CIPD Membership Secretary reported a figure of 101,634 members in 2001, an increase of 50 per cent since 1996.
6. Guest highlights Karen Legge, Tom Keenoy and Hugh Willmott as being critical analysts of HRM.
7. We are indebted to Peter Sawchuk, University of Toronto, for his insight into historical trajectories and some of the historical links between HRM and informal learning. See Bratton et al., *Workplace Learning: A Guide for Students*, Garamond Press, 2003.
8. Biotechnology refers to a range of developments such as cell culture technology, DNA technology and protein engineering technology. Nanotechnology is concerned with controlling and manipulating matter at the level of atoms and molecules. Visit the Institute of Nanotechnology at www.nano.org.uk/.

9. There are inevitably ongoing debates about the categorization of the 'knowledge worker'. See Storey and Quintas (2001, p. 346).

10. The ten schools, grouped into three categories are:

   ■ *prescriptive:* design, planning, positioning

   ■ *process:* entrepreneurial, cognitive, learning, power, cultural, environmental

   ■ *fit:* configuration.

HRM WEB LINKS

Go to www.is.lse.ac.uk/complexity/default.htm for access to the Complexity Research Programme website at the London School of Economics. www.santafe.edu/ will take you to the Santa Fe Institute, a multidisciplinary research and education centre. Visit www.aom.pace.edu/cms/ for the home page of the Critical Management Studies Interest Group of the American Academy of Management, which has links to other resources.

Appendices

CHARTERED INSTITUTE OF PERSONNEL AND DEVELOPMENT

Code of professional conduct and disciplinary procedures

The CIPD code of professional conduct

The Chartered Institute of Personnel and Development (CIPD) is the professional association specialising in the management and development of people for the United Kingdom and the Republic of Ireland.

1 Mission

The mission of the Chartered Institute of Personnel and Development is:

1.1 to lead in the development and promotion of good practice in the field of the management and development of people, for application both by professional members and by their organisational colleagues

1.2 to serve the professional interests of members

1.3 to uphold the highest ideals in the management and development of people.

2 Objects

The objects for which the Institute is established are:

2.1 The promotion of the art and science of the management and development of people for the public benefit.

3 Purpose of this code

All the CIPD members of whatever grade of membership should be concerned with the maintenance of good practice within the profession and must commit themselves to this code of professional conduct which sets out the standards of professional conduct to which members must adhere. Attached to this code is a description of the procedure which will be applied to deal with any complaints arising.

4 Standards of professional conduct

CIPD members are expected to exercise relevant competence in accordance with the Institute's professional standards and qualifications.

4.1 CIPD members provide specialist professional knowledge, advice, support and management competence in the management and development of people. In all circumstances they:

4.1.1 must endeavour to enhance the standing and good name of the profession; adherence to this code of professional conduct is an essential aspect of this

4.1.2 must seek continually to improve their performance and update and refresh their skills and knowledge

4.1.3 must within their own or any client organisation and in whatever capacity they are working, seek to achieve the fullest possible development of people for present and future organisational needs and encourage self-development by individuals

4.1.4 must within their own or any client organisation and in whatever capacity they are working, seek to adopt in the most appropriate way, the most appropriate people management processes and structures to enable the organisation to best achieve its present and future objectives

4.1.5 must promote and themselves maintain fair and reasonable standards in the treatment of people who are operating within scope of their influence

4.1.6 must promote and themselves seek to exercise employment practices that remove unfair discrimination including but not limited to gender, age, race, religion, disability and background

4.1.7 must respect legitimate needs and requirements for confidentiality

4.1.8 must use due diligence and exercise high standards of timeliness, appropriateness and accuracy in the information and advice they provide to employers and employees

4.1.9 must seek to recognise the limitations of their own knowledge and ability and must not undertake activity for which they are not yet appropriately prepared or, where applicable, qualified.

4.2 In the public interest and in the pursuit of its objects, the Chartered Institute of Personnel and Development is committed to the highest possible standards of professional conduct and competency. To this end members:

4.2.1 are required to exercise integrity, honesty, diligence and appropriate behaviour in all their business, professional and related personal activities

4.2.2 must act within the law and must not encourage, assist or act in collusion with employers, employees or others who may be engaged in unlawful conduct.

5 Complaints

Any person, whether or not a member, may complain to the Institute that a member has been guilty of conduct which is not in accordance with the provisions of this code and/or where that conduct appears likely to bring discredit to the Institute or the profession. Such conduct will be considered under the terms of the disciplinary procedure.

CIPD professional conduct disciplinary procedure

1 Procedures for complaints

1.1 Complaints may be made against a member by:
- the Institute
- another member
- a third party

1.2 Any complaint made against a member must be made in writing under confidential cover and addressed to the Secretary of the Institute at its registered office. Complainants shall set out the circumstances forming the basis of the complaint, including the relationship, if any, between the complainant and the member concerned.

1.3 The Secretary shall at his/her discretion consult with the complainant and other parties, in particular, officers and members of the Institute, including the member concerned to determine whether a prima facie case has been made. If the Secretary concludes that there is a prima facie case, he/she shall then formally notify in writing the member concerned.

1.4 If the Secretary concludes that a prima facie case has not been made, he/she shall so advise the complainant, and at the Secretary's discretion the member concerned, in writing. The complainant may challenge the decision of the Secretary in writing to the member of the Nominations and Professional Conduct Committee designated to consider such appeals (designated member). This 'preliminary appeal' process will consist solely of the consideration of the information already submitted to the Secretary, the Secretary's own advice and written representations from the complainant and the member concerned. The designated member's decision shall be final and binding and there shall be no obligation to give written reasons for the decision.

1.5 If the Secretary decides in the first instance, or the designated member of the Nominations and Professional Conduct Committee on preliminary appeal considers a prima facie case has been made, the Secretary shall then notify in writing the member concerned of the nature of the complaint and the Secretary shall request the member concerned's written response within 28 days of the date of sending out the notification. Upon receipt of the response or at the end of the period, whichever is earlier, the Secretary shall refer the complaint and the member concerned's response, if any, to the Chair of the Nominations and Professional Conduct Committee. The Chair shall then instruct the Secretary to convene, as soon as reasonably practicable, a disciplinary panel.

2 Disciplinary panel

2.1 The power of making disciplinary decisions is vested in a disciplinary panel.

2.2 Disciplinary panels shall be drawn from members of the Nominations and Professional Conduct Committee. The Chair of the Nominations and Professional Conduct Committee shall not be a member of a disciplinary panel. The nominated panel members will appoint one of their number to act as their Chair.

2.3 A disciplinary panel will consist of not more than four and not less than three members including the Chair of the panel, each of whom shall have a primary vote. A panel may co-opt additional specialist advisers should it so decide, who will not have a vote. There will also be a Secretary for each panel who will normally be the Secretary of the Institute. In the event of a tied vote, the Chair does not have a casting vote.

3 Disciplinary panel hearings

3.1 Within 14 days of receiving a response, or after the lapse of 28 days from sending notification to the member concerned whichever is the lesser, the Secretary shall fix a date and place for the complaint to be heard by the disciplinary panel, giving at least 28 days notice to the member and complainant concerned or such other period as may be determined (unless otherwise agreed between all the parties). The place where the complaint will be heard will ordinarily be the headquarters of the CIPD.

3.2 At least 14 days before the disciplinary hearing, the panel must present in writing to the member concerned and all other parties involved the document supporting the complaint. The member concerned shall also have proper opportunity to bring witnesses and introduce at the hearing any relevant evidence he/she may consider fit. The person making the complaint will normally be required to appear before the hearing and given the opportunity of an explanation. Either or both parties may be accompanied by a full member (i.e. companion, fellow, or member) of the CIPD if he/she so wishes. Such a member shall attend as a supporter or adviser but not as a representative.

3.3 The hearing can, with the agreement of the parties, take place in the absence of one of the parties if, in the opinion of the disciplinary panel, there is no alternative to proceeding in this way. With the agreement of the parties, the hearing could be conducted by correspondence.

3.4 The disciplinary panel may make such further enquiries by correspondence or call witnesses or otherwise as it may think fit. This may involve an adjournment of the panel hearing for a reasonable period.

3.5 The disciplinary panel, after considering all available submissions, will determine their decision. If the panel decides that the case has not been substantiated, the complaint will be dismissed. The Secretary will in writing inform the person making the complaint and the member concerned.

3.6 Decisions of the disciplinary panel shall be by simple majority and can be made in the absence of the member concerned, provided they have been previously informed of the date of the hearing and nature of the complaint. In the event of a tied vote, the Chair shall not have a casting vote; in these circumstances the complaint shall be regarded as dismissed.

4   Powers of the disciplinary panel

The disciplinary panel shall have the following powers:

4.1 dismiss the complaint

4.2 exercise one or more of the following disciplinary decisions, in combination or as alternative:

4.2.1 warn, admonish or reprimand any member

4.2.2 call for a written undertaking from the member as to future conduct and performance, to provide for guidance from a senior colleague and specific training, and/or arrange for regular reporting

4.2.3 direct that a statement recording the complaint should be entered on the CIPD's personal record of the respondent for a defined time

4.2.4 review the member's eligibility for Institute office

4.2.5 re-designate a member in the Institute's membership grades

4.2.6 withdraw the benefits of membership of the Institute and the use of designatory letters for a defined time

4.2.7 call for the resignation of a member

4.2.8 expel a member from the Institute

4.2.9 make recommendations to the President of the Institute regarding publication of the decision.

5   Appeal system

5.1 It is open for a member against whom a complaint has been upheld in full or in part by a disciplinary panel and against whom a disciplinary decision has been made, to lodge an appeal to an appeals panel. Such appeal must be made in writing to the Secretary of the Institute at the registered office of the CIPD within 28 days of the date of notification of the disciplinary decision. The notice must set out the full grounds on which issue is taken with the disciplinary decision. The action decided upon will, at the discretion of the disciplinary panel, normally be suspended until after the appeal is heard.

5.2 The Secretary will notify the Chair of the Nominations and Professional Conduct Committee, as Chair of the appeals panel, of the appeal, and he/she will instruct the Secretary to convene an appeals panel.

5.3 The Secretary shall fix a date and place for the case to be heard, giving at least 28 days notice to the member concerned or such other period as may be agreed between all the parties.

5.4 The appeals panel will follow the same procedure as the disciplinary panel save that the member concerned may be represented by a third party who need not be a member of the Institute. Relevant documents will be circulated to all parties before the appeal hearing. The decision of the appeals panel will be final and by a simple majority; where no such majority is obtained, the appeal fails and the original decision stands.

5.5 The appeals panel may overturn the disciplinary decision, vary or uphold it.

5.6 The member concerned will be informed in writing within 14 days of the decision of the appeals panel.

6   Appeals panel

The appeals panel will consist of the Chair of the Nominations and Professional Conduct Committee, as Chair, and four other members of that committee. In the unavoidable absence or indisposition of the Chair, that person or the panel itself may nominate another member of the panel to act as Chair. No member may serve on the appeals panel who was previously involved in the disciplinary panel, in relation to the same matter.

7   Publication of decisions

7.1 Decisions by the Secretary and upon preliminary appeal by the Chair of the Nominations and Professional Conduct Committee shall be reported to that committee.

7.2 Decisions of the disciplinary panel (subject to paragraph 5.1) and of the appeals panel will be notified to the member against whom the complaint has been made and as soon as practicable to the council, and will be effective immediately. The extent of publication will be at the discretion of the President of the Institute, based on a recommendation from the disciplinary or appeals panel. Individuals in cases which have been dismissed will not be identified, but details of such cases may nevertheless be published. Members who have been the subject of disciplinary proceedings may request the President, at his/her discretion, to publish decisions on their behalf.

8   Readmittance

Before a member is readmitted following expulsion, the matter will be referred to the Nominations and Professional Conduct Committee.

The European Union
Social Charter

The Social Charter was adopted by all Member States, except the UK, in December 1989. The Social Charter is not a legal text. It is a statement of principles by which governments agree to abide. They will be required each year to present a report on how they are implementing the Charter. Its aim is to highlight the importance of the social dimension of the single market in achieving social as well as economic cohesion in the EC.

The preamble of the Social Charter gives added weight to other international obligations such as ILO conventions. The preamble also includes a commitment to combat every form of discrimination, including discrimination on grounds of sex, colour, race, opinions and belief.

Summary of the rights set out in the Social Charter:

1. Freedom of movement throughout the Community with equal treatment in access to employment, working conditions and social protection.

2. Freedom to choose and engage in an occupation, which shall be fairly remunerated.

3. Improvement of living and working conditions, especially for part-time and temporary workers, and rights to weekly rest periods and annual paid leave.

4. Right to adequate social protection.

5. Right to freedom of association and collective bargaining.

6. Right to access to lifelong vocational training, without discrimination on grounds of nationality.

7. Right of equal treatment of men and women, especially in access to employment, pay, working conditions, education and training and career development.

8. Right to information, consultation and participation for employees, particularly in conditions of technological change, restructuring, redundancies, and for transfrontier workers.

9. Right to health protection and safety at the workplace including training, information, consultation and participation for employees.

10. Rights of children and adolescents, including a minimum working age.

11. Right for the elderly to have a decent standard of living on retirement.

12. Right of people with disabilities to programmes to help them in social and professional life.

Glossary

360° Appraisal Feedback regarding performance from all aspects of the job.

Appraisal A process that provides analysis of a person's overall capabilities and potential, allowing informed decisions to be made for particular purposes.

Assessment An important part of the appraisal process whereby data on an individual's past and current work behaviour and performance are collected and reviewed.

Assessment centre The combination of assessment techniques at a single event to make judgements about people for selection and promotion and/or to provide feedback to employees on areas for development.

Attraction Favourable interaction between potential applicants and the images, values and information about an organization.

Autonomy The extent to which a job allows employees freedom and discretion to schedule their work and decide the procedures used to complete it.

Bargaining scope The range of issues covered by the subject matter of collective agreements.

Behaviour-anchored rating scale (BARS) A performance appraisal technique with performance levels anchored by job-related behaviours.

Best Value Provides a framework or benchmark for performance management in local government service provision in the UK.

Briefing groups Groups called together on a regular and consistent basis so that organization decisions and the reasons for them may be communicated. Group members may in turn meet with another briefing group so that information is systematically communicated down the management line.

Bureaucracy An organizational structure marked by rules and procedures, hierarchy of authority and division of labour.

Business process re-engineering (BPR) A radical change of business processes by applying IT to integrate tasks.

Career management Activities and processes to match individual needs and aspirations with organization needs, set within an integrative framework.

'Careless worker' model Assumption that most accidents at work are due to an employee's failure to take safety seriously (or to protect him/herself).

Coaching A management activity to enhance the development of employees, with a particular emphasis on the transfer of learning from formal training courses into workplace activity.

Collective agreement The outcome of collective bargaining, it is an agreement between employers and trade unions respecting terms and conditions of employment. Unlike Canada and the USA, in the UK the agreement is not legally enforceable.

Collective bargaining An institutional system of negotiation in which the making, interpretation and administration of rules, and the application of the statutory controls affecting the employment relationship, are decided within union–management negotiating committees.

Communication The process by which information is exchanged between a sender and a receiver.

Competences The outcomes of work performance in an occupational area with specified performance criteria.

Competencies Underlying characteristics of a person which result in competent or effective performance taking into consideration the nature of the tasks and the organization context.

Computerized personnel information system (CPIS) The use of software to record manpower data and calculate measures such as turnover, absenteeism and staff profiles.

Cooperatives The joint ownership and management of an organization between its customers and/or employees.

Core workforce Workers with organization-specific skills and high discretionary elements in their work.

Corporate manslaughter Employers will be prosecuted for this in the event of a death resulting from the failure to provide a safe working environment.

Culture The set of values, understandings and ways of thinking that is shared by the majority of members of a work organization, and that is taught to new employees as correct.

Delayering Restructuring an organization by reducing the number of grades and levels of work.

Deskilling An initiative taken by management to redesign jobs that leads to a reduction in needed job skills due to job simplification and new technology.

Development The process of improvement or enhancement – of an organization or individuals – through learning and maturation.

Development centres The use of assessment techniques to provide feedback for development.

Developmental approach (to appraisal) An attempt to harness the potential of employees through the discussion of the development needs of employees.

Developmental humanistic A view of people which focuses on their potential for learning.

Diagnostic approach (to manpower planning) The use of manpower data to understand manpower problems so that appropriate action can be taken.

Distributive bargaining A system of activities instrumental to the attainment of one party's goals when they are in basic conflict with those of the other party, for example pay bargaining.

Downsizing The laying-off of employees to restructure the business.

e-Assessment On-line testing used for selection and other HR purposes.

e-Learning Learning through the medium of technology such as e-mail, the Internet and computer software packages.

Emergent learning Learning derived by interaction with evolving situations such as dealing with customers, and used in the formation and formulation of strategy.

Employability Ensuring that, through workplace learning, employees' skills are transferable, making them employable – and thus less dependent – from one organization to another.

Employee involvement (EI) Processes providing employees with the opportunity to influence decision-making on matters which affect them.

Employee participation Involves workers exerting a countervailing and upward pressure on management control. This does not, however, imply unity between managers and non-managers.

Employment relationship This describes the dynamic, interlocking economic, legal, social and psychological relations that exist between individuals and their work organizations.

Empowering Limited power sharing: the delegation of power or authority to subordinates.

Epistemology The study of knowledge and the justification of belief. Questions such as 'Which beliefs are justified and which are not?', 'What, if anything, can we know?' and 'Do researchers reflect reality or create it?' are at the centre of epistemology.

e-Recruitment A fast-changing facet of e-HRM which encompasses both on-line general recruitment agents (for example Monster, StepStone), and recruitment sites established by companies for advertising their own vacancies.

Ethics The code of moral principles and values that governs the behaviour of an individual or group with respect to what is right or wrong.

Expectancy theory A process theory of motivation, stating that employees will direct their work effort towards behaviours that they believe will lead to desired outcomes.

Experience-based interview The use of questions in selection interviews that examine past performance in real situations.

Experimental research This is used to provide evidence regarding cause-and-effect relationships within the workplace with as much control as possible.

Face validity How selection and assessment techniques appear to those subjected to them.

Fordism The application of Taylorist principles of job design to work performed on specialized machines, usually based on flow-line production assembly work. First applied by Henry Ford.

Foucauldian analysis Refers to the application of Michel Foucault's concepts of taxinomia, mathesis, examination and confession to HRM. The hypothesis is that HRM practices play a key role in constituting the self, in defining the nature of work, and in organizing and controlling employees.

Globalization Describes the integration of the world's economies and cultures that has occurred as a result of the global communications revolution, and through the increasing undertaking in an international market of the manufacturing of commodities and processing of information.

Goal setting The process of setting targets and objectives to improve performance (individual, team, department, organization).

Group technology The grouping of machines and workers to form a logical 'whole task' which can be performed with minimum interference.

Groupthink The tendency of members of a highly cohesive group to adhere to shared views so strongly that they totally ignore external information inconsistent with these views.

HRM auditing A process of evaluating the effectiveness of the HR function.

HRM benchmarking A form of auditing which enables organizations to gauge their own practices against those in 'excellent' organizations, to learn from other organizations about effective HR strategies, and to identify what actions need to be taken in order to improve, relative to those organizations.

Human capital theory The view that people are worth investing in as a form of capital: that people's performance and the results achieved can be considered as a return on investment and assessed in terms of cost and benefits.

Human relations movement A movement which grew out of the Hawthorne experiments conducted by Elton Mayo in the 1920s, which emphasizes the psychological and social aspects of job design.

Human resource development (HRD) A term used to indicate training and development as an organization's investment in the learning of its people as part of an HRM approach.

Human resource management (HRM) That part of the management process that specializes in the management of people in work organizations.

Human resource planning (HRP) An HRM approach to planning, set in the context of organizations' views of people as the source of competitive advantage.

Human resource strategy The patterns of decisions regarding human resource policies and practices used by management to design work and select, train and develop, appraise, motivate and control workers.

Image projection A loose model of the values, personality and attitudes of potential employees directed at appropriate labour markets.

Industrial relations The processes of regulation and control over the collective aspects of the employment relationship.

Internal equity Refers to the pay relationships between jobs within a single organization. It is translated into practice using reward techniques, and focuses on comparing jobs and individuals in terms of their relative contributions to the organization's objectives.

Japanization A term used to encapsulate the adoption of Japanese-style management techniques such as team or cellular production, just-in-time and total quality control systems in Western organizations.

Job analysis The systematic process of collecting and evaluating information about the tasks, responsibilities and context of a specific job.

Job characteristic model A job design model developed by Hackman and Oldham (1980) suggesting that five core job characteristics – skill variety, task identity, task significance, autonomy and feedback – result in positive work experience.

Job description Descriptions of tasks and responsibilities that make up a job, usually derived from job analysis.

Job design The process of combining tasks and responsibilities to form complete jobs, and the relationships of jobs in the organization.

Job enlargement The horizontal expansion of tasks in a job.

Job enrichment Processes that assign greater responsibility for scheduling, coordinating and planning work to the employees who actually produce the product.

Job evaluation A systematic process designed to determine the relative worth of jobs within a single work organization.

Job rotation The periodic shifting of a worker from one task to another to reduce monotony and/or increase skill variety.

Joint consultation The involvement of employee representatives in discussion and consideration of matters which affect employees.

Knowledge-based organization An organization that values the collection, dissemination and utilization of new knowledge, with a view to innovation and the development of what is known.

Knowledge management Management of information and knowledge to enhance organization activities.

Labour market segmentation A method of classifying the ways in which organizations seek to employ different kinds of worker.

Labour process The process by which a product is created from raw materials through the application of human labour.

Leadership A process whereby an individual exerts influence upon others in an organizational context.

Learning The process of attaining new knowledge, expertise or skills resulting from the processing and ongoing reinforcement of information and experience.

Learning climate Physical and psycho-social variables in an organization which affect the efficiency of employees in realizing learning potential.

Learning cycle A view of adult learning that emphasizes learning as a continuous process. It is usually associated with the work of Kolb (1984).

Learning movement Encompasses the recommendations, ideas and exhortations relating to HRD and learning at work, plus the structures to support these.

Learning organization A concept representing an ideal of whole organization learning by all employees, and the use of learning to transform the organization.

Learning style The way in which individuals prefer different aspects and ways of learning to others.

Learning transfer Learning from HRD activities transferred to workplace behaviour and performance.

Line manager responsibility The acceptance by line managers of responsibility for the development of subordinates.

Low-cost leadership A business strategy that attempts to increase market share by emphasizing low cost compared to competitors.

Low-quality product – low-skill equilibrium Finegold and Soskice's (1988) explanation of the UK's failure to educate and train its workforce to the same levels as its competitors.

Managerial prerogative A belief that management should have unilateral control within an organization.

Managerialist perspective An ideology concerned primarily with the maximization of employee commitment and motivation through the adoption of appropriate HRM practices.

Manpower planning Processes, techniques and activities to ensure the necessary supply of people is forthcoming to allow organization targets to be met.

Manpower planning techniques and modelling Application of statistical techniques to models of manpower stocks and flow, allowing calculation of manpower decisions.

McDonaldization (also known as 'McWork') Symbolizes the new realities of corporate-driven globalization which engulf young people in the 21st century, including simple work patterns, electronic controls, low pay, part-time and temporary employment.

Mentor A more senior or experienced member of staff who provides one-to-one, career-related guidance and encouragement to a less experienced colleague, with a focus on longer term learning and development.

Multisource feedback (MSF) Feedback from a variety of sources for appraisal and development.

Networking The process of establishing professional relations with individuals and groups both within and outside the workplace.

New unionism Is internally focused and places a renewed emphasis on the recruitment and organization of new union members. It also refers to a trade union organizing strategy.

Normative model A theoretical model that describes how managers should make choices and decisions and provides guidelines for reaching an ideal outcome for the organization.

Organizational communication The systematic provision of information to employees concerning all aspects of their employment and the wider issues relating to the organization in which they work.

Organizational learning An explanation of learning at an organizational level. Emphasis is placed on the 'potential' that individuals and work groups have to learn, and the means – through job redesign, empowerment and changing leadership style – they have to achieve these goals.

Organizational politics Those activities that are not required as part of a manager's formal role, but that influence the distribution of resources for the purpose of promoting personal objectives.

Panopticon The panopticon is a 12-sided polygon with a central observatory tower through which prison guards can observe the behaviour of inmates. For Michel Foucault, the panopticon provides the architectural image of society's disciplinary power. Over time, constant observation induces in the inmate a state of consciousness and reduces the need for discipline so that the surveillance is permanent in its effects, even when it is discontinued.

Paradigm A framework of thinking based on fundamental assumptions providing explicit and implicit views about the nature of reality.

Pay equity Pay relationships among jobs both within an organization (internal equity) and between comparative or competing organizations (external competitiveness).

Pay model A heuristic (learning device) designed to facilitate our understanding of the complex links between an organization's business strategy, reward objectives, the different reward options and techniques and the effect of markets on reward management.

Pendulum arbitration Form of arbitration that prohibits the arbitrator from recommending a compromise solution. The arbitrator must find in favour of either the employer or the income.

Performance and development plan The linking of a business aim with an individual's key areas of responsibility, the competencies that are expected to be demonstrated in performing a role and measurable objectives.

Performance appraisal Analysis of an employee's capabilities and potential drawn from assessment data of past and current work, behaviour and performance, allowing decisions to be made in relation to purpose – for example HRD needs.

Performance contracts Details of what a jobholder agrees to accomplish over time.

Performance control approach (to appraisal) Means by which employee performance can be measured, monitored and controlled.

Performance rating Judgements of performance in terms of personality attributes, results and work outcomes or behaviour within performance.

Peripheral workforce Workers outside the core workforce (for example temporary or casual workers).

Personnel management A function of management which coordinates the human resource needs of an organization, including the designation of work, employee selection, training and development, rewards, performance assessment and union–management relations.

Personnel specification Profile of the requirements of a person to fill a job used as a framework to assess applicants. Requirements may be expressed as 'essential' and 'desirable'.

Pluralist perspective A view of workplace relations which assumes that management and employees have different goals but seek a reconciliation of such differences.

Point method A quantitative method of job evaluation, and the most common technique used for this purpose. The point method develops separate scales for each compensable factor in order to develop a hierarchy of jobs, using points to determine each job's relative value, and hence its location in the pay scale.

Post-Fordism Describes the development from mass production assembly lines to more flexible manufacturing processes.

Post-industrial society/organization The thesis that posits that the modern Western industrial society is moving into a 'post-industrial' era, where traditional manual work will disappear and large bureaucratic work organizations will be replaced by smaller organizations, 'adhocracies', charactized by high levels of flexibility and participation in decision-making.

Post-modernism This refers to the flexible, anti-hierarchical organizational structures which have come to replace the 'modern' rigid, hierarchical organizational structures of the past.

Power A term denoting the ability to influence others' behaviour.

Profit-sharing A scheme through which employees are given a share of company profits.

Psychological contract A metaphor that captures a variety of largely unwritten expectations and understandings of the two parties – employees and their organization – about their mutual obligations.

Psychometric tests Techniques to measure a sample of a person's behaviour.

Qualitative research Refers to the gathering and sorting of information through a variety of techniques, including interviews, focus groups, observations and the use of archival data in organizational files, records or reports.

Quality circle A small group of employees who hold regular meetings to ensure that quality within the workplace is maintained and improved.

Realistic job previews An opportunity for applicants to obtain a realistic picture of a job through job sampling, video, shadowing and case studies.

Recruitment Processes to attract applicants within appropriate labour markets for vacant positions within an organization.

Re-engineering A cross-functional initiative by senior management involving fundamental redesign of business processes to bring about changes in organizational structure, culture, information technology, job design and the management of people.

Reliability A statistical measure of the extent to which a selection or assessment technique achieves consistency in what it is measuring over repeated use.

Research design A plan which is created by the HR researcher or professional in order to make choices about how to handle the most important HR variables and how to study them. HRM research designs usually take the form of survey research, case studies, experimental research or meta-analysis.

Return on investment (ROI) The calculation of the cost of a HR intervention, such as training or an employee participation arrangement, and its determined benefit in monetary terms.

Reward All forms of financial returns and tangible services and benefits employees receive as part of the employment relationship.

Safety policy A set of guidelines and procedures which maintain health and safety in the workplace.

Scientific management A process of determining the division of work into its smallest possible skill elements, and how the process of completing each task can be standardized to achieve maximum efficiency. Also referred to as Taylorism.

Selection Processes to establish the most suitable applicants for vacant positions within an organization from a number of applicants.

Selection interviews The oldest and most widely used method of employee selection.

Self-appraisal A review of one's own performance.

Self-managed team (SMT) A group of employees with different skills who rotate jobs and assume managerial responsibilities as they produce an entire product or service.

Shared responsibility model A view that the best way to reduce levels of occupational accidents and disease and improve health and safety at work lies with cooperation between employers and employees.

Social Charter European legislation created in 1989 to protect and improve workers' health and safety, communications, employee involvement and employment equity across Europe.

Sophisticated modernism A style of industrial relations management that encourages union membership, membership participation in trade unions, workplace union organization, and joint union–management involvement in areas of common interest in order to gain acceptance for change, to maximize cooperation, and to minimize conflict.

Sophisticated paternalism A style of industrial relations management that does not take for granted that employees accept the organization's goal (unitary perspective) and therefore management devote considerable resources in ensuring that their employees have the 'right' attitude and approach.

Standard modernism A style of industrial relations management that is pragmatic or opportunist. Trade unions and workplace union organization are recognized but union–management relations tend to be viewed primarily as a 'reactive' activity; it is assumed to be non-problematic until events prove otherwise.

Strategic HRD The process of responding to and influencing organization strategy through learning and development.

Strategic HRM The process of linking the human resource function with the strategic objectives of the organization in order to improve performance.

Strategic management Denotes a specific pattern of decisions and actions undertaken by the upper echelon of an organization in order to accomplish specific outcomes and/or performance goals.

Synergy The concept that the whole is greater than the sum of its parts. The condition that exists when a group interacts and learns and produces a group outcome that is greater than the sum of the individuals acting alone.

Systematic training model An approach to training encouraged by industrial training boards in the 1960s, based on a four-stage process of identifying training needs and specifying objectives, designing a programme, implementing training and evaluation.

Tacit knowledge Knowledge that is gained through doing rather than learned through being taught.

Taylorism A management control strategy named after F. G. W. Taylor. A systematic theory of management, its defining characteristic has been the identification and measurement of work tasks so that the completion of tasks can be standardized to achieve maximum efficiency (see also scientific management).

Teleworking Working at a distance from an employer's premises but maintaining contact via telecommunications.

Time and motion study The systematic observation, measurement and timing of movements in the completion of tasks to identify more efficient work behaviour.

Training champions Senior managers who contribute to an organization's philosophy of support for training and development.

Transferable skills Skills that can be transferred from one position to another.

Transformation process Behaviour by which an employee converts attributes, skills, knowledge and attitudes into work outcomes and results.

Transformational leadership The ability of leaders to motivate followers to believe in the vision of organizational transformation or re-engineering.

Union density A measurement of current union membership expressed as a percentage of potential union membership.

Union recognition strategy A management strategy to accept the legitimacy of a trade union role and of collective bargaining as a process for regulating the employment relationship. This contrasts with union exclusion, a strategy to curtail the role of trade unions, and union opposition, a strategy to maintain a non-union company.

Unitarist perspective A view of workplace relations which assumes that management and employees share common goals.

Upward appraisal A form of appraisal that includes feedback to subordinates.

Validity A statistical measure of the extent to which a selection or assessment technique actually measures what it sets out to measure. Criterion validity measures the results of a technique against criteria such as present success of existing employees (concurrent validity) and future performance of recruits (predictive validity).

Welfare management The acceptance by employers of responsibility for the general welfare of their employees.

Whistle-blowing Employee disclosure of illegal, immoral, or illegitimate practices on the part of the organization.

Work Physical and mental activity that is carried out at a particular place and time, according to instructions, in return for money.

Work–life balance The need to balance work and leisure/family activities.

Working arrangements Activities associated with the work–effort exchange: allocation of work, work teams, functional flexibility.

Workplace learning A metaphor for capturing formal, self-directed, collective and informal learning activities in the organization.

Works council A council set up within the workplace in order to maintain peaceful and cooperative employment relations. It will normally consist of management, employees and union representatives, and establishes two-way communication between employees and management, and unions and management.

Bibliography

Abercrombie, N. & Warde, A. (1988). *Contemporary British Society*. Cambridge: Polity Press.

Abraham, S. E., Karns, L. A., Shaw, K., & Mena, M. A. (2001). Managerial competencies and the managerial appraisal process. *Journal of Management Development*, **20**(10): 842–52.

Ackroyd, S., & Thompson, P. (1999) *Organizational Misbehaviour*. Thousand Oaks, CA: Sage.

Adams, R. (1995). Canadian industrial relations in comparative perspective. In M. Gunderson, & A. Ponak (eds), *Union–management relations in Canada* (3rd edn) (pp. 495–526). Don Mills, Ontario: Addison-Wesley.

Adams, T., & McQuillan, K. (2000). New jobs, new workers? Organizational restructuring and management hiring decisions. *Relations Industrielles/Industrial Relations*, **55**(3): 391–413.

Adamson, S. J., Doherty, N., & Viney, C. (1998). The meanings of career revisited: implications for theory and practice. *British Journal of Management*, **9**(4): 251–9.

Addison, J., Siebert, W., Wagner, J., & Wei, X. (2000). Worker participation and firm performance. *British Journal of Industrial Relations,* **38**(1): 7–48.

Advisory, Conciliation and Arbitration Service (1987). *Working Together: The Way Forward*. Leeds: ACAS.

Advisory, Conciliation and Arbitration Service (1988). *Labour Flexibility in Britain: The 1987 ACAS survey*. London: ACAS.

Agashae, Z., & Bratton, J. (2001). Leader–follower dynamics: developing a learning organization. *Journal of Workplace Learning*, **13**(3): 89–102.

Aktouf, O. (1996). *Traditional Management and Beyond*. Montreal: Morin.

Alberga, T. (1997). Time for a check-up. *People Management*, 6 February, pp. 30–2.

Albert, S., & Bradley, K. (1997). *Managing Knowledge: Experts, Agencies and Organizations*. Cambridge: Cambridge University Press.

Alliger, G., Tannenbaum, S., Bennett, W., Traver, H., & Shotland, A. (1997). A meta-analysis of the relations among training criteria. *Personnel Psychology*, **50**, 341–58.

Alvesson, M. (1996). *Communication, Power and Organization*. New York: Walter de Gruyter.

Amit, R., & Shoemaker, P. J. H. (1993). Strategic assets and organizational rent. *Strategic Management Journal*, **14**, 33–46.

Anderson, J., Gunderson, M., & Ponak, A. (1989). *Union–management Relations in Canada*. Don Mills, Ontario: Addison-Wesley.

Appelbaum, E., & Batt, R. (1994). *The New America Workplace: Transforming Systems in the United States*. Ithaca, NY: ICR/Cornell University Press.

Appelbaum, S. H, & Donna, M. (2000). The realistic downsizing preview: a management intervention in the prevention of survivor syndrome. Part I. *Career Development International*, **5**(7): 333–50.

Aries, E. (1996). *Men and Women in Interaction: Reconsidering the Differences*. New York: Oxford University Press.

Armstrong, M. (1998). *Employee Reward*. London: Institute for Personnel and Development.

Armstrong, M., & Baron, A. (1998). *Performance Management: The New Realities*. London: Institute of Personnel and Development.

Armstrong, P. (1989). Limits and possibilities for HRM in an age of management accountancy. In J. Storey (ed.), *New Perspectives on Human Resource Management* (pp. 154–66). London: Routledge.

Arnold, J. (1997). *Managing Careers into the 21st Century*. London: Paul Chapman.

Arthur, J. (1994). Effects of human resources systems on manufacturing performance and turnover. *Academy of Management Journal*, **37**, 670–87.

Arthur, W., Woehr, D. J., & Graziano, W. G. (2001). Personality testing in employment settings. *Personnel Review*, **30**(6): 657–76.

Arvey, R. D., & Campion, J. E. (1982). The employment interview: a summary and review of recent research. *Personnel Psychology*, **35**, 281–322.

Ashton, D., & Felstead, A. (1995). Training and development. In Storey, J. (ed.), *Human Resource Management* (pp. 234–53). London: Routledge.

Atkinson, J. S. (1984). Manpower strategies for flexible organizations. *Personnel Management*, August.

Atkinson, J. S. (1985). The changing corporation. In Clutterbuck, D. (ed.), *New Patterns of Work* (pp. 13–34). Aldershot: Gower.

Atkinson, J. S. (1989). Four stages of adjustment to the demographic downturn. *Personnel Management*, August, 20–4.

Atkinson, J. S., & Meager, N. (1985). Introduction and summary of main findings. In Atkinson, J. S., & Meager, N., *Changing Work Patterns* (pp. 2–11). London: National Economic Development Office.

Atwater, L. E., Waldman, D. A., Atwater, D., & Cartier, P. (2000). An upward feedback field experiment: supervisors' cynicism, reactions and commitment to subordinates. *Personnel Psychology*, **53**(2): 275–97.

Bach, S. D. (2000). From performance appraisal to performance management. In S. Bach, & K. Sisson (eds), *Personnel Management* (3rd edn). Oxford: Blackwell.

Bach, S. D. (2002). Public-sector employment relations reforms under Labour: muddling through on modernization? *British Journal of Industrial Relations*, **40**(2): 319–39.

Bacon, N., & Storey, J. (1993). Individualization of the employment relationship and the implications for trade unions. *Employee Relations*, **15**(1): 5–17.

Bacon, N., & Storey, J. (2000). New employee relations strategies in Britain: towards individualism or partnership? *British Journal of Industrial Relations*, **38**(3): 407–27.

Baglioni, G., & Crouch, C. (1991). *European Industrial Relations: The Challenge of Flexibility*. London: Sage.

Bain, G. S., & Price, R. (1983). Union growth: determinants, and density. In G. S. Bain (ed.), *Industrial Relations in Britain* (pp. 3–33). Oxford: Blackwell.

Bain, P. (1997). Human resource malpractice: the deregulation of health and safety at work in the USA and Britain. *Industrial Relations Journal*, **28**(3): 176–91.

Bain, P., & Baldry, C. (1995). Sickness and control in the office – the sick building syndrome. New Technology, *Work and Employment*, **10**(1): 19–31.

Baker, T. (1999). *Doing Well by Doing Good*. Washington: Economic Policy Institute.

Baldamus, W. (1961). *Efficiency and Effort: An Analysis of Industrial Administration*. London: Tavistock.

Baldwin, T. T., & Ford, J. K. (1988). Transfer of training: a review and directions for future research. *Personnel Psychology*, **41**, 63–105.

Ball, B. (1997). Career management competences – the individual perspective. *Career Development International*, **2**(2): 74–9.

Ball, K. (2001). The use of human resource information systems: a survey. *Personnel Review*, **30**(6): 677–93.

Bamberger, P., & Meshoulam, I. (2000). *Human Resource Management Strategy*. Thousand Oaks, CA: Sage.

Bamberger, P., & Phillips, B. (1991). Organizational environment and business strategy: parallel versus conflicting influences on human resource strategy in the pharmaceutical industry. *Human Resource Management*, **30**, 153–82.

Banker, R. D., Field, J. M., Schroeder, R. G., & Sinha, K. (1996). Impact of work teams on manufacturing performance: a longitudinal field study. *Academy of Management Journal*, **39**(4): 867–90.

Bansler, J. (1989). Trade unions and alternative technology in Scandinavia. *New Technology, Work and Employment*, **4**(2): 92–9.

Barber, A. E., & Bretz, R. (2000). Compensation, attraction and retention. In S. Rynes & B. Gerhart (eds), *Compensation in Organizations: Current Research and Practice* (pp. 32–60). San Francisco, CA: Jossey-Bass.

Barber, A. E., Wesson, M. J., Roberson, Q. M., & Taylor, M. S. (1999). A tale of two job markets: organizational size and its effects on hiring practices and job search behaviour. *Personnel Psychology*, **52**(4): 841–67.

Barclay, J. (1999). Employee selection: a question of structure. *Personnel Review*, **28**(1/2): 134–51.

Barclay, J. (2001). Improving selection interviews with structure: organisations' use of 'behavioural' interviews. *Personnel Review*, **30**(1): 81–101.

Bardram, J. E. (1997). Plans as situated action: an activity theory approach to workflow systems. http://www.daimi.aau.dk/~bardram/ECSCW97.html. Accessed 16 December 2002.

Barlow, G. (1989). Deficiencies and the perpetuation of power: latent functions in management appraisal. *Journal of Management Studies*, **26**(5): 499–517.

Barney, J. B. (1991). Firm resources and sustained competitive advantage. *Journal of Management*, **17**(1): 99–120.

Barrett, J. T. (1996). Trade unions in South Africa: dramatic change after apartheid ends. *Monthly Labor Review*, **119**(5): 37–46.

Bartholomew, D. J. (1971). The statistical approach to manpower planning. *The Statistician*, **20**, 3–26.

Bartol, K., & Locke, E. (2000). Compensation. In S. Rynes, & B. Gerhart (eds), *Compensation in Organizations: Current Research and Practice* (pp. 104–47). San Francisco, CA: Jossey-Bass.

Bass, B. M. (1985). *Leadership and Performance Beyond Expectations*. New York: Free Press.

Bassett, P. (1987). *Strike Free: New Industrial Relations in Britain*. London: Papermac.

Bassett, P. (1988). Non-unionism's growing ranks. *Personnel Management*, March, 16–19.

Batstone, E. (1984). *Working Order*. Oxford: Blackwell.

Batstone, E., & Gourlay, S. (1986). *Unions, Unemployment and Innovation*. Oxford: Blackwell.

Batstone, E., Levie, H., & Moore, R. (1987). *New Technology and the Process of Labour Regulation*. Oxford: Oxford University Press.

Bauer, T. N., Truxillo, D. M., Sanchez, R. J., Craig, J. M., Ferrera, P., & Campion, M. A. (2001). Applicant reactions to selection: development of the selection procedural justice scale (SPJS). *Personnel Psychology*, **54**(2): 387–421.

Bean, R. (1985). *Comparative Industrial Relations*. London: Croom Helm.

Beatty, R. W., & Schneier, C. E. (1996). New human resource roles to impact organizational performance: from partner to players. *Human Resource Management*, **36**(1): 29–37.

Beaumont, P. (1991). Trade unions and HRM. *Industrial Relations Journal*, **22**(4): 300–8.

Beaumont, P. (1992). *Public Sector Industrial Relations*. London: Routledge.

Becker, B., & Gerhart, B. (1996). The impact of HRM on organizational performance: progress and prospects. *Academy of Management Journal*, **39**, 779–801.

Beer, M., Spector, B., Lawrence, P. R., Quin Mills, D., & Walton, R. E. (1984). *Managing Human Assets*. New York: Fress Press.

Belanger, J., Edwards, P., & Wright, M. (1999). Best HR practice and the multinational company. *Human Resource Management Journal*, **9**(3): 53–70.

Belcourt, M., Wright, P. C., & Saks, A.M. (2000). *Managing Performance Through Training and Development* (2nd edn). Scarborough, Ontario: Nelson.

Bell, D. (1989). Why manpower planning is back in vogue. *Personnel Management*, July, 40–3.

Bendal, S. E., Bottomley, C. R., & Cleverly, P. M. (1998). Building a new proposition for staff at NatWest UK. In P. Sparrow, & M. Marchington (eds), *Human Resource Management: The New Agenda* (pp. 90–105). London: Financial Times/Pitman.

Bengtsson, L. (1992). Work organization and occupational qualification in CIM: the case of Swedish NC machine shops. *New Technology, Work and Employment*, **7**(1): 29–43.

Bennison, M. (1980). *The IMS Approach to Manpower Planning*. Brighton: IMS.

Bentham, K. (2002). Employer resistance to union certification: a case study of eight Canadian jurisdictions. *Relations Industrielles/Industrial Relations*, **57**(1): 159–87.

Berg, B. (1998). *Qualitative Research Methods for the Social Sciences*. Boston: Allyn & Bacon.

Betcherman, G., McMullen, K., Leckie, N., & Caron, C. (1994). *The Canadian Workplace in Transition*. Queen's University, Kingston, Ontario: IRC Press.

Bevan, S. (1991). *Staff retention – a manager's guide*. Report 203. Brighton: IMS.

Beynon, H. (1984). *Working for Ford*. Harmondsworth: Penguin.

Billett, S. (2001). Learning through work: workplace learning affordances and individual engagement. *Journal of Workplace Learning*, **13**(5): 209–15.

Bin Idris, A. R. & Eldridge, D. (1998). Reconceptualising human resource planning in response to institutional change. *International Journal of Manpower*, **19**(5): 343–57.

Blinder, A. (Ed.) (1990). *Paying for Productivity*. Washington, DC: Brooking Institute.

Blum, S. (1997). Preventing culture shock. *Smythe Dorward Lambert Review*, Winter/Spring, 4–5.

Blyton, P., & Turnbull, P. (1992). HRM: debates, dilemmas and contradictions. In P. Blyton, & P. Turnbull, (eds), *Reassessing Human Resource Management*. London: Sage.

Blyton, P., & Turnbull, P. (1998). *The Dynamic of Employee Relations* (2nd edn). London: Macmillan – now Palgrave Macmillan.

Boam, S., & Sparrow, P. (1992). *Designing and Achieving Competency*. Maidenhead: McGraw-Hill.

Booth, R. (1985). What's new in health and safety management? *Personnel Management*, April, 17–23.

Bosquet, M. (1980). The meaning of job enrichment. In T. Nichols (ed.), *Capital and Labour* (pp. 370–80). Glasgow: Fontana.

Bottomore, T. B., & Rubel, M. (1956). *Karl Marx: Selected Writings in Sociology and Social Philosophy*. London: Penguin.

Boud, D., & Garrick, J. (eds) (1999). *Understanding Learning at Work*. London: Routledge.

Boxall, P. F. (1992). Strategic human resource management: beginnings of a new theoretical sophistication? *Human Resource Management Journal*, **2**(3): 60–79.

Boxall, P. F. (1995). Building the theory of comparative HRM. *Human Resource Management Journal*, **5**(5): 5–17.

Boxall, P. F. (1996). The strategic HRM debate and the resource-based view of the firm. *Human Resource Management Journal*, **6**(3): 59–75.

Boydell, T. H. (1976). *Guide to the Identification of Training Needs* (2nd edn). London: BACIE.

Bramley, P. (1989). Effective training. *Journal of European Industrial Training*, **13**.

Brannen, P., Batstone, E., Fatchett, D., & White, P. (1976). *The Worker Directors*. London: Hutchinson.

Bratton, J. (1991). Japanization at work: the case of engineering plants in Leeds. *Work, Employment and Society*, **5**(3): 377–95.

Bratton, J. (1992). *Japanization at Work: Managerial Studies for the 1990s*. London: Macmillan – now Palgrave Macmillan.

Bratton, J. (1999). Gaps in the workplace learning paradigm: Labour flexibility and job design. 1st International Conference on Researching Work and Learning, University of Leeds, England.

Bratton, J. (2001). Why workers are reluctant learners: the case of the Canadian pulp and paper industry. *Journal of Workplace Learning*, **13**(7/8): 333–43.

Bratton, J., & Sinclair, L. (1987). *New Patterns of Management: Communications and Employee Involvement in Local Government in Yorkshire and Humberside*. Leeds: Leeds City Council.

Bratton, J., Grint, K., & Nelson, D. *Organizational Leadership*. Mason, OH: South-Western Thompson (in press).

Braverman, H. (1974). *Labour and Monopoly Capital*. New York: Monthly Review Press.

Brewster, C. (1993). Developing a 'European' model of human resource management. *International Journal of Human Resource Management*, **4**(4): 765–84.

Brewster, C. (1995). Towards a 'European model' of human resource management. *Journal of International Business Studies*, First Quarter, 1–21.

Brewster, C. (2001). HRM: 'the comparative dimension.' In J. Storey (ed.), *Human Resource Management: A Critical Text* (pp. 255–71). London: Thompson Learning.

Brewster, C., Larsen, H., & Mayrhofer, W. (1999). Human resource management: a strategic approach. In C. Brewster, & H. Larsen (eds), *Human Resource Management in Northern Europe*. Oxford: Blackwell.

Brewster, C., Mayrhofer, W., & Morley, M. (eds) (2000). *New Challenges for European Human Resource Management*. New York: St. Martins Press.

Brewster, C., Harris, H., & Sparrow, P. (2002). United nations. *People Management*, **8**(14): 32–4.

Broderick, R., & Boudreau, J. W. (1992). HRM, IT and the competitive edge. *Academy of Management Executive*, **6**(2): 7–17.

Broughton, A., & Gilman, M. (2001). European industrial relations in 2000: a chronicle of events. *British Journal of Industrial Relations*, **32**(5): 494–516.

Brown, J. S., & Duguid, P. (1991). Organizational learning and communities-of-practice: toward a unified view of working, learning and innovation. *Organization Science*, **2**(1): 40–7.

Brown, M. (2001). Unequal pay, unequal responses? Pay referents and their implications for pay level satisfaction. *Journal of Management Studies*, **38**(6): 879–96.

Brown, W. (ed.) (1981). *The Changing Contours of British Industrial Relations*. Oxford: Blackwell.

Brown, W. (1988). The employment relationship in sociological theory. In D. Gallie (ed.), *Employment in Britain* (pp. 33–66). Oxford: Blackwell.

Brown, W. (1989). Managing remuneration. In K. Sisson (ed.), *Personnel Management in Britain* (pp. 249–70). Oxford: Blackwell.

Brown, W. (2000). Putting partnership into practice in Britain. *British Journal of Industrial Relations*, **38**(2): 299–316.

Brown, W., Deakin, S., & Ryan, P. (1997). The effects of British industrial relations legislation. *National Institute Economic Review*, **161**, 69–83.

Brown, W., Deakin, S., Nash, D., & Oxenbridge, S. (2000). The employment contract: from collective procedures to individual rights. *British Journal of Industrial Relations*, **38**(4): 611–29.

Buchanan, D. A. (1997). The limitations and opportunities of business process re-engineering in a politicized organizational climate. *Human Relations*, **50**(1): 51–72.

Buckingham, G. (2000). Same indifference. *People Management*, **6**(4): 44–6.

Bullock, Lord (1977). Report of the Committee of Inquiry on Industrial Democracy. Cmnd 6706. London: HMSO.

Burawoy, M. (1979). *Manufacturing Consent: Changes in the Labour Process Under Monopoly Capitalism*. Chicago: Chicago University Press.

Burchell, B., Day, D., Hudson, M., Ladipo, D., Mankelow, R., Nolan, J., et al. (1999). *Job Insecurity and Work Intensification: Flexibility and the Changing Boundaries of Work*. York: Joseph Rowntree Foundation.

Burke, J. (1985). *The Day the Universe Changed*. Boston, MA: Little, Brown.

Buyens, D., & De Vos, A. (2001). Perceptions of the value of HR function. *Human Resource Management Journal*, **11**(3): 70–89.

Byers, P. Y. (ed.) (1997). *Organizational Communication: Theory and Behavior*. Boston: Allyn & Bacon.

Byrne, D. (1998). *Complexity Theory and the Social Sciences*, London: Routledge.

Cable, D. M., & Parsons, C. K. (2001). Socialization tactics and person–organization fit. *Personnel Psychology*, **54**(1): 1–23.

Caldwell, R. (2001). Champions, adaptors, consultants and synergists: the new change agents in HRM. *Human Resource Management Journal*, **11**(3): 39–52.

Callaghan, G., & Thompson, P. (2001). Edwards revisited: technical control and worker agency in call centres. *Economic and Industrial Democracy*, **22**, 13–37.

Campbell, D. J. & Lee, C. (1988). Self-appraisal in performance evaluation. *Academy of Management Review*, **13**(2): 3–8.

Campbell, M. (1999). *Learning Pays and Learning Works*. London: National Advisory Council for Education and Training Targets.

Campion, M. A., Palmer, D. K., & Campion, J. E. (1997). A review of structure in the selection interview. *Personnel Psychology*, **50**, 655–702.

Cannell, M. (2002). Class struggle. *People Management*, **8**(5): 46–7.

Cappelli, P. (1984). Competitive pressures and labor relations in the airline industry. *Industrial Relations*, **24**, 316–18.

Cappelli, P., & Chalykoff, J. (1985). The effects of management industrial relations strategy: results of a survey. Quoted in Anderson, J., Gunderson, M., & Ponak, A. (1989). *Union–management Relations in Canada*. Don Mills, Ontario: Addison-Wesley.

Cappelli, P., & Singh, H. (1992). Integrating strategic human resources and strategic management. In

D. Lewin, O. S. Mitchell, & P. Sherer (eds) *Research Frontiers in Industrial Relations and Human Resources* (pp. 165–92). Madison, WI: Industrial Relations Research Association.

Carrick, P., & Williams, R. (1999). Development centres – a review of assumptions. *Human Resource Management Journal*, **9**(2): 77–92.

Carter, A. (2001). *Executive coaching: Inspiring performance at work*. Report 379. Sussex: Institute for Employment Studies.

Caruth, D., & Handlogten, G. (2001). *Managing Compensation: A Handbook for the Perplexed*. Westport, CT: Quorum.

Castells, M. (1996). *The Rise of the Network Society*. Oxford: Blackwell.

Castells, M. (2000). Information technology and global capitalism. In W. Hutton, & A. Giddens (eds), *On the Edge: Living with Global Capitalism* (pp. 52–74). London: Jonathan Cape.

Caulkin, S. (2001). The time is now. *People Management*, **7**(17): 32–4.

Ceci, S., & Williams, W. (2000). Smart bomb. *People Management*, **6**(17): 32–6.

Centre for Labour–Management Development (2001). *Progressive Discipline*. Toronto, CLMD.

Champy, J. (1996). *Reengineering Management: The Mandate for New Leadership*. New York: HarperCollins.

Chandler, A. (1962). *Strategy and Structure*. Cambridge, MA: MIT Press.

Chapman, R. (1990). Personnel management in the 1990s. *Personnel Management*, January, 28–32.

Charlwood, A. (2002). Why do non-union employees want to unionize? Evidence from Britain. *British Journal of Industrial Relations*, **40**(3): 463–91.

Charmaz, K. (2000). Grounded theory: objectivist and constuctivist methods. In N. Denzin, & Y. Lincoln (eds), *Handbook of Qualitative Research* (2nd edn) (pp. 509–35). Thousand Oaks, CA: Sage.

Child, J. (1972). Organizational structure, environment and performance: the role of strategic choice. *Sociology*, **6**(1): 331–50.

Chiu, W., Thomson, D., Mak, W., & Lo, K. L. (1999). Re-thinking training needs analysis. *Personnel Review*, **28**(1/2): 77–90.

Chomsky, N. (1999). *Profit over People*. New York: Seven Stories Press.

Clark, J. (ed.) (1993). *Human Resource Management and Technical Change*. London: Sage.

Clark, T., & Pugh, D. (2000). Similarities and differences in European conceptions of human resource management. *International Studies of Management and Organizations*, **29**(4): 84–100.

Clark, T., Grant, D., & Heijltjes, M. (2000). Researching comparative and international human resource management. *International Studies of Management and Organization*, **29**(4): 6–23.

Clarke, L. (1997). Changing work systems, changing social relations. *Relations Industrielles/Industrial Relations*, **52**(4): 839–61.

Clarke, T. (1977). Industrial democracy: the institutional suppression of industrial conflict. In T. Clarke, & L. Clements, *Trade Unions under Capitalism*. London: Fontana.

Clarke, T., & Hermens, A. (2001). Corporate developments and strategic alliances in e-learning. *Education + Training*, **43**(4): 256–67.

Clausen, C., & Lorentzen, B. (1993). Workplace implications of FMS and CIM in Denmark and Sweden. *New Technology, Work and Employment*, **8**(1): 21–30.

Claydon, T. (1989). Union de-recognition in Britain in the 1980s. *British Journal of Industrial Relations*, **27**(2): 214–24.

Clayton, T. (1998). Problematizing partnerships: the prospects for a cooperative bargaining agenda. In P. Sparrow, & M. Marchington (eds), *Human Resource Management: The New Agenda* (pp. 180–92). London: Financial Times Management.

Clegg, H. (1976). *Trade Unionism Under Collective Bargaining*. Oxford: Blackwell.

Clegg, H. (1979). *The Changing System of Industrial Relations in Great Britain*. Oxford: Blackwell.

Clegg, S. R. (1990). *Modern Organizations: Organization Studies in the Postmodern World*. London: Sage.

Clegg, S. R., & Dunkerley, D. (1980). *Organization, Class and Control*. London: Routledge & Kegan Paul.

Clegg, S. R., & Hardy, C. (eds) (1999). *Studying Organizations: Theory and Method*. London: Sage.

Cloke, K., & Goldsmith, J. (2002). *The End of Management and the Rise of Organizational Democracy*. San Francisco, CA: Jossey-Bass.

Coates, D. (1975). *The Labour Party and the Struggle for Socialism*. Cambridge: Polity Press.

Coates, K., & Topham, T. (1980). *Trade Unions in Britain*. Nottingham: Spokesman.

Cohen, P. S. (1968). *Modern Social Theory*. New York: Basic Books.

Coleman, S., & Keep, E. (2001). Background literature review for PIU project on workforce development. Available from http://www.cabinet-office.gov.uk/innovation/2001/workforce/literaturereview.pdf.

Colling, T. (1995). Experiencing turbulence: competition, strategic choice and the management of human resources in British airways. *Human Resource Management*, **5**(5): 18–32.

Collins, J. M., & Muchinsky, P. M. (1993). An assessment of the construct validity of three job evaluation methods: a field experiment. *Academy of Management Journal*, **36**, 895–904.

Conger, J., & Kanungo, R. (eds) (1988). *Charismatic Leadership*. San Francisco: Jossey-Bass.

Conway, H. E. (1987). *Equal Pay for Work of Equal Value Legislation in Canada: An Analysis*. Ottawa: Studies in Social Policy.

Cook, M. (1994). *Personnel Selection and Productivity*. Chichester: Wiley.

Cooke, F. L. (2000) *Human resource strategy to improve organisational performance: A route for British firms?* Working Paper 9. Economic and Social Research Council Future of Work Programme. Swindon: ESRC.

Cooper, D., & Robertson, I. T. (2001). *Recruitment and Selection*. London: Thomson Learning.

Coopey, J. (1996). Crucial gaps in the 'learning organization'. In K. Starkey (ed.), *How Organizations Learn* (pp. 348–67). London: International Thomson Business.

Coriat, B. (1980). The restructuring of the assembly line: a new economy of time and control. *Capital and Class*, (11): 34–43.

Coulson, A. (1999). Local business representation: can we afford TECs and chambers? *Regional Studies*, **33**(3): 269–73.

Coupar, W., & Stevens, B. (1998). Towards a new model of industrial partnership. In P. Sparrow, & M. Marchington (eds), *Human Resource Management: A New Agenda* (pp. 145–59). London: Financial Times Management.

Coverdale Ltd (1995). *Competencies: The Current State of Play*. London: Coverdale Organisation.

Cowling, A., & Walters, M. (1990). Manpower planning – where are we today? *Personnel Review*, **19**(3): 3–8.

Coyle-Shapiro, J., & Kessler, I. (2000). Consequences of the psychological contract for the employment relationship: a large-scale survey. *Journal of Management Studies*, **37**(7): 903–30.

Craig, M. (1981). *Office Worker' Survival Handbook*. London: BSSR.

Crawford, M. (1995). *Talking Differences: On Gender and Language*. Thousand Oaks, CA: Sage.

Cressey, P. (1998). European works councils in practice. *Human Resource Management Journal*, **8**(1): 67–81.

Crossan, M. M. (1999). An organizational learning framework: from intuition to institution. *Academy of Management Review*, **24**(3): 522–38.

Crouch, C. (1982). *The Politics of Industrial Relations* (2nd edn). London: Fontana.

Cully, M., O'Reilly, A., Woodland, S., & Dix, G. (1998). The 1998 Workplace Employee Relations Survey, first findings. www.dti.gov.uk/emar.

Cully, M., Woodland, S., O'Reilly, A., & Dix, G. (1999). *Britain at Work*. London: Routledge.

Cunningham, I., & Hyman, J. (1999). Devolving human resource responsibilities to the line. *Personnel Review*, **28**(1/2): 9–27.

Cunningham, S., Ryan, Y., Stedman, L., Bagdon, K., Flew, T., & Coaldrake, P. (2000). *The Business of Borderless Education*. Canberra: Department of Education, Training and Youth Affairs.

Curnow, B. (1986). The creative approach to pay. *Personnel Management*, October, 32–6.

Daft, R. (2001). *Organization Theory and Design* (7th edn). Cincinnati, OH: South-Western.

Dalen, L. H., Stanton, N. A., & Roberts, A. D. (2001). Faking personality questionnaires in personnel selection. *Journal of Management Development*, **20**(8): 729–41.

Dancy, J. (1985). *Introduction to Contemporary Epistemology*. Oxford: Blackwell.

Daniel, W. W., & Millward, N. (1983). *Workplace Industrial Relations in Britain*. London: Heinemann.

Daniel, W. W., & Millward, N. (1993). Findings from the Workplace Industrial Relations Surveys. In J. Clark (ed.), *Human Resource Management and Technical Change* (pp. 943–77). London: Sage.

Davidow, W. H., & Malone, M. S. (1992). *The Virtual Corporation: Structuring and Revitalizing the Corporation for the 21st Century*. New York: Harper Business.

Davidson, M. J., & Cooper, C. L. (1992). *Shattering the Glass Ceiling*. London: Paul Chapman.

Davies, L. (1996). Development centres for senior managers in Yorkshire Water. *Career Development International*, **1**(6): 17–24.

Dearden, L., McIntosh, S., Myck, M., & Vignoles, A. (2001). *Basic skills, soft skills and labour marketoOutcomes: Secondary analysis of the NCDS*. Research Report 250. London: Department for Education and Employment.

Debono, J. (2001). Sexual harassment in employment: an examination of decisions looking for evidence of a sexist jurisprudence. *New Zealand Journal of Industrial Relations*, **26**(3): 329–40.

Deery, S. (1995). The demise of the trade union as a representative body? *British Journal of Industrial Relations*, **33**(4): 537–43.

Delaney, J. T., & Huselid, M. A. (1996). The impact of HRM practices on perceptions of organizational performance. *Academy of Management Journal*, **39**(4): 949–69.

Delbridge, R., & Whitfield, K. (2001). Employee perceptions of job influence and organizational participation. *Industrial Relations*, **40**(3): 472–89.

Delery, J., & Doty, H. (1996). Modes of theorizing in strategic human resource management: tests of universalistic, contingency and configurational performance predictions. *Academy of Management Journal*, **39**, 802–35.

Denham, D. (1990). Unfair dismissal law and the legitimation of managerial control. *Capital and Class*, (41): 32–41.

Denzin, N., & Lincoln, Y. (2000). *Handbook of Qualitative Research* (2nd edn). Thousand Oaks, CA: Sage.

Department for Education and Employment (1991). *Education and training for the 21st century*. White Paper. Sheffield: DfEE.

Department for Education and Employment (1998a). *The learning age: A renaissance for a new Britain*. Green Paper. Sheffield: DfEE.

Department for Education and Employment (1998b). *TECs: Meeting the challenge of the millennium*. London: DfEE.

Department for Education and Employment (1999). *Learning to succeed: A new framework for post-16 learning*. Sheffield: DfEE.

Department for Education and Employment (2000). *Labour market and skill trends*. Sheffield: DfEE.

Department of Employment (1974). *Company manpower planning*. Manpower Papers 1. London: HMSO.

Dermer, J. (ed.) (1992). *The New World Economic Order: Opportunities and Threats*. New York, Ontario: Captus.

Despres, C., & Hiltrop, J. (1995). Human resource management in the knowledge age: current practice and perspectives on the future. *Employee Relations*, **17**(1): 9–23.

Devanna, M. A., Fombrun, C. J., & Tichy, N. M. (1984). A framework for strategic human resource management. In C. J. Fombrun, N. M. Tichy, & M. A. Devanna (eds), *Strategic Human Resource Management*. New York and Chichester: Wiley.

Dex, S. (1988). Gender and the labour market. In D. Gallie (ed.), *Employment in Britain* (pp. 281–309). Oxford: Blackwell.

Dickens, C. (1859 [1952]). *A Tale of Two Cities*. London: HarperCollins.

Dickens, L. (1994). Wasted resources? Equal opportunities in employment. In K. Sisson (ed.), *Personnel Management: A Comprehensive Guide to Theory and Practice in Britain*. Oxford: Blackwell.

Dickens, L. (1998). What HRM means for gender equality. *Human Resource Management Journal*, **8**(1): 23–45.

Dietrich, M., & Roberts, J. (1997). Beyond the economics of professionalism. In J. Broadbent, M. Dietrich, & J. Roberts (eds), *The End of the Professions?* (pp. 14–33). London: Routledge.

Disney, R. (1990). Explanations of the decline in trade union density in Britain: an appraisal. *British Journal of Industrial Relations*, **28**(2): 165–77.

Dixon, N. (1992). Organizational learning: a review of the literature with implications for HRD professionals. *Human Resource Development Quarterly* **3**(1): 29–49.

Dixon, N. (1994). *The Organizational Learning Cycle: How We Can Learn Collectively*. Maidenhead: McGraw-Hill.

Donnelly, E. (1987). The training model: time for a change. *Industrial and Commercial Training*, May/June, 3–6.

Donovan, Lord (1968). Royal Commission on Trade Unions Employers' Association. Cmnd 3623. London: HMSO.

Dore, R. (1973). *British Factory, Japanese Factory*. London: Allen & Unwin.

Dowlen, A. (1996). NLP – help or hype? Investigating the uses of neuroliguistic programming in management learning. *Career Development International*, **1**(1): 27–34.

Down, S., & Smith, D. (1998). It pays to be nice to people. *Personnel Review*, **27**(2): 143–55.

Drache, D. (1995). The decline of collective bargaining: is it irreversible? Proceedings of the XXXIst ACRI/CIRA, pp. 101–22.

Drohan, M. (2000). Technology comes with a price: stress and depression. *Globe and Mail*, 11 October, p. B15.

Drucker, P. F. (1993). *Post-capitalist Society*. London: Butterworth Heinemann.

Dulewicz, V., & Higgs, M. (2000). Emotional intelligence: a review and evaluation. *Journal of Managerial Psychology*, **15**(4): 341–72.

Easterby-Smith, M., Snell, R., & Gherardi, S. (1998). Organizational learning: diverging communities of practice. *Management Learning*, **29**(3): 259–72.

Easterby-Smith, M., Burgoyne, J., & Araujo, L. (eds) (1999). *Organizational Learning and the Learning Organization*. London: Sage.

Ebbinghaus, B., & Waddington, J. (2000). United Kingdom/Great Britain. In B. Ebbinghaus, & J. Visser (eds), *The Societies of Europe: Trade Unions in Western Europe Since 1945* (pp. 705–56). London: Macmillan – now Palgrave Macmillan.

Edvinsson, L., & Malone, M. S. (1997). *Intellectual Capital*. London: Piatkus.

Edwards, J. (2000). Technological discontinuity and workforce size: an argument for selective downsizing. *International Journal of Organizational Analysis*, **8**(3): 290–308.

Edwards, P. K. (1985). *Managing Labour Relations Through the Recession*. Warwick: University of Warwick, Industrial Relations Research Unit.

Edwards, P. K., Geary, J., & Sisson, K. (2001). Employee invovement in the workplace: transformative, exploitative or limited and controlled? In J. Bélanger, G. Murray, & P-A Lapointe (eds) *Work and Employment Relations in the High Performance Workplace*. London: Cassell/Mansell.

Edwards, R. (1979). *Contested Terrain: The Transformation of the Workplace in the Twentieth Century*, London: Heinemann.

Egri, C. P., & Pinfield, L. T. (1999). Organizations and the biosphere ecologies and environments. In S. Clegg, C. Hardt, & W. Nord *Managing Organizations: Current Issues* (pp. 209–33). London: Sage.

Eisenberg, E. M., & Goodall, H. L. (1997). *Organizational Communication* (2nd edn). New York: St. Martin's Press.

Eisenhardt, K. M. (1989). Agency theory: an assessment and review. *Academy of Management Review*, **14**, 57–74.

Elger, T., & Smith, C. (1994). *Global Japanization?* London: Routledge.

Emmott, M., & Hutchinson, S. (1998). Employment flexibility: threat or promise? In P. Sparrow, & M. Marchington (eds), *Human Resource Management: A New Agenda* (pp. 229–44). London: Financial Times Management.

Eraut, M. (2000). Non-formal learning and tacit knowledge in professional work. *British Journal of Educational Psychology*, **70**: 113–36.

Etzioni, A. (1988). *The Moral Dimension*. New York: Free Press.

Eva, D., & Oswald, R. (1981). *Health and Safety at Work*. London: Pan Original.

Evans, A. L., & Lorange, P. (1989). The two logics behind human resource management. In P. Evans, Y. Doz, & A. Laurent (eds), *Human Resource Management in International Firms*. London: Macmillan – now Palgrave Macmillan.

Evered, R. D., & Selman, J. C. (1989). Coaching and the art of management. *Organizational Dynamics*, Autumn, 16–32.

Exworthy, M., & Halford, S. (1999a). Professionals and managers in a changing public sector: conflict, compromise and collaboration. In M. Exworthy, & S. Halford (eds), *Professionals and the New Managerialism in the Public Sector* (pp. 1–17). Buckingham: Open University Press.

Exworthy, M., & Halford S. (eds) (1999b) *Professionals and the New Managerialism in the Public Sector*. Buckingham: Open University Press.

Farnham, D. (1990). *Personnel in Context*. London: Institute of Personnel Management.

Faux, J., & Mishel, L. (2000). Inequality and the global economy. In W. Hutton, & A. Giddens (eds), *On the Edge: Living with Global Capitalism* (pp. 93–111). London: Jonathan Cape.

Fayol, H. (1949). *Administration Industrielle et Générale/General and Industrial Management*. London: Pitman.

Felstead, A., & Ashton, D. (2000). Tracing the links: organizational structures and skill demands. *Human Resources Management Journal*, **10**(3): 5–20.

Felstead, A., & Jewson, N. (1999). Flexible labour and non-standard employment: an agenda of issues. In A. Felstead, & N. Jewson (eds), *Global Trends in Flexible Labour* (pp. 1–20). London: Macmillan – now Palgrave Macmillan.

Felstead, A. , Jewson, N., Phizacklea, A., & Walters, S. (2002). Opportunities to work at home in the context of work–life balance. *Human Resource Management Journal*, **12**(1): 54–76.

Feltham, R. (1992). Using competencies in selection and recruitment. In S. Boam, & P. Sparrow (eds), *Designing and Achieving Competency*. Maidenhead: McGraw-Hill.

Fernie, S., Metcalfe, D., & Woodland, S. (1994). Does human resource management boost employee management relations? London School of Economics CEP Working Paper 546. London: LSE.

Field, J. (2000). *Lifelong Learning and the New Educational Order*. Stoke-on-Trent: Tentham Books.

Findlay, P., McKinlay, A., Marks, A., & Thompson, P. (2000). Flexible when it suits them: the use and abuse of teamwork skills. In S. Procter, & F. Mueller (eds), *Teamworking* (pp. 222–43). London: Macmillan – now Palgrave Macmillan.

Finegold, D., & Soskice, D. (1988). The failure of training in Britain: analysis and prescription. *Oxford Review of Economic Policy*, **4**(3): 21–53.

Fitz-enz, J. (1995). *How to Measure Human Resource Management*. New York: McGraw-Hill.

Fitz-enz, J. (2000). *The ROI of Human Capital*. New York: AMACOM.

Fitz-enz, J., & Davison, B. (2002). *How to Measure Human Resources Management* (3rd edn). New York: McGraw-Hill.

Flamholz, E. (1985). *Human Resource Accounting*. Los Angeles: Jossey-Bass.

Flynn, R. (1999). Managerialism, professionalism and quasi-markets. In M. Exworthy, & S. Halford (eds), *Professionals and the New Managerialism in the Public Sector*. Buckingham: Open University Press.

Fombrun, C. J., Tichy, N. M., & Devanna, M. A. (eds) (1984). *Strategic Human Resource Management*. New York and Chichester: Wiley.

Foresight (2000). Opportunities for industry in the application of nanotechnology. Available at: http://www.foresight.gov.uk/servlet/DocViewer/doc=359. Accessed 16 October 2000.

Fox, A. (1985). *Man Mismanagement* (2nd edn). London: Hutchinson.

Freeman, R. B., & Lazear, E. P. (1995). An economic analysis of works councils. In J. Rogers, & W. Streeck (eds), *Works Councils: Consultation, Representation and Cooperation in Industrial Relations*. Chicago: University of Chicago Press.

Freeman, R. B., & Pelletier, J. (1990). The impact of industrial relations legislation on British union density. *British Journal of Industrial Relations*, **28**(2): 141–64.

Frege, C. M. (2002). A critical assessment of the theoretical and empirical research on works councils. *British Journal of Industrial Relations*, **40**(2): 221–48.

Friedman, A. (1977). *Industry and Labour: Class Struggle at Work and Monopoly Capitalism*. London: Macmillan – now Palgrave Macmillan.

Friedson, E. (2001). *Professionalism*. Cambridge: Polity Press.

Frits, K., & MacDuffie, P. (1996). The adoption of high-involvement work practices. *Industrial Relations*, **35**(3): 423–55.

Fyfe, J. (1986). Putting people back into the manpower planning equation. *Personnel Management*, October, 64–9.

Gabriel, Y. (2000). *Storytelling in Organizations*. Oxford: Oxford University Press.

Garavan, T. N. (1997). The learning organization: a review and an evaluation. *The Learning Organization*, **4**(1): 18–29.

Garavan, T. N., & McGuire, D. (2001). Competencies and workplace learning: some reflections on the rhetoric and the reality. *Journal of Workplace Learning*, **13**(4): 144–63.

Garavan, T. N., Heraty, N., & Barnicle, B. (1999). Human resource development: current issues, priorities and dilemmas. *Journal of European Industrial Training*, **23**(4/5): 169–79.

Garavan, T. N., Morley, M., Gunnigle, P., & Collins, E. (2001). Human capital accumulation: the role of human resource development. *Journal of European Industrial Training*, **25**(2–4): 48–68.

Garrick, J. (1998). *Informal Learning in the Workplace*. London: Routledge.

Garrick, J. (1999). The dominant discourses of learning at work. In D. Boud, & J. Garrick (eds), *Understanding Learning at Work* (pp. 216–29). London: Routledge.

Garvey, B., & Williamson, B. (2002). *Beyond Knowledge Management*. Harlow: Pearson Education.

Gattiker, U. E., & Cohen, A. (1997). Gender-based wage differences. *Relations Industrielles/Industrial Relations*, **52**(3): 507–29.

Geary, J. F., & Dobbins, A. (2001). Teamworking: a new dynamic in pursuit of management control. *Human Resource Management Journal*, **11**(1): 3–23.

Gennard, J., Steele, M., & Miller, K. (1989). Trends and developments in industrial relations law: trade union discipline and non-strikers. *Industrial Relations Journal*, **20**(1): 5–15.

Gerhart, B. (2000). Compensation strategy and organizational performance. In S. Rynes, & B. Gerhart (eds), *Compensation in Organizations: Current Research and Practice* (pp. 151–94). San Francisco: Jossey-Bass.

Gewirth, A. (1991). Human rights and the prevention of cancer. In D. Poff, & W. Waluchow (eds), *Business Ethics in Canada* (2nd edn) (pp. 205–15). Scarborough, Ontario: Prentice Hall.

Gibb, S. (1998). Exploring career chaos: patterns of belief. *Career Development International*, **3**(4): 149–53.

Giddens, A. (1984). *The Constitution of Society*. Berkeley, CA: University of California Press.

Giddens, A., & Hutton, W. (2000). In conversation. In W. Hutton, & A. Giddens, *On the Edge. Living with Global Capitalism* (pp. 1–51). London: Jonathan Cape.

Giles, A., & Iain, H. (1989). The collective agreement. In J. Anderson, M. Gunderson, & A. Ponak, *Union–management Relations in Canada*, (2nd edn). Don Mills, Ontario: Addison-Wesley.

Giles, A., & Starkman, A. (2001). The collective agreement. In M. Gunderson, A. Ponack, & D. Taras (eds), *Union–management Relations in Canada* (4th edn) (pp. 272–313). Toronto: Addison-Wesley Longman.

Gilman, M., & Marginson, P. (2002). Negotiating European Works Councils: contours of constrained choice. *Industrial Relations Journal*, **33**(1): 36–51.

Gilson, C., & Wager, T. (2000). Human resource management and labour management committee: from contracts to consultation? *New Zealand Journal of Industrial Relations*, **25**(2): 169–81.

Glasbeek, H. (1991). The worker as a victim. In D. Poff, & W. Waluchow (eds), *Business Ethics in Canada* (2nd edn) (pp. 199–204). Scarborough, Ontario: Prentice Hall.

Godard, J. (1991). The progressive HRM paradigm: a theoretical and empirical re-examination. *Relations Industrielles/Industrial Relations*, **46**(2): 378–99.

Godard, J. (1994). *Industrial Relations: The Economy and Society*. Toronto: McGraw-Hill Ryerson.

Godard, J., & Delaney, J. T. (2000). Reflections on the 'high performance' paradigm's implications for industrial relations as field. *Industrial and Labor Relations Review*, **53**(3): 482–502.

Gold, J., & Hamblett, J. (1999). Emotions, values and rhetorical performance: a detailed description of a conflict within a human resource management team. In T. Abma (ed.), *Telling Tales: On Evaluation and Narrative* (pp. 131–50). Stamford, CT: JAI Press.

Gold, J., & Smith, V. (2003). Advances toward a learning movement: translations at work. *Human Resource Development International* (in press).

Gold, J., Rodgers, H., & Smith, V. (2002). A typology for the future human resource development professional. Paper presented to the Third Conference on Human Resource Development: Research and Practice across Europe, Edinburgh, January.

Gollan, P. J. (2002). So what's the news? Management strategies towards non-union employee representation at News International. *Industrial Relations Journal*, **33**(4): 316–31.

Gomez-Mejia, L., & Balkin, D. (1992). *Compensation, Organizational Strategy, and Firm Performance*. Cincinnati, OH: South-Western.

Gospel, H. F. (1994). *Markets, Firms and the Management of Labour in Modern Britain*. Cambridge: Cambridge University Press.

Gospel, H. F., & Littler, C. R. (eds) (1983). *Managerial Strategies and Industrial Relations*. London: Heinemann.

Gospel, H. F., & Palmer, G. (1993). *British Industrial Relations* (2nd edn). London: Routledge.

Grant, D., & Oswick, C. (1998). Of believers, atheists and agnostics: practitioner views on HRM. *Industrial Relations Journal*, **29**(3): 178–93.

Gratton, L. (1997). Tomorrow people. *People Management*, 24 July, 22–7.

Gratton, L. (2000). A real step change. *People Management*, **6**(6): 26–30.

Gray, G., & Guppy, N. (1999). *Success Surveys: Research Methods and Practice*. Toronto: Harcourt.

Green, F. (1997). *Review of information on the benefits of training for employees*. Research Report 7. Sheffield: Department for Education and Employment.

Green, F. (1999). Training the workers. In P. Gregg, & J. Wadsworth (eds), *The State of Working Britain*. Manchester: Manchester University Press.

Green, F., & Ashton, D. (1992). Skill shortage and skill deficiency. *Work, Employment and Society*, **6**(2): 287–301.

Green, F., Machin, S., & Wilkinson, D. (1998). Trade unions and training practices in British workplaces. *Industrial and Labour Relations Review*, **52**(2): 179–95.

Green, J. (1998). Employers learn to live with AIDS. *HR Magazine*, **43**(2): 62–7.

Gregg, P. (1973). *A Social and Economic History of Britain, 1760–1972* (7th edn). London: Harrap.

Greider, W. (2002). China is winning the new 'race to the bottom' in wages. *Canadian Centre for Policy Alternatives Monitor*, **9**(1): 30–1.

Grey, C. (1998). Against learning. Paper presented to the Emergent Fields in Management Connecting Learning and Critique Conference, Leeds University, July.

Grey, C., & Mitev, N. (1995). Reengineering organizations: a critical appraisal. *Personnel Review*, **24**(1): 6–18.

Griffiths, A., & Wall, S. (1989). *Applied Economics* (3rd edn). London: Longman.

Grint, K. (1995). *Management*. Cambridge: Polity Press.

Grint, K., & Willcocks, L. (1995). Business process re-engineering in theory and practice: business paradise regained? *New Technology, Work and Employment*, **10**(2): 99–108.

Gröjer, J.-E., & Johanson, U. (1998). Current development in human resource accounting and costing. *Accounting, Auditing and Accountability*, **11**(4): 495–505.

Grundy, T. (1994). *Strategic Learning in Action*. Maidenhead: McGraw-Hill.

Grzeda, M. M. (1999). Re-conceptualizing career change: a career development perspective. *Career Development International*, **4**(6): 305–11.

Guba, E. G., & Lincoln, Y. S. (1989). *Fourth Generation Evaluation*. London: Sage.

Guest, D. E. (1986). Worker participation and personnel policy in the UK: some case studies. *International Labour Review*, **125**(6): 406–27.

Guest, D. E. (1987). Human resource management and industrial relations. *Journal of Management Studies*, **24**(5): 503–21.

Guest, D. E. (1989). HRM: implications for industrial relations. In J. Storey (ed.), *New Perspectives on Human Resource Management* (pp. 41–55). London: Routledge.

Guest, D. E. (1990). Human resource management and the American dream. *Journal of Management Studies*, **27**(4): 377–97.

Guest, D. E. (1991). Personnel management: the end of orthodoxy? *British Journal of Industrial Relations*, **29**(2): 149–75.

Guest, D. E. (1995). Human resource management, trade unions and industrial relations. In J. Storey (ed.), *Human Resource Management: A Critical Text* (pp. 110–41). London: Routledge.

Guest, D. E. (1997). Human resource management and performance: a review and research agenda. *International Journal of Human Resource Management*, **8**(3): 263–76.

Guest, D. E. (1998). Beyond HRM: commitment and the contract culture. In P. Sparrow, & M. Marchington (eds) *Human Resource Management: The New Agenda* (pp. 37–51). London: Financial Times/Pitman.

Guest, D. E. (1999). Human resource management – the workers' verdict. *Human Resource Management Journal*, **9**(3): 5–25.

Guest, D. E. (2000). Piece by piece. *People Management*, **6**(15): 26–30.

Guest, D. E. (2001). Industrial relations and human resource management. In J. Storey (ed.), *Human Resource Management: A Critical Text* (2nd edn) (pp. 96–113). London: Thomson Learning.

Guest, D. E., & Conway, N. (2002). Communicating the psychological contract: an employer perspective. *Human Resource Management Journal,* **12**(2): 22–38.

Guest, D. E., Davey, K., & Patch, A. (1998). *The Impact of New Forms of Employment Contract on Motivation and Innovation.* London: Economic and Social Research Council.

Guest, D. E., Michie, J., Sheehan, M., & Conway, N. (2000). *Getting inside the HRM–performance relationship.* Working Paper 8. Economic and Social Research Council Future of Work Programme. Swindon: ESRC.

Gunderson, M., Ponak, A., & Taras, D. (eds) (2001). *Union–management Relations in Canada* (4th edn). Toronto: Addison Wesley Longman.

Hackman, J. R., & Oldham, G. R. (1980). *Work Redesign.* New York: Addison-Wesley.

Hakim, C. (1990). Core and periphery in employers' workforce strategies. Evidence from the 1987 ELUS survey. *Work, Employment and Society,* **4**(2): 157–88.

Hale, R. (2000). To match or mis-match? The dynamics of mentoring as a route to personal and organisational learning. *Career Development International,* **5**(4): 223– 34.

Hales, C. P. (1986). What do managers do? A critical review of the evidence. *Journal of Management Studies,* **23**(1): 88–115.

Hall, S. (1998). The great moving nowhere show. *Marxism Today,* Nov/Dec, 9–14.

Hall, S., & Jacques, M. (1989). *New Times.* London: Lawrence & Wishart.

Hamel, G., & Prahalad, C. K. (1994). *Competing for the Future.* Boston: Harvard Business School.

Hammer, M. (1997). *Beyond Reengineering.* New York: HarperCollins.

Hammer, M., & Champy, J. (1993). *Reengineering the Corporation.* London: Nicholas Brealey.

Hammer, M., & Stanton, S. (1995). *The Reengineering Revolution: A Handbook.* New York: Harper Business Press.

Handy, C. (1994 h/c; 1995 p/b). *The Age of Paradox.* Boston: Harvard Business School Press.

Handy, L., Devine, M., & Heath, L. (1996). *360° Feedback: Unguided Missile or Powerful Weapon?* Berkhamsted: Ashridge Management Research Group.

Harper, S. C. (1983). A developmental approach to performance appraisal. *Business Horizons,* September/October, 68–74.

Harri-Augstein, S., & Webb, I. M. (1995). *Learning to Change.* Maidenhead: McGraw-Hill.

Harrington, B., McLoughlin, K., & Riddell, D. (1998). Business process re-engineering in the public sector: a case study of the Contributions Agency. *New Technology, Work and Employment,* **13**(1): 43–50.

Harris, M. M. (1989). Reconsidering the employment interview: a review of recent literature and suggestions for future research. *Personnel Psychology,* **42**, 691–726.

Hassard, J., & Parker, M. (1993). *Postmodernism and Organizations.* London: Sage.

Hawkins, K. W. (1995). Effects of gender and communications content on leadership in small task-oriented groups. *Small Group Research,* **26**, 234–50.

Health and Safety Commission/Department of the Environment, Transport and the Regions (HSC/DETR) (2000). *Revitalizing health and safety.* Strategy statement. London: DETR.

Hearn, J., Sheppard, D., Tancred-Sheriff, P., & Burrell, G. (eds) (1989). *The Sexuality of Organization.* London: Sage.

Heckscher, C. (1994). Defining the post-bureaucratic type. In C. Heckscher, & A. Donnelon (eds) *The Post-bureaucratic Organisation.* Thousand Oaks, CA: Sage.

Heckscher, C., & Donnelon, A. (eds) (1994). *The Post-bureaucratic Organization.* Thousand Oaks, CA: Sage.

Heery, E. (2002). Partnership versus organizing: alternative futures for British trade unionism. *Industrial Relations Journal,* **33**(1): 20–35.

Heery, E., & Salmon, J. (2000). *The Insecure Workforce.* London: Routledge.

Helgesen, S. (1995). *The Female Advantage: Women's Ways of Leadership.* New York: Doubleday.

Heller, F., Pusic, E., Strauss, G., & Wilpert, B. (1998). *Organizational Participation: Myth and Reality.* Oxford: Oxford University Press.

Hendry, C. (2000). Strategic decision making, discourse, and strategy as a social practice. *Journal of Management Studies,* **37**(7): 955–77.

Hendry, C., & Pettigrew, A. (1990). Human resource management: an agenda for the 1990s. *International Journal of Human Resource Management*, **1**(1): 17–44.

Hepple, B. (1983). Individual labour law. In G. S. Bain (ed.), *Industrial Relations in Britain* (pp. 393–417). Oxford: Blackwell.

Herriot, P. (1989). *Recruitment in the 1990s*. London: Institute of Personnel Management.

Herriot, P. (1998). The role of human resource management in building a new proposition. In P. Sparrow, & M. Marchington (eds), *Human Resource Management: A New Agenda* (pp. 106–16). London: Financial Times Management.

Herriot, P., & Fletcher, C. (1990). Candidate-friendly, selection for the 1990s. *Personnel Management*, February, 32–35.

Herriot, P., Manning, W. E. G., & Kidd, J. M. (1997). The content of the psychological contract. *British Journal of Management*, **8**(2): 151–62.

Hertz, N. (2002). *The Silent Takeover: Global Capitalism and the Death of Democracy*. London: Arrow.

Herzberg, F. (1966). *Work and the Nature of Man*. Chicago, IL: World Publishing.

Heyes, J. (2000). Workplace industrial relations and training. In H. Rainbird (ed.), *Training in the Workplace* (pp. 148–68). Basingstoke: Palgrave – now Palgrave Macmillan.

Hill, C., & Jones, G. (2001). *Strategic Management Theory* (5th edn). Boston, MA: Houghton-Mifflin.

Hillage, J., & Moralee, J. (1996). *The return on investors*. Report 314. Brighton: Institute for Employment Studies.

Hillier, Y. (1997). Competence based qualifications in training, development and management. *Journal of Further and Higher Education*, **21**(1): 33–41.

Hirsh, W. (1990). *Succession planning: Current practice and future issues*. Report 184. Brighton: Institute of Management Studies.

Hirsh, W., & Jackson, C. (1997). *Strategies for career development: Promise, practice and pretence*. Report 305. Brighton: Institute for Employment Studies.

Hirst, P., & Thompson, G. (2000). Globalization in one country? The peculiarities of the British. *Economy and Society*, **29**(3): 335–56.

Hobsbawm, E. J. (1968). *Industry and Empire*. London: Weidenfeld & Nicolson.

Hobsbawm, E. J. (1997). *On History*. London: Weidenfeld & Nicolson.

Hochschild, A. R. (2000). Global care chains and emotional surplus value. In W. Hutton, & A. Giddens (eds), *On the Edge: Living with Global Capitalism* (pp. 130–46). London: Jonathan Cape.

Hofstede, G. (1980). *Culture's Consquences: International Differences in Work-related Values*. London: Sage.

Hogarth, T. (1993). Worker support for organizational change and technical change. *Work, Employment and Society*, **7**(2): 45–63.

Hogarth, T., Hasluck, C., Pierre, G., Winterbotham, M., & Vivien, D. (2001). *Work–life balance 2000: Results from the baseline study*. Department for Education and Employment Research Report 249. London: DfEE.

Holbeche, L. (1998). *Motivating People in Lean Organizations*. Oxford: Butterworth Heinemann.

Holbeche, L. (1999). *Aligning Human Resources and Business Strategy*. Oxford: Butterworth Heinemann.

Holman, D. (2000). A dialogical approach to skill and skilled activity. *Human Relations*, **53**(7): 957–80.

Holman, D., Pavlica, K., & Thorpe, R. (1997). Rethinking Kolb's theory of experiential learning in management education: the contribution of social constructionism and activity theory. *Management Learning*, **28**(2): 135–48.

Hom, P. W., Griffeth, R. W., Palich, L. E., & Bracker, J. S. (1999). Revisiting met expectations as a reason why realistic job previews work. *Personnel Psychology*, **52**(1): 1–16.

Hoque, K. (1999). Human resource management and performance in the UK hotel industry. *British Journal of Industrial Relations*, **37**(3): 419–43.

Hoque, K., & Noon, M. (2001). Counting angels: a comparison of personnel and HR specialists. *Human Resource Management Journal*, **11**(3): 5–22.

Huczynski, A., & Buchanan, D. (1991). *Organizational Behaviour* (2nd edn). Harlow: Pearson Education.

Huczynski, A., & Buchanan, D. (2001). *Organizational Behaviour* (4th edn). Harlow: Pearson Education.

Huffcutt, A. I., Weekly, J. A., Wiesner, W. H., DeGrout, T. G., & Jones, C. (2001). Comparison of situational and behavior description interview questions for higher-level positions. *Personnel Psychology*, **54**(3): 619–44.

Huselid, M. A. (1995). The impact of HRM practices on turnover, productivity, and corporate financial performance. *Academy of Management Journal*, **38**(3): 635–72.

Huseman, R. C., & Goodman, J. P. (1999). *Leading with Knowledge: The Nature of Competition in the 21st Century*. Thousand Oaks, CA: Sage.

Hutchinson, S., Purcell, J., & Kinnie, N. (2000). Evolving high commitment management and the experience of the RAC call centre. *Human Resource Management Journal*, **10**(1): 63–78.

Hutton, W. (1996). *The State We're In*. London: Vintage.

Hutton, W. (1997). *The State to Come*. London: Vintage.

Hutton, W., & Giddens, A. (2000). *On the Edge: Living with Global Capitalism*. London: Jonathan Cape.

Huws, U. (1997). *Teleworking: Guidelines for good practice*. Report 329. Brighton: Institute for Employment Studies.

Hyman, R. (1975). *Industrial Relations: A Marxist Introduction*. London: Macmillan – now Palgrave Macmillan.

Hyman, R. (1987). Trade unions and the law: papering over the cracks? *Capital and Class*, (31): 43–63.

Hyman, R. (1988). Flexible specialization: miracle or myth? In R. Hyman, & W. Streeck (eds), *New Technology and Industrial Relations*. Oxford: Blackwell.

Hyman, R. (1989). *Strikes* (4th edn). London: Macmillan – now Palgrave Macmillan.

Hyman, R. (1991). European unions: towards 2000. *Work, Employment and Society*, **5**(4): 621–39.

Hyman, R. (1994). Industrial relations in Western Europe: an era of ambiguity? *Industrial Relations Journal*, **33**(1): 1–24.

Hyman, R. (1997a). Editorial. *European Journal of Industrial Relations*, **3**(1): 5–6.

Hyman, R. (1997b). The future of employee representation. *British Journal of Industrial Relations*, **35**(3): 309–36.

Hyman, R., & Mason, B. (1995). *Managing Employee Involvement and Participation*. London: Sage.

Ichniowski, C., Kochan, T., Levine, D., Olson, C., & Strauss, G. (1996). What works at work: overview and assessment. *Industrial Relations*, **35**(3): 299–333.

Iles, P., & Salaman, G. (1995). Recruitment, selection and assessment. In Storey, J. (ed.), *Human Resource Management* (pp. 203–33). London: Routledge.

Industrial Relations Services (1998). *Partnership in Practice at Legal and General*. IRS Employment Trends 650. London: IRS.

Industrial Relations Services (2001). *Competency Frameworks in UK Organisations*. London: IRS.

Institute of Personnel and Development (1996). *The Lean Organisation: Managing the People Dimension*. London: IPD.

Institute of Personnel and Development (1997) *Overqualified and Underemployed?* London: IPD.

Institute of Personnel Management (1981). Representative structures, *Institute of Personnel Management*. London: IPM.

International Labour Organisation (2000). High performance working: research project overview. http://www.ilo.org/public/english/employement/skills/training/casest/overivew.htm. Accessed 2 May 2002.

Jackson, C. (1996). Understanding psychological testing. Leicester: BPS Books.

Jaffee, D. (2001). *Organization Theory: Tension and Change*. Boston: McGraw-Hill.

James, P., & Walters, D. (2002). Worker representation in health and safety: options for regulatory reform. *Industrial Relations Journal*, **33**(2): 141–56.

Jenkins, C., & Sherman, B. (1979). *The Collapse of Work*. London: Eyre Methuen.

Johanson, U. (1999). Why the concept of human resource costing and accounting does not work. *Personnel Review*, **28**(1/2): 91–107.

Johanson, U., & Nilson, M. (1996). *Human resource costing and accounting and organisational learning*. Report 1995:1. Stockholm: Personnel Economics Institute.

Johnson, C. (1988). *Measuring the Economy*. London: Penguin.

Johnson, G. (1987). *Strategic Change and the Management Process*. Oxford: Blackwell.

Johnson, R. (2001). Doubled entente. *People Management*, **7**(9): 38–9.

Johnson, S., Campbell, M., Devins, D., Gold, J., & Hamblett, J. (2000). *Learning Pays*. Sheffield: National Advisory Council for Education and Training Targets.

Jones, O. (1997). Changing the balance? Taylorism, TQM and the work organization. *New Technology, Work and Employment*, **12**(1): 13–23.

Judge, T. A., & Cable, D. M. (1997). Applicant personality, organizational culture and organization attraction. *Personnel Psychology*, **50**, 359–94.

Jurgens, U. (1989). The transfer of Japanese management concepts in the international automobile industry. In S. Wood (ed.), *The Transformation of Work?* (pp. 204–18). London: Unwin Hyman.

Kasl, E., Marsick, V., & Dechant, K. (1997). Teams as learners. *Journal of Applied Behaviour Science*, **33**(2): 227–46.

Keenoy, T. (1990). Human resource management: rhetoric, reality and contradiction. *International Journal of Human Resource Management*, **1**(3): 363–84.

Keenoy, T., & Anthony, P. (1992). HRM: metaphor, meaning and morality. In P. Blyton, & P. Turnbull (eds), *Reassessing Human Resource Management* (pp. 233–55). London: Sage.

Keep, E. (1989) Corporate training policies: the vital component. In J. Storey (ed.) *New Perspectives in Human Resource Management* (pp. 109–25). Routledge: London.

Keep, E. (1999). *Employer attitudes towards adult learning*. Skills Task Force Research Paper 15. London: Department for Education and Employment.

Keith, M. (2000). Sexual harassment case law under the Employment Contracts Act 1991. *New Zealand Journal of Industrial Relations*, **25**(3): 277–89.

Kelly, J. E. (1985). Management's redesign of work: labour process, labour markets and product markets. In D. Knights, H. Willmott, & D. Collinson (eds), *Job Design: Critical Perspectives on the Labour Process* (pp. 30–51). Aldershot: Gower.

Kelly, J. E. (1988). *Trade Unions and Socialist Politics*. London: Verso.

Kelly, J. E. (1996). Union militancy and social partnership. In P. Ackers, C. Smith, & P. Smith (eds) *The New Workplace and Trade Unionism*. London: Routledge.

Kelly, J. E. (1998). *Rethinking Industrial Relations: Mobilisation, Collectivism and Long Waves*. London: Routledge.

Kelly, J. E., & Bailey, R. (1989). Research note: British trade union membership, density and decline in the 1980s. *Industrial Relations Journal*, **20**(1): 54–61.

Kessels, J. W. M. (1996). *Corporate Education: The Ambivalent Perspective of Knowledge Productivity*. Leiden University: Centre for Education and Instruction.

Kessels, J. W. M. (2001). Learning in organisations: a corporate curriculum for the knowledge economy. *Futures*, **33** (6): 497–506.

Kessler, I. (1994). Performance pay. In K. Sisson (ed.), *Personnel Management* (2nd edn). Oxford: Blackwell.

Kessler, I. (1995). Reward systems. In J. Storey (ed.), *Human Resource Management: A Critical Text* (pp. 254–79). London: Routledge.

Kessler, I. (2001). Reward system choices. In J. Storey (ed.), *Human Resource Management: A Critical Text* (2nd edn) (pp. 206–31). London: Thomson Learning.

Kessler, S., & Bayliss, F. (1995). *Contemporary British Industrial Relations* (2nd edn). London: Macmillan – now Palgrave Macmillan.

Kettley, P. (1997). *Personal feedback: Cases in point*. Report 326. Brighton: Institute for Employment Studies.

Kidd, J., Xue, L., & Richter, F.-J. (2001). *Maximizing Human Intelligence Deployment in Asian Business*. Basingstoke: Palgrave – now Palgrave Macmillan.

Kinnie, N. J., & Arthurs, A. J. (1996). Personnel specialists' advanced use of information technology. *Personnel Review*, **25**(3): 3–19.

Kirkpatrick, D. L. (1983). Four steps to measuring training effectiveness. *Personnel Administrator*, November, 19–25.

Klein, N. (2000). *No Logo*. London: Flamingo.

Kline, T. (1999). *Remaking Teams*. San Francisco, CA: Jossey-Bass.

Knight, K., & Latreille, P. (2000). Discipline, dismissals and complaints to employment tribunals. *British Journal of Industrial Relations*, **38**(4): 533–55.

Knights, D., & Willmott, H. (eds) (1996). *Gender and the Labour Process*. Aldershot: Gower.

Kochan, T. E., & Dyer, L. (1995). HRM: an American view. In J. Storey (ed.), *Human Resource Management: A Critical Text* (pp. 332–51). London: Routledge.

Kochan, T. E., Katz, H., & McKersie, R. (1986). *The Transformation of American Industrial Relations*. New York: Basic Books.

Kochan, T. E., Batt, R., & Dyer, L. (1992). International human resource studies: a framework for future research. In D. Lewlin, O. Mitchell, & P. Sterer (eds), *Research Frontiers – Industrial Relations and Human Resources* (pp. 309–37). Madison, University of Wisconsin: Industrial Relations Association.

Kolb, D. A. (1984). *Experiential Learning*. Prentice Hall, NJ: Englewood Cliffs.

Kotter, J. (1990). *A Force for Change*. New York: Free Press.

Kotter, J. (1996). *Leading Change*. Boston, MA: Harvard Business.

KPMG (1996). *Learning Organisation Benchmarking Survey*. KPMG: London.

Kramer, R. M., & Tyler, T. R. (1996). *Trust in Organizations: Frontiers of Theory and Research*. Newbury Park, CA: Sage.

Kraut, A. (1996). An overview of organizational surveys. In A. Kraut (ed.), *Organizational Surveys* (pp. 1–17). San Francisco, CA: Jossey-Bass.

Kuttner, R. (2000). The role of governments in the global economy. In W. Hutton. & A. Giddens (eds), *On the Edge: Living with Global Capitalism* (pp. 147–63). London: Jonathan Cape.

Kydd, B., & Oppenheim, L. (1990). Using human resource management to enhance competitiveness: lessons from four excellent companies. *Human Resource Management Journal*, **29**(2): 145–66.

Lank, E. (2002). Head to head. *People Management*, **8**(4): 46–9.

Lash, S., & Urry, J. (1987). *The End of Organized Capitalism*. Cambridge: Polity Press.

Latham, G. P., Saari, L. M., Pursell, E. D., & Campion, M. A. (1980). The situational interview. *Journal of Applied Psychology*, **65**, 422–27.

Lave, J., & Wenger, E. (1991). *Situated Learning*. Cambridge: Cambridge University Press.

Lawler, E. E. (1990). *Strategic Pay: Aligning Organizational Strategies and Pay Systems*. San Francisco: Jossey-Bass.

Legge, K. (1989). Human resource management: a critical analysis. In J. Storey (ed.), *New Perspectives on Human Resource Management* (pp. 21–36). London: Routledge.

Legge, K. (1995). *Human Resource Management: Rhetorics and Realities*. Basingstoke: Macmillan – now Palgrave Macmillan.

Legge, K. (1998). The morality of HRM. In C. Mabey, D. Skinner, & T. Clark, *Experiencing Human Resource Management*. London: Sage.

Legge, K. (2001). Silver bullet or spent round? Assessing the meaning of the 'high commitment'/performance relationship. In J. Storey (ed.), *Human Resource Management* (pp. 21–36). London: Thomson-Learning.

Lepak, D. P., & Snell, S. A. (1999). The strategic management of human capital: determinants and implications of different relationships. *Academy of Management Review*, **24**(1): 1–18.

Levinson, H. (1970). Management by whose objectives? *Harvard Business Review*, July/August, 125–34.

Liff, S. (1997). Constructing HR information systems. *Human Resource Management Journal*, **7**(2): 18–31.

Liff, S. (2000). Manpower or human resource planning – what's in a name? In S. Bach, & K. Sisson (eds), *Personnel Management* (3rd edn) (pp. 93–110). Blackwell: Oxford.

Lincoln, J., & Kalleberg, A. (1992). *Culture Control and Commitment*. Cambridge: Cambridge University Press.

Lipsig-Mummé, C. (2001). Trade unions and labour relations systems in comparative perspective. In M. Gunderson, A. Ponak, & D. Taras (eds), *Union–management Relations in Canada* (4th edn) (pp. 521–38). Toronto: Addison Wesley Longman.

Littler, C. R. (1982). *The Development of the Labour Process in Capitalist Societies*. London: Heinemann.

Littler, C. R., & Salaman, G. (1984). *Class at Work: The Design, Allocation and Control of Jobs*. London: Batsford.

Lloyd, C. (1997). Microelectronics in the clothing industry: firm strategy and the skills debate. *New Technology, Work and Employment*, **12**(1): 36–47.

Locke, E. A., Feren, D. B., McCaleb, V., Shaw, K., & Denny, A. (1980). The relative effectiveness of four methods of motivating employee performance. In K. D. Duncan, M. Gruneberg, & D. Wallis (eds), *Changes in Working Life*. London: Wiley.

Long, R. J. (2002). *Strategic Compensation in Canada* (2nd edn). Scarborough, Ontario: Thomson Learning.

Loveridge, R. (1983). Labour market segmentation and the firm. In J. Edwards et al. (eds) *Manpower Planning: Strategy and Techniques in an Organisational Context* (pp. 155–75). Chichester: Wiley.

Lowe, G. (2000). *The Quality of Work*. Don Mills, Ontario: Oxford University Press.

Lowstedt, J. (1988). Prejudices and wishful thinking about computer aided design. *New Technology, Work and Employment*, **3**(1): 30–7.

Lyon, P., & Glover, I. (1998). Divestment or investment? The contradictions of HRM in relation to older employees. *Human Resource Management Journal*, **8**(1): 56–68.

Mabey, C., & Iles, P. (1991). HRM from the other side of the fence. *Personnel Management*, February, 50–3.

Mabey, C., Skinner, D., & Clark, D. (eds) (1998). *Experiencing Human Resource Management*. London: Sage.

McCarthy, A. M., & Garavan, T. N. (2001). 360° Feedback processes: performance improvement and employee career development. *Journal of European Industrial Training*, **25**(1): 5–32.

McClurg, L. N. (2001). Team rewards: how far have we come? *Human Resource Management*, **40**(1): 73–86.

McCormack, B. (2000). Workplace learning: a unifying concept. *Human Resource Development International*, **3**(3): 397–404.

McCracken, M., & Wallace, M. (2000). Towards a redefinition of strategic HRD. *Journal of European Industrial Training*, **24**(5): 281–90.

MacDuffie, J. P. (1995). Human resource bundles and manufacturing performance: organizational logic and flexible production systems in the world of auto industry. *Industrial and Labor Relations Review*, **48**, 197–221.

McGoldrick, J., & Stewart, J. (1996). The HRM–HRD nexus. In J. McGoldrick, & J. Stewart (eds), *Human Resource Development*. London: Pitman Publishing.

McGoldrick, J., Stewart, J., & Watson, S. (2001). Theorizing human resource development. *Human Resource Development International*, **4**(3): 343–56.

McGregor, D. (1957). An uneasy look at performance appraisal. *Harvard Business Review*, **35**(3): 89–94.

McGregor, D. (1960). *The Human Side of Enterprise*. New York: McGraw-Hill.

McHenry, R. (1997a). Tried and tested. *People Management*, 23 January, 32–7.

McHenry, R. (1997b). Spurring stuff. *People Management*, 24 July, 28–31.

Machin, S. (2000). Union decline in Britain. *British Journal of Industrial Relations*, **38**(4): 631–45.

Machin, S., & Vignoles, A. (2001). T*he Economic Benefits of Training to the Individual, the Firm and the Economy: The Key Issues*. London: Centre for the Economics of Education.

McIlroy, J. (1991). *The Permanent Revolution? Conservative Law and the Trade Unions*. Nottingham: Spokesman.

MacInnes, J. (1985). Conjuring up consultation. *British Journal of Industrial Relations*, **23**(1): 93–113.

MacInnes, J. (1987). *Thatcherism at Work*. Milton Keynes: Open University Press.

McKendrick, E. (1988). The rights of trade union members: part I of the Employment Act 1980. *Industrial Law Journal*, **17**(3): 141–61.

Mackie, K. S., Holahan, C., & Gottlieb, N. (2001). Employee involvement management practices, work stress, and depression in employees of a human services residential care facility. *Human Relations*, **54**(8): 1065–92.

McKinlay, A., & Taylor, P. (1998). Through the looking glass: Foucault and the politics of production. In A. McKinlay, & K. Starkey (eds), *Foucault, Management and Organizational Theory* (pp. 173–90). London: Sage.

McLoughlin, I., & Clark, J. (1988). *Technological Change at Work*. Milton Keynes: Open University Press.

McLoughlin, I., & Gourlay, S. (1992). Enterprise without unions: managing employment relations in non-union firms. *Journal of Management Studies*, **29**(5): 509–28.

McNabb, R., & Whitfield, K. (2001). Job evaluation and high performance work practices: compatible or conflictual? *Journal of Management Studies*, **38**(2): 293–312.

McShane, S. L. (1990). Two tests of direct gender bias in job evaluation ratings. *Journal of Occupational Psychology*, **63**, 129–40.

McShane, S. L. (2001). *Canadian Organizational Behaviour* (4th edn). Boston: Irwin.

Malloch, H. (1997). Strategic and HRM aspects of kaizen: a case study. *New Technology, Work and Employment*, **12**(2): 108–22.

Mankin, D. P. (2001). A model for human resource development. *Human Resource Development International*, **4**(1): 65–85.

Mannion, E., & Whittaker, P. (1996). European Passenger Services Ltd – assessment centres for recruitment and development. *Career Development International*, **1**(6): 12–16.

Marchington, M. (1980). *Responses to Participation at Work*. Aldershot: Gower.

Marchington, M. (1982). *Managing Industrial Relations*. Maidenhead: McGraw-Hill.

Marchington, M. (1987). A review and critique of research on developments in joint consultation. *British Journal of Industrial Relations*, **25**(3): 339–52.

Marchington, M. (1995). Involvement and participation. In J. Storey (ed.), *Human Resource Management: A Critical Text* (pp. 280–305). London: Routledge.

Marchington, M. (2001). Employee involvement. In J. Storey (ed.) *Human Resource Management: A Critical Text* (pp 232–52). London: Thomson Learning.

Marchington, M., & Wilding, P. (1983). Employee involvement inaction? *Personnel Management*, December, 73–82.

Marchington, M., & Wilkinson, A. (2000). Direct participation. In S. Bach, & K. Sisson (eds), *Personnel Management: A Comprehensive Guide to Theory and Practice*. Oxford: Blackwell.

Marchington, M., Goodman, J., Wilkinson, A., & Ackers, P. (1992). *Recent Developments in Employee Involvement*. Employment Department Research Series 1. London: HMSO.

Marginson, P., & Wood, S. (2000). WERS98 special issue: Editor's introduction. *British Journal of Industrial Relations*, **38**(4): 489–99.

Marsick, V., & Watkins, K. E. (1999). Envisioning new organisations for learning. In D. Boud, & J. Garrick (eds), *Understanding Learning at Work* (pp. 199–215). London: Routledge.

Martin, J. N., & Nakayama, T. K. (2000). *Intercultural Communications in Context* (2nd edn). Mountain View, CA: Mayfield.

Martinez Lucio, M. & Weston, S. (1992). Human resource management and trade union responses: bringing the politics of the workplace back into the debate. In P. Blyton, & P. Turnbull (eds), *Reassessing Human Resource Management* (pp. 215–32). London: Sage.

Maslow, A. (1954). *Motivation and Personality*. New York: Harper & Row.

Mathias, P. (1969). *The First Industrial Nation*. London: Methuen.

Matzdorf, F., Price, I., & Green, M. (1999). Barriers to organizational learning in the chartered surveying profession. *Property Management*, **18**(2): 92–113.

Mayhew, C., & Quinlan, M. (1997). Subcontracting and occupational health and safety in the residential building industry. *Industrial Relations Journal*, **28**(3): 192–205.

Mayo, A. (1991). *Managing Careers*. London: Institute of Personnel Management.

Mayo, A. (1998). Memory Bankers. *People Management*, 22 January, 34–8.

Mayo, A. (2002). A thorough evaluation. *People Management*, **8**(7): 36–9.

Mayrhofer, W., Brewster, C., Morley, M., & Gunnigle, P. (2000). Communication, consultation and the HRM debate. In C. Brewster, W. Mayrhofer, & M. Morley (eds), *New Challenges for European Human Resource Management* (pp. 222–44). London: Macmillan – now Palgrave Macmillan.

Megginson, D. (2000). Current issues in mentoring. *Career Development International*, **5**(4): 256–60.

Megginson, D., & Clutterbuck, D. (1995). *Mentoring in Action*. London: Kogan Page.

Megginson, D., & Pedler, M. (1992). *Self Development*. Maidenhead: McGraw-Hill.

Merriam, S., & Simpson, E. (1995). *A Guide to Research for Educators and Trainers of Adults*. Malabar, FL: Krieger.

Merrick, N. (2001). Wel.com aboard. *People Management*, **7**(10): 26–32.

Meyer, H. H., Kay, E., & French, J. R. P. (1965). Split roles in performance appraisal. *Harvard Business Review*, **43**, 123–29.

Mezirow, J. (1991). *Transformative Dimensions of Adult Learning*. San Francisco: Jossey-Bass.

Michie, J. (1992). Unlucky 13 for the economy. *Observer*, Sunday 5 April, p. 35.

Michie, J., & Sheehan-Quinn, M. (2001). Labour market flexibility: human resource management and corporate performance. *British Journal of Management*, **12**(4): 287–305.

Middlehurst, R., & Kennie, T. (1997). Leading professionals: towards new concepts of professionalism. In J. Broadbent, M. Dietrich, & J. Roberts (eds), *The End of the Professions?* (pp. 50–68). London: Routledge.

Miles, R., & Snow, C. (1984). Designing strategic human resources systems. *Organizational Dynamics*, Summer, 36–52.

Milkovitch, G., & Newman, J. (2002). *Compensation* (7th edn). New York: McGraw-Hill.

Miller, P. (1987). Strategic industrial relations and human resource management – distinction, definition and recognition. *Journal of Management Studies*, **24**(4): 347–61.

Mills, A., & Simmons, T. (1995). *Reading Organizational Theory*. Toronto: Garamond.

Mills, A., & Tancred, P. (eds) (1992). *Gendering Organizational Analysis*. Newbury Park, CA: Sage.

Millward, N., & Stevens, M. (1986). *British Workplace Industrial Relations 1980–1984*. Aldershot: Gower.

Millward, N., Stevens, M., Smart, D., & Hawes, W. (1992). *Workplace Industrial Relations in Transition*. Aldershot: Dartmouth Press.

Millward, N., Bryson, A., & Forth, J. (2000). *All Change at Work: British Employee Relations 1980–1998*. London: Routledge.

Mintzberg, H. (1973). *The Nature of Managerial Work*. London: Harper & Row.

Mintzberg, H. (1978). Patterns in strategy formation. *Management Science*, **24**(9): 934–48.

Mintzberg, H. (1987). Crafting strategy. *Harvard Business Review*, July/August, 66–75.

Mintzberg, H. (1989). *Mintzberg on Management*. New York: Collier/Hamilton.

Mintzberg, H. (1990). The design school: reconsidering the basic premises of strategic management. *Strategic Management Journal*, **11**, 171–95.

Mintzberg, H. (1992). Five tips for strategy. In H. Mintzberg, & J. Quinn (eds), *The Strategy Process: Concepts and Contexts*. Englewood Cliffs, NJ: Prentice Hall.

Mintzberg, H., Ahlstrand, B., & Lampel, J. (1998). *Strategic Safari: A Guided Tour Through the Wilds of Strategic Management*. New York: Free Press.

Monks, J. (1998). Foreword. In C. Mabey, C., Skinner, & D. Clark (eds) (1998). *Experiencing Human Resource Management*. London: Sage.

Monks, K., & McMackin, J. (2001). Designing and aligning an HR system. *Human Resource Management Journal*, **11**(2): 57–72.

Montgomery, J., & Kelloway, K. (2002). *Management of Occupational Health and Safety* (2nd edn). Scarborough, Ontario: Nelson Thomson Learning.

Moore, H. L. (1995). The future of work. *British Journal of Industrial Relations*, **33**(4): 657–78.

Moore, L., & Devereaux Jennings, P. (eds) (1995). *Human Resource Management on the Pacific Rim*. New York: Walter de Gruyter.

Morgan, G. (1997). *Images of Organization*. London: Sage.

Morley, M., Brewster, C., Gunnigle, P., & Mayrhofer, W. (2000). Evaluating change in European industrial relations: research evidence on trends at organizational level. In C. Brewster, W. Mayrhofer, & M. Morley (eds), *New Challenges for European Human Resource Management*. New York: St. Martin's Press.

Morrison, E. W., & Robinson, S. L. (1997). When employees feel betrayed: a model of how psychological contract violation develops. *Academy of Management Review*, **22**(1): 226–56.

Mueller, C., De Coster, S., & Estes, S. (2001). Sexual harassment in the workplace. *Work and Occupations*, **28**(4): 411–46.

Munro, A., & Rainbird, H. (2000). The new unionsism and the new bargaining agenda: UNISON–employer partnerships on workplace learning in Britain. *British Journal of Industrial Relations*, **38**(2): 223–40.

Munro-Fraser, J. (1971). *Psychology: General, Industrial, Social*. London: Pitman.

Murakami, T. (1995). Introducing team working: a motor industry case study from Germany. *Industrial Relations Journal*, **26**(4): 293–304.

Murphy, C., & Olthuis, D. (1995). The impact of work reorganization on employee attitudes towards work, the company and the union. In C. Schenk, & J. Anderson (eds), *Re-shaping Work: Union Responses to Technological Change* (pp. 76–102). Toronto, Ontario: Ontario Federation of Labour.

Murray, G. (2001). Unions: membership, structures, actions, and challenges. In M. Gunderson, A. Ponak, & D. Taras (eds), *Union–management Relations in Canada* (4th edn) (pp. 79–116). Toronto: Addison Wesley Longman.

Mwita, J. I. (2000). Performance management model. *International Journal of Public Sector Management*, **13**(1): 19–37.

National Skills Task Force (1998). *Towards a National Skills Agenda*. London: Department for Education and Employment.

National Skills Task Force (2000). *Skills for All: Research Report from the National Skills Task Force*. London: Department for Education and Employment.

Needle, D. (2000). *Business in Context* (3rd edn). London: Thompson Learning.

Neher, W. W. (1997). *Organizational Communication*. Boston: Allyn & Bacon.

Newell, S., & Shackleton, V. (2000). Recruitment and selection. In S. Bach, & K. Sisson (eds), *Personnel Management* (3rd edn) (pp. 111–36). Blackwell: Oxford.

Newton, T., & Findlay, P. (1996). 'Playing God? The performance of appraisal. *Human Resource Management Journal*, **6**(3): 42–58.

Nichols, T. (ed.) (1980). *Capital and Labour*. London: Fontana.

Nichols, T. (1986). *The British Worker Question: A New Look at Workers and Productivity in Manufacturing*. London: Routledge & Kegan Paul.

Nichols, T. (1990). Industrial safety in Britain and the 1974 Health and Safety at Work Act: the case of manufacturing. *International Journal of the Sociology of Law*, **18**, 371–42.

Nichols, T., & Beynon, H. (1977). *Living with Capitalism: Class Relations and the Modern Factory*. London: Routledge & Kegan Paul.

Nichols, T., Sugur, N., & Demir, E. (2002). Globalized management and local labour: the case of the white-goods industry in Turkey. *Industrial Relations Journal*, **33**(1): 68–85.

Nkomo, S. M. (1988). Strategic planning for human resources – let's get started. *Long Range Planning*, **21**(1): 66–72.

Noble, C. (1997). International comparisons of training policies. *Human Resource Management Journal*, **7**(1): 5–18.

Nonaka, I., & Takeuchi, H. (1995). *The Knowledge-creating Company*. Oxford: Oxford University Press.

Noon, M. (1992). HRM: A map, model or theory? In P. Blyton, & P. Turnbull (eds), *Reassessing Human Resource Management* (pp. 16–32). London: Sage.

Nutley, S. (2000). Beyond systems: HRM audits in the public sector. *Human Resource Management Journal*, **10**(2): 21–38.

Oliver, N., & Wilkinson, B. (1988). *The Japanization of British Industry*. Oxford: Blackwell.

Organisation for Economic Co-operation and Development (1996). *The Knowledge-based Economy*. Paris: OECD.

Organisation for Economic Co-operation and Development (1997). *The Internationalisation of Higher Education*. Paris: OECD.

Osterman, P. (1995). How common is workplace transformation and who adopts it? *Industrial and Labor Relations Review*, **47**, 173–87.

Ouchi, W. (1979). A conceptual framework for the design of organizational control mechanisms. *Management Science*, **25**(9): 833–48.

Ouchi, W. (1981). *Theory Z: How American Companies Can Meet the Japanese Challenge*. Reading, MA: Addison-Wesley.

Pahl, R. E. (ed.) (1988). *On Work: Historical, Comparative and Theoretical Approaches*. Oxford: Blackwell.

Palys, T. (1997). *Research Decisions: Quantitative and Qualitative Perspectives*. Toronto: Harcourt Brace.

Panteli, N., & Dawson, P. (2001). Video conferencing meetings: changing patterns of business. *New Technology, Work and Employment*, **16**(2): 88–99.

Parker, B., & Caine, D. (1996). Holonic modelling: human resource planning and the two faces of Janus. *International Journal of Manpower*, **17**(8): 30–45.

Payne, J. (2000). The contribution of individual learning accounts to the lifelong learning policies of the UK government: a case-study. *Studies in the Education of Adults*, **32**(2): 257–75.

Pearson, I. (1999). The power of information. *Foresight*, **1**(5): 413–26.

Pearson, R. (1991). *The Human Resource*. Maidenhead: McGraw-Hill.

Pedler, M., & Aspinall, K. (1996). *Perfect PLC?* Maidenhead: McGraw-Hill.

Pedler, M., Boydell, T., & Burgoyne, J. (1988). *The Learning Company Project Report*. Sheffield: Employment Department.

Pedler, M., Burgoyne, J., & Boydell, T. (1991). *The Learning Company: A Strategy for Sustainable Development*. Maidenhead: McGraw-Hill.

Pendleton, A. (1997a). The evolution of industrial relations in UK nationalized industries. *British Journal of Industrial Relations*, **35**(2): 145–72.

Pendleton, A. (1997b). What impact has privatization had on pay and employment? *Relations Industrielles/Industrial Relations*, **52**(3): 554–82.

Penn, R., Lilja, K., & Scattergood, H. (1992). Flexibility and employment patterns in the paper industry: an analysis of mills in Britain and Finland. *Industrial Relations Journal*, **23**(3): 214–23.

Penrose, E. T. (1959). *The Theory of the Growth of the Firm*. Oxford: Blackwell.

Performance and Innovation Unit (2001). *In demand: Adult skills for the 21st century*. Performance and Innovation Unit, Cabinet Office. Available from http://www.piu.gov.uk/2001/workforce/report/index.html.

Perrow, C. (1986). *Complex Organizations: A Critical Essay*. New York: Random House.

Peters, T., & Waterman, R. (1982). *In Search of Excellence*. New York: Harper & Row.

Pettigrew, A., Sparrow, P., & Hendry, C. (1988). The forces that trigger training. *Personnel Management,* December, 28–32.

Pettijohn, L. S., Parker, S., Pettijohn, C. E., & Kent, J. L. (2001). Performance appraisals: usage, criteria and observations. *Journal of Management Development*, **20**(9): 754–71.

Pfeffer, J. (1994). *Competitive Advantage Through People: Understanding the Power of the Workforce*. Boston, MA: Houghton Mifflin.

Pfeffer, J. (1998). *The Human Equation*. Boston, MA: Harvard Business School Press.

Pfeffer, J., & Salancik, G. (1977). Organizational context and the characteristics and tenure of hospital administrators. *Academy of Management Journal*, **20**, 74–88.

Pfeffer, J., & Salancik, G. (1978). *The External Control of Organizations: A Resource Dependency Perspective*. New York: Harper & Row.

Phillips, J. J. (1996). *Accountability in Human Resource Management*. Houston, TX: Gulf Publishing.

Phillips, J. M. (1998). Effects of realistic job previews on multiple organizational outcomes: a meta-analysis. *Academy of Management Journal*, **41**(6): 673–90.

Phillips, P., & Phillips, E. (1993). *Women and Work: Inequality in the Canadian Labour Market*. Toronto: Lorimer.

Phillips, R. (1995). Coaching for higher performance. *Executive Development*, **8**(7): 5–7.

Pickard, J. (1997). Vacational qualifications. *People Management*, 10 July, 26–31.

Pickard, J. (2001). When push comes to shove. *People Management*, **7**(23): 30–5.

Piore, M., & Sabel, C. (1984). *The Second Industrial Divide*. New York: Basic Books.

Pitt, G. (1998). The ins and outs of management tools. *Globe and Mail,* January 8, 11.

Plachy, R. J. (1987). Writing job descriptions that get results. *Personnel,* October, 56–63.

Platt, L. (1997). Employee work–life balance: the competitive advantage. In F. Hesselbein, M. Goldsmith, & R. Beckhard (eds), *The Drucker Foundation, the Organization of the Future*. San Francisco: Jossey-Bass.

Pollard, E., & Hillage, J. (2001). *Exploring e-learning*. Report 376. Brighton: Institute for Employment Studies.

Pollert, A. (1988). Dismantling flexibility. *Capital and Class*, (34): 42–75.

Pollert, A. (1991). *Farewell to Flexibility?* Oxford: Blackwell.

Pollitt, C. (2000). Is the emperor in his new underwear?: an analysis of the impacts of public management reform. *Public Management*, **2**(2): 181–99.

Porter, M. (1980). *Competitive Strategy*. New York: Free Press.

Porter, M. (1985). *Competitive Advantage: Creating and Sustaining Superior Performance*. New York: Free Press.

Powell, W. & DiMaggio, P. (eds) (1991). *The New Institutionalism in Organizational Analysis*. Chicago: University of Chicago Press.

Prahalad, C. K., & Hamel, G. (1990). The core competencies of the corporation. *Harvard Business Review*, **68**(May–June), 79–91.

Pratt, D. D. (1998). Alternative frames of understanding. In D. D. Pratt (ed.), *Five Perspectives on Teaching in Adult and Higher Education* (pp. 33–53). Malabar, FL: Krieger.

Premack, S. L., & Wanous, J. P. (1985). A meta-analysis of realistic job preview experiments. *Journal of Applied Psychology*, **70**(4): 706–19.

Proctor, S., & Mueller, F. (eds) (2000). *Teamworking*. Basingstoke: Macmillan – now Palgrave Macmillan.

Pryce, V., & Nicholson, C. (1988). The problems and performance of employee ownership firms. *Employment Gazette*, **96**(6): 53–8.

Psoinos, A., & Smithson, S. (2002). Employee empowerment in manufacturing: a study of organizations in the UK. *New Technology, Work and Employment*, **17**(2): 132–48.

Pulakos, E. D., & Schmitt, N. (1995). Experienced-based and situational questions: studies of validity. *Personnel Psychology*, **48**, 289–309.

Purcell, J. (1989). The impact of corporate strategy on human resource management. In J. Storey (ed.), *New Perspectives on Human Resource Management* (pp. 67–91). London: Routledge.

Purcell, J. (1995). Corporate strategy and its link with human resource management strategy. In J. Storey (ed.), *Human Resource Management: A Critical Text* (pp. 63–86). London: Routledge.

Purcell, J. (1999). Best practice and best fit: chimera or cul-de-sac? *Human Resource Management Journal*, **9**(3): 26–41.

Purcell, J. (2001). The meaning of strategy in human resource management: a critical text. In J. Storey (ed.), *Human Resource Management* (pp. 59–77). London: Thomson-Learning.

Purcell, J., & Ahlstrand, B. (1994). *Human Resource Management in the Multi-divisional Company*. Oxford: Oxford University Press.

Pye, M., Cullinane, J., & Harcourt, M. (2001). The right to refuse unsafe work in New Zealand. *New Zealand Journal of Industrial Relations*, **26**(2): 199–216.

Quah, D. (1997). Weightless economy packs a heavy punch. *Independent on Sunday*, May 18, 4.

Quinn, J. B., Anderson, P., & Finkelstein, S. (1996). Managing professional intellect: making the most of the best. *Harvard Business Review*, March–April, 71–80.

Rainbird, H. (2000). Training in the workplace and workplace learning: introduction. In H. Rainbird (ed.), *Training in the Workplace* (pp. 1–17). Basingstoke: Palgrave – now Palgrave Macmillan.

Rana, E. (2001). Low skills, low interest. *People Management*, **7**(18): 24–30.

Randell, G. (1994) Employee Appraisal. In K. Sisson (ed.), *Personnel Management* (pp. 221–52). Oxford: Blackwell.

Rarick, C. A., & Baxter, G. (1986). Behaviourally anchored rating scales (bars): an effective performance appraisal approach. *SAM Advanced Management Journal*, Winter, 36–9.

Redman, T., Snape, E., Thompson, D., & Ka-Ching Yan, F. (2000). Performance appraisal in an NHS hospital. *Human Resource Management Journal*, **10**(1): 48–62.

Reed, M. I. (1989). *The Sociology of Management*. Hemel Hempstead: Harvester Wheatsheaf.

Reed, M. I. (1993). Organizations and modernity: continuity and discontinuity in organization theory. In J. Hassard, & M. Parker (eds), *Postmodernism and Organizations* (pp. 163–82). London: Sage.

Rees, W. D. (1998). Communication. In M. Poole, & M. Warner (eds), *Handbook of Human Resource Management* (pp. 488–91). London: Thomson Business.

Reilly, B., Paci, P., & Holl P. (1995). Unions, safety committees and workplace injuries. *British Journal of Industrial Relations*, **33**(2): 275–87.

Reilly, R. R., Smither, J. W., & Vasilopoulos, N. L. (1996). A longitudinal study of upward appraisal. *Personnel Psychology*, **46**, 599–61.

Reinharz, S. (1988). Feminist distrust: problems of context and content in sociological work. In D. N. Berg, & K. K. Smith (eds), *The Self in Social Inquiry*. Newbury Park, CA: Sage.

Rendall, P. (1986). Stuck in the middle. *Chief Executive*, September.

Richbell, S. (2001). Trends and emerging values in human resource management. *International Journal of Manpower*, **22**(3): 261–8.

Riesman, C. K. (1993). *Narrative Analysis*. Thousand Oaks, CA: Sage.

Rifkin, J. (1996). *The End of Work*. New York: Tarcher/Putnam Press.

Rinehart, J., Huxley, C., & Robertson, D. (1997). *Just Another Car Factory? Lean Production and its Discontents*. Ithaca, NY: Cornell University Press.

Risher, H. (1978). Job evaluation: mystical or statistical. *Personnel*, **55**, 23–36.

Rix, M., & Gold, J. (2000). 'With a little help from my academic friend': mentoring change agents. *Mentoring and Tutoring*, **8**(1): 47–62.

Robbins, S. P. (1989). *Organizational Behavior* (4th edn). London: Prentice Hall.

Robbins, S. P. (1990). *Organization Theory* (3rd edn). Englewood Cliffs, NJ: Prentice Hall.

Robens, Lord (1972). *Safety and health at work*. Cmnd 5034. London: HMSO.

Roberts, G. (1997). *Recuitment and Selection*. London: Institute of Personnel and Development.

Robertson, I. T., Baron, H., Gibbons, P., MacIver, R., & Nyfield, G. (2000). Conscientiousness and managerial performance. *Journal of Occupational and Organizational Psychology*, **73**(2): 171–81.

Roche, W., & Geary, J. (2002). Advocates, critics and union involvement in workplace partnerships: Irish airports. *British Journal of Industrial Relations*, **40**(4): 659–88.

Rodger, A. (1970). *The Seven Point Plan* (3rd edn). London: NFER.

Rolfe, H. (1986). Skill, deskilling and new technology in the non-manual labour process. *New Technology, Work and Employment*, **1**(1): 37–49.

Rose, M. (1988). *Industrial Behaviour*. London: Penguin.

Rose, M. (2000). Target practice. *People Management*, **6**(23): 44–5.

Rousseau, D. M. (1995). *Psychological Contracts in Organizations: Understanding Written and Unwritten Agreements*. Thousand Oaks, CA: Sage.

Rousseau, D. M., & Ho, V. T. (2000). Psychological contract issues in compensation. In S. L. Rynes, & B. Gerhart (eds), *Compensation in Organizations: Current Research and Practice* (pp. 273–310). San Francisco, CA: Jossey-Bass.

Rubery, J. (1992). Pay gender, and the social dimension to Europe. *British Journal of Industrial Relations*, **30**(4): 605–21.

Rubery, J., Earnshaw, J., Marchington, M., Cooke, F. L., & Vincent, S. (2000). *Changing organisational forms and the employment relationship*. Working Paper 14. Economic and Social Research Council Future of Work Programme. Swindon: ESRC.

Rynes, S., & Gerhart, B. (eds) (2000). *Compensation in Organizations: Current Research and Practice*. San Francisco: Jossey-Bass.

Saks, A. M. (2000). *Research, Measurement, and Evaluation of Human Sources*. Scarborough, ON: Nelson/Thompson Learning.

Salaman, G. (1979). *Work Organizations: Resistance and Control*. London: Longman.

Salaman, G. (1981). *Class and the Corporation*. London: Fontana.

Salamon, M. (1987). *Industrial Relations: Theory and Practice*. London: Prentice Hall.

Salgado, J. F. (1997). The five factor model of personality and job performance in the European Community. *Journal of Applied Psychology*, **82**(1): 30–43.

Sass, R. (1982). Safety and self-respect. *Policy Options*, July–August, 17–21.

Sayer, A. (1986). New developments in manufacturing: the just-in-time system. *Capital and Class*, (30): 43–72.

Scarbrough, H. (2000). The HR implications of supply chain relations. *Human Resource Management Journal*, **10**(1): 5–17.

Scarbrough, H., & Swan, J. (2001). Explaining the diffusion of knowledge management: the role of fashion. *British Journal of Management*, **12**(1): 3–12.

Scase, R. (1999). *Britain Towards 2010: The Changing Business Environment*. Swindon: Economic and Social Research Council.

Schneider, B. (1987). The people make the place. *Personnel Psychology*, **40**, 437–53.

Schneider, B. (1999). Research in the workplace: whose knowledge is it anyway? In *Conference Proceedings: How to Keep Your Intellectual Capital*. Calgary: University of Calgary.

Schneider, R. (2001). Variety performance. *People Management*, **7**(9): 26–31.

Schön, D. A. (1983). *The Reflective Ppractitioner: How Professionals Think in Action*. London: Maurice Temple Smith.

Schonberger, R. (1982). *Japanese Manufacturing Techniques: Nine Hidden Lessons in Simplicity*. London: Collier Macmillan.

Schramm, J. (2002). A hard lesson to learn. *People Management*, **8**(8): 32–4.

Schuler, R. S. (1989). Strategic human resource management and industrial relations. *Human Relations*, **42**(2): 157–84.

Schuler, R. S. (1990). Repositioning the human resource function: transformation or demise? *Academy of Management Executive*, **4**(3): 49–60.

Schuler, R. S. (1992). Strategic human resource management: linking people with the strategic needs of the business. *Organizational Dynamics*, **21**, 18–31.

Schuler, R. S., & Jackson, S. (1987). Linking competitive strategies and human resource management practices. *Academy of Management Executive*, **1**(3): 209–13.

Schultz, T. W. (1981). *Investing in People: The Economics of Population Quality*. Berkeley, CA: University of California Press.

Scott, M. (1998). *Value Drivers*. Chichester: Wiley.

Scott, S. G., & Einstein, W. O. (2001). Strategic performance appraisal in team-based organizations: one size does not fit all. *Academy of Management Executive*, **15**(2): 107–16.

Scott, W. R. (2003). *Organizations: Rational, Natural, and Open Systems* (5th edn). Upper Saddle River, NJ: Prentice Hall.

Scullion, H. (1995). International human resource management. In J. Storey (ed.), *Human Resource Management: A Critical Text* (pp. 352–82). London: Routledge.

Scullion, H. (2001). International human resource management. In J. Storey (ed.), *Human Resource Management: A Critical Text* (pp. 288–313). London: Thompson Learning.

Sebbens, T. D. (2000). Rising tides, leaky boats: the influence of downsizing on wage levels. *New Zealand Journal of Industrial Relations*, **25**(2): 119–50.

Selwyn, N. M. (2000). *Selwyn's Law of Employment* (11th edn). London: Butterworths.

Selznick, P. (1957). *Leadership and Administration*. New York: Harper & Row.

Senge, P. (1990). *The Fifth Discipline*. New York: Doubleday.

Sennett, R. (1998). *The Corrosion of Character*. New York: Norton.

Sewell, G. (1998). The discipline of teams: the control of team-based industrial work through electronic and peer surveillance. *Administrative Science Quarterly*, **43**, 406–69.

Shalev, M. (1981). Theoretical dilemmas and value analysis in comparative industrial relations. In G. Dlugos, & K. Weiermair (eds), *Management Under Differing Value Systems*. New York: de Gruyer.

Sheffield, J., & Coleshill, P. (2001). Developing best value in a Scottish local authority. *Measuring Business Excellence*, **5**(2): 31–8.

Shenkar, O. (1995). *Global Perspectives on Human Resource Management*. Englewood Cliffs, NJ: Prentice Hall.

Shiva, V. (2000). The world on the edge. In W. Hutton, & A. Giddens (eds), *On the Edge: Living with Global Capitalism* (pp. 112–29). London: Jonathan Cape.

Shotter, J. (1993). *Cultural Politics of Everyday Life*. Toronto: University of Toronto Press.

Sianesi, B., & Van Reenan, J. (2000). *The Returns to Education: A Review of the Macro-economic Literature*. London: Centre for the Economics of Education.

Simpson, B. (1986). Trade union immunities. In R. Lewis (ed.), *Labour Law in Britain*. Oxford: Blackwell.

Singh, R. (1997). Equal opportunities for men and women in the EU: a commentary. *Industrial Relations*, **28**(1): 68–71.

Sisson, K. (ed.) (1989). *Personnel Management*. Oxford: Blackwell.

Sisson, K. (1993). In search of HRM. *British Journal of Industrial Relations*, **31**(2): 201–9.

Sisson, K. (ed.) (1994). *Personnel Management* (2nd edn). Oxford: Blackwell.

Sisson, K. (1995). Human resource management and the personnel function. In J. Storey (ed.), *Human Resource Management: A Critical Text* (pp. 87–109). London: Routledge.

Sisson, K., & Storey, J. (2000). *The Realities of Human Resource Management: Managing the Employment Relationship*. Buckingham, Oxford University Press.

Skills Task Force (2000). *Skills for All: Research Report from the National Skills Task Force*. Sudbury: Department for Education and Employment.

Sloman, M., & Reynolds, J. (2002). Developing the e-learning community. Paper presented to the Third Conference on Human Resource Development: Research and Practice Across Europe, Edinburgh, January.

Smith, Adam (1776 [1982]). *The Wealth of Nations*. Harmondsworth: Penguin.

Smith, A. R. (1980). *Corporate Manpower Planning*. London: Gower Press.

Smith, Andrew (2001). Perceptions of stress at work. *Human Resource Management Journal*, **11**(4): 74–86.

Smith, I. (1992). Reward management and HRM. In P. Blyton, & P. Turnbull (eds), *Reassessing Human Resource Management*. London: Sage.

Smith, P., & Morton, G. (1993). Union exclusion and the decollectivization of industrial relations in contemporary Britain. *British Journal of Industrial Relations*, **31**(1): 97–114.

Smith, P., & Morton, G. (2001). New Labour's reform of Britain's employment law: the devil is not only in detail but in the values and policy too. *British Journal of Industrial Relations*, **39**(1): 119–38.

Snell, S. A. (1992). Control theory in strategic human resource management: the mediating effect of administrative information. *Academy of Management Journal*, **35**, 292–327.

Snell, S. A., Youndt, M. A., & Wright, P. M. (1996). Establishing a framework for research in strategic human resource management: merging source theory and organizational learning. *Research in Personnel and Human Resources Management*, **14**, 61–90.

Sparrow, P. (1996). Too good to be true. *People Management*, 5 December, 22–7.

Sparrow, P., & Marchington, M. (1998). *Human Resource Management: The New Agenda*. London: Financial Times/Pitman.

Spychalski, A. C., Quiñones, M. A., Gaugler, B. B., & Pohley, K. (1997). A survey of assessment center practices in the United States. *Personnel Psychology*, **50**, 71–90.

Squires, G. (2001). Mangement as a professional discipline. *Journal of Management Studies*, **38**(4): 473–87.

Standing, G. (1997). Globalization, labour flexibility and insecurity: the era of market regulation. *European Journal of Industrial Relations*, **3**(1): 7–37.

Stern, E., & Sommerlad, E. (1999). *Workplace Learning,Culture and Performance*. London: Institute of Personnel and Development.

Stewart, J., & Knowles, V. (1999). The changing nature of graduate careers. *Career Development International*, **4**(7): 370–83.

Stewart, J., & Knowles, V. (2000). Graduate recruitment: implications for business and management courses in HE. *Journal of European Industrial Training*, **25**(2): 98–108.

Stewart, R. (1998). Managerial behaviour. In M. Poole, & M. Warner (eds), *Handbook of Human Resource Management* (pp. 147–63). London: Thomson Business.

Stiglitz, J. E. (2002). *Globalization and its Discontents*. New York: Norton.

Stohl, C., & Cheney, G. (2001). Participatory processes/paradoxical practices. *Management Communications Quarterly*, **14**(3): 349–407.

Stokes, A. (2001). Using tele-mentoring to deliver training to SMEs: a pilot study. *Education and Training*, **43**(6): 317–24.

Stone, T. H., & Meltz, N. M. (1988). *Human Resource Management in Canada* (2nd edn). Toronto: Human Rights Watch.

Storey, J. (ed.) (1989). *New Perspectives on Human Resource Management*. London: Routledge.

Storey, J. (1992). *Developments in the Management of Human Resources*. Oxford: Basil Blackwell.

Storey, J. (1995). Human resource management: still marching on or marching out? In J. Storey (ed.), *Human Resource Management: A Critical Text* (pp. 3–32). London: Routledge.

Storey, J. (ed.) (1995a). *Human Resource Management: A Critical Text*. London: Routledge.

Storey, J. (2001). Human resource management today: an assessment. In J. Storey (ed.), *Human Resource Management: A Critical Text* (pp. 3–20). London: Thompson Learning.

Storey, J., & Quintas, P. (2001). Knowledge management and HRM. In J. Storey (ed.), *Human Resource Management* (pp. 339–63). London: Thomson-Learning.

Storey, J., Cressey, P., Morris, T., & Wilkinson, A. (1997). Changing employment practices in UK banking: case studies. *Personnel Review*, **26**(1): 24–42.

Strauss, G. (1998). An overview. In F. Heller, E. Pusic, G. Strauss, & B. Wilpert (eds), *Organizational Participation: Myth and Reality* (pp. 8–39). Oxford: Oxford University Press.

Strebler, M., Robinson, D., & Heron, P. (1997). *Getting the best out of your competencies.* Report 334. Brighton: Institute for Employment Studies.

Stredwick, J., & Ellis, S. (1998). *Flexible Working Practices.* London: Institute of Personnel Development.

Streeck, W. (1987). The uncertainties of management in the management of uncertainty. *Work, Employment and Society*, **1**: 281–308.

Streeck, W. (1996). Comment on Ronald Dore. *Industrielle Beziehungen*, **3**, 187–96.

Streeck, W., & Visser, J. (1997). The rise of the conglomerate union. *European Journal of Industrial Relations*, **3**(3): 305–32.

Sukert, A. (2000). Marionettes of globalization: a comparative analysis of legal protections for contingent workers in the international community. *Syracuse Journal of International Law and Commerce*, **27**(2): 403–77.

Sveiby, K. E. (1997). *The New Organizational Wealth: Managing and Measuring Organizational Wealth.* San Francisco, CA: Berrett-Koehler.

Swanson, R. A. (2001). HRD and its underlying theory. *Human Resource Development International*, **4**(3): 299–312.

Swinburne, P. (2001). How to use feedback to improve performance. *People Management*, **7**(11): 46–7.

Tamkin, P., Barber, L., & Hirsh, W. (1995). *Personal development plans: Case studies of practice.* Report 280. Brighton: Institute for Employment Studies.

Tamkin, P., Barber, L., & Dench, S. (1997). *From admin to strategy: The changing face of the HR function.* Report 332. Brighton: Institute for Employment Studies.

Tan, J.-S. (1998). Communication, cross-cultural. In M. Poole, & M. Warner (eds), *Handbook of Human Resource Management* (pp. 492–97). London: Thomson Business.

Tannen, D. (1993). *You Just Don't Understand: Women and Men in Conversation.* London: Virago.

Taras, D., Ponak, A., & Gunderson, M. (2001). Introduction to Canadian industrial relations. In M. Gunderson, A. Ponak, & D. Taras (eds), *Union–management Relations in Canada* (4th edn) (pp. 1–24). Toronto: Addison Wesley Longman.

Taylor, C. (2001). Windows of opportunity. *People Management*, **7**(5): 32–6.

Taylor, H. (1991). The systematic training model: corn circles in search of a spaceship? *Management Education and Development*, **22**(4): 258–78.

Taylor, R. (2002). *Britain's World of Work – Myths and Realities.* Swindon: Economic and Social Research Council.

Taylor, S. (1998). *Employee Resourcing.* London: Institute of Personnel Development.

Teague, P., & Grahl, J. (1992). *Industrial Relations and European Integration.* London: Lawrence & Wishart.

Templer, A. J. & Cawsey, T. F. (1999). Rethinking career development in an era portfolio careers. *Career Development International*, **4**(2): 70–6.

Temporal, P. (1978). The nature of non-contrived learning and its implications for management development. *Management Education and Development*, **9**, 20–3.

Terry, M. (1995). Trade unions: shop stewards and the workplace. In P. Edwards (ed.), *Industrial Relations.* Oxford: Blackwell.

Thomas, C., & Wallis, B. (1998). Dŵr Cymru/Welsh water: a case study in partnership. In P. Sparrow, & M. Marchington (eds), *Human Resource Management: A New Agenda* (pp. 160–70). London: Financial Times.

Thompson, J. D. (1967). *Organizations in Action.* New York: McGraw-Hill.

Thompson, M. (2001). The management of industrial relations. In M. Gunderson, A. Ponak, & D. Taras (eds), *Union–management Relations in Canada* (4th edn) (pp. 117–41). Toronto, Addison Wesley Longman.

Thompson, P. (1989). *The Nature of Work* (2nd edn). London: Macmillan – now Palgrave Macmillan.

Thompson, P. (1993). Postmodernism: fatal distraction. In J. Hassard, & M. Parker (eds), *Postmodernism and Organizations* (pp. 183–203). London: Sage.

Thompson, P., & McHugh, D. (2002). *Work Organisations: A Critical Introduction* (3rd edn). Basingstoke: Palgrave Macmillan.

Thompson, P., & Wallace, T. (1996). Redesigning production through teamworking. *International Journal of Operations and Production Management*, **16**(2): 103–18.

Thompson, P., & Warhurst, C. (eds) (1998). *Workplaces of the Future*. Basingstoke: Macmillan – now Palgrave Macmillan.

Thomson, N., & Millar, C. (2001). The role of slack in transforming organizations. *International Studies of Management and Organization*, **31**(2): 65–83.

Thornhill, A., Saunders, M. N. K., & Stead, J. (1997). Downsizing, delayering – but where's the commitment. *Personnel Review*, **26**(1): 81–98.

Thurley, K., & Wood, S. (1983). Business strategy and industrial relations strategy. In K. Thurley, & S. Wood (Eds). *Industrial Relations and Management Strategy*. Cambridge: Cambridge University Press.

Thursfield, D. (2000). *Post-Fordism and Skill*. Aldershot: Ashgate.

Tichy, N., & Devanna, M. (1986). *The Transformational Leader*. New York: Wiley.

Tomaney, J. (1990). The reality of workplace flexibility. *Capital and Class*, (40): 97–124.

Torrington, D. (1998). Discipline and dismissals. In M. Poole, & M. Warner (eds), *The Handbook of Human Resource Management* (pp. 498–506). London: International Thomson Business Press.

Towers, B. (1989). Running the gauntlet: British trade unions under Thatcher, 1979–1988. *Industrial and Labor Relations Review*, **42**(2): 296–313.

Towers, B. (1992). Two speed ahead: social Europe and the UK after Maastricht. *Industrial Relations Journal*, **23**(2): 83–9.

Townley, B. (1989). Employee communication programmes. In K. Sisson (ed.) *Personnel Management* (pp. 329–55). Oxford: Blackwell.

Townley, B. (1994). *Reframing Human Resource Managment*. London: Sage

Trades Union Congress (1986). *Health and Safety at Work: TUC Course Book for Union Reps* (4th edn). London: TUC.

Trades Union Congress (1999). *Partners for Progress: New Unionism in the Workplace*. London: TUC.

Trades Union Congress (2000). *Focus on Recognition*. London: TUC.

Trades Union Congress (2002). New record high for employers recognizing unions. TUC press release, Jan 21, TUC website: www.tuc.org.uk/organization/tuc.

Trapp, R. (2001). Of mice and men. *People Management*, **7**(13): 24–32.

Trethewey, A. (1997). Organizational culture. In P. Y. Byers (ed.), *Organizational Communication: Theory and Behavior*. Boston: Allyn & Bacon.

Truss, C. (2001). Complexities and controversies in linking HRM with organizational outcomes. *Journal of Management Studies*, **38**(8): 1121–49.

Truss, C., Gratton, L., Hope-Hailey, V., Stiles, P., & Zaleska, J. (2002). Paying the piper: choice and constraint in changing HR functional roles. *Human Resource Management Journal*, **12**(2): 39–63.

Tung, R. (1988). *The New Expatriates*. Boston, MA: Ballinger.

Turnbull, P. (1986). The Japanisation of British industrial relations at Lucas. *Industrial Relations Journal*, **17**(3): 193–206.

Turner, G. (1996). Human resource accounting – whim or wisdom? *Journal of Human Resource Costing and Accounting*, **1**(1): 63–73

Tyson, D. E. (1996). *Profit Sharing in Canada: The Complete Guide to Designing and Implementing Plans That Really Work*. Toronto: Wiley.

Tyson, S. (1987). The management of the personnel function. *Journal of Management Studies*, **24**, 523–32.

Tyson, S. (1995). *Human Resource Strategy*. London: Pitman.

Tyson, S., & Brewster, C. (1991). Comparative studies and the development of human resource management. In C. Brewster, & S. Tyson (eds), *International Comparisons in Human Resource Management* (pp. 257–9). London: Pitman.

Tyson, S., & Fell, A. (1986). *Evaluating the Personnel Function*. London: Hutchinson.

Tziner, A., Joanis, C., & Murphy, K. R. (2000). A comparison of three methods of performance appraisal with regard to goal properties, goal perception and ratee satisfaction. *Group and Organization Management*, **25**(2): 175–90.

Ulrich, D. (1997). *Human Resource Champions*. Boston, MA: Harvard Business School Press.

Ulrich, D., & Beatty, R. W. (2001). From partner to players. *Human Resource Management*, **40**(4): 293–307.

Ulrich, L., & Trumbo, D. (1965). The selection interview since 1949. *Psychological Bulletin*, **63**, 100–16.

Undy, R., Ellis, V., McCarthy, W. E. J., & Halmos, A. M. (1981). *Change in Trade Unions*. London: Hutchinson.

Vallas, S. (1999). Re-thinking post-Fordism: the meaning of workplace flexibility. *Sociological Theory*, **17**(1): 68–85.

Vedd, R. (2001). Management accounting and strategic human resource management: a comparison of the UK Royal Mail and Canada Post. Paper presented at the 13th Asian-Pacific Conference on International Accounting Issues, Brazil.

Veng Seng, C., Zannes, E., & Pace, R. W. (2002). The contributions of knowledge management to workplace learning. *Journal of Workplace Learning*, **14**(4): 138–47.

Verhaar, C. H. A., & Smulders, H. R. M. (1999). Employability in practice. *Journal of European Industrial Training*, **23**(6): 268–74.

Verlander, E. G. (1985). The system's the thing. *Training and Development*, April, 20–3.

Verma, A. (1995). Employee involvement in the workplace. In M. Gunderson, & A. Ponak (eds), *Union–management Relations in Canada* (3rd edn) (pp. 281–308). Don Mills, Ontario: Addison-Wesley.

Verma, A., & Taras, D. (2001). Employee involvement in the workplace. In M. Gunderson, A. Ponak, & D. Taras (eds), *Union–management Relations in Canada* (4th edn). Don Mills, Ontario: Addison-Wesley.

Verma, A., Kochan, T., & Wood, S. (eds) (2002). Editor's Introduction. *British Journal of Industrial Relations*, **40**(3): 373–84.

Visser, J., & Waddington, J. (1996). Industrialization and politics: a century of union structural developments in three European countries. *European Journal of Industrial Relations*, **2**(1): 21–53.

Vroom, V. H. (1964). *Work and Motivation*. New York: Wiley.

Waddington, J. (1988). Business unionism and fragmentation within the TUC. *Capital and Class*, (36): 7–15.

Waddington, J. (1992). Trade union membership in Britain, 1980–1987: unemployment and restructuring. *British Journal of Industrial Relations*, **30**(2): 7–15.

Waddington, J., & Whitston, C. (1994). The politics of restructuring: trade unions on the defensive in Britain since 1979. *Relations Industrielles/Industrial Relations*, **49**(4): 794–817.

Wageman, R. (1997). Critical success factors for creating superb self-managing teams. *Organizational Dynamics*, **26**(1): 49–61.

Wagner, R. F. (1949). The employment interview: a critical summary. *Personnel Psychology*, **2**, 17–46.

Wajcman, J. (1998). *Managing Like a Man*. University Park, PA: Pennsylvania State University Press.

Wajcman, J. (2000). Feminism facing industrial relations in Britain. *British Journal of Industrial Relations*, **38**(2): 183–201.

Wallace, M. (1989). Brave new workplace: technology and work in the new economy. *Work and Occupations*, **16**(4): 363–92.

Walters, D. (1987). Health and safety and trade union workplace organization: a case study in the printing industry. *Industrial Relations Journal*, **18**(1): 40–7.

Walters, M. (ed.) (1995). *The Performance Management Handbook*. London: Institute of Personnel Development.

Walton, R. (1985). From control to commitment in the workplace. *Harvard Business Review*, March/April, 77–84.

Warde, A. (1990). The future of work. In J. Anderson, & M. Ricci (eds), *Society and Social Science: A Reader* (pp. 86–94). Milton Keynes: Open University Press.

Watson, T. (1986). *Management, Organization and Employment Strategy*. London: Routledge & Kegan Paul.

Watson, T. (1994). Recruitment and selection. In Sisson, K. (ed.), *Personnel Management*. Oxford: Blackwell.

Watson, T. (1999). Human resourcing strategies. In J. Leopold, L. Harris, & T. Watson (eds), *Strategic Human Resourcing* (pp. 17–38). London: Pitman.

Webb, D., & Collis, C. (2000). Regional development agencies and the 'new regionalism' in England. *Regional Studies*, **34**(9): 857–64.

Weber, M. (1968 [1922]). *Economy and Society*. New York: Bedminster.

Wedderburn, Lord (1986). *The Worker and the Law* (3rd edn). Harmondsworth: Penguin Books.

Weick, K., & Westley, F. (1996). Organizational learning: affirming an oxymoron. In S. Clegg, C. Hardy, & W. Nord (eds), *Handbook of Organization Studies* (pp. 190–208). London: Sage.

Welbourne, T., & Trevor, C. (2000). The roles of departmental and position power in job evaluation. *Academy of Management Journal*, **43**(4): 761–71.

Wells, D. (1993). Are strong unions compatible with the new model of human resource management? *Relations Industrielles/Industrial Relations*, **48**(1): 56–84.

Wenger, E. C., & Snyder, W. M. (2000). Communities of practice: the organizational frontier. *Harvard Business Review*, January–February, 139–45.

West, A. C. (1980). Involving employees – practical action on section one. *Journal of Occupational Psychology*, **5**(5): 538–56.

Wheatley, M. (1994). *Leadership and the New Science*. San Francisco: Berrett-Koehler.

Wheelen, T., & Hunger, J. (1995). *Strategic Management and Business Policy* (5th edn). New York: Addison-Wesley.

Whipp, R. (1999). Creative destruction: strategy and organizations. In S. Clegg, C. Hardy, & W. Nord (eds), *Managing Organizations: Current Issues* (pp. 11–25). London: Sage.

Whittaker, D. H. (1990). *Managing Innovation: A Study of British and Japanese Factories*. Cambridge: Cambridge University Press.

Whittington, R. (1993). *What is Strategy and Does it Matter?* London: Routledge.

Wickens, P. (1987). *The Road to Nissan*. London: Macmillan – now Palgrave Macmillan.

Wiggins, J. S. (ed.) (1996). *The Five-factor Model of Personality*. New York: Guildford Publications.

Williams, A. (1993). *Human Resource Management and Labour Market Flexibility*. Aldershot: Avebury.

Williams, S. (1999). Policy failure in education and training: the introduction of National Vocational Qualifications (1986–1990). *Education and Training*, **41**(5): 216–26.

Willman, P. (1996). Merger propensity and merger outcomes among British unions, 1986–95. *Industrial Relations Journal*, **27**(4): 331–7.

Willmott, H. (1984). Images and ideals of managerial work. *Journal of Management Studies*, **21**(3): 349–68.

Willmott, H. (1995). The odd couple?: re-engineering business processes; managing human relations. *New Technology, Work and Employment*, **10**(2): 89–97.

Wilson, F. (1994). Introducing new computer-based systems into Zenbank. *New Technology, Work and Employment*, **9**(2): 115–26.

Wilson, J. P., and Western, S. (2000). Performance appraisal: an obstacle to training and development. *Journal of European Industrial Training*, **24**(7): 384–90.

Wilson, N. A. B. (1973). *On the quality of working life*. Manpower Papers 7. London: HMSO.

Winter, J., Neal, J., & Waner, K. (2001). How male, female and mixed gender groups regard interaction and leadership differences in the business communication course. *Business Communication Quarterly*, **64**(3): 43–58.

Witherspoon, P. D. (1997). *Communicating Leadership*. Boston: Allyn & Bacon.

Witz, A. (1986). Patriarchy and the labour market: occupational control strategies and the medical division of labour. In D. Knights, & H. Willmott (eds), *Gender and the Labour Process* (pp. 14–35). Aldershot: Gower.

Womack, J., Jones, D., & Roos, D. (1990). *The Machine That Changed the World*. New York: Rawson Associates.

Wong, M. L. (2001). The strategic use of contingent workers in Hong Kong's economic upheaval. *Human Resource Management Journal*, **11**(4): 22–37.

Wood, S. (1995). The four pillars of HRM: are they connected? *Human Resource Management Journal*, **5**(5): 49–59.

Wood, S. (2000). The BJIR and industrial relations in the new millennium. *British Journal of Industrial Relations*, **38**(1): 1–5.

Wood, S., & Godard, J. (1999). The statutory union recognition procedure in the Employment Relations Bill: a comparative analysis. *British Journal of Industrial Relations*, **37**(2): 203–44.

Wood, S., Moore, S., & Willman, P. (2002). Third time lucky for statutory recognition in the UK. *Industrial Relations Journal*, **33**(3): 215–33.

Woodall, J. (2001). Editorial. *Human Resource Development International*, **4**(3): 287–90.

Woodruffe, C. (1992). What is meant by a competency? In S. Boam, & P. Sparrow (eds), *Designing and Achieving Competency* (pp. 16–30). Maidenhead: McGraw-Hill.

Wright, M. (1996). The collapse of compulsory unionism? Collective organization in highly unionized British companies, 1979–1991. *British Journal of Industrial Relations*, **34**(4): 497–513.

Wright, P. M., & McMahan, C. G. (1992). Theoretical perspectives for strategic human resource management. *Journal of Management*, **18**, 295–319.

Yammarino, F. J., & Atwater, L. E. (1997). Implications of self–other rating agreement for human resources management. *Organizational Dynamics*, **25**(4): 35–44.

Yanow, D. (2000). Seeing organizational learning: a 'cultural' view. *Organization*, **7**(2): 247–68.

Youndt, M. A., Snell, S. A., Dean, J. W., & Lepak, D. P. (1996). Human resource management, manufacturing strategy and firm performance. *Academy of Management Journal*, **39**, 836–66.

Yukl, G., (2002). *Leadership in Organizations* (5th edn). Englewood Cliffs, NJ: Prentice Hall.

Zhou, J., & Martocchio, J. (2001). Chinese and American managers' compensation award decisions: a comparative study. *Personnel Psychology*, **54**(1): 115–45.

Zorn, T. E., Christensen, L., & Cheney, G. (1999). *Do We Really Want Constant Change?* San Francisco: Berrett-Koehler.

Index

Author index

Subject index